D0145008

The Working Life

JOHN ALBERTI
Northern Kentucky University

PEARSON
Longman

New York   San Francisco   Boston
London   Toronto   Sydney   Tokyo   Singapore   Madrid
Mexico City   Munich   Paris   Cape Town   Hong Kong   Montreal

Senior Vice President and Publisher: Joseph Opiela
Acquisitions Editor: Susan Kunchandy
Executive Marketing Manager: Deborah Murphy
Senior Supplements Editor: Donna Campion
Production Manager: Charles Annis
Project Coordination, Text Design, and Electronic Page Makeup: Pre-Press
    Company, Inc.
Cover Design Manager: John Callahan
Cover Designer: Kay Petronio
Cover Image: Courtesy of The Stock Illustration Source
Photo Researcher: Marci Lunetta
Manufacturing Manager: Dennis J. Para
Printer and Binder: R. R. Donnelly and Sons Co.
Cover Printer: Phoenix Color Corp.

For permission to use copyrighted material, grateful acknowledgment is made to
the copyright holders on pp. 491–495, which are hereby made part of this copyright
page.

Library of Congress Cataloging-in-Publication Data
The working life / [edited by] John Alberti.
        p. cm.
    Includes bibliographical references and index.
    ISBN 0-321-09422-0
        1. Readers—Work. 2. Report writing—Problems, exercises, etc. 3. Work—
    Problems, exercises, etc. 4. English language—Rhetoric. 5. College readers.
    I. Alberti, John.

PE1127.W65W555 2004
808'.0427—dc21   2003054824

Copyright © 2004 by Pearson Education, Inc.

All rights reserved. No part of this publication may be reproduced, stored in a
retrieval system, or transmitted, in any form or by any means, electronic, mechanical, photocopying, recording, or otherwise, without the prior written permission of
the publisher. Printed in the United States.

Please visit our Web site at http://www.ablongman.com

ISBN 0-321-09422-0

1 2 3 4 5 6 7 8 9 10—DOH—06 05 04 03

Brief Contents

Detailed Contents

(handwritten marginalia: "inbetween RUR + HOW —")

Globalization?

no-need something else

Readings and Materials by Genre and Mode

Analysis/Research

- Aristotle, from *The Politics*
- Coontz, Stephanie, "The American Family"
- Iyer, Pico, "The Global Village Finally Arrives"
- Kessler-Harris, Alice, from *Women Have Always Worked*
- Schor, Juliet B., from *The Overworked American: The Unexpected Decline of Leisure*
- Smith, Adam, from *An Inquiry into the Nature and Causes of the Wealth of Nations*
- Span, Paula, "The On-Line Mystique"
- Weber, Max, from *The Protestant Ethic and the Spirit of Capitalism*

Autobiography

- Douglass, Frederick, from *The Narrative of the Life of Frederick Douglass*
- Franklin, Benjamin, from *The Autobiography of Benjamin Franklin*
- Kirn, Walter, "Summertime Dues"
- Rose, Mike, from *Lives on the Boundary*
- Welfare, Before and After: Two Essays by Anne Downey

Argument

- Aristotle, from *The Politics*
- Barber, Benjamin R., "Jihad vs. McWorld"
- Black, Bob, from "The Abolition of Work"
- Chideya, Farai, from *The Color of Our Future*
- Cohen, Randy, Letters from "The Ethicist"
- Conley, Dalton, "The Cost of Slavery"
- Galinsky, Ellen, "Do Working Parents Make the Grade?"
- Greider, William, from *One World, Ready or Not*
- Judis, John, "Value Free"

Preface for Instructors

It may be the oldest truth in composition pedagogy that we all write better about subjects that matter to us and to which we feel a deep personal connection. *The Working Life* started with this basic search for a subject to engage my writing students at Northern Kentucky University. As sometimes happens with what seem like hopeless quests, an answer was sitting right in front of me every day in class. As I thought about the lives my students lead and the paths that have brought them to college, a common thread was evident: work.

As is true for most college students in America, work and career preparation are the central motivations for why the students in my classes attend college, and work-for-pay outside of the classroom is a central part of their lives as college students. Here was a subject that every student in class could speak to and write about with a sense of personal investment, one that connected their academic lives with their lives outside of school in fundamental, inescapable ways. It was also a subject that tied my life and career as a college instructor directly into the curriculum, for as college faculty the classroom is our workplace, and there continues to be no issue more fraught within composition studies and teaching than the working lives, conditions, and employment status of college writing teachers.

As obvious as the choice of work as an organizing issue for my writing class seemed after I decided on it, it was equally strange to me that the choice would seem novel at all. Yet I quickly discovered that work as a subject is strangely underrepresented in composition textbooks and in college curricula in general. Instead, work and career preparation is addressed extensively as a practical concern on campus, whether in the forms of internship programs, career development offices, job fairs, or brochures from majors listing possible job opportunities for graduates. What seemed missing was a more theoretical and philosophical perspective on work, an approach that encouraged students to ask basic questions about how we define work and understand its cultural importance, about why work is organized the way it is from a variety of perspectives, and, perhaps most important, what kind of Working Life we want to create for ourselves, our country, and our world.

These are big, even global questions, but they are also questions that begin in the most familiar lived experiences of everyone in the writing classroom, both teachers and students. The primary courses for which this text is designed are first- and second-semester composition classes. As is probably evident from this description, *The Working Life* is not a professional or workplace writing textbook in the technical sense, nor is it primarily designed to prepare students for the specific demands of job-related writing. That said, however, one of the central guiding ideas of *The Working Life* is that in the end the distinction between "theoretical" and "practical" thinking is merely an academic convenience, that ultimately nothing is more practical than serious, engaged critical reflection. As a result, there could be no better preparation for the rhetorical and ethical challenges of workplace writing than the opportunities for students to develop their critical reading and writing skills and knowledge supplied by *The Working Life*.

More and more, college educators struggle with the increasingly vocational orientation toward higher education that drives government policies and student enrollment. Many of us rightly fear that such an orientation reduces the possibilities for intellectual, emotional, and spiritual growth in college. *The Working Life* acknowledges this vocational reality in higher education by turning it into an opportunity to use writing as a means of self-reflection and critical engagement with these social trends. *The Working Life* is not about simply adapting to the "real world" but engaging critically with that world.

Theoretical Orientation of *The Working Life*

The Working Life is informed by social constructivist theories of rhetoric and collaborative, democratic pedagogy. In other words, the text asks students to approach questions of form, genre, and rhetorical strategy not as fixed formulas or structures but as contingent, evolving social practices that change and adapt according to specific contexts and purposes. While certain tested techniques and approaches can be used successfully time and again in different situations (putting a thesis statement up front in a piece of expository writing, for example), none are universally applicable in every situation, and all need to be constantly reassessed and reexamined, a process that works best in the form of collaboration and consultation with other writers in the classroom.

Structure of the Book

The Working Life consists of one chapter on critical reading and writing and eight chapters and an epilogue of readings and other materials. Each of these eights chapters focuses on a key issue or theme related to work broadly understood:

- Work, Labor, and Career: The Meaning of Work
- Education and Work/Education as Work
- Work and Social Class
- Work and Family
- Work and Diversity
- Ethics of Work/The Work Ethic
- Work in the Global Economy
- Work in the Information Age/The Future of Work

Each chapter includes a range of textual materials:

- **Foundational Readings** are the most traditional in terms of academic approaches to the subject, featuring selections from the historical literature on work, academic studies, and serious contemporary journalism.

- **Stories of Work** and **Media Images** expand both genre and disciplinary categories to include fiction, poetry, drama, cartoons, film, visual imagery, and other media. Just as *The Working Life* challenges students to reconsider work from a variety of perspectives, these selections encourage students to broaden their range of rhetorical expertise and understanding.

- **Reading the Web: A Sample Web Site** builds on this expansive understanding of rhetoric by introducing students to the emergent and rapidly growing writing space of the Internet. As the first chapter will suggest, the Internet has refocused our attention on the visual and design aspects of writing. These web page samples are designed to encourage responsible Internet research, teach critical web reading and analysis skills, and introduce students to the web page as rhetorical space.

- **The Work of Writing/Writing as Work** sections provide opportunities to use writing as social action. Assignments suggest various levels of service learning activities, whether these are explored hypothetically in the classroom or in actual service learning programs.

The Instructors Guide features detailed descriptions and pedagogical advice about each of the selections in *The Working Life*, including suggestions for prereading exercises and discussions, strategies for promoting engaged student responses, and writing suggestions and assignments.

Whether you teach at a community college, a four-year open-enrollment state school, a small liberal arts college, or a large research university, *The Working Life* will allow your students to experience writing as an important means of investigating and making sense of one of the most deeply personal yet profoundly social issues. If one of the goals of critical pedagogy and writing instruction is to include the work of developing as a writer as part of the focus of critical investigation, I hope *The Working Life* enables you to make that connection in your classroom.

Preface for Students

Consider one of the first questions we ask when meeting someone new: "So, what do you do?" Even though the question is really pretty vague when you think about it, we all know exactly what it means, and it goes beyond simply finding out how someone earns a paycheck. The fact that work is one of the first things we want to know about someone suggests more than simple curiosity; it's really a question about identity, about who we are and how others perceive (and misperceive) us. In answering this question, we know we are providing a crucial piece of information in terms of the opinion the person we are meeting forms of us. As such, it's a question that connects to larger social values, beliefs, and even prejudices. That's why a person might prefer to answer, "I'm between jobs" rather than "I'm unemployed," or why another might say, "I'm a college professor" instead of "I'm a teacher." Like race and gender, what we do for a living (and just think about the implications of that common phrase) is a part of the way we size each other up, for better and worse.

The importance we place on the question of what we "do" leads to further questions: Why is this information so important anyway? Why does it matter so much? Why do we care whether we are called a "secretary" or an "administrative assistant"? A "sales clerk" or an "associate"? A "team leader" or a "boss"? Answering these questions involves an exploration that can lead us into fields as diverse as sociology, psychology, history, philosophy, and beyond.

Let's look at another example: think about all the aspects of work that we take for granted or think of as natural. There is the eight-hour workday, for instance, and the forty-hour work week, or even the idea of the "weekend." For most of us, these seem like definitions of "normal," full-time working conditions. Anything less is "part-time," anything more is "overtime." Yet not so long ago, "normal" for most people meant working ten or more hours per day, six days a week. The idea of working on Saturday was not seen as an imposition or a particular hardship; Saturday was no less a workday than Monday or Wednesday. To go a step further, the very idea of defining work by measures of time such as hours and minutes isn't universal (it depended on the development of inexpensive clocks and watches, for one thing), and the idea of exchanging work for money is actually a pretty recent development in human history.

These examples only begin to address the theoretical possibilities of work, because they all deal with work for pay. Let's take another step back, however, and ask some even bigger questions about what we might mean by *work*. Think of some of the varied uses of the term: A life's work. A work of art. I'm working on it. This plan won't work. We're working through a problem. Getting all worked up. You can probably think of many more, each suggesting a new way to understand this seemingly simple word.

These questions and issues may seem theoretical, but in reality, nothing is more practical than asking theoretical questions. The work of writing is a case in point. Writing is an intensely practical activity, an important way of doing work in the world, whether getting a grade in a class, applying for a job, maintaining a friendship over e-mail, or drafting a petition. Writing is also intensely theoretical in that it involves exploring and analyzing the rhetorical context of writing, including who we are writing to, what their values are, and how we want to persuade or move them to action. As we explore the meanings of the working life, we also explore the meanings and uses of the work of writing.

Thinking theoretically isn't a strange or alien activity. In fact, it's something we begin doing almost as soon as we are able to speak. Think of how young children constantly ask adults, "Why?" In a sense, the work of grown-up theorists is simply an extension of this childhood desire to question the world around us. Why, for example, do we think of forty hours as a normal work week? When did this change come about? Who helped bring it about? Although we can describe these questions as "theoretical," they have very practical implications. If the work week used to be longer in the past, for instance, then why can't it be shorter in the future? What about a twenty-hour work week? A four- or even three-day work week? We soon may realize that changing the world can start with a question as simple as "Why?"

The Structure of *The Working Life*

Each chapter asks you to explore a different aspect of the working life and different aspects of the work of writing by presenting you with a range of textual and visual materials:

- **Foundational Readings:** These are a collection of essays, journalism, and other print sources that provide an overview for reading and discussion of the topic of that chapter.

- **Reading the Web:** As a way of exploring the research possibilities of the Internet and of considering the challenges posed by writing for the web, each chapter features a web site related to the chapter topic and the issues raised in the Foundational Readings.

- **Stories of Work:** Fiction, autobiography, poetry, songs—Stories of Work expands the range of perspectives and approaches to the chapter topic by looking at the connections between the work of writing and the art of writing.

- **Images of Work:** The selections in Images of Work ask you to extend your critical reading skills to the reading of culture, especially visual culture. Images of Work can include advertisements, works of art, promotional materials, cartoons—materials that all ask you to consider how images are used to communicate, argue, and persuade.

- **The Work of Writing/Writing as Work:** Writing as Work asks you to make the connection between the work of writing you do in school and how your writing can do work in the world by suggesting assignments and activities that allow you to put your writing knowledge and skills to work in the community.

Acknowledgements

T he publication of *The Working Life* has depended on the creativity, expertise, advice, support, and encouragement of many people. I am grateful and thankful for their help in turning a promising but vague idea into the material object you hold in your hand. First of all, as a new textbook writer I relied on the professionalism, tact, and guidance of all the people at Longman who made this project possible. I wish in particular to thank Susan Kunchandy, who first encouraged me to send her a book proposal and who has championed the project from the beginning. This book would not have been possible without her. When Susan moved to another division at Longman, the project transferred smoothly to the stewardship of Joseph Opiela, who kept me on task without missing a beat. I wish also to thank, Richard Ruane, then at Longman, who helped with the first stages of the book. Rebecca Gilman in the English Composition section at Longman has provided invaluable help and advice in seeking copyright permissions and keeping me moving steadily forward. Thanks as well to Marcy Lunetta at Page to Page Publishing Services for her careful and meticulous work in securing the permissions. First Sara Wendt and later Teresa Wood helped to show me how to create the Instructor's Manual for *The Working Life* and have been more than patient in allowing me to revise deadlines. Finally, Brett Shanahan, the Project Manager for *The Working Life* at Pre-Press Company is responsible for the beautiful design of *The Working Life*. She has been a model of efficiency and responsiveness.

I am equally grateful to my colleagues at Northern Kentucky University who have provided invaluable support and who have generously shared of their knowledge and imagination. My first chair and assistant chair, Paul Reichardt and Bob Collier, allowed me to teach a writing course based on the theme of work for the first time. My current chair and friend Danny Miller has continued to provide support both material and spiritual. Our current Writing Instruction Program Director Jonathan Cullick has likewise proved a good friend and counsel. Fran Zaniello not only liked the idea of the course but also taught her own version of it and helped confirm how powerful the topic of work can be for writing students. She has provided many good ideas for readings and assignments. My fellow writing teacher Judith Blackburn was not only a philosophical co-conspirator in terms of writing pedagogy but also a role model of an instructor always willing to try new things and go in different directions. My friend and colleague Joan Ferrante, the creator of a wonderful textbook in sociology, gave me much needed advice in how to make a textbook. Most of all, I wish to thank the students in my ENG 291 Advanced Writing courses who first tried out the theme of work and read and wrote about many of the texts in *The Working Life*. As always, their generosity, insight, and tolerance served as both inspiration and validation for *The Working Life*.

Finally, my partner Kristin Dietsche and daughter Martha Dietsche-Alberti have provided love, encouragement, advice, and perhaps most of all patience throughout this long process.

I also wish to acknowledge and express my gratitude to the writing instructors across the country who read the proposal and various drafts of the manuscript. Without their endorsement of the project as well as their constructive suggestions, *The Working Life* could not have been written:

Vicki Stieha	Northern Kentucky University
Jeff E. Cravello	California State Poly University, Pomona
Antha Spreckelmeyer	University of Kansas
Pamela Katzir	Barry University
Joddy Murray	University of Syracuse
David Curtis	Belmont University
Anita Aukee Johnson	Whatcom Community College, Bellingham, WA
Lucy Schultz	University of Cincinnati
Roxanne Mountford	University of Arizona
Thomas Hallock	University of Tampa

CHAPTER 1

The Writer's Work

Working with Texts: Critical Reading and Writing

Reading and writing are work. Whether you find this statement inspiring or depressing depends on how you understand and define *work*, which is really the fundamental question *The Working Life* asks you to explore. Work can refer to doing what has to be done, bearing responsibility, shouldering the load. Work can also express a sense of accomplishment, of creating something new, as when we refer to a "work" of art.

Consider how the poet Marge Piercy, someone whose life's work is reading and writing, expresses the variety of emotions and ideas we associate with work in her poem, "To Be of Use":

The people I love the best
jump into work head first
without dallying in the shallows
and swim off with sure strokes almost out of sight.
They seem to become natives of that element,
The black sleek heads of seals
bouncing like half-submerged balls.

I love people who harness themselves, an ox to a heavy cart,
who pull like water buffalo, with massive patience,
who strain in the mud and the muck to move things forward,
who do what has to be done, again and again.

I want to be with people who submerge
in the task, who go into the fields to harvest
and work in a row and pass the bags along,
who stand in the line and haul in their places,
who are not parlor generals and field deserters
but move in a common rhythm
when the food must come in or the fire be put out.

The work of the world is common as mud.
Botched, it smears the hands, crumbles to dust.

But the thing worth doing well done
has a shape that satisfies, clean and evident.
Greek amphoras for wine or oil,
Hopi vases that held corn, are put in museums
but you know they were made to be used.
The pitcher cries for the water to carry
and a person for work that is real.

Piercy's poem expresses the idea of work as active engagement with and in the world, of work as a means of self-expression, independence, and creativity, a way of meeting the challenges of the world in a distinctive and unique way. As Piercy puts it, "work that is real." For Piercy, work is almost synonymous with life.

It is this sense of critical reading and writing as ways of doing meaningful work in the world that is at the heart of *The Working Life,* and this chapter will give you strategies for making that work a rich process of discovery, self-reflection, expression, and connection with the world.

The Work of Reading

Critical reading is not a passive activity; it is a way of doing work in the world. The best critical reading comes from active engagement, working with and sometimes against texts to find and make meaning. Such engagement starts before you pick up a text or click on a web site. It begins when you consider the work to be done and the purposes to be accomplished. Most of all, engaged reading comes from making a personal connection with the reading tasks you will do both in college and beyond.

The Work of Readers and Texts

Any reading experience consists of an encounter between two different sets of needs and motives, two different efforts to do work in the world: those of you as a reader and those of the creator or creators of the text you are reading. As a reader, you may have a number of motives and purposes that lead you to the work of reading. Some of these you may already be aware of, but others you will discover as you read:

- To fulfill an assignment.
- To find information.
- To be entertained.
- To make connections with others.

- To question the world around you.
- To explore your thoughts and feelings.

At the same time, every text you read originates in the writer's (or writers') collection of motives and purposes, some obvious and some less visible, some intentional and some accidental:

- To persuade and convince.
- To teach and inform.
- To sell.
- To amuse.
- To soothe.
- To incite to action.

Yet the crucial fact of the reading process is that none of these purposes, none of this work, can be accomplished without readers and texts working together. As many theorists have argued, texts only have meaning (some would even say texts only really exist) when they are being read. Otherwise, any piece of writing is simply a collection of inky smudges on a page. Whenever you read a book, skim a magazine, or browse a web page, you are in an important sense the cocreator of the text's meaning along with the original author(s). You and the text work together.

Sometimes this work flows easily, and sometimes it is difficult. Sometimes the work is cooperative, as when a text seems to echo and express your own thoughts and feelings. Sometimes the relationship can be antagonistic, as with a text that you disagree with or that confuses and frustrates you. And sometimes the work leads to surprising and unexpected results. In reading Marge Piercy's poem, for example, undoubtedly some in the class immediately connected with Piercy's appreciation of the virtues of hard, useful work. Others, however, may have had almost the opposite reaction, with her references to "an ox" harnessed to "a heavy cart" suggesting physical punishment and mindless drudgery. Still others may have been suspicious of poetry altogether and wondered whether there wasn't really a "hidden" meaning in the poem that it would take a teacher to puzzle out. And every once in a while a student will experience a deeper personal connection that will lead her to seek out more poetry by Marge Piercy.

Reading Is Writing

If reading is active, not passive, if it involves the reader and text in an act of cocreation, then in a very real sense reading is a kind of writing.

Web sites and hypertexts stitched together by hyperlinks have only reinforced this truth: as you choose which links to follow and in what order, you work to create the structure of the text you read, a structure that won't be identical for any two readers.

Of course, this cocreation, this cowriting that goes on in the reading process, is not arbitrary. It takes place in the field of language, and language itself—figures of speech, regional expressions, the multiple meanings of even the most common words, along with the context within which language takes place, such as the time and place when reading occurs, the particular readers involved with their varying cultural backgrounds and experiences—are all part of the dynamic, active work of reading and are all possible issues for the critical reader to consider.

Work Habits for Critical Reading

In each section of *The Working Life*, you will be presented with a variety of texts, from essays and journalism to stories, poems, and plays; from web sites, images, and pictures to cartoons, computer devices, and job application forms. Along the way, you will be given the chance to sharpen your skills in reading all these kinds of texts.

Working with Words and Images/ Words as Images: Reading in a Visual Culture

Many people have made the point that we live in a "visual" age, where the power of images increasingly supplements and even replaces traditional "print" sources. In some ways, the World Wide Web seems the ultimate embodiment of this move away from print and toward pictures as our primary means of communication. Looked at another way, however, the web moves us "back to the future" by refocusing our attention on what is really a very old issue: the visual meaning and presentation of texts.

From the beginning of writing, the visual appearance of texts has been a crucial feature of any "document," whether a Sumerian clay tablet, Egyptian hieroglyphics, a medieval illuminated text, or a modern web page. Readers have likewise always decoded texts both verbally and visually, finding and creating meaning not only in the definitions of words but also in the very real impressions created by letters that are either neatly printed, elaborately detailed, or casually scrawled, by print that is tiny and densely packed on a page or a headline that almost screams from the top of a newspaper. Think, for example, of how often we prejudge a book by skimming through its pages and noticing the size of the type and the thickness of the pages (not to mention the art on its cover, despite what the old saying tells us). Part of the work of both critical reading and writing involves becoming aware of different visual codes and conventions. Here are a few examples of different visual conventions typically encountered in college reading:

- Academic essays: This category includes papers published in scholarly journals as well as many of the traditional research papers or essays assigned in college classes. This kind of writing usually features sparse visual coding. The use of exclamation points and underlining in order to indicate emphasis is frowned upon. Part of the reasoning behind this visual minimalism is that such writing is directed at readers who already have a serious interest in the subject at hand; therefore, too many design features would be distracting. Still, even traditional academic writing makes use of the visual cues provided by paragraphs, punctuation, standardized spelling, and documentation styles.

- Textbooks: A form of academic writing, a textbook has the task of explaining information to readers who are new to a subject. As a result, textbook writers use a variety of visual cues beyond those in traditional academic writing to interest readers and to help organize information, as you will see in *The Working Life* itself: boldface headings; highlighted or boxed subsections; bulleted lists; illustrations, graphs, and diagrams.

- World Wide Web: Web pages combine conventions from both the graphic arts and print (web *pages*) traditions. Because they are still part of an emerging rhetorical tradition, the look of web pages ranges from the sparseness of academic essays to an almost overwhelming array of visual cues, in part depending on the multiple types of work done by web pages: informing, advertising, entertaining, and so on.

- E-mail and Instant Messaging (IM): Although in structure and content e-mail and IM closely resemble aspects of traditional letter writing, they also share in the visual potential of web pages, especially e-mail software that uses the same HTML code as web pages. In addition, e-mail and IM have spawned an entirely new series of visual cues in the form of shorthand acronyms for longer phrases (e.g., "FAQ" for "Frequently Asked Questions" and "IMHO" for "In my humble opinion"), creative respellings such as "GR8" and "CU" to decrease the numbers of letters needed (especially when the keyboard being used may be a cell phone), and "emoticons," sideways pictures created out of letters and punctuation marks: : -).

Learning, Choosing, and Adapting Strategies That Work for You

What follows are some general techniques, strategies, and tips to aid you in the work of critical reading, but there is no single recipe that works for every reader. Individual reading strategies vary due to learning style, gender, age, cultural background, aptitude, and interest. To extend the recipe metaphor, beginning chefs may work to master basic cooking techniques, but they then transform these techniques into unique personal styles. Some cooks may prefer using food processors and other kitchen gadgets, whereas others like doing everything by hand. Some clean up as they go and prefer an orderly workspace, whereas others thrive in an atmosphere of "organized chaos." The same is true for readers and writers.

Some Common Questions for Critical Reading: A Brief Overview

ABOUT READERS

- Why am I reading?
- What do I want to know or experience?
- What information am I looking for?
- What do I already know or believe about the subject?
- Do I want to be persuaded or supported in my opinions and beliefs?
- Do I hope to be amused or distracted?

ABOUT TEXTS

- Who created this text?
- What do I know about him/her/them?
- Why was this written?
- What work is the text trying to accomplish?
- When was this written?
- What authority claims are being made, either explicitly or implicitly?

Some Common Questions for Critical Reading: A Detailed Approach

Planning Your Work: Previewing Strategies

As with any kind of work, you need to prepare to read by thinking about your motives and purposes in reading. Actually, we do this whenever we read, whether we are aware of it or not. Sometimes our reasons are casual: we might be looking to pass the time in a waiting room or on a long airplane ride by browsing through a magazine. Other reading serves more serious, deliberate purposes, and in such cases your reading experience can be made more productive by taking a little bit of time to examine these goals:

- **Make a list of preliminary goals and purposes.** Perhaps you are looking for general background information to help familiarize yourself about a subject or issue. Maybe you want to explore a range of opinions and points of view. If you already feel strongly about a subject, you could be looking for information or authority to support your position, or you may be trying to understand how others see the situation differently. Whatever the case, be prepared to revise this list as you go along.

- **What do you already know about this topic?** Our minds integrate and process new information and ideas by relating them to what we already know and think, transforming both in the process. Ask yourself what factual information you already know (or think you know) about a subject. Where did you learn it, and how certain are you? What opinions, values, and beliefs do you already have? How strongly do you hold these beliefs, and where did you acquire them? How do you anticipate your reading might challenge or reinforce them? How easily do you think your mind could be changed?

- **What do I know about the writer(s)/creator(s) of what I am reading?** How much biographical information do you have? Is any provided with the text or web site? Is the writer/creator associated with a particular group or political perspective? How do you understand the motives of this writer/creator? What work are they trying to accomplish with their texts?

- **For web readers.** Use the "page information" command on your browser. What does it tell you about when the site was created and updated? Is this information included on the web pages as well? Web pages as well as print texts often feature a corporate "author," whether more than one person or an actual corporation or other institution. One way to determine whether the site or text represents a commercial or nonprofit organization is through the URL of the web site: ".com" or ".net" often represent businesses; ".edu" educational institutions; ".gov" government agencies; and ".org" nonprofit organizations. In any case, consider how the different potential motives implied by these address tags (for example, education versus sales) can and should affect your approach to the text.

■ **Look for visual clues.** Is there an introductory headnote (as is the case with the readings in *The Working Life*)? Does the text feature bold type? Section headings? Pop-out boxes? Charts and graphs?

■ **Look for design clues.** What impression do you get from the overall design of the text or web site? Are there primarily long or short paragraphs? For example, journalistic writing often features small, concise paragraphs, whereas academic writing tends toward longer, more expository paragraphs. How cluttered is the web site or text? What competes for your attention, and what stands out?

■ **Check the site map.** If you are looking at a web site, is there a site map that can give you a quick overview of how the site is structured?

Working with Texts: Annotating Strategies

Working with a text has both a figurative and literal meaning. While you intellectually and emotionally "work" with a text through the process of decoding and interpreting what you read, you should also physically work with the text by taking notes, writing reactions, and marking significant passages as you go. Read with a pen in hand and notebook at the ready. When marking a text, it's best to avoid highlighters. While they are useful for making text stand out, they are not very helpful when you need to respond even more actively by writing a comment in the margin or an idea in your notebook. If you are doing web reading and research, use the bookmark feature of your web browser if you are using your own computer to help you recall specific web pages.

WHAT TO MARK IN THE TEXT

■ Significant ideas, useful pieces of information, and interesting opinions.

- Places you find confusing.
- Ideas you agree and disagree with.

WHAT TO WRITE IN THE MARGINS OF THE TEXT

- Key terms or ideas in your own words.
- Your own reactions (from a long response to something as simple as "I agree!").
- Connections to other readings.

WHAT TO WRITE IN A NOTEBOOK

- Quotable material.
- Longer reactions and responses to the text.
- Future sources mentioned in the reading, bibliography, or Works Cited page.

Note: As you find ideas to use and portions of text to quote, be sure to take down accurate citation information as you go. This should include:

- Author's name.
- Full title (if an article, both article title and the name of the book or periodical from which it came).
- Publication information (where published and when; volume numbers; issue dates).
- Exact page numbers.
- Full URLs for web sites and the date you accessed them.

WHAT TO LOOK FOR ON THE WEB

- Links to explore. As you come across intriguing hyperlinks, visit them briefly to determine whether they merit further study. If so, make a quick bookmark and return to the original page. Part of the adventure of the web is following links wherever they may take you. As a researcher, you have to strike the right balance between getting off track and being open to new directions of inquiry.

Processing Your Work: Summary and Analysis

There is nothing quite like the feeling of getting to the end of a reading passage and closing the cover of a book or magazine. It's the feeling of having completed a task, of finishing a journey, of having done work. In reality, the work of critical reading is not yet done when you get to the end of the text. In order to get the most out of your work, you also should do some processing of that work, reflecting on what you've read in an organized way. While you still have pen in hand, your notebook open, or your laptop ready, do the following process and analysis work.

Summarize the reading in your own words. Write down what you see as the main points, ideas, and opinions in the text or web site.

Examine assumptions. When a newspaper story, news web site, or TV news program announces that "Most Americans are satisfied with their jobs," they may be basing that statement on a sociological study, an opinion poll, e-mail reactions they have received, or selected interviews with workers. In any case, they are also making some key assumptions: that the respondents they have heard from are representative of American workers as a whole; that "job satisfaction" means the same thing for most workers; that job satisfaction is a topic that concerns most Americans. How valid or correct these assumptions are is something every reader and viewer has to decide. Whatever you have read, the writer/creator will have made similar assumptions, often implicitly. What do you think these assumptions are, and how accurate do you take them to be?

Write down your own initial reactions. What did you agree most with or find most useful or thought provoking? What seemed most true? What did you disagree with, find confusing or irritating, think most questionable?

Usefulness. How do you think the writing fits into and contributes to the writing project you are working on?

Reliability of sources. Examine the sources and evidence cited. How reliable are they? Do you trust the sources? In the preceding example, for instance, there are several sources suggested for the statement about job satisfaction. If a survey was used, how was it conducted? How many people did it involve? Is it possible to find out how the questions were phrased? What were the actual response numbers?

Analyze tone. Language is both intellectual and emotional; appeals to both the head and the heart are parts of communication and persuasion. Write down your impression of the tone of the text. Was it confident? Angry? Distant? Friendly? How did the tone affect your reactions to the text?

Connections to other texts. Throughout *The Working Life,* you will be asked to consider how individual readings, images, and texts interrelate with others in the book. For example, a text that seems outrageous by itself may make more sense read as a satire in relation to other texts. Conversely, a very persuasive argument may seem less so in the light of other readings.

Analyze visual elements. What visuals and images—pictures, charts, illustrations, graphs—were included? As with text, visual imagery only has meaning when it is viewed and interpreted. That is, visual imagery needs to be "read" as well. Consider the composition of images and pictures. What is your eye drawn to? What is highlighted? What is in the background? What is ambiguous? What emotional response does the visual produce? How are the images connected to the text? Are they meant to reinforce ideas and opinions? Provide an example? Do they distract at all from the argument of the text?

The Work of Writing

As the kinds of activities described in "Processing Your Work" suggest, reading and writing are not two separate kinds of work. They are two parts of the same whole, the process of making meaning as a way of doing work in the world. The evidence of how embedded writing is in our day-to-day lives is all around us: whether on TV or computer screens; in magazines, newspapers, and books; in advertising, posters, and announcements that cover almost every available public space; in memos, reports, orders, and web pages. The work of writing is everywhere and assumes many different forms to do many different kinds of work.

Sometimes it might seem that writing in and for school doesn't have much impact on the world around us. Since schools, however, are very much a part of the world, they include opportunities for writing as work that has an impact on the world, whether that writing has official approval—the research paper that helps open your eyes to the seriousness of the health care coverage problem; a poem that is published in a school literary magazine; an editorial in the school paper that brings an important issue to the attention of the campus community; the creation of a collaborative web site for a campus organization—or whether the writing is "unofficial"—a thread on a listserv debating U.S. foreign policy; a collaborative web site offering student evaluations of different courses and professors on campus; graffiti placed in public spaces; even those instant messages secretly sent during a boring lecture. All these kinds of writing are highly motivated and have an effect—do some work—whether that effect is seen as positive or negative by different audiences or whether that effect is what the writer intended.

Here are a few examples of the kinds of intellectual work that writing can do, examples that you will have the opportunity to learn more about and practice in *The Working Life*. Rather than fixed types or models, think of these kinds of writing as strategies, ways of meeting specific writing challenges and contexts, tools to help you get the job done. While individual assignments may be based predominantly on one of these kinds of writing, these categories are interrelated, as you will see from the following descriptions. You can use these categories as a means of defining the work that needs to be done more clearly, but you also need to remain flexible and call on as many different types and strategies as you need.

Kinds of Writing Work

Analyzing. The work of analysis involves asking questions: about assumptions, motives, causes and effects, and meaning. These questions can be asked about the structure and purpose of a written text (the writer's motives, the persuasive strategies attempted, the organization and logic of an argument, the tone created and language used) or about a situation in the world. Analysis can also involve applying a general theory, or way of explaining a problem or issue, to a particular example of that problem or issue.

Arguing. Arguing involves the work of contrasting your own point of view with that of another and trying to convince a reader of the rightness or at least the value of your own position. Sometimes arguing can take the form of bickering and denouncing; arguing can also be a means to engage constructively with others to explore and understand the possibilities and limitations of different points of view.

Comparing/Contrasting. How do we tell whether a proposed solution has merit or not? Whether a particular concept seems sensible or outlandish? Writers will work to examine and describe similarities (comparing) and differences (contrasting) between ideas, situations, people, and positions in order to achieve a greater understanding of the subjects being considered and to help evaluate them.

Defining. Words, ideas, and concepts are by their nature slippery things, and they mean different things in different situations when used by different people. The title of Chapter 2, "The Meaning of Work: Work,

Labor, and Career," offers three examples of words that can conjure very different pictures in different people's minds. The work of defining can involve either systematically exploring the various meanings of a specific word, idea, or concept in order to appreciate the complexity of a given issue or idea or attempting to provide a stable meaning for a word, idea, or concept to accomplish some larger purpose.

Describing. Before the age of photography and the instantaneous duplication and circulation of visual images, careful verbal description, whether oral or in print, was the key means by which people passed along information about far-off places and events. Description still serves this purpose today. Experienced writers, reporters, and story-tellers know that highly detailed description plays a key role in getting and maintaining the interests of readers and listeners. In our own increasingly visual age, the art and work of verbal description has become only more important, if also more complicated. As we discussed earlier, visual images need interpretation just as much as verbal texts do. More than ever, we need to analyze closely and question the images that seem to come at us from all sides. The first step in any such analysis is careful description.

Evaluating. A form of analysis, the work of evaluating involves determining the worth or value of a particular idea, argument, or proposal by constructing a standard of judgment and then applying that standard to the work under consideration. For most students, grading may be the most familiar process of evaluation, and you know from experience that different instructors use varying standards or criteria in judging your work in class. The work of evaluating can also involve subjecting the standards themselves to critical scrutiny. In other words, even the means of evaluating can be evaluated.

Narrating. To many scholars, narrating or storytelling—the chronological, detailed description of cause and effect—is the primary form of human communication, even predating spoken language. If you think about it, narrative is the form we most often choose ourselves for our everyday communication. "You'll never believe what happened to me," we say, before launching into the story of the commute to school disrupted by a massive traffic jam, the encounter with a rude and unreasonable customer, or the chance meeting with a friend you hadn't seen for over a year. Some argue, in fact, that we can understand all forms of writing, whether a novel or a lab report, as different kinds of storytelling or narration.

Profiling. We probably encounter examples of profiling most often in journalism, whether it's a magazine story describing the main candidates in an election, a newspaper article about a local animal shelter, or a segment on a television newsmagazine about the star of the latest hit movie. Reporters, in other words, can be thought of as professional profilers. They use careful description to give us a detailed sense about a person, place, or situation.

Responding. Responding includes the activities described earlier in the section on processing your reading experience. In the larger world, responding can be part of arguing or debating, the goal being not simply to deny the views of another but to put everyone's opinions into critical perspective through comparison and contrast. The work of responding involves exploring your reactions to a particular idea or argument in order to communicate these reactions in a way that not only lets your reader know what you think in detail about what another has written or said but also places your ideas in a larger context, so that your reader can understand how your response will be useful to him or her.

Satirizing. Anyone who has seen a skit on *Saturday Night Live* or an episode of *The Simpsons* that makes fun of a popular movie, comically exaggerates the personality quirks of a celebrity or political leader, or makes a joke out of the sometimes deceptive language of advertising has encountered a form of satire. Sometimes, satire just seems like making someone or something look ridiculous simply for a laugh, but satire can also be used as an effective form of analysis, evaluation, and response. In its classical form, satire involves focusing on or exaggerating the key details of a particular person or social practice in order to show how that person or practice falls short of a specific moral or ethical ideal. In other words, satire involves using humor and careful imitation as a form of criticism, of pointing out how people or institutions fail to live up to our expectations, as when *Dilbert* imitates the language use of corporate management in order to highlight in a comic way how irrational or demeaning some workplace practices are.

Summarizing. Another way of processing the work of reading, summarizing involves describing the information, ideas, and beliefs of another in your own words. The result is not really a duplication of the work of another, but a careful description of *your own understanding* of what another person has said or written. Viewed in this way, summarizing can be understood as a crucial first step in responding or arguing, and in fact many arguments and responses include summaries of the positions being countered or reacted to.

Work Habits for Writing

As with reading, the work of writing involves exploring different strategies, techniques, and ideas about writing and then using them to develop processes that work best for you in terms of learning styles, organizational habits, personality type, available resources, and preferences. The goal of a college writing class is not to teach you *how* to write. You already know how, and there is no one "correct" way to write. The goal is to help you continue developing your writing skills and knowledge by promoting self-awareness of yourself as a writer. The more aware you become of the processes you typically use when writing, the better able you will be to evaluate those processes, try out new techniques, tricks, and strategies, and manage your time and work pace.

Common Questions for Writers: A Brief Overview

ABOUT WRITERS

- Why am I writing?
- What am I trying to accomplish?
- What do I already know, and what do I need to learn?
- What are my work specifications (i.e., length, research requirements, format, etc.)?
- How much time do I have, and how much time will I need?

ABOUT READERS

- Whom am I writing to?
- What do I know about them?
- What do I want my readers to learn, do, or experience?

Common Questions: A Detailed Approach

Planning Your Work: Preparation Strategies

For most writers, getting started is the hardest part of writing. It can seem a long, long way from the blank screen or page to the finished product. The key to getting started is taking the pressure off. You can do this by breaking down the writing task into smaller, manageable pieces, and that includes the job of getting started itself. These first strategies are all ways of beginning the project with some smaller, less intimidating tasks. Some writing textbooks refer to these techniques as "prewriting," while others resist that term because it suggests that you still aren't "writing" yet. But that lack of agreement about what to call the beginning of the writing process is the whole point, in a way. There is no "official" way to start writing. Whether you are brainstorming, making lists, skimming a text or web site, or planning out a work schedule, "writing" has begun, and you're on your way.

A note to web writers: If you are new to writing for the web, your biggest worry may be technological: how do I operate the web composing software? If a web assignment is part of your writing class, your instructor will work with you on learning the software skills you need. For planning and drafting purposes, however, old-fashioned paper will work just fine to sketch out the design of your web page. For the text part of your page, paper, pencils, pens, and a standard word processor are all you need to begin.

Analyze the assignment or task in terms of purpose: what work is to be accomplished?

For a school-based writing assignment, look for a reference to one of the writing strategies previously listed (e.g., analysis, comparison/contrast, etc.). If the assignment doesn't indicate any specific strategy, ask yourself what kinds of work you are being asked to do with your writing. These questions pertain as well to any writing task you might encounter, in or out of the classroom. For example, are you:

- Trying to demonstrate understanding of a key issue or concept? (a common writing task found on essay exams).
- Applying a concept to a specific situation or example? (another common test question).
- Trying to solve a problem?
- Forming and expressing an opinion?
- Trying to persuade your readers? Incite them? Soothe and comfort them?
- Trying to achieve greater self-awareness and understanding? (This is the work of journal keeping and diary writing.)

Analyze the assignment or task in terms of specifications: how big is the job?

Length. Many writers approach this question in a backwards way, by considering whether a given topic is capable of inspiring the writer enough to generate an essay of a given length (e.g., "how can I write five pages about the worst job I have ever had? That's only a three-page topic."). In truth, even a seemingly simple topic like the preceding one can be the basis of a book-length project, whereas a complicated subject such as globalization might be addressed in a few paragraphs in a reference work or newspaper story. The question is not what is the topic, but into how much depth and detail am I expected to go? This is the message to get from a specific page length or assigned number of words. For example, a twenty-page assignment on the future of work is asking you to do much more research and discuss the issue in greater complexity than a five-page paper on the same subject. Of course, length is a relative idea. What seems long to one writer might seem brief to another. In any case, use length guidelines as a means of determining how much time you need to spend getting information and developing your ideas.

Time. The analysis of length is linked very closely to considering how much time you have and need, and these are two very different questions. The first is easiest to determine: for school-based assignments, you will be given an overall deadline and very often intermediate deadlines for various drafts, outlines, research notes, and so forth. Other kinds of writing may come simply with a final deadline, or you may have to generate your own.

How much time you will need depends on knowing yourself as a writer. Are you someone who tends to work in short bursts of activity? In long stretches? Do you tend to procrastinate? How familiar and experienced are you with this type of writing? The newer the kind of writing work, the longer you will need to allow yourself. Will the task involve research, how much, and is it a kind of research you have done before? Whatever your answers, it's a good idea to make a time management schedule or to-do list as one of your first writing activities (it's also an easy way to get started on the project). Be realistic—allow time for the problems and setbacks that inevitably occur in any work project.

Analyze the assignment or task in terms of audience: who are your readers? The audience for your writing might be as specific as your best friend receiving your e-mail message or as varied as the range of surfers who might chance upon your web page. Even school-based assignments presume an audience, whether it is explicitly stated or not. This audience might include your instructor or the other students in the class. Sometimes a specific audience will be identified in the assignment; for example, you might be asked to write a letter to a school administrator explaining your position on the controversy surrounding clothing bearing the names and logos of colleges and universities that are manufactured in low-wage factories overseas. In a service-learning project or other nonschool writing work, audience will be a crucial issue in determining the kind of work you want your writing to do in the world. Here are some questions to consider:

- Who are your readers?
- What do you know about their beliefs, attitudes, and language styles?
- Who else besides your target audience may read your text or visit your web site?
- Which readers are you not interested in?

Analyze the assignment or task in terms of evaluation: how will you measure success? For writing that is trying to accomplish a very specific task, such as working on a grant application to secure funding for a food bank, success might be narrowly defined in terms of whether the grant is awarded or not, or it might be more broadly viewed to include learning about and gaining experience in the grant-writing process. For writing that has more complex goals, such as a research paper comparing and contrasting the meaning of work in three different cultures, success might include learning more about different cultures, exploring and revising your own attitudes about work, or honing and developing your research skills. As you can see, what constitutes "successful" writing is a complex question that can involve multiple goals and benefits, even for a writing assignment that ultimately receives a single-letter grade. Even in terms of grading, success is often measured in multiple ways, as instructors typically look for a number of features working together to define success. For graded, school-based assignments, here are some questions to consider:

- What are the grading standards being used?
- How explicit are they? That is, how much detail is given in terms of what will constitute a successful paper?
- How well do you understand these standards?

Analyze yourself: where are you starting from? What do you already know or think about the topic you are working on? Use a brainstorming technique such as freewriting, listing, or clustering to explore and create ideas and connections. Write a preliminary thesis if you can, stating the point you think you will want to make with your writing. Be prepared to focus, refine, or even completely change your thesis as your writing work continues.

Conversely, what don't you know about the topic, and what do you need to find out? What information do you need from research? Where are some likely places to get this information? (See the section on research at the end of this chapter.)

Working with Texts: Drafting and Revising Strategies

Some might think of these strategies as the "real" writing stage, but drafting and revising are no more or less real than planning, research, and editing, and no more or less important. If there is a defining characteristic to these strategies, it is the shaping process, using writing, feedback, and revision to create an increasingly complete form of the final writing project.

Expect to revise as you go. Even though your goal is to draft a complete version of your writing project, keep in mind that this project is still very much in process. Many writers get stuck or suffer from writer's block because they believe that every sentence and paragraph they write must be perfect and can never be changed. Instead, use the knowledge that major changes can still be made at any part of the drafting process to help free your creativity.

When you get stuck, skip ahead. If you have trouble with a particular section of your text, whether the introduction, your thesis, a particular example, or a transition, feel free to skip ahead to another section. Often, the experience of working on other parts of your text will help you rethink or reimagine the section that is causing you trouble.

Set reasonable work goals. As we discussed previously in terms of time management, some writers can work on a draft for an hour at a time; others need to take short breaks every fifteen or twenty minutes. Some prefer to set goals in terms of pages rather than time and vice versa. The key is to know yourself. What work habits work best for you and help you get the job done? Time management is essential.

Be open to discovery and change. Some people think of writing simply as a means of recording ideas on paper that already exist in our heads. It's an attitude writers sometimes express in frustration by saying, "But I don't know what to write about." Instead, consider the work of writing as a process of creation and discovery. It's a way of finding out what we think about a particular topic or issue, of constructing "what to write about." As you write your draft, you may find your opinions changing and evolving from what you may have had in your original plans. This is what writing is all about. Again, don't be afraid to change or revise your thesis.

Revision Strategies

As we have discussed, revision is really not a separate part of the drafting process. Although your writing class might specify a date when drafts are due and ask you to participate in peer revision groups, these kinds of work are really just a more organized and focused version of what goes on in large and small ways throughout the drafting process, from the paragraph you add to the beginning of a draft to the various versions of a conclusion you might try out. Here are some guidelines for effective revision.

Revision is not editing; work on large-scale issues first. In the final editing and polishing stage, you will focus on surface-level issues such as sentence structure, punctuation, and spelling. While the project is still taking shape, however, you and your revision readers should concentrate on larger issues such as the development of ideas, clarity of your thesis, organization of your discussion, and use of details and examples. After all, there is no point spending a lot of time working on the syntax of a particular sentence until you are pretty certain that it's a keeper.

Work with others in the revision process. As the basic shape and structure of your project come together, you need to involve the other half of the writing/reading combination by getting feedback from readers and using that feedback to continue shaping your writing. In turn, you will learn much about your own writing from making comments on the work of others.

STRATEGIES FOR GIVING HELPFUL FEEDBACK

- Read the draft-in-process all the way through once and record your general impressions.
- Try and restate the thesis and main ideas of the draft. How successful you are or the troubles you have in doing this can tell the writer what still needs work.
- Mark places where you feel ideas need more explanation or specific examples, descriptions need more details, and transitions from one section to another need to be clearer.
- Use "I" statements to describe your experience as a reader. Instead of saying, "this doesn't make sense," say, "I wasn't sure what this means."

Leave enough time for effective revision. Work to produce a draft complete enough to get effective feedback before the end of your working schedule. If your class has a due date for a preliminary draft, produce as complete a draft as you can.

Working with Texts: Editing, Proofreading, and Polishing Strategies

One of the most crucial stages in the writing process comes at the very end, when many writers feel their energy flagging. This is the stage when your project is carefully checked and polished into its final presentation form. It's also the stage when the visual aspect of writing comes back into focus, whether on paper or on the web. Many student writers (and some writing instructors) think of this as the "correction" stage, and they are not completely wrong. "Correct," though, is relative when it comes to language use, depending on who your readers are and what they believe is "correct" and whether you as a writer wish to conform to those beliefs. The way we dress makes for a good analogy. We choose our clothes and alter our appearances based on the messages we want to send and the impressions we want to make on particular people. A job interview, for example, presents a different situation than a swim party or a wedding. Although many writers feel frustrated that readers might judge the quality of their thoughts and opinions on the basis of a paper's or web site's appearance, we know from our own experience as readers that this is a fact of life. Your goal is to have as much control as possible over the impression you make.

Strategies for Effective Editing, Polishing, and Proofreading

Leave enough time for careful editing, polishing, and proofreading. One of the most common problems student writers run into involves not leaving sufficient time to work carefully on the final visual presentation of writing projects. Plan to leave at least a day before a project is due to work on polishing, and make this a conscious part of your time management planning.

Work with others in editing, polishing, and proofreading. The more involved we become in our writing, the harder it is to check for style and visual presentation. We know the text too well, and our brain automatically will fill in missing words and correct incomplete sentences. That's the reason professional publications all employ editors and proofreaders to check the work of even the most experienced writers, and the writers are glad to have them do it.

Read aloud. When we read silently, we read for meaning, and as experienced readers we no longer read one word at a time. In a way similar to what happens when we read our own writing, our brains anticipate the appearance of small words like *the*, *are*, and *to*, and we will "read" them whether they are in the text or not. When reading aloud, it is easier to force ourselves to concentrate on each individual word. If you combine reading aloud with working with others, both the reader and listener(s) can hear potential problems with sentence structure and even punctuation.

Listen to your instincts, and keep a handbook close by. You don't need to be a "grammar expert" or have all the rules of comma usage memorized to be an effective proofreader. Be suspicious of any aspect of the text that feels funny, even if you can't say exactly why. Use the handbook to help confirm or deny your suspicions, and consult with other students, your instructor, or a peer tutor.

Check all documentation carefully. Plagiarism is the use of the words or ideas of another as if they were your own. While writers sometimes plagiarize in a deliberate effort to cheat or deceive, plagiarism can also result from unfamiliarity with conventions of how to cite sources or a lack of adequate care in the editing, polishing, and proofreading stage. Be sure that whenever you include the exact words from another source in your writing that you enclose these words in quotation marks and carefully note the required publication information and page number. If you are paraphrasing or summarizing the ideas of another, be sure to include page number and publication information as well. If you are in doubt as to whether a source needs to be cited and an expert consultant such as an instructor or tutor is not available, play it safe and include the reference.

The Work of Research

When many students hear the word *research*, they think of a kind of work that is somehow special or different than ordinary writing or reading, work usually connected with the assignment of something called a "research paper." In truth, just as all reading involves an imaginative engagement with a text in the cocreation of meaning, and just as all writing involves questions of audience, context, and purpose, so too the work of research is as common as an everyday conversation. "Research" is really just a form of learning. In the broadest sense, looking out the window in the morning to see what the weather is like is a kind of research. As with reading and writing, the goal of this textbook and your writing class is to help you approach research in a deliberate, organized way that will allow you to continue developing your research skills and strategies. In general, research can be broken down into three basic categories: empirical research, text-based research, and web-based research.

Empirical research. Empirical research involves getting information firsthand from experience in the world. Such research work might involve:

- Personal experience.
- Observation/reporting.
- Interviewing.
- Conducting a survey.

Text-based research. Text-based research is probably the kind associated most with writing research papers. Obviously, this is research based on your reading in books, magazines, journals, newspapers, and other print sources, usually through a library. Some typical sources and tools for text-based research include:

- Encyclopedias.
- Electronic library catalogs (increasingly available over the Internet).
- Searchable databases of periodicals and other text-based sources.

Web-based research. In many ways, web-based research is simply a variation of text-based research. Unlike libraries, however, which carefully collect and organize text-based sources, the web is an open collection of resources with no real system of classification or oversight. This expansiveness and variety is both the web's greatest strength and its greatest challenge to researchers.

Search engines. Instead of electronic library databases, the Internet relies on web sites known as search engines to help web surfers find the information they need. These search engines, such as Yahoo, Excite, Altavista, Lycos, and Hotbot, work in similar ways to a library database: the researcher types in a name, subject, or title and the search engine looks for information in hundreds of web sites. Given the sheer size and complexity of the Internet, however, search engines typically cover only a small percentage of the web (usually no more than 15 percent at best), and results will only be partially organized. Thus, the same search terms can produce very different results at different search engine sites. Keep in mind also that most search engines are themselves commercial sites. That is, unlike most libraries, the search engines' sites make money by selling advertising space, an economic incentive that may determine which sites and subjects are most likely to come up in a search.

Meta-engines. A meta search engine automatically searches the databases of many other search engines. Such meta-engines can be very useful in getting a quick overview of what might be available on the web at the beginning of a research project. Examples of meta-engines include Google, Ask Jeeves, Dogpile, and Metacrawler.

Working with Sources: Evaluating Information

Evaluating sources is really a version of critical reading, so the same general questions apply in determining the relative reliability of the sources you encounter:

- Who is writing?
- Why?
- Who is the audience?

Questions of authority and reliability. "Authority" and "reliability" are not absolute concepts. Various factors go into determining the credibility of the information or opinions found at a given source, including the crucial question of whether you are looking for information or opinion in the first place. No one of these factors guarantees accuracy or authority. Instead, each features different strengths and weaknesses. Here is a list of some of these:

- **Personal experience**

  Strength: Writer or source has immediate firsthand knowledge of the subject.

  Weakness: Relevance of the writer's experience may be limited or may not be representative of the experience of others. It may be hard to confirm whether the experience is genuine.

- **Professional credentials**

  Strengths: Writer or source has completed a formal process of education and training and has been certified by other experts.

  Weakness: Credentials are not an automatic guarantee that the information or opinions given by the source are accurate or well reasoned. An authority may also be speaking outside of his or her area of expertise.

- Use of empirical data (statistics, records, official measurements, etc).

    Strengths: Can show that a writer's opinions and beliefs are supported by more than just personal bias.

    Weakness: Empirical data is not self-evident or obvious in its meaning or relevance. Writer may distort or exaggerate the importance of evidence.

The reliability of the Internet sources. The Internet has refocused attention on the reliability of research sources because of the openness and lack of supervision of the web. However, this does not mean that the Internet is unreliable and that print texts are. A process of editorial review and supervision does not guarantee accuracy, and questions relating to bias, point of view, and motivation apply to all texts. If anything, the diversity of sources on the web reminds us always to use the skills of critical reading in all our research.

Final Thoughts

The pitcher cries for the water to carry
and a person for work that is real.

While the work of reading and writing is, to use Marge Piercy's image, "as common as mud," it as also just as elemental, more powerful than the work of machines in shaping and changing our hearts and minds. This chapter has tried to offer some strategies, tips, and advice for beginning and managing that work. As Piercy also points out, however, the real way of making the work of reading and writing "work that is real" doesn't come from a bulleted list or set of guidelines. It comes from active engagement, from the desire to "jump into work head first" and make the work real. Good luck, and let's get to work!

CHAPTER 2

Work, Labor, and Career: the Meaning of Work

The most powerful words in our vocabulary are often the simplest: *love, family, trust, success, truth.* Even though we use them hundreds of times each day without giving them much thought, words such as these signify some of our most deeply held beliefs and powerful emotions. The social critic Raymond Williams called such terms "keywords": concepts and ideas that transmit and reproduce social values, attitudes, and ways of understanding the world. A sociologist or political scientist would refer to these keywords as the "ideology" of a culture or society. Whatever we call them, no keyword is more important than *work.*

One characteristic of these keywords, however, is that they can be tricky to define precisely. Just think of *love*, for example, and the variety of ways we use this word. Trying to come up with an overall definition can seem impossible, and we often fall back on simply saying, "Well, everybody knows what it means, even if we can't really define it." In fact, it is the ability of these words to contain different, sometimes even contradictory, meanings that allow them to function as keywords. They can produce the effect of consensus, of general agreement, even if we discover that they can operate in very different ways in different situations and mean very different things to different people.

This chapter is entitled "Work, Labor, and Career" as a way of investigating the multiple meanings of *work*. Consider these three terms. In some ways, we think of them as synonyms—words that mean more or less the same thing. Yet as the following writing suggestion will show you, these words can also convey different shades of meaning, in some cases meanings that can turn them into antonyms or opposites. As you read, discuss, and write about the texts in this chapter, return to your response to this writing suggestion in order to chart the progress of your own thinking about the meanings of work.

Preparing to Read: Writing Suggestions for the Beginning of Chapter 2

Make three columns on a piece of paper or on your computer screen. List each of the three terms, *work*, *labor*, and *career*, at the top of each column, and brainstorm a list of related words and ideas you associate with each term. Try to come up with as many as possible. When you are done, compile a group or class list of responses to each word, and then go through and evaluate each response as either "positive," "negative," or "neutral." Which word had the most positive associations? Which the most negative? Pull these findings and your reactions together by writing about them.

Foundational Readings

From the *King James Bible*, Genesis 3:17–19 ■

Creation stories serve many cultural functions beyond explaining where the world came from. In their descriptions of the origins of humanity, they transmit powerful messages about cultural values related to gender identity, how society should be governed and who rightly wields authority, and the proper roles for each member of society. The creation story from Genesis serves this purpose for three of the world's great religions: Islam, Judaism, and Christianity. After their creation in a world of abundance, immortality, and leisure, Adam and Eve violate the law against eating of the tree of knowledge and are cast out of Eden into a life of pain, death, and toil, a consequence that evokes a sense of work as a curse.

[17] And unto Adam he said, Because thou hast hearkened unto the voice of thy wife, and hast eaten of the tree, of which I commanded thee, saying, Thou shalt not eat of it: cursed is the ground for thy sake; in sorrow shalt thou eat of it all the days of thy life;
[18] Thorns also and thistles shall it bring forth to thee; and thou shalt eat the herb of the field;
[19] In the sweat of thy face shalt thou eat bread, till thou return unto the ground; for out of it wast thou taken: for dust thou art, and unto dust shalt thou return. ■

Working with the Text

1. Explore and describe your own attitudes toward work in the form of an "autobiography of work" based on your own working history, whether that work has been at home, at school, or on the job. To what extent do or don't your own attitudes reflect this idea of work as punishment?

2. Describe some specific examples of common phrases, behaviors, or social practices that similarly suggest the idea of work as a kind of punishment (the phrase "Thank God it's Friday," for example, or the idea of the Monday-morning blues). Based on these examples, express how seriously you think we believe in the idea of work as punishment.

3. If work is to be thought of as a form of punishment, does this mean that we should try to avoid or embrace work? What kinds of "work ethics" does this passage imply? Discuss your own responses in relation to your observations of your own behavior and those of others.

Working with Other Connections

1. While this passage may be one of the first in the Bible to refer specifically to work, it is by no means the last. Using an index of the Bible, locate one or two other passages that you feel either reinforce or offer a contrast to this excerpt and explain the significance of your findings.

2. How do non-Genesis-based religions discuss work? Based on your own knowledge or on more formal research, find an alternative view of work from a different religious tradition.

3. "Bartleby, the Scrivener" (featured on page 55) concerns a narrator who worries about the ethical conflict between religious teachings and the demands of business in his role as employer. Use this passage to explore how the workplace is presented in Melville's story.

ARISTOTLE

From *The Politics* ■

Like the Bible, the works of the Greek philosopher Aristotle form another foundational text in the European cultural tradition, but from a distinctly non-Biblical point of view. Writing in 350 B.C.E, Aristotle does not see work as punishment in the same way that the passage from Genesis does. However, he does see work, especially manual labor, as interfering with the development of a person's intellect and moral character. In the following passage from Book Seven of The Politics, *Aristotle considers what should qualify a person to be a "citizen"—that is, a member of society who is able to take part in the political decision-making process. Before you read, you might consider your own definition of* citizen. *What are the responsibilities of the citizen? Are there any ways a person might be disqualified from this position?*

Having determined these points, we have in the next place to consider whether all ought to share in every sort of occupation. Shall every man be at once husbandman, artisan, councillor, judge, or shall we suppose the several occupations just mentioned assigned to different persons? or, thirdly, shall some employments be assigned to individuals and others common to all? The same arrangement, however, does not occur in every constitution; as we were saying, all may be shared by all, or not all by all, but only by some; and hence arise the differences of constitutions, for in democracies all share in all, in oligarchies the opposite practice prevails. Now, since we are here speaking of the best form of government, i.e., that under which the state will be most happy (and happiness, as has been already said, cannot exist without virtue), it clearly follows that in the state which is best governed and possesses men who are just absolutely, and not merely relatively to the principle of the constitution, the citizens must not lead the life of mechanics* or tradesmen, for such a life is ignoble, and inimical to virtue. Neither must they be husbandmen, since leisure is necessary both for the development of virtue and the performance of political duties. ■

Working with the Text

1. Many contemporary Americans would probably be shocked at Aristotle's assertion that "the citizens must not lead the life of mechanics or tradesmen, for such a life is ignoble, and inimical to virtue. Neither must they be husbandmen, since leisure is necessary both for the development of virtue and the performance of political duties." Try and explain what you think Aristotle means by the idea that "leisure is necessary . . . for the development of virtue." Why would he think that hard work might prevent a person from becoming a good political decision maker? To what extent do you agree or disagree with him?

2. In a small group, brainstorm some examples of contemporary beliefs or social practices that still seem to reflect the attitudes about work, leisure, and "virtue" expressed in the preceding passage. Using some of these examples, make an argument about how widespread or significant you think these beliefs are.

3. Write a response to Aristotle in the persona of a "mechanic" or "tradesman," taking issue with his assertion that your working life does not provide you with enough leisure time to become a "virtuous" person.

*mechanics: people who do manual labor.

Working with Other Connections

1. While Aristotle makes an elitist argument about the necessity of maintaining a privileged class of people with the free time to govern effectively, his claim that leisure is necessary for virtue is echoed in this chapter from a very different political point of view in "The Abolition of Work" by Bob Black. In what ways does Black's essay make you think or react differently to the selection from Aristotle?

2. In "Social Class and the Hidden Curriculum of Work" by Jean Anyon (located in Chapter 3, "Education and Work/Education as Work"), Anyon compares the kinds of schoolwork done in different schools serving students from different socioeconomic backgrounds. Based on your reading of Aristotle, which schools seem to be doing the most effective job of cultivating "virtue" in their students? (Be sure to define carefully how you understand Aristotle's definition of "virtue.")

BENJAMIN FRANKLIN

From *The Autobiography*

Benjamin Franklin was born in Boston in 1706, the youngest of eleven children, and he grew up to become one of the most famous Americans in history. Writer, printer, satirist, politician, inventor—Franklin was not only multitalented and accomplished in a variety of fields, he was also the first notable example of "the self-made man," an idea he promoted in his Autobiography. *In describing his rise from an apprentice in his brother's print shop to his key role as one of the founders of the United States, Franklin claimed that by imitating his own actions, his readers might also follow in his footsteps. The idea of being "self-made" remains an important value in American culture: the belief that with hard work and perseverance, a person can overcome any obstacle to become a "success." In this selection from what may be America's first "self-help" book, Franklin advises his readers that such success depends on a carefully organized and managed life, and he offers a detailed plan for self-improvement. In his use of a small notebook in which he keeps track of his daily affairs and moral progress, Franklin anticipates modern notebook planners and electronic personal daily assistants such as the Personal Daily Assistant (seen in Chapter 9, "Work in the Information Age/The Future of Work").*

It was about this time that I conceiv'd the bold and arduous Project of arriving at moral Perfection. I wish'd to live without committing any Fault at any time; I would conquer all that either Natural Inclination, Custom, or Company might lead me into. As I knew, or thought I knew, what was right and wrong, I did not see why I might not *always* do the one and avoid the other. But I soon found I had undertaken a Task of more Difficulty than I had imagined. While my Care was employ'd in guarding against one Fault, I was often surpriz'd by another. Habit took the Advantage of Inattention. Inclination was sometimes too strong for Reason. I concluded at length, that the mere speculative Conviction that it was our Interest to be compleatly virtuous, was not sufficient to prevent our Slipping, and that the contrary Habits must be broken and good Ones acquired and established, before we can have any Dependance on a steady uniform Rectitude of Conduct. For this purpose I therefore contriv'd the following Method.—

In the various Enumerations of the moral Virtues I had met with in my Reading, I found the Catalogue more or less numerous, as different Writers included more or fewer Ideas under the same Name. Temperance, for Example, was by some confin'd to Eating & Drinking, while by others it was extended to mean the moderating every other Pleasure, Appetite, Inclination or Passion, bodily or mental, even to our Avarice & Ambition. I propos'd to myself, for the sake of Clearness, to use rather more Names with fewer Ideas annex'd to each, than a few Names with more Ideas; and I included under Thirteen Names of Virtues all that at that time occurr'd to me as necessary or desirable, and annex'd to each a short Precept, which fully express'd the Extent I gave to its Meaning.—

These Names of Virtues with their Precepts were

1. TEMPERANCE.

Eat not to Dulness.

Drink not to Elevation.

2. SILENCE.

Speak not but what may benefit others or your self. Avoid trifling Conversation.

3. ORDER.

Let all your Things have their Places. Let each Part of your Business have its Time.

4. RESOLUTION.

Resolve to perform what you ought. Perform without fail what you resolve.

5. FRUGALITY.

Make no Expence but to do good to others or yourself: i.e., Waste nothing.

6. INDUSTRY.

Lose no Time.—Be always employ'd in something useful.—Cut off all unnecessary Actions.—

7. SINCERITY.

Use no hurtful Deceit.

Think innocently and justly; and, if you speak; speak accordingly.

8. JUSTICE.

Wrong none, by doing Injuries or omitting the Benefits that are your Duty.

9. MODERATION.

Avoid Extreams. Forbear resenting Injuries so much as you think they deserve.

10. CLEANLINESS.

Tolerate no Uncleanness in Body, Cloaths or Habitation.—

11. TRANQUILITY

Be not disturbed at Trifles, or at Accidents common or unavoidable.

12. CHASTITY.

Rarely use Venery but for Health or Offspring; Never to Dulness, Weakness, or the Injury of your own or another's Peace or Reputation.—

13. HUMILITY.

Imitate Jesus and Socrates.—

My intention being to acquire the *Habitude* of all these Virtues, I judg'd it would be well not to distract my Attention by attempting the whole at once, but to fix it on one of them at a time, and when I should be Master of that, then to proceed to another, and so on till I should have gone thro' the thirteen. And as the previous Acquisition of some might facilitate the Acquisition of certain others, I arrang'd them with that View as they stand above. *Temperance* first, as it tends to produce that Coolness & Clearness of Head, which is so necessary where constant Vigilance was to be kept up, and Guard maintained, against the unremitting Attraction of ancient Habits, and the Force of perpetual Temptations. This being acquir'd & establish'd, *Silence* would be more easy, and my Desire being to gain Knowledge at the same time that I improv'd in Virtue, and considering that in Conversation it was obtain'd rather by the Use of the Ears than of the Tongue, & therefore wishing to break a Habit I was getting into of Prattling, Punning & Joking, which only made me acceptable to trifling Company, I gave *Silence* the second Place. This, and the next, *Order*, I expected would allow me more Time for attending to my Project and my Studies; RESOLUTION once become habitual, would keep me firm in my Endeavours to obtain all the subsequent Virtues; *Frugality* & *Industry*, by freeing me from my remaining Debt, & producing Affluence & Independance would make more easy the Practice of *Sincerity* and *Justice*, &c. &c.. Conceiving then that agreeable to the Advice of Pythagoras in his Golden Verses, daily Examination would be necessary, I contriv'd the following Method for conducting that Examination.

I made a little Book in which I allotted a Page for each of the Virtues. I rul'd each Page with red Ink so as to have seven Columns, one for each Day of the Week, marking each Column with a Letter for the Day. I cross'd these Columns with thirteen red Lines, marking the Beginning of each Line with the first Letter of one of the Virtues, on which Line & in its proper Column I might mark by a little black Spot every Fault I found upon Examination, to have been committed respecting that Virtue upon that Day.

FORM OF THE PAGES

TEMPERANCE.						
Eat not to Dulness.						
Drink not to Elevation.						
S	M	T	W	T	F	S

	S	M	T	W	T	F	S
T							
S	••	•			•	•	
O	•	•	•			•	•
R			•				
F		•			•		
I			•				
S							
J							
M							
Cl.							
T							
Ch							
H							

I determined to give a Week's strict Attention to each of the Virtues successively. Thus in the first Week my great Guard was to avoid every the least Offence against Temperance, leaving the other Virtues to their ordinary Chance, only marking every Evening the Faults of the Day. Thus if in the first Week I could keep my first Line marked T clear of Spots, I suppos'd the Habit of that Virtue so much strengthen'd and its opposite weaken'd, that I might venture extending my Attention to include the next, and for the following Week keep both Lines clear of Spots. Proceeding thus to the last, I could go thro' a Course compleat in Thirteen Weeks, and four Courses in a Year.—And like him who having a Garden to weed, does not attempt to eradicate all the bad Herbs at once, which would exceed his Reach and his Strength, but works on one of the Beds at a time, & having accomplish'd the first proceeds to a second; so I should have, (I hoped) the encouraging Pleasure of seeing on my Pages the Progress I made in Virtue, by clearing successively my Lines of their Spots, till in the End by a Number of Courses, I should be happy in viewing a clean Book after a thirteen Weeks daily Examination.

The Precept of *Order* requiring that *every Part of my Business should have its allotted Time,* one Page in my little Book contain'd the following Scheme on Employment for the Twenty-four Hours of a natural Day.

The Morning Question, What Good Shall I do this Day?	5	Rise, wash, and address *Powerful Goodness;* contrive Day's Business and take the Resolution of the Day; prosecute the present Study: and breakfast?—
	6	
	7	
	8	
	9	Work.
	10	
	11	
	12	Read, or overlook my Accounts, and dine.
	1	
	2	
	3	Work.
	4	
	5	
Evening Question, What Good have I done to day?	6	Put Things in their Places, Supper, Musick, or Diversion, or Conversation, Examination of the Day.
	7	
	8	
	9	
	10	
	11	
	12	
	1	Sleep—
	2	
	3	
	4	

I enter'd upon the Execution of this Plan for Self Examination, and continu'd it with occasional Intermissions for some time. I was surpriz'd to find myself so much fuller of Faults than I had imagined, but I had the Satisfaction of seeing them diminish. To avoid the Trouble of renewing now & then my little Book, which by scraping out the Marks on the Paper of old Faults to make room for new Ones in a new Course, became full of Holes: I transferr'd my Tables & Precepts to the Ivory Leaves of a Memorandum Book, on which the Lines were drawn with red Ink that made a durable Stain, and on those Lines I mark'd my Faults with a black Lead Pencil, which Marks I could easily wipe out with a wet Sponge. After a while I went thro' one Course only in a Year, and afterwards only one in several Years; till at length I omitted them entirely, being employ'd in Voyages & Business abroad with a Multiplicity of Affairs, that interfered. But I always carried my little Book with me. My Scheme of ORDER, gave me the most Trouble, and I found, that tho' it might be practicable where a Man's Business was such as to leave him the Disposition of his Time, that of a Journey-man Printer for instance, it was not possible to be exactly observ'd by a Master, who must mix with the World, and often receive People of Business at their own Hours.—*Order* too, with regard to Places for Things, Papers, &c. I found extreamly difficult to acquire. I had not been early accustomed to it, & having an exceeding good Memory, I was not so sensible of the Inconvenience attending Want of Method. This Article therefore cost me so much painful Attention & my Faults in it vex'd me so much, and I made so little Progress in Amendment, & had such frequent Relapses, that I was almost ready to give up the Attempt, and content my self with a faulty Character in that respect. Like the Man who in buying an Ax of a Smith my Neighbour, desired to have the whole of its Surface as bright as the Edge; the Smith consented to grind it bright for him if he would turn the Wheel. He turn'd while the Smith press'd the broad Face of the Ax hard & heavily on the Stone, which made the Turning of it very fatiguing. The Man came every now & then from the Wheel to see how the Work went on; and at length would take his Ax as it was without farther Grinding. No, says the Smith, Turn on, turn on; we shall have it bright by and by; as yet 'tis only speckled. Yes, says the Man; but—*I think I like a speckled Ax best.*—And I believe this may have been the Case with many who having for want of some such Means as I employ'd found the Difficulty of obtaining good, & breaking bad Habits, in other Points of Vice & Virtue, have given up the Struggle, & concluded that *a speckled Ax was best.* For something that pretended to be Reason was every now and then suggesting to me, that such extream Nicety as I exacted of my self might be a kind of Foppery in Morals, which if it were known would make me ridiculous; that a perfect Character might be attended with the Inconvenience of being envied and hated; and that a benevolent Man should allow a few Faults in himself, to keep his Friends in Countenance. In Truth I found myself incorrigible with respect to *Order;* and now I am grown old, and my Memory bad, I feel very sensibly the want of it. But on the whole, tho' I never arrived at the Perfection I had been so ambitious of obtaining, but fell far short of it, yet I was by the Endeavour made a better and a happier Man than I otherwise should have been, if I had not attempted it; As those who aim at perfect Writing by imitating the engraved Copies, tho' they never reach the wish'd for Excellence of those Copies, their Hand is mended by the Endeavour, and is tolerable while it continues fair & legible.— ■

Working with the Text

1. Try Franklin's project for yourself. Work in a group to come up with a list of contemporary versions of the virtues that Franklin describes. Then devise a daily, hour-by-hour schedule that you think fits your working and school life and write an essay recommending your plan, perhaps in imitation of Franklin's distinctive eighteenth-century writing style. If you want to take this experiment even further, spend a week trying to follow your plan and

write up the results along with your conclusions about what these results say about the practicality and effectiveness of leading such an organized life.

2. At the end of the selection, Franklin concludes, "tho' I never arrived at the Perfection I had been so ambitious of obtaining, but fell far short of it, yet I was by the Endeavour made a better and a happier Man than I otherwise should have been." Readers of Franklin have long argued about how serious or satirical Franklin is in making his recommendations, given that he admits to failure while also claiming to have been improved by the experience. Use specific evidence from the text to explain how serious or satirical you think Franklin is being in his advice.

3. The extreme version of the idea of the "self-made" person implies that the kind of discipline and organization Franklin recommends will enable us to overcome any social disadvantage. Based on your observations and experiences, write a critique of the "self-made" person concept that addresses potential problems with this idea.

Working with Connections

1. Horatio Alger's *Ragged Dick* novels were directly inspired by the self-made example of people like Franklin. What connections can you find between the preceding excerpt from Franklin's life and the selection from Alger's *Ragged Dick* on page 49.

2. In the excerpt from her book *Nickel and Dimed: On (Not) Getting by in America* (in Chapter 4, "Work and Social Class"), Barbara Ehrenreich describes a group of professional house cleaners who face social obstacles related to access to health care and other resources that she implies cannot be overcome through individual effort alone. Write either as Ehrenreich responding to Franklin's plan or as Franklin commenting on Ehrenreich's book.

3. Even though his *Autobiography* is addressed specifically to his son, Franklin focuses little on his family life in his book, thus suggesting how gender roles affect the idea of the self-made person. Use the issues raised by Juliet B. Schor in *The Overworked American* or in Deb Casey's poem "ZOOOOOOOM A Familiar Story: Drop-off/Pick-up Panic" (both in Chapter 5, "Work and Family") to discuss how family responsibilities would complicate Franklin's ideal of a perfectly organized life.

BOB BLACK ▄

From The Abolition of Work

*Is work necessary? While there are many arguments about what consti-
tutes meaningful work and just working conditions, we might think there
would be general agreement that work is an inevitable part of life. Our
assumptions, however, may just depend on how exactly we define the
idea of "work." In "The Abolition of Work," Bob Black asks us to rethink
our basic assumptions about the value of work and the importance of a
job by making an extreme argument for the abolition of work and the
promotion of play, an argument he says is both "joking and serious." Bob
Black is a former lawyer who was involved in various kinds of political
activism in the 1970s before becoming a leading proponent of the Zero
Work Movement, dedicated to challenging many of our fundamental
beliefs about work in the modern world.*

*Before reading Black's essay, write about your reactions to the title,
"The Abolition of Work." What do you think Black means by this idea?
What would a world without work look like? What practical or philosoph-
ical questions does the idea of "The Abolition of Work" raise for you?*

No one should ever work.

Work is the source of nearly all the misery in the world. Almost any evil you'd
care to name comes from working or from living in a world designed for work.
In order to stop suffering, we have to stop working.

That doesn't mean we have to stop doing things. It does mean creating a
new way of life based on play; in other words, a ludic revolution. By "play" I
mean also festivity, creativity, conviviality, commensality, and maybe even art.
There is more to play than child's play, as worthy as that is. I call for a collective
adventure in generalized joy and freely interdependent exuberance. Play isn't
passive. Doubtless we all need a lot more time for sheer sloth and slack than we
ever enjoy now, regardless of income or occupation, but once recovered from
employment-induced exhaustion nearly all of us want to act.

The ludic life is totally incompatible with existing reality. So much the worse
for "reality," the gravity hole that sucks the vitality from the little in life that still
distinguishes it from mere survival. Curiously—or maybe not—all the old ideologies are conservative because they believe in work. Some of them, like Marxism
and most brands of anarchism, believe in work all the more fiercely because
they believe in so little else.

Liberals say we should end employment discrimination. I say we should end
employment. Conservatives support right-to-work laws. Following Karl Marx's
wayward son-in-law Paul Lafargue I support the right to be lazy. Leftists favor full
employment. Like the surrealists—except that I'm not kidding—I favor full
un*employment. Trotskyists agitate for permanent revolution. I agitate for permanent revelry. But if all the ideologues (as they do) advocate work—and not

only because they plan to make other people do theirs—they are strangely reluctant to say so. They will carry on endlessly about wages, hours, working conditions, exploitation, productivity, profitability. They'll gladly talk about anything but work itself. These experts who offer to do our thinking for us rarely share their conclusions about work, for all its saliency in the lives of all of us. Among themselves they quibble over the details. Unions and management agree that we ought to sell the time of our lives in exchange for survival, although they haggle over the price. Marxists think we should be bossed by bureaucrats. Libertarians think we should be bossed by businessmen. Feminists don't care which form bossing takes, so long as the bosses are women. Clearly these ideology-mongers have serious differences over how to divvy up the spoils of power. Just as clearly, none of them have any objection to power as such and all of them want to keep us working.

You may be wondering if I'm joking or serious. I'm joking *and* serious. To be ludic is not to be ludicrous. Play doesn't have to be frivolous, although frivolity isn't triviality; very often we ought to take frivolity seriously. I'd like life to be a game—but a game with high stakes. I want to play *for keeps*.

The alternative to work isn't just idleness. To be ludic is not to be quaaludic. As much as I treasure the pleasure of torpor, it's never more rewarding than when it punctuates other pleasures and pastimes. Nor am I promoting the managed time-disciplined safety-valve called "leisure"; far from it. Leisure is nonwork for the sake of work. Leisure is the time spent recovering from work and in the frenzied but hopeless attempt to forget about work. Many people return from vacations so beat that they look forward to returning to work so they can rest up. The main difference between work and leisure is that at work at least you get paid for your alienation and enervation.

I am not playing definitional games with anybody. When I say I want to abolish work, I mean just what I say, but I want to say what I mean by defining my terms in non-idiosyncratic ways. My minimum definition of work is forced *labor*, that is, compulsory production. Both elements are essential. Work is production enforced by economic or political means, by the carrot or the stick. (The carrot is just the stick by other means.) But not all creation is work. Work is never done for its own sake, it's done on account of some product or output that the worker (or, more often, somebody else) gets out of it. This is what work necessarily is. To define it is to despise it. But work is usually even worse than its definition decrees. The dynamic of domination intrinsic to work tends over time toward elaboration. In advanced work-riddled societies, including all industrial societies whether capitalist of "communist," work invariably acquires other attributes which accentuate its obnoxiousness.

Usually—and this is even more true in "communist" than capitalist countries, where the state is almost the only employer and everyone is an employee—work is employment, i.e., wage-labor, which means selling yourself on the installment plan. Thus 95% of Americans who work, work for somebody (or some*thing*) else. In the USSR or Cuba or Yugoslavia or Nicaragua or any other alternative model which might be adduced, the corresponding figure approaches 100%. Only the embattled Third World peasant bastions—Mexico, India, Brazil, Turkey—temporarily shelter significant concentrations of agriculturists who perpetuate the traditional arrangement of most laborers in the last several millennia, the payment of taxes (= ransom) to the state or rent to parasitic landlords in return for being otherwise left alone. Even this raw deal is beginning to look good. *All* industrial (and office) workers are employees and under the sort of surveillance which ensures servility.

But modern work has worse implications. People don't just work, they have "jobs." One person does one productive task all the time on an or-else basis. Even if the task has a quantum of intrinsic interest (as increasingly many jobs don't) the monotony of its obligatory exclusivity drains its ludic potential. A "job" that might engage the energies of some people, for a reasonably limited time, for the fun of it, is just a burden on those who have to do it for forty hours a week with no say in how it should be done, for the profit of owners who contribute nothing to the project, and with no opportunity for sharing tasks or spreading the work among those who actually have to do it. This is the real world of work: a world of bureaucratic blundering, of sexual harassment and discrimination, of bonehead bosses exploiting and scapegoating their subordinates who—by any rational/technical criteria—should be calling the shots. But capitalism in the real world subordinates the rational maximization of productivity and profit to the exigencies of organizational control.

The degradation which most workers experience on the job is the sum of assorted indignities which can be denominated as "discipline." Foucault has complexified this phenomenon but it is simple enough. Discipline consists of the totality of totalitarian controls at the workplace—surveillance, rote-work, imposed work tempos, production quotas, punching-in and -out, etc. Discipline is what the factory and the office and the store share with the prison and the school and the mental hospital. It is something historically original and horrible. It was beyond the capacities of such demonic dictators of yore as Nero and Genghis Khan and Ivan the Terrible. For all their bad intentions they just didn't have the machinery to control their subjects as thoroughly as modern despots do. Discipline is the distinctively diabolical modern mode of control, it is an innovative intrusion which must be interdicted at the earliest opportunity.

Such is "work." Play is just the opposite. Play is always voluntary. What might otherwise be play is work if it's forced. This is axiomatic. Bernie de Koven has defined play as the "suspension of consequences." This is unacceptable if it implies that play is inconsequential. The point is not that play is without consequences. This is to demean play. The point is that the consequences, if any, are gratuitous. Playing and giving are closely related, they are the behavioral and transactional facets of the same impulse, the play-instinct. They share an aristocratic disdain for results. The player gets something out of playing; that's why he plays. But the core reward is the experience of the activity itself (whatever it is). Some otherwise attentive students of play, like Johan Huizinga (*Homo Ludens*), *define* it as gameplaying or following rules. I respect Huizinga's erudition but emphatically reject his constraints. There are many good games (chess, baseball,

Monopoly, bridge) which are rule-governed but there is much more to play than game-playing. Conversation, sex, dancing, travel—these practices aren't rule-governed but they are surely play if anything is. And rules can be *played with* at least as readily as anything else.

Work makes a mockery of freedom. The official line is that we all have rights and live in a democracy. Other unfortunates who aren't free like we are have to live in police states. These victims obey orders or else, no matter how arbitrary. The authorities keep them under regular surveillance. State bureaucrats control even the smaller details of everyday life. The officials who push them around are answerable only to higher-ups, public or private. Either way, dissent and disobedience are punished. Informers report regularly to the authorities. All this is supposed to be a very bad thing.

And so it is, although it is nothing but a description of the modern workplace. The liberals and conservatives and Libertarians who lament totalitarianism are phonies and hypocrites. There is more freedom in any moderately deStalinized dictatorship than there is in the ordinary American workplace. You find the same sort of hierarchy and discipline in an office or factory as you do in a prison or a monastery. In fact, as Foucault and others have shown, prisons and factories came in at about the same time, and their operators consciously borrowed from each other's control techniques. A worker is a part-time slave. The boss says when to show up, when to leave, and what to do in the meantime. He tells you how much work to do and how fast. He is free to carry his control to humiliating extremes, regulating, if he feels like it, the clothes you wear or how often you go to the bathroom. With a few exceptions he can fire you for any reason, or no reason. He has you spied on by snitches and supervisors, he amasses a dossier on every employee. Talking back is called "insubordination," just as if a worker is a naughty child, and it not only gets you fired, it disqualifies you for unemployment compensation. Without necessarily endorsing it for them either, it is noteworthy that children at home and in school receive much the same treatment, justified in their case by their supposed immaturity. What does this say about their parents and teachers who work?

Let's pretend for a moment that work doesn't turn people into stultified submissives. Let's pretend, in defiance of any plausible psychology and the ideology of its boosters, that it has no effect on the formation of character. And let's pretend that work isn't as boring and tiring and humiliating as we all know it really is. Even then, work would *still* make a mockery of all humanistic and democratic aspirations, just because it usurps so much of our time. Socrates said that manual laborers make bad friends and bad citizens because they have no time to fulfill the responsibilities of friendship and citizenship. He was right. Because of work, no matter what we do, we keep looking at our watches. The only thing "free" about so-called free time is that it doesn't cost the boss anything. Free time is mostly devoted to getting ready for work, going to work, returning from work, and recovering from work. Free time is a euphemism for the peculiar way labor, as a factor of production not only transports itself at its own expense to and from the workplace, but assumes primary responsibility for its own maintenance and repair. Coal and steel don't do that. Lathes and typewriters don't do that. No wonder Edward G. Robinson in one of his gangster movies exclaimed, "Work is for saps!"

Both Plato and Xenophon attribute to Socrates and obviously share with him an awareness of the destructive effects of work on the worker as a citizen and as a human being. Herodotus identified contempt for work as an attribute of the classical Greeks at the zenith of their culture. To take only one Roman example, Cicero said that "whoever gives his labor for money sells himself and puts himself in the rank of slaves." His candor is now rare, but contemporary primitive societies which we are wont to look down upon have provided spokesmen who have enlightened Western anthropologists. The Kapauku of West Irian, according to Pospisil, have a conception of balance in life and accordingly work only every other day, the day of rest designed "to regain the lost power and health." Our ancestors, even as late as the eighteenth century when they were far along the path to our present predicament, at least were aware of what we have forgotten, the underside of industrialization. Their religious devotion to "St. Monday"—thus establishing a de facto five-day week 150–200 years before its legal consecration—was the despair of the earliest factory owners. They took a long time in submitting to the tyranny of the bell, predecessor of the time clock. In fact it was necessary for a generation or two to replace adult males with women accustomed to obedience and children who could be molded to fit industrial needs. Even the exploited peasants of the *ancien regime* wrested substantial time back from their landlord's work. According to Lafargue, a fourth of the French peasants' calendar was devoted to Sundays and holidays, and Chayanov's figures from villages in Czarist Russia—hardly a progressive society—likewise show a fourth or fifth of peasants' days devoted to repose. Controlling for productivity, we are obviously far behind these backward societies. The exploited *muzhiks* would wonder why any of us are working at all. So should we.

To grasp the full enormity of our deterioration, however, consider the earliest condition of humanity, without government or property, when we wandered as hunter-gatherers. Hobbes surmised that life was then nasty, brutish and short. Others assume that life was a desperate unremitting struggle for subsistence, a war waged against a harsh Nature with death and disaster awaiting the unlucky or anyone who was unequal to the challenge of the struggle for existence. Actually, that was all a projection of fears for the collapse of government authority over communities unaccustomed to doing without it, like the England of Hobbes during the Civil War. Hobbes' compatriots had already encountered alternative forms of society which illustrated other ways of life—in North America, particularly—but already these were too remote from their experience to be understandable. (The lower orders, closer to the condition of the Indians, understood it better and often found it attractive. Throughout the seventeenth century, English settlers defected to Indian tribes or, captured in war, refused to return to the colonies. But the Indians no more defected to white settlements than West Germans climb the Berlin Wall from the west.) The "survival of the fittest" version—the Thomas Huxley version—of Darwinism was a better account of economic conditions in Victorian England than it was of natural selection, as the anarchist Kropotkin showed in his book *Mutual Aid, A Factor in Evolution*. (Kropotkin was a scientist who'd had ample involuntary opportunity for fieldwork whilst exiled in Siberia: he knew what he was talking about.) Like most social and political theory, the story Hobbes and his successors told was really unacknowledged autobiography.

The anthropologist Marshall Sahlins, surveying the data on contemporary hunter-gatherers, exploded the Hobbesian myth in an article entitled "The Original Affluent Society." They work a lot less than we do, and their work is hard to distinguish from what we regard as play. Sahlins concluded that "hunters and gatherers work less than we do; and, rather than a continuous travail, the food quest is intermittent, leisure abundant, and there is a greater amount of sleep in the daytime per capita per year than in any other condition of society." They worked an average of four hours a day, assuming they were "working" at all. Their "labor," as it appears to us, was skilled labor which exercised their physical and intellectual capacities; unskilled labor on any large scale, as Sahlins says, is impossible except under industrialism. Thus it satisfied Friedrich Schiller's definition of play, the only occasion on which man realizes his complete humanity by giving full "play" to both sides of his twofold nature, thinking and feeling. Play and freedom are, as regards production, coextensive. Even Marx, who belongs (for all his good intentions) in the productivist pantheon, observed that "the realm of freedom does not commence until the point is passed where labor under the compulsion of necessity and external utility is required." He never could quite bring himself to identify this happy circumstance as what it is, the abolition of work—it's rather anomalous, after all, to be pro-worker and anti-work—but we can.

What I've said so far ought not to be controversial. Many workers are fed up with work. There are high and rising rates of absenteeism, turnover, employee theft and sabotage, wildcat strikes, and overall goldbricking on the job. There may be some movement toward a conscious and not just visceral rejection of work. And yet the prevalent feeling, universal among bosses and their agents and also widespread among workers themselves, is that work itself is inevitable and necessary.

I disagree. It is now possible to abolish work and replace it, insofar as it serves useful purposes, with a multitude of new kinds of free activities. To abolish work requires going at it from two directions, quantitative and qualitative. On the one hand, on the quantitative side, we have to cut down massively on the amount of work being done. At present most work is useless or worse and we should simply get rid of it. On the other hand—and I think this is the crux of the matter and the revolutionary new departure—we have to take what useful work remains and transform it into a pleasing variety of game-like and craft-like pastimes, indistinguishable from other pleasurable pastimes except that they happen to yield useful end-products. Surely that shouldn't make them *less* enticing to do. Then all the artificial barriers of power and property could come down. Creation could become recreation. And we could all stop being afraid of each other.

I don't suggest that most work is salvageable in this way. But then most work isn't worth trying to save. Only a small and diminishing fraction of work serves any useful purpose independent of the defense and reproduction of the work-system and its political and legal appendages. Twenty years ago, Paul and Percival Goodman estimated that just five percent of the work then being done—presumably the figure, if accurate, is lower now—would satisfy our minimal needs for food, clothing, and shelter. Theirs was only an educated guess but the main point is quite clear: directly or indirectly, most work serves the unproductive purposes of commerce or social control. Right off the bat we can liberate tens of millions of salesmen, soldiers, managers, cops, stockbrokers, clergymen, bankers, lawyers, teachers, landlords, security guards, ad-men and everyone who works for them. There is a snowball effect since every time you idle some bigshot you liberate his flunkeys and underlings also. Thus the economy *implodes.*

Forty percent of the workforce are white-collar workers, most of whom have some of the most tedious and idiotic jobs ever concocted. Entire industries, insurance and banking and real estate for instance, consist of nothing but useless paper-shuffling. It is no accident that the "tertiary sector," the service sector, is growing while the "secondary sector" (industry) stagnates and the "primary sector" (agriculture) nearly disappears. Because work is unnecessary except to those whose power it secures, workers are shifted from relatively useful to relatively useless occupations as a measure to assure public order. Anything is better than nothing. That's why you can't go home just because you finish early. They want your *time,* enough of it to make you theirs, even if they have no use for most of it. Otherwise why hasn't the average work week gone down by more than a few minutes in the past fifty years?

Next we can take a meat-cleaver to production work itself. No more war production, nuclear power, junk food, feminine hygiene deodorant—and above all, no more auto industry to speak of. An occasional Stanley Steamer or Model T might be all right, but the auto-eroticism on which such pestholes as Detroit and Los Angeles depend is out of the question. Already, without even trying, we've virtually solved the energy crisis, the environmental crisis and assorted other insoluble social problems.

Finally, we must do away with far and away the largest occupation, the one with the longest hours, the lowest pay and some of the most tedious tasks. I refer to *housewives* doing housework and child-rearing. By abolishing wage-labor and achieving full unemployment we undermine the sexual division of labor. The nuclear family as we know it is an inevitable adaptation to the division of labor imposed by modern wage-work. Like it or not, as things have been for the last century or two, it is economically rational for the man to bring home the bacon, for the woman to do the shitwork to provide him with a haven in a heartless world, and for the children to be marched off to youth concentration camps called "schools," primarily to keep them out of Mom's hair but still under control, but incidentally to acquire the habits of obedience and punctuality so necessary for workers. If you would be rid of patriarchy, get rid of the nuclear family whose unpaid "shadow work," as Ivan Illich says, makes possible the work-system that makes *it* necessary. Bound up with this no-nukes strategy is the abolition of childhood and the closing of the schools. There are more full-time students than full-time workers in this country. We need children as teachers, not students. They have a lot to contribute to the ludic revolution because they're better at playing than grown-ups are. Adults and children are not identical but they will become equal through interdependence. Only play can bridge the generation gap.

What I really want to see is work turned into play. A first step is to discard the notions of a "job" and an "occupation." Even activities that already have some ludic content lose most of it by being reduced to jobs which certain people, and only those people, are forced to do to the exclusion of all else. Is it not odd that farm workers toil painfully in the fields while their air-conditioned masters go home every weekend and putter about in their gardens? Under a system of permanent revelry, we will witness the Golden Age of the dilettante which will put the Renaissance to shame. There won't be any more jobs, just things to do and people to do them.

The secret of turning work into play, as Charles Fourier demonstrated, is to arrange useful activities to take advantage of whatever it is that various people at various times in fact enjoy doing. To make it possible for some people to do the things they could enjoy, it will be enough just to eradicate the irrationalities and distortions which afflict these activities when they are reduced to work. I, for instance, would enjoy doing some (not too much) teaching, but I don't want coerced students and I don't care to suck up to pathetic pedants for tenure.

Second, there are some things that people like to do from time to time, but not for too long, and certainly not all the time. You might enjoy baby-sitting for a few hours in order to share the company of kids, but not as much as their parents do. The parents meanwhile, profoundly appreciate the time to themselves that you free up for them, although they'd get fretful if parted from their progeny for too long. These differences among individuals are what make a life of free play possible. The same principle applies to many other areas of activity, especially the primal ones. Thus many people enjoy cooking when they can practice it seriously at their leisure, but not when they're just fuelling up human bodies for work.

Third, other things being equal, some things that are unsatisfying if done by yourself or in unpleasant surroundings or at the orders of an overlord are enjoyable, at least for a while, if these circumstances are changed. This is probably true, to some extent, of all work. People deploy their otherwise wasted ingenuity to make a game of the least inviting drudge-jobs as best they can. Activities that appeal to some people don't always appeal to all others, but everyone at least potentially has a variety of interests and an interest in variety. As the saying goes, "anything once." Fourier was the master at speculating about how aberrant and perverse penchants could be put to use in post-civilized society, what he called Harmony. He thought the Emperor Nero would have turned out all right if as a child he could have indulged his taste for bloodshed by working in a slaughterhouse. Small children who notoriously relish wallowing in filth could be organized in "Little Hordes" to clean toilets and empty the garbage, with medals awarded to the outstanding. I am not arguing for these precise examples but for the underlying principle, which I think makes perfect sense as one dimension of an overall revolutionary transformation. Bear in mind that we don't have to take today's work just as we find it and match it up with the proper people, some of whom would have to be perverse indeed.

If technology has a role in all this, it is less to automate work out of existence than to open up new realms for re/creation. To some extent we may want to return to handicrafts, which William Morris considered a probable and desirable upshot of communist revolution. Art would be taken back from the snobs and collectors, abolished as a specialized department catering to an elite audience, and its qualities of beauty and creation restored to integral life from which they were stolen by work. It's a sobering thought that the Grecian urns we write odes about and showcase in museums were used in their own time to store olive oil. I doubt our everyday artifacts will fare as well in the future, if there is one. The point is that there's no such thing as progress in the world of work; if anything it's just the opposite. We shouldn't hesitate to pilfer the past for what it has to offer, the ancients lose nothing yet we are enriched.

So the abolitionists will be largely on their own. No one can say what would result from unleashing the creative power stultified by work. Anything can happen. The tiresome debater's problem of freedom vs. necessity, with its theological overtones, resolves itself practically once the production of use-values is coextensive with the consumption of delightful play-activity.

Life will become a game, or rather many games, but not—as it is now—a zero/sum game. An optimal sexual encounter is the paradigm of productive play. The participants potentiate each other's pleasures, nobody keeps score, and everybody wins. The more you give, the more you get. In the ludic life, the best of sex will diffuse into the better part of daily life. Generalized play leads to the libidinization of life. Sex, in turn, can become less urgent and desperate, more playful. If we play our cards right, we can all get more out of life than we put into it; but only if we play for keeps.

Workers of the world . . . RELAX! ■

Working with the Text

1. In making up your own mind about what Black writes, identify and write about three specific statements he makes that you find most persuasive or relevant to your own experience. Now identify and write about three specific statements that you most disagree with.

2. We can categorize Black's essay as a manifesto, or a statement of core beliefs and a call to action. As a way of exploring Black's ideas further, turn his essay into a list of what you see as his main beliefs and what specific action you think he is urging us to take.

3. Black deliberately tries to shake up our thinking by reversing the usual order of importance we assign to the ideas of "work" and "play," arguing instead that play is more important than work. Come up with another pair of opposing terms related to work and

try your hand at writing an argument that makes the same kind of reversal that Black does.

4. Black claims he is being both "joking and serious" at the same time in his essay. Could you write an equally playful response to Black, expressing your reaction to his ideas?

Working with Connections

1. Kathryn Carmony's "Surfing the Classifieds" is an equally playful critique of contemporary work-for-pay practices. What aspects of Carmony's satire most reinforce the arguments made by Black?

2. Black says he agrees with the claim of Socrates, the famous Greek philosopher immortalized by his student Plato and who equally influenced Aristotle, that "manual laborers make bad friends and bad citizens because they have no time to fulfill the responsibilities of friendship and citizenship." In what ways does Black's argument cause you to think differently about the selection from Aristotle? What would your strongest counterargument be to both philosophers of work?

3. In "Summertime Dues" (in Chapter 7, "Ethics of Work/The Work Ethic"), the novelist Walter Kirn describes the not very positive values he feels he learned from his summer jobs as a youth. Write what you think Black's response would be to Kirn's essay in the form of a letter to the editor of the periodical that published it, either in your own voice or in an imitation of Black's style.

Reading the Web

MONSTER.COM

■

Monster.com is an Internet business that helps connect job seekers with employers. Beyond offering a job-finding service, the company also promotes and markets a particular attitude, almost an ideology or philosophy, toward work and the "job market." On the next page is an example of the company home page from 2002.

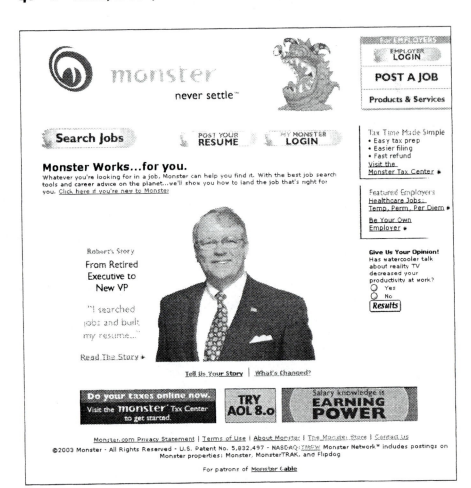

Working with the Text

1. What attitudes, assumptions, and ideas about work do you think the web site wants to project, and what about the page leads you to feel this way? Among the components you might consider:

   ■ The name of the web site and the cartoon monsters that act as logos for the company. What levels of seriousness or playfulness do these images project? What do you think the strategies are behind these images, and how successful do you find them? Do they make you more or less receptive to the web site?

   ■ What kinds of people do you think the home page is trying to attract? Do you feel that you are a part of that audience? Why or why not?

   ■ How clear are the services being offered by the web site? Would you feel confident navigating the site?

2. Visit a current version of Monster.com and explore the web site with a particular eye to services aimed at college students. How do the images and language used express a particular view of what college students are like, and how accurate or successful do you find this view?

3. How might the commercial motives driving the web site affect the presentation they offer to their visitors? How does the site seem to fit into the larger rhetorical strategy of the company's overall marketing campaign, as evidenced by other advertising (print ads, television commercials) you might be familiar with.

Work on the Web

1. Working as a team, write a critique of either the web page illustrated here or a current version of Monster.com. You may choose to write a critique aimed at giving the company feedback on how successful you think their appeal to college students is, or you may aim your critique at other college students, offering them a guide and interpretation to the web site.

2. Working as a team, design an alternative home page offering visitors your own ideas and attitudes about finding a job. Consider whether you want your own home page to function as a revision, a radically different alternative, or a satirical parody of the Monster.com page.

Stories of Work

HORATIO ALGER
From *Ragged Dick*
■

Horatio Alger (1832–1899) was an enormously popular writer of novels for young people in the late nineteenth century whose most famous stories describe how poor boys manage, through "luck and pluck," to overcome hardship and transform themselves into "respectable" members of society. In many ways, these fictional success stories embody the myth of the self-made man we have seen in Benjamin Franklin's Autobiography, *and Alger's novels inspired the phrase "rags to riches." Alger published over 100 of these stories between 1867 and his death in 1899. This excerpt is the conclusion to his first and perhaps most famous novel,* Ragged Dick. *At the beginning of the novel, Dick is a boy of fourteen living on the streets of New York and earning a meager living as a shoeshine boy. Unable to read or write but blessed with a strong moral*

*character and "enterprise" (a favorite word of Alger's), Dick sets out to
turn himself into a prosperous, middle-class success.*

Dick now began to look about for a position in a store or countingroom. Until
he should obtain one he determined to devote half the day to blacking boots,
not being willing to break in upon his small capital. He found that he could
earn enough in half a day to pay all his necessary expenses, including the
entire rent of the room. Fosdick desired to pay his half; but Dick steadily
refused, insisting upon paying so much as compensation for his friend's services as instructor.

It should be added that Dick's peculiar way of speaking and use of slang terms
had been somewhat modified by his education and his intimacy with Henry
Fosdick. Still he continued to indulge in them to some extent, especially when he
felt like joking, and it was natural to Dick to joke, as my readers have probably
found out by this time. Still his manners were considerably improved, so that he
was more likely to obtain a situation than when first introduced to our notice.

Just now, however, business was very dull, and merchants, instead of hiring
new assistants, were disposed to part with those already in their employ. After
making several ineffectual applications, Dick began to think he should be
obliged to stick to his profession until the next season. But about this time something occurred which considerably improved his chances of preferment.

This is the way it happened.

As Dick, with a balance of more than a hundred dollars in the savings bank,
might fairly consider himself a young man of property, he thought himself justified in occasionally taking a half holiday from business, and going on an excursion. On Wednesday afternoon Henry Fosdick was sent by his employer on an
errand to that part of Brooklyn near Greenwood Cemetery. Dick hastily dressed
himself in his best, and determined to accompany him.

The two boys walked down to the South Ferry, and, paying their two cents
each, entered the ferry-boat. They remained at the stern, and stood by the rail-
ing, watching the great city, with its crowded wharves, receding from view.
Beside them was a gentleman with two children,—a girl of eight and a little boy
of six. The children were talking gayly to their father. While he was pointing out
some object of interest to the little girl, the boy managed to creep, unobserved,
beneath the chain that extends across the boat, for the protection of passengers, and, stepping incautiously to the edge of the boat, fell over into the foam-
ing water.

At the child's scream, the father looked up, and, with a cry of horror, sprang
to the edge of the boat. He would have plunged in, but, being unable to swim,
would only have endangered his own life, without being able to save his child.

"My child!" he exclaimed in anguish,—"who will save my child? A thousand—
ten thousand dollars to any one who will save him!"

There chanced to be but few passengers on board at the time, and nearly all
these were either in the cabins or standing forward. Among the few who saw
the child fall was our hero.

Now Dick was an expert swimmer. It was an accomplishment which he had possessed for years, and he no sooner saw the boy fall than he resolved to rescue him. His determination was formed before he heard the liberal offer made by the boy's father. Indeed, I must do Dick the justice to say that, in the excitement of the moment, he did not hear it at all, nor would it have stimulated the alacrity with which he sprang to the rescue of the little boy.

Little Johnny had already risen once, and gone under for the second time, when our hero plunged in, He was obliged to strike out for the boy, and this took time. He reached him none too soon. Just as he was sinking for the third and last time, he caught him by the jacket. Dick was stout and strong, but Johnny clung to him so tightly, that it was with great difficulty he was able to sustain himself.

"Put your arms round my neck," said Dick.

The little boy mechanically obeyed, and clung with a grasp strengthened by his terror. In this position Dick could bear his weight better. But the ferry-boat was receding fast. It was quite impossible to reach it. The father, his face pale with terror and anguish, and his hands clasped in suspense, saw the brave boy's struggles, and prayed with agonizing fervor that he might be successful. But it is probable, for they were now midway of the river, that both Dick and the little boy whom he had bravely undertaken to rescue would have been drowned, had not a row-boat been fortunately near. The two men who were in it witnessed the accident, and hastened to the rescue of our hero.

"Keep up a little longer," they shouted, bending to their oars, "and we will save you."

Dick heard the shout, and it put fresh strength into him. He battled manfully with the treacherous sea, his eyes fixed longingly upon the approaching boat.

"Hold on tight, little boy," he said. "There's a boat coming."

The little boy did not see the boat. His eyes were closed to shut out the fearful water, but he clung the closer to his young preserver, Six long, steady strokes, and the boat dashed along side. Strong hands seized Dick and his youthful burden, and drew them into the boat, both dripping with water.

"God be thanked!" exclaimed the father, as from the steamer he saw the child's rescue. "That brave boy shall be rewarded, if I sacrifice my whole fortune to compass it."

"You've had a pretty narrow escape, young chap," said one of the boatmen to Dick. "It was a pretty tough job you undertook."

"Yes," said Dick. "That's what I thought when I was in the water. If it hadn't been for you, I don't know what would have 'come of us."

"Anyhow you're a plucky boy, or you wouldn't have dared to jump into the water after this little chap. It was a risky thing to do."

"I'm used to the water," said Dick, modestly. "I didn't stop to think of the danger, but I wasn't going to see that little fellow drown without tryin' to save him."

The boat at once headed for the ferry wharf on the Brooklyn side. The captain of the ferry-boat, seeing the rescue, did not think it necessary to stop his boat, but kept on his way. The whole occurrence took place in less time than I have occupied in telling it.

The father was waiting on the wharf to receive his little boy, with what feeling of gratitude and joy can be easily understood. With a burst of happy tears he clasped him to his arms. Dick was about to withdraw modestly, but the gentleman perceived the movement, and, putting down the child, came forward, and, clasping his hand, said with emotion, "My brave boy, I owe you a debt I can never repay. But for your timely service I should now be plunged into an anguish which I cannot think of without a shudder."

Our hero was ready enough to speak on most occasions, but always felt awkward when he was praised.

"It wasn't any trouble," he said, modestly. "I can swim like a top."

"But not many boys would have risked their lives for a stranger," said the gentleman. "But," he added with a sudden thought, as his glance rested on Dick's dripping garments, "both you and my little boy will take cold in wet clothes. Fortunately I have a friend living close at hand, at whose house you will have an opportunity of taking off your clothes, and having them dried."

Dick protested that he never took cold; but Fosdick, who had now joined them, and who, it is needless to say, had been greatly alarmed at Dick's danger, joined in urging compliance with the gentleman's proposal, and in the end our hero had to yield. His new friend secured a hack, the driver of which agreed for extra recompense to receive the dripping boys into his carriage, and they were whirled rapidly to a pleasant house in a side street, where matters were quickly explained, and both boys were put to bed.

"I aint used to goin' to bed quite so early," thought Dick, "This is the queerest excursion I ever took."

Like most active boys Dick did not enjoy the prospect of spending half a day in bed; but his confinement did not last as long as he anticipated.

In about an hour the door of his chamber was opened, and a servant appeared, bringing a new and handsome suit of clothes throughout.

"You are to put on these," said the servant to Dick; "but you needn't get up till you feel like it."

"Whose clothes are they?" asked Dick.

"They are yours."

"Mine! Where did they come from?"

"Mr. Rockwell sent out and bought them for you. They are the same size as your wet ones."

"Is he here now?"

"No. He bought another suit for the little boy, and has gone back to New York. Here's a note he asked me to give you."

Dick opened the paper, and read as follows,—

"Please accept this outfit of clothes as the first instalment of a debt which I can never repay. I have asked to have your wet suit dried, when you can reclaim it. Will you oblige me by calling to-morrow at my counting room, No. —, Pearl Street.

"Your friend,
"J<small>AMES</small> R<small>OCKWELL</small>."

When Dick was dressed in his new suit, he surveyed his figure with pardonable complacency. It was the best he had ever worn, and fitted him as well as if it had been made expressly for him.

"He's done the handsome thing," said Dick to himself; "but there wasn't no 'casion for his givin' me these clothes. My lucky stars are shinin' pretty bright now. Jumpin' into the water pays better than shinin' boots; but I don't think I'd like to try it more'n once a week."

About eleven o'clock the next morning Dick repaired to Mr. Rockwell's counting-room on Pearl Street. He found himself in front of a large and handsome warehouse. The counting-room was on the lower floor. Our hero entered, and found Mr. Rockwell sitting at a desk. No sooner did that gentleman see him than he arose, and, advancing, shook Dick by the hand in the most friendly manner.

"My young friend," he said, "you have done me so great a service that I wish to be of some service to you in return. Tell me about yourself, and what plans or wishes you have formed for the future."

Dick frankly related his past history, and told Mr. Rockwell of his desire to get into a store or counting-room, and of the failure of all his applications thus far. The merchant listened attentively to Dick's statement, and, when he had finished, placed a sheet of paper before him, and, handing him a pen, said, 'Will you write your name on this piece of paper?"

Dick wrote, in a free, bold hand, the name Richard Hunter, He had very much improved his penmanship, as has already been mentioned, and now had no cause to be ashamed of it.

Mr. Rockwell surveyed it approvingly.

"How would you like to enter my counting-room as clerk, Richard?" he asked.

Dick was about to say "Bully," when he recollected himself, and answered, "Very much."

"I suppose you know something of arithmetic, do you not?"

"Yes, sir."

"Then you may consider yourself engaged at a salary of ten dollars a week. You may come next Monday morning."

"Ten dollars!" repeated Dick, thinking he must have misunderstood.

"Yes; will that be sufficient?"

"It's more than I can earn," said Dick, honestly.

"Perhaps it is at first," said Mr. Rockwell, smiling; "but I am willing to pay you that. I will besides advance you as fast as your progress will justify it."

Dick was so elated that he hardly restrained himself from some demonstration which would have astonished the merchant; but he exercised self-control, and only said, "I'll try to serve you so faithfully, sir, that you won't repent having taken me into your service."

"And I think you will succeed," said Mr. Rockwell, encouragingly. "I will not detain you any longer, for I have some important business to attend to. I shall expect to see you on Monday morning."

Dick left the counting-room, hardly knowing whether he stood on his head or his heels, so overjoyed was he at the sudden change in his fortunes. Ten dollars a week was to him a fortune, and three times as much as he had expected to obtain at first. Indeed he would have been glad, only the day before, to get a place at three dollars a week. He reflected that with the stock of clothes which he had now on hand, he could save up at least half of it, and even then live better than he had been accustomed to do; so that his little fund in the savings bank, instead of being diminished, would be steadily increasing. Then he was to be advanced if he deserved it. It was indeed a bright prospect for a boy who, only a year before, could neither read nor write, and depended for a night's lodging upon the chance hospitality of an alley-way or old wagon. Dick's great ambition to "grow up 'spectable" seemed likely to be accomplished after all.

"I wish Fosdick was as well off as I am," he thought generously. But he determined to help his less fortunate friend, and assist him up the ladder as he advanced himself.

When Dick entered his room on Mott Street, he discovered that some one else had been there before him, and two articles of wearing apparel had disappeared.

"By gracious!" he exclaimed; "somebody's stole my Washington coat and Napoleon pants. Maybe it's an agent of Barnum's, who expects to make a fortun' by exhibitin' the valooable wardrobe of a gentleman of fashion."

Dick did not shed many tears over his loss, as, in his present circumstances, he never expected to have any further use for the well-worn garments. It may be stated that he afterwards saw them adorning the figure of Micky Maguire; but whether that estimable young man stole them himself, he never ascertained. As to the loss, Dick was rather pleased that it had occurred. It seemed to cut him off from the old vagabond life which he hoped never to resume. Henceforward he meant to press onward, and rise as high as possible.

Although it was yet only noon, Dick did not go out again with his brush. He felt that it was time to retire from business. He would leave his share of the public patronage to other boys less fortunate than himself. That evening Dick and Fosdick had a long conversation. Fosdick rejoiced heartily in his friend's success, and on his side had the pleasant news to communicate that his pay had been advanced to six dollars a week.

"I think we can afford to leave Mott Street now," he continued. "This house isn't as neat as it might be, and I should like to live in a nicer quarter of the city."

"All right," said Dick. "We'll hunt up a new room tomorrow. I shall have plenty of time, having retired from business. I'll try to get my reg'lar customers to take Johnny Nolan in my place. That boy hasn't any enterprise. He needs somebody to look out for him."

"You might give him your box and brush, too, Dick."

"No," said Dick; "I'll give him some new ones, but mine I want to keep, to remind me of the hard times I've had, when I was an ignorant boot-black, and never expected to be anything better."

"When, in short, you were 'Ragged Dick.' You must drop that name, and think of yourself now as"—

"Richard Hunter, Esq.," said our hero, smiling.

"A young gentleman on the way to fame and fortune," added Fosdick.

Working with the Text

1. At the end of the novel, Dick keeps his old shoeshine kit to remind him of "'when I was an ignorant boot-black, and never expected to be anything better.'" The idea of "bettering" oneself is central to Alger's novel and is still an influential idea in contemporary American society. In what ways does Dick see James Rockwell, for example, his future employer, as "better" than he is? Apply the concept to yourself: how much do modern college students see education as a way to "better" themselves, and what do they mean by the idea of becoming "better"? What are the potential problems in the idea of "bettering" yourself?

2. Alger writes that "Dick's great ambition" is to "'grow up 'spectable.'" How would you define what Dick means in modern terms? What does "respectability" mean today for you and society in general? Are there terms you think we would use instead?

2. Dick's success in this passage depends on both his own daring and on chance. Many critics have suggested that Alger's novels promote the belief that good luck will come to those who deserve it. How true do you think this is? What role do you see luck playing in achieving your own goals?

Working with Connections

1. Benjamin Franklin's *Autobiography* is an obvious influence on the story of *Ragged Dick*. However, what differences in terms of goals, methods of achieving them, or attitude can you find between the two texts?

2. As part of a larger project, read the rest of *Ragged Dick* and write about what you find most inspiring and least convincing in the novel as a whole.

HERMAN MELVILLE

Bartleby, the Scrivener
A Story of Wall-Street

The American writer Herman Melville (1819–1891) is best known as the author of Moby-Dick, or The Whale, *a novel now considered a masterpiece of world literature. His stories mix symbolism, ironic humor, and imaginative wordplay to examine issues relating to philosophy, religion, social justice, colonialism, and politics. One of his persistent themes is work, whether the work of sailors in the whaling industry or, as in "Bartleby the Scrivener," copyists or "scriveners" in a Manhattan law office. Written at the beginning of the era of corporations and office jobs, when the narrator of the story treats the word* employé *as a new word in English, "Bartleby the Scrivener" asks its readers to consider the human costs and moral assumptions behind the then-new work arrangements of employer/employee by considering the case of Bartleby, a mysterious figure who for reasons he only hints at refuses to follow the rules of his workplace.*

I am a rather elderly man. The nature of my avocations for the last thirty years has brought me into more than ordinary contact with what would seem an interesting and somewhat singular set of men, of whom as yet nothing that I know of has ever been written:—I mean, the law-copyists, or scriveners. I have known very many of them, professionally and privately, and if I pleased, could relate divers histories, at which good-natured gentlemen might smile, and sentimental souls might weep. But I waive the biographies of all other scriveners for a few passages in the life of Bartleby, who was a scrivener the strangest I ever saw or heard of. While of other law-copyists I might write the complete life, of Bartleby nothing of that sort can be done. I believe that no materials exist for a full and satisfactory biography of this man. It is an irreparable loss to literature. Bartleby was one of those beings of whom nothing is ascertainable, except from the original sources, and, in his case those are very small. What my own astonished eyes saw of Bartleby, *that* is all I know of him, except, indeed, one vague report which will appear in the sequel.

Ere introducing the scrivener, as he first appeared to me, it is fit I make some mention of myself, my *employés,* my business, my chambers, and general surroundings; because some such description is indispensable to an adequate understanding of the chief character about to be presented.

Imprimis: I am a man who, from his youth upwards, has been filled with a profound conviction that the easiest way of life is the best. Hence, though I belong to a profession proverbially energetic and nervous, even to turbulence, at times, yet nothing of that sort have I ever suffered to invade my peace. I am one of those unambitious lawyers who never addresses a jury, or in any way draws down public applause; but in the cool tranquillity of a snug retreat, do a snug business among rich men's bonds and mortgages and title-deeds. All who know me, consider me an eminently *safe* man. The late John Jacob Astor, a personage little given to poetic enthusiasm, had no hesitation in pronouncing my first grand point to be prudence; my next, method. I do not speak it in vanity, but simply record the fact, that I was not unemployed in my profession by the late John Jacob Astor; a name which, I admit, I love to repeat, for it hath a rounded and orbicular sound to it, and rings like unto bullion. I will freely add, that I was not insensible to the late John Jacob Astor's good opinion.

Some time prior to the period at which this little history begins, my avocations had been largely increased. The good old office, now extinct in the State of New-York, of a Master in Chancery, had been conferred upon me. It was not a very arduous office, but very pleasantly remunerative. I seldom lose my temper; much more seldom indulge in dangerous indignation at wrongs and outrages; but I must be permitted to be rash here and declare, that I consider the sudden and violent abrogation of the office of Master in Chancery, by the new Constitution, as a —— premature act; inasmuch as I had counted upon a life-lease of the profits, whereas I only received those of a few short years. But this is by the way.

My chambers were up stairs, at No. — Wall-street. At one end they looked upon the white wall of the interior of a spacious sky-light shaft, penetrating the building from top to bottom. This view might have been considered rather tame than otherwise, deficient in what landscape painters call "life." But if so, the view from the other end of my chambers offered, at least, a contrast, if nothing more. In that direction my windows commanded an unobstructed view of a lofty brick wall, black by age and everlasting shade; which wall required no spy-glass to bring out its lurking beauties, but for the benefit of all near-sighted spectators, was pushed up to within ten feet of my window panes. Owing to the great height of the surrounding buildings, and my chambers being on the second floor, the interval between this wall and mine not a little resembled a huge square cistern.

At the period just preceding the advent of Bartleby, I had two persons as copyists in my employment, and a promising lad as an office-boy. First, Turkey; second, Nippers; third, Ginger Nut. These may seem names, the like of which are not usually found in the Directory. In truth they were nicknames, mutually conferred upon each other by my three clerks, and were deemed expressive of their respective persons or characters. Turkey was a short, pursy Englishman of about my own age, that is, somewhere not far from sixty. In the morning, one might say, his face was of a fine florid hue, but after twelve o'clock, meridian—his dinner hour—it blazed like a grate full of Christmas coals; and continued blazing—but, as it were, with a gradual wane—till 6 o'clock, P.M., or thereabouts; after which, I saw no more of the proprietor of the face, which, gaining its meridian with the sun, seemed to set with it, to rise, culminate, and decline the following day, with the like regularity and undiminished glory. There are many singular coincidences I have known in the course of my life, not the least among which was the fact, that exactly when Turkey displayed his fullest beams from his red and radiant countenance, just then, too, at that critical moment, began the daily period when I considered his business capacities as seriously disturbed for the remainder of the twenty-four hours. Not that he was absolutely idle, or averse to business then; far from it. The difficulty was, he was apt to be altogether too energetic. There was a strange, inflamed, flurried, flighty recklessness of activity about him. He would be incautious in dipping his pen into his inkstand. All his blots upon my documents, were dropped there after twelve o'clock, meridian. Indeed, not only would he be reckless, and sadly given to making blots in the afternoon, but some days he went further, and was rather noisy. At such times, too, his face flamed with augmented blazonry, as if cannel coal had been heaped on anthracite. He made an unpleasant racket with his chair; spilled his sand-box; in mending his pens, impatiently split them all to pieces, and threw them on the floor in a sudden passion; stood up, and leaned over his table, boxing his papers about in a most indecorous manner, very sad to behold in an elderly man like him. Nevertheless, as he was in many ways a most valuable person to me, and all the time before twelve o'clock, meridian, was the quickest, steadiest creature, too, accomplishing a great deal of work in a style not easily to be matched—for these reasons, I was willing to overlook his eccentricities, though indeed, occasionally, I remonstrated with him. I did this very gently, however, because, though the civilest, nay, the blandest and most reverential of men in the morning, yet in the afternoon he was disposed, upon provocation, to be slightly rash with his tongue, in fact, insolent. Now, valuing his morning services as I did, and resolved not to lose them; yet, at the same time made uncomfortable by his inflamed ways after twelve o'clock; and being a man of peace, unwilling by my admonitions to call forth unseemly retorts from him; I took upon me, one Saturday noon (he was always worse on Saturdays), to hint to him, very kindly, that perhaps now that he was growing old, it might be well to abridge his labors; in short, he need not come to my chambers after twelve o'clock, but, dinner over, had best go home to his lodgings and rest himself till tea-time. But no; he insisted upon his afternoon devotions. His countenance became intolerably fervid, as he oratorically assured me—gesticulating with a long ruler at the other end of the room—that if his services in the morning were useful, how indispensable, then, in the afternoon?

"With submission, sir," said Turkey, on this occasion, "I consider myself your right-hand man. In the morning I but marshal and deploy my columns; but in the afternoon I put myself at their head, and gallantly charge the foe, thus!"—and he made a violent thrust with the ruler.

"But the blots, Turkey," intimated I.

"True,—but, with submission, sir, behold these hairs! I am getting old. Surely, sir, a blot or two of a warm afternoon is not to be severely urged against gray hairs. Old age—even if it blot the page—is honorable. With submission, sir, we *both* are getting old."

This appeal to my fellow-feeling was hardly to be resisted. At all events, I saw that go he would not. So I made up my mind to let him stay, resolving, nevertheless, to see to it, that during the afternoon he had to do with my less important papers.

Nippers, the second on my list, was a whiskered, sallow, and, upon the whole, rather piratical-looking young man of about five and twenty. I always deemed him the victim of two evil powers—ambition and indigestion. The ambition was evinced by a certain impatience of the duties of a mere copyist, an unwarrantable usurpation of strictly professional affairs, such as the original drawing up of legal documents. The indigestion seemed betokened in an occasional nervous testiness and grinning irritability, causing the teeth to audibly grind together over mistakes committed in copying; unnecessary maledictions, hissed, rather than spoken, in the heat of business; and especially by a continual discontent with the height of the table where he worked. Though of a very ingenious mechanical turn, Nippers could never get this table to suit him. He put chips under it, blocks of various sorts, bits of pasteboard, and at last went so far as to attempt an exquisite adjustment by final pieces of folded blotting-paper. But no invention would answer. If, for the sake of easing his back, he brought the table lid at a sharp angle well up towards his chin, and wrote there like a man using the steep roof of a Dutch house for his desk:—then he declared that it stopped the circulation in his arms. If now he lowered the table to his waist-bands, and stooped over it in writing, then there was a sore aching in his back. In short, the truth of the matter was, Nippers knew not what he wanted. Or, if he wanted any thing, it was to be rid of a scrivener's table altogether. Among the manifestations of his diseased ambition was a fondness he had for receiving visits from certain ambiguous-looking fellows in seedy coats, whom he called his clients. Indeed I was aware that not only was he, at times, considerable of a ward-politician, but he occasionally did a little business at the Justices' courts, and was not unknown on the steps of the Tombs. I have good reason to believe, however, that one individual who called upon him at my chambers, and who, with a grand air, he insisted was his client, was no other than a dun, and the alleged title-deed, a bill. But with all his failings, and the annoyances he caused me, Nippers, like his compatriot Turkey, was a very useful man to me; wrote a neat, swift hand; and, when he chose, was not deficient in a gentlemanly sort of deportment. Added to this, he always dressed in a gentlemanly sort of way; and so, incidentally, reflected credit upon my chambers. Whereas with respect to Turkey, I had much ado to keep him from being a reproach to me. His clothes were apt to look oily and smell of eating-houses. He wore his pantaloons very loose and baggy in summer. His coats were execrable; his hat not to be handled. But while the hat was a thing of indifference to me, inasmuch as his natural civility and deference, as a dependent Englishman, always led him to doff it the moment he entered the room, yet his coat was another matter. Concerning his coats, I reasoned with him; but with no effect. The truth was, I suppose, that a man with so small an income, could not afford to sport such a lustrous face and a lustrous coat at one and the same time. As Nippers once observed, Turkey's money went chiefly for red ink. One winter day I presented Turkey with a highly-respectable looking coat of my own—a padded gray coat, of a most comfortable warmth, and which buttoned straight up from the knee to the neck. I thought Turkey would appreciate the favor, and abate his rashness and obstreperousness of afternoons. But no. I verily believe that buttoning himself up in so downy and blanket-like a coat had a pernicious effect upon him; upon the same principle that too much oats are bad for horses. In fact, precisely as a rash, restive horse is said to feel his oats, so Turkey felt his coat. It made him insolent. He was a man whom prosperity harmed.

Though, concerning the self-indulgent habits of Turkey I had my own private surmises, yet touching Nippers I was well persuaded that whatever might be his faults in other respects, he was, at least, a temperate young man. But indeed, nature herself seemed to have been his vintner, and at his birth charged him so thoroughly with an irritable, brandy-like disposition, that all subsequent pota-tions were needless. When I consider how, amid the stillness of my chambers, Nippers would sometimes impatiently rise from his seat, and stooping over his table, spread his arms wide apart, seize the whole desk, and move it, and jerk it, with a grim, grinding motion on the floor, as if the table were a perverse volun-tary agent, intent on thwarting and vexing him; I plainly perceive that for Nippers, brandy and water were altogether superfluous.

It was fortunate for me that, owing to its peculiar cause—indigestion—the irri-tability and consequent nervousness of Nippers, were mainly observable in the morning, while in the afternoon he was comparatively mild. So that Turkey's paroxysms only coming on about twelve o'clock, I never had to do with their eccentricities at one time. Their fits relieved each other like guards. When Nippers' was on, Turkey's was off; and *vice versa*. This was a good natural arrangement, under the circumstances.

Ginger Nut, the third on my list, was a lad some twelve years old. His father was a carman, ambitious of seeing his son on the bench instead of a cart, before he died. So he sent him to my office as student at law, errand-boy, and cleaner and sweeper, at the rate of one dollar a week. He had a little desk to himself, but he did not use it much. Upon inspection, the drawer exhibited a great array of the shells of various sorts of nuts. Indeed, to this quick-witted youth the whole noble science of the law was contained in a nut-shell. Not the least among the employments of Ginger Nut, as well as one which he discharged with the most alacrity, was his duty as cake and apple purveyor for Turkey and Nippers. Copying law papers being proverbially a dry, husky sort of business, my two scriveners were fain to moisten their mouths very often with Spitzenbergs to be had at the numerous stalls nigh the Custom House and Post Office. Also, they sent Ginger Nut very frequently for that peculiar cake—small, flat, round, and very spicy—after which he had been named by them. Of a cold morning when business was but dull, Turkey would gobble up scores of these cakes, as if they were mere wafers—indeed they sell them at the rate of six or eight for a penny—the scrape of his pen blending with the crunching of the crisp particles in his mouth. Of all the fiery afternoon blunders and flurried rashnesses of Turkey, was his once moistening a ginger-cake between his lips, and clapping it on to a mortgage for a seal. I came within an ace of dismissing him then. But he molli-fied me by making an oriental bow, and saying—"With submission, sir, it was generous of me to find you in stationery on my own account."

Now my original business—that of a conveyancer and title hunter, and drawer-up of recondite documents of all sorts—was considerably increased by receiving the master's office. There was now great work for scriveners. Not only must I push the clerks already with me, but I must have additional help. In answer to my advertisement, a motionless young man one morning, stood upon my office threshold, the door being open, for it was summer. I can see that figure now—pallidly neat, pitiably respectable, incurably forlorn! It was Bartleby.

After a few words touching his qualifications, I engaged him, glad to have among my corps of copyists a man of so singularly sedate an aspect, which I thought might operate beneficially upon the flighty temper of Turkey, and the fiery one of Nippers.

I should have stated before that ground glass folding-doors divided my premises into two parts, one of which was occupied by my scriveners, the other by myself. According to my humor I threw open these doors, or closed them. I resolved to assign Bartleby a corner by the folding-doors, but on my side of them, so as to have this quiet man within easy call, in case any trifling thing was to be done. I placed his desk close up to a small side-window in that part of the room, a window which originally had afforded a lateral view of certain grimy back-yards and bricks, but which, owing to subsequent erections, commanded at present no view at all, though it gave some light. Within three feet of the panes was a wall, and the light came down from far above, between two lofty buildings, as from a very small opening in a dome. Still further to a satisfactory arrangement, I procured a high green folding screen, which might entirely isolate Bartleby from my sight, though not remove him from my voice. And thus, in a manner, privacy and society were conjoined.

At first Bartleby did an extraordinary quantity of writing. As if long famishing for something to copy, he seemed to gorge himself on my documents. There was no pause for digestion. He ran a day and night line, copying by sunlight and by candle-light. I should have been quite delighted with his application, had he been cheerfully industrious. But he wrote on silently, palely, mechanically.

It is, of course, an indispensable part of a scrivener's business to verify the accuracy of his copy, word by word. Where there are two or more scriveners in an office, they assist each other in this examination, one reading from the copy, the other holding the original. It is a very dull, wearisome, and lethargic affair. I can readily imagine that to some sanguine temperaments it would be altogether intolerable. For example, I cannot credit that the mettlesome poet Byron would have contentedly sat down with Bartleby to examine a law document of, say five hundred pages, closely written in a crimpy hand.

Now and then, in the haste of business, it had been my habit to assist in comparing some brief document myself, calling Turkey or Nippers for this purpose. One object I had in placing Bartleby so handy to me behind the screen, was to avail myself of his services on such trivial occasions. It was on the third day, I think, of his being with me, and before any necessity had arisen for having his own writing examined, that, being much hurried to complete a small affair I had in hand, I abruptly called to Bartleby. In my haste and natural expectancy of instant compliance, I sat with my head bent over the original on my desk, and my right hand sideways, and somewhat nervously extended with the copy, so that, immediately upon emerging from his retreat, Bartleby might snatch it and proceed to business without the least delay.

In this very attitude did I sit when I called to him, rapidly stating what it was I wanted him to do—namely, to examine a small paper with me. Imagine my surprise, nay, my consternation, when, without moving from his privacy, Bartleby in a singularly mild, firm voice, replied, "I would prefer not to."

I sat awhile in perfect silence, rallying my stunned faculties. Immediately it occurred to me that my ears had deceived me, or Bartleby had entirely misunderstood my meaning. I repeated my request in the clearest tone I could assume. But in quite as clear a one came the previous reply, "I would prefer not to."

"Prefer not to," echoed I, rising in high excitement, and crossing the room with a stride. "What do you mean? Are you moon-struck? I want you to help me compare this sheet here—take it," and I thrust it towards him.

"I would prefer not to," said he.

I looked at him steadfastly. His face was leanly composed; his gray eye dimly calm. Not a wrinkle of agitation rippled him. Had there been the least uneasiness, anger, impatience, or impertinence in his manner; in other words, had there been anything ordinarily human about him, doubtless I should have violently dismissed him from the premises. But as it was, I should have as soon thought of turning my pale plaster-of-paris bust of Cicero out of doors. I stood gazing at him awhile, as he went on with his own writing, and then reseated myself at my desk. This is very strange, thought I. What had one best do? But my business hurried me. I concluded to forget the matter for the present, reserving it for my future leisure. So, calling Nippers from the other room, the paper was speedily examined.

A few days after this, Bartleby concluded four lengthy documents, being quadruplicates of a week's testimony taken before me in my High Court of Chancery. It became necessary to examine them. It was an important suit, and great accuracy was imperative. Having all things arranged I called Turkey, Nippers, and Ginger Nut from the next room, meaning to place the four copies in the hands of my four clerks, while I should read from the original. Accordingly, Turkey, Nippers, and Ginger Nut had taken their seats in a row, each with his document in his hand, when I called to Bartleby to join this interesting group.

"Bartleby! quick, I am waiting."

I heard a slow scrape of his chair legs on the uncarpeted floor, and soon he appeared standing at the entrance of his hermitage.

"What is wanted?" said he, mildly.

"The copies, the copies," said I hurriedly. "We are going to examine them. There"—and I held towards him the fourth quadruplicate.

"I would prefer not to," he said, and gently disappeared behind the screen.

For a few moments I was turned into a pillar of salt, standing at the head of my seated column of clerks. Recovering myself, I advanced towards the screen, and demanded the reason for such extraordinary conduct.

"*Why* do you refuse?"

"I would prefer not to."

With any other man I should have flown outright into a dreadful passion, scorned all further words, and thrust him ignominiously from my presence. But there was something about Bartleby that not only strangely disarmed me, but in a wonderful manner touched and disconcerted me. I began to reason with him.

"These are your own copies we are about to examine. It is labor saving to you, because one examination will answer for your four papers. It is common usage. Every copyist is bound to help examine his copy. Is it not so? Will you not speak? Answer!"

"I prefer not to," he replied in a flute-like tone. It seemed to me that while I had been addressing him, he carefully revolved every statement that I made; fully comprehended the meaning; could not gainsay the irresistible conclusion; but, at the same time, some paramount consideration prevailed with him to reply as he did.

"You are decided, then, not to comply with my request—a request made according to common usage and common sense?"

He briefly gave me to understand that on that point my judgment was sound. Yes: his decision was irreversible.

It is not seldom the case that, when a man is browbeaten in some unprecedented and violently unreasonable way, he begins to stagger in his own plainest faith. He begins, as it were, vaguely to surmise that, wonderful as it may be, all the justice and all the reason is on the other side. Accordingly, if any disinterested persons are present, he turns to them for some reinforcement for his own faltering mind.

"Turkey," said I, "what do you think of this? Am I not right?"

"With submission, sir," said Turkey, in his blandest tone, "I think that you are."

"Nippers," said I, "what do *you* think of it?"

"I think I should kick him out of the office."

(The reader of nice perceptions will here perceive that, it being morning, Turkey's answer is couched in polite and tranquil terms, but Nippers replies in ill-tempered ones. Or, to repeat a previous sentence, Nippers' ugly mood was on duty, and Turkey's off.)

"Ginger Nut," said I, willing to enlist the smallest suffrage in my behalf, "what do *you* think of it?"

"I think, sir, he's a little *luny*," replied Ginger Nut, with a grin.

"You hear what they say," said I, turning towards the screen, "come forth and do your duty."

But he vouchsafed no reply. I pondered a moment in sore perplexity. But once more business hurried me. I determined again to postpone the consideration of this dilemma to my future leisure. With a little trouble we made out to examine the papers without Bartleby, though at every page or two Turkey deferentially dropped his opinion that this proceeding was quite out of the common; while Nippers, twitching in his chair with a dyspeptic nervousness, ground out between his set teeth occasional hissing maledictions against the stubborn oaf behind the screen. And for his (Nippers's) part, this was the first and the last time he would do another man's business without pay.

Meanwhile Bartleby sat in his hermitage, oblivious to every thing but his own peculiar business there.

Some days passed, the scrivener being employed upon another lengthy work. His late remarkable conduct led me to regard his ways narrowly. I observed that he never went to dinner; indeed that he never went any where. As yet I had never of my personal knowledge known him to be outside of my office. He was a perpetual sentry in the corner. At about eleven o'clock though, in the morning, I noticed that Ginger Nut would advance toward the opening in Bartleby's screen, as if silently beckoned thither by a gesture invisible to me where I sat. The boy would then leave the office jingling a few pence, and reappear with a handful of ginger-nuts which he delivered in the hermitage, receiving two of the cakes for his trouble.

He lives, then, on ginger-nuts, thought I; never eats a dinner, properly speaking; he must be a vegetarian then; but no; he never eats even vegetables, he eats nothing but ginger-nuts. My mind then ran on in reveries concerning the probable effects upon the human constitution of living entirely on ginger-nuts. Ginger-nuts are so called because they contain ginger as one of their peculiar constituents, and the final flavoring one. Now what was ginger? A hot, spicy thing. Was Bartleby hot and spicy? Not at all. Ginger, then, had no effect upon Bartleby. Probably he preferred it should have none.

Nothing so aggravates an earnest person as a passive resistance. If the individual so resisted be of a not inhuman temper, and the resisting one perfectly harmless in his passivity; then, in the better moods of the former, he will endeavor charitably to construe to his imagination what proves impossible to be solved by his judgment. Even so, for the most part, I regarded Bartleby and his ways. Poor fellow! thought I, he means no mischief; it is plain he intends no insolence; his aspect sufficiently evinces that his eccentricities are involuntary. He is useful to me. I can get along with him. If I turn him away, the chances are he will fall in with some less indulgent employer, and then he will be rudely treated, and perhaps driven forth miserably to starve. Yes. Here I can cheaply purchase a delicious self-approval. To befriend Bartleby; to humor him in his strange wilfulness, will cost me little or nothing, while I lay up in my soul what will eventually prove a sweet morsel for my conscience. But this mood was not invariable with me. The passiveness of Bartleby sometimes irritated me. I felt strangely goaded on to encounter him in new opposition, to elicit some angry spark from him answerable to my own. But, indeed, I might as well have essayed to strike fire with my knuckles against a bit of Windsor soap. But one afternoon the evil impulse in me mastered me, and the following little scene ensued:

"Bartleby," said I, "when those papers are all copied, I will compare them with you."

"I would prefer not to."

"How? Surely you do not mean to persist in that mulish vagary?"

No answer.

I threw open the folding-doors near by, and turning upon Turkey and Nippers, exclaimed in an excited manner—

"He says, a second time, he won't examine his papers. What do you think of it, Turkey?"

It was afternoon, be it remembered. Turkey sat glowing like a brass boiler, his bald head steaming, his hands reeling among his blotted papers.

"Think of it?" roared Turkey; "I think I'll just step behind his screen, and black his eyes for him!"

So saying, Turkey rose to his feet and threw his arms into a pugilistic position. He was hurrying away to make good his promise, when I detained him, alarmed at the effect of incautiously rousing Turkey's combativeness after dinner.

"Sit down, Turkey," said I, "and hear what Nippers has to say. What do you think of it, Nippers? Would I not be justified in immediately dismissing Bartleby?"

"Excuse me, that is for you to decide, sir. I think his conduct quite unusual, and, indeed, unjust, as regards Turkey and myself. But it may only be a passing whim."

"Ah," exclaimed I, "you have strangely changed your mind, then—you speak very gently of him now."

"All beer," cried Turkey; "gentleness is effects of beer—Nippers and I dined together to-day. You see how gentle I am, sir. Shall I go and black his eyes?"

"You refer to Bartleby, I suppose. No, not to-day, Turkey," I replied; "pray, put up your fists."

I closed the doors, and again advanced towards Bartleby. I felt additional incentives tempting me to my fate. I burned to be rebelled against again. I remembered that Bartleby never left the office.

"Bartleby," said I, "Ginger Nut is away; just step around to the Post Office, won't you?" (it was but a three minutes walk,) "and see if there is any thing for me."

"I would prefer not to."

"You *will* not?"

"I *prefer* not."

I staggered to my desk, and sat there in a deep study. My blind inveteracy returned. Was there any other thing in which I could procure myself to be ignominiously repulsed by this lean, penniless wight?—my hired clerk? What added thing is there, perfectly reasonable, that he will be sure to refuse to do?

"Bartleby!"

No answer.

"Bartleby," in a louder tone.

No answer.

"Bartleby," I roared.

Like a very ghost, agreeably to the laws of magical invocation, at the third summons, he appeared at the entrance of his hermitage.

"Go to the next room, and tell Nippers to come to me."

"I would prefer not to," he respectfully and slowly said, and mildly disappeared.

"Very good, Bartleby," said I, in a quiet sort of serenely severe self-possessed tone, intimating the unalterable purpose of some terrible retribution very close at hand. At the moment I half intended something of the kind. But upon the whole, as it was drawing towards my dinner-hour, I thought it best to put on my hat and walk home for the day, suffering much from perplexity and distress of mind.

Shall I acknowledge it? The conclusion of this whole business was, that it soon became a fixed fact of my chambers, that a pale young scrivener, by the name of Bartleby, had a desk there; that he copied for me at the usual rate of four cents a folio (one hundred words); but he was permanently exempt from examining the work done by him, that duty being transferred to Turkey and Nippers, out of compliment doubtless to their superior acuteness; moreover, said Bartleby was never on any account to be dispatched on the most trivial errand of any sort; and that even if entreated to take upon him such a matter, it was generally understood that he would prefer not to—in other words, that he would refuse point-blank.

As days passed on, I became considerably reconciled to Bartleby. His steadiness, his freedom from all dissipation, his incessant industry (except when he chose to throw himself into a standing revery behind his screen), his great stillness, his unalterableness of demeanor under all circumstances, made him a valuable acquisition. One prime thing was this—*he was always there;*—first in the morning, continually through the day, and the last at night. I had a singular confidence in his honesty. I felt my most precious papers perfectly safe in his hands. Sometimes to be sure I could not, for the very soul of me, avoid falling into sudden spasmodic passions with him. For it was exceeding difficult to bear in mind all the time those strange peculiarities, privileges, and unheard of exemptions, forming the tacit stipulations on Bartleby's part under which he remained in my office. Now and then, in the eagerness of dispatching pressing business, I would inadvertently summon Bartleby, in a short, rapid tone, to put his finger, say, on the incipient tie of a bit of red tape with which I was about compressing some papers. Of course, from behind the screen the usual answer, "I prefer not to," was sure to come; and then, how could a human creature with the common infirmities of our nature, refrain from bitterly exclaiming upon such perverseness—such unreasonableness? However, every added repulse of this sort which I received only tended to lessen the probability of my repeating the inadvertence.

Here it must be said that, according to the custom of most legal gentlemen occupying chambers in densely-populated law buildings, there were several keys to my door. One was kept by a woman residing in the attic, which person weekly scrubbed and daily swept and dusted my apartments. Another was kept by Turkey for convenience sake. The third I sometimes carried in my own pocket. The fourth I knew not who had.

Now, one Sunday morning I happened to go to Trinity Church, to hear a celebrated preacher, and finding myself rather early on the ground, I thought I would walk round to my chambers for a while. Luckily I had my key with me; but upon applying it to the lock, I found it resisted by something inserted from the inside. Quite surprised, I called out; when to my consternation a key was turned from within; and thrusting his lean visage at me, and holding the door ajar, the apparition of Bartleby appeared, in his shirt-sleeves, and otherwise in a strangely tattered dishabille, saying quietly that he was sorry, but he was deeply engaged just then, and—preferred not admitting me at present. In a brief word or two, he moreover added, that perhaps I had better walk round the block two or three times, and by that time he would probably have concluded his affairs.

Now, the utterly unsurmised appearance of Bartleby, tenanting my lawchambers of a Sunday morning, with his cadaverously gentlemanly nonchalance yet withal firm and self-possessed, had such a strange effect upon me, that incontinently I slunk away from my own door, and did as desired. But not without sundry twinges of impotent rebellion against the mild effrontery of this unaccountable scrivener. Indeed, it was his wonderful mildness chiefly, which not only disarmed me, but unmanned me, as it were. For I consider that one, for the time, is sort of unmanned when he tranquilly permits his hired clerk to dictate to him, and order him away from his own premises. Furthermore, I was full of uneasiness as to what Bartleby could possibly be doing in my office in his shirt-sleeves, and in an otherwise dismantled condition on a Sunday morning. Was any thing amiss going on? Nay, that was out of the question. It was not to be thought of for a moment that Bartleby was an immoral person. But what could he be doing there?—copying? Nay again, whatever might be his eccentricities, Bartleby was an eminently decorous person. He would be the last man to sit down to his desk in any state approaching to nudity. Besides, it was Sunday; and there was something about Bartleby that forbade the supposition that he would by any secular occupation violate the proprieties of the day.

Nevertheless, my mind was not pacified; and full of a restless curiosity, at last I returned to the door. Without hindrance I inserted my key, opened it, and entered. Bartleby was not to be seen. I looked round anxiously, peeped behind his screen; but it was very plain that he was gone. Upon more closely examining the place, I surmised that for an indefinite period Bartleby must have ate, dressed, and slept in my office, and that too without plate, mirror, or bed. The cushioned seat of a rickety old sofa in one corner bore the faint impress of a lean, reclining form. Rolled away under his desk, I found a blanket; under the empty grate, a blacking box and brush; on a chair, a tin basin, with soap and a ragged towel; in a newspaper a few crumbs of ginger-nuts and a morsel of cheese. Yet, thought I, it is evident enough that Bartleby has been making his home here, keeping bachelor's hall all by himself. Immediately then the thought came sweeping across me, What miserable friendlessness and loneliness are here revealed! His poverty is great; but his solitude, how horrible! Think of it. Of a Sunday, Wall-Street is deserted as Petra; and every night of every day it is an emptiness. This building, too, which of week-days hums with industry and life, at nightfall echoes with sheer vacancy, and all through Sunday is forlorn. And here Bartleby makes his home; sole spectator of a solitude which he has seen all populous—a sort of innocent and transformed Marius brooding among the ruins of Carthage!

For the first time in my life a feeling of overpowering stinging melancholy seized me. Before, I had never experienced aught but a not-unpleasing sadness. The bond of a common humanity now drew me irresistibly to gloom. A fraternal melancholy! For both I and Bartleby were sons of Adam. I remembered the bright silks and sparkling faces I had seen that day, in gala trim, swan-like sailing down the Mississippi of Broadway; and I contrasted them with the pallid copyist, and thought to myself, Ah, happiness courts the light, so we deem the world is gay; but misery hides aloof, so we deem that misery there is none. These sad fancyings—chimeras, doubtless, of a sick and silly brain—led on to other and more special thoughts, concerning the eccentricities of Bartleby. Presentiments of strange discoveries hovered round me. The scrivener's pale form appeared to me laid out, among uncaring strangers, in its shivering winding sheet.

Suddenly I was attracted by Bartleby's closed desk, the key in open sight left in the lock.

I mean no mischief, seek the gratification of no heartless curiosity, thought I; besides, the desk is mine, and its contents too, so I will make bold to look within. Every thing was methodically arranged, the papers smoothly placed. The pigeon holes were deep, and removing the files of documents, I groped into their recesses. Presently I felt something there, and dragged it out. It was an old bandanna handkerchief, heavy and knotted. I opened it, and saw it was a savings' bank.

I now recalled all the quiet mysteries which I had noted in the man. I remembered that he never spoke but to answer; that, though at intervals he had considerable time to himself, yet I had never seen him reading—no, not even a newspaper; that for long periods he would stand looking out, at his pale window behind the screen, upon the dead brick wall; I was quite sure he never visited any refectory or eating house; while his pale face clearly indicated that he never drank beer like Turkey, or tea and coffee even, like other men; that he never went any where in particular that I could learn; never went out for a walk, unless indeed that was the case at present; that he had declined telling who he was, or whence he came, or whether he had any relatives in the world; that though so thin and pale, he never complained of ill health. And more than all, I remembered a certain unconscious air of pallid—how shall I call it?—of pallid haughtiness, say, or rather an austere reserve about him, which has positively awed me into my tame compliance with his eccentricities, when I had feared to ask him to do the slightest incidental thing for me, even though I might know, from his long-continued motionlessness, that behind his screen he must be standing in one of those dead-wall reveries of his.

Revolving all these things, and coupling them with the recently discovered fact that he made my office his constant abiding place and home, and not forgetful of his morbid moodiness; revolving all these things, a prudential feeling began to steal over me. My first emotions had been those of pure melancholy and sincerest pity; but just in proportion as the forlornness of Bartleby grew and grew to my imagination, did that same melancholy merge into fear, that pity into repulsion. So true it is, and so terrible too, that up to a certain point the thought or sight of misery enlists our best affections; but, in certain special cases, beyond that point it does not. They err who would assert that invariably this is owing to the inherent selfishness of the human heart. It rather proceeds from a certain hopelessness of remedying excessive and organic ill. To a sensitive being, pity is not seldom pain. And when at last it is perceived that such pity cannot lead to effectual succor, common sense bids the soul be rid of it. What I saw that morning persuaded me that the scrivener was the victim of innate and incurable disorder. I might give alms to his body; but his body did not pain him; it was his soul that suffered, and his soul I could not reach.

I did not accomplish the purpose of going to Trinity Church that morning. Somehow, the things I had seen disqualified me for the time from church-going. I walked homeward, thinking what I would do with Bartleby. Finally, I resolved upon this;—I would put certain calm questions to him the next morning, touching his history, &c., and if he declined to answer them openly and unreservedly (and I supposed he would prefer not), then to give him a twenty dollar bill over and above whatever I might owe him, and tell him his services were no longer required; but that if in any other way I could assist him, I would be happy to do so, especially if he desired to return to his native place, wherever that might be, I would willingly help to defray the expenses. Moreover, if, after reaching home, he found himself at any time in want of aid, a letter from him would be sure of a reply.

The next morning came.

"Bartleby," said I, gently calling to him behind his screen.

No reply.

"Bartleby," said I, in a still gentler tone, "come here; I am not going to ask you to do anything you would prefer not to do—I simply wish to speak to you."

Upon this he noiselessly slid into view.

"Will you tell me, Bartleby, where you were born?"

"I would prefer not to."

"Will you tell me *any thing* about yourself?"

"I would prefer not to."

"But what reasonable objection can you have to speak to me? I feel friendly towards you."

He did not look at me while I spoke, but kept his glance fixed upon my bust of Cicero, which, as I then sat, was directly behind me, some six inches above my head.

"What is your answer, Bartleby?" said I, after waiting a considerable time for a reply, during which his countenance remained immovable, only there was the faintest conceivable tremor of the white attenuated mouth.

"At present I prefer to give no answer," he said, and retired into his hermitage.

It was rather weak in me I confess, but his manner on this occasion nettled me. Not only did there seem to lurk in it a certain calm disdain, but his perverseness seemed ungrateful, considering the undeniable good usage and indulgence he had received from me.

Again I sat ruminating what I should do. Mortified as I was at his behavior, and resolved as I had been to dismiss him when I entered my office, nevertheless I strangely felt something superstitious knocking at my heart, and forbidding me to carry out my purpose, and denouncing me for a villain if I dared to breathe one bitter word against this forlornest of mankind. At last, familiarly drawing my chair behind his screen, I sat down and said: "Bartleby, never mind then about revealing your history; but let me entreat you, as a friend, to comply as far as may be with the usages of this office. Say now you will help to examine papers to-morrow or next day: in short, say now that in a day or two you will begin to be a little reasonable:—say so, Bartleby."

"At present I would prefer not to be a little reasonable," was his mildly cadaverous reply.

Just then the folding-doors opened, and Nippers approached. He seemed suffering from an unusually bad night's rest, induced by severer indigestion than common. He overheard those final words of Bartleby.

"*Prefer not*, eh?" gritted Nippers—"I'd *prefer* him, if I were you, sir," addressing me—"I'd *prefer* him; I'd give him preferences, the stubborn mule! What is it, sir, pray, that he *prefers* not to do now?"

Bartleby moved not a limb.

"Mr. Nippers," said I, "I'd prefer that you would withdraw for the present."

Somehow, of late I had got into the way of involuntarily using this word "prefer" upon all sorts of not exactly suitable occasions. And I trembled to think that my contact with the scrivener had already and seriously affected me in a mental way. And what further and deeper aberration might it not yet produce? This apprehension had not been without efficacy in determining me to summary measures.

As Nippers, looking very sour and sulky, was departing, Turkey blandly and deferentially approached.

"With submission, sir," said he, "yesterday I was thinking about Bartleby here, and I think that if he would but prefer to take a quart of good ale every day, it would do much towards mending him, and enabling him to assist in examining his papers."

"So you have got the word, too," said I, slightly excited.

"With submission, what word, sir?" asked Turkey, respectfully crowding himself into the contracted space behind the screen, and by so doing, making me jostle the scrivener. "What word, sir?"

"I would prefer to be left alone here," said Bartleby, as if offended at being mobbed in his privacy.

"*That's* the word, Turkey," said I—"*that's* it."

"Oh, *prefer*? oh yes—queer word. I never use it myself. But, sir, as I was saying, if he would but prefer—"

"Turkey," interrupted I, "you will please withdraw."

"Oh certainly, sir, if you prefer that I should."

As he opened the folding-door to retire, Nippers at his desk caught a glimpse of me, and asked whether I would prefer to have a certain paper copied on blue paper or white. He did not in the least roguishly accent the word prefer. It was plain that it involuntarily rolled from his tongue. I thought to myself, surely I must get rid of a demented man, who already has in some degree turned the tongues, if not the heads of myself and clerks. But I thought it prudent not to break the dismission at once.

The next day I noticed that Bartleby did nothing but stand at his window in his dead-wall revery. Upon asking him why he did not write, he said that he had decided upon doing no more writing.

"Why, how now? what next?" exclaimed I, "do no more writing?"

"No more."

"And what is the reason?"

"Do you not see the reason for yourself?" he indifferently replied.

I looked steadfastly at him, and perceived that his eyes looked dull and glazed. Instantly it occurred to me, that his unexampled diligence in copying by his dim window for the first few weeks of his stay with me might have temporarily impaired his vision.

I was touched. I said something in condolence with him. I hinted that of course he did wisely in abstaining from writing for a while; and urged him to embrace that opportunity of taking wholesome exercise in the open air. This, however, he did not do. A few days after this, my other clerks being absent, and being in a great hurry to dispatch certain letters by the mail, I thought that, having nothing else earthly to do, Bartleby would surely be less inflexible than usual, and carry these letters to the post-office. But he blankly declined. So, much to my inconvenience, I went myself.

Still added days went by. Whether Bartleby's eyes improved or not, I could not say. To all appearance, I thought they did. But when I asked him if they did, he vouchsafed no answer. At all events, he would do no copying. At last, in replying to my urgings, he informed me that he had permanently given up copying.

"What!" exclaimed I; "suppose your eyes should get entirely well—better than ever before—would you not copy then?"

"I have given up copying," he answered, and slid aside.

He remained as ever, a fixture in my chamber. Nay—if that were possible—he became still more of a fixture than before. What was to be done? He would do nothing in the office: why should he stay there? In plain fact, he had now become a millstone to me, not only useless as a necklace, but afflictive to bear. Yet I was sorry for him. I speak less than truth when I say that, on his own account, he occasioned me uneasiness. If he would but have named a single relative or friend, I would instantly have written, and urged their taking the poor fellow away to some convenient retreat. But he seemed alone, absolutely alone in the universe. A bit of wreck in the mid Atlantic. At length, necessities connected with my business tyrannized over all other considerations. Decently as I could, I told Bartleby that in six days' time he must unconditionally leave the office. I warned him to take measures, in the interval, for procuring some other abode. I offered to assist him in this endeavor, if he himself would but take the first step towards a removal. "And when you finally quit me, Bartleby," added I, "I shall see that you go not away entirely unprovided. Six days from this hour, remember."

At the expiration of that period, I peeped behind the screen, and lo! Bartleby was there.

I buttoned up my coat, balanced myself; advanced slowly towards him, touched his shoulder, and said, "The time has come; you must quit this place; I am sorry for you; here is money; but you must go."

"I would prefer not," he replied, with his back still towards me.

"You *must.*"

He remained silent.

Now I had an unbounded confidence in this man's common honesty. He had frequently restored to me sixpences and shillings carelessly dropped upon the floor, for I am apt to be very reckless in such shirt-button affairs. The proceeding then which followed will not be deemed extraordinary.

"Bartleby," said I, "I owe you twelve dollars on account; here are thirty-two; the odd twenty are yours.—Will you take it?" and I handed the bills towards him.

But he made no motion.

"I will leave them here then," putting them under a weight on the table. Then taking my hat and cane and going to the door I tranquilly turned and added—"After you have removed your things from these offices, Bartleby, you will of course lock the door—since every one is now gone for the day but you—and if you please, slip your key underneath the mat, so that I may have it in the morning. I shall not see you again; so good-bye to you. If, hereafter in your new place of abode I can be of any service to you, do not fail to advise me by letter. Good-bye, Bartleby, and fare you well."

But he answered not a word; like the last column of some ruined temple, he remained standing mute and solitary in the middle of the otherwise deserted room.

As I walked home in a pensive mood, my vanity got the better of my pity. I could not but highly plume myself on my masterly management in getting rid of Bartleby. Masterly I call it, and such it must appear to any dispassionate thinker. The beauty of my procedure seemed to consist in its perfect quietness. There was no vulgar bullying, no bravado of any sort, no choleric hectoring, and striding to and fro across the apartment, jerking out vehement commands for Bartleby to bundle himself off with his beggarly traps. Nothing of the kind. Without loudly bidding Bartleby depart—as an inferior genius might have done—I *assumed* the ground that depart he must; and upon that assumption built all I had to say. The more I thought over my procedure, the more I was charmed with it. Nevertheless, next morning, upon awakening, I had my doubts,—I had somehow slept off the fumes of vanity. One of the coolest and wisest hours a man has, is just after he awakes in the morning. My procedure seemed as sagacious as ever,—but only in theory. How it would prove in practice—there was the rub. It was truly a beautiful thought to have assumed Bartleby's departure; but, after all, that assumption was simply my own, and none of Bartleby's. The great point was, not whether I had assumed that he would quit me, but whether he would prefer so to do. He was more a man of preferences than assumptions.

After breakfast, I walked down town, arguing the probabilities *pro* and *con*. One moment I thought it would prove a miserable failure, and Bartleby would be found all alive at my office as usual; the next moment it seemed certain that I should find his chair empty. And so I kept veering about. At the corner of Broadway and Canal-street, I saw quite an excited group of people standing in earnest conversation.

"I'll take odds he doesn't," said a voice as I passed.

"Doesn't go?—done!" said I, "put up your money."

I was instinctively putting my hand in my pocket to produce my own, when I remembered that this was an election day. The words I had overheard bore no reference to Bartleby, but to the success or non-success of some candidate for the mayoralty. In my intent frame of mind, I had, as it were, imagined that all Broadway shared in my excitement, and were debating the same question with me. I passed on, very thankful that the uproar of the street screened my momentary absent-mindedness.

As I had intended, I was earlier than usual at my office door. I stood listening for a moment. All was still. He must be gone. I tried the knob. The door was locked. Yes, my procedure had worked to a charm; he indeed must be vanished. Yet a certain melancholy mixed with this: I was almost sorry for my brilliant success. I was fumbling under the door mat for the key, which Bartleby was to have left there for me, when accidentally my knee knocked against a panel, producing a summoning sound, and in response a voice came to me from within—"Not yet; I am occupied."

It was Bartleby.

I was thunderstruck. For an instant I stood like the man who, pipe in mouth, was killed one cloudless afternoon long ago in Virginia, by summer lightning; at his own warm open window he was killed, and remained leaning out there upon the dreamy afternoon, till someone touched him, when he fell.

"Not gone!" I murmured at last. But again obeying that wondrous ascendancy which the inscrutable scrivener had over me, and from which ascendancy, for all my chafing, I could not completely escape, I slowly went down stairs and out into the street, and while walking round the block, considered what I should next do in this unheard-of perplexity. Turn the man out by an actual thrusting I could not; to drive him away by calling him hard names would not do; calling in the police was an unpleasant idea; and yet, permit him to enjoy his cadaverous triumph over me—this too I could not think of. What was to be done? or, if nothing could be done, was there anything further that I could *assume* in the matter? Yes, as before I had prospectively assumed that Bartleby would depart, so now I might retrospectively assume that departed he was. In the legitimate carrying out of this assumption, I might enter my office in a great hurry, and pretending not to see Bartleby at all, walk straight against him as if he were air. Such a proceeding would in a singular degree have the appearance of a home-thrust. It was hardly possible that Bartleby could withstand such an application of the doctrine of assumption. But upon second thoughts the success of the plan seemed rather dubious. I resolved to argue the matter over with him again.

"Bartleby," said I, entering the office, with a quietly severe expression, "I am seriously displeased. I am pained, Bartleby. I had thought better of you. I had imagined you of such a gentlemanly organization, that in any delicate dilemma a slight hint would suffice—in short, an assumption. But it appears I am deceived. Why," I added, unaffectedly starting, "you have not even touched that money yet," pointing to it, just where I had left it the evening previous.

He answered nothing.

"Will you, or will you not, quit me?" I now demanded in a sudden passion, advancing close to him.

"I would prefer *not* to quit you," he replied, gently emphasizing the *not*.

"What earthly right have you to stay here? Do you pay any rent? Do you pay my taxes? Or is this property yours?"

He answered nothing.

"Are you ready to go on and write now? Are your eyes recovered? Could you copy a small paper for me this morning? or help examine a few lines? or step round to the post-office? In a word, will you do anything at all, to give a coloring to your refusal to depart the premises?"

He silently retired into his hermitage.

I was now in such a state of nervous resentment that I thought it but prudent to check myself at present from further demonstrations. Bartleby and I were alone. I remembered the tragedy of the unfortunate Adams and the still more unfortunate Colt in the solitary office of the latter; and how poor Colt, being dreadfully incensed by Adams, and imprudently permitting himself to get wildly excited, was at unawares hurried into his fatal act—an act which certainly no man could possibly deplore more than the actor himself. Often it had occurred to me in my ponderings upon the subject, that had that altercation taken place in the public street, or at a private residence, it would not have terminated as it did. It was the circumstance of being alone in a solitary office, up stairs, of a building entirely unhallowed by humanizing domestic associations—an uncarpeted office, doubtless, of a dusty, haggard sort of appearance;—this it must have been, which greatly helped to enhance the irritable desperation of the hapless Colt.

But when this old Adam of resentment rose in me and tempted me concerning Bartleby, I grappled him and threw him. How? Why, simply by recalling the divine injunction: "A new commandment give I unto you, that ye love one another." Yes, this it was that saved me. Aside from higher considerations, charity often operates as a vastly wise and prudent principle—a great safeguard to its possessor. Men have committed murder for jealousy's sake, and anger's sake, and hatred's sake, and selfishness' sake, and spiritual pride's sake; but no man that ever I heard of ever committed a diabolical murder for sweet charity's sake. Mere self-interest, then, if no better motive can be enlisted, should, especially with high-tempered men, prompt all beings to charity and philanthropy. At any rate, upon the occasion in question, I strove to drown my exasperated feelings towards the scrivener by benevolently construing his conduct. Poor fellow, poor fellow! thought I, he don't mean any thing; and besides, he has seen hard times, and ought to be indulged.

I endeavored also immediately to occupy myself, and at the same time to comfort my despondency. I tried to fancy that in the course of the morning, at such time as might prove agreeable to him, Bartleby, of his own free accord, would emerge from his hermitage, and take up some decided line of march in the direction of the door. But no. Half-past twelve o'clock came; Turkey began to glow in the face, overturn his inkstand, and become generally obstreperous; Nippers abated down into quietude and courtesy; Ginger Nut munched his noon apple; and Bartleby remained standing at his window in one of his profoundest dead-wall reveries. Will it be credited? Ought I to acknowledge it? That afternoon I left the office without saying one further word to him.

Some days now passed, during which, at leisure intervals I looked a little into "Edwards on the Will," and "Priestley on Necessity." Under the circumstances, those books induced a salutary feeling. Gradually I slid into the persuasion that these troubles of mine touching the scrivener, had been all predestined from eternity, and Bartleby was billeted upon me for some mysterious purpose of an all-wise Providence, which it was not for a mere mortal like me to fathom. Yes, Bartleby, stay there behind your screen, thought I; I shall persecute you no more; you are harmless and noiseless as any of these old chairs; in short, I never feel so private as when I know you are here. At last I see it, I feel it; I penetrate to the predestinated purpose of my life. I am content. Others may have loftier parts to enact; but my mission in this world, Bartleby, is to furnish you with office-room for such period as you may see fit to remain.

I believe that this wise and blessed frame of mind would have continued with me, had it not been for the unsolicited and uncharitable remarks obtruded upon me by my professional friends who visited the rooms. But thus it often is, that the constant friction of illiberal minds wears out at last the best resolves of the more generous. Though to be sure, when I reflected upon it, it was not strange that people entering my office should be struck by the peculiar aspect of the unaccountable Bartleby, and so be tempted to throw out some sinister observations concerning him. Sometimes an attorney having business with me, and calling at my office, and finding no one but the scrivener there, would undertake to obtain some sort of precise information from him touching my whereabouts; but without heeding his idle talk, Bartleby would remain standing immovable in the middle of the room. So after contemplating him in that position for a time, the attorney would depart, no wiser than he came.

Also, when a Reference was going on, and the room full of lawyers and witnesses, and business driving fast; some deeply occupied legal gentleman present, seeing Bartleby wholly unemployed, would request him to run round to his (the legal gentleman's) office and fetch some papers for him. Thereupon, Bartleby would tranquilly decline, and yet remain idle as before. Then the lawyer would give a great stare, and turn to me. And what could I say? At last I was made aware that all through the circle of my professional acquaintance, a whisper of wonder was running round, having reference to the strange creature I kept at my office. This worried me very much. And as the idea came upon me of his possibly turning out a long-lived man, and keeping occupying my chambers, and denying my authority; and perplexing my visitors; and scandalizing my professional reputation; and casting a general gloom over the premises; keeping soul and body together to the last upon his savings (for doubtless he spent but half a dime a day), and in the end perhaps outlive me, and claim possession of my office by right of his perpetual occupancy: as all these dark anticipations crowded upon me more and more, and my friends continually intruded their relentless remarks upon the apparition in my room; a great change was wrought in me. I resolved to gather all my faculties together, and for ever rid me of this intolerable incubus.

Ere revolving any complicated project, however, adapted to this end, I first simply suggested to Bartleby the propriety of his permanent departure. In a calm and serious tone, I commended the idea to his careful and mature consideration. But having taken three days to meditate upon it, he apprised me, that his original determination remained the same; in short, that he still preferred to abide with me.

What shall I do? I now said to myself, buttoning up my coat to the last button. What shall I do? what ought I to do? what does conscience say I *should* do with this man, or rather ghost. Rid myself of him, I must; go, he shall. But how? You will not thrust him, the poor, pale, passive mortal,—you will not thrust such a helpless creature out of your door? you will not dishonor yourself by such cruelty? No, I will not, I cannot do that. Rather would I let him live and die here, and then mason up his remains in the wall. What then will you do? For all your coaxing, he will not budge. Bribes he leaves under your own paper-weight on your table; in short, it is quite plain that he prefers to cling to you.

Then something severe, something unusual must be done. What! surely you will not have him collared by a constable, and commit his innocent pallor to the common jail? And upon what ground could you procure such a thing to be done?—a vagrant, is he? What! he a vagrant, a wanderer, who refuses to budge? It is because he will *not* be a vagrant, then, that you seek to count him *as* a vagrant. That is too absurd. No visible means of support: there I have him. Wrong again: for indubitably he *does* support himself, and that is the only unanswerable proof that any man can show of his possessing the means so to do. No more then. Since he will not quit me, I must quit him. I will change my offices; I will move elsewhere; and give him fair notice, that if I find him on my new premises I will then proceed against him as a common trespasser.

Acting accordingly, next day I thus addressed him: "I find these chambers too far from the City Hall; the air is unwholesome. In a word, I propose to remove my offices next week, and shall no longer require your services. I tell you this now, in order that you may seek another place."

He made no reply, and nothing more was said.

On the appointed day I engaged carts and men, proceeded to my chambers, and having but little furniture, every thing was removed in a few hours. Throughout, the scrivener remained standing behind the screen, which I directed to be removed the last thing. It was withdrawn; and being folded up like a huge folio, left him the motionless occupant of a naked room. I stood in the entry watching him a moment, while something from within me upbraided me.

I re-entered, with my hand in my pocket—and—and my heart in my mouth.

"Good-bye, Bartleby; I am going—good-bye, and God some way bless you; and take that," slipping something in his hand. But it dropped upon the floor, and then,—strange to say—I tore myself from him whom I had so longed to be rid of.

Established in my new quarters, for a day or two I kept the door locked, started at every footfall in the passages. When I returned to my rooms after any little absence, I would pause at the threshold for an instant, and attentively listen, ere applying my key. But these fears were needless. Bartleby never came nigh me.

I thought all was going well, when a perturbed looking stranger visited me, inquiring whether I was the person who had recently occupied rooms at No. — Wall-street.

Full of forebodings, I replied that I was.

"Then sir," said the stranger, who proved a lawyer, "you are responsible for the man you left there. He refuses to do any copying; he refuses to do any thing; he says he prefers not to; and he refuses to quit the premises."

"I am very sorry, sir," said I, with assumed tranquillity, but an inward tremor, "but, really, the man you allude to is nothing to me—he is no relation or apprentice of mine, that you should hold me responsible for him."

"In mercy's name, who is he?"

"I certainly cannot inform you. I know nothing about him. Formerly I employed him as a copyist; but he has done nothing for me now for some time past."

"I shall settle him then,—good morning, sir."

Several days passed, and I heard nothing more; and though I often felt a charitable prompting to call at the place and see poor Bartleby, yet a certain squeamishness of I know not what withheld me.

All is over with him, by this time, thought I at last, when through another week no further intelligence reached me. But coming to my room the day after, I found several persons waiting at my door in a high state of nervous excitement.

"That's the man—here he comes," cried the foremost one, whom I recognized as the lawyer who had previously called upon me alone.

"You must take him away, sir, at once," cried a portly person among them, advancing upon me, and whom I knew to be the landlord of No. — Wall-street. "These gentlemen, my tenants, cannot stand it any longer; Mr. B——" pointing to the lawyer, "has turned him out of his room, and he now persists in haunting the building generally, sitting upon the banisters of the stairs by day, and sleeping in the entry by night. Every body is concerned; clients are leaving the offices; some fears are entertained of a mob; something you must do, and that without delay."

Aghast at this torrent, I fell back before it, and would fain have locked myself in my new quarters. In vain I persisted that Bartleby was nothing to me—no more than to any one else. In vain:—I was the last person known to have anything to do with him, and they held me to the terrible account. Fearful then of being exposed in the papers (as one person present obscurely threatened), I considered the matter, and at length said, that if the lawyer would give me a confidential interview with the scrivener, in his (the lawyer's) own room, I would that afternoon strive my best to rid them of the nuisance they complained of.

Going up stairs to my old haunt, there was Bartleby silently sitting upon the banister at the landing.

"What are you doing here, Bartleby?" said I.

"Sitting upon the banister," he mildly replied.

I motioned him into the lawyer's room, who then left us.

"Bartleby," said I, "are you aware that you are the cause of great tribulation to me, by persisting in occupying the entry after being dismissed from the office?"

No answer.

"Now one of two things must take place. Either you must do something, or something must be done to you. Now what sort of business would you like to engage in? Would you like to re-engage in copying for some one?"

"No; I would prefer not to make any change."

"Would you like a clerkship in a dry-goods store?"

"There is too much confinement about that. No, I would not like a clerkship; but I am not particular."

"Too much confinement," I cried, "why, you keep yourself confined all the time!"

"I would prefer not to take a clerkship," he rejoined, as if to settle that little item at once.

"How would a bar-tender's business suit you? There is no trying of the eye-sight in that."

"I would not like it at all; though, as I said before, I am not particular."

His unwonted wordiness inspirited me. I returned to the charge.

"Well then, would you like to travel through the country collecting bills for the merchants? That would improve your health."

"No, I would prefer to be doing something else."

"How then would going as a companion to Europe, to entertain some young gentleman with your conversation—how would that suit you?"

"Not at all. It does not strike me that there is any thing definite about that. I like to be stationary. But I am not particular."

"Stationary you shall be then," I cried, now losing all patience, and for the first time in all my exasperating connections with him fairly flying into a passion. "If you do not go away from these premises before night, I shall feel bound—indeed, I *am* bound—to—to—to quit the premises myself!" I rather absurdly concluded, knowing not with what possible threat to try to frighten his immobility into compliance. Despairing of all further efforts, I was precipitately leaving him, when a final thought occurred to me—one which had not been wholly unindulged before.

"Bartleby," said I, in the kindest tone I could assume under such exciting circumstances, "will you go home with me now—not to my office, but my dwelling—and remain there till we can conclude upon some convenient arrangement for you at our leisure? Come, let us start now, right away."

"No: at present I would prefer not to make any change at all."

I answered nothing; but effectually dodging every one by the suddenness and rapidity of my flight, rushed from the building, ran up Wall-street towards Broadway, and jumping into the first omnibus was soon removed from pursuit. As soon as tranquillity returned I distinctly perceived that I had now done all that

I possibly could, both in respect to the demands of the landlord and his tenants, and with regard to my own desire and sense of duty, to benefit Bartleby, and shield him from rude persecution. I now strove to be entirely care-free and quiescent; and my conscience justified me in the attempt; though indeed it was not so successful as I could have wished. So fearful was I of being again hunted out by the incensed landlord and his exasperated tenants, that, surrendering my business to Nippers, for a few days I drove about the upper part of the town and through the suburbs, in my rockaway; crossed over to Jersey City and Hoboken, and paid fugitive visits to Manhattanville and Astoria. In fact I almost lived in my rockaway for the time.

When again I entered my office, lo, a note from the landlord lay upon the desk. I opened it with trembling hands. It informed me that the writer had sent to the police, and had Bartleby removed to the Tombs as a vagrant. Moreover, since I knew more about him than any one else, he wished me to appear at that place, and make a suitable statement of the facts. These tidings had a conflicting effect upon me. At first I was indignant; but at last almost approved. The landlord's energetic, summary disposition, had led him to adopt a procedure which I do not think I would have decided upon myself; and yet as a last resort, under such peculiar circumstances, it seemed the only plan.

As I afterwards learned, the poor scrivener, when told that he must be conducted to the Tombs, offered not the slightest obstacle, but in his pale unmoving way, silently acquiesced.

Some of the compassionate and curious bystanders joined the party; and headed by one of the constables arm in arm with Bartleby, the silent procession filed its way through all the noise, and heat, and joy of the roaring thoroughfares at noon.

The same day I received the note I went to the Tombs, or, to speak more properly, the Halls of Justice. Seeking the right officer, I stated the purpose of my call, and was informed that the individual I described was indeed within. I then assured the functionary that Bartleby was a perfectly honest man, and greatly to be compassionated, however unaccountably eccentric. I narrated all I knew, and closed by suggesting the idea of letting him remain in as indulgent confinement as possible till something less harsh might be done—though indeed I hardly knew what. At all events, if nothing else could be decided upon, the alms-house must receive him. I then begged to have an interview.

Being under no disgraceful charge, and quite serene and harmless in all his ways, they had permitted him freely to wander about the prison, and especially, in the inclosed grass-platted yards thereof. And so I found him there, standing all alone in the quietest of the yards, his face towards a high wall, while all around, from the narrow slits of the jail windows, I thought I saw peering out upon him the eyes of murderers and thieves.

"Bartleby!"

"I know you," he said, without looking round,—"and I want nothing to say to you."

"It was not I that brought you here, Bartleby," said I, keenly pained at his implied suspicion. "And to you, this should not be so vile a place. Nothing reproachful attaches to you by being here. And see, it is not so sad a place as one might think. Look, there is the sky, and here is the grass."

"I know where I am," he replied, but would say nothing more, and so I left him.

As I entered the corridor again, a broad meat-like man, in an apron, accosted me, and jerking his thumb over my shoulder, said—"Is that your friend?"

"Yes."

"Does he want to starve? If he does, let him live on the prison fare, that's all."

"Who are you?" asked I, not knowing what to make of such an unofficially speaking person in such a place.

"I am the grub-man. Such gentlemen as have friends here, hire me to provide them with something good to eat."

"Is this so?" said I, turning to the turnkey.

He said it was.

"Well then," said I, slipping some silver into the grub-man's hands (for so they called him). "I want you to give particular attention to my friend there; let him have the best dinner you can get. And you must be as polite to him as possible."

"Introduce me, will you?" said the grub-man, looking at me with an expression which seemed to say he was all impatience for an opportunity to give a specimen of his breeding.

Thinking it would prove of benefit to the scrivener, I acquiesced; and asking the grub-man his name, went up with him to Bartleby.

"Bartleby, this is Mr. Cutlets; you will find him very useful to you."

"Your sarvant, sir, your sarvant," said the grub-man, making a low salutation behind his apron. "Hope you find it pleasant here, sir; nice grounds—cool apartments, sir—hope you'll stay with us some time—try to make it agreeable. May Mrs. Cutlets and I have the pleasure of your company to dinner, sir, in Mrs. Cutlets' private room?"

"I prefer not to dine to-day," said Bartleby, turning away. "It would disagree with me; I am unused to dinners." So saying, he slowly moved to the other side of the inclosure, and took up a position fronting the dead-wall.

"How's this?" said the grub-man, addressing me with a stare of astonishment. "He's odd, ain't he?"

"I think he is a little deranged," said I, sadly.

"Deranged? deranged is it? Well, now, upon my word, I thought that friend of yourn was a gentleman forger; they are always pale and genteel-like, them forgers. I can't help pity 'em—can't help it, sir. Did you know Monroe Edwards?" he added, touchingly, and paused. Then, laying his hand pityingly on my shoulder, sighed, "he died of consumption at Sing-Sing. So you weren't acquainted with Monroe?"

"No, I was never socially acquainted with any forgers. But I cannot stop longer. Look to my friend yonder. You will not lose by it. I will see you again."

Some few days after this, I again obtained admission to the Tombs, and went through the corridors in quest of Bartleby; but without finding him.

"I saw him coming from his cell not long ago," said a turnkey, "may be he's gone to loiter in the yards."

So I went in that direction.

"Are you looking for the silent man?" said another turnkey passing me. "Yonder he lies—sleeping in the yard there. 'Tis not twenty minutes since I saw him lie down."

The yard was entirely quiet. It was not accessible to the common prisoners. The surrounding walls, of amazing thickness, kept off all sounds behind them. The Egyptian character of the masonry weighed upon me with its gloom. But a soft imprisoned turf grew under foot. The heart of the eternal pyramids, it seemed, wherein, by some strange magic, through the clefts, grass-seed, dropped by birds, had sprung.

Strangely huddled at the base of the wall, his knees drawn up, and lying on his side, his head touching the cold stones, I saw the wasted Bartleby. But nothing stirred. I paused; then went close up to him; stooped over, and saw that his dim eyes were open; otherwise he seemed profoundly sleeping. Something prompted me to touch him. I felt his hand, when a tingling shiver ran up my arm and down my spine to my feet.

The round face of the grub-man peered upon me now. "His dinner is ready. Won't he dine to-day, either? Or does he live without dining?"

"Lives without dining," said I, and closed the eyes.

"Eh!—He's asleep, aint he?"

"With kings and counsellors," murmured I.

* * * * *

There would seem little need for proceeding further in this history. Imagination will readily supply the meagre recital of poor Bartleby's interment. But ere parting with the reader, let me say, that if this little narrative has sufficiently interested him, to awaken curiosity as to who Bartleby was, and what manner of life he led prior to the present narrator's making his acquaintance, I can only reply, that in such curiosity I fully share, but am wholly unable to gratify it. Yet here I hardly know whether I should divulge one little item of rumor, which came to my ear a few months after the scrivener's decease. Upon what basis it rested, I could never ascertain; and hence, how true it is I cannot now tell. But inasmuch as this vague report has not been without a certain suggestive interest to me, however sad, it may prove the same with some others; and so I will briefly mention it. The report was this: that Bartleby had been a subordinate clerk in the Dead Letter Office at Washington, from which he had been suddenly removed by a change in the administration. When I think over this rumor, hardly can I express the emotions which seize me. Dead letters! does it not sound like dead men? Conceive a man by nature and misfortune prone to a pallid hopelessness, can any business seem more fitted to heighten it than that of continually handling these dead letters, and assorting them for the flames? For by the cart-load they are annually burned. Sometimes from out the folded paper the pale clerk takes a ring:—the finger it was meant for, perhaps, moulders in the grave; a bank-note sent in swiftest charity:—he whom it would relieve, nor eats nor hungers any more; pardon for those who died despairing; hope for those who died unhoping; good tidings for those who died stifled by unrelieved calamities. On errands of life, these letters speed to death.

Ah, Bartleby! Ah, humanity! ■

Working with the Text

1. Although the story is entitled "Bartleby, the Scrivener," the narrative seems as much about the lawyer telling the story as his stubborn copyist. What do you think Melville wants us to think about this lawyer? Find descriptions that you feel make us sympathetic to the lawyer and others that make us view him critically. If Melville is satirizing the lawyer, what particular qualities about him are being satirized?

2. "Nothing so aggravates an earnest person as a passive resistance," the lawyer tells us. Consider Bartleby's actions in the story as a form of protest. What do you think Bartleby is objecting to, and what specific effects does he have on the lawyer? Compare Bartleby's form of protest with that of his fellow employees, Turkey and Nippers.

3. The lawyer/narrator is baffled by Bartleby's response of "I prefer not to," but in one way at least Bartleby's position makes perfect sense: who would prefer to spend their days copying endless legal documents over by hand? Bartleby's response along with the lawyer's various failed attempts to motivate him raise questions about what makes people do unpleasant work, why we behave the ways we do on the job, and other "assumptions" about how a workplace should operate. Working in a group, compile a list of the various assumptions about the workplace that Bartleby challenges in the story.

4. Write your own version of a "Bartleby" story set in a contemporary workplace. Who would your employer/narrator be, and how exactly would his or her mysterious employee drive him or her crazy?

Working with Connections

1. Imagine that the lawyer were to write a letter to Randy Cohen's "The Ethicist" column (from Chapter 7, "Ethics of Work/The

Work Ethic") asking for advice on how to handle Bartleby. Write that letter and what you think Cohen's response might be.

2. Melville's story was made into a movie in 2001 by Jonathan Parker (now available on video) that transplants the story into the present-day world of work. Before you watch the movie, write about and discuss how you might update Bartleby's story. What kind of contemporary work would he do? What point would you want to make about work through the story? What form would his resistance take, and how would it be met? After watching the movie, discuss the different choices made by the class and by the filmmakers. How well do you think they captured the spirit of Melville's story? How does their adaptation make you rethink the story and the issues involved?

KATHRYN CARMONY

Surfing the Classifieds

A Quick Reference Guide

Most of us have at one time or another searched for a job in the classi-fied pages of the local newspaper. Experienced job hunters learn that the language of these advertisements can be read as a kind of code that tries to hide the negative aspects of the job being listed. In "Surfing the Classifieds," Kathryn Carmony sarcastically decodes the "real" meaning of the language found in many job ads. Before reading, brainstorm "code words" that members of the class have come across in their own job-hunting experiences. Carmony is a web designer, artist, and humorist who lives in Indianapolis.

What it says . . .	**. . . and what it means.**
advancement opportunity	Shit job
entry level	*Really* a shit job
no experience necessary	The mother of all shit jobs
administrative assistant	Shit job with a title
Room to grow!	Your worst nightmare of a shit job
ground floor opportunity	Shit job with a company that will file bankruptcy within a year
progressive company	Employees get to wear business casual every other Friday

team player	Must deal with dangerously territorial co-workers with rabid personalities
upbeat personality	Must neither threaten us with any kind of lawsuit nor use the drug & alcohol rehab benefit within the first year
Word processing skills essential	There's a crippling case of carpal tunnel syndrome in your future
Public relations	Receptionist
professional appearance important	A $20K/year job that requires a $100K/year wardrobe
time-management skills critical	Before we downsized, four people were doing this job
money-motivated	We'll dangle that carrot 'til you drop
some travel required	You'll learn to call Motel 6 home, but we'll leave the light on for ya
pleasant telephone manner	Be the voice of 1-900-SUCK
Earn up to $300/hour!	*Be* 1-900-SUCK
Salary range $24,000 to $32,000	The salary is $24,000
Jeans job!	Minimum wage temp job in concentration camp conditions
Will train	Prior conviction of a felony or two no problem
Must have tools	Must have balls
Must meet lifting requirements	Must have big, burly balls
BA required, master's preferred	Must be an MA willing to work for a BA's salary
civil service	This job was filled from the inside six months ago
non-profit	Exactly
Women & minorities encouraged to apply	White males need not waste the stamp
Executive level	Women & minorities need not waste the stamp
outstanding benefits	Inadequate health insurance
drug-free environment	Periodically, we'll make you pee in a cup
smoke-free environment	But you're free to huddle outside the building in sub-zero temperatures, smoking your lungs out

Employee stock purchase plan	With all your discretionary income from this minimum-wage job, you can buy the company!
Tons of variety!	We took all the heinous tasks no other employee would do and rolled them into one job
Top-notch communications skills	Telemarketing
Previous telephone experience	Evidently all men, women, children and most chimpanzees in the developed world are qualified for this job
Must have Macintosh experience	And maybe you own a Yugo and a Betamax, too
Sense of humor helpful . . .	. . . because God knows you're going to need it
Beautiful offices in attractive location	Brand new ticky-tacky windowless building where the picture frames all match the carpeting, located in suburbia
Secretary	Woman-only job with the responsibilities of management and wages of a migrant worker
Executive secretary to CEO	Much more powerful position than the CEO, at one-billionth his salary
Dedicated	You're looking at a minimum of 80 hours/week from now until we force you into early retirement
salary commensurate	We'll pay you whatever the hell we feel like
salary negotiable	We'll take the lowest bidder
competitive salary	We'll pay you up to 10% more than your last job, and not one penny more
competitive starting salary	Ten cents above minimum wage
pleasant atmosphere	A staff of pod people
professional atmosphere	Zombie pod people
fun, creative atmosphere	Pod people from hell
dynamic atmosphere	Zombie pod people from hell
If *your* good at communicating . . .	Obviously we could use your help
Eighty-percent of the good jobs are never published!	*And we don't know where they are either!*
Good speaking personality	Must have a personality that speaks good?

Must truly love answering the phone	Must be a brain-dead masochist
good attitude and personality	Even though this job offers no intrinsic or extrinsic reward whatsoever, we'd like you to be damned happy about it
Must be very conscientious of your work	Try not to let this boring job zone you into a coma
Attention to detail required	Try to stay sober
"OPPORTUNITY UNLEASHED!"	Run!
"THE SKY'S THE LIMIT!"	Run away, fast!
"STOP LOOKING!"	Run, run, run!
"TASTE SUCCESS!"	Eat shit!
Send application, resume, cover letter, references, official transcripts, and non-returnable writing samples	What, no blood sample?
Gal Friday	Anyone who actually applies for this job *deserves* it
self-starter	(Open to very broad interpretation since no one really knows what this means) ▪

Working with the Text

1. Which of Carmony's satirical definitions rang the most true for you? Write about a job experience you have had that connects to that definition.

2. Carmony's piece invites imitation. Working in groups, build on the brainstorming exercise described in the introduction to Carmony's piece to come up with additional job descriptions or workplace terms that need similar decoding and invent your own definitions. You could also take aim at the language of school-work: course descriptions, paper assignments, test questions, grading standards, and so on.

3. By making fun of and criticizing certain kinds of social institutions and behaviors, satire implies a set of moral and ethical values that the satirist believes society should live up to but doesn't. Based on what she makes fun of in the language of job ads, write about what you think Carmony's main objections are to the contemporary American workplace and what values she thinks are being violated or ignored.

Working with Connections

1. Carmony's satire of the language of job ads shares a lot in common with the way Scott Adams makes fun of the corporate workplace in *Dilbert*. To what extent do you think Carmony and Adams share the same points of view, and in what ways might they differ?

2. Walter Kirn, in his "Summertime Dues" (in Chapter 7, "The Ethics of Work/The Work Ethic"), argues that what he learned from his summer jobs as a teenager were not exactly wholesome values. In many ways, he takes a similar approach to Carmony's in revealing what summer work was "really" about. Write about the extent to which you agree and disagree with their assessment of working conditions.

3. The advertisement reproduced in Chapter 6, "Work and Diversity," provides an opportunity for decoding both textual and visual cues about the workplace. How might you decode this visual job ad in the style of Carmony?

Media Images

SCOTT ADAMS
Dilbert
■

The workplace has always been a rich source for parody and humor. Even when depictions of the workplace are meant in fun, however, what we laugh at can reveal just as much about our values, beliefs, and ideals as what we take seriously. Reading this Dilbert *cartoon by Scott Adams making fun of the workplace can raise questions about just what our laughter means.*

Scott Adams's cartoon Dilbert *has grown into one of the most popular comics in America by satirizing the corporate workplace, focusing in particular on the plight of office workers attempting to deal with maddening orders and instructions from clueless bosses. The image of the character of Dilbert, with his blank eyes and upturned tie, has become an instantly recognizable icon for frustrated employees everywhere. The success of the comic strip has led to an animated television series and a series of books by Scott Adams that deal with workplace management, such as* The Dilbert Principle: A Cubicle's-Eye View of Bosses, Meetings, Management Fads and Other Workplace Afflictions *(1997).*

Working with the Text

1. What are the objects of Scott Adams' humor in the *Dilbert* strip? What values, beliefs, and attitudes about work are revealed by our laughing at the situation depicted.

2. In addition to Adams's keen ability to observe the absurdities of the workplace, his drawing style also functions as part of the humor and satire of the strip. How does Adams extend his critique of the corporate workplace through the visual presentation of his characters? What do you see as the most effective details of the characters and why?

3. On the one hand, the popularity of *Dilbert* might suggest that there are many employees unhappy with corporate work, an unhappiness that could potentially turn into demands for change. On the other, *Dilbert* has also been embraced by many corporations, and Scott Adams has licensed the use of *Dilbert* images to companies such as IBM and the Lockheed Marietta Corporation. How do you understand the purpose of *Dilbert* cartoons? Do they help people cope with their jobs or do they urge them to change what they find dehumanizing about them? Rather than approaching this as a yes/no question, what would the arguments be for each side?

THE WORK OF WRITING/WRITING AS WORK

One focus of this chapter on "Work, Labor, and Career" has been definitions. From the opening exercise at the beginning of the chapter asking you to define these three terms through the various readings, you have been challenged to question the fundamental meanings of "keywords" we often take for granted, whether work, play, or success. As writers such as Bob Black have argued, our beliefs and ideas about work have real consequences in the ways we structure our lives and organize our labor.

The connections between how we define work and the ways in which work gets done in the world are crucial outside of the writing classroom as well. In any collective work enterprise, whether it is a corporation or a charity, a school or a homeless shelter, the work of that enterprise needs to be broken down, defined, and organized. One basic yet crucial component of this process is the job description. In any organization, a job description defines the responsibilities and authority of each person who works there. More than just a list of duties, a job description can explain how the person doing that job fits in the decision-making structure of the organization, how his or her performance will be evaluated, and how the person will be paid or compensated. Even the title of the position can be crucial in terms of conveying the importance of the work being done.

Writing in the World

1. As a class, in groups, or as individuals, locate an organization that is willing to let you interview a personnel director or some other person involved in hiring or in finding volunteers. Interview that person about how they develop their job descriptions. Ask to look at some sample job descriptions. In a paper or presentation for your class, review these job descriptions and make recommendations for improving them, based on your interview and your own experiences as an employee.

2. As a class or in groups, work with your instructor to locate local nonprofit organizations in need of volunteers to write job descriptions for their group. Work out a contract with that organization, spelling out exactly what kind of writing work you will do and when it will be completed. Then, conduct interviews and do research into the work of the organization in order to write the needed job descriptions. For class, write about your experiences working on these descriptions. Who were your audiences? What legal concerns did you have to address? What revisions were asked for?

CHAPTER 3

Education and Work/ Education as Work

Have you ever felt under pressure to justify your plan of study in college when asked by a parent or other family member, "So, what's your major?" Even if you don't have one yet, you may feel compelled to offer some possible candidates. Chances are, unless you are in a major that has a specific career path attached to it such as accounting or education, you will be asked, "So, what are you going to do with that?" (As an English major, I found that replying "I'm thinking of law school" usually satisfied the questioner, and it wasn't really a lie—the truth was I was thinking of a lot of things.)

Questions like these about college suggest that there is a strong connection in our society between education and work. As was noted in the Preface, concerns about work and career are the major motivations that drive many students to go to college, but even before college the connection is evident in many ways, from programs designed to help children learn about future careers to the structure of the school day itself, which teaches us to show up at a set time, follow a specific work schedule, and learn the rules of a complex organization. No wonder many people describe school as the main job of young people, even as more and more teenagers work outside of school as well.

Clearly, formal education has a lot to do with career preparation, but is that or should that be the primary function of school? As students, are you preparing for a job or a life, and what is the relationship between the two? Conversely, what kind of an education do we get from work? Is there a difference between what work and school are supposed to teach us and what they really teach us?

Preparing to Read: Writing Suggestions for the Beginning of Chapter 3

1. What are your goals as a college student? Make a list of what you hope to learn from college. Next, look at the general-studies courses for your college and the requirements for your major or

one you are thinking about. How well do or don't they fit your own personal goals? What changes would you suggest? Find the official educational goals of your college or university and compare them with your own. Where do you agree or disagree?

2. Write about the job or work experiences that you feel taught you about the most positive and negative aspects of work. This may involve a single experience or multiple jobs. Would you recommend these experiences to others? How well did they relate to what you were studying in school?

Foundational Readings

JEAN ANYON   ■

From *Social Class and the Hidden Curriculum of Work*

Education is often promoted as the great equalizer in society, the main means for overcoming differences in income and opportunity. While schools can be powerful agents for changing the lives of individuals and for transforming societies, they can also serve to maintain levels of inequality and social division. In the late 1970s, Jean Anyon, currently the chairperson of the Department of Education at Rutgers University in New Jersey, conducted a study to look at the differences among public schools in neighborhoods ranging from working class to wealthy. While she did find expected differences in terms of teaching resources and school facilities connected to how affluent the districts were, she argues in the essay based on her research that the most striking and important differences among these schools have to do with the way classes are taught and the expectations teachers have for their students. Writing for fellow teachers and education professors, Anyon makes the case that the way teachers teach and schools are run have to do with the assumptions made about the kinds of work students will do as adults, and that these assumptions can hinder the ideal of social mobility.

Scholars in political economy and the sociology of knowledge have recently argued that public schools in complex industrial societies like our own make available different types of educational experience and curriculum knowledge to students in different social classes. Bowles and Gintis[1] for example, have argued that students in different social-class backgrounds are rewarded for classroom behaviors that correspond to personality traits allegedly rewarded in the different occupational strata—the working classes for docility and obedi-

---

[1] S. Bowles and H. Gintis, *Schooling in Capitalist America: Educational Reform and the Contradictions of Economic Life* (New York: Basic Books, 1976).

ence, the managerial classes for initiative and personal assertiveness. Basil Bernstein, Pierre Bourdieu, and Michael W. Apple,[2] focusing on school knowledge, have argued that knowledge and skills leading to social power and regard (medical, legal, managerial) are made available to the advantaged social groups but are withheld from the working classes, to whom a more "practical" curriculum is offered (manual skills, clerical knowledge). While there has been considerable argumentation of these points regarding education in England, France, and North America, there has been little or no attempt to investigate these ideas empirically in elementary or secondary schools and classrooms in this country.[3]

This article offers tentative empirical support (and qualification) of the above arguments by providing illustrative examples of differences in student *work* in classrooms in contrasting social class communities. The examples were gathered as part of an ethnographical study of curricular, pedagogical, and pupil evaluation practices in five elementary schools. The article attempts a theoretical contribution as well and assesses student work in the light of a theoretical approach to social-class analysis. . . . It will be suggested that there is a "hidden curriculum" in schoolwork that has profound implications for the theory—and consequence—of everyday activity in education. . . .

THE SAMPLE OF SCHOOLS

. . . The social-class designation of each of the five schools will be identified, and the income, occupation, and other relevant available social characteristics of the students and their parents will be described. The first three schools are in a medium-sized city district in northern New Jersey, and the other two are in a nearby New Jersey suburb.

The first two schools I will call *working-class schools*. Most of the parents have blue-collar jobs. Less than a third of the fathers are skilled, while the majority are in unskilled or semiskilled jobs. During the period of the study (1978–1979), approximately 15 percent of the fathers were unemployed. The large majority (85 percent) of the families are white. The following occupations are typical: platform, storeroom, and stockroom workers; foundrymen, pipe welders, and boilermakers; semiskilled and unskilled assemblyline operatives; gas station attendants, auto mechanics, maintenance workers, and security guards. Less than 30 percent of the women work, some part-time and some full-time, on assembly lines, in storerooms and stockrooms, as waitresses, barmaids, or sales clerks. Of the fifth-grade parents, none of the wives of the skilled workers had jobs. Approximately 15 percent of the families in each school are at or below the

---

[2] B. Bernstein, *Class, Codes and Control, Vol. 3. Towards a Theory of Educational Transmission,* 2d ed. (London: Routledge & Kegan Paul, 1977); P. Bourdieu and J. Passeron, *Reproduction in Education, Society and Culture* (Beverly Hills, Calif.: Sage, 1977); M. W. Apple, *Ideology and Curriculum* (Boston: Routledge & Kegan Paul, 1979).

[3] But see, in a related vein, M. W. Apple and N. King, "What Do Schools Teach?" *Curriculum Inquiry* 6 (1977): 341–58; R. C. Rist, *The Urban School: A Factory for Failure* (Cambridge, Mass.: MIT Press, 1973).

federal "poverty" level;[4] most of the rest of the family incomes are at or below $12,000, except some of the skilled workers whose incomes are higher. The incomes of the majority of the families in these two schools (at or below $12,000) are typical of 38.6 percent of the families in the United States.[5]

The third school is called the *middle-class school*, although because of neighborhood residence patterns, the population is a mixture of several social classes. The parents' occupations can be divided into three groups: a small group of blue-collar "rich," who are skilled, well-paid workers such as printers, carpenters, plumbers, and construction workers. The second group is composed of parents in working-class and middle-class white-collar jobs: women in office jobs, technicians, supervisors in industry, and parents employed by the city (such as firemen, policemen, and several of the school's teachers). The third group is composed of occupations such as personnel directors in local firms, accountants, "middle management," and a few small capitalists (owners of shops in the area). The children of several local doctors attend this school. Most family incomes are between $13,000 and $25,000, with a few higher. This income range is typical of 38.9 percent of the families in the United States.[6]

The fourth school has a parent population that is at the upper income level of the upper middle class and is predominantly professional. This school will be called the *affluent professional school*. Typical jobs are: cardiologist, interior designer, corporate lawyer or engineer, executive in advertising or television. There are some families who are not as affluent as the majority (the family of the superintendent of the district's schools, and the one or two families in which the fathers are skilled workers). In addition, a few of the families are more affluent than the majority and can be classified in the capitalist class (a partner in a prestigious Wall Street stock brokerage firm). Approximately 90 percent of the children in this school are white. Most family incomes are between $40,000 and $80,000. This income span represents approximately 7 percent of the families in the United States.[7]

In the fifth school the majority of the families belong to the capitalist class. This school will be called the *executive elite school* because most of the fathers are top executives (for example, presidents and vice-presidents) in major United States–based multinational corporations—for example, AT&T, RCA, Citibank,

---

[4] The U.S. Bureau of the Census defines *poverty* for a nonfarm family of four as a yearly income of $6,191 a year or less. U.S. Bureau of the Census, *Statistical Abstract of the United States: 1978* (Washington, D.C.: U.S. Government Printing Office, 1978), 465, table 754.

[5] U.S. Bureau of the Census. "Money Income in 1977 of Families and Persons in the United States," *Current Population Reports* Series P-60, no. 118 (Washington, D.C.: U.S. Government Printing Office, 1979), p. 2, table A.

[6] Ibid.

[7] This figure is an estimate. According to the Bureau of the Census, only 2.6 percent of families in the United States have money income of $50,000 or over. U.S. Bureau of the Census, *Current Population Reports* Series P-60. For figures on income at these higher levels, see J. D. Smith and S. Franklin. "The Concentration of Personal Wealth, 1922–1969," *American Economic Review* 64 (1974): 162–67.

American Express, U.S. Steel. A sizable group of fathers are top executives in financial firms on Wall Street. There are also a number of fathers who list their occupations as "general counsel" to a particular corporation, and these corporations are also among the large multinationals. Many of the mothers do volunteer work in the Junior League, Junior Fortnightly, or other service groups; some are intricately involved in town politics; and some are themselves in well-paid occupations. There are no minority children in the school. Almost all the family incomes are over $100,000, with some in the $500,000 range. The incomes in this school represent less than 1 percent of the families in the United States.[8]

Since each of the five schools is only one instance of elementary education in a particular social class context, I will not generalize beyond the sample. However, the examples of schoolwork which follow will suggest characteristics of education in each social setting that appear to have theoretical and social significance and to be worth investigation in a larger number of schools. . . .

The Working-Class Schools

In the two working-class schools, work is following the steps of a procedure. The procedure is usually mechanical, involving rote behavior and very little decision making or choice. The teachers rarely explain why the work is being assigned, how it might connect to other assignments, or what the idea is that lies behind the procedure or gives it coherence and perhaps meaning or significance. Available textbooks are not always used, and the teachers often prepare their own dittos or put work examples on the board. Most of the rules regarding work are designations of what the children are to do; the rules are steps to follow. These steps are told to the children by the teachers and are often written on the board. The children are usually told to copy the steps as notes. These notes are to be studied. Work is often evaluated not according to whether it is right or wrong but according to whether the children followed the right steps.

The following examples illustrate these points. In math, when two-digit division was introduced, the teacher in one school gave a four-minute lecture on what the terms are called (which number is the divisor, dividend, quotient, and remainder). The children were told to copy these names in their notebooks. Then the teacher told them the steps to follow to do the problems, saying, "This is how you do them." The teacher listed the steps on the board, and they appeared several days later as a chart hung in the middle of the front wall: "Divide, Multiply, Subtract, Bring Down." The children often did examples of two-digit division. When the teacher went over the examples with them, he told them what the procedure was for each problem, rarely asking them to conceptualize or explain it themselves: "Three into twenty-two is seven; do your subtraction and one is left over." During the week that two-digit division was introduced (or at any other time), the investigator did not observe any discussion of the idea of grouping involved in division, any use of manipulables, or any attempt to relate two-digit division to any other mathematical process. Nor was

---

[8] Smith and Franklin, "The Concentration of Personal Wealth."

there any attempt to relate the steps to an actual or possible thought process of the children. The observer did not hear the terms *dividend, quotient,* and so on, used again. The math teacher in the other working-class school followed similar procedures regarding two-digit division and at one point her class seemed confused. She said, "You're confusing yourselves. You're tensing up. Remember, when you do this, it's the same steps over and over again—and that's the way division always is." Several weeks later, after a test, a group of her children "still didn't get it," and she made no attempt to explain the concept of dividing things into groups or to give them manipulables for their own investigation, Rather, she went over the steps with them again and told them that they "needed more practice."

In other areas of math, work is also carrying out often unexplained fragmented procedures. For example, one of the teachers led the children through a series of steps to make a 1-inch grid on their paper *without* telling them that they were making a 1-inch grid or that it would be used to study scale. She said, "Take your ruler. Put it across the top. Make a mark at every number. Then move your ruler down to the bottom. No, put it across the bottom. Now make a mark on top of every number. Now draw a line from . . ." At this point a girl said that she had a faster way to do it and the teacher said, "No, you don't; you don't even know what I'm making yet. Do it this way or it's wrong." After they had made the lines up and down and across, the teacher told them she wanted them to make a figure by connecting some dots and to measure that, using the scale of 1 inch equals 1 mile. Then they were to cut it out. She said, "Don't cut it until I check it."

In both working-class schools, work in language arts is mechanics of punctuation (commas, periods, question marks, exclamation points), capitalization, and the four kinds of sentences. One teacher explained to me, "Simple punctuation is all they'll ever use." Regarding punctuation, either a teacher or a ditto stated the rules for where, for example, to put commas. The investigator heard no classroom discussion of the aural context of punctuation (which, of course, is what gives each mark its meaning). Nor did the investigator hear any statement or inference that placing a punctuation mark could be a decision-making process, depending, for example, on one's intended meaning. Rather, the children were told to follow the rules. Language arts did not involve creative writing. There were several writing assignments throughout the year, but in each instance the children were given a ditto, and they wrote answers to questions on the sheet. For example, they wrote their "autobiography" by answering such questions as "Where were you born?" "What is your favorite animal?" on a sheet entitled "All About Me."

In one of the working-class schools, the class had a science period several times a week. On the three occasions observed, the children were not called upon to set up experiments or to give explanations for facts or concepts. Rather, on each occasion the teacher told them in his own words what the book said. The children copied the teacher's sentences from the board. Each day that preceded the day they were to do a science experiment, the teacher told them to copy the directions from the book for the procedure they would carry out the next day and to study the list at home that night. The day after each experiment, the teacher went over what they had "found" (they did the experiments as a class, and each was actually a class demonstration led by the teacher). Then the teacher wrote what they "found" on the board, and the children copied that in their notebooks. Once or twice a year there are science projects. The project is chosen and assigned by the teacher from a box of 3-by-5-inch cards. On the card the teacher has written the question to be answered, the books to use, and how much to write. Explaining the cards to the observer, the teacher said, "It tells them exactly what to do, or they couldn't do it."

Social studies in the working-class schools is also largely mechanical, rote work that was given little explanation or connection to larger contexts. In one school, for example, although there was a book available, social studies work was to copy the teacher's notes from the board. Several times a week for a period of several months the children copied these notes. The fifth grades in the district were to study United States history. The teacher used a booklet she had purchased called "The Fabulous Fifty States." Each day she put information from the booklet in outline form on the board and the children copied it. The type of information did not vary: the name of the state, its abbreviation, state capital, nickname of the state, its main products, main business, and a "Fabulous Fact" ("Idaho grew twenty-seven billion potatoes in one year. That's enough potatoes for each man, woman, and . . ."). As the children finished copying the sentences, the teacher erased them and wrote more. Children would occasionally go to the front to pull down the wall map in order to locate the states they were copying, and the teacher did not dissuade them. But the observer never saw her refer to the map; nor did the observer ever hear her make other than perfunctory remarks concerning the information the children were copying. Occasionally the children colored in a ditto and cut it out to make a stand-up figure (representing, for example, a man roping a cow in the Southwest). These were referred to by the teacher as their social studies "projects."

Rote behavior was often called for in classroom work. When going over math and language arts skills sheets, for example, as the teacher asked for the answer to each problem, he fired the questions rapidly, staccato, and the scene reminded the observer of a sergeant drilling recruits: above all, the questions demanded that you stay at attention: "The next one? What do I put here? . . . Here? Give us the next." Or "How many commas in this sentence? Where do I put them . . . The next one?"

The four fifth-grade teachers observed in the working-class schools attempted to control classroom time and space by making decisions without consulting the children and without explaining the basis for their decisions. The teacher's control thus often seemed capricious. Teachers, for instance, very often ignored the bells to switch classes—deciding among themselves to keep the children after the period was officially over to continue with the work or for disciplinary reasons or so they (the teachers) could stand in the hall and talk. There were no clocks in the rooms in either school, and the children often asked,

"What period is this?" "When do we go to gym?" The children had no access to materials. These were handed out by teachers and closely guarded. Things in the room "belonged" to the teacher: "Bob, bring me my garbage can." The teachers continually gave the children orders. Only three times did the investigator hear a teacher in either working-class school preface a directive with an unsarcastic "please," or "let's" or "would you." Instead, the teachers said, "Shut up," "Shut your mouth," "Open your books," "Throw your gum away—if you want to rot your teeth, do it on your own time." Teachers made every effort to control the movement of the children, and often shouted, "Why are you out of your seat??!!" If the children got permission to leave the room, they had to take a written pass with the date and time. . . .

Middle-Class School

In the middle-class school, work is getting the right answer. If one accumulates enough right answers, one gets a good grade. One must follow the directions in order to get the right answers, but the directions often call for some figuring, some choice, some decision making. For example, the children must often figure out by themselves what the directions ask them to do and how to get the answer: what do you do first, second, and perhaps third? Answers are usually found in books or by listening to the teacher. Answers are usually words, sentences, numbers, or facts and dates; one writes them on paper, and one should be neat. Answers must be given in the right order, and one cannot make them up.

The following activities are illustrative. Math involves some choice: one may do two-digit division the long way or the short way, and there are some math problems that can be done "in your head." When the teacher explains how to do two-digit division, there is recognition that a cognitive process is involved; she gives you several ways and says, "I want to make sure you understand what you're doing—so you get it right"; and, when they go over the homework, she asks the *children* to tell how they did the problem and what answer they got.

In social studies the daily work is to read the assigned pages in the textbook and to answer the teacher's questions. The questions are almost always designed to check on whether the students have read the assignment and understood it: who did so-and-so; what happened after that; when did it happen, where, and sometimes, why did it happen? The answers are in the book and in one's understanding of the book; the teacher's hints when one doesn't know the answers are to "read it again" or to look at the picture or at the rest of the paragraph. One is to search for the answer in the "context," in what is given.

Language arts is "simple grammar, what they need for everyday life." The language arts teacher says, "They should learn to speak properly, to write business letters and thank-you letters, and to understand what nouns and verbs and simple subjects are." Here, as well, actual work is to choose the right answers, to understand what is given. The teacher often says, "Please read the next sentence and then I'll question you about it." One teacher said in some exasperation to a boy who was fooling around in class, "If you don't know the answers to the questions I ask, then you can't stay in this *class!* [pause] You *never* know the answers to the questions I ask, and it's not fair to me—and certainly not to you!"

Most lessons are based on the textbook. This does not involve a critical perspective on what is given there. For example, a critical perspective in social studies is perceived as dangerous by these teachers because it may lead to controversial topics; the parents might complain. The children, however, are often curious, especially in social studies. Their questions are tolerated and usually answered perfunctorily. But after a few minutes the teacher will say, "All right, we're not going any farther. Please open your social studies workbook." While the teachers spend a lot of time explaining and expanding on what the textbooks say, there is little attempt to analyze how or why things happen, or to give thought to how pieces of a culture, or, say, a system of numbers or elements of a language fit together or can be analyzed. What has happened in the past and what exists now may not be equitable or fair, but (shrug) that is the way things are and one does not confront such matters in school. For example, in social studies after a child is called on to read a passage about the pilgrims, the teacher summarizes the paragraph and then says, "So you can see how strict they were about everything." A child asks, "Why?" "Well, because they felt that if you weren't busy you'd get into trouble." Another child asks, "Is it true that they burned women at the stake?" The teacher says, "Yes, if a woman did anything strange, they hanged them. [sic] What would a woman do, do you think, to make them burn them? [sic] See if you can come up with better answers than my other [social studies] class." Several children offer suggestions, to which the teacher nods but does not comment. Then she says, "Okay, good," and calls on the next child to read.

Work tasks do not usually request creativity, Serious attention is rarely given in school work on *how* the children develop or express their own feelings and ideas, either linguistically or in graphic form. On the occasions when creativity or self-expression is requested, it is peripheral to the main activity or it is "enrichment" or "for fun." During a lesson on what similes are, for example, the teacher explains what they are, puts several on the board, gives some other examples herself, and then asks the children if they can "make some up." She calls on three children who give similes, two of which are actually in the book they have open before them. The teacher does not comment on this and then asks several others to choose similes from the list of phrases in the book. Several do so correctly, and she says, "Oh good! You're picking them out! See how good we are?" Their homework is to pick out the rest of the similes from the list.

Creativity is not often requested in social studies and science projects, either. Social studies projects, for example, are given with directions to "find information on your topic" and write it up. The children are not supposed to copy but to "put it in your own words." Although a number of the projects subsequently went beyond the teacher's direction to find information and had quite expressive covers and inside illustrations, the teacher's evaluative comments had to do with the amount of information, whether they had "copied," and if their work was neat.

The style of control of the three fifth-grade teachers observed in this school varied from somewhat easygoing to strict, but in contrast to the working-class schools, the teachers' decisions were usually based on external rules and regulations—for example, on criteria that were known or available to the children. Thus, the teachers always honor the bells for changing classes, and they usually evaluate children's work by what is in the textbooks and answer booklets.

There is little excitement in schoolwork for the children, and the assignments are perceived as having little to do with their interests and feelings. As one child said, what you do is "store facts up in your head like cold storage—until you need it later for a test or your job." Thus, doing well is important because there are thought to be *other,* likely rewards: a good job or college.[9]

Affluent Professional School

In the affluent professional school, work is creative activity carried out independently. The students are continually asked to express and apply ideas and concepts. Work involves individual thought and expressiveness, expansion and illustration of ideas, and choice of appropriate method and material. (The class is not considered an open classroom, and the principal explained that because of the large number of discipline problems in the fifth grade this year they did not departmentalize. The teacher who agreed to take part in the study said she is "more structured" this year than she usually is.) The products of work in this class are often written stories, editorials and essays, or representations of ideas in mural, graph, or craft form. The products of work should not be like everybody else's and should show individuality. They should exhibit good design, and (this is important) they must also fit empirical reality. Moreover, one's work should attempt to interpret or "make sense" of reality. The relatively few rules to be followed regarding work are usually criteria for, or limits on, individual activity. One's product is usually evaluated for the quality of its expression and for the appropriateness of its conception to the task. In many cases, one's own satisfaction with the product is an important criterion for its evaluation. When right answers are called for, as in commercial materials like SRA (Science Research Associates) and math, it is important that the children decide on an answer as a result of thinking about the idea involved in what they're being asked to do. Teacher's hints are to "think about it some more."

The following activities are illustrative. The class takes home a sheet requesting each child's parents to fill in the number of cars they have, the number of television sets, refrigerators, games, or rooms in the house, and so on. Each child is to figure the average number of a type of possession owned by the fifth grade. Each child must compile the "data" from all the sheets. A calculator is available in the classroom to do the mechanics of finding the average. Some

---

[9] A dominant feeling, expressed directly and indirectly by teachers in this school, was boredom with their work. They did, however, in contrast to the working-class schools, almost always carry out lessons during class times.

children decide to send sheets to the fourth-grade families for comparison. Their work should be "verified" by a classmate before it is handed in.

Each child and his or her family has made a geoboard. The teacher asks the class to get their geoboards from the side cabinet, to take a handful of rubber bands, and then to listen to what she would like them to do. She says, "I would like you to design a figure and then find the perimeter and area. When you have it, check with your neighbor. After you've done that, please transfer it to graph paper and tomorrow I'll ask you to make up a question about it for someone. When you hand it in, please let me know whose it is and who verified it. Then I have something else for you to do that's really fun. [pause] Find the average number of chocolate chips in three cookies. I'll give you three cookies, and you'll have to *eat* your way through, I'm afraid!" Then she goes around the room and gives help, suggestions, praise, and admonitions that they are getting noisy. They work sitting, or standing up at their desks, at benches in the back, or on the floor. A child hands the teacher his paper and she comments, "I'm not accepting this paper. Do a better design." To another child she says, "That's fantastic! But you'll never find the area. Why don't you draw a figure inside [the big one] and subtract to get the area?"

The school district requires the fifth grade to study ancient civilization (in particular, Egypt, Athens, and Sumer). In this classroom, the emphasis is on illustrating and re-creating the culture of the people of ancient times. The following are typical activities: the children made an 8mm film on Egypt, which one of the parents edited. A girl in the class wrote the script, and the class acted it out. They put the sound on themselves. They read stories of those days. They wrote essays and stories depicting the lives of the people and the societal and occupational divisions. They chose from a list of projects, all of which involved graphic representations of ideas: for example, "Make a mural depicting the division of labor in Egyptian society."

Each child wrote and exchanged a letter in hieroglyphics with a fifth grader in another class, and they also exchanged stories they wrote in cuneiform. They made a scroll and singed the edges so it looked authentic. They each chose an occupation and made an Egyptian plaque representing that occupation, simulating the appropriate Egyptian design. They carved their design on a cylinder of wax, pressed the wax into clay, and then baked the clay. Although one girl did not choose an occupation but carved instead a series of gods and slaves, the teacher said, "That's all right, Amber, it's beautiful." As they were working the teacher said, "Don't cut into your clay until you're satisfied with your design."

Social studies also involves almost daily presentation by the children of some event from the news. The teacher's questions ask the children to expand what they say, to give more details, and to be more specific. Occasionally she adds some remarks to help them see connections between events.

The emphasis on expressing and illustrating ideas in social studies is accompanied in language arts by an emphasis on creative writing. Each child wrote a rebus story for a first grader whom they had interviewed to see what kind of story the child liked best. They wrote editorials on pending decisions by the school board and radio plays, some of which were read over the school intercom from the office and one of which was performed in the auditorium. There is no language arts textbook because, the teacher said, "The principal wants us to be creative." There is not much grammar, but there is punctuation. One morning when the observer arrived, the class was doing a punctuation ditto. The teacher later apologized for using the ditto. "It's just for review," she said. "I don't teach punctuation that way. We use their language." The ditto had three unambiguous rules for where to put commas in a sentence. As the teacher was going around to help the children with the ditto, she repeated several times, "Where you put commas depends on how you say the sentence; it depends on the situation and what you want to say." Several weeks later the observer saw another punctuation activity. The teacher had printed a five-paragraph story on an oak tag and then cut it into phrases. She read the whole story to the class from the book, then passed out the phrases. The group had to decide how the phrases could best be put together again. (They arranged the phrases on the floor.) The point was not to replicate the story, although that was not irrelevant, but to "decide what you think the best way is." Punctuation marks on cardboard pieces were then handed out, and the children discussed and then decided what mark was best at each place they thought one was needed. At the end of each paragraph the teacher asked, "Are you satisfied with the way the paragraphs are now? Read it to yourself and see how it sounds." Then she read the original story again, and they compared the two.

Describing her goals in science to the investigator, the teacher said, "We use ESS (Elementary Science Study). It's very good because it gives a hands-on experience—so they can make *sense* out of it. It doesn't matter whether it [what they find] is right or wrong. I bring them together and there's value in discussing their ideas."

The products of work in this class are often highly valued by the children and the teacher. In fact, this was the only school in which the investigator was not allowed to take original pieces of the children's work for her files. If the work was small enough, however, and was on paper, the investigator could duplicate it on the copying machine in the office.

The teacher's attempt to control the class involves constant negotiation. She does not give direct orders unless she is angry because the children have been too noisy. Normally, she tries to get them to foresee the consequences of their actions and to decide accordingly. For example, lining them up to go see a play written by the sixth graders, she says, "I presume you're lined up by someone with whom you want to sit. I hope you're lined up by someone you won't get in trouble with." . . .

One of the few rules governing the children's movement is that no more than three children may be out of the room at once. There is a school rule that anyone can go to the library at any time to get a book. In the fifth grade I observed, they sign their name on the chalkboard and leave. There are no passes. Finally, the children have a fair amount of officially sanctioned say over what happens in the class. For example, they often negotiate what work is to be done. If the teacher wants to move on to the next subject, but the children say they are not ready, they want to work on their present projects some more, she very often lets them do it.

Executive Elite School

In the executive elite school, work is developing one's analytical intellectual powers. Children are continually asked to reason through a problem, to produce intellectual products that are both logically sound and of top academic quality. A primary goal of thought is to conceptualize rules by which elements may fit together in systems and then to apply these rules in solving a problem. Schoolwork helps one to achieve, to excel, to prepare for life.

The following are illustrative. The math teacher teaches area and perimeter by having the children derive formulas for each. First she helps them, through discussion at the board, to arrive at $A = W \times L$ as a formula (not *the* formula) for area. After discussing several, she says, "Can anyone make up a formula for perimeter? Can you figure that out yourselves? [pause] Knowing what we know, can we think of a formula?" She works out three children's suggestions at the board, saying to two, "Yes, that's a good one," and then asks the class if they can think of any more. No one volunteers. To prod them, she says, "If you use rules and good reasoning, you get many ways. Chris, can you think up a formula?"

She discusses two-digit division with the children as a decision-making process. Presenting a new type of problem to them, she asks, "What's the *first* decision you'd make if presented with this kind of example? What is the first thing you'd *think*? Craig?" Craig says, "To find my first partial quotient." She responds, "Yes, that would be your first decision. How would you do that?" Craig explains, and then the teacher says, "OK, we'll see how that works for you." The class tries his way. Subsequently, she comments on the merits and shortcomings of several other children's decisions. Later, she tells the investigator that her goals in math are to develop their reasoning and mathematical thinking and that, unfortunately, "there's no *time* for manipulables."

While right answers are important in math, they are not "given" by the book or by the teacher but may be challenged by the children. Going over some problems in late September the teacher says, "Raise your hand if you do not agree." A child says, "I don't agree with sixty-four." The teacher responds, "OK, there's a question about sixty-four. [to class] Please check it. Owen, they're disagreeing with you. Kristen, they're checking yours." The teacher emphasized this repeatedly during September and October with statements like "Don't be afraid to say you disagree. In the last [math] class, somebody disagreed, and they were right. Before you disagree, check yours, and if you still think we're wrong, then we'll check it out." By Thanksgiving, the children did not often speak in terms of right and wrong math problems but of whether they agreed with the answer that had been given.

There are complicated math mimeos with many word problems. Whenever they go over the examples, they discuss how each child has set up the problem.

The children must explain it precisely. On one occasion the teacher said, "I'm more—just as interested in *how* you set up the problem as in what answer you find. If you set up a problem in a good way, the answer is *easy* to find."

Social studies work is most often reading and discussion of concepts and independent research. There are only occasional artistic, expressive, or illustrative projects. Ancient Athens and Sumer are, rather, societies to analyze. The following questions are typical of those that guide the children's independent research. "What mistakes did Pericles make after the war?" "What mistakes did the citizens of Athens make?" "What are the elements of a civilization?" "How did Greece build an economic empire?" "Compare the way Athens chose its leaders with the way we choose ours." Occasionally the children are asked to make up sample questions for their social studies tests. On an occasion when the investigator was present, the social studies teacher rejected a child's question by saying, "That's just fact. If I asked you that question on a test, you'd complain it was just memory! Good questions ask for concepts."

In social studies—but also in reading, science, and health—the teachers initiate classroom discussions of current social issues and problems. These discussions occurred on every one of the investigator's visits, and a teacher told me, "These children's opinions are important—it's important that they learn to reason things through." The classroom discussions always struck the observer as quite realistic and analytical, dealing with concrete social issues like the following: "Why do workers strike?" "Is that right or wrong?" "Why do we have inflation, and what can be done to stop it?" "Why do companies put chemicals in food when the natural ingredients are available?" and so on. Usually the children did not have to be prodded to give their opinions. In fact, their statements and the interchanges between them struck the observer as quite sophisticated conceptually and verbally, and well-informed. Occasionally the teachers would prod with statements such as, "Even if you don't know [the answers], if you think logically about it, you can figure it out." And "I'm asking you [these] questions to help you think this through."

Language arts emphasizes language as a complex system, one that should be mastered. The children are asked to diagram sentences of complex grammatical construction, to memorize irregular verb conjugations (he lay, he has lain, and so on . . .), and to use the proper participles, conjunctions, and interjections in their speech. The teacher (the same one who teaches social studies) told them, "It is not enough to get these right on tests; you must use what you learn [in grammar classes] in your written and oral work. I will grade you on that."

Most writing assignments are either research and essays for social studies or experiment analyses and write-ups for science. There is only an occasional story or other "creative writing" assignment. On the occasion observed by the investigator (the writing of a Halloween story), the points the teacher stressed in preparing the children to write involved the structural aspects of a story rather than the expression of feelings or other ideas. The teacher showed them a film-strip, "The Seven Parts of a Story," and lectured them on plot development, mood setting, character development, consistency, and the use of a logical or appropriate ending. The stories they subsequently wrote were, in fact, well-structured, but many were also personal and expressive. The teacher's evaluative comments, however, did not refer to the expressiveness or artistry but were all directed toward whether they had "developed" the story well.

Language arts work also involved a large amount of practice in presentation of the self and in managing situations where the child was expected to be in charge. For example, there was a series of assignments in which each child had to be a "student teacher." The child had to plan a lesson in grammar, outlining, punctuation, or other language arts topic and explain the concept to the class. Each child was to prepare a worksheet or game and a homework assignment as well. After each presentation, the teacher and other children gave a critical appraisal of the "student teacher's" performance. Their criteria were: whether the student spoke clearly, whether the lesson was interesting, whether the student made any mistakes, and whether he or she kept control of the class. On an occasion when a child did not maintain control, the teacher said, "When you're up there, you have authority and you have to use it. I'll back you up." . . .

The executive elite school is the only school where bells do not demarcate the periods of time. The two fifth-grade teachers were very strict about changing classes on schedule, however, as specific plans for each session had been made. The teachers attempted to keep tight control over the children during lessons, and the children were sometimes flippant, boisterous, and occasionally rude. However, the children may be brought into line by reminding them that "It is up to you." "You must control yourself," "you are responsible for your work," you must "set your own priorities." One teacher told a child, "You are the only driver of your car—and only you can regulate your speed." A new teacher complained to the observer that she had thought "these children" would have more control.

While strict attention to the lesson at hand is required, the teachers make relatively little attempt to regulate the movement of the children at other times. For example, except for the kindergartners the children in this school do not have to wait for the bell to ring in the morning; they may go to their classroom when they arrive at school. Fifth graders often came early to read, to finish work, or to catch up. After the first two months of school, the fifth-grade teachers did not line the children up to change classes or to go to gym, and so on, but, when the children were ready and quiet, they were told they could go—sometimes without the teachers.

In the classroom, the children could get materials when they needed them and took what they needed from closets and from the teacher's desk They were in charge of the office at lunchtime. During class they did not have to sign out or ask permission to leave the room; they just got up and left. Because of the pressure to get work done, however, they did not leave the room very often. The teachers were very polite to the children, and the investigator heard no sarcasm, no nasty remarks, and few direct orders. The teachers never called the children "honey" or "dear" but always called them by name. The teachers were expected to be available before school, after school, and for part of their lunchtime to provide extra help if needed. . . .

The foregoing analysis of differences in schoolwork in contrasting social class contexts suggests the following conclusion: the "hidden curriculum" of schoolwork is tacit preparation for relating to the process of production in a particular way. Differing curricular, pedagogical, and pupil evaluation practices emphasize different cognitive and behavioral skills in each social setting and thus contribute to the development in the children of certain potential relationships to physical and symbolic capital, to authority, and to the process of work. School experience, in the sample of schools discussed here, differed qualitatively by social class. These differences may not only contribute to the development in the children in each social class of certain types of economically significant relationships and not others but would thereby help to *reproduce* this system of relations in society. In the contribution to the reproduction of unequal social relations lies a theoretical meaning and social consequence of classroom practice.

The identification of different emphases in classrooms in a sample of contrasting social class contexts implies that further research should be conducted in a large number of schools to investigate the types of work tasks and interactions in each to see if they differ in the ways discussed here and to see if similar potential relationships are uncovered. Such research could have as a product the further elucidation of complex but not readily apparent connections between everyday activity in schools and classrooms and the unequal structure of economic relationships in which we work and live. ■

Working with the Text

1. As carefully as you can, reconstruct a typical day from your elementary school, paying particular attention to the details that Anyon describes in her school visits: what the classroom looked like; how students were seated; how many and what the rules were; the type of assignments, and so on. Based on your findings, how do you think Anyon would classify your school, and what do you think about this classification?

2. Describe two courses from your school experiences that you feel best and least prepared you for the work you do now and the work you may be planning to do. Be as specific as you can about which particular practices and activities you think influenced you positively or negatively.

3. Anyon refers in her title to the "hidden" curriculum of work. How specifically do you remember your schools discussing work possibilities with you? How helpful or discouraging were these discussions?

4. Choose one or two of your college courses and describe a "hidden curriculum of work" for these courses. Compare experiences with your classmates, or if some of you share other courses, you

may want to collaborate on this assignment. Do you see an over-all trend that cuts across different courses, or do different courses seem to have different "curricula of work"?

Working with Connections

1. James Traub describes a movement to create "online" universities where students attend college over the Internet. Based on his descriptions, graduates of which of the schools that Anyon describes do you believe would be most attracted to online education and why?

2. What kinds of schools must the characters in Scott Adams's *Dilbert* have attended (from Chapter 2, "Work, Labor and Career: The Meaning of Work")?

RON NIXON
Caution: Children at Work

Many people think of "child labor" as something from the 19thcentury or as a practice found only in so-called "third world" countries. Most of us would probably say that the proper place for children is in school, not at work, even if part of the purpose of school is to prepare children for the workplace. In "Caution: Children at Work," however, investigative journalist Ron Nixon describes how child labor is still very much a part of the modern American economy, thus providing a different, often dangerous, form of "education" for the children described here.

Ron Nixon lives in Virginia and writes for the Roanoke Times *as well as national news magazines such as* The Nation *and* The Progressive, *where this article originally appeared.*

The next time you buy fresh fruit or vegetables from the supermarket, think about the true costs. Rosa Rubina will. Her five-year-old son Jacob lost his hand while helping to grade and package watermelons in Tifton, Georgia. The boy's hand was caught in a conveyor belt and ripped off. "I saw his arm wasn't there and his hand was stuck in the conveyer belt. I went crazy," Rubina remembers.

Even though the boy was rushed to a nearby hospital and eventually to Atlanta, doctors were unable to save his hand. Today, because of the injury, the child keeps to himself, "He doesn't go out," Rubina says. "Some days he asks me, 'Ma are you still gonna love me with one hand?'"

Accidents like Jacob's are becoming all too common for children in the workplace. Thousands of young people are injured, some even killed, on the job each year in the United States. A report by the National Institute for Occupational Safety and Health found that 64,000 children, ages fourteen through seventeen, were treated in hospitals for work-related injuries in 1992. Another report by the Institute found that from 1980 to 1989, 670 sixteen- and seventeen-year-olds died in work-related accidents.

These statistics tell only part of the story. Thousands of children like Jacob Rubina are not counted in the data gathered by the Department of Labor and other agencies because they work in largely unreportable jobs or help out their parents on the farm where they aren't listed as workers. This problem is particularly acute for minority youth. "Though they are less likely to work than their white counterparts, minority children often work in more dangerous and unreportable jobs," says Charles Geszeck of the Government Accounting Office, the investigative wing of Congress.

Nowhere are the dangers of children working more apparent than in agriculture. On any given day during the harvest season, children as young as five are in the field picking cucumbers, tomatoes, strawberries, and other hand-harvested fruits. Growers say that they don't hire children, but in 1992, on a tour of ten farms in Ohio, the Associated Press found dozens of children working. Many of these farms were selling their crops to major agriculture corporations like Vlasic Foods, Heinz USA, and Dean Foods. According to the American Friends Service Committee and the United Farm Workers, between 800,000 and 1.5 million children work in agriculture.

While agriculture is not the only industry that employs large numbers of children, it is certainly the most dangerous. In fact, agriculture is the second most dangerous occupation after mining, according to a 1995 report by the National Safety Council. Yet agriculture is less regulated than any other industry, particularly when it comes to children.

Consider the following:

■ Hazardous work is prohibited in farming only until age sixteen (compared with age eighteen in nonagricultural occupations), and all work on family farms is exempt.

■ A section of the Fair Labor Standards Act, the law regulating child labor, allows agricultural industries to obtain waivers that will allow them to use ten- and eleven-year-olds for hand-harvested products if the companies can show that not using the ten- and eleven-year-olds "would cause severe economic disruption to the industry."

■ A child fourteen years of age or younger can use knives, machetes, operate machinery, and be exposed to pesticides. Children in other occupations cannot.

■ Children in agriculture can work more than forty hours a week, even during a school term, although children in other industries are prohibited from doing so. Young farmworkers can also work an unlimited number of hours before school.

"In no other industry could you get away with this," says Diane Mull of the Association of Farmworker Opportunities Program in Virginia. "For just about every labor standard in the book, agriculture is exempt."

Parents like Rosa Rubina have little choice but to expose their children to a dangerous environment. Like most migrant families, the Rubinas and their children work side by side, or the children play in the fields while their parents work.

"I tried to get the children into day care but there was a long waiting list," says Rosa Rubina. She is not alone. According to the federal Migrant Head Start program, in 1990 only 23,000 out of millions of migrant children were provided day care.

Children left in the field unsupervised can get into serious trouble, says Francisco Rivera, an attorney with the Florida Department of Labor. "I used to work for Florida Legal Services, and children are out in the field all the time. Three years ago a minor was run over in the field by a tractor. Another year two kids drowned. They were playing in some ditches on a Saturday while their parents worked."

"I don't know what else to do," says Juan Hernandez, whose nine-year-old son helps him pick cucumbers in Fremont, Ohio. "If he wasn't doing this he'd be running around. We have to watch him."

Lack of child care isn't the only reason that children work on the farm, of course. Poverty makes hard choices for many farmworkers. The average farmworker's annual wage is about $4,600. Since many farmworkers are paid by the number of fruits or vegetables they pick, "everyone in the family needs to work just to make a living," says Diane Mull. "It perpetuates a cycle of poverty. Kids work and don't go to school and they don't make much money, so they stay poor."

Farm industry representatives disagree. "Housewives in Boston may not understand it, but there is nothing wrong with fourteen-year-olds getting their hands dirty and learning some discipline," says Scottie Butler, general counsel for the Florida Farm Bureau.

But children who work in agricultural jobs face more serious problems than dirty hands. Farmworker children are often two or more years below grade level in reading and math skills, and their dropout rate is 45 percent, compared with 29 percent for non-farmworkers. In Florida, many children from Mexico, Honduras, Guatemala, and Haiti drop out of school to work on farms for $4 or $5 an hour. Many have no illusions about their future.

"Once you start working in the groves, you never come out," says a fifteen-year-old farmworker who asked not to be named. "But if I don't pick I don't eat."

Exposure to pesticides represents the greatest threat to the health of children in agriculture, says Valerie Wilks, formerly of the Farmworker Justice Fund in Washington, D.C. Children in agriculture are exposed to a range of chemicals each year. And children tend to be more susceptible to pesticides because they absorb more pesticides per pound of body weight and because of their developing nervous system and organs. Furthermore, children in the fields may eat contaminated dirt or pesticide-treated crops. Yet according to a lawsuit filed in 1979 by Public Citizen, a Ralph Nader group, the Department of Labor published regulations that permitted ten- and eleven-year-olds in potato and strawberry fields to be exposed to the residues of some twenty-five pesticides, including many that produce birth defects, impair growth, and damage the reproductive system.

A report in 1990 of migrant children in New York found that more than 40 percent had been sprayed with pesticides. Another 40 percent had worked in the fields while the fields were still wet. Still, the EPA has not felt a need to set standards for child exposure to pesticides. Current regulations are established for adults. According to the GAO report, "the EPA regulations for protecting workers against pesticide hazards are based on adult exposure only and give no special consideration to children." Even so, the EPA's own data show that 300,000 pesticide-related illnesses occur among adults and children each year.

In 1994 only 200 children nationwide were found working illegally, according to Bob Cuccia, a spokesperson for the Department of Labor. "Food processors know that they are being targeted, so they are being good," said Cuccia. But the National Child Labor Committee says more than 110,000 children work illegally on U.S. farms. "And even this may be an undercount," says Jeffrey Newman of the Committee.

It may be impossible for the Department of Labor to know the exact number of children working on farms. A provision in the annual appropriations bill forbids the Department of Labor and the Occupational Safety and Health Administration from inspecting farms that claim fewer than ten workers, This provision is supposed to keep small farms from being subjected to the same laws as giant agribusiness. But to exploit this provision, some growers allow an independent contractor to hire workers. This keeps the grower from having to comply with worker-safety or child-labor laws.

"So you could have fifty or sixty people, including children, working on a farm and only ten people on the employer's books," says Mull. Another tactic that growers use to circumvent the laws is to register an entire family as working under the social security number of the head of a household, says Mull. "This also give the illusion that there are only a few workers being employed, when in reality there could be hundreds."

There is little regulatory agencies can do to help. In addition to being barred from inspecting farms that claim fewer than ten workers, labor officials have to ask a grower's permission to inspect a farm. "This makes it more difficult to measure the problem of child labor in agriculture," says Jesus Martinez, a district director for the U.S. Labor Department.

Despite urgings from regulatory officials and farm-labor organizations, Congress has been unwilling to change the laws to protect farmworkers and their kids. Politicians from farming states are loath to take on agribusiness, and agribusiness wants to keep it that way. Last year, according to the Center for Responsive Politics, the agriculture industries gave millions to a conservative Congress bent on undoing reforms that date back to the New Deal era, including restrictions on child labor. The American Farm Bureau and a trade association made up of state agriculture commissioners have lobbied Congress not to strengthen laws and regulations governing farmworkers.

Last year Congress took the first step in what many child advocates fear will be an all-out assault on child-labor laws. The House of Representatives passed a bill allowing youths under the age of eighteen to load paper compactors even though a report by the National Institute for Occupational Health Science found numerous injuries resulting from the operation of these balers. The Food Marketing Institute, the lead trade organization behind the baler repeal, gave $173,369 to legislators from 1991 to 1994, according to Federal Election Commission records. Other opponents of child-labor laws and regulations have joined an anti-regulation task force called Project Relief, which gave $10.5 million to legislators, mostly Republicans, during the 1994 elections.

Due to budget cuts, the Consumer Product Safety Commission, charged with collecting data on young injured farmworkers, has decided to stop collecting data on injuries caused by farming equipment like tractors and pesticides in its reports on consumer products. "We can't spend our limited resources on things that we aren't sure are considered consumer products," says Art McDonald of the Commission.

The absence of such data could have a crippling effect on efforts to prevent injury to young agricultural workers, advocates say. "The research isn't there because nobody cares," says Mull. "These are migrant children who are just a source of cheap labor. It's a national disgrace." ■

Working with the Text

1. Write about what you find most surprising or shocking about this story. If you aren't surprised by what Nixon reports here, write about your experiences with child labor or your past study of modern child labor.

2. A farm industry representative quoted by Nixon argues that the children engaged in farm work are "learning some discipline," while a young farm worker says that, "Once you start working in the fields, you never come out." Based on the information in this story, write about what you think child farm workers are learning about work from their experiences.

3. As a society, we have mixed feelings about children and work. While many would object to the exploitation of children reported here, a part-time job or work at home or on a family farm is often seen as an important part of a child's education. What do you see as the appropriate mix of schoolwork and other kinds of work? What should children be learning about work, and what are the best ways to teach them?

4. Ron Nixon's article originally appeared in 1996. As a research project, find the most current information you can about the issues he describes here. What is the current state of legislation and discussion about this issue? What positions or changes in the law would you argue for?

Working with Connections

1. In the transcript of their discussion (in Chapter 8: Work in the Global Economy), filmmaker Michael Moore and Nike founder and CEO Phil Knight argue about whether the use of child labor can ever be justified. What might Moore and Knight say about the kinds of child labor Nixon describes?

2. Chapter 8: Work in the Global Economy features a debate about the harms and benefits of low-wage factory work in other countries. "Caution: Children at Work" suggests that these global concerns are also a part of the American work force. Combine the information and ideas from the debate in Chapter 8 with Nixon's article to construct your own debate about the issue of child farm labor in the United States.

The Role of Technology in Higher Education

Technology is definitely changing the nature of higher education, but there is a widespread debate as to whether these changes are for the better or for the worse. One common and persuasive argument made for the increased use of computers in the classroom and college courses offered over the Internet points to the increasingly technology-driven information economy and the need for employees and entrepreneurs familiar with computer technology. Others, however, argue that in our rush to embrace computers and meet the needs of the workplace, we may be losing sight of other important purposes for school and education that are not directly connected to economic needs. The three readings in this section offer glimpses into this debate, from an overview of developments in computer-aided education to an interview with a strong proponent of online, career-oriented education to a confirmed skeptic who believes that computer technology may be a distraction from our real social needs.

ROBERT CWIKLIK ■

A Different Course

In this newspaper article written for the Wall Street Journal, *freelance writer and reporter Robert Cwiklik reports on the growth of online learning in higher education and discusses various predictions about how computer technology will transform college life. Cwiklik has written books and articles on a wide range of subjects, including many books of history and biography for children and young adults.*

The Internet could unleash a new force into university life: star power.

Ten years from now, talented university professors may develop whole courses in the form of multimedia lessons distributed well beyond their host universities to masses of students over the Internet, says Jonathan Zittrain, director of Harvard's Berkman Center for Internet and Society. Such products, which Mr. Zittrain likens to "textbooks on steroids," could combine video lectures with coordinated demonstrations on virtual blackboards and create a new class of academic celebrities, with top professors building world-wide reputations.

Star teachers and pumped-up multimedia texts are just two aspects of the future that experts envision for higher education. Of course, the prognosticators differ on specific points in their forecasts. Some see the private sector muscling in on education; some envision a rethinking of the traditional campus; and most see the school library eclipsed by online stacks. But all these forecasts seem to revolve around one agreed-upon premise: In the future, geography is going to matter a lot less.

"Education will change from a place-centered enterprise to an 'education where you need it,'" says Douglas Van Houweling, chief executive of University Corporation for Advanced Internet Development, the Washington-based consortium of universities and private-sector partners established to implement Internet2, a project aimed at enhancing the capacities of the global computer network.

"A decade from now," says Dr. Van Houweling, "it wouldn't surprise me if the majority of education took place in people's homes, in people's offices, on the production line, wherever it is needed."

AT THEIR CONVENIENCE

Workers seeking advanced training but lacking the time to pursue on-campus studies, or undergraduates without the means or desire to live on-campus, would be able to tap into, say, a video of a professor's latest lecture "asynchronously"—meaning, not necessarily at the time it was delivered—from their home or workplace desktops.

Such access, while freeing students from rigid class schedules, would also enable them to rewind and review difficult points or fast-forward past obvious ones. And while the lecture runs in the top left corner of their computer screens, students could perhaps watch a graphical display of an important concept in a window on the top right—a combination virtual blackboard and slide projector. Meanwhile, on the bottom left, germane links to other lectures in the course, or in other courses, could be displayed. On the bottom right, students could perhaps monitor live commentary on the class from other students in a chat room, or compose an e-mail query to their instructor.

Glimpses of that vision can be found on the Internet today. Scores of universities now offer online courses that count toward degrees. Their efforts have generally been greeted with enthusiasm as ways of extending educational opportunities beyond the campus.

As a rule, Internet-based courses today aren't nearly as flashy as the predictions. Michael P. Lambert, executive director of the Distance Education and

Training Council, a Washington nonprofit group that tracks such efforts, says that most online courses, while making use of e-mail and chat rooms, still amount to "glorified study guides" delivering lessons via pages and pages of plain text. Still, some of the advanced features experts envision are already showing up in universities' online offerings. For example, Stanford University, in Stanford, Calif., offers video lectures with synchronized slide demonstrations. Other advanced features are in the planning stages.

But schools may not be the only institutions delivering online education down the road. Because information technology makes it possible to deliver big chunks of the campus experience without the campus, private-sector players are already contending for a bigger slice of the shifting higher-education market.

Ten years down the road, "universities will not enjoy the monopoly they've had in the past," says Daniel E. Atkins, dean of the School of Information at the University of Michigan, in Ann Arbor. Apollo Group Inc., a Phoenix-based education holding company, already offers online accredited degree programs, mainly in business-related subjects, through its wholly owned University of Phoenix. And Kaplan Educational Centers, the standardized-test-preparation unit of *Washington Post* Co., recently announced plans to create an online law school, offering courses taught by teachers also employed at various brick-and-mortar law schools, with the goal of becoming fully accredited.

Both the University of Phoenix and the Kaplan efforts are aimed at working professionals. Some experts say private-sector initiatives in higher education will probably continue to focus on such students, leaving basic instruction in such academic strongholds as science and the humanities largely to universities. Chris Thomsen, director of a commission on technology and education at Stanford University, says that while it "may sound pretty naive," he sees "no threat" that corporations will eclipse universities in such traditional domains.

Mr. Zittrain, of Harvard, says that either of two possible new university models may emerge in response to marketplace changes ushered in by new technologies. On the one hand, elite universities could attempt to leverage their prestige into brand-name dominance of an exploding online market, overwhelming competitors of inferior cachet. That could lead to big changes in the traditional campus: Mr. Zittrain says that students, instead of attending classrooms for an academic year, may make single annual visits to campuses, perhaps a month long, to establish personal contacts with professors and classmates.

Even students who stay on campus year round could have a vastly different experience with teachers. Dr. Van Houweling's Internet2 project is working to enhance the Web's capacity to transmit, among other things, live multimedia productions online. As these enhanced capacities are rolled out over the next few years, he says, universities will increasingly import lectures from faculty all over the world "to get the best" available instruction in a given field.

"The way it feels to be on the campus will change," Dr. Van Houweling says. "It won't any longer be dominated by the faculty who actually live on that campus."

GOING IT ALONE

Then there's another possible model: Mr. Zittrain says individual professors may try to offer their own courses over the Internet, separate from any single institution. Such a strategy, if successful, "could eliminate the university from the calculus," he says. For instance, he says, new accrediting methods could develop to give an online course by a professor with the stature of, say, Harvard Law School's Alan Dershowitz, the status of an accredited university course of today.

Naturally, there could be significant drawbacks to these scenarios. For instance, to the extent that the market power of top universities is driven by their very exclusivity, distribution of their courses over the Internet may threaten to "dilute it" in the eyes of many people, Mr. Zittrain says.

Professors as online celebrities may also pose a danger, says Paul Saffo, director of the Institute for the Future, a Palo Alto, Calif., research and consulting firm. "Does it set in motion a star-making machine that corrupts academia in the same way that TV corrupted football or baseball with outrageous salary differences?"

And what does that mean for professors who aren't stars online? Mr. Zittrain says that even if some instructors develop highly popular online course modules, he says, such offerings are "still going to require some intermediary" to interact with students—to respond to their e-mail queries and grade assignments and tests, among other things. But functioning as such an intermediary may involve "more craft and less art" than current modes of classroom instruction, he says.

Indeed, there are already shadows in the bright dawn of this new educational approach. Some professors are grousing that electronic courses consume a startlingly huge chunk of their time in responding to students' e-mailed queries—far more time, they suggest, than similar queries raised in a classroom, where an answer to one student may satisfy several others as well.

"TOO SIMPLISTIC"

To some, such complaints are just one example of why the Internet won't displace brick-and-mortar universities. The notion that Internet-based distance learning "will suddenly take over all of higher education is far too simplistic," says Robert McClintock, director of the institute for Learning Technologies at Columbia University in New York. He says the Internet will probably be a boon for continuing education, or professional-retraining initiatives, but argues that the full richness of a higher education can't be captured online.

"A great deal of pedagogy is in small groups in seminars," he says, and amounts to "conversation with a thoughtful person."

"That's not a commodity," he adds.

Some experts aren't swayed by such arguments. Mr. Thomsen of Stanford, for example, says collegiate chat rooms will offer ample opportunities for student-teacher interactions.

Mr. Zittrain says that watching old forms survive and new ones take root in academia's networked future "will be a kind of Darwinian experiment." But a consensus view already appears to be solidifying among experts about the probable fate of one current academic structure: the university library.

"Natural forces," such as the costs of maintaining huge collections of books and other documents, are driving a gradual conversion of these materials to digital form and the eventual development of an online "universal library," says Dr. Atkins of the University of Michigan, who is also director of the university's digital-library project. "In a decade," he says, "a threshold of collections with most everything you need will perhaps be available" online.

A universal online library would most likely be modeled on electronic commerce, Dr. Atkins says. A commercial service would probably search a network of individual online libraries to find the document sought, post terms and fees, and deliver it to the user.

But the universal library will also be a place "where knowledge work is done," says Dr. Atkins. For instance, he says tools are being developed to permit researchers to collaborate online, either in real time or asynchronously, with colleagues the world over, and to utilize sophisticated scientific instruments at remote locations, such as the Hubble Space Telescope, from their own desktops.

WEAKER CENTER

Indeed, just as the Internet may make access to instruction less campus-dependent, it could do the same for academic research, potentially diluting the power of big university research centers. "If the Net allows for rich collaboration without the need for geographic proximity, the university as a geographic center is weakened," says Mr. Zittrain.

But Dr. McClintock says an all-encompassing online library would hardly eliminate the need for physical libraries, if only to house a collection of "canonical texts" required to verify digitized versions. These hard copies "may become sort of like the gold in Fort Knox," he says. "We may not want to consult it much, but we're all glad it's there."

Moreover, Dr. McClintock says that despite the potential power of an online library to foster learning and research collaboration, "a vital campus will still be important" for research and the generation of knowledge.

To illustrate this, Dr. McClintock says he likes to remind people that the Redmond, Wash., headquarters of Microsoft Corp.—symbol, to some, of the high-tech barbarians poised to storm academia's ramparts—resembles nothing so much as a campus. "And they call it that," he says. ■

Working with the Text

1. Write about your own experiences using computers as part of a course, especially if you or someone you know has taken a course either completely or partly online. Investigate the online courses offered at your college. How attractive do they seem to you? What would your concerns be?

2. Throughout his article, Cwiklik reports on various predictions made by educators and technology specialists as to just how

much computers and online learning will transform college education. Work in groups to make a list of these possibilities, and then write your own prediction about how you think online education will change your present college or university over the next ten to twenty years.

3. Cwiklik is writing for the *Wall Street Journal*, a daily newspaper that focuses especially on covering business issues for investors and managers. Based on your reading of the article, what kinds of work outside of college do online courses seem to be preparing students for? Are these different kinds of work than "traditional" courses seem most connected to?

JAMES TRAUB

From The Next University. Drive-Thru U.: Higher Education for People Who Mean Business

James Traub is a journalist who has written several books and articles on higher education, including City on a Hill: Testing the American Dream at City College. *In this article written for the* New Yorker *magazine, Traub investigates the University of Phoenix, a new kind of "college" aimed at working students and run according to a business model. In talking with the founder of the school, Traub raises questions about whether the school and others like it are too dedicated to the needs of worker training.*

At the University of Phoenix, which describes itself as the second-largest private university in the United States, terms that normally have a clear and literal meaning are used in an oddly evanescent way; this seems especially true of the language that evokes our most romantic feelings about higher education. The university has, for example, a "bookstore" on the ground floor of its central administration building. The store is a boutique offering backpacks, T-shirts, coffee mugs, beer glasses, and ties, all bearing the school logo; the only books are textbooks, which you have to order from someone standing behind a counter. The U. of P.'s "library" can be found, as Kurt Slobodzian, the librarian, likes to say, "wherever there's a computer"; students can access thousands of journals via the On-line Collection. And the word "campus" is understood, at the University of Phoenix, to mean "site," or even "outlet." The university is a franchise operation, with forty-seven sites all over the West and in Michigan, Florida, and Louisiana; most of them consist of an office building, or merely a few floors of a building, just off a highway exit ramp. When I was talking to the director of the university's "distance learning" program I noticed that he was using the word "campus" to apply to himself and three other people, who ran the program from a suite of offices. The University of Phoenix is, in fact, a para-university. It has the operational core of higher education—students, teachers, classrooms, exams, degree-granting programs—without a campus life, or even an intellectual life. There are no tenured professors, and the most recent issue of the university's only academic journal contained but a single academic article, about copyright law.

You cannot get a rise out of the university's top officials by pointing any of this out. William Gibbs, a former Price Waterhouse manager, who is the president of the U. of P., said to me, "The people who are our students don't really want the education. They want what the education provides for them—better jobs, moving up in their career, the ability to speak up in meetings, that kind of stuff. They want it to *do* something for them."

Apparently, it does. Enrollment may be flat at élite institutions, but the U. of P. has grown from three thousand students to forty thousand over the last decade. It offers accredited bachelor's-degree programs in business, nursing, and education, and an M.B.A. as well. The university is also the principal subsidiary of a profit-making company called the Apollo Group. Since late 1994, when the company first offered shares on the NASDAQ exchange, Apollo stock has increased in value from two dollars to thirty-five dollars, on a split-adjusted basis. One broker I spoke to said that most of his customers were professors at Arizona State, who had concluded that the U. of P. delivered pretty much the same product they did, only more efficiently. The University of Phoenix is competing not with the Ivy League but with the big state schools and the small, unheralded private colleges, where most students enroll. It's a Darwinian world out there: some two hundred colleges have closed during the last ten years.

College, for most of us, means greenswards, dreamy spires, professors with elbow patches, old volumes in the stacks; but no more than several dozen colleges answer to this description. Higher education in America is now a vast industry that accommodates two-thirds of America's high-school graduates, or more than fourteen million people. Most of the nation's thirty-seven hundred colleges see themselves as market-driven institutions trying to satisfy customer demand. As I drove around Phoenix, I kept hearing ads on the radio for Ottawa University, a Kansas institution that has three campuses in Arizona and others in Singapore, Malaysia, and Hong Kong. "Ottawa," the announcer said, "majors in *you*."

Almost half of America's freshmen attend community colleges, institutions with no residential facilities and, often, no campus. According to a study conducted by Arthur Levine, the president of Teachers College, at Columbia University, only a sixth of America's college students fit the stereotype: full-time students, living on campus. Levine says that a survey of the five-sixths who do not has found that "they wanted the kind of relationship with a college that they had with their bank, their supermarket, and their gas company. They say, 'I want terrific service, I want convenience, I want quality control. Give me classes twenty-four hours a day, and give me in-class parking, if possible.' These are students who want stripped-down classes. They don't want to buy anything they're not using." Such students understand clearly that higher education has become an indispensable passport to a better life.

In a 1994 book entitled "Dogmatic Wisdom," a history professor named Russell Jacoby faults critics on both the left and the right for focussing on the intellectual melodramas that agitate a tiny number of institutions—"canon wars" and battles over "speech codes"—while ignoring the "narrow practicality" that dominates educational practice at almost all the others. Jacoby quotes a Department of Education study showing that of a million bachelor's degrees awarded in 1991 seven thousand three hundred were in philosophy and religion, twelve thousand in foreign languages, and about two hundred and fifty thousand in business. The institution that sees itself as a steward of intellectual culture is becoming increasingly marginal; the others are racing to accommodate the new student. And the University of Phoenix, according to Arthur Levine, "is the first of the new breed."

John Sperling, the founder of the University of Phoenix and the chairman of the Apollo Group, is a blunt, ornery seventy-six-year-old from the Ozarks. In the company's bland and studiously polite environment, he stands out for his willingness to call an idiot an idiot. Sperling is an economic historian by profession, and, like many economists, he considers himself one of the few rational people on earth. Among the people he counts as idiots are those who believe that market forces can be ignored; during one of several conversations, he observed that the principal effect of the war on drugs was that it forced users to commit crimes. Along with George Soros and Peter Lewis, Sperling helped finance the Arizona referendum to permit the medical use of marijuana.

Sperling himself had a classical education—a B.A. in history at Reed, a master's in history at Berkeley, and a D. Phil. in economic history at Cambridge. He recalls his time at Berkeley as among the happiest years of his life. He was, however, far too restless to stick with the academic routine. In the early seventies, while teaching courses in the humanities at San Jose State, Sperling won a government contract to offer a variety of classes to teachers and police officers, and that was the beginning of what he considers his real education. "They were the best students I ever had," he told me. "They really fell in love with education. It wasn't long before they said, "We'd like to get a degree.' So I went to the administration, and they said, 'No way.' I said, 'I'm bringing you students.' And they said, "We don't need no stinking students.'"

Sperling developed a program with twenty-five hundred teachers and police at the University of San Francisco and two other colleges in California, but he claims that the regional accrediting body said, "Either get rid of these programs or we'll pull your accreditation for the whole university." Sperling came to see higher education as a closed system whose gates were manned by the accrediting agencies—a racket designed to squelch the forms of individual choice.

Sperling reached the Wild West of the free-market system in 1976, when he went to Phoenix, visited a local law firm, and drew up a charter for a new university and, just like that, the University of Phoenix opened for business. He targeted the niche market that he had already begun serving—the adult learner. The University of Phoenix would accept anybody who was twenty-three or older and was working. Students had to have sixty college credits when they arrived, so the need for general education, liberal arts, and all the other stuff that takes up so much time and money at college could be dispensed with. Sperling wanted to provide a useful and profitable service, not replicate higher education. What interested him was not so much what to teach this population as *how* to deliver it. "Higher education is one of the most inefficient mechanisms for the transfer of knowledge that have ever been invented," Sperling said. "I decided to go back to my economics and conceive of education as a production function, in which you specify the learning outcomes that you want—they're your product—and then do a regression and figure out the most efficient way of producing them."

Just as the Ivy league model was developed two centuries ago to accommodate aspiring clerics, so the University of Phoenix is shaped by the needs of working adults in the corporate economy. And because it was created all at once it's a highly rational institution. Classes are held at night, from six to ten. Courses consist of five or six weekly sessions, taken one at a time and one right after another. Each degree program is identical from one campus to the next. Laura Palmer Noone, whose title is vice-president for academic affairs—elsewhere she would be called "provost"—says, "What we have found is that adults don't want all that much flexibility; they want it to be simple."

One of Sperling's early insights was that adults also put very little stock in academic opinion. He concluded, "You were going to have to draw your faculty from the world they were familiar with—the world of work. If you had a Ph.D. that didn't mean shit." Marketing would be taught by a marketing executive, and accounting by an accountant. In a vocational setting, these teachers had the credentials that mattered. The "practitioner" system also, and not incidentally, allowed the university to deliver coursework far more cheaply than its competitors, since it paid its instructors an average of about a thousand dollars for each five-week course. Many of the teachers, and especially the businessmen, say they do their nighttime job for the sheer satisfaction of it. Hugh McBride, the executive director and chair of the graduate business programs, told me, "It's really a joy to have someone say, 'You know, Hugh, I used that last week in the company.'" . . .

The University of Phoenix is still one of the few for-profit academic institutions established to date; but the distinction between profit-making companies and educational institutions is becoming increasingly moot. Several education experts I spoke to volunteered the idea that a new kind of institution would come into being as the result of an alliance between a state-university system, a "content provider," like Disney, and a technology firm, like Motorola. The fastest-growing sector of higher education is, in fact, the "corporate university," which typically provides training for middle and upper management. A 1994 book by Stan Davis and Jim Botkin entitled "The Monster Under the Bed" observes that the increase in "classroom contact hours" for corporate employees in one year, 1992, exceeded the enrollment growth at all the colleges built between 1960 and 1990. The authors foresee the business model, with its focus on "competition, service, and standards," supplanting the current educational model.

This may be a bit premature, but the line between corporate training and academic education has clearly blurred. One day, I drove into Tempe, a suburb just beyond Phoenix (itself a sprawling suburb), to visit Motorola University, a gleaming facility on landscaped grounds that looks more like a university than the University of Phoenix does. Motorolans, as they are known, were taking courses in Behavioral Interviewing and Developing Your Human Potential, along with some in recondite aspects of computer-chip design. The curriculum sounded a lot like the one at the University of Phoenix, and, in fact, the U. of P. offers several of its courses on the campus. Motorola does not provide an academic degree, as some corporate universities do, but Arizona State offers a master's in Management of Technology on the Motorola campus, using teachers from both institutions. In Phoenix, if not yet in Boston or New York, the corporate university is part of a web, not of a pecking order—one of several kinds of "providers" filling in different aspects of a "learner's" needs. Arthur Levine, of Teacher's College, predicts that several generations from now "we'll still have some number of residential colleges and some number of research universities, but most of the rest will disappear." Corporations may simply make postsecondary education an in-house function. Non-élite institutions, Levine suggests, will be reduced largely to examining and certifying students for workplace readiness.

Like any successful business, the University of Phoenix is oriented toward growth, and in recent years it has begun to expand into the realm of the conventional university. The number of credits required for admission has dropped from sixty to zero. The U. of P. has created a General Studies department, which offers courses not only in Oral Communications but in Philosophy and Religion. (Bill Gibbs, though, says that he would like to see the Religion course focus on such practical advice as how to do business among different bodies of believers.) In effect, it is now taking responsibility for the entire undergraduate education of many of its students. The administration hired William Pepicello, who has a Ph.D. in linguistics from Brown and a manner that is identifiably academic, to establish a Gen. Ed. curriculum and embody the school's new identity. Last year, the U. of P. sought permission from accreditors to offer undergraduate degrees in whatever subjects it wished, and to establish a doctoral program. Both of these proposals were rejected—a decision that infuriated many at the school. The general view in Phoenix is that the forces of convention which have been trying to throttle John Sperling for a quarter of a century still have the upper hand in academe. An alternative point of view is that there are still standards for an academic education, and the university may have been threatening to transgress them. Stephen Spangehl, an official of the North Central Association, which is the regional accrediting body, declines to give specific reasons for the decision but says that the group was concerned about, among other things, the university's lack of rigorous academic assessment. "They seem more concerned about customer satisfaction," Spangehl says. "Our focus has always been on learning."

It's that sort of curt dismissal that makes John Sperling furious. "Jesus, they're disgusting," he said when I asked him about the decision. But he was moving ahead, looking for new markets. He had recently returned from a trip to the Far East. There were, he said, a million potential customers for information-systems training in Malaysia alone, and the China market was incalculable. The Apollo Group was making a big push into distance learning, and that may well be the growth market for postsecondary education. Moreover, the whole public-school market was opening up. Jorge Klor de Alva, a former anthropology professor at Berkeley, who is now the chair of the U. of P.'s academic cabinet, told me that the advent of school vouchers "will create huge opportunities for private, for-profit schools." Apollo could own a chain of schools, provide management services, and market curricular material. Once you conceive of education as a product, and regress from the needs of the consumer, a whole world of possibilities presents itself.

Sperling himself seems unable to decide whether he has created a superior model for higher education or a viable alternative to the existing one. As we were having dinner one evening, he started going on about the uselessness of classical education. "One of my favorite books is 'Tom Jones,'" he said. "I read 'Tom Jones' for the sheer pleasure, but I didn't go out and rut with some maid in the canebrakes. It's all part of what happens up here." He pointed to his head, but he sounded so thoroughly exasperated that he might as well have been talking about his appendix. "The University of Phoenix causes you to *apply* what you've learned *the next day at work*." Then, lest I get the wrong idea, he reminded me of how deeply he had loved Berkeley.

"Why don't you want all your students to have the experience you had?" I asked.

"Because they can't afford to."

"Wouldn't it be good if they could?"

Sperling gave me a weary look, and said, "I'm not involved in social reform." He had once tried to build a chain of technical schools for inner-city youth, he told me, and when that failed he had vowed never again to create something there wasn't a demand for. "Microsoft is a much more powerful force shaping the world than Harvard or Yale or Princeton," he said. "So if you can't beat 'em, join 'em." ■

Working with the Text

1. According to Traub, the University of Phoenix relies on a business-oriented, customer-service model in designing their educational programs. What do you see as the benefits and drawbacks of thinking of students as "customers" and colleges as "businesses"? Compose a letter for the school newspaper arguing that your present school either should or shouldn't follow more of a business model.

2. Traub quotes a prediction by Arthur Levine that in the future a few residential and research colleges will exist, but "'most of the rest will disappear.' Corporations may simply make postsec-

ondary education an in-house function. Non-élite institutions . . . will be reduced largely to examining and certifying students for workplace readiness." Do you find this possibility hopeful or depressing, and why do you feel this way?

3. Traub's interview with John Sperling, the founder of the University of Phoenix, raises the question of what students value in a college education beyond career preparation. Sperling suggests some students are only interested in career preparation or improvement and that others "'can't afford'" the liberal arts experience he had as a graduate student at the University of California, Berkeley. Do you think Sperling is right when he implies that many students are only interested in learning "practical" information? What do you value about college beyond job preparation? How satisfied are you with how well your present school meets your educational desires, and what changes would you recommend?

NEIL POSTMAN

Of Luddites, Learning, and Life

In this article written for the journal TECHNOS Quarterly, *Neil Postman seriously questions the importance of computer technology in contemporary education, arguing instead that the most important challenges facing educators have little to do with the state of information technology.*

Neil Postman is the head of the Department of Culture and Communication at New York University and has written many books and articles about education and the effects (both positive and negative) of mass media in the culture, including Amusing Ourselves to Death: Public Discourse in the Age of Show Business.

LUDDITES

I think it is a fair guess to say that my role in the pages of TECHNOS is to serve as the resident Luddite. If this is so, then there are two things you need to know. The first is that I do not regard my association with Luddism as, in any way, a disgrace. As perhaps readers will know, the Luddite movement flourished in England between 1811 and 1818 as a response to the furious growth of machines and factories. Notwithstanding the excesses of their zeal, the Luddites seemed to be the only group in England that could foresee the catastrophic effects of the factory system, especially on children. They did not want their children to be deprived of an education—indeed, of childhood itself—for the purpose of their being used to fuel the machines of industry. As William Blake put it, they did not want their children to labor in the "dark Satanic Mills."

It is true that the Luddites busted up some textile machinery from which their unsavory reputation originates, but when did we decide to mock or despise people who try to protect their children and preserve their way of life?

The second thing you need to know is that despite the respect I have for them, I am not at all a Luddite. I have, for example, no hostility toward new technologies and certainly no wish to destroy them, especially those technologies, like computers, that have captured the imagination of educators. Of course, I am not enthusiastic about them, either. I am indifferent to them. And the reason I am indifferent to them is that, in my view, they have nothing whatever to do with the fundamental problems we have to solve in schooling our young. If I do harbor any hostility toward these machines, it is only because they are distractions. They divert the intelligence and energy of talented people from addressing the issues we need most to confront.

Let me begin, then, to make my case by telling you about a conversation I had with an automobile salesman who was trying to get me to buy a new Honda Accord. He pointed out that the car was equipped with cruise control, for which there was an additional charge. As is my custom in thinking about the value of technology, I asked him, "What is the problem to which cruise control is the answer?" The question startled him, but he recovered enough to say, "It is the problem of keeping your foot on the gas." I told him I had been driving for 35 years and had never found that to be a problem. He then told me about the electric windows. "What is the problem," I asked, "to which electric windows are the answer?" He was ready for me this time. With a confident smile, he said, "You don't have to wind the windows up and down with your arm." I told him that this, too, had never been a problem, and that, in fact, I rather valued the exercise it gave me.

I bought the car anyway, because, as it turns out, you cannot get a Honda Accord without cruise control and electric windows—which brings up the first point I should like to mention. It is that, contrary to conventional wisdom, new technologies do not, by and large, *increase* people's options but do just the opposite. For all practical purposes, you cannot go to Europe anymore by boat, which I can report is a thrilling and civilized way to go. Now you have to take an airplane. You cannot work for a newspaper unless you use a word processor, which eliminates me, since I do all of my composing with a pen and yellow pad and do not wish to change. You cannot buy records anymore; you must use CDs. I can go on with a thousand examples which demonstrate the point that new technologies drive old technologies out of business; which is to say that there is an imperialistic thrust to technology, a strong tendency to get everyone to conform to the requirements of what is new. Now, this is not always a bad thing, although sometimes it is very bad. I bring it up to call attention to the fact that what we too easily call "progress" is always problematic. The word comes trippingly to the tongue, but when you examine what it means, you discover that technology is always a Faustian bargain. It giveth and it taketh away. And we would all be clearer about what we are getting into if there were less cheerleading about, let us say, the use of computers in the classroom and more sober analysis of what may be its costs intellectually and socially.

A second point my Honda story illuminates is that new technologies may not always solve significant problems or any problem at all. But because the technologies are *there,* we often invent problems to justify our using them. Or sometimes we even pretend we are solving one problem when, in fact, the reason for building and employing a new technology is altogether different. There are two expensive examples I can think of on this point. The first concerns the construction of the superconducting supercollider in Texas. It was justified by no less a person than Stephen Hawking, who told us that the research the supercollider would permit would give us entry to the mind of God. Since Hawking is an avowed atheist, he cannot possibly believe this; but even if he were not, it is equally sure he does not believe it. Nonetheless, it was good public relations. A Christian nation would be likely to go for it (though its Congress, after a $2 billion investment, did not), since the mysterious ways of the Lord have always been a serious problem for most of us. This is not to say that there aren't some interesting problems in cosmology that the supercollider might have solved. But since the people who would have been required to pay for this machine did not have any background or interest in these problems, it was best to talk about the mind of God.

The second example is the information superhighway that President Clinton and especially Vice President Gore are so ardently promoting. I have not yet heard a satisfactory answer to the question "What is the problem to which this $50 billion investment is the solution?" I suspect that an honest answer would be something like this: "There *is* no social or intellectual problem, but we can stimulate the economy by investing in new technologies." That is not at all a bad answer, but it is not the answer the vice president has given. He is trying to sell the idea by claiming that it solves the problem of giving more people greater access to more information faster, including providing them with 500 TV channels (or even a thousand).

LEARNING

This leads me directly to the question of schools and technology. In reading Lewis Perelman's book, *School's Out,* and the work of those who are passionate about the educational value of new technologies, I find that their enthusiasm is almost wholly centered on the fact that these technologies will give our students greater access to more information faster, more conveniently, and in more various forms than has ever been possible. That is their answer to the question "What is the problem to which the new technologies are the solution?" I would suggest a modification of the question by putting it this way: "What was the 19th-century problem to which these technologies are an irrelevant solution?" By putting it this way, I mean to say that the problem of getting information to people fast and in various forms was the main technological thrust of the 19th century, beginning with the invention of telegraphy and photography in the 1840s. It would be hard not to notice that the problem was solved and is therefore no longer something that any of us needs to work at, least of all, become worked up about. If anyone argues that technology can give people access to more information outside of the classroom than could possibly be given inside the classroom, then I would say that has been the case for almost 100 years. What else is new?

In other words, the information-giving function of the schools was rendered obsolete a long time ago. For some reason, more than a few technophiles (like Perelman) have just noticed this and are, in some cases, driven to favor eliminating our schools altogether. They err in this, I think, for a couple of reasons. One is that their notion of what schools are for is rather limited. Schools are not now and in fact have never been *largely* about getting information to children. That has been on the schools' agenda, of course, but has always been way down on the list.

One of the principal functions of school is to teach children how to behave in groups. The reason for this is that you cannot have a democratic, indeed, civilized, community life unless people have learned how to participate in a disciplined way as part of a group. School has never been about individualized learning. It has always been about how to learn and how to behave as part of a community. And, of course, one of the ways this is done is through the communication of what is known as social values. If you will read the first chapter of Robert Fulghum's *All I Ever Really Needed to Know I Learned in Kindergarten*, you will find an elegant summary of the important business of schools. The summary includes the following: Share everything, play fair, don't hit people, put things back where you found them, clean up your own mess, wash your hands before you eat, and, of course, flush. The only thing wrong with Fulghum's book is that no one has learned all these things, along with an affection for one's country, at kindergarten's end. We have ample evidence that it takes many years of teaching these values in school before they have been accepted and internalized. Some would say that this function of schooling is the most difficult task educators must achieve. If it is not, then the function of providing the young with narratives that help them to find purpose and meaning in learning and life surely is.

By a narrative I mean a story of human history that gives meaning to the past, explains the present, and provides guidance for the future. If there is a single problem that plagues American education at the moment, it is that our children no longer believe, as they once did, in some of the powerful and exhilarating narratives that were the underpinning of the school enterprise. I refer to such narratives as the story of our origins in which America is brought forth out of revolution, not merely as an experiment in governance but as part of God's own plan—the story of America as a moral light unto the world. Another great narrative tells of America as a melting pot where the teeming masses, from anywhere, yearning to be free, can find peace and sustenance. Still another narrative—sometimes referred to as the Protestant Ethic—tells of how hard work is one of the pathways to a fulfilled life. There are many other such narratives on which the whole enterprise of education in this country has rested. If teachers, children, and their parents no longer believe in these narratives, then schools become houses of detention rather than attention.

LIFE

What I am driving at is that the great problems of education are of a social and moral nature and have nothing to do with dazzling new technologies. In fact, the new technologies so loudly trumpeted in TECHNOS and in other venues are themselves not a solution to anything, but a problem to be solved. The fact is that our children, like the rest of us, are now suffering from information glut, not information scarcity. In America there are 260,000 billboards, 17,000 newspapers, 12,000 periodicals, 27,000 video outlets for renting tapes, 400 million television sets, and well over 400 million radios, not including those in automobiles. There are 40,000 new book titles published every year, and every day in America 41 million photographs are taken. And, just for the record (thanks to the computer), over 60 billion pieces of advertising junk mail come into our mailboxes every year. Everything from telegraphy and photography in the 19th century to the silicon chip in the 20th has amplified the din of information. From millions of sources all over the globe, through every possible channel and medium—light waves, air waves, ticker tapes, computer banks, telephone wires, television cables, satellites, and printing presses—information pours in. Behind it in every imaginable form of storage—on paper, on video and audio tape, on disks, film, and silicon chips—is an even greater volume of information waiting to be retrieved. Information has become a form of garbage. It comes indiscriminately, directed at no one in particular, disconnected from usefulness. We are swamped by information, have no control over it, and don't know what to do with it.

And in the face of all of this, there are some who believe it is time to abandon schools.

Well, if anyone is wondering whether or not the schools of the future have any use, here is something for them to contemplate. The role of the school is to help students learn how to ignore and discard information so that they can achieve a sense of coherence in their lives; to help students cultivate a sense of social responsibility; to help students think critically, historically, and humanely; to help students understand the ways in which technology shapes their consciousness; to help students learn that their own needs sometimes are subordinate to the needs of the group. I could go on for another three pages in this vein without any reference to how machinery can give students access to information. Instead, let me summarize in two ways what I mean. First, I'll cite a remark made repeatedly by my friend Alan Kay, who is sometimes called "the father of the personal computer." Alan likes to remind us that any problems the schools cannot solve without machines, they cannot solve with them. Second, and with this I shall come to a close: If a nuclear holocaust should occur some place in the world, it will not happen because of insufficient information; if children are starving in Somalia, it's not because of insufficient information; if crime terrorizes our cities, marriages are breaking up, mental disorders are increasing, and children are being abused, none of this happens because of a lack of information. These things happen because we lack something else. It is the "something else" that is now the business of schools. ■

Working with the Text

1. What does Postman see as the true purposes of education? How much do you agree with his description of these goals? How might you revise or add to these purposes?

2. Postman argues, "new technologies do not, by and large, *increase* people's options but do just the opposite." As a way of deciding whether you agree or disagree with him, examine the examples he offers to prove his point. How successful do you think he is? Come up with your own examples to either reinforce or challenge his point.

3. According to Postman, "The fact is that our children, like the rest of us, are now suffering from information glut, not information scarcity." Think of examples from your own experience that demonstrate Postman's point and come up with advice for teachers and parents on how to help students deal with "information glut."

Working on Connections: The Role of Technology in Higher Education

1. Based on these readings, work in groups to identify what you see as the key issues and questions we face in relation to the impact of computers and the Internet on higher education. What developments do you anticipate, and do you see these as positive or negative? To expand your project, locate additional sources of information for one or more of the key issues that you identify. This research can involve searching the Internet, working in the library, or interviewing people on campus with experience or expertise in computers and online learning.

2. Of all the voices we hear in these readings, John Sperling (interviewed by James Traub in "Drive-Thru U.") seems the most enthusiastic about online learning, and Neil Postman seems the most skeptical. Devise a debate between these two men on some specific issues related to the role of technology in higher education. What questions do you want to ask, and how do you think they would answer them?

Reading the Web

Comparing College Web Sites:
Three Views on School and Work

The "Focus on the Future of College Work" section asks you to think about how computer technology will transform higher education, especially in relation to the career interests of students and the economic needs of businesses. The following samples from the web sites of three different institutions of higher education will allow you to explore further the changing relationship between college work and the world of work by providing you with examples of how different schools present themselves to prospective students and others interested in the purpose of higher education. The first school represented, the University of Phoenix, was the particular subject of James Traub's article, "The Next University. Drive-Thru U.: Higher Education for People Who Mean Business." A for-profit enterprise, the University of Phoenix approaches education from a business perspective, both in the way it is run and in how it prepares students. The next school, Portland State University, is a public four-year university. The final school, Mount San Antonio College, is a two-year public community college in Southern California. For each school you are provided with the home page and "mission statement," or statement of core values and educational purpose, as they appeared in the fall of 2002. As you look at these web pages, keep the following questions in mind:

1. How do the designs of the different web pages signal the audiences each school is trying to reach? What kinds of potential students would be attracted to each site? What message is being sent to other members of the community, including businesses, parents, government, and so forth?
2. How do these sites represent the relationship between college work and the world of work? How much does each present college primarily as career preparation? What similar ideas do you see expressed across each web site, and where do you see differences?
3. How do you think the "for-profit" nature of the University of Phoenix might affect their sense of purpose and educational mission as compared to the not-for-profit state schools?

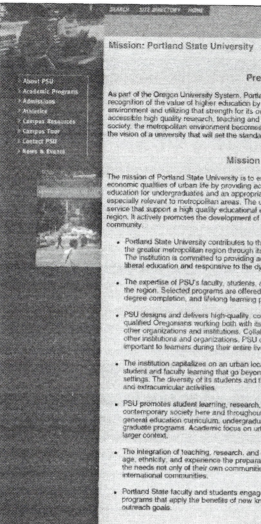

SEARCH SITE DIRECTORY HOME

PORTLAND STATE UNIVERSITY

Mission: Portland State University

> About PSU
> Academic Programs
> Admissions
> Athletics
> Campus Resources
> Campus Tour
> Contact PSU
> News & Events

Preamble

As part of the Oregon University System, Portland State University's vision is to enhance recognition of the value of higher education by continually strengthening the metropolitan environment and utilizing that strength for its own growth toward standards of excellence in accessible high quality research, teaching and outreach programs. As a microcosm of the global society, the metropolitan environment becomes a laboratory for Portland State in this vision. It is the vision of a university that will set the standard for institutions located in an urban setting.

Mission Statement

The mission of Portland State University is to enhance the intellectual, social, cultural and economic qualities of urban life by providing access throughout the life span to a quality liberal education for undergraduates and an appropriate array of professional and graduate programs especially relevant to metropolitan areas. The university conducts research and community service that support a high quality educational environment and reflect issues important to the region. It actively promotes the development of a network of educational institutions to serve the community.

- Portland State University contributes to the creation and communication of knowledge in the greater metropolitan region through its teaching, research, and outreach programs. The institution is committed to providing access to programs defined by the traditions of liberal education and responsive to the dynamics of employment and market requirements.

- The expertise of PSU's faculty, students, and staff enriches programs extending beyond the region. Selected programs are offered throughout the state, including professional, degree completion, and lifelong learning programs.

- PSU designs and delivers high-quality, cost-effective academic and service programs to all qualified Oregonians working both with its own resources and through partnerships with other organizations and institutions. Collaborating with K-12, community colleges, and other institutions and organizations, PSU demonstrates its commitment to address issues important to learners during their entire lives.

- The institution capitalizes on an urban location with diverse and unique opportunities for student and faculty learning that go beyond the traditional classroom and laboratory settings. The diversity of its students and their communities enhances academic programs and extracurricular activities.

- PSU promotes student learning, research, and community involvement relevant to contemporary society here and throughout the world through its unique interdisciplinary general education curriculum, undergraduate degree programs, and professional and graduate programs. Academic focus on urban issues includes the study of societies in their larger context.

- The integration of teaching, research, and outreach at PSU offers students of a diverse age, ethnicity, and experience the preparation to become responsible citizens attuned to the needs not only of their own communities but those of regional, national and international communities.

- Portland State faculty and students engage in national and international research programs that apply the benefits of new knowledge to the institution's learning and outreach goals.

3/5/99

TUESDAY FEBRUARY 25, 2003

Welcome to
Mt. San Antonio College

About Mt. SAC   Academics

Alumni Information   College Information

Community Education   Faculty / Staff Information

Mountie Sports   News & Press

Online Resources   Student Services

[HOME | AFFILIATES | ALUMNI | COMMUNITY | FACULTY / STAFF | STUDENTS | SEARCH]

MT. SAN ANTONIO COLLEGE
1100 N. GRAND AVENUE, WALNUT, CA 91789
909-594-5611

WEDNESDAY JUNE 25 2003

Mission Statement

To provide accessible and affordable quality learning opportunities in response to the needs and interests of the individuals and organizations.

To provide quality transfer, career, and life-long learning programs that prepare students with the knowledge and skills needed for success in an interconnected world.

To advance the state's and region's economic growth and global competitiveness through education, training, and services that contribute to continuous workforce improvement.

BACK TO ABOUT MT. SAC

· ADMINISTRATION · ADMISSIONS · MT. SAC FOUNDATION · CLASSES · EMPLOYMENT · STUDENTS · SPORTS ·

MT. SAN ANTONIO COLLEGE
1100 N. GRAND AVENUE, WALNUT, CA 91789
909.594.5611

Information Security Standards | Feedback | Mt. SAC Privacy Statement | Terms of Use | Web Statistics

This page current as of Tuesday March 25, 2003   Copyright © 2003 Mt. San Antonio College. All Rights Reserved.

Working with the Texts

1. Visit the current versions of each of the web sites represented here. How have they been updated or changed? Explore each web site further as a way of expanding your reaction to the preliminary questions above related to how each school portrays the relationship between college and career.

2. Compare these web sites with your own school's web site and mission statement. Which of these web sites does your school most resemble? What do you most agree and disagree with in your college's mission statement?

3. What do you think the proper relationship is between college work and preparation for the working world? How career oriented should a college curriculum be? Working collaboratively with other students, create a web site for prospective college students reviewing the different perspectives on this issue and advising them on what to look for in a college to best meet their needs and philosophies.

Stories of Work

MARK TWAIN (SAMUEL CLEMENS)
From *The Adventures of Tom Sawyer* ■

Mark Twain (the pen name used by Samuel Clemens) is one of America's most famous satirists and storytellers. His work includes autobiography, travel writing, and essays, but he is probably best known for the novels he wrote about Tom Sawyer and Huckleberry Finn, two boys growing up in Hannibal, Missouri in the decade before the Civil War. Based in part on Twain's own boyhood experiences in Hannibal, both The Adventures of Tom Sawyer *and* Adventures of Huckleberry Finn *are more than just humorous reminiscences or adventure stories. Twain used his novels as a means of social satire and criticism as well. In this excerpt from* The Adventures of Tom Sawyer, *Tom, a mischievous boy from a middle-class family, attends a special assembly of his Sunday School with his half-brother Sid and cousin Mary. Since Twain's time, Tom Sawyer has come to represent a mythic type of the American boy: full of imagination and energy, unwilling to follow rules, perpetually in trouble, but possessing a good heart and clever mind that gets him in and out of scrapes. As you read, think about what Twain is saying about the formal institutions of education and what we are supposed to admire about Tom.*

The sun rose upon a tranquil world, and beamed down upon the peaceful village like a benediction. Breakfast over, Aunt Polly had family worship; it began with a prayer built from the ground up of solid courses of Scriptural quotations, welded together with a thin mortar of originality; and from the summit of this she delivered a grim chapter of the Mosaic Law, as from Sinai.

Then Tom girded up his loins, so to speak, and went to work to 'get his verses'. Sid had learned his lesson days before. Tom bent all his energies to the memorising of five verses; and he chose part of the Sermon on the Mount, because he could find no verses that were shorter. At the end of half an hour, Tom had a vague general idea of his lesson, but no more, for his mind was traversing the whole field of human thought, and his hands were busy with distracting recreations. Mary took his book to hear him recite, and he tried to find his way through the fog.

'Blessed are the—a—a——'

'Poor——'

'Yes—poor; blessed are the poor—a—a——'

'In spirit——'

'In spirit; blessed are the poor in spirit, for they—they——'

'Theirs——'

'For *theirs*. Blessed are the poor in spirit, for *theirs*—is the kingdom of heaven. Blessed are they that mourn, for they—they—'

'Sh——'

'For they—a——'

'S, H, A——'

'For they S, H—— Oh, I don't know what it is!'

'*Shall!*'

'Oh, *shall!* for they shall—for they shall—a—a—shall mourn—a—a—blessed are they that shall—they that—a—they that shall mourn, for they shall—a—shall *what*? Why don't you tell me, Mary?—what do you want to be so mean for?'

'Oh, Tom, you poor, thick-headed thing, I'm not teasing you. I wouldn't do that. You must go and learn it again. Don't you be discouraged, Tom, you'll manage it—and if you do, I'll give you something ever so nice. There, now, that's a good boy.'

'All right! What is it, Mary? tell me what it is.'

'Never you mind, Tom. You know if I say it's nice, it *is* nice.'

'You bet you that's so, Mary. All right, I'll tackle it again.'

And he did 'tackle it again'; and under the double pressure of curiosity and prospective gain, he did it with such spirit that he accomplished a shining success. Mary gave him a brand-new 'Barlow' knife, worth twelve and a half cents; and the convulsion of delight that swept his system shook him to his foundations. True, the knife would not cut anything, but it was a 'sure enough' Barlow, and there was inconceivable grandeur in that—though where the western boys ever got the idea that such a weapon would possibly be counterfeited to its injury is an imposing mystery, and will always remain so, perhaps. Tom contrived to scarify the cupboard with it, and was arranging to begin on the bureau, when he was called off to dress for Sunday-school.

Mary gave him a tin basin of water and a piece of soap, and he went outside the door and set the basin on a little bench there; then he dipped the soap in the water and laid it down; turned up his sleeves; poured out the water on the ground gently, and then entered the kitchen, and began to wipe his face diligently on the towel behind the door. But Mary removed the towel and said:

'Now ain't you ashamed, Tom? You mustn't be so bad. Water won't hurt you.'

Tom was a trifle disconcerted. The basin was refilled, and this time he stood over it a little while, gathering resolution; took in a big breath and began. When he entered the kitchen presently, with both eyes shut and groping for the towel with his hands, an honourable testimony of suds and water was dripping from his face. But when he emerged from the towel he was not yet satisfactory, for the clean territory stopped short at his chin and his jaws like a mask; below and beyond this line there was a dark expanse of unirrigated soil that spread downward in front and backward around his neck. Mary took him in hand, and when she was done with him he was a man and a brother, without distinction of colour, and his saturated hair was neatly brushed, and its short curls wrought into a dainty and symmetrical general effect. (He privately smoothed out the curls, with labour and difficulty, and plastered his hair close down to his head; for he held curls to be effeminate, and his own filled his life with bitterness.) Then Mary got out a suit of his clothing that had been used only on Sundays during two years— they were simply called his 'other clothes'—and so by that we know the size of his wardrobe. The girl 'put him to rights' after he had dressed himself; she buttoned his neat roundabout up to his chin, turned his vast shirt-collar down over his shoulders, brushed him off, and crowned him with his speckled hat. He now looked exceedingly improved and uncomfortable. He was fully as uncomfortable as he looked; for there was a restraint about whole clothes and cleanliness that galled him. He hoped that Mary would forget his shoes, but the hope was blighted; she coated them thoroughly with tallow, as was the custom, and brought them out. He lost his temper, and said he was always being made to do everything he didn't want to do. But Mary said persuasively:

'Please, Tom—that's a good boy.'

So he got into his shoes, snarling. Mary was soon ready, and the three children set out for Sunday-school, a place that Tom hated with his whole heart; but Sid and Mary were fond of it.

Sabbath-school hours were from nine to half-past ten; and then church service. Two of the children always remained for the sermon voluntarily; and the other always remained, too—for stronger reasons. The church's high-backed uncushioned pews would seat about three hundred persons; the edifice was but a small, plain affair, with a sort of pine-board tree-box on top of it for a steeple. At the door Tom dropped back a step and accosted a Sunday-dressed comrade.

'Say, Bill, got a yaller ticket?'

'Yes.'

'What'll you take for her?'

'What'll you give?'

"Piece of lickrish and a fish-hook.'

"Less see 'em.'

Tom exhibited. They were satisfactory, and the property changed hands. Then Tom traded a couple of white alleys for three red tickets, and some small trifle or other for a couple of blue ones. He waylaid other boys as they came, and went on buying tickets of various colours ten or fifteen minutes longer. He entered the church, now, with a swarm of clean and noisy boys and girls, proceeded to his seat and started a quarrel with the first boy that came handy. The teacher, a grave, elderly man, interfered; then turned his back a moment, and Tom pulled a boy's hair in the next bench, and was absorbed in his book when the boy turned around; stuck a pin in another boy, presently, in order to hear him say 'Ouch!' and got a new reprimand from his teacher. Tom's whole class were of a pattern—restless, noisy, and troublesome. When they came to recite their lessons, not one of them knew his verses perfectly, but had to be prompted all along. However, they worried through, and each got his reward in small blue tickets, each with a passage of Scripture on it; each blue ticket was pay for two verses of the recitation. Ten blue tickets equalled a red one, and could be exchanged for it; ten red tickets equalled a yellow one; for ten yellow tickets the Superintendent gave a very plainly bound Bible (worth forty cents in those easy times) to the pupil. How many of my readers would have the industry and application to memorise two thousand verses, even for a Doré Bible? And yet Mary had acquired two Bibles in this way; it was the patient work of two years: and a boy of German parentage had won four or five. He once recited three thousand verses without stopping; but the strain upon his mental faculties was too great, and he was little better than an idiot from that day forth—a grievous misfortune for the school, for on great occasions before company, the Superintendent (as Tom expressed it) had always made this boy come out and 'spread himself'. Only the older pupils managed to keep their tickets and stick to their tedious work long enough to get a Bible, and so the delivery of one of these prizes was a rare and noteworthy circumstance; the successful pupil was so great and conspicuous for that day that on the spot every scholar's heart was fired with a fresh ambition that often lasted a couple of weeks. It is possible that Tom's mental stomach had never really hungered for one of those prizes, but unquestionably his entire being had for many a day longed for the glory and the *éclat* that came with it.

In due course the Superintendent stood up in front of the pulpit, with a closed hymn-book in his hand and his forefinger inserted between its leaves, and commanded attention. When a Sunday-school superintendent makes his customary little speech, a hymn-book in the hand is as necessary as is the inevitable sheet of music in the hand of a singer who stands forward on the platform and sings a solo at a concert—though why is a mystery; for neither the hymn-book nor the sheet of music is ever referred to by the sufferer. This superintendent was a slim creature of thirty-five, with a sandy goatee, and short sandy hair; he wore a stiff standing-collar whose upper edge almost reached his ears, and whose sharp points curved forward abreast the corners of his mouth—a fence that compelled a straight look-out ahead, and a turning of the whole body when a side view was required. His chin was propped on a spreading cravat, which was as broad and as long as a bank-note, and had fringed ends; his boot toes were turned sharply up, in the fashion of the day, like sleigh-runners—an effect patiently and laboriously produced by the young men by sitting with their toes pressed against a wall for hours together. Mr. Walters was very earnest of mien, and very sincere and honest at heart; and he held sacred things and places in such reverence, and so separated them from worldly matters, that unconsciously to himself his Sunday-school voice had acquired a peculiar intonation which was wholly absent on weekdays. He began after this fashion:

'Now, children, I want you all to sit up just as straight and pretty as you can, and give me all your attention for a minute or two. There, that is it. That is the way good little boys and girls should do. I see one little girl who is looking out of the window—I am afraid she thinks I am out there somewhere—perhaps up in one of the trees making a speech to the little birds. [Applausive titter.] I want to tell you how good it makes me feel to see so many bright, clean little faces assembled in a place like this, learning to do right and be good.'

And so forth, and so on. It is not necessary to set down the rest of the oration. It was of a pattern which does not vary, and so it is familiar to us all.

The latter third of the speech was marred by the resumption of fights and other recreations among certain of the bad boys, and by fidgetings and whisperings that extended far and wide, washing even to the bases of isolated and incorruptible rocks like Sid and Mary. But now every sound ceased suddenly with the subsidence of Mr. Walters' voice, and the conclusion of the speech was received with a burst of silent gratitude.

A good part of the whispering had been occasioned by an event which was more or less rare—the entrance of visitors; Lawyer Thatcher, accompanied by a very feeble and aged man, a fine, portly, middle-aged gentleman with iron-grey hair, and a dignified lady who was doubtless the latter's wife. The lady was leading a child. Tom had been restless and full of chafings and repinings, conscience-smitten, too—he could not meet Amy Lawrence's eye, he could not brook her loving gaze. But when he saw this small new-comer his soul was all ablaze with bliss in a moment. The next moment he was 'showing off' with all his might—cuffing boys, pulling hair, making faces, in a word, using every art that seemed likely to fascinate a girl, and win her applause. His exultation had but one alloy—the memory of his humiliation in this angel's garden; and that record in sand was fast washing out under the waves of happiness that were sweeping over it now. The visitors were given the highest seat of honour, and as soon as Mr. Walters' speech was finished, he introduced them to the school. The middle-aged man turned out to be a prodigious personage: no less an one than the county judge—altogether the most august creation these children had ever looked upon; and they wondered what kind of material he was made of; and they half wanted to hear him roar, and were half afraid he might, too. He was from Constantinople, twelve miles away—so he had travelled and seen the world—these very eyes had looked upon the County Court House, which was said to have a tin roof. The awe which these reflections inspired was attested by the impressive silence and the ranks of staring eyes. This was the great Judge

Thatcher, brother of their own lawyer. Jeff Thatcher immediately went forward to be familiar with the great man, and be envied by the school. It would have been music to his soul to hear the whisperings.

'Look at him, Jim! he's going up there. Say look! he's a going to shake hands with him; he *is* shaking hands with him. By jinks, don't you wish you was Jeff?'

Mr. Walters fell to 'showing off' with all sorts of official bustlings and activities, giving orders, delivering judgments, discharging directions here, there, everywhere that he could find a target. The librarian 'showed off', running hither and thither with his arms full of books and making a deal of the splutter and fuss that insect authority delights in. The young lady teachers 'showed off'—bending sweetly over pupils that were lately being boxed, lifting pretty warning fingers at bad little boys and patting good ones lovingly. The young gentleman teachers 'showed off' with small scoldings and other little displays of authority and fine attention to discipline; and most of the teachers, of both sexes, found business up at the library by the pulpit; and it was business that frequently had to be done over again two or three times (with much seeming vexation). The little girls 'showed off' in various ways, and the little boys 'showed off' with such diligence that the air was thick with paper wads and the murmur of scufflings. And above it all the great man sat and beamed a majestic judicial smile upon all the house, and warmed himself in the sun of his own grandeur, for he was 'showing off' too. There was only one thing wanting to make Mr. Walters' ecstasy complete, and that was a chance to deliver a Bible prize and exhibit a prodigy. Several pupils had a few yellow tickets, but none had enough—he had been around among the star pupils inquiring. He would have given worlds, now, to have that German lad back again with a sound mind.

And now at this moment, when hope was dead, Tom Sawyer came forward with nine yellow tickets, nine red tickets, and ten blue ones, and demanded a Bible! This was a thunderbolt out of a clear sky. Walters was not expecting an application from this source for the next ten years. But there was no getting around it—here were the certified checks, and they were good for their face. Tom was therefore elevated to a place with the Judge and the other elect, and the great news was announced from headquarters. It was the most stunning surprise of the decade; and so profound was the sensation that it lifted the new hero up to the judicial one's altitude, and the school had two marvels to gaze upon in place of one. The boys were all eaten up with envy; but those that suffered the bitterest pangs were those who perceived too late that they themselves had contributed to this hated splendour by trading tickets to Tom for the wealth he had amassed in selling whitewashing privileges. These despised themselves, as being the dupes of a wily fraud, a guileful snake in the grass.

The prize was delivered to Tom with as much effusion as the Superintendent could pump up under the circumstances; but it lacked somewhat of the true gush, for the poor fellow's instinct taught him that there was a mystery here that could not well bear the light, perhaps; it was simply preposterous that *this* boy had warehoused two thousand sheaves of Scriptural wisdom on his premises—

a dozen would strain his capacity, without a doubt. Amy Lawrence was proud and glad, and she tried to make Tom see it in her face; but he wouldn't look. She wondered; then she was just a grain troubled; next a dim suspicion came and went—came again; she watched; a furtive glance told her worlds—and then her heart broke, and she was jealous, and angry, and the tears came and she hated everybody; Tom most of all, she thought.

Tom was introduced to the Judge; but his tongue was tied, his breath would hardly come, his heart quaked—partly because of the awful greatness of the man, but mainly because he was *her* parent. He would have liked to fall down and worship him, if it were in the dark. The Judge put his hand on Tom's head and called him a fine little man, and asked him what his name was. The boy stammered, gasped, and got it out.

'Tom.'

'Oh, no, not Tom—it is——'

'Thomas.'

'Ah, that's it. I thought there was more to it, maybe. That's very well. But you've another one I dare say, and you'll tell it to me, won't you?'

'Tell the gentleman your other name, Thomas,' said Walters, 'and say *sir*. You mustn't forget your manners.'

'Thomas Sawyer—sir.'

'That's it! that's a good boy. Fine boy. Fine, manly little fellow. Two thousand verses is a great many—very, very great many. And you never can be sorry for the trouble you took to learn them; for knowledge is worth more than anything there is in the world; it's what makes great men and good men; you'll be a great man and a good man yourself some day, Thomas, and then you'll look back and say, "It's all owing to the precious Sunday-school privileges of my boyhood; it's all owing to my dear teachers that taught me to learn; it's all owing to the good Superintendent, who encouraged me and watched over me, and gave me a beautiful Bible, a splendid, elegant Bible, to keep and have it all for my own, always; it's all owing to right bringing up!" That is what you will say, Thomas; and you wouldn't have any money for those two thousand verses—no, indeed you wouldn't. And now you wouldn't mind telling me and this lady some of the things you've learned—no, I know you wouldn't—for we are proud of little boys that learn. Now no doubt you know the names of all the twelve disciples. Won't you tell us the names of the first two that were appointed?'

Tom was tugging at a button and looking sheepish. He blushed now, and his eyes fell. Mr. Walters's heart sank within him. He said to himself, It is not possible that the boy can answer the simplest question—why *did* the Judge ask him? Yet he felt obliged to speak up and say:

'Answer the gentleman, Thomas—don't be afraid.'

Tom still hung fire.

'Now, I know you'll tell *me*,' said the lady. 'The names of the first two disciples were——'

'David and Goliath!'

Let us draw the curtain of charity over the rest of the scene. ■

Working with the Text

1. Mr. Walters, the school superintendent, describes the purpose of education as "learning to do right and be good." How does the school seem to define "doing right" and "being good"? Find a passage that you feel suggests Twain's attitude toward these professed goals and the effectiveness of the teaching methods used to attain them.

2. The assembly is staged before two prominent members of the community, the "great Judge Thatcher" and his wife. While Tom defies almost all of the rules of his school as well as most authority figures, he remains in awe of the Judge and longs to meet him, a decidedly unrebellious attitude. How much is or isn't Tom Sawyer really rebelling against society's expectations of him?

3. Even though Tom does poorly at learning the "official" lessons of the school, he does manage to figure out how to meet Judge Thatcher and receive a prize Bible, suggesting he has learned something at school after all. Make a list of the "official" and "unofficial" lessons Tom seems to have learned at school. Compare this list with your own experiences as a student: what are the "official" and "unofficial" ways school has prepared you for the world?

4. Tom's rebelliousness is very much linked to gender in this story. How would this story be different if Tom were a girl in the mid-nineteenth century? Rewrite the events of this chapter reflecting what differences you think this change in gender would make.

Working with Connections

1. In many ways, Tom Sawyer seems the opposite of Ragged Dick (from Chapter 2: The Meaning of Work: Work, Labor, Career), yet both characters were popular depictions of boyhood from late-nineteenth-century America. They seem to represent conflicting ideas about how children, especially boys, should behave and about the meaning of success: being rebellious versus being obedient; conforming to "respectable" ideals versus defying authority, and so forth. Continue this list of seemingly contradictory ideals presented by Tom and Dick and write about how you understand them. Are they necessarily opposed to each other? Which do you think reflect more typical values?

2. While Tom always gets into trouble and ignores most of the adult advice given him, his story suggests that in the end things will work out all right for him. Compare the fictional misadventures of Tom Sawyer with the real life situations Mike Rose describes in *Lives on the Boundary*. In what ways does a comparison of the two stories highlight the issue of class privilege that the character of Tom takes for granted?

MIKE ROSE
■

From *Lives on the Boundary*

Most high schools use some form of "tracking" in assigning students to classes. While some students take "normal" classes, others choose or are placed in "College Prep," "AP," or "Advanced" tracks. While this kind of differentiation can help schools meet the specific needs of individual students, these tracks also run the risk of withholding opportunity or of becoming self-fulfilling prophecies. In this excerpt from his educational autobiography, Lives on the Boundary, *Mike Rose tells his own story of trying to overcome obstacles in his high school that he didn't even recognize at the time. Placed into the Vocational Education track because of a clerical error, Rose relates a student's-eye view of how frustrating and confusing school can be, even after a teacher switches him to the College Prep track. In reflecting on the chain of circumstances, some planned, others lucky, that led him eventually to pursue a college degree, Rose raises important questions about how school shapes our expectations of the future for good and ill.*

Mike Rose is a teacher, writer, and scholar who has focused on the roles played by social class, ethnicity, and culture in how students negotiate the educational system, especially the writing and language demands of college work. He is currently professor of Education at the University of California, Los Angeles.

It took two buses to get to Our Lady of Mercy. The first started deep in South Los Angeles and caught me at midpoint. The second drifted through neighborhoods with trees, parks, big lawns, and lots of flowers. The rides were long but were livened up by a group of South L.A. veterans whose parents also thought that Hope had set up shop in the west end of the county. There was Christy Biggars, who, at sixteen, was dealing and was, according to rumor, a pimp as well. There were Bill Cobb and Johnny Gonzales, grease-pencil artists extraordinaire, who left Nembutal-enhanced swirls of "Cobb" and "Johnny" on the corrugated walls of the bus. And then there was Tyrrell Wilson. Tyrrell was the coolest kid I knew. He ran the dozens like a metric halfback, laid down a rap that outrhymed and outpointed Cobb, whose rap was good but not great—the curse of a moderately soulful kid trapped in white skin. But it was Cobb who would sneak a radio onto the bus, and thus underwrote his patter with Little Richard, Fats Domino, Chuck Berry, the Coasters, and Ernie K. Doe's mother-in-law, an awful woman who was "sent from down below." And so it was that Christy and Cobb and Johnny G. and Tyrrell and I and assorted others picked up along the way passed our days in the back of the bus, a funny mix brought together by geography and parental desire.

Entrance to school brings with it forms and releases and assessments. Mercy relied on a series of tests, mostly the Stanford-Binet, for placement, and somehow the results of my tests got confused with those of another student named Rose. The other Rose apparently didn't do very well, for I was placed in the vocational track, a euphemism for the bottom level. Neither I nor my parents realized what this meant. We had no sense that Business Math, Typing, and English-Level D were dead ends. The current state of reports on the schools criticizes parents for not involving themselves in the education of their children. But how would someone like Tommy Rose, with his two years of Italian schooling, know what to ask? And what sort of pressure could an exhausted waitress apply? The error went undetected, and I remained in the vocational track for two years. What a place.

My homeroom was supervised by Brother Dill, a troubled and unstable man who also taught freshman English. When his class drifted away from him, which was often, his voice would rise in paranoid accusations, and occasionally he would lose control and shake or smack us. I hadn't been there two months when one of his brisk, face-turning slaps had my glasses sliding down the aisle. Physical education was also pretty harsh. Our teacher was a stubby ex-lineman who had played old-time pro ball in the Midwest. He routinely had us grabbing our ankles to receive his stinging paddle across our butts. He did that, he said, to make men of us. "Rose," he bellowed on our first encounter; me standing geeky in line in my baggy shorts. "'Rose'? What the hell kind of name is that?"

"Italian, sir," I squeaked.

"Italian! Ho. Rose, do you know the sound a bag of shit makes when it hits the wall?"

"No, sir."

"Wop!"

Sophomore English was taught by Mr. Mitropetros. He was a large, bejeweled man who managed the parking lot at the Shrine Auditorium. He would crow and preen and list for us the stars he'd brushed against. We'd ask questions and glance knowingly and snicker, and all that fueled the poor guy to brag some more. Parking cars was his night job. He had little training in English, so his lesson plan for his day work had us reading the district's required text, *Julius Caesar*, aloud for the semester. We'd finish the play way before the twenty weeks was up, so he'd have us switch parts again and again and start again: Dave Snyder, the fastest guy at Mercy, muscling through Caesar to the breathless squeals of Calpurnia, as interpreted by Steve Fusco, a surfer who owned the school's most envied paneled wagon. Week ten and Dave and Steve would take on new roles, as would we all, and render a water-logged Cassius and a Brutus that are beyond my powers of description.

Spanish I—taken in the second year—fell into the hands of a new recruit. Mr. Montez was a tiny man, slight, five foot six at the most, soft-spoken and delicate. Spanish was a particularly rowdy class, and Mr. Montez was as prepared for it as a doily maker at a hammer throw. He would tap his pencil to a room in which Steven Fusco was propelling spitballs from his heavy lips, in which Mike Dweetz was taunting Bill Hawk, a half-Indian, half-Spanish, reed-thin, quietly explosive boy. The vocational track at Our Lady of Mercy mixed kids traveling in from South L.A. with South Bay surfers and a few Slavs and Chicanos from the harbors of San Pedro. This was a dangerous miscellany: surfers and hodads and South-Central blacks all ablaze to the metronomic tapping of Hector Montez's pencil.

One day Billy lost it. Out of the corner of my eye I saw him strike out with his right arm and catch Dweetz across the neck. Quick as a spasm, Dweetz was out of his seat, scattering desks, cracking Billy on the side of the head, right behind the eye. Snyder and Fusco and others broke it up, but the room felt hot and close and naked. Mr. Montez's tenuous authority was finally ripped to shreds, and I think everyone felt a little strange about that. The charade was over, and when it came down to it, I don't think any of the kids really wanted it to end this way. They had pushed and pushed and bullied their way into a freedom that both scared and embarrassed them.

Students will float to the mark you set. I and the others in the vocational classes were bobbing in pretty shallow water. Vocational education has aimed at increasing the economic opportunities of students who do not do well in our schools. Some serious programs succeed in doing that, and through exceptional teachers—like Mr. Gross in *Horace's Compromise*—students learn to develop hypotheses and troubleshoot, reason through a problem, and communicate effectively—the true job skills. The vocational track, however, is most often a place for those who are just not making it, a dumping ground for the disaffected. There were a few teachers who worked hard at education; young Brother Slattery, for example, combined a stern voice with weekly quizzes to try to pass along to us a skeletal outline of world history. But mostly the teachers had no idea of how to engage the imaginations of us kids who were scuttling along at the bottom of the pond.

And the teachers would have needed some inventiveness, for none of us was groomed for the classroom. It wasn't just that I didn't know things—didn't know how to simplify algebraic fractions, couldn't identify different kinds of clauses, bungled Spanish translations—but that I had developed various faulty and inadequate ways of doing algebra and making sense of Spanish. Worse yet, the years of defensive tuning out in elementary school had given me a way to escape quickly while seeming at least half alert. During my time in Voc. Ed., I developed further into a mediocre student and a somnambulant problem solver, and that affected the subjects I did have the wherewithal to handle: I detested Shakespeare; I got bored with history. My attention flitted here and there. I fooled around in class and read my books indifferently—the intellectual equivalent of playing with your food. I did what I had to do to get by, and I did it with half a mind.

But I did learn things about people and eventually came into my own socially. I liked the guys in Voc. Ed. Growing up where I did, I understood and admired physical prowess, and there was an abundance of muscle here. There was Dave Snyder, a sprinter and halfback of true quality. Dave's ability and his quick wit gave him a natural appeal, and he was welcome in any clique, though he always kept a little independent. He enjoyed acting the fool and could care less about studies, but he possessed a certain maturity and never caused the faculty much trouble. It was a testament to his independence that he included me among his friends—I eventually went out for track, but I was no jock. Owing to the Latin alphabet and a dearth of *R*s and *S*s, Snyder sat behind Rose, and we started exchanging one-liners and became friends.

There was Ted Richard, a much-touted Little League pitcher. He was chunky and had a baby face and came to Our Lady of Mercy as a seasoned street fighter. Ted was quick to laugh and he had a loud, jolly laugh, but when he got angry he'd smile a little smile, the kind that simply raises the corner of the mouth a quarter of an inch. For those who knew, it was an eerie signal. Those who didn't found themselves in big trouble, for Ted was very quick. He loved to carry on what we would come to call philosophical discussions: What is courage? Does God exist? He also loved words, enjoyed picking up big ones like *salubrious* and *equivocal* and using them in our conversations—laughing at himself as the word hit a chuckhole rolling off his tongue. Ted didn't do all that well in school—baseball and parties and testing the courage he'd speculated about took up his time. His textbooks were *Argosy* and *Field and Stream*, whatever newspapers he'd find on the bus stop—from the *Daily Worker* to pornography—conversations with uncles and hobos or businessmen he'd meet in a coffee shop, *The Old Man and the Sea*. With hindsight, I can see that Ted was developing into one of those rough-hewn intellectuals whose sources are a mix of the learned and the apocryphal, whose discussions are both assured and sad.

And then there was Ken Harvey. Ken was good-looking in a puffy way and had a full and oily ducktail and was a car enthusiast . . . a hodad. One day in religion class, he said the sentence that turned out to be one of the most memorable of the hundreds of thousands I heard in those Voc. Ed. years. We were talking about the parable of the talents, about achievement, working hard, doing the best you can do, blah-blah-blah, when the teacher called on the restive Ken Harvey for an opinion. Ken thought about it, but just for a second, and said (with studied, minimal affect), "I just wanna be average." That woke me up. Average?! Who wants to be average? Then the athletes chimed in with the clichés that make you want to laryngectomize them, and the exchange became a platitudinous melee. At the time, I thought Ken's assertion was stupid, and I wrote him off. But his sentence has stayed with me all these years, and I think I am finally coming to understand it.

Ken Harvey was gasping for air. School can be a tremendously disorienting place. No matter how bad the school, you're going to encounter notions that don't fit with the assumptions and beliefs that you grew up with—maybe you'll hear these dissonant notions from teachers, maybe from the other students, and maybe you'll read them. You'll also be thrown in with all kinds of kids from all kinds of backgrounds, and that can be unsettling—this is especially true in places of rich ethnic and linguistic mix, like the L.A. basin. You'll see a handful of students far excel you in courses that sound exotic and that are only in the curriculum of the elite: French, physics, trigonometry. And all this is happening while you're trying to shape an identity, you body is changing, and your emotions are running wild. If you're a working-class kid in the vocational track, the options you'll have to deal with this will be constrained in certain ways: You're defined by your school as "slow"; you're placed in a curriculum that isn't designed to liberate you but to occupy you, or, if you're lucky, train you, though the training is for work the society does not esteem; other students are picking up the cues from your school and your curriculum and interacting with you in particular ways. If you're a kid like Ted Richard, you turn your back on all this and let your mind roam where it may. But youngsters like Ted are rare. What Ken and so many others do is protect themselves from such suffocating madness by taking on with a vengeance the identity implied in the vocational track. Reject the confusion and frustration by openly defining yourself as the Common Joe. Champion the average. Rely on your own good sense. Fuck this bullshit. Bullshit, of course, is everything you—and the others—fear is beyond you: books, essays, tests, academic scrambling, complexity, scientific reasoning, philosophical inquiry.

The tragedy is that you have to twist the knife in your own gray matter to make this defense work. You'll have to shut down, have to reject intellectual stimuli or diffuse them with sarcasm, have to cultivate stupidity, have to convert boredom from a malady into a way of confronting the world. Keep your vocabulary simple, act stoned when you're not or act more stoned than you are, flaunt ignorance, materialize your dreams. It is a powerful and effective defense—it neutralizes the insult and the frustration of being a vocational kid and, when perfected, it drives teachers up the wall, a delightful secondary effect. But like all strong magic, it exacts a price.

My own deliverance from the Voc. Ed. world began with sophomore biology. Every student, college prep to vocational, had to take biology, and unlike the other courses, the same person taught all sections. When teaching the vocational group, Brother Clint probably slowed down a bit or omitted a little of the fundamental biochemistry, but he used the same book and more or less the same syllabus across the board. If one class got tough, he could get tougher. He was young and powerful and very handsome, and looks and physical strength were high currency. No one gave him any trouble.

I was pretty bad at the dissecting table, but the lectures and the textbook were interesting: plastic overlays that, with each turned page, peeled away skin, then veins and muscle, then organs, down to the very bones that Brother Clint, pointer in hand, would tap out on our hanging skeleton. Dave Snyder was in big trouble, for the study of life—versus the living of it—was sticking in his craw. We worked out a code for our multiple-choice exams. He'd poke me in the back: once for the answer under *A*, twice for *B*, and so on; and when he'd hit the right one, I'd look up to the ceiling as though I were lost in thought. Poke: cytoplasm. Poke, poke: methane. Poke, poke, poke: William Harvey. Poke, poke, poke, poke: islets of Langerhans. This didn't work out perfectly, but Dave passed the course, and I mastered the dreamy look of a guy on a record jacket. And something else happened. Brother Clint puzzled over this Voc. Ed. kid who was racking up 98s and 99s on his tests. He checked the school's records and discovered the error. He recommended that I begin my junior year in the College Prep program. According to all I've read since, such a shift, as one report put it, is virtually impossible. Kids at that level rarely cross tracks. The telling thing is how chancy both my placement into and exit from Voc. Ed. was; neither I nor my parents had anything to do with it. I lived in one world during spring semester, and when I came back to school in the fall, I was living in another.

Switching to College Prep was a mixed blessing. I was an erratic student. I was undisciplined. And I hadn't caught onto the rules of the game: Why work hard in a class that didn't grab my fancy? I was also hopelessly behind in math. Chemistry was hard; toying with my chemistry set years before hadn't prepared me for the chemist's equations. Fortunately, the priest who taught both chemistry and second-year algebra was also the school's athletic director. Membership on the track team covered me; I knew I wouldn't get lower than a C. U.S. history was taught pretty well, and I did okay. But civics was taken over by a football coach who had trouble reading the textbook aloud—and reading aloud was the center-piece of his pedagogy. College Prep at Mercy was certainly an improvement over the vocational program—at least it carried some status—but the social science cur-riculum was weak, and the mathematics and physical sciences were simply beyond me. I had a miserable quantitative background and ended up copying some assignments and finessing the rest as best I could. Let me try to explain how it feels to see again and again material you should once have learned but didn't.

You are given a problem. It requires you to simplify algebraic fractions or to multiply expressions containing square roots. You know this is pretty basic material because you've seen it for years. Once a teacher took some time with you, and you learned how to carry out these operations. Simple versions, any-way. But that was a year or two or more in the past, and these are more com-plex versions, and now you're not sure. And this, you keep telling yourself, is ninth- or even eighth-grade stuff.

Next it's a word problem. This is also old hat. The basic elements are as familiar as story characters: trains speeding so many miles per hour or shadows of buildings angling so many degrees. Maybe you know enough, have sat through enough explanations, to be able to begin setting up the problem: "If one train is going this fast . . ." or "This shadow is really one line of a triangle. . . ." Then: "Let's see . . ." "How did Jones do this?" "Hmmmm." "No." "No, that won't work." Your attention wavers. You wonder about other things: a football game, a dance, that cute new checker at the market. You try to focus on the problem again. You scribble on paper for a while, but the tension wins out and your attention flits elsewhere. You crumple the paper and begin daydreaming to ease the frustration.

The particulars will vary, but in essence that is what a number of students go through, especially those in so-called remedial classes. They open their text-books and see once again the familiar and impenetrable formulas and diagrams and terms that have stumped them for years. There is no excitement here. *No excitement.* Regardless of what the teacher says, this is not a new challenge. There is, rather, embarrassment and frustration and, not surprisingly, some anger in being reminded once again of longstanding inadequacies. No wonder so many students finally attribute their difficulties to something inborn, organic: "That part of my brain just doesn't work." Given the troubling histories many of these students have, it's miraculous that any of them can lift the shroud of hope-lessness sufficiently to make deliverance from these classes possible.

Through this entire period, my father's health was deteriorating with cruel momentum. His arteriosclerosis progressed to the point where a simple nick on his shin wouldn't heal. Eventually it ulcerated and widened. Lou Minto would come by daily to change the dressing. We tried renting an oscillating bed—which we placed in the front room—to force blood through the constricted arteries in my father's legs. The bed hummed through the night, moving in place to ward off the inevitable. The ulcer continued to spread, and the doctors finally had to amputate. My grandfather had lost his leg in a stockyard accident. Now my father too was crippled. His convalescence was slow but steady, and the doctors placed him in the Santa Monica Rehabilitation Center, a sun-bleached building that opened out onto the warm spray of the Pacific. The place gave him some strength and some color and some training in walking with an artificial leg. He did pretty well for a year or so until he slipped and broke his hip. He was confined to a wheelchair after that, and the confinement con-tributed to the diminishing of his body and spirit.

I am holding a picture of him. He is sitting in his wheelchair and smiling at the camera. The smile appears forced, unsteady, seems to quaver, though it is frozen in silver nitrate. He is in his mid-sixties and looks eighty. Late in my junior year, he had a stroke and never came out of the resulting coma. After that, I would see him only in dreams, and to this day that is how I join him. Sometimes the dreams are sad and grisly and primal: my father lying in a bed soaked with his suppuration, holding me, rocking me. But sometimes the dreams bring him back to me healthy: him talking to me on an empty street, or buying some pic-tures to decorate our old house, or transformed somehow into someone strong and adept with tools and the physical.

Jack MacFarland couldn't have come into my life at a better time. My father was dead, and I had logged up too many years of scholastic indiffer-ence. Mr. MacFarland had a master's degree from Columbia and decided, at twenty-six, to find a little school and teach his heart out. He never took any cre-dentialing courses, couldn't bear to, he said, so he had to find employment in a private system. He ended up at Our Lady of Mercy teaching five sections of senior English. He was a beatnik who was born too late. His teeth were stained, he tucked his sorry tie in between the third and fourth buttons of his shirt, and his pants were chronically wrinkled. At first, we couldn't believe this guy, thought he slept in his car. But within no time, he had us so startled with work that we didn't much worry about where he slept or if he slept at all. We wrote three or four essays a month. We read a book every two to three weeks, starting with the *Iliad* and ending up with Hemingway. He gave us a quiz on the reading every other day. He brought a prep school curriculum to Mercy High.

MacFarland's lectures were crafted, and as he delivered them he would pace the room jiggling a piece of chalk in his cupped hand, using it to scribble on the board the names of all the writers and philosophers and plays and novels he was weaving into his discussion. He asked questions often, raised everything from Zeno's paradox to the repeated last line of Frost's "Stopping by Woods on a Snowy Evening." He slowly and carefully built up our knowledge of Western intellectual history—with facts, with connections, with speculations. We learned about Greek philosophy, about Dante, the Elizabethan world view, the Age of Reason, existentialism. He analyzed poems with us, had us reading sections from John Ciardi's *How Does a Poem Mean?*, making a potentially difficult book accessible with his own explanations. We gave oral reports on poems Ciardi didn't cover. We imitated the styles of Conrad, Hemingway, and *Time* magazine. We wrote and talked, wrote and talked. The man immersed us in language.

Even MacFarland's barbs were literary. If Jim Fitzsimmons, hung over and irritable, tried to smart-ass him, he'd rejoin with a flourish that would spark the indomitable Skip Madison—who'd lost his front teeth in a hapless tackle—to flick his tongue through the gap and opine, "good chop," drawing out the single "o" in stinging indictment. Jack MacFarland, this tobacco-stained intellectual, brandished linguistic weapons of a kind I hadn't encountered before. He was this *egghead*, for God's sake, keeping some pretty difficult people in line. And from what I heard, Mike Dweetz and Steve Fusco and all the notorious Voc. Ed. crowd settled down as well when MacFarland took the podium. Though a lot of guys groused in the schoolyard, it just seemed that giving trouble to this particular teacher was a silly thing to do. Tomfoolery, not to mention assault, had no place in the world he was trying to create for us, and instinctively everyone knew that. If nothing else, we all recognized MacFarland's considerable intelligence and respected the hours he put into his work. It came to this: The troublemaker would look foolish rather than daring. Even Jim Fitzsimmons was reading *On the Road* and turning his incipient alcoholism to literary ends.

There were some lives that were already beyond Jack MacFarland's ministrations, but mine was not. I started reading again as I hadn't since elementary school. I would go into our gloomy little bedroom or sit at the dinner table while, on the television, Danny McShane was paralyzing Mr. Moto with the atomic drop, and work slowly back through *Heart of Darkness*, trying to catch the words in Conrad's sentences. I certainly was not MacFarland's best student; most of the other guys in College Prep, even my fellow slackers, had better backgrounds than I did. But I worked very hard, for MacFarland had hooked me. He tapped my old interest in reading and creating stories. He gave me a way to feel special by using my mind. And he provided a role model that wasn't shaped on physical prowess alone, and something inside me that I wasn't quite aware of responded to that. Jack MacFarland established a literacy club, to borrow a phrase of Frank Smith's, and invited me—invited all of us—to join.

There's been a good deal of research and speculation suggesting that the acknowledgment of school performance with extrinsic rewards—smiling faces, stars, numbers, grades—diminishes the intrinsic satisfaction children experience by engaging in reading or writing or problem solving. While it's certainly true that we've created an educational system that encourages our best and brightest to become cynical grade collectors and, in general, have developed an obsession with evaluation and assessment, I must tell you that venal though it may have been, I loved getting good grades from MacFarland. I now know how subjective grades can be, but then they came tucked in the back of essays like bits of sci-entific data, some sort of spectroscopic readout that said, objectively and publicly, that I had made something of value. I suppose I'd been mediocre for too long and enjoyed a public redefinition. And I suppose the workings of my mind, such as they were, had been private for too long. My linguistic play moved into the world; like the intergalactic stories I told years before on Frank's berry-splattered truck bed, these papers with their circled, red B-pluses and A-minuses linked my mind to something outside it. I carried them around like a club emblem.

One day in the December of my senior year, Mr. MacFarland asked me where I was going to go to college. I hadn't thought much about it. Many of the students I teach today spent their last year in high school with a physics text in one hand and the Stanford catalog in the other, but I wasn't even aware of what "entrance requirements" were. My folks would say that they wanted me to go to college and be a doctor, but I don't know how seriously I ever took that; it seemed a sweet thing to say, a bit of supportive family chatter, like telling a gan-gly daughter she's graceful. The reality of higher education wasn't in my scheme of things: No one in the family had gone to college; only two of my uncles had completed high school. I figured I'd get a night job and go to the local junior college because I knew that Snyder and Company were going there to play ball. But I hadn't even prepared for that. When I finally said, "I don't know," MacFarland looked down at me—I was seated in his office—and said, "Listen, you can write."

My grades stank. I had A's in biology and a handful of B's in a few English and social science classes. All the rest were C's—or worse. MacFarland said I would do well in his class and laid down the law about doing well in the others. Still, the record for my first three years wouldn't have been acceptable to any four-year school. To nobody's surprise, I was turned down flat by USC and UCLA. But Jack MacFarland was on the case. He had received his bachelor's degree from Loyola University, so he made calls to old professors and talked to somebody in admissions and wrote me a strong letter. Loyola finally accepted me as a probationary student. I would be on trial for the first year, and if I did Okay, I would be granted regular status. MacFarland also intervened to get me a loan, for I could never have afforded a private college without it. Four more years of religion classes and four more years of boys at one school, girls at another. But at least I was going to college. Amazing.

In my last semester of high school, I elected a special English course fashioned by Mr. MacFarland, and it was through this elective that there arose at Mercy a fledgling literati. Art Mitz, the editor of the school newspaper and a very smart guy, was the kingpin. He was joined by me and by Mark Dever, a quiet boy who wrote beautifully and who would die before he was forty. MacFarland occasionally invited us to his apartment, and those visits became the high point of our apprenticeship: We'd clamp on our training wheels and drive to his salon.

He lived in a cramped and cluttered place near the airport, tucked away in the kind of building that architectural critic Reyner Baham calls a *dingbat*. Books were all over: stacked, piled, tossed, and crated, underlined and dog eared, well worn and new. Cigarette ashes crusted with coffee in saucers or spilled over the sides of motel ashtrays. The little bedroom had, along two of its walls, bricks and boards loaded with notes, magazines, and oversized books. The kitchen joined the living room, and there was a stack of German newspapers under the sink. I had never seen anything like it: a great flophouse of language furnished by City Lights and Café le Metro. I read every title. I flipped through paperbacks and scanned jackets and memorized names: Gogol, *Finnegan's Wake*, Djuna Barnes, Jackson Pollock, *A Coney Island of the Mind*, F. O. Matthiessen's *American Renaissance*, all sorts of Freud, *Troubled Sleep*, Man Ray, *The Education of Henry Adams*, Richard Wright, *Film as Art*, William Butler Yeats, Marguerite Duras, *Redburn*, *A Season in Hell*, *Kapital*. On the cover of Alain-Fournier's *The Wanderer* was an Edward Gorey drawing of a young man on a road winding into dark trees. By the hotplate sat a strange Kafka novel called *Amerika*, in which an adolescent hero crosses the Atlantic to find the Nature Theater of Oklahoma. Art and Mark would be talking about a movie or the school newspaper, and I would be consuming my English teacher's library. It was heady stuff. I felt like a Pop Warner athlete on steroids.

Art, Mark, and I would buy stogies and triangulate from MacFarland's apartment to the Cinema, which now shows X-rated films but was then L.A.'s premier art theater, and then to the musty Cherokee Bookstore in Hollywood to hobnob with beatnik homosexuals—smoking, drinking bourbon and coffee, and trying out awkward phrases we'd gleaned from our mentor's bookshelves. I was happy and precocious and a little scared as well, for Hollywood Boulevard was thick with a kind of decadence that was foreign to the South Side. After the Cherokee, we would head back to the security of MacFarland's apartment, slaphappy with hipness.

Let me be the first to admit that there was a good deal of adolescent passion in this embrace of the avant-garde: self-absorption, sexually charged pedantry, an elevation of the odd and abandoned. Still it was a time during which I absorbed an awful lot of information: long lists of titles, images from expressionist paintings, new wave shibboleths, snippets of philosophy, and names that read like Steve Fusco's misspellings—Goethe, Nietzsche, Kierkegaard. Now this is hardly the stuff of deep understanding. But it was an introduction, a phrase book, a Baedeker to a vocabulary of ideas, and it felt good at the time to know all these words. With hindsight I realize how layered and important that knowledge was.

It enabled me to do things in the world. I could browse bohemian bookstores in far-off, mysterious Hollywood; I could go to the Cinema and see events through the lenses of European directors; and, most of all, I could share an evening, talk that talk, with Jack MacFarland, the man I most admired at the time. Knowledge was becoming a bonding agent. Within a year or two, the persona of the disaffected hipster would prove too cynical, too alienated to last. But for a time it was new and exciting: It provided a critical perspective on society, and it allowed me to act as though I were living beyond the limiting boundaries of South Vermont. ■

Working with the Text

1. According to Rose, "Vocational education has aimed at increasing the economic opportunities of students who do not do well in our schools," yet the vocational education program he found himself in seemed to have different goals. How would you describe the function of the Voc Ed track at Rose's high school?

2. Rose recognizes that he has a rare perspective that comes from spending time in both the Voc Ed and College Prep tracks, a situation few students experience. Which of his insights about his experience in these two tracks do you find most valuable? What are the pros and cons of having a "tracking" system in high school? If your own high school also had "tracks," what was your experience of them?

3. Jack MacFarland became a mentor and an important role model for Rose. What did Rose find most inspiring about him and worthy of imitation? What was your own response to his character?

4. In telling his own story, Rose draws vivid portraits of several of his classmates and uses their stories to express different opinions about the role of education. Try your hand at writing detailed descriptions of memorable members of your own high school class and what you think their experiences can teach us about the positive and negative impact of school. You may use different names or even combine different people into a single "composite" student.

Working with Connections

1. The use of "tracking" in education raises the question of whether a single school might contain more than one of the school types described in Jean Anyon's *Social Class and the Hidden Curriculum of Work*. To what extent do the Voc Ed and College Prep

tracks described by Rose suggest different class-based educational programs, and to what extent do they seem to belong to the same social-class-based teaching style?

2. Rose relied on the help of Jack MacFarland in deciding on a college to attend. Based on your reading of the web sites in the section on "Reading the Web" and the college ads in "Media Images," which schools seemed most aimed at attracting students like Rose or his classmates?

Media Images

MATT GROENING   ■

"Life in School"

Now most famous as the creator of The Simpsons, *cartoonist Matt Groening has produced the alternative comic strip* Life in Hell *for almost twenty years. The strip features the trials and tribulations of two very un-Disney-like rabbits, Bongo and Binky, and displays the same irreverent, caustic take on modern life found in* The Simpsons. *In this comic, Binky suggests the difference between the "official" and "unofficial" lessons learned in school.*

©1983 by Matt Groening. All Rights Reserved.

Working with the Text

1. Choose one of Binky's "secret" answers that you most agree or disagree with and write about the personal experiences that lead you to feel this way.

2. Write a "teacher's eye" version of this same strip in response to the student question "Why are we in school?"

3. Based on Binky's thoughts, speculate about what Groening implies should happen in school.

Working with Connections

1. Compare Binky's assessment of school with Mark Twain's representation of the Sunday school assembly in *The Adventures of Tom Sawyer*. How have things changed or stayed the same in terms of what each writer is satirizing about school then and now?

2. According to your reading of Anyon's essay, which kinds of schools would Groening's comic most apply to and why?

THE WORK OF WRITING/WRITING AS WORK

In Mike Rose's *Lives on the Boundary*, we read about his struggle to understand the educational system and the importance of finding a mentor figure. One important role a college student can play is that of mentor for young people who have much to learn about what opportunities and challenges await them and how they need to prepare for them. This mentoring involves not just teaching skills, but shaping attitudes, expectations, and a sense of possibility. As a class, you can work with a local elementary school to develop a college mentoring program, whether by pairing your writing class with a class at the school, working individually, or in small teams. Working with a local school will allow you to apply what you have learned from Jean Anyon's "Social Class and the Hidden Curriculum of Work" in thinking about what attitudes you think are already being formed at that school. Which schools in your area seemed most and least focused on sending students to college? How difficult is it to enroll at your college or university? Remember, in designing your projects it is important to work with the faculty at the local school to find out what their needs and expectations are. Among the projects you might consider:

1. Write and design brochures and other materials aimed at introducing children to higher education. Think about how best to

engage the children emotionally as well as intellectually. Decide what attitudes you want to cultivate, and what behaviors you hope to encourage.

2. Write, prepare, and make presentations about college- to elementary-age children, either at an elementary school or on your college campus. As you work, keep in mind the discussion carried on in many of the readings in this chapter about whether children should be encouraged more to play and experiment or to become focused and disciplined.

3. Prepare a guided tour of your campus for local schoolchildren. In preparing your tour, consider your knowledge of your audience and their experiences. What would they find most immediately attractive about your school? What specific impressions do you hope they take away from the experience?

CHAPTER 4

Work and Social Class

Ask most Americans what their social class is, and they will probably reply, "middle class." It's an identity many of us are comfortable with, something right in the center, neither too rich nor too poor. But what exactly is this middle? How do we define it? If we go by family income, there is actually a pretty wide range to the middle. In 1998, for example, the U.S. Census Bureau defined the median income for all households in the United States at almost $39,000. This means that half of all households made less than $39,000, and half made more, although the bottom 50 percent includes household incomes from $0 to $39,000, while the upper 50 percent extends from $39,000 to the millions per year made by a person like Bill Gates, the founder of Microsoft.

Social class can also mean more than just how much money a person makes. It can also refer to the kinds of work a person does, the lifestyle a person lives, even details like the kinds of clothes a person wears, the food they eat, and the television shows they watch. We can find these differences reflected in our everyday language. Consider what people do for a living and some of the words we use to describe different kinds of work: blue collar, white collar, and pink collar; a desk job; an office job; "skilled" and "unskilled" labor; minimum-wage work. You can probably add your own terms to the list.

We can also argue over just how many social classes there are. Are there two classes (the haves and the have-nots)? Three (rich, middle, and poor)? What about the term "working-class"? And can classes have their own subdivisions, as in "upper middle class," or "working poor"? What different purposes do these various classification systems and definitions serve? What does each reveal about our society, and what might they conceal?

There are even bigger questions connected to the division of labor and the idea of social class, questions that connect our day-to-day lives on the job and in the classroom to major issues of social policy. For example, do we see the different social classes living in conflict or co-existence with one another? How do we reconcile or balance a belief in equality of opportunity with wide differences in economic resources and social privileges? Finally, what difference does class make? Do our social-class backgrounds stay with us our entire lives, or can people change class identities? What is involved in "moving up" the class ladder? What is gained and what is lost? These are especially important questions for any college student, since a college education is seen as a gateway (at times an entrance, at other times a barrier) from one class to another. The readings and texts in this section will encourage you to think about what social class is, how it is defined, and what it's consequences are.

Preparing to Read: Writing Suggestions for the Beginning of Chapter 4

1. Work in small groups to come up with your own definitions of social classes. How many do you think there are? What are their defining characteristics? As you read, write, and work in the chapter, consider how you might want to revise these initial definitions as you go along.

2. Define your own social-class identity. Why did you choose the one you did? Does thinking and writing about your social class make you uncomfortable in any way? Why or why not? Do you think it's helpful or not to discuss social class? Again, as you work with this chapter, consider how you might want to revise your answer as you consider different ideas and viewpoints about social class.

Foundational Readings

ADAM SMITH

From *An Inquiry into the Nature and Causes of the Wealth of Nations*

Published in 1776, Adam Smith's An Inquiry into the Nature and Causes of the Wealth of Nations *(or simply,* The Wealth of Nations, *as it is commonly referred to) is perhaps the most famous book on economics ever written. In fact, Smith's book is credited with virtually inventing the modern study of economics. Smith was born in Scotland in 1723 and became a professor at Glasgow University and later traveled in Europe as the tutor to a Scottish Duke. Smith was influenced by movements in both Great Britain and France that sought to bring a more scientific, empirical approach to the study of nature and human society. In* The Wealth of Nations, *Smith described what he saw as the basic laws governing the creation of economic wealth in societies. His is one of the first descriptions of what we now call the "free-market" system of economics, and Smith argued that this kind of economy works best when governments interfere as little as possible with its "natural" operations. Smith's ideas still influence business and government policy decisions to this day, and they have provoked many counterarguments and critiques. In this passage from the beginning of* The Wealth of Nations, *Smith describes and argues for the advantages of "the division of labor," a means of organizing work that defines most of our current economic system and in many ways is a foundation for the formation of contemporary social classes.*

CHAPTER I: *Of the Division of Labour*

The greatest improvement in the productive powers of labour, and the greater part of the skill, dexterity, and judgment with which it is any where directed, or applied, seem to have been the effects of the division of labour.

The effects of the division of labour, in the general business of society will be more easily understood, by considering in what manner it operates in some particular manufactures. It is commonly supposed to be carried furthest in some very trifling ones; not perhaps that it really is carried further in them than in others of more importance: but in those trifling manufactures which are destined to supply the small wants of but a small number of people, the whole number of workmen must necessarily be small; and those employed in every different branch of the work can often be collected into the same workhouse, and placed at once under the view of the spectator. In those great manufactures, on the contrary, which are destined to supply the great wants of the great body of the people, every different branch of the work employs so great a number of workmen, that it is impossible to collect them all into the same workhouse. We can seldom see more, at one time, than those employed in one single branch. Though in such manufactures, therefore, the work may really be divided into a much greater number of parts, than in those of a more trifling nature, the division is not near so obvious, and has accordingly been much less observed.

To take an example, therefore, from a very trifling manufacture; but one in which the division of labour has been very often taken notice of, the trade of the pin-maker; a workman not educated to this business (which the division of labour has rendered a distinct trade), nor acquainted with the use of the machinery employed in it (to the invention of which the same division of labour has probably given occasion), could scarce, perhaps, with his utmost industry, make one pin in a day, and certainly could not make twenty. But in the way in which this business is now carried on, not only the whole work is a peculiar trade, but it is divided into a number of branches, of which the greater part are likewise peculiar trades. One man draws out the wire, another straights it, a third cuts it, a fourth points it, a fifth grinds it at the top for receiving the head; to make the head requires two or three distinct operations; to put it on, is a peculiar business, to whiten the pins is another; it is even a trade by itself to put them into the paper; and the important business of making a pin is, in this manner, divided into about eighteen distinct operations, which, in some manufactories, are all performed by distinct hands, though in others the same man will sometimes perform two or three of them. I have seen a small manufactory of this kind where ten men only were employed, and where some of them consequently performed two or three distinct operations. But though they were very poor, and therefore but indifferently accommodated with the necessary machinery, they could, when they exerted themselves, make among them about twelve pounds of pins in a day. There are in a pound upwards of four thousand pins of a middling size. Those ten persons, therefore, could make among them upwards of forty-eight thousand pins in a day. Each person, therefore, making a tenth part of forty-eight thousand pins, might be considered as making four thousand eight hundred pins in a day. But if they had all wrought separately and independently, and without any of them having been educated to this peculiar business, they certainly could not each of them have made twenty, perhaps not one pin in a day; that is, certainly, not the two hundred and fortieth, perhaps not the four thousand eight hundredth part of what they are at present capable of performing, in consequence of a proper division and combination of their different operations.

In every other art and manufacture, the effects of the division of labour are similar to what they are in this very trifling one; though, in many of them, the labour can neither be so much subdivided, nor reduced to so great a simplicity of operation. The division of labour, however, so far as it can be introduced, occasions, in every art, a proportionable increase of the productive powers of labour. The separation of different trades and employments from one another, seems to have taken place, in consequence of this advantage. This separation too is generally carried furthest in those countries which enjoy the highest degree of industry and improvement; what is the work of one man, in a rude state of society, being generally that of several in an improved one. In every improved society, the farmer is generally nothing but a farmer; the manufacturer, nothing but a manufacturer. The labour too which is necessary to produce any one complete manufacture, is almost always divided among a great number of hands. How many different trades are employed in each branch of the linen and woollen manufactures, from the growers of the flax and the wool, to the bleachers and smoothers of the linen, or to the dyers and dressers of the cloth! The nature of agriculture, indeed, does not admit of so many subdivisions of labour, nor of so complete a separation of one business from another, as manufactures. It is impossible to separate so entirely, the business of the grazier from that of the corn-farmer, and the trade of the carpenter is commonly separated from that of the smith. The spinner is almost always a distinct person from the weaver; but the ploughman, the harrower, the sower of the seed, and the reaper of the corn, are often the same. The occasions for those different sorts of labour returning with the different seasons of the year, it is impossible that one man should be constantly employed in any one of them. This impossibility of making so complete and entire a separation of all the different branches of labour employed in agriculture, is perhaps the reason why the improvement of the productive powers of labour in this art, does not always keep pace with their improvement in manufactures. The most opulent nations, indeed, generally excel all their neighbours in agriculture as well as in manufactures; but they are commonly more distinguished by their superiority in the latter than in the former. Their lands are in general better cultivated, and having more labour and expence bestowed upon them, produce more, in proportion to the extent and natural fertility of the ground. But this superiority of produce is seldom much more than in proportion to the superiority of labour and expence. In agriculture, the labour of the rich country is not always much more productive than that of the poor; or, at least, it is never so much more productive, as it commonly is in manufactures. The corn of the rich country, therefore, will not always, in the same degree of goodness, come cheaper to market than that of the poor. The corn of Poland, in the same degree of goodness, is as cheap as that of France, notwithstanding the superior opulence and improvement of the latter country. The corn of France is, in the corn provinces, fully as good, and in most years nearly about the same price with the corn of England, though, in opulence and improvement, France is perhaps inferior to England. The corn-lands of England, however, are better cultivated than those of France, and the corn-lands of France are said to be much better cultivated than those of Poland. But though the poor country, notwithstanding the inferiority of its cultivation, can, in some measure, rival the rich in the cheapness and goodness of its corn, it can pretend to no such competition in its manufactures; at least if those manufactures suit the soil, climate, and situation of the rich country. The silks of France are better and cheaper than those of England, because the silk manufacture, at least under the present high duties upon the importation of raw silk, does not so well suit the climate of England as that of France. But the hard-ware and the coarse woollens of England are beyond all comparison superior to those of France, and much cheaper too in the same degree of goodness. In Poland there are said to be scarce any manufactures of any kind, a few of those coarser household manufactures excepted, without which no country can well subsist.

This great increase of the quantity of work, which, in consequence of the division of labour, the same number of people are capable of performing, is owing to three different circumstances; first, to the increase of dexterity in every particular workman; secondly, to the saving of the time which is commonly lost in passing from one species of work to another; and lastly, to the invention of a great number of machines which facilitate and abridge labour, and enable one man to do the work of many.

First, the improvement of the dexterity of the workman necessarily increases the quantity of the work he can perform, and the division of labour, by reducing every man's business to some one simple operation, and by making this operation the sole employment of his life, necessarily increases very much the dexterity of the workman. A common smith who, though accustomed to handle the hammer, has never been used to make nails, if upon some particular occasion he is obliged to attempt it, will scarce, I am assured, be able to make above two or three hundred nails in a day, and those too very bad ones. A smith who has been accustomed to make nails, but whose sole or principal business has not been that of a nailer, can seldom with his utmost diligence make more than the eight hundred or a thousand nails in a day. I have seen several boys under twenty years of age who had never exercised any other trade but that of making nails, and who, when they exerted themselves, could make, each of them, upwards of two thousand three hundred nails in a day. The making of a nail, however, is by no means one of the simplest operations. The same person blows the bellows, stirs or mends the fire as there is occasion, heats the iron, and forges every part of the nail: In forging the head too he is obliged to change his tools. The different operations into which the making of a pin, or of a metal button, is subdivided, are all of them much more simple, and the dexterity of the person, of whose life it has been the sole business to perform them, is usually much greater. The rapidity with which some of the operations of those manufacturers are performed, exceeds what the human hand could, by those who had never seen them, be supposed capable of acquiring.

Secondly, the advantage which is gained by saving the time commonly lost in passing from one sort of work to another, is much greater than we should at first view be apt to imagine it. It is impossible to pass very quickly from one kind of work to another, that is carried on in a different place, and with quite different tools. A country weaver, who cultivates a small farm, must lose a good deal of time in passing from his loom to the field, and from the field to his loom. When the two trades can be carried on in the same workhouse, the loss of time is no doubt much less. It is even in this case, however, very considerable. A man commonly saunters a little in turning his hand from one sort of employment to another. When he first begins the new work he is seldom very keen and hearty; his mind, as they say, does not go to it, and for some time he rather trifles than applies to good purpose. The habit of sauntering and of indolent careless application, which is naturally, or rather necessarily acquired by every country workman who is obliged to change his work and his tools every half hour, and to apply his hand in twenty different ways almost every day of his life; renders him almost always slothful and lazy, and incapable of any vigorous application even on the most pressing occasions. Independent, therefore, of his deficiency in point of dexterity, this cause alone must always reduce considerably the quantity of work which he is capable of performing.

Thirdly, and lastly, every body must be sensible how much labour is facilitated and abridged by the application of proper machinery. It is unnecessary to give any example. I shall only observe, therefore, that the invention of all those machines by which labour is so much facilitated and abridged, seems to have been originally owing to the division of labour. Men are much more likely to discover easier and readier methods of attaining any object, when the whole attention of their minds is directed towards that single object, than when it is dissipated among a great variety of things. But in consequence of the division of labour, the whole of every man's attention comes naturally to be directed towards some one very simple object. It is naturally to be expected, therefore, that some one or other of those who are employed in each particular branch of labour should soon find out easier and readier methods of performing their own particular work, wherever the nature of it admits of such improvement. A great part of the machines made use of in those manufactures in which labour is most subdivided, were originally the inventions of common workmen, who, being each of them employed in some very simple operation, naturally turned their thoughts towards finding out easier and readier methods of performing it. Whoever has been much accustomed to visit such manufactures, must frequently have been shewn very pretty machines, which were the inventions of such workmen, in order to facilitate and quicken their own particular part of the work. In the first fire-engines, a boy was constantly employed to open and shut alternately the communication between the boiler and the cylinder, according as the piston either ascended or descended. One of those boys, who loved to play with his companions, observed that, by tying a string from the handle of the valve, which opened this communication, to another part of the machine, the valve would open and shut without assistance, and leave him at liberty to divert himself with his play-fellows. One of the greatest improvements that has been made upon this machine, since it was first invented, was in this manner the discovery of a boy who wanted to save his own labour.

All the improvements in machinery, however, have by no means been the inventions of those who had occasion to use the machines. Many improvements have been made by the ingenuity of the makers of the machines, when to make them became the business of a peculiar trade; and some by that of those who are called philosophers or men of speculation, whose trade it is, not to do any thing, but to observe every thing; and who, upon that account, are often capable of combining together the powers of the most distant and dissimilar objects. In the progress of society, philosophy or speculation becomes, like every other employment, the principal or sole trade and occupation of a particular class of citizens. Like every other employment too, it is subdivided into a great number of different branches, each of which affords occupation to a peculiar tribe or class of philosophers; and this subdivision of employment in philosophy, as well as in every other business, improves dexterity, and saves time. Each individual becomes more expert in his own peculiar branch, more work is done upon the whole, and the quantity of science is considerably increased by it.

It is the great multiplication of the productions of all the different arts, in consequence of the division of labour, which occasions, in a well-governed society, that universal opulence which extends itself to the lowest ranks of the people. Every workman has a great quantity of his own work to dispose of beyond what he himself has occasion for; and every other workman being exactly in the same situation, he is enabled to exchange a great quantity of his own goods for a great quantity, or, what comes to the same thing, for the price of a great quantity of theirs. He supplies them abundantly with what they have occasion for, and they accommodate him as amply with what he has occasion for, and a general plenty diffuses itself through all the different ranks of the society.

Observe the accommodation of the most common artificer or day-labourer in a civilized and thriving country, and you will perceive that the number of people of whose industry a part, though but a small part, has been employed in procuring him this accommodation, exceeds all computation. The woollen coat, for example, which covers the day-labourer, as coarse and rough as it may appear, is the produce of the joint labour of a great multitude of workmen. The shepherd, the sorter of the wool, the wool-comber or carder, the dyer, the scribbler, the spinner, the weaver, the fuller, the dresser, with many others, must all join their different arts in order to complete even this homely production. How many merchants and carriers, besides, must have been employed in transporting the materials from some of those workmen to others who often live in a very distant part of the country! How much commerce and navigation in particular, how many ship-builders, sailors, sail-makers, rope-makers, must have been employed in order to bring together the different drugs made use of by the dyer, which often come from the remotest corners of the world! What a variety of labour too is necessary in order to produce the tools of the meanest of those workmen! To say nothing of such complicated machines as the ship of the sailor, the mill of the fuller, or even the loom of the weaver, let us consider only what a variety of labour is requisite in order to form that very simple machine, the shears with which the shepherd clips the wool. The miner, the builder of the furnace for smelting the ore, the feller of the timber, the burner of the charcoal to be made use of in the smelting-house, the brick-maker, the brick-layer, the workmen who attend the furnace, the mill-wright, the forger, the smith, must all of them join their different arts in order to produce them. Were we to examine, in the same manner, all the different parts of his dress and household furniture, the coarse linen shirt which he wears next his skin, the shoes which cover his feet, the bed which he lies on, and all the different parts which compose it, the kitchen-grate at which he prepares his victuals, the coals which he makes use of for that purpose, dug from the bowels of the earth, and brought to him perhaps by a long sea and a long land carriage, all the other utensils of his kitchen, all the furniture of his table, the knives and forks, the earthen or pewter plates upon which he serves up and divides his victuals, the different hands employed in preparing his bread and his beer, the glass window which lets in the heat and the light, and keeps out the wind and the rain, with all the knowledge and art requisite for preparing that beautiful and happy invention, without which these northern parts of the world could scarce have afforded a very comfortable habitation, together with the tools of all the different workmen employed in producing those different conveniencies; if we examine, I say, all these things, and consider what a variety of labour is employed about each of them, we shall be sensible that without the assistance and cooperation of many thousands, the very meanest person in a civilized country could not be provided, even according to, what we very falsely imagine, the easy and simple manner in which he is commonly accommodated. Compared, indeed, with the more extravagant luxury of the great, his accommodation must no doubt appear extremely simple and easy; and yet it may be true, perhaps, that the accommodation of an European prince does not always so much exceed that of an industrious and frugal peasant, as the accommodation of the latter exceeds that of many an African king, the absolute master of the lives and liberties of ten thousand naked savages. ■

Working with the Text

1. What does Smith see as the primary advantages of the division of labor?

2. In paragraph 6, Smith argues, "by reducing every man's business to some one simple operation and by making this operation the sole employment of his life, necessarily increases very much the dexterity of the workman." Imagine a conversation between Smith and a workman (or woman) who makes pins not according to the division of labor that Smith advocates. How would Smith try to persuade this worker that he or she would be better off by focusing on doing one specific task over and over rather than many different tasks? What questions or challenges might the workman make?

3. Describe an example of the division of labor from your own work experience and evaluate how well you think the system works. What are its advantages and disadvantages? What is Smith correct about? What problems does he not describe?

4. Try applying the division of labor to the work of writing an essay. Acting as the "philosophers" described by Smith in paragraph 9, first define the separate tasks that you see in writing an essay and then assign each task to specific members of the class. How well does this system work? What advantages and disadvantages do you see?

Working with Connections

1. Apply the concept of the division of labor to the schools Jean Anyon describes in "Social Class and the Hidden Curriculum of Work" (from Chapter 3, Education and Work/Education as Work). What different kinds of divisions of labor are students being prepared for in each school?

2. In *Women Have Always Worked* (from Chapter 5, Work and Family), Alice Kessler-Harris describes the creation of a "women's sphere" of work in the nineteenth century, the same period when industrialization was spreading the idea of the division of labor. How do you see the division of labor affecting the way work is organized in the home and among family members? Are there areas of work where the division of labor is not, cannot, or should not be applied?

GREGORY MANTSIOS ■

Media Magic: Making Class Invisible

It is a commonplace to say that the media—television, radio, the Internet, movies—have a tremendous influence on our society, both positive and negative. Television news, for example, can show and tell us about places and peoples we would otherwise have little or no personal contact with or extensive knowledge of. On the other hand, this lack of firsthand experience can make us vulnerable to accepting stereotypes or to remaining unaware of how biases inevitably shape every news broadcast. Strangely, however, while most of us would agree with the above statement, we also tend to minimize the impact of the media on our own individual thinking and value systems. In "Media Magic: Making Class Invisible," the sociologist Gregory Mantsios challenges us to consider how the news media affect (or in his view erase) our understanding of social-class issues by arguing that most news reports are slanted against the experiences and interests of the poor and in favor of the wealthiest Americans. Mantsios is Director of Worker Education and the Labor Resource Center at Queens College of the City University of New York.

Of the various social and cultural forces in our society, the mass media is arguably the most influential in molding public consciousness. Americans spend an average twenty-eight hours per week watching television. They also spend an undetermined number of hours reading periodicals, listening to the radio, and going to the movies. Unlike other cultural and socializing institutions, ownership and control of the mass media is highly concentrated. Twenty-three corporations own more than one-half of all the daily newspapers, magazines, movie studios, and radio and television outlets in the United States.[1] The number of media companies is shrinking and their control of the industry is expanding. And a relatively small number of media outlets is producing and packaging the majority of news and entertainment programs. For the most part, our media is national in nature and single-minded (profit-oriented) in purpose. This media plays a key role in defining our cultural tastes, helping us locate ourselves in history, establishing our national identity, and ascertaining the range of national and social possibilities. In this essay, we will examine the way the mass media shapes how people think about each other and about the nature of our society.

The United States is the most highly stratified society in the industrialized world. Class distinctions operate in virtually every aspect of our lives, determining the nature of our work, the quality of our schooling, and the health and safety of our loved ones. Yet remarkably, we, as a nation, retain illusions about living in an egalitarian society. We maintain these illusions, in large part, because the media hides gross inequities from public view. In those instances when inequities are revealed, we are provided with messages that obscure the nature of class realities and blame the victims of class-dominated society for their own plight. Let's briefly examine what the news media, in particular, tells us about class.

ABOUT THE POOR

The news media provides meager coverage of poor people and poverty. The coverage it does provide is often distorted and misleading.

The Poor Do Not Exist

For the most part, the news media ignores the poor. Unnoticed are forty million poor people in the nation—a number that equals the entire population of Maine, Vermont, New Hampshire, Connecticut, Rhode Island, New Jersey, and New York combined. Perhaps even more alarming is that the rate of poverty is increasing twice as fast as the population growth in the United States. Ordinarily, even a calamity of much smaller proportion (e.g., flooding in the Midwest) would garner a great deal of coverage and hype from a media usually eager to declare a crisis, yet less than one in five hundred articles in the *New York Times* and one in one thousand articles listed in the *Readers Guide to Periodic Literature* are on poverty. With remarkably little attention to them, the poor and their problems are hidden from most Americans.

When the media does turn its attention to the poor, it offers a series of contradictory messages and portrayals.

The Poor Are Faceless

Each year the Census Bureau releases a new report on poverty in our society and its results are duly reported in the media. At best, however, this coverage emphasizes annual fluctuations (showing how the numbers differ from previous years) and ongoing debates over the validity of the numbers (some argue the number should be lower, most that the number should be higher). Coverage like this desensitizes us to the poor by reducing poverty to a number. It ignores the human tragedy of poverty—the suffering, indignities, and misery endured by millions of children and adults. Instead, the poor become statistics rather than people.

The Poor Are Undeserving

When the media does put a face on the poor, it is not likely to be a pretty one. The media will provide us with sensational stories about welfare cheats, drug addicts, and greedy panhandlers (almost always urban and Black). Compare these images and the emotions evoked by them with the media's treatment of middle-class (usually white) "tax evaders," celebrities who have a "chemical dependency," or wealthy businesspeople who use unscrupulous means to "make a profit." While the behavior of the more affluent offenders is considered an "impropriety" and a deviation from the norm, the behavior of the poor is considered repugnant, indicative of the poor in general, and worthy of our indignation and resentment.

The Poor Are an Eyesore

When the media does cover the poor, they are often presented through the eyes of the middle class. For example, sometimes the media includes a story about community resistance to a homeless shelter or storekeeper annoyance with panhandlers. Rather than focusing on the plight of the poor, these stories are about middle-class opposition to the poor. Such stories tell us that the poor are an inconvenience and an irritation.

The Poor Have Only Themselves to Blame

In another example of media coverage, we are told that the poor live in a personal and cultural cycle of poverty that hopelessly imprisons them. They routinely center on the Black urban population and focus on perceived personality or cultural traits that doom the poor. While the women in these stories typically exhibit an "attitude" that leads to trouble or a promiscuity that leads to single motherhood, the men possess a need for immediate gratification that leads to drug abuse or an unquenchable greed that leads to the pursuit of fast money. The images that are seared into our mind are sexist, racist, and classist. Census figures reveal that most of the poor are white, not Black or Hispanic, that they live in rural or suburban areas, not urban centers, and hold jobs at least part of the year.[2] Yet, in a fashion that is often framed in an understanding and sympathetic tone, we are told that the poor have inflicted poverty on themselves.

The Poor Are Down on Their Luck

During the Christmas season, the news media sometimes provides us with accounts of poor individuals or families (usually white) who are down on their luck. These stories are often linked to stories about soup kitchens or other charitable activities and sometimes call for charitable contributions. These "Yule time" stories are as much about the affluent as they are about the poor: they tell us that the affluent in our society are a kind, understanding, giving people—which we are not.* The series of unfortunate circumstances that have led to impoverishment are presumed to be a temporary condition that will improve with time and a change in luck.

Despite appearances, the messages provided by the media are not entirely disparate. With each variation, the media informs us what poverty is not (i.e., systemic and indicative of American society) by informing us what it is. The media tells us that poverty is either an aberration of the American way of life (it doesn't exist, it's just another number, it's unfortunate but temporary) or an end product of the poor themselves (they are a nuisance, do not deserve better, and have brought their predicament upon themselves).

By suggesting that the poor have brought poverty upon themselves, the media is engaging in what William Ryan has called "blaming the victim."[3] The media identifies in what ways the poor are different as a consequence of deprivation, then defines those differences as the cause of poverty itself. Whether blatantly hostile or cloaked in sympathy, the message is that there is something fundamentally wrong with the victims—their hormones, psychological makeup, family environment, community, race, or some combination of these—that accounts for their plight and their failure to lift themselves out of poverty.

But poverty in the United States is systemic. It is a direct result of economic and political policies that deprive people of jobs, adequate wages, or legitimate support. It is neither natural nor inevitable: there is enough wealth in our nation to eliminate poverty if we chose to redistribute existing wealth or income. The plight of the poor is reason enough to make the elimination of poverty the nation's first priority. But poverty also impacts dramatically on the nonpoor. It has a dampening effect on wages in general (by maintaining a reserve army of unemployed and underemployed anxious for any job at any wage) and breeds crime and violence (by maintaining conditions that invite private gain by illegal means and rebellion-like behavior, not entirely unlike the urban riots of the 1960s). Given the extent of poverty in the nation and the impact it has on us all, the media must spin considerable magic to keep the poor and the issue of poverty and its root causes out of the public consciousness.

---

*American households with incomes of less than $10,000 give an average of 5.5 percent of their earning to charity or to a religious organization, while those making more than $100,000 a year give only 2.9 percent. After changes in the 1986 tax code reduced the benefits of charitable giving, taxpayers earning $500,000 or more slashed their average donation by nearly one-third. Furthermore, many of these acts of benevolence do not help the needy. Rather than provide funding to social service agencies that aid the poor, the voluntary contributions of the wealthy go to places and institutions that entertain, inspire, cure, or educate wealthy Americans—art museums, opera houses, theaters, orchestras, ballet companies, private hospitals, and elite universities. (Robert Reich, "Secession of the Successful," *New York Times Magazine,* February 17, 1991, p. 43.)

ABOUT EVERYONE ELSE

Both the broadcast and the print news media strive to develop a strong sense of "we-ness" in their audience. They seek to speak to and for an audience that is both affluent and like-minded. The media's solidarity with affluence, that is, with the middle and upper class, varies little from one medium to another. Benjamin DeMott points out, for example, that the New York Times understands affluence to be intelligence, taste, public spirit, responsibility, and a readiness to rule and "conceives itself as spokesperson for a readership awash in these qualities."[4] Of course, the flip side to creating a sense of "we," or "us," is establishing a perception of the "other." The other relates back to the faceless, amoral, undeserving, and inferior "underclass." Thus, the world according to the news media is divided between the "underclass" and everyone else. Again the messages are often contradictory.

The Wealthy Are Us

Much of the information provided to us by the news media focuses attention on the concerns of a very wealthy and privileged class of people. Although the concerns of a small fraction of the populace, they are presented as though they were the concerns of everyone. For example, while relatively few people actually own stock, the news media devotes an inordinate amount of broadcast time and print space to business news and stock market quotations. Not only do business reports cater to a particular narrow clientele, so do the fashion pages (with $2,000 dresses), wedding announcements, and the obituaries. Even weather and sports news often have a class bias. An all news radio station in New York City, for example, provides regular national ski reports. International news, trade agreements, and domestic policies issues are also reported in terms of their impact on business climate and the business community. Besides being of practical value to the wealthy, such coverage has considerable ideological value. Its message: the concerns of the wealthy are the concerns of us all.

The Wealthy (as a Class) Do Not Exist

While preoccupied with the concerns of the wealthy, the media fails to notice the way in which the rich as a class of people create and shape domestic and foreign policy. Presented as an aggregate of individuals, the wealthy appear without special interests, interconnections, or unity in purpose. Out of public view are the class interests of the wealthy, the interlocking business links, the concerted actions to preserve their class privileges and business interests (by running for public office, supporting political candidates, lobbying, etc.). Corporate lobbying is ignored, taken for granted, or assumed to be in the public interest. (Compare this with the media's portrayal of the "strong arm of labor" in attempting to defeat trade legislation that is harmful to the interests of working people.) It is estimated that two-thirds of the U.S. Senate is composed of millionaires.[5] Having such a preponderance of millionaires in the Senate, however, is perceived to be neither unusual nor antidemocratic; these millionaire senators are assumed to be serving "our" collective interests in governing.

The Wealthy Are Fascinating and Benevolent

The broadcast and print media regularly provide hype for individuals who have achieved "super" success. These stories are usually about celebrities and superstars from the sports and entertainment world. Society pages and gossip columns serve to keep the social elite informed of each others' doings, allow the rest of us to gawk at their excesses, and help to keep the American dream alive. The print media is also fond of feature stories on corporate empire builders. These stories provide an occasional "insider's" view of the private and corporate life of industrialists by suggesting a rags to riches account of corporate success. These stories tell us that corporate success is a series of smart moves, shrewd acquisitions, timely mergers, and well thought out executive suite shuffles. By painting the upper class in a positive light, innocent of any wrongdoing (labor leaders and union organizations usually get the opposite treatment), the media assures us that wealth and power are benevolent. One person's capital accumulation is presumed to be good for all. The elite, then, are portrayed as investment wizards, people of special talent and skill, whom even their victims (workers and consumers) can admire.

The Wealthy Include a Few Bad Apples

On rare occasions, the media will mock selected individuals for their personality flaws. Real estate investor Donald Trump and New York Yankees owner George Steinbrenner, for example, are admonished by the media for deliberately seeking publicity (a very un-upper class thing to do); hotel owner Leona Helmsley was caricatured for her personal cruelties; and junk bond broker Michael Milkin was condemned because he had the audacity to rob the rich. Michael Parenti points out that by treating business wrongdoings as isolated deviations from the socially beneficial system of "responsible capitalism," the media overlooks the features of the system that produce such abuses and the regularity with which they occur. Rather than portraying them as predictable and frequent outcomes of corporate power and the business system, the media treats abuses as if they were isolated and atypical. Presented as an occasional aberration, these incidents serve not to challenge, but to legitimate, the system.[6]

The Middle Class Is Us

By ignoring the poor and blurring the lines between the working people and the upper class, the news media creates a universal middle class. From this perspective, the size of one's income becomes largely irrelevant: what matters is that most of "us" share an intellectual and moral superiority over the disadvantaged. As *Time* magazine once concluded, "Middle America is a state of mind."[7] "We are all middle class," we are told, "and we all share the same concerns": job security, inflation, tax burdens, world peace, the cost of food and housing, health care, clean air and water, and the safety of our streets. While the concerns of the wealthy are quite distinct from those of the middle class (e.g., the wealthy worry about investments, not jobs), the media convinces us that "we [the affluent] are all in this together."

The Middle Class Is a Victim

For the media, "we" the affluent not only stand apart from the "other"—the poor, the working class, the minorities, and their problems—"we" are also victimized by the poor (who drive up the costs of maintaining the welfare roles), minorities (who commit crimes against us), and workers (who are greedy and drive companies out and prices up). Ignored are the subsidies to the rich, the crimes of corporate America, and the policies that wreak havoc on the economic well-being of middle America. Media magic convinces us to fear, more than anything else, being victimized by those less affluent than ourselves.

The Middle Class Is Not a Working Class

The news media clearly distinguishes the middle class (employees) from the working class (i.e., blue collar workers) who are portrayed, at best, as irrelevant, outmoded, and a dying breed. Furthermore, the media will tell us that the hardships faced by blue collar workers are inevitable (due to progress), a result of bad luck (chance circumstances in a particular industry), or a product of their own doing (they priced themselves out of a job). Given the media's presentation of reality, it is hard to believe that manual, supervised, unskilled, and semiskilled workers actually represent more than 50 percent of the adult working population.[8] The working class, instead, is relegated by the media to "the other."

In short, the news media either lionizes the wealthy or treats their interests and those of the middle class as one in the same. But the upper class and the middle class do not share the same interests or worries. Members of the upper class worry about stock dividends (not employment), they profit from inflation and global militarism, their children attend exclusive private schools, they eat and live in a royal fashion, they call on (or are called upon by) personal physicians, they have few consumer problems, they can escape whenever they want from environmental pollution, and they live on streets and travel to other areas under the protection of private police forces.*[9]

The wealthy are not only a class with distinct life-styles and interests, they are a ruling class. They receive a disproportionate share of the country's yearly income, own a disproportionate amount of the country's wealth, and contribute a disproportionate number of their members to governmental bodies and decision-making groups—all traits that William Domhoff, in his classic work *Who Rules America,* defined as characteristic of a governing class.[10]

This governing class maintains and manages our political and economic structures in such a way that these structures continue to yield an amazing pro-

*The number of private security guards in the United States now exceeds the number of public police officers. (Robert Reich, "Secession of the Successful," *New York Times Magazine,* February 17, 1991, p. 42.)

portion of our wealth to a minuscule upper class. While the media is not above referring to ruling classes in other countries (we hear, for example, references to Japan's ruling elite),[11] its treatment of the news proceeds as though there were no such ruling class in the United States.

Furthermore, the news media inverts reality so that those who are working class and middle class learn to fear, resent, and blame those below, rather than those above, them in the class structure. We learn to resent welfare, which accounts for only two cents out of every dollar in the federal budget (approximately $10 billion) and provides financial relief for the needy,* but learn little about the $11 billion the federal government spends on individuals with incomes in excess of $100,000 (not needy),[12] or the $17 billion in farm subsidies, or the $214 billion (twenty times the cost of welfare) in interest payments to financial institutions.

Middle-class whites learn to fear African Americans and Latinos, but most violent crime occurs within poor and minority communities and is neither interracial† nor interclass. As horrid as such crime is, it should not mask the destruction and violence perpetrated by corporate America. In spite of the fact that 14,000 innocent people are killed on the job each year, 100,000 die prematurely, 400,000 become seriously ill, and 6 million are injured from work-related accidents and diseases, most Americans fear government regulation more than they do unsafe working conditions.

Through the media, middle-class—and even working-class—Americans learn to blame blue collar workers and their unions for declining purchasing power and economic security. But while workers who managed to keep their jobs and their unions struggled to keep up with inflation, the top 1 percent of American families saw their average incomes soar 80 percent in the last decade.[13] Much of the wealth at the top was accumulated as stockholders and corporate executives moved their companies abroad to employ cheaper labor (56 cents per hour in El Salvador) and avoid paying taxes in the United States. Corporate America is a world made up of ruthless bosses, massive layoffs, favoritism and nepotism, health and safety violations, pension plan losses, union busting, tax evasions, unfair competition, and price gouging, as well as fast buck deals, financial speculation, and corporate wheeling and dealing that serve the interests of the corporate elite, but are generally wasteful and destructive to workers and the economy in general.

* * *

*A total of $20 billion is spent on welfare when you include all state funding. But the average state funding also comes to only two cents per state dollar.

†In 92 percent of the murders nationwide the assailant and the victim are of the same race (46 percent are white/white, 46 percent are black/black), 5.6 percent are black on white, and 2.4 percent are white on black. (FBI and Bureau of Justice Statistics, 1985–1986, quoted in Raymond S. Franklin, *Shadows of Race and Class,* University of Minnesota Press, Minneapolis, 1991, p, 108.)

It is no wonder Americans cannot think straight about class. The mass media are neither objective, balanced, independent, nor neutral. Those who own and direct the mass media are themselves part of the upper class, and neither they nor the ruling class in general have to conspire to manipulate public opinion. Their interest is in preserving the status quo, and their view of society as fair and equitable comes naturally to them. But their ideology dominates our society and justifies what is in reality a perverse social order—one that perpetuates unprecedented elite privilege and power on the one hand and widespread deprivation on the other. A mass media that did not have its own class interests in preserving the status quo would acknowledge that inordinate wealth and power undermines democracy and that a "free market" economy can ravage a people and their communities. ■

NOTES

1. Martin Lee and Norman Solomon, *Unreliable Sources,* Lyle Stuart (New York, 1990), p. 71. See also Ben Bagdikian, *The Media Monopoly,* Beacon Press (Boston, 1990).
2. Department of Commerce, Bureau of the Census, "Poverty in the United States: 1992," *Current Population Reports, Consumer Income,* Series P60–185, pp. xi, xv, 1.
3. William Ryan, *Blaming the Victim,* Vintage (New York, 1971).
4. Benjamin Demott, *The Imperial Middle,* William Morrow (New York, 1990), p. 123.
5. Fred Barnes, "The Zillionaires Club," *The New Republic,* January 29, 1990, p. 24.
6. Michael Parenti, *Inventing Reality,* St. Martin's Press (New York, 1986), p. 109.
7. *Time,* January 5, 1979, p. 10.
8. Vincent Navarro, "The Middle Class—A Useful Myth," *The Nation,* March 23, 1992, p. 1.
9. Charles Anderson, *The Political Economy of Social Class,* Prentice Hall (Englewood Cliffs, N.J., 1974), p. 137.
10. William Domhoff, *Who Rules America,* Prentice Hall (Englewood Cliffs, N.J., 1967), p. 5.
11. Lee and Solomon, *Unreliable Sources,* p. 179.
12. *Newsweek,* August 10, 1992, p. 57.
13. *Business Week,* June 8, 1992, p. 86.

Working with the Text

1. Mantsios argues, "media play a key role in defining our cultural tastes, helping us locate ourselves in history, establishing our national identity, and ascertaining the range of national and social possibilities." Consider Mantsios's assertion in the light of your own experience. Choose one or more of the areas of influence that Mantsios defines in the above quotation and write about specific ways you think the media have influenced you in this area. Can you remember a television program that had a profound effect on you, for example, in shaping your likes or dislikes in terms of fashion or culture? How did the way television news reported on an important political or social event (e.g., a presi-

dential election; protests against the World Trade Organization; the tragedies of September 11, 2001; the war in Iraq) affect your understanding of that event?

2. Work in small groups to test Mantsios's claims about how television news represents the experiences of different social classes. Watch a variety of newscasts, both national and local (different groups in class might be assigned to cover different programs), and take careful notes about how poverty and affluence are portrayed on these various news shows. Pay particular attention to the images shown, the language and diction used, the attitudes expressed through intonation and emphasis, and the types of stories told. Write up and present your conclusions in terms of how well each program does or does not support Mantsios's conclusions.

3. Mantsios argues, "The news media strive to develop a strong sense of 'we-ness' in their audience," a sense of us against them that urges viewers to identify with a "universal middle class." Watch the news looking for images or representations of people you feel most closely match your own background. Who seems most like you? What roles are they playing? If no one seems very much like you, who comes the closest, and what are the crucial differences? How does this analysis affect your view of the media?

Working with Connections

1. Write a television news story reporting on the experiences of the women Barbara Ehrenreich describes in the excerpt from *Nickel and Dimed*. Consider who you think your viewers are and the impression you want to create. What visuals will you want to use in your story? You might also write two versions of this story: one in the manner Mantsios describes as typical of mainstream media and the other in the way you think is most accurate and fair.

2. What commercials are shown during various newscasts, and what can they tell us about whom the broadcasters and their sponsors think are the main viewers of their programs? Do you notice different advertisers for different kinds of newscasts (e.g., national versus local; cable versus broadcast; channel versus channel)? Do these differences translate into differences in how the news is covered?

MICHAEL ZWEIG ■

From *The Working Class Majority: America's Best Kept Secret*

In this excerpt from the first chapter of his book, economist Michael Zweig argues against the popular idea that most people in the United States are "middle class." In so doing, he reviews different ways of defining class, such as income, type of work, and lifestyle. In the end, however, he argues for using "power" as the best way of understanding class and applies his definition to employment statistics in order to make his claim about a "working class majority." Zweig received his PhD in economics from the University of Michigan and is currently a professor at the State University of New York at Stony Brook.

WHAT ARE CLASSES?

I first learned about class growing up in Detroit and its suburbs. Long before I knew what classes were, I experienced them. Before I had the words and concepts, I saw for myself profound differences in different parts of town.

I went to grade school and junior high in Detroit with the children of auto workers. For high school, my classmates were children of top auto executives in suburban Bloomfield Hills. My parents had found a house in one of the first subdivisions in the area, a corner of one of the finest public school districts in Michigan, where huge estates stood in sharp contrast to the housing I had known before. Other differences soon emerged. The auto plants closed on the first day of deer season so thousands of workers could head into the woods of northern Michigan, but others in Bloomfield Hills took their kids hunting for moose in northern Canada or on safari to Africa. A young teenager I knew in Detroit who killed an old woman was put away, but a small group of my new classmates who beat a truck driver to death by the side of the road on a lark received barely two weeks' social probation at school. Whether we are aware of it or not, even when we don't have the words to explain it, the American experience is an experience of intense class difference.

A population as large and diverse as ours contains many divides. In recent decades, we have arrived at better understandings of race, ethnicity, gender, and sexual orientation, helping us to make progress toward overcoming discrimination. But as public awareness of these issues has developed, knowledge of class differences has all but disappeared.

It wasn't always so. At the end of the nineteenth and far into the twentieth century, newspapers were filled with stories of pitched class struggle. General strikes. The army called out to put down rebellious workers. Mass picketing and factory occupations in the course of union organizing drives. In cartoons, fat capitalist plutocrats with cigars in their mouths and dollar signs for eyes were denounced as enemies of the common man.

More recently, the general view is that class, if it ever was important, is a thing of the past. No one argues that capitalism is a thing of the past, of course. Instead, we often hear that the relative decline of manufacturing and the tremendous growth of service industries have changed the basic facts of life in capitalist society. The relative decline of blue collar factory employment and the rise of white collar service jobs is supposed to show that the working class is history. The fact that we no longer see pitched battles between masses of workers and squads of armed goons hired by the company to kill the union organizers is taken as proof that class struggle is over, that we've outgrown that sordid past. In short, the conventional wisdom is that post-industrial society is not industrial society.

True. But also not true. Life in the United States today is dramatically different from life thirty or sixty or a hundred years ago; many of the changes do correspond with changes in the economy. Yet much remains the same. A telephone operator today can tell you stories of speed-up and harassment by supervisors that equal anything reported by her grandfather who worked on the auto assembly line. And both are just as adamant about union representation. A temp services bookkeeper today is as subject to the whims of his employer as was the garment worker at the turn of the twentieth century. The political power of the economic elite today is at least as great as it was in the 1920s, and perhaps even greater, since it is less effectively challenged by other class interests. And while service jobs have certainly grown as a share of the labor force, nearly 2 million more people were working to produce goods (in mining, manufacturing, and construction) in 1998 than in 1970, over 25 million people.

Despite all the changes in the economy, it remains as true today as it was forty and eighty years ago that the majority of Americans are working class people. To see this clearly, we first need to understand what classes make up modern capitalist society. The way to do that is to assess power.

Class is about the power some people have over the lives of others, and the powerlessness most people experience as a result. This way of approaching class is different from looking at income or status or lifestyle. When Americans do talk about class, these are the measures that usually come up, and for good reason. The working class does have different income, status, and lifestyles from those of the middle class and capitalist class. But if we leave the matter there, we miss the basic reason that classes exist in the first place.

Classes are groups of people connected to one another, and made different from one another, by the ways they interact when producing goods and services. This production process is based in the workplace, but extends into the political and cultural dynamics of society as well, where the rules and expectations that guide the economy are laid down, largely in accord with the needs of the economically powerful. Class is not a box that we "fit" into, or not, depending on our own personal attributes. Classes are not isolated and self-contained. What class we are in depends upon the role we play, as it relates to what others do, in the complicated process in which goods and services are made. These roles carry with them different degrees of income and status, but their most fundamental feature is the different degrees of power each has. The heart of class is not about lifestyle. It is about economics.

Clearly, it makes a difference whether you own the factory or are a hired hand. It makes a difference whether you are the CEO at the bank or the technician who repairs the ATMs. The chief difference is a difference of power: power to determine and control the processes that go on in the factory and the bank, and beyond that, power in the larger society, especially political power.

Power is complicated; it has many sources and is exercised in many ways. Some people have the power to determine which goods and services will be made, how and by whom. Some set government policy and use the government to control others, through the police, through regulations, through the military. Others have cultural power to shape which ideas and values tend to dominate our thinking. Elections involve still another type of power.

A person with power in one of these parts of life doesn't necessarily have power in another. But power isn't random, either. We can find patterns in the exercise of power, spill-over from one area of society to another. Economic and political power are related and reinforce one another. The power to affect our culture comes from control over economic and political resources, but influencing the culture tends to strengthen one's economic and political power as well.

Some power is obvious and some is invisible. The power that we can see we tend to identify with individuals. My supervisor has power. The President of the United States has power. A media critic of the *New York Times* and a program officer at the National Endowment for the Arts have power. I have power, and you do, too, in the aspects of our lives that we can control or influence. Most of us are acutely aware of power in its visible, individual forms.

But other kinds of power are easy to miss. The power of inertia tends to perpetuate existing ways of doing things and existing relationships. We aren't necessarily aware, day to day, of the power that limits alternatives, the power of a kinds of social automatic pilot, invisible as long as everyone goes along with the program. Invisible force fields of power are built into the structures that hold society together, giving it shape, setting the paths for our opportunity, and setting the limits as well. We tend to take these contours for granted, internalize them, think of them as the natural order. But when some group of people seriously challenges this kind of power, in politics, in the culture, in assertions of new ways to organize the economy, what had been invisible roars into full view: "the powers that be" step out to demolish the threat.

Classes arise in these relationships of social power, visible and invisible. Class is first and foremost a product of power asserted in the production process. This means power over what goes on at work: who will do which tasks at what pace for what pay, and the power to decide what to produce, how to produce it, and where to sell it. But beyond that, production power involves setting the rules for how markets work and the laws governing property rights. Production power includes organizing an educational system that will generate a workforce with the skills and work habits required to keep production going. Production power extends into many aspects of our lives beyond the job.

We will see shortly that the majority of the population in the United States belongs to the working class. The working class does not exist in isolation, of course; it draws its existence from its relationship to other classes, other people also engaged in making and distributing goods and services. First and foremost among these other classes is the capitalist class, those who own and operate the major corporations. What is important about capitalists is not simply that they own all that is made in their factories and offices. They have the power to control the work lives of their employees, most of whom are working class people. Their economic power finds its way into enormous influence in politics as well.

In a capitalist society, the "powers that be" are largely the capitalists. For the most part, capitalists set the terms of production, in all the senses just described, and more. They own the businesses, so, of course, they have the power to make the rules. And, owning the businesses, they have the money and social status, and, with these, power to influence the political and cultural life of the country. Their influence tends to define everyone's opportunities and limits according to what will be good for capitalists, what will continue, broaden, and deepen their power. Sometimes this power is visible; when it is not, it just is, baked in the cake.

When I talk about the working class, on the other hand, I am talking about people who have a common situation in these social structures, but one without much power. To be in the working class is to be in a place of relative vulnerability— on the job, in the market, in politics and culture.

On the job, most workers have little control over the pace and content of their work. They show up, a supervisor shows them the job, and they do it. The job may be skilled or unskilled, white collar or blue collar, in any one of thousands of occupations. Whatever the particulars, most jobs share a basic powerlessness in relation to the authority of the owner and the owner's representatives who are there to supervise and control the workforce.

Capitalists and workers are not the only classes in America. There is also a middle class, made up of professional people, supervisors and managers, and small business owners. We will see that it makes sense to put some people who are technically capitalists, those who own small businesses, into the middle class rather than the capitalist class, because of the very real differences in power that separate large and small business.

To understand class, we need to measure it. This is hard to do, because class is not a simple category. But we can get close to the structure of classes by looking at the structure of occupations. The jobs we do give a strong indication of the place we occupy, on the job and off, in the class structure. So before we examine the ways class works in the larger society, we will look at the work people do for a living.

Although I have measured class by looking at the labor force, people not in the labor force are also in classes. Non-working spouses typically share the class position of their working mate. Children share the class position of their parents, and retired people typically retain the class standing they had in their working life. The relative sizes of different classes in the labor force closely reflect the class composition of society as a whole.

Before looking at the working class, let's look at the capitalists, the class with whom workers are most directly engaged.

THE CAPITALIST CLASS

Capitalists and their managers own and control businesses of all sizes. In a strict sense, *anyone* who makes a living by owning a business is a capitalist, even if she employs only a couple of people, even if he is self-employed and has no one working for him. But it makes sense to distinguish between big and small capitalists, to recognize the difference in power they have over their workers, in the market and in the political arena. Ross Perot and David Rockefeller don't belong in the same class as the guy who has a small plumbing business and employs an occasional helper when work is steady. In 1995 (the latest year for which these data are available), 22.5 million businesses existed in the United States. Most were small, even tiny. About 60 percent of businesses had less than $25,000 in gross receipts, and all these very small businesses put together, 13.3 million of them, took in just 0.5 percent of all business revenue. Seventy percent of all businesses had no employees at all except for the owner.

The overwhelming majority of these small businesses are sole proprietorships, in which the business owner does not incorporate. Any business profits are mixed in with the owner's other income and reported on his or her federal income tax form using Schedule C. Millions of these self-employed "small business people" have working class jobs as their main source of support; their business activity is just another source of personal income, often much smaller than their job income. Sometimes a working class person will be forced to connect to an employer as an independent contractor, as when a hairdresser rents a chair in a salon whose owner has complete control over work hours and pay. For tax purposes, the "independent" hairdresser is a small business owner, but the reality is quite different.

On the other end of the scale are the incorporated businesses, or corporations. Even most of these are on the small side. Of the nearly 4.3 million corporations operating in 1994, only 18 percent, 766,000 companies, had gross receipts above a million dollars. But the receipts going to this 18 percent added up to 94 percent of all corporate receipts that year.

Clearly it is appropriate to make distinctions among capitalists, separating big business from small entrepreneurs. No clear, bright line separates the small business of the middle class entrepreneur and the big business of the capitalist class. A company employing fifteen people might be big in a town of five hundred residents; its owner might have a respected role in the local community and its political and social life. But in a larger city, such a business would disappear in the scheme of things, from the point of view of those who hold serious power. So there is no simple rule to differentiate big from small business. Any attempt has to take into account the overall social setting of the business. Still, the distinction is worth pursuing to get a clearer picture of the diverse interests of "the business community."

To begin, I call any business "small" if its owner works side by side with the employees and supervises them directly. This owner is in the middle class. The business becomes "big" and the owner a member of the capitalist class only when the owner no longer works directly with the workers, exercises control over the workforce through at least one layer of middle management, and becomes occupied full-time with running the business as a senior strategist and source of authority, largely removed from the production process itself. Again, there is no hard and fast rule to separate theses types of businesses, but experience suggests that 20 employees is a reasonable cutoff, beyond which a small business becomes big.

By this measure, there were 881,000 big businesses in the United States in 1995, each employing 20 or more people. These were only 13 percent of all businesses that had any employees beyond the owner, but they had 75 percent of all employees and accounted for 77 percent of the country's nongovernment payroll. The owners and top managers of these companies form the capitalist class. They are no more than 2 percent of the labor force. Most of these businesses are big fish in small ponds, holding sway in a local area but wielding little market or political power on a national or even regional scale.

To get a handle on the scope of big business and the capitalist class on a national scale, we can learn from how the business community itself approaches the question. One way is to look at the Small Business Administration, a part of the U.S. Department of Commerce that provides technical and financial assistance to small businesses. According to the rules of the SBA, established by Congress, any business with fewer than 500 employees is a small business. This number indicates that the government views "big business" as a relatively tiny number of corporations. In 1995, by the standards of the SBA, there were only 16,000 big businesses in the United States, 0.2 percent of all businesses with any employees, and .07 percent of all businesses in the country. Yet they employed 20 percent of all business employees, and paid over a quarter of the country's private payroll.

We can reasonably consider these 16,000 big businesses to be the national economic elite. Their directors and senior officers exercise considerable power, not only within the companies they control but in the larger society, which is affected by their decisions and opinions on strategies for investment, collective bargaining, and foreign affairs.

Even within this elite, power is concentrated in the very largest financial, manufacturing, service, and transportation companies. At the end of 1998, there were 10,508 banks in the United States (not counting the separate branches many banks have): 9,303 commercial banks and 1,205 savings banks (not counting credit unions). Banks are typically ranked in size by the amount of assets each controls. Thousands of banks are small businesses in small towns, important there but nowhere else. But the twenty-five largest commercial banks had assets ranging from $32 billion (Union Bank of California) to $317 billion (Nationsbank). They were only 0.3 percent of all commercial banks, but this tiny fraction controlled 46.9 percent of all commercial bank assets in the country.

Even among these very richest and most powerful institutions, power is concentrated in the uppermost tier: the five biggest banks controlled half the assets of the top twenty-five.

Similar concentrations occur in farming. When we think of agriculture, most of us think of the family farm, the backbone of rural America. In 1992, of the nearly 2 million farms operating in the United States, 29 percent were under 50 acres, but they accounted for just over 1 percent of all farmland. By contrast, fewer than 4 percent of farms were larger than 2,000 acres, but they covered over half the farmland in the Untied States. In 1992, almost half the farms in the country sold crops worth less than $10,000 for the entire year, taking in a total of less than 2 percent of all farm sales. The biggest operations, with 1992 sales of a million dollars or more, were fewer than 1 percent of all farms, but they took in a third of all farm revenue.

These lopsided holdings are more than matched in manufacturing. In 1995, 390,000 manufacturing enterprises were operating in the United States. Two-thirds of these plants were small businesses employing fewer than 20 people; together they employed only 8 percent of the manufacturing labor force. At the other end of the scale, there were 6,000 manufacturing companies that each employed 500 workers. These big businesses were 1.5 percent of the total, but they employed 34 percent of the manufacturing workforce. Ninety-six percent of manufacturing corporations had under $10 million in assets in 1995, and together they took in only 12 percent of all corporate manufacturing revenue. But the 1,324 largest manufacturing corporations had assets in excess of $250 million apiece. They were less than 0.5 percent of all manufacturing corporations, but they took in 71 percent of all manufacturing corporations' revenues, and 83 percent of the profit.

These concentrations of power dominate industries we encounter in everyday life. The top three soft-drink makers have over 90 percent of their market. The top five music album producers have 84 percent. Ninety percent of the cigarettes sold in this country are made by three companies, while four companies dominate residential telephone service, and so on. Huge corporate mergers will almost surely continue well into the twenty-first century, and the 1999 repeal of laws limiting mergers in the financial industry will certainly usher in a wave of consolidations in the banking sector.

Given the stark pattern of concentration of business assets in the relatively few largest corporations, it makes sense to consider big business as a distinct force in the economy, and to consider the people who run these big businesses as a distinct class with more economic and political power than others. The average board of directors of a big business operating on a national scale includes about 15 people. There are, then, a total of about 240,000 positions on the boards of directors of the 16,000 national-scale big businesses in the United States. These are the senior corporate officers, and the outside directors who represent major suppliers, customers, sources of credit, and other links to the rest of the corporate world.

Most directors sit only on one company's board, but some sit on the boards of two or five or even more corporations at the same time, forming intricate patterns of interlocking directorships among the major corporations. One detailed study of the directors of the 800 largest corporations in the United States found that 15 percent of directors sat on more than one company's board. Taking these multiple director positions into account, we can identify 200,000 or so individuals who together constitute the governing boards of national-scale corporations. They are the "captains of industry" who dominate the U.S. economy, the two-tenths of one percent of the private sector workforce who are the core of the capitalist class.

From among these directors, a few tens of thousands sit on two or more boards and form a pattern of interlocking directorships among the major banks and non-financial corporations. This network, together with the top-level political and cultural leaders aligned with it, can fairly be called the "ruling class." Its members have substantial power but, like all classes, the ruling class is not a monolithic unit and it is not all-powerful. The ruling class is limited by competition among corporations and by the organized power of other classes, both within the United States and abroad. Its members also have factional disputes among themselves, regional differences and differences based on the interests of specific industries. But they have enough coherence of interest and outlook, and enough similarities to differentiate them from the rest of society, that we can identify a ruling class within the larger capitalist class. The entire U.S. ruling class could easily be seated in Yankee Stadium, which holds 57,000 people.

Understanding the structure and size of the capitalist class helps us to understand the middle class. "The middle class" is under constant discussion in American political life. As the working class has disappeared from polite conversation, the middle class has come to be accepted as the social position most Americans are in. Politicians appeal to the middle class. Tax cuts are designed for the middle class. Downsizing afflicts the middle class. Even union leaders almost always refer to their members as middle class.

Most people think of the middle class in terms of income and lifestyle. In short, the middle class has a middling income. Its members are not the rich, who are a fringe group of celebrities and business millionaires: nor are they the poor, the fringe at the bottom of society who are chronically unemployed, on welfare, outside the mainstream, "the underclass." The middle class are those people who, in Bill Clinton's phrase, "work hard and play by the rules," going to work every day just to get by. The common man, everywoman.

Just where to draw the line between the poor, the middle class, and the rich is arbitrary in this way of thinking. The middle class itself often gets divided into an "upper middle class," a "lower middle," and even a "middle middle." Rather than get sidetracked by the many possible income dividing lines that are sometimes used, we will get a better understanding of classes if we define them in a very different way.

Let's ask: What is the middle class in the middle of? If we answer this question in terms of power instead of income, we see that the middle class is in between the two great social forces in modern society, the working class and the capitalist class. These two classes are connected at work, in the production of goods and services. But they have sharply opposing interests, in production and in politics. The middle class is caught in the middle of these conflicting roles and interests. In the context of the sharp conflicts that arise between labor and capital, the middle class is caught in the crossfire. A look at the lives of small business owners, supervisors, and professional people will help make the point clear.

Small Business Owners

First, let's return to small business owners. They are caught between big businesses on the one hand, which impose intense restrictions on their ability to compete, grow, and make money, and workers on the other, who press for wages, working conditions, and social policies that are often beyond the capacity of a small business to finance.

As is typical of the middle class in general, small business owners share common ground with big business in the defense of property interests and hostility to organized labor, but they also have common ground with workers in their desire to find relief from the discipline of the marketplace dominated by big business. Small entrepreneurs are not in the working class, of course, even though they work hard and many have themselves been in the working class in the past, especially in the building trades. Entrepreneurs have more independence than workers—that's the whole point of being your own boss. And to their workers they are the boss.

In short, small business owners are caught in the middle. They share with working people a common vulnerability to market forces dominated by large corporations, but they share with those same big businesses an interest in keeping the power of working people to a minimum.

Supervisors and Managers

Supervisors and middle managers make up another large part of the middle class. Think about a foreman or supervisor. This person is the company's front line of management, there to make sure the work gets done, responsible for pushing the workforce to perform. Foremen and supervisors are often promoted from the ranks of the workers themselves, often have a detailed knowledge of the work, and sometimes even continue to work alongside those they are supervising. But they are an extension of management, although at the lowest level, with layers of management above pushing them to perform, just as they push the workforce below.

The foreman has a notoriously nasty job. He or she takes grief both from the workers being supervised and also from those in higher management who are suspicious of any laxness in the performance of managerial duties. This is what supervisors at all levels are in the middle of. This distinction has long been recognized in labor law, which usually requires supervisors to be in a different bargaining unit from nonsupervisory employees, and in the way the Department of Labor reports wages and other information separately for "supervisory" and "nonsupervisory" employees.

Of course, class position is based on the reality of the work situation, not the job title. I had a student who was an "assistant manager" at a shoe store in a local mall. All this meant was that she had a key to open up the store in the morning (so the boss didn't have to come in early), and she had the authority to count the money. These extra duties brought her a slightly higher wage than her co-workers, but she didn't manage anything. She was in the working class despite her managerial title.

Some workers do take on what may seem like supervisory duties. "Lead workers," for example, give direction to co-workers with less experience or skill and often get premium pay for their abilities. These more senior workers are not middle class managers, however. They don't discipline fellow workers or act in other ways as direct representatives of management authority, duties that are central parts of any supervisor's work life.

Professionals

A third section of the middle class is made up of the millions of professional people such as doctors, lawyers, college professors, and accountants. These people tend to have considerable authority and flexibility in their jobs, whether they are self-employed or work in a corporate department. They often put in long hours, and they do their work in accordance with rules that guide their actions. But on the whole they function within professional associations that exert considerable influence in setting the rules and standards to which the members of the profession are subject. In this way, the discipline professionals face is not the same as that experienced by workers.

Young professionals just starting their careers can be subject to intense supervision and long hours and have no control over their work. Medical residents or first-year associates in a law firm may experience these conditions. At universities, young adjuncts face conditions much closer to those of the working class than to those of tenured professors. But worker-like conditions do not put young professionals into the working class. Rather, the conditions are part of an apprenticeship, or even hazing. The hope and expectation are that full professional status will come. One's sense of class, and the reality of class, is therefore not just a question of one's current work setting. It is related to the trajectory of future prospects connected to the current work.

If a medical resident were told that she would have to live that life for the next forty years, she would think differently about her situation and her supervisors and employers. People with new Ph.D. degrees may be willing to put up with temporary employment for a year or two before settling into a tenure track job with an academic future. But in recent years, as it has become apparent that tens of thousands of adjuncts will *never* find a regular place in the professional life of the university, their attitudes as adjuncts have been changing. Their militancy and interest in union protections have increased, and their feelings of estrangement from the regular professorate have grown as well.

In recent years, even managers have been subject to the discipline of capitalist labor relations. When the *New York Times* ran a week-long series called

"Downsizing in America" in 1996, the stories were those of middle managers as well as skilled workers. During the corporate restructuring of the early nineties, millions of workers lost their jobs. But in fact production workers were not losing jobs any faster than in the 1980s. What had changed was the increase in layoffs for managers and supervisors, long cushioned from the discipline of the labor market.

The fervor the media had for this story reminded me of the 1968 garbage strike in New York City. After many days of growing piles of garbage on the sidewalks, a TV reporter tried to convey the seriousness of the situation: the rats, he said, had been seen leaving Harlem, crossing over the Triboro Bridge into largely white areas of Queens.

Rats shouldn't go into Queens. But neither should they have been in Harlem in the first place, and it wasn't news when they were. It is of course a serious matter that middle managers and professional people are being treated badly, stripped of their dignity at work, and subject to the raw power of capitalist authority. But for working class people, such treatment is no news at all.

The fact that middle class professionals are increasingly exposed to capitalist power does not, however, immediately put them into the working class. This could happen if the basic nature of the work and work relations in a profession changes drastically enough. That is what happened to skilled craftsmen as mass production drew them into capitalist work settings in the last part of the nineteenth century. It was this proletarianization of skilled craft work that led these workers to form the first long-lasting trade unions, the basis of the American Federation of Labor.

Some teachers, social workers, and other professionals I place in the middle class already think of themselves as workers. Others resist any association with people who are not professional and identify more closely with the capitalist class in their values and political leanings. In politics, as in economics, people in the middle class are in the middle, more or less strongly identifying themselves with labor or with capital, depending on their particular situation and depending on the relative power of working class movements compared with the power capitalists can demonstrate.

THE WORKING CLASS

The working class is large and diverse. Pursuing our economic approach to class, we can get a picture of it by looking carefully at the occupational structure of the U.S. economy. But the specific work of the job is not the only question to consider. Since class is a matter of relationships and power, not job title, a person with the same job will be in one or another class depending on the circumstances of the work. A truck driver who owns his own rig, for example, is in the middle class as a small entrepreneur, but a truck driver employed by a freight shipper is in the working class. A plumber operating as an independent contractor counts in the middle class, but the same plumber working for someone else is in the working class.

The U.S. Department of Labor publishes detailed information about the numbers of people employed in hundreds of different occupations. These occupations are grouped into nine broad categories: executive, administrative, and managerial; professional specialty; technicians and related support; sales; administrative support; services; precision production, craft, and repair; operators, fabricators, and laborers; and farming, forestry, and fishing. After examining the detailed occupational content of each job title in each category, I have assigned employees to the working class or to the middle and capitalist class according to the degree of authority and independence the employee typically has on the job. The results are shown in Table 1.

For example, in 1996 15.4 million people were employed in sales occupations. Of these, 4.5 million are supervisors and proprietors and therefore belong in the middle class. The 2.9 million retail cashiers, on the other hand, all belong in the working class. Another 4.9 million retail and personal services sales workers—sales assistants in shops and stores—are also in the working class. But stock traders and real estate agents, also counted by the Department of Labor in the broad "sales" category, have enough authority and independence to be counted in the middle class. By going through each occupation in the sales category in this way, I conclude that of these 15.4 million people, 6.8 million are in the working class, and 8.6 million in the middle class.

TABLE 1
The Working Class Majority (millions of persons, 1996)

Occupational Category	Total	Working class (no.)	Working class (%)
Executive, administrative, and managerial	17.7	—	—
Professional specialty	18.8	1.5	8
Technicians and related support	3.9	2.9	74
Sales	15.4	6.8	44
Administrative support	18.3	17.6	96
Services	17.2	15.8	92
Precision production, craft, and repair	13.6	12.6	93
Operators, fabricators, and laborers	18.2	18.2	100
Farming, forestry, and fishing	3.6	2.0	55
Unemployed	7.2	5.4	75
Total	133.9	82.8	62

Table 1 shows that service occupations are overwhelmingly working class. These include firefighters, dental assistants and nursing aides, private guards and police officers, hairdressers and cosmetologists, janitors, and waiters. But service occupations also include some middle class positions such as supervisors and restaurant chefs (though not short-order cooks, who are typically working class).

The professional specialty category divides the other way: only 8 percent are working class. People counted as professionals hold such jobs as engineers (not technicians), computer scientists (not computer operators), schoolteachers (not aides), doctors, lawyers, university professors, and the like. These are middle class people, given the degree of independence and authority they typically have at work. But this broad category also includes some working class people. For example, the Department of Labor includes respiratory, speech, and physical therapists among professional specialists. Given the specifics of these jobs and their place in the medical treatment system, I think it is appropriate to count these therapists as highly trained and skilled working class people, even with their professional qualifications, except when they are self-employed. Similarly, the Labor Department counts all nurses as professionals, but the conditions of their work lead me to believe that perhaps half are working class, while the other half have the authority and independence that characterize middle class jobs.

Of the remaining six occupational categories, four are fairly homogeneous, two are mixed. The "executive, administrative, and managerial" category includes no working class people. These are such jobs as property managers, financial managers, and educational administrators. At the other extreme, all "operators, fabricators, and laborers" are working class—machine operators, bus and truck drivers (other than self-employed), freight and stock handlers, equipment cleaners, and so on. Almost all the administrative support personnel are working class: secretaries, information clerks, file clerks and other records processing occupations, postal clerks and mail carriers, computer equipment operators, and teacher aides, among others. The middle class is found among the supervisors.

Similarly, nearly all the "precision production, craft, and repair" jobs are in working class hands. Middle class positions are held mostly by self-employed construction trades people and by supervisors.

The two smallest occupational groups are more divided in class terms. In farming, fishing, and forestry, 45 percent are middle class, mostly farm operators and managers. And about a quarter of technicians are middle class people: computer programmers, pilots and flight engineers, and legal assistants (except clerical). The rest of the technician jobs are working class—radiological technicians, LPNs, drafting occupations, chemical technicians (but not chemists or chemical engineers, who are middle class).

In addition to those working in 1996, the labor force included 7.2 million unemployed people who were actively looking for work but had no job of any kind. Data are available showing the last-held occupation of the unemployed. Not surprisingly, the unemployed tend to be from those occupational groups with a larger concentration of working class jobs. If we assume that the unemployed in each occupational group have the same class composition as those who are working in that occupational group, we find that 75 percent of the unemployed are working class people.

Once each occupational group is analyzed and separated into working class and middle class jobs, it is a simple matter to add up the pieces and find the total class composition of the labor force. In 1996, the labor force numbered 133.9 million people (employed or unemployed but actively looking for work). Of these, 82.8 million were working class; 51.1 million were middle class and above. In other words, the working class is 62 percent of the labor force. This is why I say we live in a country with a working class majority.

By the way, the Department of Labor comes up with an even larger number for what might be considered the working class than I do. The Department notes that 82 percent of the 100 million non-farm, private sector employees in the United States in 1996 were "nonsupervisory" employees. This includes such professionals as doctors, accountants, teachers, and airline pilots, whom I count as middle class.

It may seem surprising that so many people are in the working class, given the declining relative size of manufacturing in the U.S. economy. But images of the working class too closely identified with goods-producing blue collar workers miss the point. Only 21 percent of people counted by the Department of Labor as "nonsupervisory employees" in the non-farm private sector are in goods-producing industries (mining, construction, and manufacturing). Over 70 percent of all private sector nonsupervisory employees hold white collar jobs in wholesale and retail trade, finance, insurance, and real estate, and a wide variety of business, persona, and health-related service industries. But even in 1950, in the heyday of American manufacturing strength, no more than a third of the nonagricultural workforce was employed in manufacturing.

Old images of the working class need correction in other ways, too. Identifying the working class with factories may foster the notion that "working class" means men, or even just white men. Think again: less than half the working class labor force, about 46 percent, are white men. Minorities have always been an integral part of the working class, a good number of women have always worked in factories, and today women are a slightly higher percentage of the working class workforce than they are of the labor force as a whole. In 1996, women were 46.2 percent of the employed workforce. Sorting through the data by detailed occupational category to look at gender composition, I find that women were 47.4 percent of the working class, and 43.5 percent of the middle class (Table 2).

But this does not mean that women have broken out of traditional job categories in a big way. Women are still grossly underrepresented in the more skilled blue collar jobs that traditionally have been held by men. In 1996 women held 24 percent of the working class jobs among operators, fabricators, and laborers, but only a 9 percent of the working class jobs among precision production, craft, and repair workers. At the other extreme, women held 87 percent of working class jobs in the professional specialties (these were mainly nurses), 80 percent of working class jobs doing administrative support, and 65 percent of working class jobs in sales.

TABLE 2

Composition of Employed Labor Force by Race and Gender (1996)

	Women (%)	Black (%)	Hispanic (%)
Employed labor force	46.2	10.7	9.2
Working class	47.4	12.6	11.3
Managerial/supervisory/ professional occupations	43.5	7.8	5.3

In the middle class also, women tended to work in the traditional female occupations. Women held fewer than 4 percent of middle class positions in precision production, craft, and repair—they are not often supervisors or independent contractors in these lines of work. Women were also underrepresented among middle class positions in sales (37 percent) and services (38 percent). In executive, administrative, and managerial positions, women held their share of jobs, as they did in middle class positions among technicians.

Women were over-represented in middle class positions, relative to their share in the total labor force, in professional specialties (just over 50 percent), but here, too, the distribution is uneven. Women dominate middle class positions among nurses, teachers, librarians, and social workers, but not among architects, engineers, and scientists. Women had 60 percent of the supervisor jobs in administrative support, but 80 percent of the working class jobs in that field.

Women may be relatively over-represented among managers compared with men in some occupations, but that doesn't mean that women have broken any glass ceilings. In no occupational category except farming did women constitute as large a percentage of managers as they did among the working class in that occupation.

If we look at racial and ethnic composition, we see that blacks and Hispanics are over-represented in the working class and underrepresented in the middle class, patterns similar to women, but even more pronounced. In 1996 blacks were 10.7 percent of the total employed labor force, but they were 12.6 percent of the working class and only 7.8 percent of the middle class. Hispanics were 9.2 percent of all those with jobs, but held only 5.3 percent of middle class positions and 11.3 percent of working class jobs. (Unfortunately, data for Asian and other minorities are not available.)

Breaking the data down further, we find that both blacks and Hispanics have more than their share of lower-level, lower-paying jobs, the service occupations and operators, fabricators, and laborers. In 1996, among farm workers, Hispanics were 29.6 percent of the working class (blacks, on the other hand, were only 5.6 percent of farm workers). Blacks were underrepresented in the better working class jobs: only 7.9 percent of professional specialty jobs (mostly nurses) and 8.1 percent of precision production, craft, and repair. Hispanics were significantly underrepresented among the working class in professional specialty jobs (3.2 percent), technicians (6.5 percent), administrative support (8.3 percent), and sales (9.1 percent).

We see from all these numbers that women, blacks, and Hispanics are a larger proportion of the working class than they are of the labor force as a whole. They are by no means absent from middle class positions of authority, but, in general, women and minorities are in the lower-paid sections of the working class and in the lower ranks of management and professional life, compared with men or white people. Following this pattern, women and minorities are also found among the capitalists, but their businesses are small by national standards. The largest black-owned business in 1998 had sales under $400 million.

A look at census data showing the number of people of different races, genders, and nationalities in hundreds of occupations reveals a surprisingly mixed labor force at all levels. Economist Doug Henwood writes, "The largest occupational category for white men in 1990 [the single occupation employing the largest number of people] was salaried managers and administrators, a title that also appears on the top ten list for black men (#8), Hispanic men (#7), and white women (#6). Secretary is the leading job label for white women—but it's also number one for Hispanic women and number three for black women. Truck driving is the leading employer of black men—but it's second for both Hispanics and whites. 'Janitors and cleaners' is the biggest occupation for Hispanic men, and second for black men—but sixth for white men. More black women are nurses aides and orderlies than any other occupation—but it's the ninth biggest employer of white women. The privileged titles usually appear higher and more often for whites, especially men, but there's no shortage of awful jobs for white folks either."

If we look at the class structure of the United States, then, we see that neither the working nor the middle class is uniform in gender, racial, or ethnic composition. Each class represent s a mosaic. Looking at the mosaic another way, we see that gender, racial, and ethnic groups are also not uniform. Each is divided by class. This complex set of relationships and identities is what we have to sort through to make sense of and then influence the politics and economics of U.S. society.

CLASS AMBIGUITIES

The majority of people are in the working class, those who do the direct work of production and who typically have little control over their jobs and no supervisory authority over others. The working class is the clear majority of the labor force, 62 percent. At the top of the class order, controlling the big business apparatus, is the capitalist class, about 2 percent of the labor force. A small fraction of the capitalist class operates on a national scale, and an even smaller network of several tens of thousands of interlocking directors among the largest of businesses is the core of the national ruling class. Between the capitalist class and the working class is the middle class, about 36 percent of the labor force.

While each of these classes is distinct from the others, all members of a particular class do not, of course, have the same degree of power, the same income, status, or lifestyle as others in the class. Each class is diverse—in skill, authority, occupation, race, gender, ethnicity, and every other characteristic human beings possess. It even happens that individuals in one class can have attributes most often identified with another class, as when some skilled workers make more money than some professionals, or some managers work longer hours and have more stress than some production workers. Because some working class people go in and out of business, with small stores or contracting outfits that mostly serve their working class neighbors, a degree of overlap exists between working class and middle class experience. In many neighborhoods, there is more than a little personal identification across this porous class boundary.

Faced with such diversity and apparent incoherence, it may be tempting to give up the idea that class is a meaningful category and just focus on each individual, or fall back to the common belief that there are simply the rich, the poor, and the broad middle class in between. But an analogy with water—though a bit of a stretch—will help explain why it makes sense to keep class categories as I am defining them, despite the variety of individual experience within each class.

Water takes different forms, ice, liquid, and steam, even though in each state it is still H_2O. Each state is distinct, yet within each wide variations can occur. Liquid water can be cold or hot or lukewarm. Ice can take different forms too, and under different conditions of pressure and volume, steam can vary in temperature and other properties. The three states of water are even fuzzy at the edges, when it is not clear exactly what is going on. Is slush ice or liquid? How many bubbles have to form at the bottom of a pan of water, and how many have to rise to the top and roil the surface, before we say the water is boiling? Yet these variations within states of water, and ambiguities at the edges, don't stop us from knowing that water takes different forms, even if it's all H_2O.

Thinking along these lines tells us about class as well. We are all people. The capitalist, the worker, the doctor, all flesh and blood, all with hopes for ourselves and our children, most of us trying to do the best we can. But this underlying sameness, which is terribly important to remember and respect, in no way means that we are all equally powerful or that no systematic differences exist among us. Our different class standings cause us to act differently, live differently, have different experiences and life chances, despite our underlying resemblance in a common humanity.

Within classes, people are different. An unskilled factory sweeper is in the same class as a radiology technician, a postal letter carrier, a bank teller, a machinist. The professionals, managers, and entrepreneurs of the middle class vary widely not only in the content of their work but in their social status, income, power. Among capitalists, too, are the big and the small, national and local power brokers, the well-connected and the relatively isolated. But despite the variations among people within each class, it still makes sense to view the world as made up of distinct classes, because, in the end, workers do not have the power of the middle class, let along the capitalists, either big or small.

In the last decade of the twentieth century nonstandard work arrangements spread. Instead of holding a regular job, more and more people were working as temps, as independent contractors, as franchise operators. These new work relations were often forced on people after they had lost a regular job to downsizing or a company move or failure. These new arrangements usually brought with them a reduction in living standards, increased insecurity, an end to employer-provided pensions and insurance. Depending on how narrowly or broadly we define "temporary" or "contingent" jobs, in 1997 anywhere from 1.9 to 4.4 percent of the labor force was in nonstandard employment. Fewer than half were employed part-time.

The largest category of people with nonstandard work relations in 1997 was independent contractors, consultants, and free-lance workers. Many of these were professionals and people involved in managerial or sales work and thus part of the middle class. But some "independent contractors" and "franchise operators" are not the middle class people their titles suggest.

In 1998, forty thousand limousine drivers (car service, not taxi) were working in New York City. Some were in traditional employee status, but many were independent contractors, forced to lease their cars from car service companies. In these lease arrangements, which have the appearance of a business contract between two independent parties, the driver takes on the status of a franchise holder, but in reality is completely controlled by the car service company.

What class does the "independent" limo driver belong to? The question is not rhetorical; the answer controls whether the drivers can organize a union and force the company to negotiate a collective bargaining agreement. In 1997, when drivers at one company wanted to organize, the company claimed they were independent contractors, no employees, and so not protected by labor law that gives workers the right to organize unions and requires their employer to negotiate in good faith. But the National Labor Relations Board, the federal agency that decides these disputes, dismissed the company's claim and ordered a union representation election. The drivers overwhelmingly voted the union in.

The story of these limousine drivers is repeated wherever employers try to mask power relations with the veneer of a professional or entrepreneurial title bestowed on workers. Class is not in the name. Class is in the power relationships people experience.

In which class is a secretary who also has a Mary Kay franchise on the side, supplying and managing three other women? What do we call an electrician who works for his city's board of education but also has his own contracting business? In what class do we put a family with a husband who works in an auto plant and a wife who is a pediatrician? Is a person who owns a machine shop employing twenty-five people on two shifts, who works side by side with his employees on the floor two mornings a week while taking care of the business the rest of the time, a capitalist or in the middle class as a small businessman?

The ambiguity of such borderline cases, and the wide variety of experience within classes, is testimony to the fact that classes are not simply boxes or static categories into which we pigeonhole people. Classes are formed in the dynamics of power and wealth creation and are by their nature a bit messy. Classes are more complicated, more interesting, and more real than the arbitrary income levels used to define class in the conventional wisdom. ■

Working with the Text

1. What does Zweig mean by "visible" and "invisible" power? Can you come up with additional examples of your own to test both your understanding and his ideas?

2. What are the advantages and disadvantages you see in using power as Zweig defines it as the main means of defining social class? Try applying Zweig's ideas about power to your own work experience or that of a parent. In what ways does Zweig cause you to think differently about that experience?

3. Zweig defines the "middle" of middle class as meaning having to negotiate and manage relations between the working class and the capitalist class. How does Zweig's view of what it means to be "middle class" clarify or challenge your own associations with the term, "middle class"?

4. Zweig suggests that thinking of most people in the United States as working class rather than middle class would mean a change in thinking for most Americans. How would the idea of a "working class majority" affect your own thinking about work in the United States? What other possible consequences could it have?

Working with Connections

1. Both Michael Zweig and Gregory Mantsios describe three different social classes in the United States, but while Zweig focuses particularly on the working class, Mantsios mainly uses the term "wealthy," "middle class," and "poor" to discuss media representations of social class. What similarities and differences does Zweig's definition of social class have with Mantsios? How might the purpose each is trying to achieve in their writings affect the definitions of the social classes they use? Based on your comparison, write about what you find to be the most useful understanding of what social class means.

2. Using information from Zweig and the other readings in this chapter, write a guide for entering college students explaining how to tell what social class you belong to and what that will mean for your college career.

Reading the Web

Justice for Janitors Web Site

Justice for Janitors <http://www.seiu.org/building/janitors> is the name of an organizing campaign run by the Service Employees International Union (SEIU). The campaign began in Denver, Colorado in 1985, and as its name suggests, it focuses on organizing custodial workers and gaining official legal recognition for them as a union. The campaign has focused special attention on the needs of immigrant workers, who often face barriers of language, social class, and fear in trying to achieve better working conditions.

In addition to providing information about the campaign, the Justice for Janitors web site also functions as part of the effort to gain broader public support for the organization. Thus, while the Justice for Janitors campaign is focused on working class issues, its web site also works to appeal to citizens from across the class spectrum. As you visit the Justice for Janitors web site, think about how it both conveys information and tries to speak to a broad audiennce. The following questions can be helpful in guiding your visit:

1. Who does the presumed audience of the site seem to be? Do you think you belong to this audience interms of any social group you identify with?
2. Who would and would not be attracted to this site?
3. How would you evaluate this site as a research source?

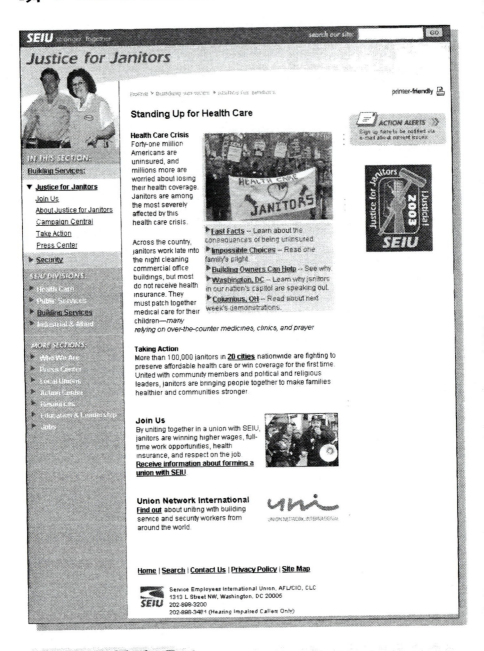

Working with the Text

1. One of the most striking features of the union's campaign is its name: Justice for Janitors. The use of alliteration, or the repetition of the "j" sound, makes the name easy to remember. Beyond that, the use of "janitors" deliberately goes against the trend (parodied by Kathryn Carmony in "Surfing the Classifieds" from Chapter 2,

Work, Labor, Career, The Meaning of Work) of renaming jobs to make them seem more "professional" and middle class—for example, salespeople become customer service representatives or associates, secretaries become administrative assistants, or, in this case, janitors become custodial engineers. What is the effect of using the older term, "janitor"? What associations do you have with that word? Why do you think the SEIU has embraced this term? How does the use of this term relate to social class identification or pride?

2. In addition to its specific organizing campaigns, Justice for Janitors has also created a series of events meant to raise awareness of the program, from Justice for Janitors Day (June 15) to an "American Dream Tour" in 2002. Read more about these activities on the web site and discuss how effective you think they are in terms of the audiences they are trying to reach and the messages you think they are trying to send.

3. The layout of the Justice for Janitors site uses images sparingly; one result is that we tend to pay more attention to them. Analyze the images that have been included in the web site, such as the man and woman in the upper left hand corner, in terms of the impression they create about the campaign and the people it serves. What preconceptions might they be trying to reinforce or challenge with their use of images?

Working with Connections

1. In some ways, the Justice for Janitors web site seems almost a response to the criticism by Gregory Mantsios in "Media Magic" that most media fail to provide a working class or poor person's perspective on the news. Choose a story about the Justice for Janitors movement included on its web site and locate versions of the story as covered by several mainstream media sources such as CNN, *Newsweek*, the *New York Times*, and others to determine the key differences in terms of how these stories are reported. In what ways do these differences confirm Mantsios's original argument, and in what ways would you modify Mantsios's analysis?

2. The Justice for Janitors movement in Los Angeles inspired a motion picture made in 2001, *Bread and Roses*, directed by Ken Loach, a British film maker famous for dealing with working class life and labor issues. Watch the film either inside or outside of

class and consider how the film uses the techniques of movie story telling both to inform its audience about the Justice for Janitors movement and build sympathy for its characters. Who do you think the audience for the film was? How effective is a movie like *Bread and Roses* in creating more awareness about the Justice for Janitors campaign?

Stories of Work

BARBARA EHRENREICH ■

From *Nickel and Dimed: On (Not) Getting By in America*

Concerned about the effects of welfare reforms that are cutting off benefits and requiring former recipients to survive in the labor market, Barbara Ehrenreich spent 1998 trying to find out if it were possible to get by in the United States working full-time at near minimum wage. Her project involved moving to a city and trying to survive and locate affordable housing by finding a job that required little or no experience. She worked as a waiter in Key West, Florida, a housecleaner and nurse's aid in Portland, Maine, and a Wal-Mart employee in Minneapolis, Minnesota. She writes about her experiences and the conclusions she reached about the difficulty, if not impossibility, of living on the minimum wage in her book Nickel and Dimed: On (Not) Getting By in America. *In this excerpt from the chapter entitled, "Scrubbing in Maine," Ehrenreich describes her first day on the job working for "The Maids," a housecleaning service.*

The Friday of my first week at The Maids is unnaturally hot for Maine in early September—95 degrees, according to the digital time-and-temperature displays offered by banks that we pass. I'm teamed up with the sad-faced Rosalie and our leader, Maddy, whose sullenness, under the circumstances, is almost a relief after Liza's relentless good cheer. Liza, I've learned, is the highest-ranking cleaner, a sort of supervisor really, and said to be something of a snitch, but Maddy, a single mom of maybe twenty-seven or so, has worked for only three months and broods about her child care problems. Her boyfriend's sister, she tells me on the drive to our first house, watches her eighteen-month-old for $50 a week, which is a stretch on The Maids' pay, plus she doesn't entirely trust the sister, but a real day care center could be as much as $90 a week. After polishing off the first house, no problem, we grab "lunch"—Doritos for Rosalie and a bag of Pepperidge Farm Goldfish for Maddy—and head out into the exurbs for what our instruction sheet warns is a five-bathroom spread and a first-timer to boot. Still, the size of the place makes us pause for a moment, buckets in hand, before searching out an appropriately humble entrance.[1] It sits there like a beached ocean liner, the prow cutting through swells of green turf, windows without number. "Well, well," Maddy says, reading the owner's name from our instruction sheet. "Mrs. W. and her big-ass house. I hope she's going to give us lunch."

Mrs. W. is not in fact happy to see us, grimacing with exasperation when the black nanny ushers us into the family room or sunroom or den or whatever kind of specialized space she is sitting in. After all, she already has the nanny, a cooklike person, and a crew of men doing some sort of finishing touches on the construction to supervise. No, she doesn't want to take us around the house, because she already explained everything to the office on the phone, but Maddy stands there, with Rosalie and me behind her, until she relents. We are to move everything on all surfaces, she instructs during the tour, and get underneath and be sure to do every bit of the several miles, I calculate, of baseboards. And be mindful of the baby, who's napping and can't have cleaning fluids of any kind near her.

Then I am let loose to dust. In a situation like this, where I don't even know how to name the various kinds of rooms, The Maids' special system turns out to be a lifesaver. All I have to do is keep moving from left to right, within rooms and between rooms, trying to identify landmarks so I don't accidentally do a room or a hallway twice. Dusters get the most complete biographical overview, due to the necessity of lifting each object and tchotchke individually, and I learn that Mrs. W. is an alumna of an important women's college, now occupying herself by monitoring her investments and the baby's bowel movements. I find special charts for this latter purpose, with spaces for time of day, most recent fluid intake, consistency, and color. In the master bedroom, I dust a whole shelf of books on pregnancy, breastfeeding, the first six months, the first year, the first two years—and I wonder what the child care-deprived Maddy makes of all this. Maybe there's been some secret division of the world's women into breeders and drones, and those at the maid level are no longer supposed to be reproducing at all. Maybe this is why our office manager, Tammy, who was once a maid herself, wears inch-long fake nails and tarty little outfits—to show she's advanced to the breeder caste and can't be sent out to clean anymore.

It is hotter inside than out, un-air-conditioned for the benefit of the baby, I suppose, but I do all right until I encounter the banks of glass doors that line the side and back of the ground floor. Each one has to be Windexed, wiped, and

[1] For the affluent, houses have been swelling with no apparent limit. The square footage of new homes increased by 39 percent between 1971 and 1996, to include "family rooms," home entertainment rooms, home offices, bedrooms, and often a bathroom for each family member ("Détente in the Housework Wars," *Toronto Star*, November 20, 1999). By the second quarter of 1999, 17 percent of new homes were larger than three thousand square feet, which is usually considered the size threshold for household help, or the point at which a house becomes unmanageable to the people who live in it ("Molding Loyal Pamperers for the Newly Rich," *New York Times*, October 24, 1999).

buffed—inside and out, top to bottom, left to right, until it's as streakless and invisible as a material substance can be. Outside, I can see the construction guys knocking back Gatorade, but the rule is that no fluid or food item can touch a maid's lips when she's inside a house. Now, sweat, even in unseemly quantities, is nothing new to me. I live in a subtropical area where even the inactive can expect to be moist nine months out of the year. I work out, too, in my normal life and take a certain macho pride in the *V*s of sweat that form on my T-shirt after ten minutes or more on the StairMaster. But in normal life fluids lost are immediately replaced. Everyone in yuppie-land—airports, for example—looks like a nursing baby these days, inseparable from their plastic bottles of water. Here, however, I sweat without replacement or pause, not in individual drops but in continuous sheets of fluid soaking through my polo shirt, pouring down the backs of my legs. The eyeliner I put on in the morning—vain twit that I am—has long since streaked down onto my cheeks, and I could wring my braid out if I wanted to. Working my way through the living room(s), I wonder if Mrs. W. will ever have occasion to realize that every single doodad and *objet* through which she expresses her unique, individual self is, from another vantage point, only an obstacle between some thirsty person and a glass of water.

When I can find no more surfaces to wipe and have finally exhausted the supply of rooms, Maddy assigns me to do the kitchen floor. OK, except that Mrs. W. is *in* the kitchen, so I have to go down on my hands and knees practically at her feet. No, we don't have sponge mops like the one I use in my own house; the hands-and-knees approach is a definite selling point for corporate cleaning services like The Maids. "We clean floors the old-fashioned way—*on our hands and knees*" (emphasis added), the brochure for a competing firm boasts. In fact, whatever advantages there may be to the hands-and-knees approach—you're closer to your work, of course, and less likely to miss a grimy patch—are undermined by the artificial drought imposed by The Maids' cleaning system. We are instructed to use less than half a small bucket of lukewarm water for a kitchen and all adjacent scrubbable floors (breakfast nooks and other dining areas), meaning that within a few minutes we are doing nothing more than redistributing the dirt evenly around the floor. There are occasional customer complaints about the cleanliness of our floors—for example, from a man who wiped up a spill on his freshly "cleaned" floor only to find the paper towel he employed for this purpose had turned gray. A mop and a full bucket of hot soapy water would not only get a floor cleaner but would be a lot more dignified for the person who does the cleaning. But it is this primal posture of submission—and of what is ultimately anal accessibility—that seems to gratify the consumers of maid services.[2]

I don't know, but Mrs. W.'s floor is hard—stone, I think, or at least a stonelike substance—and we have no knee pads with us today. I had thought in my mid-

---

[2] In *Home Comforts: The Art and Science of Keeping House* (Scribner, 1999), Cheryl Mendelson writes, "Never ask hired housecleaners to clean your floors on their hands and knees; the request is likely to be regarded as degrading" (p. 501).

dle class innocence that knee pads were one of Monica Lewinsky's prurient fantasies, but no, they actually exist, and they're usually a standard part of our equipment. So here I am on my knees, working my way around the room like some fanatical penitent crawling through the stations of the cross, when I realize that Mrs. W. is staring at me fixedly—so fixedly that I am gripped for a moment by the wild possibility that I may have once given a lecture at her alma mater and she's trying to figure out where she's seen me before. If I were recognized, would I be fired? Would she at least be inspired to offer me a drink of water? Because I have decided that if water is actually offered, I'm taking it, rules or no rules, and if word of this infraction gets back to Ted, I'll just say I thought it would be rude to refuse. Not to worry, though. She's just watching that I don't leave out some stray square inch, and when I rise painfully to my feet again, blinking through the sweat, she says, "Could you just scrub the floor in the entryway while you're at it?"

I rush home to the Blue Haven at the end of the day, pull down the blinds for privacy, strip off my uniform in the kitchen—the bathroom being too small for both a person and her discarded clothes—and stand in the shower for a good ten minutes, thinking all this water is *mine*. I have paid for it, in fact, I have earned it. I have gotten through a week at The Maids without mishap, injury, or insurrection. My back feels fine, meaning I'm not feeling it at all; even my wrists, damaged by carpal tunnel syndrome years ago, are issuing no complaints. Coworkers warned me that the first time they donned the backpack vacuum they felt faint, but not me. I am strong and I am, more than that, good. Did I toss my bucket of filthy water onto Mrs. W.'s casual white summer outfit? No. Did I take the wand of my vacuum cleaner and smash someone's Chinese porcelain statues or Hummel figurines? Not once. I was at all times cheerful, energetic, helpful, and as competent as a new hire can be expected to be. If I can do one week, I can do another, and might as well, since there's never been a moment for job-hunting. The 3:30 quitting time turns out to be a myth; often we don't return to the office until 4:30 or 5:00. And what did I think? That I was going to go out to interviews in my soaked and stinky postwork condition? I decide to reward myself with a sunset walk on Old Orchard Beach.

On account of the heat, there are still a few actual bathers on the beach, but I am content to sit in shorts and T-shirt and watch the ocean pummel the sand. When the sun goes down I walk back into the town to find my car and am amazed to hear a sound I associate with cities like New York and Berlin. There's a couple of Peruvian musicians playing in the little grassy island in the street near the pier, and maybe fifty people—locals and vacationers—have gathered around, offering their bland end-of-summer faces to the sound. I edge my way through the crowd and find a seat where I can see the musicians up close—the beautiful young guitarist and the taller man playing the flute. What are they doing in this rinky-dink blue-collar resort, and what does the audience make of this surprise visit from the dark-skinned South? The melody the flute lays out over the percussion is both utterly strange and completely familiar, as if it had been imprinted in the minds of my own peasant ancestors centuries ago and forgotten until this very moment. Everyone else seems to be as transfixed as I am. The musicians wink and smile at each other as they play, and I see then that they are the secret emissaries of a worldwide lower-class conspiracy to snatch joy out of degradation and filth. When the song ends, I give them a dollar, the equivalent of about ten minutes of sweat.

The superwoman mood does not last. For one thing, while the muscles and joints are doing just fine, the skin has decided to rebel. At first I think the itchy pink bumps on my arms and legs must be poison ivy picked up at a lockout. Sometimes an owner forgets we are coming or forgets to leave a key under the mat or changes his or her mind about the service without thinking to notify Ted. This is not, for us, an occasion for joy like a snow day for the grade-school crowd, because Ted blames us for his customers' fecklessness. When owners forget we are coming, he explains at one of our morning send-off meetings, it "means something," like that they're dissatisfied and too passive-aggressive to tell us. Once, when I am with Pauline as my team leader, she calls Ted to report a lockout and his response, she reports ruefully, is, "Don't do this to me." So before we give up and declare a place a lockout, we search like cat burglars for alternative points of entry, which can mean trampling through overgrowth to peer into windows and test all the doors. I haven't seen any poison ivy, but who knows what other members of the poison family (oak, sumac, etc.) lurk in the flora of Maine?

Or maybe the cleaning fluids are at fault, except that then the rash should have begun on my hands. After two days of minor irritation, a full-scale epidermal breakdown is under way. I cover myself with anti-itch cream from Rite Aid but can manage to sleep only for an hour and a half at a time before the torment resumes. I wake up realizing I can work but probably shouldn't, if only because I look like a leper. Ted doesn't have much sympathy for illness, though; one of our morning meetings was on the subject of "working through it." Somebody, and he wasn't going to name names, he told us, was out with a migraine. "Now if I get a migraine I just pop two Excedrins and get on with my life. That's what you have to do—work through it." So it's in the spirit of a scientific experiment that I present myself at the office, wondering if my speckled and inflamed appearance will be enough to get me sent home. Certainly I wouldn't want anyone who looks like me handling my children's toys or bars of bathroom soap. But no problem. Must be a latex allergy, is Ted's diagnosis. Just stay out of the latex gloves we use for particularly nasty work; he'll give me another kind to wear.

I should, if I were going to stay in character, find an emergency room after work and try to cop a little charitable care. But it's too much. The itching gets so bad at night that I have mini-tantrums, waving my arms and stamping my feet to keep from scratching or bawling. So I fall back on the support networks of my real-life social class, call the dermatologist I know in Key West, and bludgeon him into prescribing something sight unseen. The whole episode—including anti-itch cream, prednisone, prednisone cream, and Benadryl to get through the nights—eats up $30. It's still unseasonably hot, and I often get to look out on someone's azure pool while I vacuum or scrub, frantic with suppressed itching. Even the rash-free are affected by the juxtaposition of terrible heat and cool, inaccessible water. In the car on one of the hottest days, after cleaning a place with pool, pool house, and gazebo, Rosalie and Maddy and I obsess about immersion in all imaginable forms—salt water versus fresh, lakes versus pools, surf versus smooth, glasslike surfaces. We can't even wash our hands in the houses, at least not after the sinks have been dried and buffed, and when I do manage to get a wash in before the sinks are offlimits, there's always some filthy last-minute job like squeezing out the rags used on floors once we get out of a house. Maybe I picked up some bug at a house or maybe it's the disinfectant I squirt on my hands, straight from the bottle, in an attempt at cleanliness. Three days into the rash, I make another trip to Old Orchard Beach and wade into the water with my clothes on (I didn't think to bring a bathing suit from Key West to Maine), trying to pretend that it's an accident when a wave washes over me and that I'm not just some pathetic street person using the beach as a bathtub.

There's something else working against my mood of muscular elation. I had been gloating internally about my ability to keep up with, and sometimes out-work, women twenty or thirty years younger than myself, but it turns out this comparative advantage says less about me than it does about them. Ours is a physical bond, to the extent that we bond at all. One person's infirmity can be a teammate's extra burden; there's a constant traffic in herbal and over-the-counter solutions to pain. If I don't know how my coworkers survive on their wages or what they make of our hellish condition, I do know about their back pains and cramps and arthritic attacks. Lori and Pauline are excused from vacuuming on account of their backs, which means you dread being assigned to a team with them. Helen has a bum foot, which Ted, in explaining her absence one day, blames on the cheap, ill-fitting shoes that, he implies, she perversely chooses to wear. Marge's arthritis makes scrubbing a torture; another woman has to see a physical therapist for her rotator cuff. When Rosalie tells me that she got her shoulder problem picking blueberries as a "kid"—she still is one in my eyes, of course—I flash on a scene from my own childhood, of wandering through fields on an intense July day, grabbing berries by the handful as I go. But when Rosalie was a kid she worked in the blueberry fields of northern Maine, and the damage to her shoulder is an occupational injury.

So ours is a world of pain—managed by Excedrin and Advil, compensated for with cigarettes and, in one or two cases and then only on weekends, with booze. Do the owners have any idea of the misery that goes into rendering their homes motel-perfect? Would they be bothered if they did know, or would they take a sadistic pride in what they have purchased—boasting to dinner guests, for example, that their floors are cleaned only with the purest of fresh human tears? In one of my few exchanges with an owner, a pert muscular woman whose desk reveals that she works part-time as a personal trainer, I am vacuuming and she notices the sweat. "That's a real workout, isn't it?" she observes, not unkindly, and actually offers me a glass of water, the only such offer I ever encounter. Flouting the rule against the ingestion of anything while inside a house, I take it, leaving an inch undrunk to avoid the awkwardness of a possible refill offer. "I tell all my clients," the trainer informs me, "'If you want to be fit, just fire your cleaning lady and do it yourself.'" "Ho ho," is all I say, since we're not just chatting in the gym together and I can't explain that this form of exercise is totally asymmetrical, brutally repetitive, and as likely to destroy the musculoskeletal structure as to strengthen it.

Self-restraint becomes more of a challenge when the owner of a million-dollar condo (that's my guess anyway, because it has three floors and a wide-angle view of the fabled rockbound coast) who is (according to a framed photograph on the wall) an acquaintance of the real Barbara Bush takes me into the master bathroom to explain the difficulties she's been having with the shower stall. Seems its marble walls have been "bleeding" onto the brass fixtures, and can I scrub the grouting extra hard? That's not your marble bleeding, I want to tell her, it's the worldwide working class—the people who quarried the marble, wove your Persian rugs until they went blind, harvested the apples in your lovely fall-themed dining room centerpiece, smelted the steel for the nails, drove the trucks, put up this building, and now bend and squat and sweat to clean it.

Not that I, even in my more histrionic moments, imagine that I am a member of that oppressed working class. My very ability to work tirelessly hour after hour is a product of decades of better-than-average medical care, a high-protein diet, and workouts in gyms that charge $400 or $500 a year. If I am now a productive fake member of the working class, it's because I haven't been working, in any hard physical sense, long enough to have ruined my body. But I will say this for myself: I have never employed a cleaning person or service (except, on two occasions, to prepare my house for a short-term tenant) even though various partners and husbands have badgered me over the years to do so. When I could have used one, when the kids were little, I couldn't afford it; and later, when I could afford it, I still found the idea repugnant. Partly this comes from having a mother who believed that a self-cleaned house was the hallmark of womanly virtue. Partly it's because my own normal work is sedentary, so that the housework I do—in dabs of fifteen minutes here and thirty minutes there—functions as a break. But mostly I rejected the idea, even after all my upper-middle-class friends had, guiltily and as covertly as possible, hired help for themselves, because this is just not the kind of relationship I want to have with another human being.[3]

---

[3] In 1999, somewhere between 14 and 18 percent of households employed an outsider to do the cleaning and the numbers are rising dramatically. Mediamark Research reports a 53 percent increase, between 1995 and 1999, in the number of households using a hired cleaner or service once a month or more, and Maritz Marketing finds that 30 percent of the people who hired help in 1999 had done so for the first time that year.

Managers of the new corporate cleaning services, such as the one I worked for, attribute their success not only to the influx of women into the workforce but to the tensions over housework that arose in its wake. When the trend toward hiring out was just beginning to take off, in 1988, the owner of a Merry Maids franchise in Arlington, Massachusetts, told the *Christian Science Monitor,* "I kid some women. I say, 'We even save marriages. In this new

Let's talk about shit, for example. It happens, as the bumper sticker says, and it happens to a cleaning person every day. The first time I encountered a shit-stained toilet as a maid, I was shocked by the sense of unwanted intimacy. A few hours ago, some well-fed butt was straining away on this toilet seat, and now here I am wiping up after it. For those who have never cleaned a really dirty toilet, I should explain that there are three kinds of shit stains. There are remnants of landslides running down the inside of toilet bowls. There are the splash-back remains on the underside of toilet seats. And, perhaps most repulsively, there's sometimes a crust of brown on the rim of a toilet seat, where a turd happened to collide on its dive to the water. You don't want to know this? Well, it's not something I would have chosen to dwell on myself, but the different kinds of stains require different cleaning approaches. One prefers those that are interior to the toilet bowl, since they can be attacked by brush, which is a kind of action-at-a-distance weapon. And one dreads the crusts on the seats, especially when they require the intervention of a Dobie as well as a rag.

Or we might talk about that other great nemesis of the bathroom cleaner—pubic hair. I don't know what it is about the American upper class, but they seem to be shedding their pubic hair at an alarming rate. You find it in quantity in shower stalls, bathtubs, Jacuzzis, drains, and even, unaccountably, in sinks. Once I spent fifteen minutes crouching in a huge four-person Jacuzzi, maddened by the effort of finding the dark little coils camouflaged against the egg-plant-colored ceramic background but fascinated by the image of the pubes of the economic elite, which must by this time be completely bald.

There are worse things that owners can do, of course, than shit or shed. They can spy on us, for example. When I ask a teammate why the rule against cursing in houses, she says that owners have been known to leave tape recorders going while we work. Video cameras are another part of the lore, positioned near valuables to catch a cleaner in an act of theft. Whether any of this is true or not, Ted encourages us to imagine that we are under surveillance at all times in each house.[4] Other owners set traps for us. In one house, I am reprimanded by the team leader for failing to vacuum far enough under the Persian rugs scattered around on the hardwood floors, because this owner likes to leave little mounds of dirt there just so she can see if they're still there when we're done. More commonly, owners will arrange to be home when we come so they can check up on us while we work. I am vacuuming the home of a retired couple

eighties period you expect more from the male partner, but very often you don't get the cooperation you would like to have. The alternative is to pay somebody to come in'" ("Ambushed by Dust Bunnies," *Christian Science Monitor,* April 4, 1988). Another Merry Maids franchise owner has learned to capitalize more directly on housework-related spats; he closes 30–35 percent of his sales by making follow-up calls Saturdays between 9:00 and 11:00 A.M.—which is "prime time for arguing over the fact that the house is a mess" ("Homes Harbor Dirty Secrets," *Chicago Tribune,* May 5, 1994).

[4] At the time, I dismissed this as a scare story, but I have since come across ads for concealable video cameras, like the Tech-7 "incredible coin-sized camera" designed to "get a visual record of your babysitter's actions" and "watch employees to prevent theft."

and happen to look into a room I've completed, where I see the female owner's enormous purple-encased butt staring up at me from the floor. I wouldn't have thought she was agile enough, but she's climbed under a desk to search out particles of overlooked dust.

I would say more about the houses themselves, but I lack the vocabulary for all the forms of wall finishings, flooring materials, fight fixtures, fireplace equipment, porches, and statuary we encounter. On the subject of interior decorating, my general feeling has long been that it's too bad we're fur-less and have to live indoors. The various consequences of this infirmity—as manifested in architecture, furniture, etc.—have never managed to engage my attention. Far more useful to me, for understanding the tics, pretensions, and insecurities of the owner class, are books and other print-related artifacts. I learn that one of our owners is a Scientologist; another proudly claims descent from one of the same Scottish clans my own ancestors belonged to. Still another has framed a certificate announcing that she is listed in the *Who's Who of American Women*. As for books, at the low end of the literacy spectrum, which is where most of our clients dwell, I find Grisham and Limbaugh; at the high end, there's a lot of Amy Tan and I once even spotted an Ondaatje. Mostly, though, books are for show, and real life—judging from the quantity of food stains and tossed items of clothing—goes on in the room that houses the large-screen TV. The only books that seriously offend me are the antique ones, no doubt purchased in bulk, that are sometimes deployed on end tables for purposes of quaintness and "authenticity"—as if the owners actually spent their spare moments reading a 1920 title like *Bobsledding in Vermont: One Boy's Adventure*. But time pressures inevitably curtail my literary investigations. The real issue for a maid is the *number* of books per shelf. if that number is greater than twelve, we can treat them as a single mass and dust around them; otherwise each one must be removed and dusted separately.

Not all of our owners are rich. Maybe a quarter to a third of the houses look to be merely middle-class and some of these—probably because they lack interim help to do the light cleaning between our visits every week or two—are seriously dirty. But class is a relative thing. Once, after polishing up two houses in which the number of occupants clearly exceeded the number of bathrooms—an unmistakable sign of financial impairment, along with the presence of teddy bears in decorative roles—I asked Holly, my team leader of the day, whether the next house on our list was "wealthy." Her answer: "If we're cleaning their house, they're wealthy."

It is undeniably fall when I find myself being assigned, day after day, to Holly's team. There's fog in the morning now and the farm stands are pushing pumpkins. On the radio in our company car the classic rock station notes the season by playing "Maggie May" several times a day—*It's late September and I really should be BACK at school.* Other people are going out to their offices or classrooms; we stay behind, Cinderella-like, in their usually deserted homes. On the pop station, it's Pearl Jam's hypnotic "Last Kiss," so beautifully sad, it makes bereavement seem like an enviable condition. Not that we ever comment on what the radio brings us or on any other part of the world outside The Maids and its string of client houses. In this, the most dutiful and serious of all the teams I have been on, the conversation, at least in the morning, is all about the houses that lie ahead. *Murphy—isn't that the one that took four hours the first time? Yeah, but it's OK once you get past the master bath, which you've gotta use mold killer on* . . . And so on. Or we pass around our routing sheet and study the day's owners' "Hot Buttons," as sketched in by Tammy. Typical "Hot Buttons" are baseboards, windowsills, and ceiling fans—never, of course, poverty, racism, or global warming.

But the relevant point about Holly is that she is visibly unwell—possibly whiter, on a daily basis, than anyone else in the state. We're not just talking Caucasian here; think bridal gowns, tuberculosis, and death. All I know about her is that she is twenty-three, has been married for almost a year, and manages to feed her husband, herself, and an elderly relative on $30–$50 a week, which is only a little more than what I spend on food for myself. I'd be surprised if she weighs more than ninety-two pounds before breakfast, assuming breakfast is even on her agenda. During an eight-to-nine-hour shift, I never see her eat more than one of those tiny cracker sandwiches with peanut butter filling, and you would think she had no use for food at all if it weren't for the fact that every afternoon at about 2:30 she starts up a food-fantasy conversation in the car. "What did you have for dinner last night, Marge?" she'll ask, Marge being our oldest and most affluent team member, who—thanks to a working commercial fisherman husband—sometimes brings reports from such fine-dining spots as T.G.I. Friday's. Or we'll drive by a Dairy Queen and Holly will say, "They have great foursquares"—the local name for a sundae—"there, you know. With four kinds of sauce. You get chocolate, strawberry, butterscotch, and marshmallow and any kind of ice cream you want. I had one once and let it get a little melted and, oh my *God*," etc.

Today, though, even Marge, who normally chatters on obliviously about the events in her life ("It was the *biggest* spider" or "So she just puts a little mustard right in with the baked beans . . ."), notices how shaky Holly looks. "Is it just indigestion or is there nausea?" she asks. When Holly admits to nausea, Marge wants to know if she's pregnant. No answer. Marge asks again, and again no answer. "I'm *talking* to you, Holly, *answer* me." It's a tense moment, with Marge prying and Holly just as rudely stonewalling, but Holly, as team leader, prevails.

There are only the three of us—Denise is out with a migraine—and at the first house I suggest that Marge and I do all the vacuuming for the day. Marge doesn't chime in on my offer, but it doesn't matter since Holly says no way. I resolve to race through dusting so I can take over as much as possible from Holly. When I finish, I rush to the kitchen, only to find a scene so melodramatic that for a second I think I have walked out of *Dusting*, the videotape, and into an entirely different movie. Holly is in a distinctly un-team-leader-like position, standing slumped over a counter with her head on her arms. "I shouldn't be here today," she says, looking up wanly. "I had a big fight with my husband. I didn't want to go to work this morning but he said I had to." This confidence is so completely out of character that I'm speechless. She goes on. The problem is probably that she's pregnant. It's been seven weeks and the nausea is out of control, which is why she can't eat anything and gets so weak, but she wants it to be a secret until she can tell Ted herself.

Very tentatively and mindful of the deep reserve of rural Mainers, as explained to me by a sociologist acquaintance, I touch her arm and tell her she shouldn't be doing this. Even if she were feeling OK she probably shouldn't be around the chemicals we use. She should go home. But all I can talk her into is taking the Pure Protein sports bar I always carry in my bag in case my sandwich lets me down. At first she refuses it. Then, when I repeat the offer, she says, "Really?" and finally takes it, picking off little chunks with trembling fingertips and cramming them into her mouth. Also, would I mind doing the driving for the rest of the day because she doesn't trust herself on account of the dizziness?

For the first time in my life as a maid I have a purpose more compelling than trying to meet the aesthetic standards of the New England bourgeoisie. I will do the work of two people, if necessary three. The next house belongs to a woman known to Holly and Marge as a "friggin' bitch," who turns out to be Martha Stewart or at least a very dedicated acolyte thereof. Everything about it enrages me, and some of it would be irritating even if I were just dropping by for cocktails and not toiling alongside this pale, undernourished child: the brass plaque on the door announcing the date of construction (mid-eighteenth century), the wet bar with its ostentatious alignment of single-malt Scotches, the four-poster king-sized bed with canopy, the Jacuzzi so big you have to climb stairs to get into it and probably safe for diving when filled. I whiz through the bathrooms and even manage to complete the kitchen while the others are still on their initial tasks. Then Marge shows up in the kitchen and points out the row of copper pots and pans hanging from a rack near the ceiling. According to our instructions, she informs me, every one of them has to be taken down and polished with the owner's special polish.

OK. The only way to get to them is to climb up on the kitchen counter, kneel there, and reach up for them from that position. These are not pots for cooking, I should point out, just decorative pots deployed to catch stray beams of sunlight or reflect the owners' no doubt expensively buffed and peeled faces. The final pot is unexpectedly heavy—they are arranged in size order—and as I grasp it from my crouching position on the countertop, it slips from my hand and comes crashing down into a fishbowl cunningly furnished with marbles. Fish fly, marbles skitter all over the floor, and water—which in our work is regarded as a dangerous contaminant—soaks everything, including a stack of cookbooks containing *Cucina Simpatica*, a number of works set in Provence, and, yes, Martha Stewart herself. No one gets mad at me, not even Ted, back in the office, who is bonded for this sort of thing. My punishment is seeing Holly's face, when she rushes into the kitchen to see what the crash was, completely polarized with fear.

After the accident, Holly decides we can take a convenience store break. I buy myself a pack of cigarettes and sit out in the rain to puff (I haven't inhaled for years but it helps anyway) while the others drink their Cokes in the car. Have to get over this savior complex, I instruct myself, no one wants to be rescued by a klutz. Even my motives seem murky at the moment. Yes, I want to help Holly and everyone else in need, on a worldwide basis if possible. I am a "good person," as my demented charges at the nursing home agree, but maybe I'm also just sick of my suddenly acquired insignificance. Maybe I want to "be somebody," as Jesse Jackson likes to say, somebody generous, competent, brave, and perhaps, above all, noticeable.

Maids, as an occupational group, are not visible, and when we are seen we are often sorry for it.[5] On the way to the Martha Stewart–ish place, when Holly and Marge were complaining about her haughtiness in a past encounter, I had ventured to ask why so many of the owners seem hostile or contemptuous toward us. "They think we're stupid," was Holly's answer. "They think we have nothing better to do with our time." Marge too looked suddenly sober. "We're nothing to these people," she said. "We're just maids." Nor are we much of anything to anyone else. Even convenience store clerks, who are $6-an-hour gals themselves, seem to look down on us. In Key West, my waitress's polo shirt was always a conversation starter: "You at Jerry's?" a clerk might ask. "I used to work at the waffle place just up the boulevard from there." But a maid's uniform has the opposite effect. At one place where we stopped for refreshments, an actual diner with a counter, I tried to order iced tea to take out, but the waitress just kept standing there chatting with a coworker, ignoring my "Excuse me's." Then there's the supermarket. I used to stop on my way home from work, but I couldn't take the stares, which are easily translatable into: What are *you* doing here? And, No wonder she's poor, she's got a beer in her shopping cart! True, I don't look so good by the end of the day and probably smell like eau de toilet and sweat, but it's the brilliant green-and-yellow uniform that gives me away, like prison clothes on a fugitive. Maybe, it occurs to me, I'm getting a tiny glimpse of what it would be like to be black.

And look at me now, sitting on a curb at a gas station, puffing into the endless slow rain, so sweat-soaked already that it doesn't matter. Things don't get any more squalid than this, is my thought. But they can—they can!—and they

---

[5] This invisibility persists at the macroscopic level. The Census Bureau reports that there were 550,000 domestic workers in 1998, up 10 percent since 1996, but this may be a considerable underestimate, since so much of the servant economy is still underground, or at least very low to the ground, where few data collectors ever venture. In 1993, for example, the year when Zoë Baird lost her chance to be attorney general for paying her undocumented nanny off the books, it was estimated that fewer than 10 percent of those Americans who paid a house-cleaner more than $1,000 a year reported these payments to the IRS. Sociologist Mary Romero offers an example of how severe the undercounting can be: the 1980 census found only 1,063 "private household workers" in El Paso, although at the same time that city's Department of Planning, Research, and Development estimated their numbers at 13,400 and local bus drivers estimated that half of the 28,300 bus trips taken daily were taken by maids going to and returning from work (*Maid in the U.S.A.*, p. 92). The honesty of employers has increased since the Baird scandal, but most experts believe that household workers remain largely uncounted and invisible to the larger economy.

do. At the next house, I am getting my toilet brush out of its Ziploc bag when the liquid that's been accumulating in the bag all day spills on my foot—100 percent pure toilet juice leaking through the laces and onto my sock. In ordinary life, if someone were to, say, piss on your foot, you'd probably strip off the shoe and the sock and throw them away. But these are the only shoes I have. There's nothing to do but try to ignore the nasty stuff soaking my foot and, as Ted exhorts us, work through it. ■

Working with the Text

1. Based on Ehrenreich's written testimony, prepare a report describing the main problems faced by the women working for "The Maids" and suggesting your ideas for improving their working conditions. Different groups in the class might prepare reports for different audiences: for the management of "The Maids"; for the employees of "The Maids"; for a government committee looking into workplace conditions of domestic workers; for the audience of a television news program; and so on.

2. Although a member of the professional middle class herself, Ehrenreich expresses anger toward some of the middle-class homeowners whose houses she is cleaning. To what extent did you share or not share her anger? What lesson do you think Ehrenreich would want one of these homeowners to take away from her book?

3. Although operating "undercover" as an investigative reporter (Ehrenreich revealed her project to her coworkers at the end of each of her jobs), Ehrenreich also wants to help her coworkers beyond reporting on their lives and making them more visible. She expresses frustration with her efforts and herself after her attempts to come to Holly's aid result in damaging one of the homes they are cleaning. In questioning her own motives, she reports, "I am a 'good person,' as my demented charges at the nursing home agree, but maybe I'm also just sick of my suddenly acquired insignificance." How do you understand Ehrenreich's motives? Write her a letter of advice explaining how you think she should have handled the situation with Holly.

4. In response to a question from Ehrenreich, Holly offers her own analysis of social class: "'If we're cleaning their house, they're wealthy.'" Explore your own reactions to Holly's comment by elaborating on her definition of "wealthy" in ways you think she would agree with. How do you think the homeowners she includes in that description would react?

Working with Connections

1. Explore the Justice for Janitors web site to look for issues raised by Ehrenreich. What strategies is the Justice for Janitors using to address these issues? Are there issues raised by Ehrenreich that you do not see addressed in the Justice for Janitors web site, and vice versa?

2. The work Ehrenreich does here relates to divisions of labor based not only on class but on gender as well, from the fact that professional house cleaning services mainly employ women to the name of the company ("The Maids") to Ehrenreich's reporting no encounters or supervision from male members of the households she works for (so that hiring a housecleaning service itself seems to be "women's work.") Use information from Alice Kessler-Harris's *Women Have Always Worked* (in Chapter 5, Work and Family) as well as the long footnote Ehrenreich includes to construct your own argument about what Ehrenreich's experiences can tell us about the current status of women in the workforce.

BERTOLT BRECHT
Questions from a Worker Who Reads ■

Bertolt Brecht was born in Germany in 1898 and became one of the twentieth century's most famous and influential playwrights and theater theorists. Brecht also wrote poems, essays, and song lyrics, and all of his work was grounded in his radical political beliefs and his desire to use art as a means of combating economic inequality and social injustice. He fled Nazi Germany in 1933, eventually moving to the United States in 1941. He subsequently left the United States in 1947 under attack for his radical political views, and finally returned to Germany where he died in Berlin in 1956.

In "Questions from a Worker Who Reads," Brecht both challenges the stereotype that working-class people do not read or think and asks us to consider whose accomplishments are left out of our history books.

Who built Thebes of the seven gates?
In the books you will find the name of kings.
Did the kings haul up the lumps of rock?
And Babylon, many times demolished.
Who raised it up so many times? In what houses
Of gold-glittering Lima did the builders live?
Where, the evening that the Wall of China was finished

Did the masons go? Great Rome
Is full of triumphal arches. Who erected them? Over whom
Did the Caesars triumph? Had Byzantium, much praised in song,
Only palaces for its inhabitants? Even in fabled Atlantis
The night the ocean engulfed it
The drowning still bawled for their slaves.

The young Alexander conquered India.
Was he alone?
Caesar beat the Gauls.
Did he not have even a cook with him?
Philip of Spain wept when his armada
Went down. Was he the only one to weep?
Frederick the Second won the Seven Years' War. Who
Else won it?

Every page a victory.
Who cooked the feast for the victors?
Every ten years a great man.
Who paid the bill?

So many reports.
So many questions. ■

Working with the Text

1. Brecht's poem is composed of a series of rhetorical questions, or
   questions that imply their own answers. What answers does
   Brecht assume we will understand in his poem? How could you
   form them into a coherent statement about the relationships
   among work, social class, and how history is written?

2. How do you understand the title of the poem, especially the reference to a "worker who reads"? How ironic or sarcastic do you
   see Brecht as being in this description? Who do you think he
   includes and excludes in his category of "worker" and why?
   What do you think he is saying about the reading habits of workers, and what of the assumptions made by others of those they
   think of as "workers"? In a way, these questions are all about
   audience. Who do you think Brecht sees as his potential readers?
   Who might be in on the joke, and whom do you think is meant to
   be criticized? How do you see yourself in relation to the audience
   for the poem?

3. Choose a spectacular achievement other than one mentioned in "Questions for a Worker Who Reads" and write your own version of the poem. This achievement could be a historical event (a war, for example, or the passing of an important law), an engineering feat (the construction and naming of an important building, or the creation of the "information superhighway," for example), or an impressive accomplishment (for example, landing a person on the moon or winning a sports championship). If you want, you could choose an event or accomplishment of international or national significance, or one close to home or important mainly in your community. When you have finished, share your poem with the class and reflect on how the process of writing the poem caused you to examine how work is organized and how credit is given.

Working with Connections

1. Brecht's poem asks you to think about the relationship between ideas about work, literacy, and education. What connections can you see between these ideas in "Questions for a Worker Who Reads" and the kinds of school curricula described in "Social Class and the Hidden Curriculum of Work" (from Chapter 3, Education and Work/Education as Work)?

2. Which of the other authors in this chapter do you think of as fitting Brecht's reference to a "worker who reads"? Write about why you think so and speculate about what that writer would think about Brecht's poem.

Poetry Inspired by the Triangle Shirtwaist Company Fire

On March 25, 1911, a fire broke out on the eighth, ninth, and tenth floors of a building occupied by the Triangle Shirtwaist Company in New York City. By the time the fire was over, 146 workers—126 women and 20 men—had died. The average age of the victims was nineteen. Many perished in the fire, while dozens of others leapt to their deaths in a desperate attempt to escape the blaze.

Like many clothing makers of the time, the Triangle Shirtwaist Company employed hundreds of garment workers, mostly women, many from immigrant families struggling to survive in turn-of-the-

century New York. They worked in rooms with poor ventilation and lighting and inadequate safety features. Only one year before the fire, the Triangle Shirtwaist Company had been one of the targets of a city-wide strike by garment workers for better wages and working conditions. While the workers at Triangle won some small pay increases, the company successfully resisted efforts to make the workshop safer.

At the Triangle Shirtwaist Company, there were no sprinkler systems or fire drills, and the heavy metal doors opened inward. One door was kept locked, supposedly to prevent theft on the part of the workers. New York City Fire Department ladders and hoses could only reach the seventh floors of buildings. The owners of the Triangle Shirtwaist Company were eventually brought to trial because of these conditions but were acquitted of wrongdoing by jurors who identified more with these businessmen than the young immigrant women who died in the fire. Nevertheless, the Triangle Shirtwaist Fire became a watershed in the history of workers' rights and the labor movement. Although sometimes omitted from history textbooks, memories of the fire have survived both through the efforts of labor historians and the oral and literary traditions of the descendants of the Triangle victims.

The following poems represent contemporary responses to the Triangle Fire. The first text, however, is a 1911 newspaper account of the fire from the New York Call, a socialist newspaper dedicated to labor issues. This piece provides both firsthand testimony about the fire and an example of the journalistic writing of the time, when many newspapers still openly proclaimed their political orientations and journalists strove for what we might see today as "literary" effects in an attempt to move their readers. The story is followed by poems from contemporary poets written in response to the fire. These writers use their poetry to preserve memory of the fire, pay tribute to the workers who died there, and explore the ways we can use history as a means to think about the present and the future.

ALLEN, CARRIE W. ■

Triangle Shop Like Other Hell-Holes, from *The New York Call,* Tuesday, March 28, 1911

"It's horrible for women to meet such a fate as that. I've done this work as special police all these years just to keep my girl from going into such a hell-hole of a factory as that," the man in the cadet-blue uniform said.

"When the shirtwaist girls were on strike, did you arrest them?" a woman asked. "Of course I did. I am hired to protect the property of the people who pay me, and when there is a strike it's my duty to arrest the strikers. I don't like it, but it's only by doing this work that I have been able to educate my girl and give her a chance," the special officer replied.

As he spoke, a hideous little bundle was slowly lowered from a window on the ninth floor of what had been the scab shop of the Triangle Waist Company. It swirled and flapped grotesquely in the wind as it made its lonely journey to the street.

On the Washington place side, where months before shirtwaist girls had tramped wearily back and forth picketing the Triangle, dead girls with broken bodies and staring eyes lay in crumpled heaps upon the pavement.

The pickets had been clubbed and arrested by the New York police. Now the bluecoats helped the firemen bear the dead girls across the street, laying the little pitiful bodies in the rude brown coffins brought to receive them.

"Tenderness for the dead, brutality for the living," the woman thought.

Huge searchlights cast their white rays into every nook and corner of the desolated building which a few hours before had teemed with the activity and life of hundreds of girls.

High up on the corner "The Triangle" blazed forth in shining letters above the three-sided trade mark of the waist company.

BUNDLES OF THE DEAD

On the eighth and ninth floors the firemen went about their ghastly work of sorting out the dead girls from the heaps of twisted metal which marked where the rows of machines had been.

One by one the bundles were put over the window ledges and started on their journey in the street, casting fantastic shadows as they swirled about, and traveled slowly down.

One—a very little one—made its way falteringly and reluctantly, clinging to each ledge and projection as if in fear. Ever and anon, as the feet tarried on the ledge, the specter face would turn upward as if to seek the answer to the tragedy in the cold, black sky overhead. Then limply falling away and spinning round and round, it kept up a goblin dance as it went down, down, down, and finally lay in eternal quiet upon the ground.

As the woman watched the little figure's shadowy dance, everything was blotted out, except the triangle and the little specter dangling in the air.

Upon the three sides of the triangle these words blazed forth: Greed, Avarice, Profit, and all the center was made up of human bones and skulls.

The triangle, symbol of the profit system, was the answer to the little questioning specter dangling helplessly in the air.

HELL HOLES ALL

As they bore the little incinerated girl across the street, the special officer brushed away a tear and said "God! What hell holes these factories are. Hundreds more just like this. I'm glad I've saved my girl from going into a hell hole like that."

Tomorrow, the next day, and perhaps the next, meetings will be held, resolutions passed, and investigations made. Then the murderers will be exonerated, and the public will be calmly told that no person is to blame, that the fault lies with the law.

The public will lose interest, all the good people will return whence they came and pursue the even tenor of their ways conscious of duty well done. No real help will come to the workers from above, and so far as uptown New York is concerned, the tragedy will go on.

It is up to the working class to prove that they are not a spineless, shapeless mass, but a living, breathing force, demanding that Blanck & Harris, the proprietors of the Triangle, shall be held responsible for the death of their comrades. It is up to the working class to see that this pair, who save their worthless lives, shall not be whitewashed, but shall be brought to account for the scores of shirtwaist girls for whose lives they had no care.

This tragedy will not be in vain if the workers of this city are aroused to an understanding of their class interests, and will use their collective strength not only to wipe out the death traps of this city, but to go steadily on to their greater work of wiping out the profit system, which saps the vitality from the workers, and annually exacts a heavy toll of human life.

Havdallah
Mary Fell

This is the great divide
by which God split
the world:
on the Sabbath side
he granted rest,
eternal toiling
on the workday side.

But even one
revolution of the world
is an empty promise
where bosses
where bills to pay
respect no heavenly bargains.
Until each day is ours

let us pour
darkness in a dish
and set it on fire,
bless those who labor
as we pray, praise God
his holy name,
strike for the rest.

Sister in the Flames
Carol Tarlen

Sister
of the flames
take my hand
I will hold you in the cradle
of my billowing skirt
in the ache of my shoulders
the center of my palm
our sisters already dance
on the sidewalk nine
floors below the fire
is leaping through my hair
the air will lick our thighs
Sister together now fly
the sky is an unlocked door
and the machines are burning

from Rituals of Spring
Safiya Henderson-Holmes

colors of spring
pale blues, pale pinks, yellows, magentas, lavender, peach,

secret thoughts of spring
falling in love under a full moon, forever young
with money enough to buy a flower or two,
time enough to smell it
yes, from bareness to fullness a flower will bloom
anytime, everytime spring enters a room
and here, near these machines, hundreds of flowering
girls

shirtwaist factory room 1911
crowded, hard, fast, too fast, closed windows,
locked doors, smell of piss, of sweat,
of wishes being cut to bits,
needle stabs, electric shocks, miscarriages over silk,
fading paisley, fading magenta,
falling in love will get you fired, forever old,
never fast enough, buying flowers is wasteful
so hurry, hurry, grind your teeth and soul
six dollars a week send to grandfather,
four dollars a week send to aunt ruth, sleep over the
machine and you're done for, way before you open your

eyes ma'am, madam, miss, mrs. mother, girlie
hundreds of flowering green spring girls in rows
waiting with needles in hand for spring to show

Sear
Chris Llewellyn

July 1982
Always adding. Revising this manuscript.
I plant *direct quotations* on the page,
arranging line-breaks, versification.

Newspaper files: Frances Perkins speaks
from the street, *I felt I must sear it
not only on my mind but on my heart
forever.* One mother, *When will it be
safe to earn our bread?* Their words.
Yet some call that schmaltz, soap-opera

Sentiment, Victorian melodrama. Riding
in the subway, smoke fizzes in my ears and
in my room, electric heater coils glow
Cs and Os in the box. To write about *them*
yet not interfere, although I'm told
a poet's task is to create a little world.

A testimony: Two tried to say together
on the ledge, but one suddenly twisted
and plunged, a burning bundle. The other
looked ahead, arms straight out, speaking
and shouting *as if addressing an invisible
audience.* She gestured an embrace then

Jumped. Her name was Celia
Weintraub. She lived
on Henry Street. ■

Working with the Text

1. Choose and write about the poem that creates the biggest
   impression on you in relation to the Triangle Shirtwaist factory
   fire. What specifically makes this poem so effective for you?
   Which lines or images make the biggest impact and why?

2. Read the poems before doing further research on the fire. Then visit the excellent web site at Cornell University dedicated to the fire <http://www.ilr.cornell.edu/trianglefire/> to learn more about the historical event. Now reread the poems and write about how your experience of the poems changed after doing further research about the fire. More theoretically, reflect on the various strengths and uses of different types of writing—nonfiction academic history writing, journalism, poetry—in conveying a sense of and ideas about a historical event.

3. While poems are different from essays, they still can express a point of view, make an argument, and work to persuade a reader. Choose one of the poems and write about what kind of argument the poem is making about the fire and how the poet conveys this argument or point of view.

Working with Connections

1. Do research into a contemporary industrial tragedy, such as the Thailand toy factory fire discussed in the selection from William Greider's One World Ready or Not (in Chapter 8, Work in the Global Economy). Based on your research and your understanding of the Triangle Shirtwaist factory fire, draw conclusions about the similarities and differences of the causes of these fires. How did people from labor organizers to factory owners argue about the Triangle fire? How do these arguments relate to arguments about the contemporary tragedy?

2. Based on your research in the previous question, write your own poetry expressing your feelings, ideas, and responses to the modern tragedy.

Media Images

The Phoenix Companies, Inc. Advertisement from the *New York Times Sunday Magazine*

The Phoenix Companies, Inc. provides affluent individuals and families with products and services designed to help them preserve, increase, and pass along through inheritance their wealth. Some of these products and services include life insurance, annuities, trust funds, and investment advice. This ad, featuring their slogan, "Money. It's Just Not What It Used to Be," appeared in the Sunday New York Times Magazine in early 2003. As with all advertising, the purpose is both to gain more clients and to promote the image of The Phoenix Companies, Inc. to the magazine's readership in general. Before studying the ad in detail, consider first what some of the challenges might be in designing an ad aimed primarily at the needs and problems of wealthy people but that will be seen by a more general audience. Are there any attitudes or values they might want to appeal to? Any they might want to avoid?

As you then read and examine the ad, pay close attention to your own reactions. Do you feel included or excluded from the target audience? Does it make you more or less sympathetic to the "accumulation, preservation and transfer needs" of the target audience, and how do you think your reactions fit into the overall rhetorical strategy of the ad campaign?

Devoted children (Share of estate: 33%)
Delighted Alma Mater (Share of estate: 67%)
Charity still begins at home, but philanthropy goes far beyond it. That's why our wealth management products and services
Money. It's just not what it used to be.
help meet the accumulation, preservation and transfer needs of today's most successful people.
Talk to your financial advisor about Phoenix.
PHOENIX WEALTH MANAGEMENT
LIFE • ANNUITIES • INVESTMENTS
PhoenixWealthManagement.com

Working with the Text

1. Although The Phoenix Companies, Inc. provides a wide range of investment and other financial products and services, the ad focuses primarily on two issues: passing wealth along to one's children and contributing to charity. Why might these two issues represent a good rhetorical strategy for the ad? How does it contribute to or counteract beliefs about the wealthy? What were your own reactions?

2. Children are often featured in advertisements, and The Phoenix Companies, Inc. ad is no exception. How do you read the visual images of the three children in this ad? What does their clothing represent? Where do you think the ad is set? An expensive ad such as this is very carefully assembled, so no detail is too small to notice and comment on, such as the teddy bear held by the girl on the left, or the necklaces just visible underneath the boy's shirt and tie. What messages do you think they are intended to send and how successful did you find them?

3. Write about in what ways you do or do not find yourself part of the intended audience for the ad. What seems most strange, and what most familiar? In what ways do the images in the ad represent a life to aspire to? As an alternative exercise, write a letter to The Phoenix Companies, Inc., expressing your opinion of the ad, exchange letters in class, and try writing a reply to the letter you receive as you think The Phoenix Companies, Inc. might.

Working with Connections

1. In what ways does this ad fit in with or suggest we need to modify Gregory Mantsios's argument in "Media Magic" about how the media work to make class invisible? Does the fact that the ad openly addresses itself to the wealthy make us more or less aware of class differences and inequality?

2. Working in groups, create a "response" ad to this one targeted at the financial and economic concerns of a different class. Decide what the goal of your response will be in relation to the original ad—critical, sarcastic, sympathetic, corrective—who your target audience will be, what kinds of language use to imitate, parody, or change from the original, and what you want your ad to accomplish.

THE WORK OF WRITING/WRITING AS WORK

Many of the writers in this chapter discuss not only the difficulties involved in defining social classes but also the resistance to talking about social class at all in American society. Yet every writer in this chapter, whether academics, reporters, novelists, poets, or memoirists, makes the case that understanding social class and the division of labor is critical to understanding how work is organized in the United States and how power and authority, opportunity and advantage, are distributed. As Jean Anyon argues (in "Social Class and the Hidden Curriculum of Work" in Chapter 3, Education and Work/Education as Work), while school curricula may reflect the realities of social class, they may not always address the topic openly. A students and writers studying the issue of social class, you can bring what you have learned about this issue a well as your rhetorical skills to bear on the question of how best to introduce the subject of social class into school.

1. Working in conjunction with local primary and/or secondary school teachers, develop materials for a unit on social class appropriate to a particular grade level. As a preliminary activity, use writing to reflect on whether and how you have learned about social class in your own education history. How do you think this education has related to your own class identify, as you understand it? Investigate the demographics of the school with which you will be working. How would you describe the class identitries of the students and their families? What is a daily class like in the school?

   Next, identify the specific learning objectives and experiences you want students to have. What key concepts do you want students of this particular age to understand and why? What materials and activities would help students make a lasting connection to the issues of social class? What historical figures and issues do you want to introduce them to? As you work, always keep in mind the sensitivity to the language of social class discussed in this chapter, especially the weight given to terms such as *higher* or *lower*. How can you help students develop an understanding of class without feeling stigmatized or without stigmatizing others?

   Finally, work on processing your experience by writing about what developing this unit has taught you about the issues of social class.

2. As a more focused project, use your experiences working with the essay by Gregory Mantsios, the Justice for Janitors web site, the advertisement for The Phoenix Companies, Inc., and other media sources to develop a unit on how to look for class issues in the mass media. Again, you will need to consider the age, development, and demographic make-up of the students with whom you will be working.

CHAPTER 5

Work and Family

F or most of human history, family has been the center of work, and for billions of people around the world, it remains so today. Whether we talk about hunter/gatherer cultures, traditional small farming societies, or nomadic peoples, the family has been the focus of productive, economic, and social activity. Family ties and relationships have been the basis of how human societies were and are organized for thousands of years, and the idea of family has involved extended and complex patterns of kinship and affiliation. Traditionally, to know your place in the family system has been to know your place in the world, including the working world.

In industrialized societies like the United States, however, the relationship between work and family has been divided and subdivided over the last 200 years. Rather than extended kinship systems, for many Americans the term *family* means what has come to be called the nuclear family, consisting primarily of two parents and their children. Even though only about 25 percent of Americans actually live in nuclear families like this, the idea of the nuclear family still dominates much of our thinking about family. Historians have suggested that such a compact family unit developed in tandem with an economy built on the division of labor and the need to be able to move workers quickly from region to region of the country when needed.

The major impact, though, of industrialized and factory-based work has been to separate the workplace from the home, a separation reflected in our everyday language practices. We commonly speak of "going to work," and when we ask people, "Where do you work?" we see that as a separate question from "Where do you live?" We talk about the need to balance work and family life and often see these two areas of our lives as being in conflict with each other. Even though work is done both in the home and "on the job" (another phrase expressing the separation of work and family), we usually mean the latter when asking about what someone does "for a living."

Historically, the consequences of this separation and the potential conflict between home and work have been and continue to be experienced most strongly by women. When the contemporary feminist movement arose in the late 1960s and early 1970s, it pointed out that in many ways this historical separation of the workplace and the home made invisible the real work that many women did. "Working" had come to mean only "work for pay," and people (primarily women) who "took care" of the home were seen as "not working." As more and more women have entered the for-pay workforce over the last thirty years, however, the potential conflicts inherent in our working lives have gained increasing national attention, as we discuss and argue about the needs to nurture children and create strong family bonds but also make a living and develop meaningful careers.

These conflicts are by no means only issues for women, though, because the same feminist movement that criticized the denigration of housework also raised important questions about the associations we make between gender and work, between "women's work" and "men's work," and between the work of mothers and fathers. If women pursuing careers in the business world caused society to consider the impossible time demands made by our jobs and our families, it also suggested we rethink the costs of the traditionally male pattern of devoting a life to the workplace while shortchanging family life. The question of gender and work also makes us rethink how traditional assumptions and ideas might limit our sense of possibility and individual fulfillment.

This chapter asks you to use writing to explore these and other issues related to work and family. Before you begin working with the texts included here, spend some time considering the following questions:

1. How do you personally define "family"? How broad a range of living arrangements and possibilities do you include in your definition and why? Who might disagree with you and why?

2. If you have come to college directly or almost directly from high school, what are your personal goals for a mix of family and work life? What potential challenges or difficulties do you anticipate? How have your goals been influenced by the relationship between work and home life in your own family? Do you hope to follow in your family's footsteps, or do you want something different for yourself?

3. If you are returning to college after time away from school, how have you experienced the relationship between work and family life? What are your own plans for the future? How does returning to college relate to your experience and your hopes for work and family life?

4. Explore the changing definitions of "men's" and "women's" work. Working in groups, brainstorm what types of work you think have been traditionally associated with these terms and how you think these terms operate now. Use your findings to reflect on your

own ideas and values about this subject. Write about whether you think we should or shouldn't maintain distinctions of work based on gender. How do you think an ideal society would view the relationship between work and gender? Reconvene in groups to discuss the range of opinions you find in your class on this subject. Where do you find points of agreement and contention?

Foundational Readings

ALICE KESSLER-HARRIS
■

From *Women Have Always Worked*
The Meaning of Women's Work

How have we developed our ideas about the relationship between home and work life? Where did our common beliefs and stereotypes about gender and work originate? These are some of the key questions historian Alice Kessler-Harris has addressed throughout her career in books such as Out to Work: A History of Wage-Earning Women in the United States *and* Women Have Always Worked, *from which this excerpt is taken. In the chapter reprinted here, Kessler-Harris describes the dramatic changes in the working lives of the common peoples of Europe, the American colonies, and later the United States from the sixteenth through the early twentieth centuries, changes that transformed these societies from primarily agricultural to the industrialized, compartmentalized world we know today. In particular, she focuses on how notions of "men's" and "women's" work developed and evolved during this time, and she reflects on the complex effects, both negative and positive, these changes had on the lives of women.*

Alice Kessler-Harris received her Ph.D. from Rutgers University and is currently R. Gordon Hoxie Professor of American History at Columbia University.

Dotha Bushnell lived on a Connecticut farm in the early 1800s, among the last of generations of American women who worked in households that produced all of the necessities of survival. Her son, Horace, lamenting the disappearing past, wept over the "frugal, faithful, pious housewife" who lived in an age when "the house was a factory on the farm; the farm a grower and producer for the house." All of a household's members were harnessed together "into the producing process, young, old, male and female, from the boy that rode the plough horse to the grandmother knitting under her spectacles."

Nobody then or now could wonder if Dotha Bushnell worked. In preindustrial societies, nearly everybody worked, and almost nobody worked for wages. But with industrialization, the harness yoking household members together loosened. As production began to move out of the household into factories, offices, and stores, those who got paid for the new jobs were clearly workers. At the same time, the kinds of work women did at home changed dramatically. The remaining tasks of the household, such as caring for children, food preparation, cleaning, and laundering, were not so clearly defined as work. In separating the job necessary to maintain the household from the job done for pay, the industrial revolution effected not only a shift in the tasks assigned to workers of either sex, but a shift in perceptions of what constituted work. Women who maintained the home and did not collect wages were no longer considered workers. Their home roles appeared as something other than work.

Sharp distinctions in male and female jobs contrast with the preindustrial period when both men and women did what could, in one sense, be called domestic work. As servants, slaves, or family members, their tasks revolved around the household that constituted the center of production. Among family members, women as well as men derived identity, self-esteem, and a sense of order from their household places. For slaves and servants, whose work lives centered in other people's families, household tasks were nevertheless the source of survival. For the most part, the core family and its extended members consumed the goods and food produced in this unit, trading what little there was left to make up for shortages.

There seems to have been a rhythm to the work performed in this preindustrial environment, in harmony with the seasons in the countryside and with family needs in both town and country. By the sixteenth century, much of Europe had what we would now call an unemployment problem: too many workers and too few jobs. To feed, clothe, and shelter the population at minimal levels required fewer workers than the numbers of people available. As a result, work was spread out. The evidence suggests that traditional role divisions, which assigned to women internal household tasks and care of gardens, dairies, and domestic animals, allowed men a good deal more freedom than their wives. Men, more than women, benefited from a growing labor surplus. Women's tasks tended to be less seasonal and more regular. Over the span of a year, men had less onerous regular responsibility.

The transition from this relatively self-sufficient domestic economy to dependence on trade took hundreds of years and developed at different speeds in different areas. The first inroads occurred when the commercial revolution of the thirteenth century created a market for manufactured goods and encouraged craftsmen and their families to concentrate their energies on producing for cash. These artisan families, who had previously made and sold their own products, began to produce for merchants who bought in bulk and sold to distant places. In these family industries, women, who were excluded from formal apprenticeships, could nevertheless become skilled in crafts. And they were partners in every other sense of the word. In most places the law acknowledged a wife's right to the business if a husband died. The garden plot still produced food supplies, and wives and widows supervised and trained young unmarried women to perform household work. If labor within these artisan families seemed relatively balanced, it was far from idyllic. Work within the household, in the shop, and on the farm was always hard. Poor crop yields or sickness could bring even comfortable households to the edge of starvation.

As trade developed in the seventeenth and eighteenth centuries, however, a subtle change came over family industry. Merchants, who had at first been content to take what was available and sell it, soon began to demand products made to their own specifications. Instead of gathering the products of local artisans, they "put out" their own orders to cottages throughout the countryside. Workers lost control over what they made. They still retained control over their time. People who worked in their own cottages would not be rushed. They did more or less work as other tasks called, and sometimes they wasted materials. As orders increased, however, merchants required faster and more reliable production. Effective supervision of workers could be obtained only if the labor force were concentrated in one place. And toward the end of the eighteenth century, the development of steam-powered machinery required a labor force able to move where the machines were, adding urgency to the demand for a factory work force.

Slowly and painfully the laboring poor were persuaded to give up their own loosely jointed and self-imposed definitions of work. In sixteenth- and seventeenth-century England, land that had been held in common for generations, as well as some that had traditionally been leased by families, was taken over by large landowners for their own use. This process, called enclosure, meant that some farm families were forcibly ejected while others no longer had common pasture. Ultimately, they could not survive on the land. Driving men, women, and children from farms made them available for work in towns. But they were reluctant workers. Employers could persuade them to show up for work regularly only by holding back wages or tying them to contracts that ran for as long as twenty-one years. Sometimes employers beat inattentive workers, especially children. Frequently the state passed laws to help employers create a reliable work force. In England and France, harsh laws against vagrancy forced people to take jobs against their own inclinations. Those who would not submit might be branded or jailed and later deported to colonies in far-off places.

WORK IN THE COLONIES

As in the old world, workers in the colonies did not easily submit to the idea of working by someone else's rhythms. In early Virginia this proved to be a special problem. Historian Edmund Morgan describes how Virginia's first colonists starved rather than bow to what they saw as the harsh discipline of the Virginia Company. They chose to work only six to eight hours a day, spending the rest of their time "bowling in the streets." These work patterns, reminiscent of English habits, lasted until the Virginia Company imposed a quasi-military regime.

The northern colonists required less pressure. Because their land was not owned by an outside company, and because many of them had come to America for common religious reasons, most early New Englanders shared an incentive to work. Puritan religion equated hard work with godliness, and salvation with the visible demonstration of God's bounty, so New England colonists drove themselves to accumulate earthly goods. Material reality enforced religious injunction. Unlike Virginia settlers, the Plymouth and Massachusetts Bay colonists had no company in England to call on for supplies in their early years. Throughout the colonial period, they suffered from severe labor shortages which only their own efforts could offset. And lacking appropriate raw materials to trade with England, they relied far more on homespun yarn and hand-woven fabrics than the southern colonies, which quickly developed tobacco and hemp as resources for trading.

Since all the colonies relied more or less on household production, women's work was necessary and recognized. Colonies initially gave plots of land to settlers and their families. In Maryland and South Carolina, women who were heads of families got allotments equal to those of men. For a few brief years, Salem gave "maid lots" to unmarried women, and Pennsylvania granted them seventy-five acres each. But opposition to unmarried women holding land developed early. Historian Julia Spruill cites a bill passed by the Maryland Assembly in 1634, and then vetoed by the proprietor. The legislators would have decreed of an unmarried woman that "unlesse she marry within seven years after land shall fall to hir, she must either dispose away of hir land, or else she shall forfeit it to the next of kinne, and if she have but one Mannor, whereas she cannot alienate it, it is gonne unless she git a husband."

Without land, women had no source of sustenance except employment or marriage. Fearful that such women would become dependent, the colonists quickly passed laws that bound people who had no visible means of support out to work. Women, it was thought, were especially prone to vice and immorality, and colonies as different as Massachusetts and Virginia paid special attention to those women who, having no homes in the conventional sense, might fall into bad habits. Harsh economic considerations undoubtedly motivated the colonists. Since pregnancy was a likely result of immorality, and there were few jobs for unwed mothers with small children, such women were likely to need public relief. Afraid of the potential costs, communities were especially careful to refuse female transients permission to settle.

The assumption that women could and should participate in the production of necessary goods persisted well into the eighteenth century, and in many areas even later. When the colonists became concerned about having adequate supplies of cloth and yarn in the revolutionary period, they appealed to women's patriotic sentiments to increase supplies. George Washington wrote to his friend General Lafayette that he would not force the introduction of manufactures to the prejudice of agriculture. But, he added, "I conceive much might be done in the way of women, children, and others without taking one really necessary hand from tilling the earth."

In contrast to much of Europe, where the imposition of work discipline required breaking old habits, in America colonists had already accepted an emphasis on work and industry before the onset of industrialization. This eased the task of disciplining a labor force for factory work. Where the Puritans had seen material prosperity as a demonstration of God's grace, the people of the early nineteenth century saw it as a manifestation of self-control and right living. Religious injunction was thus supplemented by new ideas of individualism, which made each person accountable for his or her success. Egalitarian notions that had emerged in the revolutionary period enhanced these ideas. Theoretically, at least, success was now plausible for even the lowliest people, slaves, people of color, and women excepted. Benjamin Franklin, who saw wealth as its own reward, urged people to depend "chiefly on two words: industry and frugality; that is waste neither time nor money, but make the best of both."

THE SUCCESS ETHIC

The emphasis on individual achievement inherent in an ideology that glorified success threatened to eliminate entirely the older notion that individual well-being was intimately bound to the well-being of the community. It was one thing to spin and weave for the public good—and to reap material rewards incidentally. It was quite another to work for others for the sake of their profit alone. By the time Andrew Jackson became president of the United States in 1829, it seemed clear that those workers who could afford to own a small shop or a piece of land, quickly rejected the routinization of the factory for a promised independence.

White American workers had some advantages over workers in older European societies. Relatively cheap, available land encouraged free workers to save money and move west. Employers were willing to let them go since a steady influx of immigrants replaced them. For these workers, the promise of independence and of upward mobility provided incentives to work hard. Yet these incentives did not always produce the kind of work force employers felt they needed.

To integrate native- and foreign-born peasants, farmers, skilled artisans, and day laborers into a changing society required, as historian Herbert Gutman has pointed out, a continual process of acculturation. Each generation had to be taught to shed its old patterns and habits and to adopt those required of steady routine workers. To accomplish this, factory owners quickly resorted to old-country methods of discipline. Factories might be located in idyllic country settings, like Dover, New Hampshire, or North Andover, Massachusetts, but their morning and evening bells called people to work with the same insistence as those in any of Manchester, England's satanic mills. Fines and locked gates forced workers to adhere to the factory rules. To obtain jobs, workers frequently had to agree to serve at least one year or to forfeit two weeks of wages. Employers ruthlessly blacklisted those of whom they disapproved. Bonuses went to those who showed up regularly for work and did not drink. Six-day work weeks protected workers against the "temptations" of leisure, and manufacturers even tried to regulate how time was spent on the seventh day.

The most extreme coercion occurred within slavery. In the South, employers occasionally offered slaves the chance to purchase their freedom by dint of learning a skilled craft. Men might become blacksmiths or carpenters, while women might learn fancy sewing or hire themselves out as cooks. More often, however, slaves got no reward for hard work, and extreme punishment for slacking off. The cruelty of many masters measures the resistance slaves demonstrated to their lives of toiling for others.

Free white Americans believed strongly enough in the work ethic and in the possibilities for success to create the institutional support systems needed to sustain them. By the 1830s, a number of states funded public elementary school systems. Working men's groups, as well as social reformers, advocated free schools on the grounds that they would help educate the populace to the high levels demanded by democratic government. Designed to teach basic literacy and elementary arithmetic, the schools also instilled regular habits, cleanliness, and attention to detail: all mechanisms for creating an efficient work force. By and large, instruction was by drill and by rote. Most public schools soon aimed to reproduce the situation children would face at work. Teachers enforced discipline by shame, and children, according to historian Michael Katz, were "programmed from an early age to compete with one another." By teaching competition and individualism, the schools helped ensure that children of working people "would not grow up to form a cohesive and threatening class force."

Like schools, Protestant churches exalted success. For them it offered evidence of morality. In the words of one famous preacher, "No man in this land suffers from poverty unless it be more than his fault—unless it be his *sin*." Some clerics justified low wages and poverty as necessary to strengthen character. They offered solace in the form of a better world to come. As late as 1877, Henry Ward Beecher, perhaps the nation's best-known preacher, earned the undying enmity of the labor movement when he thundered his opposition to the railroad strikes of that year. Workers should bear their poverty more nobly, he argued. After all, "is not a dollar a day enough to buy bread with? Water costs nothing, and a man who cannot live on bread is not fit to live." The legal system confirmed what ideology left undone. It criminalized "conspiracies" among workers who formed trade unions to improve their bargaining power and threatened jail for the debtor and starvation for those who did not succeed in the competitive struggle.

Few people escaped the harsh constraints of working life. Increasingly, expectations of long days and minimal wages drove out notions of humane work. Time after work, or leisure time, became the pleasurable moments in individual lives. Competition replaced notions of cooperative work. As the nineteenth century moved into the twentieth, technology reduced the work process to ever simpler levels. Wage work became increasingly more monotonous and alienating. The home remained the last refuge of all that was nurturing and caring.

These changes were justified in terms of the success ethic. If hard work was a way of "making it," it could be tolerated, even glorified. But success for men was not success for women. Sociologist Alice Rossi has captured the dilemma succinctly. From the perspective of a white male, she argues, "American society in 1820 was an open vista of opportunity: by dint of hard work he could hope to improve his position in society; if he did not succeed in one locality, he could move on to another, carrying his skills with him. . . ." At least in theory, the hard-working white male, with the emotional and financial support of a family, had access to newly available jobs in medicine, law, and the professions. Whether or not many actually succeeded in these terms was less important than the myth that they could.

But for women, black or white, the notion that success could be achieved by individual effort had the opposite effect. For black women, it perpetuated an endless cycle of hard work, with economic and social discrimination preventing the promised rewards from materializing. At the same time, white women, excluded from paid work and with the production of necessities within the home diminishing by the year, were, in Rossi's words, "effectively cut off from participation in the significant work of their society." How then was woman's labor to be rewarded if not by tangible demonstrations of her productive capacity? To those women for whom industrialization brought an end to the unity of work and home, women's virtue came to be measured in terms of her support-ive functions in the home.

WOMAN'S SEPARATE SPHERE

A thicket of biological and social arguments emerged over a period of several decades to justify woman's exclusion from paid labor and her relegation to what Americans were pleased to call her "separate sphere." While black women, still largely slave and largely rural, continued to toil ceaselessly, urbanized white women faced a new set of demands. Appeals to women's natural inferiority, her small brain, her lack of physical stamina, and her delicate sensibilities were used to justify the social roles women were forced to adopt as the industrial revolution spread. The rhetoric hid what should have been apparent by the nineteenth century. Depriving women of paid labor had created a financially dependent strata. Dependence in turn spawned a series of behavioral characteristics, per-sonality traits, and cultural expectations that were reinforced by persistent dis-crimination against women who sought paid labor.

The arguments for a "separate sphere" drew strength from the changing needs of the paid work force. If urban working men did not require wives to labor with them on the land, they did require supportive environments to help them maintain the competitive pace. A dependent wife not only confirmed a man's ability to make money, but also offered the clean socks, prepared meals, and disciplined children that hard-working husbands had no time to participate in creating. By the nineteenth century, economic expectations of urban middle-class women had shrunk. Instead of producing goods in the home, middle-class women would spend their time engaged in caring for children and ministering to the emotional needs of family members.

This "separate sphere" must have been attractive to many women. For women who needed to work for pay, the kinds of jobs available were of the most menial sort. Ivy Pinchbeck, a historian of eighteenth-century England, has pointed out that the industrial revolution offered for the first time to free women from the burden of two jobs. Instead of bearing responsibility for producing some of the goods to be used in the home and for running the household, women could devote their attention to the latter task alone. From that perspective, and in a time when the task of maintaining a household included a wide variety of chores, the possibility of not having to engage in paid employment must have seemed appealing indeed.

Women who maintained households and did not work for wages retained a pocket of freedom. Barren as it sometimes was, home was a refuge from harsh factory discipline or its alternative: the relentless pressure of paid domestic service. In one of those curious moral trade-offs, women became the guardians of moral values at home—enabling men to assume competitive roles. Women's task was to preserve the humane, nurturing, collective, and caring aspects of an individualistic and competitive world. Women who stayed in their homes worked. Yet they were, and have remained in diminishing numbers, among the few people with the possibility of working at their own pace, by their own lights. The kind of work for which they were trained left them relatively free of the hierarchical, competitive, aggressive, and status-ridden world for which men were socialized. Work done for self and family at least retained the possibility of being creative, individualized, and nonalienating. Although it was often hard and could become rote, work in one's own home offered a freedom that toiling in someone else's house or factory never did.

The costs of this trade-off were not small, just different for women than for men. The home itself reproduced some of the dominant-subordinate relationships to which the work force subjected people. "True" women were expected, in historian Barbara Welter's definition, to be pious, pure, submissive, and domestic. Since the "lady" was defined in reference to her father or husband, dependence was assured. Societal institutions confirmed these ideas. Laws deprived a woman of her property upon marriage, gave a husband claim to all of a wife's wages, and turned over the children to him should she commit any impropriety or ask for a divorce. A "lady's" family was to be the only sphere in which she could shine, her only occupation. Schools included her only peripherally in the lower grades and generally excluded her from advanced academic study. Those women forced by necessity into paid employment found themselves relegated to the most menial and poorest paid tasks: a confirmation of the injunction that they ought not to be in the work force at all.

In the absence of an identity derived from wage work, woman's identity was grounded in her home role. Especially for middle-class women, status, even self-esteem, came through men, giving truth to the old saying: man does, woman is. While many, perhaps most, women derived gratification from husbands and children, the evidence indicates that substantial numbers of women hungered for greater self-determination and resented their inability to achieve in their own right. Margaret Fuller wrote in 1843, "Many women are considering within themselves what they need that they have not, and what they can have if they find they need it." Yet lacking opportunities for economic self-sufficiency, only a few exceptional women could achieve success by male standards. Some of the most successful, like Sarah Josepha Hale, a widow who edited a widely read magazine called *Godey's Lady's Book,* and the author Sarah Payson Willis Parton (better known as Fanny Fern), earned their livings by advocating a female reticence they did not themselves practice.

BREAD AND ROSES

For most ordinary women, the unappealing nature of wage work made confinement to the hearth an attractive alternative. Increasing specialization of labor in the late nineteenth and early twentieth centuries produced barren work experiences for most men and women. Women in the paid labor force retained sufficient connection with expectations of freedom and cooperation to demand not merely adequate wages, but some joy in life. Marching down the streets of Lawrence, Massachusetts, in 1912, striking women carried banners that proclaimed, "We want bread and roses too." Poet James Oppenheimer, watching the parade, immortalized the words in a poem that went on to say, "hearts starve as well as bodies."

The particular expectations women brought into the labor force, stemming from their different experiences, have in some ways been used to keep women in subservient positions. As one nineteenth-century mill manager wrote, "Women are not captious and do not clan as the men do, against the overseers." But the same sensitivities and expectations enable women to make demands for more humane working conditions where men might not. The ways in which women have worked involve a constant tension between the two areas of women's lives: the home and the marketplace. This tension is the crux of our understanding of women's working lives.

To describe women's household work as merely auxiliary to paid work in the labor force, or to talk about some women as "not working" ignores both the value of housework in sustaining the labor force, and its relationship to the wage-working lives of women. Wage work and household work are two sides of the same coin. Scratch one side deeply enough and the other will be blemished.

Classifying what women did at home and in the marketplace as either "non-work" or auxiliary work became a way of avoiding a confrontation with how women worked. What they did at home, because it was unpaid, could easily be shunted aside. And when they began to move into industry in large numbers, their low pay and menial conditions were justified by considering their wage work as mere preparation for home roles. Defining women's work this way was useful. It confirmed women's status as subordinate or auxiliary to that of men. The household was forced to rely on male income, since women's wages were insufficient to sustain households. And, women were less likely to seek wage work as jobs were not attractive anyway. These conditions also ensured a continuing supply of cheap labor at times of labor shortage.

Though many women were drawn into the labor force for a while, most managed to drift in and out of it in response to family needs. Up until 1900, less than 20 percent of all women over fourteen were in the paid labor force at any one time. Black women, who rarely had the option of working only at home, engaged in paid labor at about three times the rate of even immigrant women. The numbers of native-born white women earning wages did not begin to increase dramatically until after World War I. Up until the 1960s, though many women worked for wages at some point in their lives, especially as young adults, the normal expectation was for women to be unpaid housewives. With some major exceptions for black women and recent immigrants, paid labor did not constitute the focus of most women's lives. Almost all women could hope that they would be free of wage work for a while.

That is no longer the case. Since World War II, changes in technology and the structure of the work force have multiplied the likelihood that women will work outside their families. The argument that family needs dictate that a woman stay home has broken down, and in 1979 more than half of all adult women in America worked for wages. This new reality has raised questions about household tasks. Who should do them and under what circumstances? Do family needs still require that women take less demanding jobs than their husbands? Is it possible to alter all jobs so that both partners can share economic responsibility as well as family work? Can families alter to accommodate the changing personal needs of their members?

The issues that emerge from these questions are all around us: equal pay for equal work, affirmative action, day care centers, new kinds of families. Much of the debate on these issues is related to outdated notions of work for women.

This book will define work in the manner of a commission appointed by the United States Department of Health, Education and Welfare in 1973. Work, the commission wrote in its final report, is "an activity that produces something of value for other people." Whether the product is then sold or distributed at no cost never figures in the definition, and later in its report, the commission explicitly includes housework. The report also cites some familiar examples of the rewards of work. Work is a source of identity, helping all of us to locate ourselves within the society and to feel a sense of value as contributing members. It enhances self-esteem, offering a sense of mastery over self and society, Work provides economic security and, a frequent correlate, family stability. It can help create a sense of order and structure. Within its sphere, people decide where and how to live. Without work, rootlessness threatens and, as in periods of economic depression, vagrancy replaces community building.

The kind of work women have done over the past two hundred years has created sensibilities that differ from those of men. Can women now leave their own sphere without giving up what is best in their lives? Is it possible for women simultaneously to join the work force on an equal basis with men and to alter it in ways that accord with their own sensibilities? ■

Working with the Text

1. As women entered the paid workforce in increasing numbers over the last thirty years, many people saw this as a "new" development, assuming that the ideal of the stay-at-home housewife was the norm up until then. As Kessler-Harris shows, however, the roles men and women have played in the economic life of Europe and the United States have varied considerably over history, and that opportunities for women in particular have expanded and contracted. Write about what you found to be the most surprising aspects or facts about the historical development of work. How does or doesn't this new perspective fit in with your preexisting ideas about gender and work?

2. Define what Kessler-Harris describes as the key components of the "success ethic" that she says developed in the United States. What does she describe as its various economic and religious underpinnings? Use this review in your own definition of how you see the success ethic operating today. What ideas and values have persisted? What have changed?

3. Although largely defining the emerging "woman's sphere" of the nineteenth century as a place of limited opportunities for women, Kessler-Harris also argues for positive aspects of housework as a refuge from the competitive, rigidly managed world of for-pay work. Try applying her observations to some of our contemporary beliefs and arguments about the role and value of housework today.

4. Kessler-Harris ends her chapter with an assertion followed by a series of questions:

> The kind of work women have done over the past two hundred years has created sensibilities that differ from those of men. Can women now leave their own sphere without giving up what is best in their lives? Is it possible for women simultaneously to join the work force on an equal basis with men and to alter it in ways that accord with their own sensibilities?

After first defining for yourself what you believe Kessler-Harris means by these "different sensibilities," explore your own reactions to her final questions by listing what you see as the main issues that would lead to "yes" or "no" answers to each. Use the results of your analysis to write a response based on your answer to either question.

Working with Connections

1. How does the information about the historical development of working patterns in Europe and the United States contribute to the discussion of low-wage factory labor in the contemporary global economy in the debate over sweatshops found in Chapter 8, Work in the Global Economy?

2. Kessler-Harris points out how the definition of the word *work* has changed according to different developments in how work was organized. How might this historical information inform the discussion of the negative connotations of *work* described in Bob Black's "The Abolition of Work" found in Chapter 2, Work, Labor, Career: the Meaning of Work?

STEPHANIE COONTZ ────────────────────────────■

The American Family

The phrase "traditional family values" has become a cliché in contemporary political discourse. While part of its popularity has to do with how flexibly it can be interpreted by different people, for many the phrase conjures up almost mythic images of the 1950s suburban nuclear family, with a dad going off to work each morning and a mom staying home to tend to the house and the needs of the children. Schools were clean, the streets were safe, and drug abuse and teenage pregnancy were unheard of.

Unheard of perhaps, but not absent from the scene. So argues historian Stephanie Coontz, who in her books The Way We Never Were: American Families and the Nostalgia Trap *and* The Way We Really Are: Coming to Terms with America's Changing Families *has argued that our view of the supposedly wholesome state of American families in the past is indeed a myth. Instead, Coontz works to show that in most aspects family life, and especially life for women, has been steadily improving since the beginning of the twentieth century and that many developments that some have pointed to with alarm, such as the increasing numbers of mothers in the workplace or the rising divorce rate, are examples of rising expectations for our quality of life.*

Stephanie Coontz studied at the University of California, Berkeley, and the University of Washington and is currently teaching history and family studies at Evergreen State College in Olympia, Washington.

As the century comes to an end, many observers fear for the future of America's families. Our divorce rate is the highest in the world, and the percentage of unmarried women is significantly higher than in 1960. Educated women are having fewer babies, while immigrant children flood the schools, demanding to be taught in their native language. Harvard University reports that only 4 percent of its applicants can write a proper sentence. There is an epidemic of sexually transmitted diseases among men. Many streets in urban neighborhoods are littered with cocaine vials. Youths call heroin "happy dust." Even in small towns, people have easy access to addictive drugs, and drug abuse by middle class wives is skyrocketing. Police see 16-year-old killers, 12-year-old prostitutes, and gang members as young as 11. America at the end of the 1990s? No, America at the end of the 1890s.

The litany of complaints may sound familiar, but the truth is that many things were worse at the start of this century than they are today. Then, thousands of children worked full-time in mines, mills and sweatshops. Most workers labored 10 hours a day, often six days a week, which left them little time or energy for family life. Race riots were more frequent and more deadly than those experienced by recent generations. Women couldn't vote, and their wages were so low that many turned to prostitution. In 1900 a white child had one chance in three of losing a brother or sister before age 15, and a black child had a fifty-fifty chance of seeing a sibling die. Children's-aid groups reported widespread abuse and neglect by parents. Men who deserted or divorced their wives rarely paid child support. And only 6 percent of the children graduated from high school, compared with 88 percent today.

Why do so many people think American families are facing worse problems now than in the past? Partly it's because we compare the complex and diverse families of the 1990s with the seemingly more standard-issue ones of the 1950s, a unique decade when every long-term trend of the 20th century was temporarily reversed. In the 1950s, for the first time in 100 years, the divorce rate fell while marriage and fertility rates soared, creating a boom in nuclear-family living. The percentage of foreign-born individuals in the country decreased. And the debates over social and cultural issues that had divided Americans for 150 years were silenced, suggesting a national consensus on family values and norms.

Some nostalgia for the 1950s is understandable: Life looked pretty good in comparison with the hardships of the Great Depression and World War II. The GI Bill gave a generation of young fathers a college education and a subsidized mortgage on a new house. For the first time, a majority of men could support a family and buy a home without pooling their earnings with those of other family members. Many Americans built a stable family life on these foundations.

But much nostalgia for the 1950s is a result of selective amnesia—the same process that makes childhood memories of summer vacations grow sunnier with each passing year. The superficial sameness of 1950s family life was achieved through censorship, coercion and discrimination. People with unconventional beliefs faced governmental investigation and arbitrary firings. African Americans and Mexican Americans were prevented from voting in some states by literacy tests that were not administered to whites. Individuals who didn't follow the rigid gender and sexual rules of the day were ostracized.

Leave it to Beaver did not reflect the real-life experience of most American families. While many moved into the middle class during the 1950s, poverty remained more widespread than in the worst of our last three recessions. More children went hungry, and poverty rates for the elderly were more than twice as high as today's.

Even in the white middle class, not every woman was as serenely happy with her lot as June Cleaver was on TV. Housewives of the 1950s may have been less rushed than today's working mothers, but they were more likely to suffer anxiety and depression. In many states, women couldn't serve on juries or get loans or credit cards in their own names.

And not every kid was as wholesome as Beaver Cleaver, whose mischievous antics could be handled by Dad at the dinner table. In 1955 alone, Congress discussed 200 bills aimed at curbing juvenile delinquency. Three years later, *LIFE* reported that urban teachers were being terrorized by their students. The drugs that were so freely available in 1900 had been outlawed, but many children grew up in families ravaged by alcohol and barbiturate abuse.

Rates of unwed childbearing tripled between 1940 and 1958, but most Americans didn't notice because unwed mothers generally left town, gave their babies up for adoption and returned home as if nothing had happened. Troubled youths were encouraged to drop out of high school. Mentally handicapped children were warehoused in institutions like the Home for Idiotic and Imbecilic Children in Kansas, where a woman whose sister had lived there for most of the 1950s once took me. Wives routinely told pollsters that being disparaged or ignored by their husbands was a normal part of a happier-than-average marriage. Denial extended to other areas of life as well. In the early 1900s doctors refused to believe that the cases of gonorrhea and syphilis they saw in young girls could have been caused by sexual abuse. Instead, they reasoned, girls could get these diseases from toilet seats, a myth that terrified generations of mothers and daughters. In the 1950s, psychiatrists dismissed incest reports as Oedipal fantasies on the part of children. Spousal rape was legal throughout the period, and wife beating was not taken seriously by authorities. Much of what we now label child abuse was accepted as a normal part of parental discipline. Physicians saw no reason to question parents who claimed that their child's broken bones had been caused by a fall from a tree. Things were much worse at the turn at the last century than they are today. Most workers labored 10 hours a day, six days a week, leaving little time for family life.

There are plenty of stresses in modern family life, but one reason they seem worse is that we no longer sweep them under the rug. Another is that we have higher expectations of parenting and marriage. That's a good thing. We're right to be concerned about inattentive parents, conflicted marriages, antisocial values, teen violence and child abuse. But we need to realize that many of our worries reflect how much better we want to be, not how much better we used to be.

Fathers in intact families are spending more time with their children than at any other point in the past 100 years. Although the number of hours the average woman spends at home with her children has declined since the early 1900s, there has been a decrease in the number of children per family and an increase in individual attention to each child. As a result, mothers today, including working moms, spend almost twice as much time with each child as mothers did in the 1920s. People who raised children in the 1940s and 1950s typically report that their own adult children and grandchildren communicate far better with their kids and spend more time helping with homework than they did—even as they complain that other parents today are doing a worse job than in the past.

Despite the rise in youth violence from the 1960s to the early 1990s, America's children are also safer now than they've ever been. An infant was four times more likely to die in the 1950s than today. A parent then was three times more likely than a modern one to preside at the funeral of a child under the age of 15, and 27 percent more likely to lose an older teen to death.

If we look back over the last millennium, we can see that families have always been diverse and in flux. In each period, families have solved one set of problems only to face a new array of challenges. What works for a family in one economic and cultural setting doesn't work for a family in another. What's helpful at one stage of a family's life may be destructive at the next stage. If there is one lesson to be drawn from the last millennium of family history, it's that families are always having to play catch-up with a changing world.

Many of our worries today reflect how much better we want to be, not how much better we used to be. Take the issue of working mothers. Families in which mothers spend as much time earning a living as they do raising children are nothing new. They were the norm throughout most of the last two millennia. In the 19th century, married women in the United States began a withdrawal from the workforce, but for most families this was made possible only by sending their children out to work instead. When child labor was abolished, married women began reentering the workforce in ever larger numbers.

For a few decades, the decline in child labor was greater than the growth of women's employment. The result was an aberration: the male breadwinner family. In the 1920s, for the first time a bare majority of American children grew up in families where the husband provided all the income, the wife stayed home full-time, and they and their siblings went to school instead of work. During the 1950s, almost two thirds of children grew up in such families, an all-time high. Yet that same decade saw an acceleration of workforce participation by wives and mothers that soon made the dual-earner family the norm, a trend not likely to be reversed in the next century.

What's new is not that women make half their families' living, but that for the first time they have substantial control over their own income, along with the social freedom to remain single or to leave an unsatisfactory marriage. Also new is the declining proportion of their lives that people devote to rearing children, both because they have fewer kids and because they are living longer. Until about 1940, the typical marriage was broken by the death of one partner within a few years after the last child left home. Today, couples can look forward to spending more than two decades together after the children leave. The growing length of time partners spend with only each other for company has made many individuals less willing to put up with an unhappy marriage, while women's economic independence makes it less essential for them to do so. It is no wonder that divorce has risen steadily since 1900. Disregarding a spurt in 1946, a dip in the 1950s and another peak around 1980, the divorce rate is just where you'd expect to find it, based on the rate of increase from 1900 to 1950. Today, 40 percent of all marriages will end in divorce before a couple's 40th anniversary. Yet despite this high divorce rate, expanded life expectancies mean that more couples are reaching that anniversary than ever before. Families and individuals in contemporary America have more life choices than in the past. That makes it easier for some to consider dangerous or unpopular options. But it also makes success easier for many families that never would have had a chance before—interracial, gay or lesbian, and single-mother families, for example. And it expands horizons for most families.

Women's new options are good not just for themselves but for their children. While some people say that women who choose to work are selfish, it turns out that maternal self-sacrifice is not good for children. Kids do better when their mothers are happy with their lives, whether their satisfaction comes from being a full-time homemaker or from having a job.

Largely because of women's new roles at work, men are doing more at home. Although most men still do less housework than their wives, the gap has been halved since the 1960s. Today, 49 percent of couples say they share child-care equally, compared with 25 percent in 1985. The biggest problem is not that our families have changed too much but that our institutions have changed too little.

Men's greater involvement at home is good for their relationships with their partners, and also good for their children. Hands-on fathers make better parents than men who let their wives do all the nurturing and childcare: They raise sons who are more expressive and daughters who are more likely to do well in school, especially in math and science.

In 1900, life expectancy was 47 years, and only 4 percent of the population was 65 or older. Today, life expectancy is 76 years, and by 2025, about 20 percent of Americans will be 65 or older. For the first time, a generation of adults must plan for the needs of both their parents and their children. Most Americans are responding with remarkable grace. One in four households gives the equivalent of a full day a week or more in unpaid care to an aging relative, and more than half say they expect to do so in the next 10 years. Older people are less likely to be impoverished or incapacitated by illness than in the past, and they have more opportunity to develop a relationship with their grandchildren.

Even some of the choices that worry us the most are turning out to be manageable. Divorce rates are likely to remain high, but more noncustodial parents are staying in touch with their children. Child-support receipts are up. And a lower proportion of kids from divorced families are exhibiting problems than in earlier decades. Stepfamilies are learning to maximize children's access to supportive adults rather than cutting them off from one side of the family. Husbands today are doing more housework. Out-of-wedlock births are also high, however, and this will probably continue because the age of first marriage for women has risen to an all-time high of 25, almost five years above what it was in the 1900s. Women who marry at an older age are less likely to divorce, but they have more years when they are at risk—or at choice for a nonmarital birth.

Nevertheless, births to teenagers have fallen from 50 percent of all nonmarital births in the 1950s to just 30 percent today. A growing late 1990s proportion of women who have a nonmarital birth are in their twenties and thirties and usually have more economic and educational resources than unwed mothers of the past. While two involved parents are generally better than one, a mother's personal maturity, along with her educational and economic status, is a better predictor of how well her child will turn out than her marital status. We should no longer assume that children raised by single parents face debilitating disadvantages.

As we begin to understand the range of sizes, shapes and colors that today's families come in, we find that the differences within family types are more important than the differences between them. No particular family form guarantees success, and no particular form is doomed to fail. How a family functions on the inside is more important than how it looks from the outside.

The biggest problem facing most families as this century draws to a close is not that our families have changed too much but that our institutions have changed too little. America's work policies are 50 years out of date, designed for a time when most moms weren't in the workforce and most dads didn't understand the joys of being involved in childcare. Our school schedules are 150 years out of date, designed for a time when kids needed to be home to help with the milking and haying. And many political leaders feel they have to decide whether to help parents stay home longer with their kids or invest in better childcare, preschool and afterschool programs, when most industrialized nations have long since learned it's possible to do both.

So America's social institutions have some Y2K bugs to iron out. But for the most part, our families are ready for the next millennium. ■

Working with the Text

1. Which of Coontz's arguments about family life in the past and present did you find most surprising? Why did you find this information so surprising, and how has Coontz affected your understanding and opinions about family life?

2. Interview a parent, grandparent, or other relative about some of the issues relating to family life in the past and present that Coontz discusses. For example, you might ask them to compare their relationships with their own parents to the relationships they have with their children in terms of attitude, emotional warmth, and openness of communication, or you could explore the differences in married life then and now in relation to gender equality and the division of labor in the home. Compare your findings with Coontz's results to see if they support or modify her argument.

3. One of Coontz's research strategies is to explore less frequently discussed though plausible explanations for what are regarded as problems with modern family life. In discussing the reasons behind increasing divorce rates, for example, she argues that increased expectations for intimacy and friendship in marriage as well as longer life spans may be as much of a cause for divorce as a decline in moral values. In other words, people may be expecting more out of marriage than ever before because they are living longer, which could be seen as an overall positive development. Work in groups to look at another contemporary social issue relating to work and family life that is generally seen as a "problem" and brainstorm various possible explanations, both positive and negative. These hypotheses could form the basis of a research project aimed at testing their validity.

Working with Connections

1. In *The Overworked American*, Juliet B. Schor points to the shrinking amount of leisure time available in the United States as a major source of stress for workers and their families. How could Coontz use the information in Schor's article to strengthen her argument about the real meaning of changes in American family life over the last fifty years? In what ways might Schor's argument cause Coontz to revise her essay?

2. Molly Martin's interview with Nina Saltman, a woman who has worked as a carpenter in the construction business since the late 1960s (in Chapter 6, Work and Diversity), includes Saltman's description of the changing attitudes toward work and gender she has experienced during that time. How might Saltman's story provide examples of the changing expectations for the roles of women that Coontz points to as a positive development since the 1950s?

JULIET B. SCHOR

From *The Overworked American: The Unexpected Decline of Leisure*

Do you find yourself constantly racing through your day, running from school to work to home and back again? Do you find that your commitments and responsibilities seem to grow endlessly, leaving you little time to relax and read a good book, leaf through a magazine, or simply chat with friends and family over a long meal? Do you find it difficult even to find time to sleep? Boston College sociologist and economist Juliet Schor has been studying what she sees as the increasing work hours of Americans and the consequences of these work habits on family and community life as well as the environment in books such as The Overspent American: Upscaling, Downshifting and the New Consumer *and* The Overworked American: The Unexpected Decline of Leisure, *from which this excerpt is taken. In it, Schor offers evidence that while Americans are able to buy from the greatest array of consumer goods and products in the world, they also have the least amount of leisure time of any industrialized nation.*

In the last twenty years the amount of time Americans have spent at their jobs has risen steadily. Each year the change is small, amounting to about nine hours, or slightly more than one additional day of work. In any given year such a small increment has probably been imperceptible. But the accumulated increase over two decades is substantial. When surveyed, Americans report that they have only sixteen and a half hours of leisure a week, after the obligations of job and household are taken care of. Working hours are already longer than they were forty years ago. If present trends continue, by the end of the century Americans will be spending as much time at their jobs as they did back in the nineteen twenties.

The rise of worktime was unexpected. For nearly a hundred years, hours had been declining. When this decline abruptly ended in the late 1940s, it marked the beginning of a new era in worktime. But the change was barely noticed. Equally surprising, but also hardly recognized, has been the deviation from Western Europe. After progressing in tandem for nearly a century, the United States veered off into a trajectory of declining leisure, while in Europe work has been disappearing. Forty years later, the differences are large. U.S. manufacturing employees currently work 320 more hours—the equivalent of over two months—than their counterparts in West Germany or France.

The decline in Americans' leisure time is in sharp contrast to the potential provided by the growth of productivity. Productivity measures the goods and services that result from each hour worked. When productivity rises, a worker can either produce the current output in less time, or remain at work the same number of hours and produce more. Every time productivity increases, we are presented with the possibility of either more free time or more money. That's the productivity dividend.

Since 1948, productivity has failed to rise in only five years. The level of productivity of the U.S. worker has more than doubled. In other words, we could now produce our 1948 standard of living (measured in terms of marketed goods and services) in less than half the time it took in that year. We actually could have chosen the four-hour day. Or a working year of six months. Or, *every worker in the United States could now be taking every other year off from work—with pay.* Incredible as it may sound, this is just the simple arithmetic of productivity growth in operation.

But between 1948 and the present we did not use any of the productivity dividend to reduce hours. In the first two decades after 1948, productivity grew rapidly, at about 3 percent a year. During that period, worktime did not fall appreciably. Annual hours per labor force participant fell only slightly. And on a per-capita (rather than a labor force) basis, they even rose a bit. Since then, productivity growth has been lower, but still positive, averaging just over 1 percent a year. Yet hours have risen steadily for two decades. In 1990, the average American owns and consumes more than twice as much as he or she did in 1948, but also has less free time.

How did this happen? Why has leisure been such a conspicuous casualty of prosperity? In part, the answer lies in the difference between the markets for consumer products and free time. Consider the former, the legendary American market. It is a veritable consumer's paradise, offering a dazzling array of products varying in style, design, quality, price, and country of origin. The consumer is treated to GM versus Toyota, Kenmore versus GE, Sony, or Magnavox, the Apple versus the IBM. We've got Calvin Klein, Anne Klein, Liz Claiborne, and Levi-Strauss; McDonald's, Burger King, and Colonel Sanders. Marketing experts and advertisers spend vast sums of money to make these choices appealing—even irresistible. And they have been successful. In cross-country comparisons, Americans have been found to spend more time shopping than anyone else. They also spend a higher fraction of the money they earn. And with the explosion of consumer debt, many are now spending what they haven't earned.

After four decades of this shopping spree, the American standard of living embodies a level of material comfort unprecedented in human history. The American home is more spacious and luxurious than the dwellings of any other nation. Food is cheap and abundant. The typical family owns a fantastic array of household and consumer appliances: we have machines to wash our clothes and dishes, mow our lawns, and blow away our snow. On a per-person basis, yearly income is nearly $22,000 a year—or sixty-five times the average income of half the world's population.

On the other hand, the "market" for free time hardly even exists in America. With few exceptions, employers (the sellers) don't offer the chance to trade off income gains for a shorter work day or the occasional sabbatical. They just pass on income, in the form of annual pay raises or bonuses, or, if granting increased vacation or personal days, usually do so unilaterally. Employees rarely have the chance to exercise an actual choice about how they will spend their productivity dividend. The closest substitute for a "market in leisure" is the travel and other leisure industries that advertise products to occupy our free time. But this indirect effect has been weak, as consumers crowd increasingly expensive leisure spending into smaller periods of time.

Nor has society provided a forum for deliberate choice. The growth of worktime did not occur as a result of public debate. There has been little attention from government, academia, or civic organizations. For the most part, the issue has been off the agenda, a nonchoice, a hidden trade off. It was not always so. As early as 1791, when Philadelphia carpenters went on strike for the ten-hour day, there was public awareness about hours of work. Throughout the nineteenth century, and well into the twentieth, the reduction of worktime was one of the nation's most pressing social issue. Employers and workers fought about the length of the working day, social activists delivered lectures, academics wrote treatises, courts handed down decisions, and government legislated hours of work. Through the Depression, hours remained a major social preoccupation. Today these debates and conflicts are long forgotten. Since the 1930s, the choice between work and leisure has hardly been a choice at all, at least in any conscious sense.

In its starkest terms, my argument is this: Key incentive structures of capitalist economies contain biases toward long working hours. As a result of these incentives, the development of capitalism led to the growth of what I call "long hour jobs." The eventual recovery of leisure came about because trade unions and social reformers waged a protracted struggle for shorter hours. Some time between the Depression and the end of the Second World War, that struggle collapsed. As the inevitable pressures toward long hours reasserted themselves, U.S. workers experienced a new decline that now, at the century's end, has created a crisis of leisure time. I am aware that these are strong claims which overturn most of what we have been taught to believe about the way our economy works. . . .

Ironically, the tendency of capitalism to expand work is often associated with a growth in joblessness. In recent years, as a majority have taken on the extra month of work, nearly one-fifth of all participants in the labor force are unable to secure as many hours as they want or need to make ends meet. While many employees are subjected to mandatory overtime and are suffering from overwork, their co-workers are put on involuntary part-time. In the context of my story, these irrationalities seem to make sense. The rational, and humane, solution—reducing hours to spread the work—has practically been ruled out of court.

In speaking of "long hour jobs" exclusively in terms of the capitalist marketplace, I do not mean to overlook those women who perform their labor in the privacy of their own homes. Until the late nineteenth century, large numbers of single and married women did participate in the market economy, either in farm labor or through various entrepreneurial activities (taking in boarders, sewing at home, and so on). By the twentieth century, however, a significant percentage of married women, particularly white women, spent all their time outside the market nexus, as full-time "domestic laborers," providing goods and, increasingly, services for their families. And they, too, have worked at "long hour jobs."

Studies of household labor beginning in the 1910s and continuing through to the 1970s show that the amount of time a full-time housewife devoted to her work remained virtually unchanged for over fifty years—despite dramatic changes in household technology, As homes, like factories, were "industrialized," refrigerators, laundry machines, vacuum cleaners, and microwaves took up residence in the American domicile. Ready-made clothes and processed food supplanted the home-produced variety. Yet with all these labor-saving innovations, no labor has been saved. Instead, housework expanded to fill the available time. Norms of cleanliness rose. Standards of mothering grew more rigorous. Cooking and baking became more complicated. At the same time, a variety of cheaper and more efficient ways of providing household services failed in the market, and housewives continued to do their own.

The stability of housewives' hours was due to a particular bias in the incentives of what we may term the "labor market for housewives." Just as the capitalist labor market contains structural biases toward long hours, so too has the housewife's situation. . . . And in neither case has technology automatically saved labor. It has taken women's exodus from the home itself to reduce their household labor. As women entered paid employment, they cut back their hours of domestic work significantly—but not by enough to keep their total working time unchanged. According to my estimates, when a woman takes a paying job, her schedule expands by at least twenty hours a week. The overwork that plagues many Americans, especially married women, springs from a combination of full-time male jobs, the expansion of housework to fill the available hours, and the growth of employment among married women.

However scarce academic research on the rising workload may be, what we do know suggests it has contributed to a variety of social problems. For example, work is implicated in the dramatic rise of "stress." Thirty percent of adults say that they experience high stress nearly every day; even higher numbers report high stress once or twice a week. A third of the population says that they are rushed to do the things they have to do—up from a quarter in 1965. Stress-related diseases have exploded, especially among women, and jobs are a major factor. Workers' compensation claims related to stress tripled during just the first half of the 1980s. Other evidence also suggests a rise in the demands placed on employees on the job. According to a recent review of existing findings, Americans are literally working themselves to death—as jobs contribute to heart disease, hypertension, gastric problems, depression, exhaustion, and a variety of other ailments. Surprisingly, the high-powered jobs are not the most dangerous. The most stressful workplaces are the "electronic sweatshops" and assembly lines where a demanding pace is coupled with virtually no individual discretion.

Sleep has become another casualty of modern life. According to sleep researchers, studies point to a "sleep deficit"' among Americans, a majority of whom are currently getting between 60 and 90 minutes less a night than they should for optimum health and performance. The number of people showing up at sleep disorder clinics with serious problems has skyrocketed in the last decade. Shiftwork, long working hours, the growth of a global economy (with its attendant continent-hopping and twenty-four-hour business culture), and the accelerating pace of life have all contributed to sleep deprivation. If you need an alarm clock, the experts warn, you're probably sleeping too little.

The juggling act between job and family is another problem area. Half the population now says they have too little time for their families. The problem is particularly acute for women: in one study, half of all employed mothers reported it caused either "a lot" or an "extreme" level of stress. The same proportion feel that "when I'm at home I try to make up to my family for being away at work, and as a result I rarely have any time for myself." This stress has placed tremendous burdens on marriages. Two-earner couples have less time together, which researchers have found reduces the happiness and satisfaction of a marriage. These couples often just don't have enough time to talk to each other. And growing numbers of husbands and wives are like ships passing in the night, working sequential schedules to manage their child care. Among young parents the prevalence of at least one partner working outside regular daytime hours is now close to one half. But this "solution" is hardly a happy one. According to one parent: "I work 11–7 to accommodate my family—to eliminate the need for babysitters. However, the stress on myself is tremendous."

A decade of research by Berkeley sociologist Arlie Hochschild suggests that many marriages where women are doing the "second shift" are close to the breaking point. When job, children, and marriage have to be attended to, it's often the marriage that is neglected. The failure of many men to do their share at home creates further problems. A twenty-six-year-old legal secretary in California reports that her husband "does no cooking, no washing, no anything else. How do I feel? Furious. If our marriage ends, it will be on this issue. And it just might."

Serious as these problems are, the most alarming development may be the effect of the work explosion on the care of children. According to economist Sylvia Hewlett, "child neglect has become endemic to our society."' A major problem is that children are increasingly left alone, to fend for themselves while their parents are at work. Nationwide, estimates of children in "self"—or, more accurately, "no"—care range up to seven million. Local studies have found figures of up to one-third of children caring for themselves. At least half a million preschoolers are thought to be left at home part of each day. One 911 operator reports large numbers of frightened callers: "It's not uncommon to hear from a child of six or seven who has been left in charge of even younger siblings."

Even when parents are at home, overwork may leave them with limited time, attention, or energy for their children. One working parent noted, "My child has severe emotional problems because I am too tired to listen to him. It is not quality time; it's bad quantity time that's destroying my family." Economist Victor Fuchs has found that between 1960 and 1986, the time parents actually had available to be with children fell ten hours a week for whites and twelve for blacks. Hewlett links the "parenting deficit" to a variety of problems plaguing the country's youth: poor performance in school, mental problems, drug and alcohol use, and teen suicide. According to another expert, kids are being "cheated out of childhood. . . . There is a sense that adults don't care about them."

Of course, there's more going on here than lack of time. Child neglect, marital distress, sleep deprivation and stress-related illnesses all have other causes. But the growth of work has exacerbated each of these social ailments. Only by understanding why we work as much as we do, and how the demands of work affect family life, can we hope to solve these problems.

The past forty years should provide a warning. They have brought us nothing in the way of leisure time and a saner pace of life. The bias of the system is strongly toward the status quo. But time poverty is straining the social fabric. Continued growth threatens environmental balance, and gender equality requires new work patterns. Despite these obstacles, I am hopeful. By understanding how we came to be caught up in the cycle of work-and-spend, perhaps we can regain a reasonable balance between work and leisure. ■

Working with the Text

1. What does Schor see as the connections between the rise in consumer culture in the United States (the growth in the number and quality of consumer products; the amount of time Americans spend shopping; the money spent on consumer goods) and the decline in leisure hours? Can you explain in your own words why Schor thinks capitalism has shown a bias toward developing "long hour jobs"?

2. How does Schor seem to be defining the idea of "leisure time"? Using her sense of the term, examine your own daily schedule and those of your friends and family members to determine how much leisure time you have. Conduct some interviews to determine how satisfied or dissatisfied people you know are with the amount of leisure time they currently have. Do they feel too stressed? Would they like to slow down? What do they see as the greatest motivating factors in terms of keeping busy?

3. Schor argues that the increase in working hours and the decrease in leisure has occurred without public debate—she calls it a "nonchoice"—yet it is a development that has potentially serious social consequences. Looking ahead in your own life, what do you see as the ideal balance between work and leisure time? Work in groups to expand your discussion to the level of national policy. What goals should the nation set in terms of balancing work and leisure time and why?

Working with Connections

1. In "Focus on the Future of College Work: The Role of Technology in Higher Education" (in Chapter 3, Education and Work/Education as Work), the essays discuss how technology can make college more convenient for busy students, especially students with demanding jobs. How does the increasing difficulty of combining school, work, and personal time exemplify the "time bind" that Schor is describing? Use the information and arguments provided by Schor to judge whether distance education helps relieve the time stress many students experience or further raises the demands and expectations of how much time college students can and should be expected to spend on the job? What do you think Schor might say about distance education?

2. A the conclusion of the excerpt here, Schor writes,

> The past forty years should provide a warning. They have brought us nothing in the way of leisure time and a saner pace of life. The bias of the system is strongly toward the status quo. But time poverty is straining the social fabric. Continued growth threatens environmental balance, and gender inequality requires new work patterns. Despite these obstacles, I am hopeful. By understanding how we came to be caught up in the cycle of work-and-spend, perhaps we can regain a reasonable balance between work and leisure.

Extend the discussion by surveying and/or interviewing full-time employees that you know about their views on the "reasonable balance between work and leisure." For example, how do they feel about the forty-hour work week? Is it too long? What alternatives would they prefer? What do they most value about their "leisure" time? How would they describe their ideal working situation?

ELLEN GALINSKY

Do Working Parents Make the Grade?

In discussing how to balance the demands of the workplace and the home, parents, scholars, and political figures often worry about the effect these potentially conflicting responsibilities have on the children of American workers. Are stay-at-home parents better caregivers than working parents? What is the proper mix of quantity and quality time? One source of opinions on this topic that often gets left out of the mix is the voices of children themselves, says Ellen Galinsky, a teacher, researcher, and writer who is the President and Co-Founder of the Families and Work Institute, a nonprofit organization that studies the relationship between work and family life. In her 1999 book, Ask the Children, *Galinsky and her research team interviewed over 1,000 children in the third through twelfth grades to ask them how they felt about their parents' working lives and the impact work had on their family relationships. In this essay from* Newsweek *magazine, Galinsky summarizes some of her key findings, many of which may surprise you and challenge some of our long-held assumptions about the impact of work on the emotional lives of children. Before you read, do a quick brainstorming exercise and compile a list of what you think the key issues might be that children bring up in discussing the impact of work on their relationships with their mothers and fathers.*

Whenever I mention that I am studying how kids see their working parents, the response is electric. People are fascinated. Parents want to know what I have found, but inevitably they are nervous, too. Sometimes they say, "I wonder what other people's children would say. I'm not sure that I'm ready to hear what mine have to say!"

Why has a comprehensive, in-depth study of this question never been conducted? Because we have been afraid to ask, afraid to know. But now I feel the time is right. The answers of children are illuminating, not frightening. They help us see that our assumptions about children's ideas are often at odds with reality. Ultimately, this information will help us be better parents—and better employees, too. In fact, adding children's voices to our national conversation about work and family life will change the way we think about them forever.

Many of the debates we've been having about work and family miss the mark. For example, we have been locked in a longstanding argument about whether it is "good or bad" for children if their mothers work. Numerous observational studies have found that having a working mother doesn't harm children, yet the debate still rages. Another way to assess this issue is to see whether children of mothers who are not employed and children of working mothers differ in the way they feel they are being parented. In our "Ask the Children" study, we had a representative group of more than 1,000 children in grades three through 12 to evaluate their parents in 12 areas strongly linked to children's healthy development, school readiness and school success. In their responses—rendered in actual letter grades—having a mother who worked was never once predictive of how children assess their mothers' parenting skills. We also found that while the amount of time children and parents spend together is very important, most children don't want more time with their parents. Instead, they give their mothers and fathers higher grades if the time they do spend together is not rushed but focused and rich in shared activities.

It may seem surprising that children whose mothers are at home caring for them full time fail to see them as more supportive. But a mother who is employed can be there for her child or not, just as mothers who are not employed can be. Indeed, children of nonworking fathers see their dads less positively when it comes to making them feel important and loved and to participating in important events in the children's lives. Fathers who work part time are less likely to be seen as encouraging their children's learning. Perhaps fathers who work less than full time or who are unemployed are feeling financial and role strain, which could affect how they interact with their children.

That children can appreciate the efforts of working parents is clear. Said one 12-year-old son of working parents: "If parents wish to provide some of the better things in life, both parents need to work and share the home and children responsibilities." A 15-year-old girl whose father works full time and whose mother does not said: "Your children may not like you working now, but it will pay off later on."

The problem isn't that mothers (and fathers) work: it is how we work and how work affects our parenting. For example, we asked the children in this study, "If you were granted one wish to change the way that your mother's or your father's work affects your life, what would that wish be?" We also asked more than 600 parents to guess what their child's response would be. Taken together, 56 percent of parents assume that their children would wish for more time together and less parental time at work. And 50 percent of parents with children up to 18 years old say they feel that they have too little time with their child—fathers (56 percent) even more so than mothers (44 percent).

But only 10 percent of children wish that their mothers would spend more time with them, and 15.5 percent say the same thing about their fathers. And surprisingly, children with employed mothers and those with mothers at home do not differ on whether they feel they have too little time with Mom.

What the largest proportion of children (23 percent) say that they want is for their mothers and their fathers to make more money. I suspect that money is seen as a stress-reducer, given children's other answers. The total number of children who wish that their parents would be less stressed or less tired by work is even larger: 34 percent make this wish for their mothers and 27.5 percent for their fathers. Sympathy for working parents comes through loud and clear: "I would like to thank the parents of America for working so hard to earn money," says one 15-year-old girl. "I know that a working parent goes through so much for their children."

The study also reveals what children learn from their parents about the world of work. Only about two in five children think their parents like their work a lot, compared with 62.5 percent of parents who say they do. That's probably because many of us have said to our kids, "I have to go to work." Or "I wish I didn't have to leave." We seem to talk around children rather than with them about our jobs. And our reluctance to talk to our children about our work has meant that young people are getting haphazard rather than intentional information, sometimes blaming themselves for distress we pick up on the job, and not fully appreciating the potential of their own future careers.

As a result, many children play detective to figure out what is going on in our jobs that upsets or elates us. They study our moods at the end of the workday. One of our young subjects says you can tell if your parents are in a bad mood "because you get a short and simple answer. If they had a bad day, they won't talk. Or they will just go off by themselves."

What makes a good parent? Through our interviews with parents and children, eight critical parenting skills emerged. We then asked the children in our national survey to grade their own mothers and dads on those criteria. They are:

1. Making the child feel important and loved
2. Responding to the child's cues and clues
3. Accepting the child for who he or she is, but expecting success
4. Promoting strong values
5. Using constructive discipline
6. Providing routines and rituals to make life predictable and create positive neural patterns in developing brains
7. Being involved in the child's education
8. Being there for the child

Which of these skills earned parents the highest—and lowest—grades? Among children in the seventh through the 12th grades, mothers are given the highest grades for being there when the child is sick (81 percent gave their mothers an A) and for raising their children with good values (75 percent). They receive the lowest grades for controlling their tempers when their children make them angry (only 29 percent gave their mothers an A) and for knowing what is really going on in their children's lives (35 percent). The age of the child makes a difference. Younger children consistently rate their parents more favorably than older ones, which no doubt reflects the way teenagers separate emotionally from their parents.

Money also matters. In analysis after analysis, the children's perception of their families' economic health is strongly linked to how they rate their moms' and dads' parenting skills. Although the public often views the problems of children as primarily moral in nature, our analyses show that families that do not have to worry about putting bread on the table may have more to give to their children emotionally. They also may be able to raise their children in more positive, cohesive communities.

These findings illustrate why it is so important to ask the children rather than to rely on our own assumptions. The issue of time with children has typically been framed in the public debate as a mothers' issue. But when we ask the children, we see that fathers need to be front and center in this discussion, as well.

Children in the seventh through the 12th grades judge their fathers less favorably than their mothers in some important respects, such as making their child feel important and loved and being someone whom the child can go to if upset. Teenagers are more likely than their younger counterparts to want more time with their fathers. Thirty-nine percent of children 13 through 18 years old feel they have too little time with their fathers, compared with 29 percent of children 8 through 12 years old.

We found that the quantity of time with mothers and fathers does matter a great deal. Children who spend more time with their mothers and fathers on workdays and nonworkdays see their parents more positively, feel that their parents are more successful at managing work and family responsibilities, and see their parents as putting their families first. "I think that if the parents spend more time with their children, they will become better people in life," says a 12-year-old boy whose father works part time while his mom stays home.

But to move beyond simply cataloging the number of hours children and parents spend together, we looked at what parents and children do while they are together, such as eating a meal, playing a game or sport or exercising, doing homework (together) and watching TV. For all these activities, the same patterns holds: the more frequently parents and children engaged in them together, the more positive the assessment parents got from their children.

But spending time together isn't enough. Many children said their interactions with parents feel rushed and hurried, and they gave their mothers and fathers lower marks as a result. More than two in five (44.5 percent) children feel that their time with their mother is rushed, while 37 percent feel their time with their father is rushed. Some mentioned mornings as particularly hectic times for their families. One 12-year-old girl said of her mother: "She's rushing and telling me to rush . . . And my backpack weighs a ton, so if she walks me to school, it's like running down the street. I'm like, 'wait up . . .'"

Predictably, children are more likely to see their parents positively if their time together is calmer. For example: of children 8 through 18 years of age who rate their time with their mothers as very calm, 86 percent give their mothers an A for making them feel important and loved, compared with 63 percent of those who rate their time with their mothers as very rushed. And 80 percent of children who feel their time with their fathers is very calm give them an A for "appreciating me for who I am," compared with only 50.5 percent of those who rate their time with their fathers as very rushed.

The flip side of feeling rushed and distracted with children is concentration and focus. In one-on-one interviews, we asked parents to describe moments when they felt particularly successful at home. Over and over, we heard the word "focus." The mother of a 12-year-old says: "It's the time you spend with your children [when] you are really focused on them that's good; not a distracted time."

Of children in the seventh through 12th grades, 62 percent say that mothers find it "very easy" and 52 percent say that fathers find it very easy to focus on them when they are together. And children are very attuned to the times when their parents are truly focused on them: "They're not just saying normal things like 'uh huh . . . uh hmmm.' They seem to be very intent on what I'm saying, they're not just looking away," said a 10-year-old boy. Some children even have "tests" of whether their parent is focusing on them. For example, one 13-year-old boy throws nonsense statements—like "a goldfish on the grass"—into the middle of a sentence to check out whether his parents are really listening to him.

Every analysis we conducted revealed that when children feel that their mothers and fathers can focus on them, they are much more likely to feel that their parents manage their work and family responsibilities more successfully and put their families before their work. And they give their parents much higher marks for all of the parenting skills we examined.

So, is it quantity time or quality time? Clearly, the words we're using to describe time within the family are wrong. To change the debate, we need new words. Since "focus" is the word that parents use to describe the quality of time they treasure most, I suggest we use it. And since parents and children highly value the quantity of time they spend being together, whether sharing a meal or just being around each other in a nonrushed way, we need a phrase for that, too. Children need focused times and hang-around times.

I hope that, as a result of this book, the conversations around work and family will change. When parents and children talk together about these issues, reasonable changes can be made. Children will tell us how some things could be better. Yes, they will still try to push our guilt buttons. Yes, they will still read our moods and plead their case for what they want because kids will be kids. But we are the adults, and we set the tone for our relationships with our children.

I repeat the wisdom of a 12-year-old child: "Listen. Listen to what your kids say, because you know, sometimes it's very important. And sometimes a kid can have a great idea and it could even affect you." So let's ask the children. ■

Working with the Text

1. Galinsky writes, "Many of the debates we've been having about work and family miss the mark," suggesting that her findings may surprise her readers. Take a look at the list you may have brainstormed before reading the essay about your own assumptions as to what some of these "debates" might be and locate the findings in Galinsky's work that most surprise you. What are the key ways in which Galinsky's essay challenges you to rethink the issue of family and work life?

2. Galinsky reports that the issue of whether mothers worked outside or inside the home had little or no impact on how much time their children felt their mothers devoted to them. Share this finding with men and women of different ages and record their reac-

tions. What assumptions do Galinsky's findings challenge? How willing were different respondents to accept Galinsky's work? Do you observe any patterns to these reactions based on age, gender, work background, or family life?

3. According to Galinsky, "the largest proportion of children (23 percent) say that they want . . . their mothers and father to make more money." She suggests this wish stems from children seeing money as a "stress-reducer." Discuss how likely you find Galinsky's explanation and work in groups to come up with other possible explanations. As a way of testing your explanations, you might locate Galinsky's book, *Ask the Children*, and see if the more complete work offers evidence to support your hypotheses.

4. At the end of her essay, Galinsky suggests that we need to change the vocabulary we use to discuss work and family issues. For example, instead of discussing quantity time or quality time, Galinsky suggests using the word *focus*, a term that many of the children she spoke with used. Based on Galinsky's essay, how would you define what *focus* means in this context? What difference in emphasis does it bring that is missed in the discussion of quality and quantity time? If you were writing advice to new parents, how would you explain this concept to them?

Working with Connections

1. In the excerpt from *Women Have Always Worked*, Alice Kessler-Harris describes the origins of the idea of the "separate spheres" of men's work and women's work, a division that was strongly based on differing family responsibilities. In what ways do Galinsky's interviews with children challenge or reinforce the idea of strongly separated roles for mothers and fathers, women and men in the raising of children? Would you say Galinsky's work had stronger implications for mothers or fathers and why?

2. In the excerpt from *Nickel and Dimed* (in Chapter 4, Work and Social Class), Barbara Ehrenreich describes her experiences working as a housecleaner, a job she is told in another part of the book is friendly to working mothers because the workday ends at 3:30. How "family friendly" does the work Ehrenreich describes seem? How might the example of low wage work Ehrenreich describes add to the discussion of the impact of work on family life that Galinsky discusses? What would need to change about the housecleaning job to allow workers to "focus" more on their families?

Reading the Web

Families and Work Institute Web Site
<http://www.familiesandwork.org/index.html>

The Families and Work Institute describes itself as a "non-profit organiza-tion that addresses the changing nature of work and family life." Its pres-ident is Ellen Galinsky, author of "Do Working Parents Make the Grade?" from the section on Foundational Readings. As you search through this web site, consider the audiences the site is trying to reach. What evi-dence can you find suggesting who might be interested in this site?

Families and **Work** Institute

Home

More About Us

Work-Life Research

Funders

FWI Speaks

Community
Mobilization Forums
- Subscribe to the
EC PEN listserv

The Fatherhood
Project ®

Publications

Press Room

FAQ

Contact FWI

Get Acrobat
Reader
Click on this image
to get the free
Adobe® Acrobat®
Reader to view the
PDF documents
found on this site.

- Click here for our free Salute to Educators guide to communicating with children in times of global uncertainty, *Coping and Contributing in the Aftermath of Crisis, Tragedy and Trauma*

- Major New Study is the First to Ask Young People What They Would Do to Stop Violence in Their Lives — *"Youth and Violence: Students Speak out for a More Civil Society"* from FWI and The Colorado Trust

- **Special Greeting from FWI**

- **FWI Designs Exciting New Activities for Youth Exploring Work and Family Life for Ms. Foundation's Take Our Daughters And Sons To Work™ Day, April 24th!**

- *9/11 As History* lesson plans covering American Values, Resiliency and Diversity; an educational resource to be used throughout the year

- Save the date! The 2003 Work-Life Conference, **Work-Life at a Crossroads: Providing Leadership on Tough Issues**, is scheduled for June 17-18, 2003 with a special pre-conference session on June 16

- We are currently accepting nominations for the **Moving into the Future Awards** to honor innovative thinkers who are making a difference in their workplaces. Whether it's a new program or a small change, let us know how you, a friend, or a colleague has found a new and creative way of moving work into the future!

- MetLife Foundation Tri-Connecting Award Winners and Finalists

- Major Study from FWI, "Feeling Overworked: When Work Becomes Too Much" Download the **Executive Summary** at no cost or purchase the **full study here**

- New Publication from FWI:

the ASK THE CHILDREN
Youth and Violence

9·11
AS HISTORY

Salute to
Educators

Publication Catalog

Hands-on Advice for Working
Parents

Parenting and work-life expert Ellen Galinsky brings together

useful suggestions for dealing with work stress, overscheduled children, managing summer vacation, constructive discipline and many other issues. This book is a wealth of information based on Ellen's years of experience in research and her conversations with parents and children. A must-have for anyone with questions about how to navigate work and family.

For more tips on managing work and family, don't miss Families and Work Institute's new Ask FWI series!

MetLife Foundation
Tri-Connecting Award

Please Remember
FWI in Your
Charitable Giving

Join FWI's
Corporate
Leadership Circle

FWI Speaks

BACK TO TOP

Working with the Text

1. Explore the question of possible audiences for this web site by imagining what different visitors might find when searching the site for information. First, create a set of different roles for you and members of the class to assume when going through the site. These roles may or may not connect directly to your own life experiences and situations. You may also approach these roles as group projects. Some examples of these roles might include:

   ■ A single working mother trying to manage work and child-care needs.

   ■ A two-parent, two-job family wondering about the right balance of work and family life, money needs, and emotional needs.

   ■ A father wishing to spend more time with his children.

   ■ A member of a nontraditional household, such as a blended family or a gay or lesbian family, concerned that most discussion of work and family issues focuses on the conventional heterosexual nuclear family structure.

   ■ A single employee without a life partner or children wondering what effect or benefit "family-friendly" company policies might have on him or her.

   These are just some examples; you may generate your own in class in relation to a specific assignment or project you are working on. You may also make them more particular by providing specific details about social-class situation, region, profession or type of work, or family structure.

2. Once you have determined your role, work up a list of specific questions or issues you would have about work and family life, and then explore the web site to see what it has to offer a person in that role. What information do and don't you find? What information provided by the web site did you find most helpful? What information was needed? How friendly was the organization of the site in terms of the person in the role you were imagining? Were there links to other organizations and sources of information, and where they useful to the person in the role you were assuming?

3. Finally, write an evaluation of this site addressed to a person in the role you assumed, making recommendations about the benefits of exploring this site and offering advice about how that person can best use that site.

Stories of Work

DEB CASEY

ZOOOOOOOM: A Familiar Story: Drop-off/Pick-up Panic

Perhaps the only way to truly understand the exhaustion, worry, and resourcefulness that are the everyday lives of many working mothers is to experience it for yourself. Rather than try to explain what her day feels like in an essay, Deb Casey has written a prose poem to try and accomplish the next best thing: provide an experience in language of her "Familiar Story" (familiar in the sense both of a common story and in the root word that connects familiar *and* family*). As you read, notice how Casey uses both the verbal and visual aspects of written language (boldface, punctuation, capital letters) to create a stop-and-go sense of hurry up and wait.*

Deb Casey teaches in the Academic Learning Services department at the University of Oregon. She has published poems in the North American Review, *the* Massachusetts Review, *and the* Northwest Review.

ZOOOM: morning frenzy, the held-breath beginning to each work day. (Zip past the entire get-up, dress-feed-comb/brush-assemble struggle, the tension between adults as to who is doing what, and who isn't.) **BEGIN** at the car: load, fasten, dash back for forgotten items. Check watch: two minutes past the sure parking spot. Accelerate. Stay calm. Sing, babble, wiggle, jounce, offer a finger to chew, look at the *"Look"* commands: back, sideways; **DRIVE.** Five miles to campus. **Park.** (First spot easy.) Unbelt, gather children (*stay close!* to the oldest), deliver one: sign in, situate, converse with Lead Teacher (casual mother), glance to clock, *Ooops!: Got to go . . .* Be thankful: almost past the tearful goodbyes with this daughter. **Re-situate:** baby into seat (again), kiss the sweet lips, eager eyes (careful not to bend legs backward in haste). Turn around. Now the real struggle. Twenty minutes gone in that drop-off (and the center opens no earlier). Circle. Lot after lot. Seeth. No parking. No options—no *good* options. Give up. **Park** on the fringe. Prepare for the hike. Gather bags, umbrella, baby stuff, books. Adjust Baby in the front pack, distribute weight. **Stride!** (And be thankful the umbrella isn't necessary, no hand left.) Trudge. **DELIVER** baby to grad-student in father's office. (Take advantage of his morning-empty space.) Whisk out the baby decor: padded play place, fur, jump-seat, chewables. Nurse. Insistently: here. Now. Greet care taker. Make fast small-talk. Say goodbyes. Breathe—no, not yet. Ignore the sudden squawk, tears, of a baby who wants you. No, don't: acknowledge the uneasiness. **Return.** Console. Promise. Leave again. NOW breathe. Find a bathroom—forget it: late. Run. (Forget, too, figuring how on earth you'll regroup bodies with the car, where it is compared to all three of our stations. **Skip** the logistics of breastfeeding connections and so on. Get to the day's close.) **DEPARTURE:** Get edgy as meeting runs late. **Fidget.** Lose all train of thought. Try not to be obvious as you pack-up, already overdue. Dash across the quad, and up three flights (fast!), present the breast, **FEED,** hear her contented warble, relax, sooth her moist cheek, soft fontanel, **marvel** again: how wide her *feed-me*-bird-mouth glomps around the nipple (See: we working mothers are not oblivious), keep her attached as you try to move smoothly, quickly (the easy minute up), **gather** her pieces. Sweater her snug, hug closely as you run to the car, urging all the bulk of you to advance a bit faster, imagining you'll find your older daughter parked on the curb: *"her time was up."* Don't exaggerate. No guilt: you called apologizing, think no more of it. Get to the car. Strap Baby in. Try to hush her yelps. Promise (again): *soon . . .* Remember what you should have brought home from the office. Try not to catch your mind sliding forward, backward. Don't think what you'd like is a drink. A moment . . . Watch the road, **shift, sing, juggle, jiggle,** finger-rub the baby's gums. Zoom. Grab Baby (gently!): up and over (watch the head). Find Older Daughter. Apologize to Lead Teacher. Concentrate on this reunion time: **focus**—while urging Daughter toward her cubby and out of the action. (And don't wrinkle the painting.) Keep Baby from the breast position temptation. **Give up:** sling Baby over hip, guide to nipple, button Older Daughter's sweater, one-handed, gather other drawings, praise (sincerely), pat, burp, sign-out (Don't forget!), get them out and loaded (again) into the car and belted and grinning, or grumbling (whatever), **DRIVE.** Sing. (What's in the fridge?) Shift. ■

Working with the Text

1. Beyond simply recounting the events of her day, Casey also highlights some key moments that express her various attitudes and feelings about her life as a working mother. Locate what you see as these crucial places in "ZOOOOOOOM" and write about what you think Casey is saying and your own reactions to these ideas.

2. Try writing a prose poem in the style of "ZOOOOOOOM." You might choose your own work/school day as the subject, or you might try rewriting "ZOOOOOOOM" from the perspective of either the older daughter or the baby. As you work on your piece, think about where you want to use the visual aspects of language to highlight key issues, images, and ideas.

3. The father of the children is mentioned briefly in the poem ("**DELIVER** baby to grad-student in father's office"). Based on "ZOOOOOOOM," what do you imagine the father's day is like? How involved do you assume he is in the child-care responsibilities of the family, and why do you make those assumptions?

What in the poem makes you think this way? What assumptions are based on personal experience or observation?

Working with Connections

1. Connect images from "ZOOOOOOOM" with ideas and arguments from Schor about the time squeeze being felt by American working families. How does Schor's argument about decreasing leisure time help explain parts of the day Casey describes?

2. Examine some of the predictions about the future found in Nicholas Negroponte's "An Age of Optimism" (from Chapter 9, Work in the Information Age/The Future of Work) to see how well they do or don't account for the specific work issues faced by working mothers. Can you find connections between specific parts of the day described by Casey and predictions made by Negroponte about how technology will affect the work day of the future?

Welfare, Before and After:
Two Essays by Annie Downey

The Welfare Reform Act of 1996 dramatically changed government programs designed to aid the poor, nowhere more so than in the dismantling of the Aid to Families with Dependent Children program and the establishment of state-based welfare-to-work programs for parents living below the poverty line. Since 1996, discussion and debate has centered on whether these changes in the welfare system have fostered greater economic independence or abandoned families struggling to make ends meet. In these two essays, Annie Downey—a single mother of two—describes her life shortly after first losing her welfare benefits in 1997 and then after two years of supporting herself and her children solely on her minimum wage income. As she describes her feelings and frustrations, Downey also acknowledges the emotional dimension of the debate over welfare, emotions connected to feelings and attitudes about gender roles, motherhood, and work.

Downey published these pieces in Hip Mama *magazine and on the* Hip Mama *web site http://www.hipmama.com, a publication dedicated to mothers interested in challenging conventional ideas and forms of motherhood.*

ANNIE DOWNEY

Is There Life After Welfare?

Desperately seeking a new story on $5.50 an hour

I am a single mother of two children, each with a different father. I am a hussy, a welfare rider—burden to everyone and everything. I am anything you want me to be—a faceless number who has no story.

My daughter's father has a job and makes over two grand a month; my son's father owns blue-chip stock in AT&T, Disney, and Campbell's. I call the welfare office, gather old bills, look for day care, write for my degree project, graduate with my son slung on my hip, breast-feeding.

At the welfare office they tell me to follow one of the caseworkers into a small room without windows. The caseworker hands me a packet and a pencil. There is an older woman with graying hair and polyester pants with the same pencil and packet. I glance at her, she looks at me, we are both ashamed. I try hard to fill out the packet correctly, answering all the questions. I am nervous. There are so many questions that near the end I start to get careless. I just want to leave. I hand the caseworker the packet in an envelope; she asks for my pencil, does not look at me. I exit unnoticed. For five years I've exited unnoticed. I can't imagine how to get a job. I ride the bus home.

After a few weeks a letter arrives assigning me to "Group 3." I don't even finish reading it. I put my son in his stroller and walk to the food shelf.

My grandmother calls later to tell me that I confuse sex with love. I tell her that I am getting a job. She asks what kind. I say, "Any job."

"Oh, Annie," she says. "Don't do that. You have a degree. Wait."

I say, "I can't, Gram, I've got to feed my kids, I have no one to fall back on." She is silent. I grasp the cord. I know I cannot ask for help.

It is 5 a.m. My alarm wakes up my kids. I try nursing my son back to sleep, but my daughter keeps him up with her questions: "Don't go out without telling me. Who's going to take care of us when you leave? What time is it?" I want to cry. It is still dark and I am exhausted. I've had three hours of sleep. I get ready for work, put some laundry in the washer, make breakfast, set out clothes for the kids, make lunches. I carry my son; my daughter follows. They cling to me. They cry when I leave. I see their faces pressed against the porch window and the sitter trying to get them inside.

I slice meat for $5.50 an hour for nine hours five days a week. I barely feed my kids, I barely pay the bills.

I struggle against welfare. I struggle against this faceless number I have become. I want my story. I want my life. But without welfare I would have nothing. On welfare I went from teen mom to woman with an education. I published two magazines, became an editor, a teacher. Welfare, along with Section 8 housing grants and Reach Up, gave my children a life. My daughter loves and does well in school. My son is round, and at 20 months speaks wondrous sentences about the moon and stars. Welfare gave me what was necessary to be a mother.

Still, I cannot claim it. There is too much shame in me. The disgusted looks in the grocery lines, the angry voices of Oprah panelists, the unmitigated rage of the blue and white collar. I never buy expensive ice cream in pints. I don't do drugs. I don't own a hot tub. But the voices won't be stilled.

I am one of 12 million who are 1 percent of the federal budget. I am one of the 26 percent of AFDC recipients who are mothers and the 36.6 percent who are white. I am one of the 68 percent of teen mothers who were sexually abused. I am $600 a month below the poverty level for a family of three. I am a hot political issue. I am 145-65-8563. Group 3.

I have brown hair and eyes. I write prose. My mother has been married and divorced twice. I have never been married. I love Pablo Neruda's poetry, Louise Gluck's essays. I love my stepfather but not my real father. My favorite book is *Love in the Time of Cholera* by Gabriel García Marquez. My favorite movie, *The Color Purple*.

I miss my son's father. I love jazz. I've always wanted to learn how to ballroom dance. I am not a number. I have a story, I have a life, I have a face. ■

ANNIE DOWNEY
The Journey to Not

This is poverty, this is the journey to not. Who am I now? Tired and alone. I am no longer a welfare hussy. I am a single mother working full-time for low wages, too distracted to parent—no medical—no humor—just given up—to a vacuum of wants never fulfilled—a vacuum of needs I cannot provide for. No one tells you this is how it will continue, after the degree, after you find daycare, after you find a real job—*after Welfare*—that you go from being real poor with benefits to being real poor with nothing at all.

Welcome to working class existence. There is no beauty here, no rage of satisfaction, of rising above the stigma. I miss my foodstamp booklets and the prejudice of those behind me in line. I miss the idea that I was going somewhere even though I was poor. I was going to school, I was on my way to a better life. Now—I write my checks, budget my way month to month, and there is no rage, just a dim confusion. I have become like everybody else, lost in the crowd, tired, working class, barely making it.

There is no time in this world for self-improvement; you're lucky if you get a good night's sleep. The B.A. I worked so hard for and went 26,000 dollars into debt for couldn't land me a job at the fast food joint.

Where do you go if you can't find Jesus? Where do you go if you have no prejudice against the welfare mommies? Where do you go if you don't listen to Rush Limbaugh, and feel better that you are not some lazy person sucking off the system. I finally understand the working class rage against welfare. Welfare provides the working class a way to feel better than somebody, anybody. Dignity in the crap jobs with the crap wages, barely making it. The working class knows that they will never be rich *there is no American dream—there is no better life* this is as good as it gets. No longer can you work hard enough and grab hold of a piece of the

American Pie, like stories you hear screamed out of the mouths of old Republican men. The stories about after the Depression—after World War II—after they booted women and racial minorities out of their jobs—it's just not the way it works. Now the story goes like this: three months before you're able to collect retirement pension they'll fire you and in your late fifties you'll get turned down for a job at a Quick Stop, scared shitless that your unemployment compensation is about to run out.

This is Welfare Reform, the road to the Working Poor, millions of tired mommies unable to take care of our children, to no longer strive for higher education that will produce jobs at living wages—without medical, without second income, without childcare benefits—this is the journey to not—this is the trail of tears—this is where we carry our children's dead soul—back from daycare to an empty house—and tell our children to go watch T.V.—go to sleep—mommie's tired—there's no story tonight—I can't help you with your homework—I'm so tired baby—maybe tomorrow—just let me lay down—let me reach the end of this road.

I have lost my voice, my rebellious rage, my sassy self, will it come again? Will I rage against the dying of this light—the light of my American Dream—or will I shuffle headbent into formation—afraid to lose my job—my children? ▪

Working with the Text

1. Who do you see as the primary audiences for Downey's essays, and what purposes do you think she has in relation to each? Whom does she wish to offer sympathy to? Whom does she wish to challenge? You might start by asking yourself what you think she would like you as a reader to do, think, or feel after reading these essays.

2. What are the major changes or developments in ideas, attitudes, and feelings between the first essay and the second? What were her greatest fears in 1997, and what were they in 1999? What concerned you the most after reading the second essay?

3. Throughout both essays, Downey describes the feeling of being judged by others—people she knows, strangers, commentators, and politicians—each of whom is quick to offer advice about what she should be doing. Work in groups to explore similar reactions among yourselves. Did you find yourself thinking about advice you would give her, in either a friendly or angry way? Compile lists of the most common reactions and suggestions readers had for Downey, and then write what you think Downey's response might be to these comments.

4. In both essays, Downey repeatedly refers to her college education—an education she credits welfare programs with helping her achieve—as well as her age, race, artistic preferences, and other descriptors that she implies might go against stereotypes of welfare

recipients. Discuss what these stereotypes might be and how effective you find Downey's attempts to complicate or refute them.

Working with Connections

1. Imagine Annie Downey visiting the Families and Work Institute web site. What information do you think she would be looking for? What at the web site would she find helpful? What might she find frustrating? Compose a letter written by Downey to the web site offering suggestions for making the site even more useful to women in her situation.

2. In *Women Have Always Worked,* Alice Kessler-Harris discusses the origins of many of our contemporary ideas about the relation of gender to work and the "proper" areas of responsibility for mothers and fathers. Locate connections between the reactions Downey has experienced from others in relation to being a single mother on welfare to these historical sources of modern ideas and attitudes. Which of these beliefs and attitudes seem to be having the strongest impact on Downey's life?

3. As a longer research project, use Downey's essays as a case study to examine arguments about the impact of the Welfare Reform Act. What were the main arguments offered for and against the act in 1996? What are the main arguments about its current success or failure now? In what ways does Downey's story support, refute, or complicate the argument? Based on your interpretation of Downey's experiences as well as your research, make an argument for what you think future welfare policy should be.

Media Images

Working Mother and Dadmag.com Web Sites ■

How much do our associations of work and gender still conform to the "separate spheres" idea that Alice Kessler-Harris describes in Women Have Always Worked? *Even though it seems as if American society has moved beyond the rigid nineteenth-century belief that the world of for-pay work was strictly the province of men and that housework and child care were the main responsibility of women, how strongly do these concepts of a division of labor according to gender still influence our thinking, behavior, and social institutions? One fruitful place to look for evidence of our complicated thinking about these issues is the mass media. Following you will find the home pages for two magazines devoted to parents, Working Mother and Dadmag.com. Examine these web pages closely to look for similarities and crucial differences between the way these publications address the subject of parenting from the perspectives of men and women. What parental concerns do both magazines address? What questions seem to be emphasized more based on assumptions about the different responsibilities of mothers and fathers? How centrally are work and family issues foregrounded in each publication?*

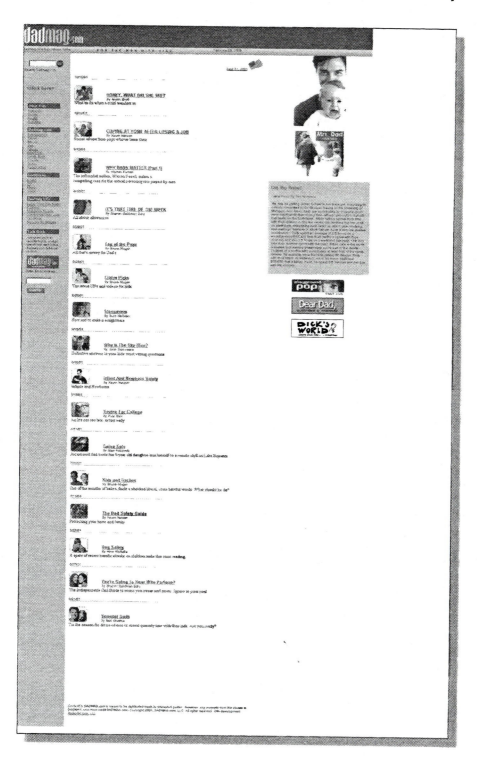

Working with the Text

1. Compare the titles of the main stories featured in each magazine. What concerns, anxieties, or responsibilities are featured in each? What different emphases based on gender can you notice? For example, what significance do you see in *Working Mother* featuring recipes on its cover, while *Dadmag.com* includes a feature on saving for college? What would be the effect of switching these stories from one magazine to the other?

2. What work issues are highlighted in each magazine? What child-care issues? Can you discern any difference in how these subjects appear to be approached based on gender?

3. Visit a local magazine rack and survey the magazines devoted to parenting, including any specifically aimed at mothers or fathers. Who seems to be the target audiences for these magazines? How might this targeting affect the treatment of work issues in them? Why do there seem to be so many more parenting magazines aimed at women than men?

4. In looking at these two magazine covers, it might seem more logical to pair *Working Mother* with *Working Father*. However, there is no *Working Father* magazine currently being published in the US. Speculate on the possible reasons for this. As a group project, outline an inaugural issue of *Working Father* magazine. Who would your target audience be? What topics would you cover in your first issue? Design a home page for the magazine.

THE WORK OF WRITING/WRITING AS WORK

Many of the readings in this chapter discuss the possible conflicts involved in balancing the demands of work and family life as well as possible solutions and options available to working parents. Unfortunately, the hectic pace of trying to fulfill these various responsibilities can make it difficult for families of various kinds to investigate the options and resources available to them. A need continually exists for research writers to explore, compile, and distribute information about these resources and options in accessible, well-organized texts, whether in print or online.

As a research project, work in groups and with your instructor to target a local business, organization, or school (including your own college) that would benefit from having materials about family/work resources made available to the people who work there. In some cases, you may find the need for existing materials and information to be updated and revised. As part of this project, you should plan to:

- Identify the business, organization, or school that could use your services. (As a secondary option, you could pursue this project as a classroom-based exercise and choose a target institution for the sake of example.) In either case, you would need to investigate the needs of the organization and the people who work there or are clients or members of the organization (a church group, for example). This research could involve looking up data about the demographics of the people involved (age, family status, etc.) and conducting interviews with the people who would be using the information you would provide.

- Research available resources for working families. These resources can include local nonprofit organizations, day-care and preschool facilities, government assistance programs, and existing programs within the organization (such as on-site child care or flex-time programs).

- Decide on a format for your writing. Are you working to produce a print brochure? A longer booklet? A web site? Some combination of these? Your choice of format will help determine the choices you make in composing your text.

- Organize these various sources of information into textual information that is both logically and visually easy to access. Consider the strategic use of headlines, bulleted items, and lists, for example, as well as what kinds of organizational strategies work best with different formats.

- Show drafts of your materials to members of your target audiences and interview them to find out how helpful they find what you have produced. What other information do they need? How might the organizational strategy be revised to make the material more useful?

CHAPTER 6

Work and Diversity

<p>
Diversity" has become what some call a *buzzword:* a term that condenses a wide variety of important and sometimes controversial issues—issues that generate a lot of "buzz," or discussion and debate—into one all-purpose word that can mean different things to different people. To some, for example, "diversity" suggests the colorful patchwork quilt of American society, where people of different ethnic backgrounds, racial identities, genders, sexual orientations, and physical abilities combine to form a common society while celebrating our unique personal identities. To others, "diversity" involves the struggles to overcome oppression and injustice based on these differences in order to create a truly democratic society. To still others, "diversity" can be either a threatening term, implying the dissolving of society into conflicting groups that share no common identity, or a word that is used in so many different situations by so many different people to refer to so many different ideas that it has lost useful meaning.
</p>

In some ways, "diversity" seems like a new idea, a product of the social justice movements of the 1960s and 1970s, or a term associated with recent "hot button" issues such as affirmative action, gay people serving in the military, or the Americans with Disabilities Act. Some versions of the American past hold that until the last part of the twentieth century, the U.S. workplace was largely the province of white-identifying men of European ethnic backgrounds, and that it was only the result of the civil rights movements that led to the diversification of the workforce and the rise of "diversity issues."

In reality, however, the American workforce has always been diverse, just as has the American population. Ever since European colonists and colonizers arrived on these shores, for example, indentured servants from Europe and enslaved peoples from Africa were a crucial part of the labor force. As the United States industrialized in the early nineteenth century, some of the first factory workers were girls and young women, many from immigrant families. Chinese workers were brought into the nation in large numbers in the second half of the nineteenth century to help build the railroads, and immigrants of all kinds have always been an important part of the workforce, also ensuring that a variety of languages have always been a part of the U.S. workplace. And of course the workplace has always been diverse in terms of what we now call sexual orientation, however hidden or persecuted gay and lesbian workers may have been or continue to be.

What the civil rights movements of the last fifty years have done is foster a new recognition of the diversity of the American workplace as part of the struggle for social justice in society and on the job. In this chapter, you will be asked to think, discuss, and write about a "diverse" range of issues related to diversity in the workplace, including:

■ The impact, challenges, and opportunities represented by the changing demographics of the U.S. workforce and U.S. population. Census projections, for example, suggest that by the middle of this century, non-Hispanic European-Americans will make up barely more than half the U.S. population, while Latino and Hispanic people will be almost one-fourth the population. What kinds of adaptations in terms of revising conceptions, prejudices, and expectations will Americans of all backgrounds face in creating a just and fair workforce?

■ The continuing efforts for recognition and inclusion in the workforce being made by people who have previously been excluded, marginalized, or exploited, from the women's rights movement, the gay and lesbian rights movement, and the ability rights movement.

■ The new recognition of the diversity that has always been a part of the American workplace and the ways this recognition challenges us to rethink our stereotypes and myths about the U.S. workforce.

As you prepare to approach this chapter, you might work in class on the following questions to investigate what your current ideas, attitudes, and questions about work and diversity might be:

1. Either individually or in pairs, brainstorm the image of what you think of as the "typical student" at your school. After seeing what others in the class come up with, do a "diversity inventory" of your school, investigating the school's web site to see what information you can come up with about the different major demographic factors that go into making up the student population, including age, gender, race/ethnicity, physical ability, sexual orientation, or other local diversity factors that you can think of. How does your research relate to the "typical student" models you brainstormed? What surprises did you find?

2. Make two lists: diversity characteristics you personally think are most and least significant in terms of the workplace (you may want to designate some specific kinds of workplaces and make several such lists). Write about why you put which factors in each category. Share your list(s) with others in the class in small groups or on the class discussion board, looking for points of agreement and disagreement.

3. Using U.S. Census information (available at http://www.census. gov/), look at some key demographic trends for the United States over the next twenty-five years. What do see as the biggest potential challenges or issues?

Foundational Readings

LISA BELKIN
Showdown at Yazoo Industries

The changing demographics of the American workplace are having a profound effect on labor organizing, according to New York Times *reporter Lisa Belkin in this article written for the* New York Times Magazine *in 1996. Where once the majority of union members and prospective union members in working-class jobs were men of European ethnic backgrounds, the potential union members of the present and future are often female and nonwhite, including recent immigrants to the United States. In "Showdown at Yazoo Industries," Belkin chronicles the attempt to organize the largely African-American and majority female workforce of a factory in Mississippi that manufactures electrical systems for the automobile industry. In telling this story, Belkin highlights the efforts of many labor unions to recruit a younger, more diverse pool of organizers by targeting college students and featuring workshops specifically designed to appeal to a new generation.*

It is the day before the union vote at the auto parts plant in Yazoo City, Miss., and Joanne Bunuan, emblem of the last hope of the labor movement in the United States, looks tired. She paces the length of Suite 122 of the Comfort Inn, which also doubles as her union office, wearing denim shorts, a vivid red T-shirt that says, "Union, Yes!" and a pair of floppy slippers decorated with neon-colored puppies. Exhaustion (or, perhaps, the slippers) has the unlikely effect of making her look even younger than her 23 years. She has slept for 9 hours during the past 48, and her meals today will be, in order, from McDonald's, Burger King and Pizza Hut.

Marc Panepinto, who at the grizzled age of 30 is a union organizing old-timer and Bunuan's immediate boss, sits on the couch across from her, beneath a wall-size chart filled with hundreds of color-coded Post-It notes. He, too, could use some sleep. He knows, without looking, that the layers of notes show a vote that is too close to call, despite two months of nearly nonstop work to bring a union to Yazoo Industries. He worries that Bunuan (pronounced buh-NEW-in), 17 months out of college, is feeling the pressure of running her first campaign from start to finish. He worries that the company has something up its sleeve at the 11th hour. He worries that the sky is alarmingly blue, with no sign of clouds, a bad omen because he believes that rain brings good luck. He worries that there is something he is forgetting to worry about.

Suddenly, the door to the suite is flung open by Cathy Lowenberg and Paula Tusiani, both only six months out of college and both training, under Bunuan's tutelage, to be union organizers, too. They are back from the Sunflower Supermarket, where Bunuan, with determined optimism, had sent them to order a "Union, Yes!" cake for the hoped-for victory party the next day. Out of breath, and trying not to giggle, they explain that while at the market they spotted another cake, one that they assume could only have been ordered for the company. Decorated with two white plastic cowboy boots, it reads: "The Union Is a Game! And a Damned Good Show. Give Them a Boot in the [expletive], and Kick 'Em Out the Door. Vote No."

Bunuan and Panepinto are fairly certain of when the cake is to be served—at the company's Thanksgiving luncheon, scheduled for this afternoon, the day before the union vote. Although the company describes the luncheon as an annual gesture of appreciation to its workers, the organizers see it as nothing more than bribery with turkey and sweet potatoes, not to mention a potential violation of the rules of the National Labor Relations Board, which prohibit a company from campaigning in the 24 hours before an election. Bunuan looks at Panepinto. Panepinto looks at Bunuan. They don't seem as tired anymore. When they speak, it is almost in unison: "So, go get that cake."

If the American Labor Movement has a future—and the debate is fevered and fractious over whether it does—then it is in the young, exuberant, inexperienced hands of people like Joanne Bunuan. Bunuan is a union organizer at a pivotal moment for organized labor. More accurately, she is an organizer because it is a pivotal moment for organized labor. Relegated to bit-player status in a pro-business era, battered by scandals and mismanagement within its leadership, hemorrhaging by an estimated one million members in the past six years, the labor movement in the United States is trying to reinvent itself. In 1970, nearly 30 percent of all American workers in private industry were union members. Today, that figure is just under 11 percent, the lowest since the 1930's.

Finding their membership back at Depression-era levels, union leaders have been adopting Depression-era tactics, specifically the grass-roots formation of new locals. They take inspiration from the fact that it is a terrible time to be a worker. Real wages in the United States have declined 28 percent since 1973, and eight million industrial jobs have been lost since 1980, a reflection of the weakness of unions in a changing economy, but also a spark of hope for their rebirth. In 1994, nearly half of the campaigns overseen by the N.L.R.B. resulted in union victories.

"It's a crossroads," says Stanley Aronowitz, a professor of sociology at the graduate center of the City University of New York and author of several books on work and labor. "They're saying, 'We've been down so long, we might as well fight.' And it will be a fierce fight, because they have nothing left to lose."

To organize, you must have organizers, and that is where Bunuan comes in. John Sweeney, a legend in the annals of organizing, was elected president of the 40-year-old A.F.L.-C.I.O. last October, largely on the promise of a huge organizing push. One of his first acts was to give the equivalent of a blank check to the Organizing Institute, the branch of the A.F.L.-C.I.O. created in 1989 at the earliest signs of this sea change. In 1990, the Organizing Institute spent less than $400,000 to recruit and train 25 organizers. Last year it spent $2.8 million to deploy 150 new organizers, one of whom was Bunuan. This year, it may spend as much as $4 million for some 320 organizers.

Because studies show that white, male organizers have the least success in workplaces, which are increasingly not white and not male, most of these new troops will be women and members of minorities. And because organizing is a life only someone with few other obligations can lead, nearly all of them will be young, often recruited straight out of college, and comfortable with the fact that home is whatever hotel room they are in. Beyond that, they will be a diverse lot, if the group at the Yazoo City Comfort Inn is any gauge. They will include long-time union zealots like Panepinto, who grew up "talking union" with his father, a construction worker, then went on to earn a master's degree in labor relations at the University of Illinois and to graduate from the Organizing Institute's first class. They will also include new converts like Bunuan, who moved to West Roxbury, Mass., from the Philippines when she was a year old; whose parents, a day-care provider and an office worker, distrusted unions; whose only career goal while at the University of Massachusetts at Amherst was to "help people, but not by giving them handouts," and who stumbled on the Organizing Institute near the end of her senior year when she signed up for an interview only because it was required for a career-planning course.

They will be people like Cathy Lowenberg, the daughter of a white father and a mother of Japanese, Spanish and Korean ancestry, who has always identified with the outsiders and the have-nots and who, as a student at the University of Washington, helped organize a protest to make the history of people of color a required part of the curriculum. But there will also be people like Paula Tusiani, the daughter of a business executive, who for most of her life knew only wealth and privilege living on the North Shore of Long Island and whose parents, when she first announced her organizing plans, wondered where they had gone wrong.

They will, more often than not, never have worked in most of the industries they set out to organize. None of the organizers in Yazoo City, for instance, have any experience in an auto parts plant, and they never did come to understand the exact meanings of the station names that the workers used, like Pull to Seat and Regular Engine. But at the same time, they will not care that they do not know. "We are aggressively organizing industries we never organized before," says Bunuan of her employer, the Laborers' International Union of North America, an A.F.L.-C.I.O. group whose 750,000 members work mostly in construction, not the auto industry, and which in the past year has gone after health care workers and poultry processors. "We feel pretty much free to organize anyone who wants to be organized."

They will, more likely than not, do that organizing with only a sketchy knowledge of the historical trends that brought their cause to this nadir in the first place. Bunuan was not yet born in the 1960's, when baby boomers began seeking different types of jobs from the ones their blue-collar, union-proud parents had. She was barely in elementary school during the 1970's, when the United States solidified the trend from an economy based in manufacturing, where unions were strong, to one based in service, where unions were weak, and when manufacturing jobs continued to migrate to the Deep South, where unions were few, and overseas, where unions were irrelevant. She was only 9 years old in 1981, when President Ronald Reagan fired 11,400 striking members of the Professional Air Traffic Controllers Organization, a move that management across the country took as permission to play hardball with unions.

And although she has certainly heard of Jimmy Hoffa, the Teamster president who went to prison in 1967 and disappeared in 1975, she sees him as a relic of a long-passed era, not as part of a documented pattern of union corruption, one almost as old as the modern union. She was just entering high school, for instance, in 1986, when the Federal Government indicted Jackie Presser, then president of the Teamsters, on charges of embezzlement and racketeering, a case that would eventually bring to light stories of murders, car bombings and cash taken away in suitcases by couriers for the mob. In short, she had no reason to be paying attention during the decades when unions, to much of the American public, came to stand not for uplifting workers but for strikes, violence, impotence and greed.

Although the young organizers may not fully understand how these forces lined up against them, they will do daily battle with them nonetheless. Union campaigns are brutal affairs, with a veneer of civility over a deep, wide layer of animosity. They do not allow for compromise, because there is no such thing as a little bit of a union, and along the way, workers will find deep-seated beliefs that they did not know they had. The union organizers will tell them that management is abusing them and that their lives would be better if they would stand together and negotiate as a group for their rights. The company bosses will tell them that the union is misleading them and that all a union will bring is membership dues to a bunch of outsiders who will make a lot of new rules.

The union will call management "heartless"; management will portray the union as "outsiders." Family members will stop speaking to one another, as will co-workers and friends. Some of the most unlikely people will become leaders, and some of those people will be fired. When each campaign is over, win or lose, the factory will never be exactly the same again, the workers will be inestimably changed, and the organizers will be altered, too. Everything will be different, including, over time, the whole of the American labor movement.

Bunuan is driving her rental car along an unpaved, unmarked road on the outskirts of Yazoo City, a community of 12,427 people, an hour north of Jackson. She passes acres of cotton fields, which had been lush and white when she arrived back in September, but which now, in late November, are scruffy and gray. Bunuan came to Yazoo in the first place because 80 of the 310 Yazoo Industries workers walked off their jobs to protest wages, and a colleague of Bunuan's, passing through the region, happened to see a report of the walkout on the local news. Bunuan and a scouting team came to town the next morning.

Piecing together what they could on the privately held company, they talked to the workers and learned that labor discontent was not new at the 16-year-old plant, a division of Hood Cable, which annually manufactures a reported $16 million worth of electrical systems for Cadillacs and Corvettes. In 1989 there had been another walkout, and the workers had even elected a person to speak with management on their behalf, but their representative was promoted to supervisor and the effort went nowhere. Wages for line workers, the organizers learned, were between $5.55 and $5.70 an hour, which initially sounded low but which they would gradually discover was a solid wage in this community. The company, one of the area's largest employers, provided no pension and no seniority, the organizers were told, and its work force is mostly black and female, groups that tend to be more sympathetic to unions. So the organizing campaign began.

Bunuan has spent the months since then doing what she is doing now, driving around looking for workers. With her is Beatrice Griffin, herself a worker at the plant, and the kind of companion Bunuan likes best—an unswayable union supporter. In fact, Griffin says she has already suffered for her cause. When the union first came to town, Griffin was working in the office, close to management, handling paperwork, not electrical wire. One morning, she says, she was told by her supervisor to wear a "Proud to Be Union-Free" T-shirt but she refused. Three days later, she was taken from her $6.40-an-hour office job and given a $5.55-an-hour position on the line. The company says she was demoted because her work was unsatisfactory.

Bunuan and Griffin pass a house as gray as the surrounding fields, and Griffin says: "Stop. I think that's Jo Ann Richardson's car." Organizers never call ahead. They simply show up. Bunuan looks around for growling dogs, her only real fear in this job, then heads toward the worker's door. As she does, her steps lengthen, so she strides rather than walks, and her shoulders square into her ready-to-tackle-all-comers stance. Richardson, a wiry woman in white sweat pants and a pink sweatshirt, answers Bunuan's knock.

When Bunuan starts to speak, she no longer sounds like herself. Instead of her usual Boston-tinged tones, her words take on a down-home Mississippi drawl. "I was hopin' we could talk for a bit about the union," she says. And her grammar slips, too. "If it ain't too much trouble, could we come in?" she asks Richardson. She says she doesn't plan the transformation, it just happens. "I think wherever I go I pick up the accent," she says. "If I'm talking to someone in a very kind of college accent, it just doesn't play right at all."

Most of her job as an organizer is about talking. The talking is done during visits, called "house calls." Research has shown that among campaigns in which workers are not visited in their homes, the win rate is 37 percent, but when they are visited in their homes at least once, the win rate jumps to 61 percent, which is why Bunuan and her team of organizers make visit after visit after visit. They go back to an address again and again, until the object of their search is found. They stop by late at night and early in the morning. They figure out who their target is dating, or where their target's mother lives, and they try those places too. They fight for each vote, face to face, one worker at a time.

One purpose of each house call is to teach workers about unions—what a union does and what it can do for them. Another is to teach the organizer about the workplace—who in the plant is related to whom, who is friendly with whom, who talks to whom, who stands where on the factory floor and who stands near them. Bunuan has never been inside the Yazoo Industries building, a squat brick-and-chrome structure that looks like an elementary school. And she has never seen the lines of workers that twist bundles of wires together in ways that will eventually run radios and power windows. Over the weeks, however, she has formed a mental map, and on it Regular Engine is in favor of the union, Bay 6 is against and Pull to Seat is unsure. Day shift in general is strong in its support, while night shift is equally strong in its opposition.

Similarly, Bunuan is a newcomer to Yazoo City itself, never having heard of this place before the campaign. Yet she has mapped the emotional landscape, too, and knows that Denise Boddy's mother and stepfather are both in management at the plant, so Denise is probably a lost cause, and that Deborah Pepper has a relationship with a Gates man and that all the sisters in the Gates family are pro-union.

As she talks, she does so with the knowledge that hers is not the only voice these people are hearing. The company's counterattack began two days after she arrived in Yazoo City, and it came as no surprise. The plant used its long-time labor law firm, Kullman, Inman, Bee, Downing & Banta of New Orleans, as a consultant in its campaign, a common practice in the years since the air-traffic controllers' strike, and the campaign run by that firm was rich with the images and trends that have been the undoing of unions in recent years.

"The union is a third party, an outsider, a big business that exists only because it takes dues money" is how Sid Lewis, the company's lawyer, sums up the message he tries to give to workers at the company's weekly anti-union meetings. "To stay in business they need to get more members. They're salesmen and they're trying to push their product. That's what this is all about."

The company repeated that message in a storm of letters and leaflets mailed to workers' homes. "The union wants one thing," said one version, mailed Oct. 11. "A part of your paycheck every month. For what? Keep them out. Vote No!" Another mailing said: "$ $ $ Money $ $ $. This is what the Laborers is all about—getting a piece of your paycheck. . . . And with the risk of strikes, you could go without pay, unemployment benefits, food stamps—and you could have to pay for your own health insurance, which costs a family of four $300 each month. Can you afford to risk paying for your own health insurance? . . . Keep your money. Vote No."

In still another mailing, the financial statement of the Laborers' local in Jackson was enclosed with a letter that said: "The union doesn't want you to know about 1) Union salaries. 2) Union administrative and office expenses. 3) Union money paid to the International union. 4) Union fees. 5) Union fines. 6) Union dues. 7) Union "other receipts." 8) Union $300 initiation fees. 9) Union buildings and cars. 10) Union cash in the bank. Your money pays for their big expenses. Don't be fooled. Vote No!"

Shortly after that, the weekly pay envelope of every worker contained the following message: "One bird in your hand . . . is worth two in the bush. . . . Suppose you had not gotten this paycheck due to a union strike? Be safe instead of sorry! Vote No." Bunuan has seen these mailings and she knows what is said in the meetings, because workers tell her. What she hears worries her. More than one supervisor, she has been told, has warned that the plant will close if the union comes in, that the company was recording workers' pro-union activities and that the union was not to be trusted because it was composed mostly of Mexicans and other foreigners. Bunuan hears that she, in particular, is regularly described as "young," with the implication that she is too inexperienced to be trusted.

Lewis calls nearly all the claims "nonsense." The company never threatened to close the plant, he says, no one was being spied on, "and the only reference to Mexico," he says, was when he told employees that "we need to stay competitive because a lot of jobs are going to Mexico. That's simply a fact." As for the descriptions of Bunuan, he says, she "is very young. And I think something like that is an issue for the workers. In my mind, I'm thinking, if I'm an employee: 'I've got 10 years on this kid. What can this kid do for me?' "

As she goes door to door, Bunuan hears echoes of the company's arguments in workers' questions. She has had practice fielding those questions, first at the role-playing sessions at the Organizing Institute, and the challenge is not to find the answers but to keep them from sounding too pat. "Why does the union require such hefty dues?" Dues are not hefty, she answers, only $16 a month, and they do not start until the first contract is signed. "Why does the union spend so much money paying people to organize?" If asked directly, she will say she makes $28,000 a year (more than twice what the average line worker at Yazoo makes, plus benefits and expenses), and those organizers who are not on staff receive $400 a week, on the theory that the only way to find good people is to pay them. "Can the union promise to pay workers' salaries if there is a strike?" No, but strikes occur in only 2 percent of all contract negotiations. "Can the union guarantee that a union contract will include a raise?" No, the union cannot guarantee anything, but groups have more power than individuals.

It is too simple, however, to say that all workers' concerns about unions are planted by the company, and Bunuan wrestles daily with doubts and hostilities whose roots are far more personal. Over the weeks of this campaign, for instance, she has spent hours talking with Linnie Williams, who has been a station operator on the Corvette line for 13 years and whose two brothers, both union members at other companies, have urged her to vote no. One of her brothers, she says, received a raise of 50 cents an hour, followed by a commensurately large raise in his union dues.

"I know what I do for a job," she says to Bunuan. "I go out and make a product. What do you folks do for a job? Do you go out and make anything? No. You make your living off of hard-working people like me."

Her brothers, she says, tell her that unions bring corruption, and she says she won't give money "to fill union bosses' pockets." Bunuan answers that "like any other organizations, there can be some bad people, and it's the workers' job" to vote carefully for their leaders. "There's corrupt politicians; there's corrupt preachers," she continues by way of example. It turns out to be the wrong example for a Catholic from Massachusetts to use with a Baptist from Mississippi. "The union is not no church," Williams says. "I know when I go to church, I give my tithe and I get my blessings. A union is not going to give me my blessings, my strength, my life."

From conversations like these, Bunuan tries to decipher how each worker will vote and who can be swayed, assigning them a number that will determine their place on the chart on the Comfort Inn wall. Those in the "one" column are actively working for the union, "twos" are people who seem to be in favor, "threes" seem undecided, "fours" are probable "no" votes, and "fives" are actively working to stop the union.

Sometimes, the predictions are easy. Just before her visit to Richardson, for instance, she stops in on Karen Anderson, who is expecting her fourth child in February and lives in an old house with a refrigerator out front and a striking lack of furniture inside. The only decoration is a small plastic radio shaped like a TV set, with a photo of New England foliage inside the faux screen—the Christmas gift the company sent to its workers last year. While her daughters play nearby, Anderson complains to Bunuan that she has not yet received her disability payment from her maternity leave with her youngest child, who is now 2. She has little hope, she says, that she will be any more successful this time. "Would a union help me with that?" she asks. They would try, Bunuan answers, and feels no need to ask directly what Anderson's vote will be. As Bunuan leaves, she mentally makes Anderson a "two."

Sometimes, however, as with Linnie Williams, the predictions are more challenging. Although Williams's questions are hostile, Bunuan sees a pinhole of promise, mostly because Williams comes to the weekly union meetings and reads the union literature in great detail, sometimes highlighting areas of particular interest, usually about the possibility of strikes. After one 45-minute house call, Williams says to Bunuan, "Maybe the union can be a good thing," and on subsequent visits she even says, "Uh-huh, I'm still with you," leaving the organizer hopeful but uncertain.

And sometimes, predictions are completely impossible. Shondra Garner, for instance. A shy woman, about the same age as Bunuan, she blossomed into a leader during the early weeks of the campaign, under the persistent coaxing of Bunuan and Lowenberg. She came to the weekly union meetings, she passed out leaflets in front of the plant and she even rode along on house calls. To Bunuan's team, she became something rare and risky during an organizing campaign—she became a friend. Then suddenly, a week before the election, her involvement stopped. She began to miss meetings, she was never home when the organizers came by and she became unwilling to listen when other pro-union workers approached her in the plant. "She's talking against the union," Griffin told Bunuan, and Bunuan became determined to find Garner. "It's my obsession," Bunuan says, as if finding Garner and saying just the right words to bring her around would somehow bring all the other "no" votes around as well.

In fact, it is Garner they are looking for when they spot Jo Ann Richardson's car and knock on her door. With some reluctance, Richardson lets them in. "I'm busy," she says, sweeping her hand over the worn linoleum floor covered with newspapers in places where Richardson is completing a pre-Christmas art project, applying gold spray paint to plain wooden picture frames.

"So how are ya feelin'?" Bunuan asks, stepping around the newspapers and taking a seat in front of the television set so that Richardson is not distracted by the program. "How are ya feelin' about the vote?"

"I'll be glad when the vote comes," Richardson says. "I'll be glad when this is over."

"Why is that?"

"I'm just tired of it, that's all." She fidgets and looks eager to end the conversation.

"Do you think you're worth more than $5.55 or $5.70 an hour?" Bunuan asks, trying to get Richardson to talk.

"Yeah, but just because we get a union doesn't mean we're gonna get no raise."

Bunuan knows that in recent days, the company has been stressing that the union cannot make promises, that all contracts are subject to negotiation and that the workers could possibly end up with less than they have now.

"It's no guarantee," she says.

Griffin, who is sitting next to Bunuan, joins in. "But without a union, ain't nobody gonna give you no raise."

"I don't know that," Richardson says.

Bunuan leans forward. "You've been there 10 years, right, Jo Ann? In those 10 years, did they ever guarantee you a raise?" she asks.

"No," Richardson says. "They ain't guaranteed us nothing. They can't guarantee us nothing and you can't guarantee us nothing. I know what I got now. I don't know what I get with you."

Bunuan feels a vote slipping away. "With the union, you're negotiating those raises," she says. "You have a say in that. And they have to negotiate with you. If the union weren't gonna do no good, if they weren't gonna get you those raises, if they weren't gonna get you that contract, the company wouldn't care at this point. They wouldn't spend the money on the 'vote no' buttons, taking you off the line to have meetings for an hour, giving you doughnuts at those meetings."

"We make an O.K. wage," Richardson says. "At least we have a wage. Some people around town don't even have that."

"Some people don't, but some have more. How much do you think you're worth?" Bunuan asks, then she tells Richardson about the last big campaign she worked on, at the Sanderson Farms chicken plant in Hazlehurst, Miss., where the union won and wages increased by 30 cents an hour. What she doesn't tell her is how close that election was—a vote of 223 to 195, a margin of 28 votes, meaning that 14 votes the other way could have brought defeat. And she certainly doesn't tell her that the memory of that near loss is responsible for today's frantic house-calling pace.

"If the union comes in, it's fine with me, and if it don't come in, it's fine with me," Richardson says, showing Griffin and Bunuan to the door.

Bunuan moves her from a "three" to a "four."

The American Legion Post No. 201 of Yazoo City was founded in 1961, and the building looks as if it has not been painted since then. There are handwritten signs on the walls, so faded as to be almost unreadable, that say, "Please No Profanity" and "Please Respect Our Ladies." At the front of the room there is another sign, placed there minutes ago by Bunuan, who is setting up for this afternoon's rally. This sign says, "Last Meeting Before Victory."

Around her, the room is filling up with workers arriving straight from the plant and talking about the company's Thanksgiving meal: turkey, ham, stuffing, yams, rolls, apple strudel and, someone says, "a cake that said something about how they'll kick our [expletive]." The original cake, Bunuan knows, is wrapped in packing tape and hidden in the Comfort Inn's refrigerator. Apparently, custom-order cakes are easy to replace at the Sunflower Supermarket.

Linnie Williams is not at this rally; Bunuan had quietly hoped that she would be, that maybe she would truly come around, despite her brothers' warnings. Of the workers who are here, some have not come from the job, because they have no job left to come from. They have been fired since the union campaign began. By Bunuan's count, 11 people have been dismissed and 5 people have been demoted in the two months since she arrived. Yazoo Industries' lawyer, Sid Lewis, says the "actions in question had nothing to do with the union activities of the employees, if any, and were all due to other circumstances," but Bunuan believes otherwise.

Firings are a common event during union drives. Academic studies estimate that they occur in one out of every four campaigns. Federal law prohibits companies from terminating workers in retaliation, but since appeals of such dismissals can take years and the only penalty a company faces is reinstatement of the employee with back pay, it is a law with few teeth. "A few well-placed firings, even if they're illegal, can stop a union campaign in its tracks," says Patricia A. Greenfield, director of the Labor Relations and Research Center at the University of Massachusetts at Amherst.

It was during the chicken plant campaign in Hazelhurst that Bunuan saw her first workers fired. She was devastated. Her boss, Panepinto, was on that campaign, too, and he offered her his way of coping with the firings. "I feel bad, but I don't feel guilty," he said. "Because I didn't do it. I've never fired a worker in my entire life. Companies fire people. And if you're on an organizing campaign and someone is discharged for trying to exercise their rights and to make something better, that was management that did that."

"If you get distracted on dealing with the terminations, it takes away from the campaign. The best way to get that person's job back is to win the election and then bargain that person's job back."

Bunuan's emotional armor, new and fragile as it was, was tested a year later, here in Yazoo City when the first firings in this campaign began. Organizers advise all their supporters to stick scrupulously to plant rules, to make it difficult for the company to find a pretext on which to fire them, but there are always lapses.

Mary Henderson, for instance, a 28-year-old employee with one year's tenure, was distributing handbills at the gate one Monday morning until 6:50 A.M., then she left the leaflet line and clocked in at the plant. She looked in her handbag for her protective wraparound glasses, she says, and when she saw they were missing, she went out to her car, found them and came back within minutes. Her supervisor, she says, was waiting.

"They said, 'I got you now,'" Henderson says, speaking so quietly she can barely be heard. "They said: 'You're fired. Your work here is done. You clocked in and then left.' But I did the same thing before, many times. Everyone had done it. I wasn't even late. My record is clean. I always bring an excuse, and I have never had a write-up. The only thing I did was be involved with the union."

As the list of dismissals grew, Bunuan turned once again to Panepinto, who told her a story that had been told to him by a friend, an organizer who had been a teacher in El Salvador. Sometimes she would teach rural peasants to read and write, she said, and then government soldiers would come after she had gone and kill some of those newly educated villagers. "She said: 'I felt bad about that, but we had to do it. We had to teach people what their rights were and had to help them to improve their conditions.' That statement crystallized it for me. It's a small price to pay when people are trying to better themselves."

Bunuan took that story and repeated it to Lowenberg and Tusiani when they felt their own levels of guilt at encouraging workers to be visible in their support even if it increased the chances that they would be fired. But although she delivered the same message in many of the same words, she feared they did not have the same impact. She was not even sure she believed them herself. Earlier in this campaign, Lowenberg knocked on the door of a young female worker, but the woman's mother answered and would not let Lowenberg in. "Where will you be when this is all over?" the mother demanded of Lowenberg. "You want her to stick her neck out, but how about you? When this is all over, you'll still have a job. Do you think about that?"

Bunuan certainly does, but she tries not to now, even as she sees some of the fired workers take their seats among the crowd of 75 people in the

American Legion hall. Instead, she picks up the microphone and tries to project only confidence.

"Let's ask y'all, are we gonna win tomorrow?" she says.

"Yes."

"I can't hear you."

"Yes."

"Y'all are better people for going through what you have the past few months," she says. "I just want to give y'all a hand for that."

Then she asks if any of the workers have anything to add.

"We all black," says Ben Sims, who has been at Yazoo Industries for two years and who has been so affected by his experience with the union that he has approached Bunuan about becoming a full-time organizer himself. "We all been slaves. Remember Dr. Martin Luther King. Remember Malcolm X. And remember, you are black and you are not a slave."

The rally ends with a prayer, given not by Bunuan but by another worker. "Our heavenly father," she says—to shouts of "Say it, sister!" and "Amen!"—"we are here to try to get a union. To try to better ourselves from our hell hole out there. Touch all who are in doubt, Jesus. It's union time. Amen."

Bunuan feels the collective weight of every historical trend against the union as she and Ben Sims drive around Yazoo City looking for Shondra Garner. It is the night before the vote and they are running out of time.

Bunuan has been hearing secondhand hints of what Garner is thinking, but what she hears does not make her understand. "She says the union lies," Sharon Cole, a friend of Garner's and a union supporter, tells Bunuan. "She says the union said they got a wage increase of $4 an hour at another plant, but it was only 30 cents."

Bunuan does not believe that any union representative ever said anything about a $4-an-hour raise.

"She says she was fooled but now a few people she knows told her about the unions and how they really are," says Sims, who talked to Garner at work earlier in the day, at Bunuan's urging. "She says her friends say the union went and lied."

Bunuan feels helpless in the face of these nameless friends. She has to find Garner and somehow win her back.

They stop first at the public housing project on Woolwine, a collection of drab, unwelcoming single-story bungalows directly across the street from the Yazoo Industries plant. This is where they think Garner's mother lives. But there is no sign of Shondra's maroon '83 Camry, so they drive over to Battle Street, an equally grim neighborhood, where Garner once lived and can sometimes be found. The car is not there, either, but Bunuan and Sims walk to the door of the darkened apartment and pound loudly. "If she's asleep, let's wake her up," Bunuan says. No one answers.

Next is Magnolia, at another housing project. This is the address Garner uses, but she never seems to be there. Bunuan drives slowly past the house. The Camry is parked near the back of the building, in the shadows. She starts to back up, and as she does she sees a face at the window. Bunuan is sure it's Garner, but when she and Sims knock on the door, it is her sister who answers. "She's not here," she says when asked about Garner. "I don't know where she is. She's not coming back here tonight. I can't get her no message."

The mystery of Shondra Garner is the mystery of many workers Bunuan meets on the campaign. Bunuan would never know for certain what changed Garner's mind, just as she would never really know what arguments reached, or failed to reach, each of the hundreds of other workers she has met in Yazoo City. As much talking and listening as the organizers do, they can only guess at what is going on in each worker's head. Even as they calibrate the "twos" and the "fours" they know that some people are lying outright and that others are agreeing with them only for the moment, because it is easier than arguing. Even though they describe the workers as "frightened" or "angry" or "confused," they cannot feel that fear, anger or confusion themselves. With their rental cars and expense accounts, the organizers can't completely understand the details and decisions of the workers' lives.

As if by way of illustration, Bunuan yawns with exhaustion as she drives away from Shondra's sister's house, this campaign's last house call.

"Tired?" Sims asks.

"Tired," Bunuan says, waiting for sympathy. Sims laughs instead.

"You're always laughing at jokes I didn't know I was making," she says.

"You say you're tired," Sims says, kindly but matter-of-factly. "You be tired, and I be the one running behind that line all day."

Later, at the Comfort Inn, Bunuan arrives to find that Panepinto has just done a new tally of the wall, and his estimate is that the union will win by a vote of 153 to 140, meaning that if the house callers guessed wrong, and seven people they ranked as "twos" are really "fours," then the union will lose.

"Our goal was to move five people today," Bunuan says. "If we did that, we'd be very comfortable."

"Very comfortable," Panepinto warns, "is an extreme statement."

"O.K. We'd be comfortable."

"We're never comfortable. If you get comfortable, you get lazy."

"Five votes and we win," Bunuan offers.

"We'd have a shot at winning," Panepinto says.

They leave the hotel at midnight for the night-shift rally, which is very different from the day-shift version earlier in the afternoon. From the first weeks of the campaign, the organizers have met with hostility from the night shift, which was not involved in the walkout and shows little sympathy for the union. It is half the size of the day shift, and more tightly knit, and the organizers feel they never found a way to burrow in and grab hold.

Few workers from the night shift have come to the weekly union meetings held just for them at 12:30 in the morning. As a result, the organizers had few night-shift workers to take along on house calls to smooth the way with other night-shift workers. Their hostility puzzles Bunuan, because Yazoo Industries does not pay night differential, meaning the workers would be very likely to feel underpaid and angry, but house calls have showed they do not. Bunuan has essentially given up on the night shift, but she is still surprised when only seven people come to this last midnight rally, a showing so depressing that Bunuan worries that it will scare off some of those who actually showed up.

She ends things quickly and returns to the hotel to give final instructions to Lowenberg and Tusiani. They are about to drive one hour south to Jackson, to the nearest Kinko's Copy shop, where they will spend the rest of the night producing the leaflet they will hand out at the factory gate the next morning, the last leaflet before the vote. Bunuan stays behind, supposedly to get some rest. She knows she should be sleeping. But she can't stop staring at the Post-Its on the wall.

It does not rain on the morning of the vote, but it is foggy and freezing. Two union organizers crawl across the lawn to sneak a pro-union bumper sticker onto the plant manager's car, and they return soaked with dew. The freshly spray-painted bed sheets that say, "What Are You Worth?" and "You Deserve Better" are fluttering slightly, not from any breeze but because the volunteers who hold them are trembling in the cold.

Despite the fact that her teeth are chattering as she paces outside the plant at 5:50 A.M., Bunuan refuses to put a jacket over her red "Union, Yes!" T-shirt. If she did, then everyone else would, too, and she has spent days pleading with workers to wear those shirts this morning as a final demonstration of support. She clings to the hope that the T-shirts, and the solidarity they stand for, might be the last word in the debate for one or two workers, the thing that sticks in their minds and maybe changes them. She would rather freeze for an hour this morning than kick herself for weeks afterward.

She is losing her voice, but she raises what is left of it to lead the group of organizers and workers in a determined chant: "What time is it?" "Union time." "What time is it?" "Union time." The line of cars, headlights on in the predawn mist, grows longer, and she stops each one to hand out a flier. "Ya gonna come on out and help us leaflet, now?" she asks every driver in a red T-shirt. Many of them do, and soon there are more than 50 people hollering and celebrating at the Yazoo Industries gate.

Linnie Williams drives in, wearing a white T-shirt, and for a moment, Bunuan feels even more of a chill. Williams clearly has not changed her mind after all. What Bunuan could not know is that Williams never came close to changing her mind. "I told them what they wanted to hear," she would say later about her hot-and-cold behavior. "I said, 'Yeah, I'm gonna join the union,' because then I don't have to be bothered by them anymore."

It is the first morning in a long time that there are no counter-chants coming from the steps of the plant. All week, about a dozen workers in anti-union shirts have been in front of the factory when the organizers arrive, dancing and shouting things with a far better beat than the ones favored by the pro-union group: "Pork chop, pork chop, greasy, greasy. We'll beat the union, easy, easy." The day before the vote, they had even worn cheerleader skirts and carried pompons. "Go back," they yelled, "go back. Go back to the woods. We don't need no union and we know you're no good." They drove Bunuan crazy.

But this morning, possibly because of the Federal regulations limiting the company's campaign in the hours before the election, they are not there. The only shouts, the only jolts of energy, all come from the union. There are more red T-shirts than Bunuan had expected, and more people distributing leaflets. For the first time, she truly believes her side will win.

At 6:50, the workers leave the line and walk toward the factory to clock in. It is the moment Bunuan always hates, as she watches them turn from "empowered grown-ups, my equals" into "drones at the whim of some boss." A few workers, including Griffin, have taken the day off and stay with the organizers, but the enthusiasm of moments earlier is gone. They are all about to leave, when at 6:59, Shondra Garner in her Camry comes barreling past, not stopping to take a leaflet, and not looking at Bunuan. She beeps the thinning crowd out of the way and drives on through.

The voting begins at 12:30 P.M., and only the N.L.R.B. representative and two workers chosen as observers are allowed in the room where the ballots are being marked. The organizers fill the hours with superstition and last-minute details. They send an anonymous fax to the company that simply says, "D.O.G.," which stands for "Death or Glory," and which Laborers' International organizers have faxed to companies since there were fax machines, although no one seems to know why. They send Tusiani to the Sunflower market with an intern to tell the bakery that only the intern can pick up the union's victory cake later that day. They field calls from workers inside the plant who tell them which "twos" are absent; they find those workers and drive them in to vote. They also give rides to those fired during the campaign, whose votes will be sealed in separate envelopes and counted only if the union wins an appeal of their dismissal.

At 3:30, they go back to the plant to leaflet the night shift. It is a sobering experience. Almost no one is wearing the union's shirts, and only one worker joins the leaflet line. Bunuan's voice is completely gone, and Griffin takes up the chants. Bunuan is pleased with the symbolism—the workers taking on the role of leaders—but there simply aren't enough people to make any significant noise. Things improve a bit as the day-shift workers come out and join the chant, and someone pulls a car onto a grassy area near the leafletters, opens the doors and turns up the volume on the radio so everyone can dance. But almost immediately, an anti-union group forms on the steps and all but drowns out that effort. Few cars, if any, are stopping for leaflets. Panepinto says leadenly: "It's over. We're going to lose. We're going to get beat up on second shift."

At 4 P.M., when the last of the night-shift workers have entered the building, Panepinto calls the group together and begins to prepare them for defeat. "This will be an ugly, ugly loss," he says. "I have never seen a campaign where so many workers have their lives invested in this."

Bunuan refuses to accept his pessimism. "I still think we're going to do it," she says. "This morning's vote is locked in. These night-shift folks don't change that. These people now are people we never counted on. It feels bad, but we knew this was coming. It doesn't change how great it felt this morning."

"There are more highs and lows in a day in this job than most people get in a career," Panepinto says, not convinced but seeing no purpose in a debate.

The vote begins at 4:15 P.M. and ends at 5:30, just after the sun sets. As Bunuan and Panepinto march up the steps and into the plant, a group of pro-union workers prays in the parking lot. "Don't let them come back here in the dark with nothing, Lord," someone says.

The organizers are led by the company's lawyer into the plant's lunchroom, where the N.L.R.B. representative stands behind a table, on top of which is a cardboard box. About two dozen plant managers, in white anti-union shirts, are in a semicircle around the table. Bunuan and Panepinto walk past them, saying nothing, and stand at the front of the group. The representative explains the voting procedure, makes a list of the votes that the union or the company plans to challenge and opens the box. As he reads the votes, the two observers—one worker chosen by the company, one by the union—record them on paper. Linnie Williams is the observer chosen to represent the company.

The union is behind from the start and never pulls ahead. The final vote is 160 against, 146 for, a difference of 14 votes. The numbers do not include the 15 challenged votes still sealed in envelopes, meaning that technically, this is still a contested election and not a loss for the union. But since only 13 of those votes, by Bunuan's count, are expected to be pro-union, a union victory is not very likely. Someone runs to the lunchroom door to shout the news to the workers on the line, and moments later there is pandemonium as more than 100 people leave their stations and run, screaming wildly, toward the front of the factory. Bunuan and Panepinto get caught in the crowd and cannot reach their troops who stand on the other side of the parking lot, waiting for news. But the pro-union workers don't really need their leaders to tell them what happened. The realization dawns as dozens of people in white shirts stream onto the factory steps and begin to dance.

Bunuan spends the rest of the evening at the American Legion hall, consoling the workers, taking statements that could be used to challenge the company's conduct and therefore overturn the election, and promising to return to Yazoo City for another vote as soon as N.L.R.B. rules allow. Eventually, the crowd goes home, and Bunuan does, too, or more accurately, to the hotel room that has come to pass for home. "We fought a good fight," Panepinto tells her, "but you can't pull the lever for people. You can't step in the box for folks."

They have planes to catch in the morning (a brief stay at home, then back to Mississippi to organize some chicken plants), and they have a lot to pack, but first, there is one thing left to do. They go to the hotel refrigerator, remove the purloined cake and carry it back to the union office. There, using a plastic knife from a fast-food restaurant, they hack the cake to bits. ■

Working with the Text

1. What are the reasons that Belkin argues, "If the American labor movement has a future . . . then it is in the young, exuberant, inexperienced hands of people like Joanne Bunuan"? What specific developments in the workplace and in the demographics of workers does Belkin see as calling for new approaches to labor organizing? How do each of the adjectives she uses to describe Belkin—"young, exuberant, inexperienced"—relate to the larger issues Belkin discusses in this article?

2. Why do unions think that people like Bunuan, Cathy Lowenberg, and Paula Tusiani will have more success at convincing the workers at Yazoo Industries to vote for a union than traditional, more experienced organizers? What specific new strategies and potential assets do these young people bring?

3. In describing how Bunuan's accent and speech patterns change when she visits workers, Belkin writes that Bunuan "says she doesn't plan the transformation. It just happens." Why do you think this change occurs in the way Bunuan talks, and what effects, both positive and negative, could it have? Can you think of similar transformations in speech pattern and accent that have happened to you or that you have witnessed? What were the circumstances, and how aware were you of what was going on? How do you understand this transformation in hindsight?

Working with Connections

1. Visit the AFL-CIO web site to learn more about the Organizing Institute (http://www.aflcio.org/orginst/index.htm). How and how well is the Institute addressing issues of diversity, in terms of both content and design layout? As a college student and target audience for the Institute, what do you find most appealing about the presentation? What suggestions for revision could you make to the web designers?

2. As a research project, find out as much as you can about the organizing drive in 1996 described in Belkin's article and its aftermath. How did local news organizations (newspapers, radio and television news) cover the story? What points of view were represented? You can use Gregory Mantsios's "Media Magic: Making Class Invisible" (in Chapter 4, Work and Social Class) for ideas about what to look for in analyzing media stories about the organizing drive.

FARAI CHIDEYA

From *The Color of Our Future: Race for the 21st Century*

Ever since the phrase "affirmative action" was created during the administration of Lyndon B. Johnson to refer to a range of government programs and policies that sought to increase the racial, ethnic, and gender diversity of workplaces, schools, and political institutions, it has acted as a cultural lightning rod, promoting intense debates between those who see these varied programs as an important part of challenging and overcoming discrimination in American society and those who argue that such policies risked substituting one kind of discrimination for another. In 1995, national attention focused on the University of California system, where the Board of Regents dramatically changed over twenty years of admissions policy by eliminating any considerations of race and ethnicity from the admissions process. In this excerpt of a chapter from her book, The Color of Our Future: Race for the 21st Century, *the journalist Farai Chideya investigates the impact of the board's decision by interviewing a range of students on the Berkeley campus who hold varying views on affirmative action. In so doing, she makes her own pro-affirmative action position clear and raises questions about how our social identities of race, gender, class, and ethnicity mold and shape our opinions and attitudes.*

Chideya has been a print and television reporter for a wide range of networks and publications, ranging from MTV to Newsweek, CNN, *and ABC news. She currently edits the news web site she founded,* PopandPolitics.com, *a cyber journal about politics and culture aimed at a young, multicultural audience. She is also the author of* Don't Believe the Hype: Fighting Cultural Misinformation About African-Americans.

I feel sorry for the white students, because they don't have anyplace that's their own, except maybe the frats.
—TON DANG, VIETNAMESE AMERICAN JUNIOR,
UNIVERSITY OF CALIFORNIA AT BERKELEY

October 12, 1995: The bodies are packed in tighter than at a rock concert: the mood is edgy and expectant. The location is Sproul Plaza, the University of California at Berkeley's main courtyard and thoroughfare. It's bustling even on normal days, as students rush between classes, stop to buy lunch from a cart, or sit, sun, and gossip on Sproul Hall's marble steps. But today the bustle has become a jostle. Today, thousands of students, faculty, administrators, and onlookers have gathered to protest the end of affirmative action at a school once known as one of the most liberal in the nation—and one of the most diverse. The heads of all nine campuses of the University of California—including UCLA and Berkeley—supported affirmative action. But the Board of Regents set a meeting during the middle of the summer and ended the program with one vote.

I've come to Berkeley to witness the end of an era. Only a few decades after the Civil Rights movement forced us to try to find solutions for discrimination, the nation's focus has turned to dismantling the few limited programs we bothered to set up. On one level, Berkeley's liberal reputation makes it an unlikely site for the demise of affirmative action. But on another, it's just the kind of volatile environment where major social changes occur. While most colleges are still wrestling with black-white racial tensions, the University of California at Berkeley is over 40 percent Asian and only 30 percent white. Berkeley is one of the most selective universities in the country; it's also state run. And California is not just any state. With over 30 million residents, it's the most populous in the nation. And over 40 percent of its residents are nonwhite, a number that is steadily increasing.

Soon California will have no racial majority. The battle over affirmative action, over what helps and hurts racial "equality," is no dry academic matter here. It is a matter of intense personal self-interest, and often one of clashing individual and group demands. Asian Americans, one of the fastest-growing groups in California and America as a whole, have been torn by the question of affirmative action. The community is heterogeneous—rich, poor, U.S.-born, refugee, immigrant. But overall, Asian Americans have the highest education rate in the country, regardless of income, and they tend to lose out rather than benefit from affirmative action policies. Black and Latino Californians, the latter of which will one day become the dominant ethnic group within the state, still often attend subpar public schools and are the most likely to be hurt by affirmative action's end. It's easy to guess the problems which lie ahead if a rapidly growing number of California's children are not receiving an education that prepares them for the upper echelons of the state's schools and workforce. The result will be—and many argue, already is—a bifurcated society, stratified by both race and class, with a white minority holding the power and a brown majority filling the low-wage, low-skill job pool. But the most powerful group in the state, and for now the majority, is white Americans.

PROTESTING A DONE DEAL

By the time Berkeley students returned to campus in the fall, the Regents' vote was a done deal—a deft political move made without student input or administration consent. A small group of student activists immediately began planning a massive rally: leader Rona Fernandez, a tough, introspective Filipina writer and union organizer who'd graduated from Cal the year before; Josh Franco, a well-heeled white eighteen-year-old freshman from L.A.; and José Palafox, a junior who transferred from a community college. Short and wiry, with buzz-cut black hair and worn Converse tennis shoes, José is a Mexican immigrant who's been told to his face by classmates that "you probably got in here because of affirmative action or something. . . . It's really sad because we as Chicanos, or other oppressed people in this country, have to be on the defensive." The young Chicano-studies major and punk-rock musician worries about divisions in the activists' ranks. He hears disgruntled anti-white murmurings among some of the black and Latino students. "I plead for more unity," says José, "and that has brought problems with some of the activists. It's like, 'No, we don't want to deal with them. Fuck them.' And I know where that [sentiment] is coming from, but it's a dead-end road."

José is caught in the California equivalent of double jeopardy, squeezed by anti-affirmative-action referendums on one side and anti-immigrant legislation on the other. A couple of weeks ago he picked up the school newspaper and read about the proposals to strip legal immigrants of financial aid benefits. He's a legal resident whose mother and father earn poverty-level wages. The fact that the bill will probably not succeed (I later learn it fails) doesn't ease the hurt that people are debating the measure. "It's like debating whether slavery is good or not," José sighs. Many of the students he lives with in Casa Joaquim Murrieta would be affected by any curbs on funding for immigrants. The Chicano dorm is a large, plain house nestled among the spit-shined mansions of Berkeley's fraternity row. It's named for a Mexican martyr—a Robin Hood-like bandit who fought against and stole from the whites who'd taken Mexican land until he was executed. Today, forty-five Mexican-American and Latino students sleep, share cooking and cleaning duties, offer support to each other, and fight fiery intellectual battles with each other in the co-op. José knows that Mexican Americans are already the dominant ethnicity in Los Angeles; one day, they will be the largest in the entire state of California as well. But without access to adequate schooling, he worries they'll become a permanent underclass in the state they demographically dominate.

Josh Franco agrees. He's one of the handful of whites deeply involved with the protest. The night before, the freshman sits in a dimly lit graduate student office the organizers have commandeered as a place to paint signs for the following day. "I love it here," says Josh of the school he's attended for a mere matter of weeks. Handsome, curly-haired, and introspective, he's trying to find his place within a campus divided. Josh describes his best friend as a "Republican frat boy. He's convinced Berkeley is just separatist cliques of every type. . . . But the only way this problem is going to be solved is if we can all make sacrifices and pull together. I grew up very wealthy. My dad is a doctor; I went to prep school. But I don't like being handed everything in life. It doesn't seem right to revel in advantages if everyone doesn't have it."

Josh sits next to another volunteer, Sascha Bittner. Sascha can't make signs. Her delicate face, surrounded by a halo of blond curls, tends to loll unpredictably to the side. She's been disabled since birth, so she uses a motorized wheelchair (equipped with cell phone) to get around. Because her speech is difficult to understand, she writes on my notepad in painstaking print: "After the egregious decision by the Regents, I decided I had to get involved somehow." I tell her to go ahead and talk; I'll listen. So the twenty-two-year-old junior (who participates in a program Berkeley runs to insure access to students with disabilities) tells me why she felt she had to support the affirmative action march. "For me, because I have a disability, I think I have empathy with other minorities." I ask her if the solidarity is reciprocal. "I think I support them more than they support me. But look at Christopher Reeve. Anyone can become disabled. There's certainly some difference between all minorities, but there's a commonality as well: discrimination."

"FOCUS NOT ON THE TOP, BUT ON THE BOTTOM"

The day of the protest, I wander through Sproul Plaza talking to students instead of listening to the speeches. Predictably, most of those who've shown up support affirmative action; a handful have come to support the Regents; and many have shown up just to see what the fuss is all about. One of the last is a stunning twenty-three-year-old junior with brown skin, almond eyes, and cheekbones sharp enough to cut steel. Ché—half Swedish, half black American—was born and raised in Sweden and came to the United States in 1983. While many of the black kids at Berkeley were making their way through urban schools, Ché says he was receiving lessons from a private tutor on African-American culture, paid for by the Swedish government. He thinks affirmative action is a great idea in concept, but "when you look at the effects, I'm against it. It lets people in, but the dropout rate is really high. It doesn't mean they [affirmative action admits] are underqualified in terms of intellect, but in terms of knowledge." The solution, Ché says "is not to focus on the top but on the bottom"—on ensuring that students in preschool and elementary schools get a decent education. "But," he shrugs his shoulders, "that's too much of a long-term solution for American politics."

The crowd has swollen to over three thousand students, staff, and faculty members. Though she's worked her ass off to make this protest a success, activist Rona Fernandez is far from convinced that the numbers of Sproul Plaza represent any real long-term commitment to fighting the Regents' decision. The entire day's events have been planned by only a tiny handful of the campus community, and she suspects that tomorrow the same few will be back to square one. "If you do activism, you see the same one hundred people," she says. "Berkeley students have more racial awareness than in most places, but they're cynical. The black students, Chicanos, Asians, and Latinos, are all separate. I would like to see them be more politicized."

Raichelle Jordan, a black twenty-six-year-old psychology major standing at the base of the steps, agrees with Fernandez. She doesn't see a lot of cohesiveness among the black students who have the most to lose, while she does see a growing cohesion among those who oppose affirmative action. "Berkeley has become a lot more conservative," she says. "People want me to jeopardize my future. If I flunk out, people will say, 'See!'" Her friend Christina Battle, a black twenty-seven-year-old junior who's also majoring in psychology, adds, "My main reason for picking this campus was diversity. Now a lot of people are going to go without a good education."

Max Lau, a tall twenty-three-year-old senior, came with a large contingent from Cal BiGay, a gay Asian-American group. Chinese by ethnicity, Latino (he was raised in Brazil) by acculturation, Max realizes that Berkeley, for all of its tensions, provides an extraordinarily rare campus environment. At how many schools could he comfortably assert his identity as an Asian-Latino-American gay man? "Living in California, in Berkeley especially, it's like we live in a different country," he admits. But he's troubled by the way the Asian-American community is torn by the issue of affirmative action. "The whole model minority theory pits ethnic groups against each other. A lot of my Asian-American friends are very apolitical, conservative. They try to segregate themselves from blacks, but only by being together will these things end." Asian Americans probably have the most complex vantage point on affirmative action. On the one hand, they tend not to benefit from affirmative action in education. They have the highest college graduation rate of any racial group, including whites. But on the other hand, despite the fact that Asians are more highly educated than whites, they earn less on average; and in recent years, greater numbers of Asian Americans have begun to benefit from affirmative action programs for businesses.

Shu Ming Cheer, the head of the Asian Students Union, is trying to puzzle through these contradictions. Shu Ming supports affirmative action—she's also a member of Asian Pacific Islander Students for Affirmative Action—but many of her friends don't. They're not helped by affirmative action in admissions; they receive no benefit and tend to have the highest high school GPAs and test scores. So how does Shu Ming defend affirmative action to other Asian Americans? "Usually, to me, I think of affirmative action as being long-term. I mean, short-term we are very well represented here at UCs or whatnot. But long-term, when we look at graduate level or tenured professors, we're really underrepresented and, to me, there's definitely a glass ceiling." She also thinks that socioeconomies affect the "meritocracy" more than most people would like to admit. "I mean when I was in high school, I took a prep course and that raised my SAT score by two hundred points and that's not because of my intelligence or anything. It's based on the fact that my parents could afford it. And grades are also based on the fact that you have the privilege of going to a school with AP courses and if you don't have to work, say, twenty hours a week to support your family." But Shu Ming's arguments don't hold much water with Asian Americans who routinely get better grades and test scores than not only blacks and Latinos but whites. Organizing Asian Americans for any cause, let alone affirmative action, is "really hard," she says. What many Americans fail to realize are the deep cultural biases—and histories of animosity—between different Asian nations, including the Chinese and Japanese. Feeling a sense of Asian-American unity requires that students let go of the tensions between their cultures. But at Berkeley, many students belong to ethnic affinity groups like Chinese, Filipino, Vietnamese, and Pacific Islander associations, but they don't join broader-based groups like the Asian Students Union.

AFFIRMATIVE ACTION AND MORALITY

So who wins, now that affirmative action is gone, and who loses? Whites have generally been the biggest opponents of affirmative action, and people tend to assume they'll benefit the most when programs are killed. That's probably true in most of the country, but not at the UC schools. Asian Americans, already the biggest group on campus, will gain the most new admissions slots. But the groups who lose are just what we expect. Two years after the Regents' decision, the numbers start coming in for UC graduate school admissions. (Undergraduate admissions will change the following year.) The numbers are stark. Black admissions at Berkeley's law school dropped by 81 percent. Fourteen African Americans were admitted, and none of them chose to attend. Latino admissions dropped by half. It's not just that admissions went down; applications did as well. Talented black and Latino students apparently decided to go somewhere where their race wasn't such an obvious bone of contention.

I look at the group of people organizing the October 12 protest and see what I expect to: a bunch of nonwhites, mostly black and Latino; women of a variety of races. Then there's Sascha and a tiny cluster of white men. With a few exceptions, like Josh, the group of people gathering here is the group that must: people directly threatened by the end of affirmative action. Discrimination is about demographics, affirmative action is about demographics, and the way these issues are playing out at Berkeley are all about the demographics of power. Even though I support affirmative action, I can easily understand the abstract moral arguments against it. But what I find disturbing—what's always been the crux of racial (and gender) struggles—is the way in which we deny that self-interest creates morality. Most people who argue for abolishing affirmative action say that theirs is a pure moral position, that they simply endorse each American being judged as an individual, not a race. They argue affirmative action punishes them for discrimination committed in the past, but they won't admit that they're still benefiting from educational and employment advantages accorded whites. By the same token, nonwhites and women who believe in affirmative action claim they've got a pure moral position as well: that no just society would allow itself to continually favor whites and men over all others. The sad truth about affirmative action is that, on the simplest level, both of these pure moral positions are right. Endorsing individual achievement is crucial; so is endorsing a society that allows and encourages achievement from all members. But can we really make moral decisions about concepts like "equality" and "opportunity" in a vacuum, where we forget not only America's history but the discrimination that continues to this day? Even the staunchest anti-affirmative-action crusaders can't do it.

As a contributing editor of *Vibe* magazine, I commissioned an interview with the hottest figure in the affirmative action debate, California businessman Ward

Connerly. As a member of the Board of Regents, he helped dismantle affirmative action at Berkeley. He went on to push through Proposition 209, a ballot dismantling affirmative action across the state. And even though he has decried the idea of "preferences" and "special consideration" for nonwhite students, he didn't hesitate to put in a letter requesting special consideration of an application to UC Davis law school. He told a moving story about the woman he championed, someone who fought her way through the educational system after an accident left her disabled. "And so I felt like, hey, this is a person who needs some special consideration," Connerly told the reporter for *Vibe*. But when asked how he could reconcile his belief that a disabled student deserved special consideration, but that students facing hardship because of race did not, Connerly dodged the question—and made a blanket statement reaffirming his moral absolutism. Discrimination "is wrong all of the time," he said. "Moral judgments are not relative."

Connerly's actions—many would say, his hypocrisy—illustrate that we can't argue these issues as abstractions. The most common criticism of affirmative action is that it tries to make up for "past discrimination." First of all, that's a misreading of the definition of affirmative action. The federal government defines the program as "action taken first to remedy patterns which show flagrant underutilization of minorities or women as a consequence of past discrimination perpetuated in *present . . . systems*, and secondly, to prevent future . . . discrimination which would prolong these patterns. [emphasis mine]" The focus is not on the past but on the present and future—on people (blacks, women, Latinos) who've historically experienced job discrimination and *still* are to this day. If the discrimination weren't ongoing, affirmative action wouldn't be needed. But just look at the numbers. Black family income, on average, rarely tops 60 percent of white income. And *The Bell Curve*, which advocated against affirmative action, compared blacks and whites of what they termed "equal IQ." They found the blacks were more highly educated than the whites, yet they still earned hundreds of dollars less.

And what about the perception that reverse discrimination has reached epidemic proportions? Of the more than three thousand discrimination cases decided by federal courts between 1990 and 1994, only one hundred claimed reverse discrimination. Of those one hundred, only six were actually proven. Or what about the argument that affirmative action is bad because it embraces what critics call "group rights"? Well, our government has no problem making distinctions between groups of adult citizens for any number of reasons. The U.S. military tells a large proportion of its armed forces—women—that members of their gender cannot go into combat, despite the fact that the opportunity to engage in combat is a crucial part of attaining higher rank. The federal government tells adult U.S. citizens between the ages of eighteen and twenty that they are not allowed to consume alcohol. Everything from homeowner tax credits to Social Security benefits is based upon the concept of aiding groups when there is a compelling state interest to do so. Some opponents of affirmative action think race is the only category *not* worthy of being considered under that same standard.

Do we even know what affirmative action is? According to a 1995 study, up to half of all Americans don't have the foggiest idea. The first programs were initiated by President John F. Kennedy and institutionalized by Richard Nixon. Today, it's almost impossible to define. There are state, local, federal, and private programs that encompass everything from minority internships to funds for female business owners. Says Troy Duster, a Berkeley sociology professor who is himself considered an expert on the issues, "There are no experts on affirmative action, only pretenders. There's nobody in this country who understands the gender and racial issues, the public and the private. The people who know about fire and police departments don't know what's going on at Texaco [which paid $187 million to settle a massive discrimination suit filed by black employees]."

In 1998, some persuasive evidence emerged that affirmative action both serves higher education well and often helps whites as well as "minorities." *The Shape of the River*, a book by the former presidents of Princeton and Harvard, documents these benefits. Authors William G. Bowen and Derek Bok analyzed a database tracking forty-five thousand students who attended twenty-eight of the nation's top colleges. They found that black students who attended the most selective schools were more likely to graduate and to get high-paying jobs than black students with similar test scores who attended less competitive schools. And the black college graduates at these top schools were more likely than their white counterparts to take leadership positions in their local communities. Bowen and Bok say that affirmative action benefits whites by giving them a hands-on experience of integration, knowledge that most professionals today can't do business without. Ironically, another study supporting affirmative action comes from the state where programs were abolished by popular vote in 1998. A study of admissions at the public universities in Washington found that white students made up three-quarters of "special admissions," which take into account race, income, and socioeconomic factors. Nonetheless, the majority-white voter pool dismantled affirmative action at state colleges.

All of this illustrates that when it comes to affirmative action, we can't argue abstractions. We *must* argue realities. The only way to understand affirmative action is to understand our history, our current socioeconomics—and the reasons why Americans of different backgrounds feel so strongly about their positions. If I weren't a black person raised to empathize with the struggles of other African Americans, I'd probably feel a lot less passionate about the battles over affirmative action. And for those who don't have strong opinions either way, the fairness of the media's coverage is critically important. We don't have a balanced debate. We've ceded the moral high ground to those who argue that programs like affirmative action, designed to foster equality, are actually thwarting it. Lost somewhere in the rhetoric and abstractions are the stories of the people with the most to lose, people like LaShunda Prescott.

SEVEN YEARS OF HARD TIME

LaShunda entered UC Berkeley in the fall of 1988. What happened over the course of the next seven years is an incredible tale of hardship and determination—and an illustration of how hollow the hypothetical debates over "qualifications" ring when measured against the reality of race and income.

Who knows if LaShunda would have qualified to enter UC Berkeley had affirmative action not existed? She was the valedictorian at Castlemont, her high school in inner-city Oakland, but even the best education her school had to offer didn't prepare her for the academic rigors of Berkeley. While she was struggling to learn new concepts in her first semester math and science classes, she says, the other kids from private and public prep schools were coasting, reviewing old material.

Oakland's East Fourteenth Street corridor, the violence-plagued neighborhood where LaShunda grew up, is just miles away but worlds apart from the manicured lawns of Berkeley. A brown-skinned woman with close-cropped natural hair and mischief in her eyes, LaShunda lost the first boy she ever had a crush on to gunfire. Her two brothers, one older than she, one younger, still carry inside their bodies the bullets that she thanks God did not kill them. Her father, a traumatized Vietnam vet, drank and smoked crack to block out the graphic flashbacks. Her sister is a recovering crack addict with two young daughters. The day her sister went to jail, LaShunda found one of her nieces abandoned and sobbing. It also happened to be the day of one of her engineering mid-terms. She flunked.

LaShunda never complains about the hard hand life's dealt her, nor have her trials eroded what can only be called her joie de vivre. Her speech, peppered with colloquialisms, her walk, even the ease with which she allows emotion to register on her face, all illustrate that she has not let life shut her off or shut her down. Despite her packed academic schedule, she's taking an elective class on black women's history. It inspired a desire to pull together an anthology of young black women's writing. "Do you remember [Toni Morrison's] *The Bluest Eye?*" she says, recalling the book where a black girl named Pecola goes insane because she wants so desperately to be white. "I never wanted the blue eyes, but I wanted the long hair. Pecola is the victim in the book. When I write, I want to make Pecola not a victim. I want to give her back her beauty."

LaShunda's seven years at Berkeley include time away from school after she was expelled for failing her classes, and the extra time it's taken to make the work up. Though she's had to step into the role of mommy, had to take exams just after her brother was shot and her grandmother died, and had to study in an apartment without hot water or heat, she never wraps herself in the mantle of victimization. She also wants to make one thing clear: though she may have moved heaven and earth to get to where she is, she considers herself no better than other African Americans who haven't made it out of the 'hood. "Sometimes I don't like telling my story because I'm not"—she affects a TV newscaster's voice—"'that black girl from the ghetto that made it.' I'm not the exception."

She rightly fears being cast into the role of "the exception that proves the rule"—the hardworking black youth who proves that if she can triumph over adversity, we don't need to change the playing field to get rid of the adversity in the first place. While everybody else is talking about how to save the tiniest vestige of affirmative action, LaShunda feels the problem of inequality is far larger and more profound. A new student at Berkeley came from her old high school and reported the changes: some of the good teachers are burning out, some of the new teachers are terrible, and there aren't even enough books to go around. "You know, people act like we're complaining. And I'm like, that shit is so . . . !" She trails off. "That's why I get mad with this affirmative action thing, 'cause I'm like we are sitting here begging for crumbs. How few of us do you see up here [at Berkeley]? We are protesting and begging them to be able to go to this school, and instead of protesting, what we need to do is go to Castlemont, make sure the kids are proficient, help them learn how to start up businesses."

THE FUTURE OF AMERICA'S MOST POPULOUS STATE

LaShunda sees something that a lot of people don't—at least not yet. California is becoming increasingly black and brown. And if something isn't done to make sure that black and Latino students have a shot at getting a good education, it's going to tear the state apart. Schools like Castlemont (and Fremont High) aren't giving smart kids the education they deserve, making it hard for them to compete at schools like Berkeley. Many urban blacks and Latinos attend segregated schools; in fact, according to the Justice Department, two-thirds of black students still do. And the Supreme Court hasn't helped matters either, ruling that remedies for segregation (like magnet schools) and school funding discrepancies between urban and suburban schools shouldn't be widely implemented. We seem to have given up on providing equal opportunity at the primary and secondary levels; now the end of affirmative action is cutting students off at the college level as well.

In a nutshell, affirmative action hinges on two issues: the inherent quality of the student (or worker) and the readiness to get the education (or job). Students like LaShunda tend to get lower test scores than whites and Asians. The first fork in the road is why they score lower: nature or nurture. Some, like Charles Murray, argue that blacks and Latinos are inherently less intelligent. If you don't believe books like *The Bell Curve* (which came under attack three years after it was published for errors and failing to have its findings reviewed by other social scientists), then you probably believe that blacks and Latinos have the potential to learn just as much as anyone else does, but they haven't reached their full potential because of poor schooling. Again we reach a fork in the road: what to do with these undereducated students. If we go by current qualifications alone, these students are less qualified. There's no point in arguing that they're not. (Take LaShunda's evaluation of how she stacked up versus other first-year engineering students.) But do you take smart kids who are "less qualified" because of a bad education and tell them they shouldn't ever get a better one? At its best, affirmative action provides a means of allowing these students to finally get the chance to compete—and to catch up. If they aren't offered the chance to run the race, they certainly won't be able to finish.

Racial discrepancies in education are going to hit states like California particularly hard. California, already 40 percent nonwhite, will be majority-minority much sooner than most of the nation. To have a majority nonwhite state where the education, and the jobs, and the power remained concentrated among whites would be nothing less than economic apartheid—far from the "equal opportunity" anti-affirmative-action forces claim they seek. Berkeley's chancellor, Chang Lin Tien, argued for the necessity of widespread educational opportunity after the Regents' vote. The campus publication *The Berkeleyan* carried his statement, along with a large photo of him seated stiffly with his hands clasped firmly together. No doubt the pose was designed to look authoritative, but it conveyed a sense of nervousness, even dread. Tien vowed that the Regents' decision would not end his "belief that excellence and diversity go hand in hand. . . . Our workforce and student population must reflect the ethnic, racial and gender composition of the world around us. . . . Today the fate of youngsters in California's elementary schools is in our hands. We must be sure to send a message to the next generation of undergraduates that our doors will be open to them if they are committed to their studies and excel academically."

It's easy to argue that making sure kids of all races have access to the universities is in the state's best interest. But given the rancor of the affirmative action debates, it's an argument we rarely hear. In fact, it seems like race is one of the only things UC admissions officers *can't* consider when they choose who to let in. "SP-1," the technical name for the Regents' vote barring affirmative action, stated that race could no longer be a factor in undergraduate admissions— though whether or not your parents were alumni, whether or not you are an athlete, and whether or not your are disabled, for example, are all categories that can be considered. So can socioeconomics: consideration for students who have "suffered disadvantage economically or in terms of their social environment (such as an abusive or otherwise dysfunctional home or a neighborhood of unwholesome or antisocial influences)." The policy was set to take full effect with the admission of the class of 1997, but fewer blacks and Latinos began applying to Berkeley immediately. In 1996, the year before the affirmative action ban officially took effect, the percentage of black applicants fell by 8 percent; for Hispanics, the figure was 6 percent.

LaShunda is precisely the kind of student Berkeley's affirmative action program was set up to help, someone whose race, gender, and socioeconomic background have all made it harder for her to get the education she deserves. But why should a talented young white man give up his space at the school even for someone as deserving as she is? That question is at the heart of the current affirmative action debate, and we can all understand the moral reasoning behind arguing that the white guy shouldn't have to pay. The opponents of affirmative action have wrapped themselves in the mantle of morality, saying they simply want each person judged as an individual. But a closer look reveals they aren't the champions of pure equality they claim to be. They're more than happy to advocate for the special admissions needs of some students—as long as those students are politically well connected.

In 1996, the *Los Angeles Times* broke what should have come as shocking allegations: top schools like Berkeley and UCLA routinely received requests from politically well-connected Californians, and many of those requests were honored. One regent sent thirty-two admissions requests to UCLA, including one for a friend's son whose grades and SAT scores were below the school's standards. He was admitted. A state assemblywoman lobbied for a school transfer that was approved even though the student had both low test scores and had missed the admissions deadline. Terry Lightfoot, a spokesman for the UC President, admitted: "In some cases . . . you had students who had been denied admittance on one or two occasions, who were then granted admission solely on the basis of who these students were connected with." Connerly, of course, put in a letter. And even Governor Wilson, the self-styled champion of the meritocracy, put in two special requests, though both his candidates were denied. But Connerly's hypocrisy on affirmative action goes deeper. He made the emphatic statement that being seen as an "affirmative action businessman" would be just as degrading as drinking from "colored only" water fountains in the pre–Civil Rights Deep South. Yet he drank from the fountain, and drank deep. During the six years before he voted to overturn affirmative action as a member of the UC Regents, he accepted fully one million dollars in state contracts for minority business owners. LaShunda Prescott wants to be a business owner one day too. She won't have the advantage of the programs Ward Connerly used to make his way.

Some of LaShunda's fellow students are as vehemently and vocally opposed to affirmative action as any national spokesperson. One of them is Steve Mohebi. A tall, nineteen-year-old Persian American, he has long sweeping eyelashes, olive skin, thick dark hair, and a Semitic nose. Persian- and Arab Americans, and Indians and other South Asians, don't fit into the narrow boundaries of American racial classifications. Mohebi has more freedom than most students to define his place within the racial power struggles, and he's made a clear choice to identify with and advocate for conservative whites.

We meet a few days after the October 12 protest. Black Republican presidential candidate Alan Keyes is coming to speak on campus that afternoon at the behest of the Berkeley College Republicans, a group Steve is the vice president of. Keyes is a political anomaly, an outsider desperately trying to squirm his way into the bosom of the GOP. A favorite of the religious right, Keyes will rarely capture more than 1 or 2 percent of the vote in Republican primaries but spends his media time on favorite issues: decrying abortion and welfare and promoting values and prayer. Regardless of how in sync his message is with the Republican ideal, Steve doesn't think Keyes has a chance. "It's a racist society," he says. Party officials "are going to advance whoever can get the votes. If you're going to advance a minority candidate, the constituency is not there. [Colin] Powell is what they call a whitewashed black guy. He gets criticism from blacks—he seems to distance himself from the black population. He's the only guy who has a glimmer of hope because he's shunned his ethnicity. America is highly racist, mostly against blacks," he admits. "For a black candidate to have any prayer of winning, he's going to have to distance himself from the black community."

Steve's own organization, the Berkeley College Republicans, has by his count three hundred and fifty dues-paying members and a mailing list of seven hundred. The largest racial group on Cal's campus is also the largest within the organization—Asian Americans. But he doesn't think an Asian American has much of a shot at being nominated for president either. That doesn't bother him terribly much, because he feels that the racism that shapes the American socio-economic and cultural system pales in comparison to the new ill of reverse racism.

"We all know the double standard. A white male club would be firebombed. A black woman's club is OK," he says. The debate over affirmative action is the one arena in which "you can have white males band together and say, 'We're being screwed.' The affirmative action vote is a step in the right direction. My friends and I had chilled champagne bottles waiting for [the announcement of] the Regents' vote."

"You might say," he smiles, "that our position was, 'Ban affirmative action by any means necessary.'"

Steve had some experience with discrimination. He grew up in Seattle and Silicon Valley, arriving in America as an infant after his family fled the Iranian revolution. His father was an ambassador to Israel under the Shah. "He was aristocracy," Steve says. Immigrating to the United States "was a socioeconomic rude awakening"—no more servants, no more chauffeur, no more royal treatment. But his family did well. His father now does import-export; his mother is a homemaker. One of his two brothers studies artificial intelligence and the other went to college at the ripe age of fourteen. But Steve's family lived through racism as well. During the tense, economically tight days of the U.S. hostage crisis in 1980, which Americans looked at them and saw the face of the Ayatollah—a man the Mohebis hated. But Steve says the in-your-face racism his family experienced didn't foster any solidarity with blacks. "Ninety-nine percent of Persians are conservative. They're racist, mostly against blacks. They don't support welfare. 'To hell with these ethnic groups.'" I point out that the largest group of women on welfare are whites. "Persians don't know that," he says.

It's one of many times that the facts about race in America seem almost immaterial to Steve. He says he's become convinced that "racism will always exist to some extent"—and that it circumscribes everything from the political ambitions to the job prospects of blacks and other groups. But "in some situations it may be OK to let it go," he says. He talks one moment about the racism of the present, then uses the rhetoric of "past discrimination" to describe affirmative action. "It's bad to penalize the white males of today for what happened in the past. What do you tell a guy who didn't get his place in grad school? We need eighteen percent Chicanos? Your qualified but you just can't get in? . . .

Read Shelby Steele—why should black people have to accept the stigma" of being labeled affirmative action recipients? He believes the "mental advantage" blacks will receive from giving up affirmative action will far outweigh "this hand-out welfare thing."

The idea that affirmative action is a "handout welfare thing" is often reinforced by what we read in the papers and see on TV. Instead of staying neutral in this political debate, the news media—often accused of having a liberal bias—chose sides by mimicking the language of its opponents. Headlines in *The New York Times, Washington Post,* and *Wall Street Journal* screamed "preference" and "bias" when talking about affirmative action. When racial code words masquerade as journalistic objectivity, it has a profound effect on the American public. In 1992, pollster Lou Harris found that Americans supported affirmative action 70 percent to 24 percent, but decried racial "preferences" by a margin of 48 to 46 percent. A *Los Angeles Times* poll found a similar split: people opposed "preferences" for blacks and women by 72 and 70 percent respectively; only 29 percent and 24 percent opposed affirmative action for blacks and women. Or look at a *Washington Post* poll that contained a double dose of bias, asking: Do you "favor preferences for blacks and other minorities to make up for past discrimination?" The words "preference" and "past discrimination" both tilt this question. Yet to this day, national papers like *The New York Times* use the word "preference" in headlines when talking about affirmative action, reinforcing the most negative vision of the program.

Steve says the issue of affirmative action is poisoning Berkeley's atmosphere. "White America is mad at black America for taking handouts," says Steve. "Everybody's racist to a certain extent. [But] however racist you are when you enter Berkeley, you will be ten times more when you graduate. It's appalling to hear people brag about taking handouts." Steve's words echo those of Charles Murray and Richard Herrnstein. They wrote in *The Bell Curve* that white students resent black [and in schools like Cal, Latino] students because they "are in fact getting a large edge in the admissions process and often in scholarship assistance. . . . [They] 'don't belong there' academically."

Steve sees the professors as enemies, too. "They've been here for twenty or thirty years. They're liberal." He's fairly pleased with the student body, which is divided but "more conservative than liberal. But there's so much leftist rhetoric," he claims, "it's hard for them to voice opinions." Far from being a cultural melting pot, Berkeley in Mohebi's eyes is a place where even the dorms are "segregated. Unit 2 is far away. It's cheaper. It's Chicano. Chicanos are financially less sound than other groups. Foothill is expensive. There are a high amount of Asians. They've got their cell phones. A lot of them are from Taiwan."

Right now, the Berkeley College Republicans are targeting the Greek system for membership. "The frats are white guy clubs," he says. "Minorities are not welcome." I ask if this is a problem. "Not if there are clubs on the other side. The Chinese Students Association has all-Chinese-guy dances and they don't invite other people." While many conservatives decry Balkanization as a byproduct of multiculturalism, Steve seems to find it comforting, if it means no one need interact with people they don't like. "I'm not sure I believe in a cohesive American culture," he says. "American culture is a patchwork quilt—more patches than quilt." He has no desire to recruit more blacks for the Berkeley Republicans, for example. "I'm not convinced that would be a good place to concentrate our efforts. I think we're strong as we are."

Is there any solution to the affirmative action conundrum? Education. "It's cost-inefficient for the government to police discrimination. We should spend more money on education," he says. Of course, providing education to blacks and Latinos was precisely the point of the University of California's affirmative action program. Are Steve's beliefs a paradox? If so, he doesn't have to puzzle it out. He doesn't feel the need to. The inequality isn't his problem.

AHISTORICAL EQUALITY

Mohebi, like many opponents of affirmative action, justifies his position as a simple quest for individual fairness. But does fairness constitute ignoring decades—even centuries—of both government- and privately sanctioned discrimination? Or does the fairness truly come into play when we chose to do something about it?

Troy Duster, the Berkeley sociology professor who has studied affirmative action, compares our current situation to two real-life case studies: South Africa under apartheid and India under the caste system. Yes, he realizes their situations have many differences from our own. But we share a common, current reality—those societies (and ours) are dealing with how to redress ongoing discrimination on the one hand while dealing with the protests of individuals who've benefited from that discrimination in the past.

Those who claim eliminating affirmative action is simply "fair" are being ahistorical, Duster argues. In South Africa, whites forcibly removed blacks from their farms and ranches, corralled them into impoverished "homelands," and refused to pay for running water or even minimally sufficient schools. By the time forty-five years of apartheid ended, whites (less than 10 percent of the population) had ten times the wealth of blacks (over 80 percent of the population). Duster writes, "In 1992, when the writing was on the wall and apartheid's days were numbered, the corporate managers at Telkom, South Africa's national telephone company, an organization with more than fifty-eight thousand employees, did a quick review of the racial composition of its corporate structure. In late 1993, they found one more black manager than many expected—this is, they found one. By the second half of 1995, Telkom employed eighty-three black managers and has since embarked upon an aggressive affirmative action program to recruit and hire more." What was the reaction to this significant, though still *very* modest, bit of progress? "More than five thousand white workers have threatened to strike to protest the new policy." If affirmative action is about group versus individual, so is the history of race that precedes it. No doubt these workers were not protesting when they were judged as a group before—as a white group accorded tremendous privilege. Now that their seniority is entrenched, they demand to be treated as individuals alone.

At the heart of the debate over affirmative action is our belief in a meritocracy. But one of the conundrums we face in puzzling a way out of racial discrimination is how to judge the *potential* for achievement when individuals have not yet been given the tools to succeed. Many black South Africans who didn't have the same education and training as whites could assume prominent positions should they be given the opportunity to get education and training. Of course, that requires money, time—and the political will to devote both to changing the status quo. It would be foolhardy, in South Africa or Berkeley, California, to place blacks in positions where they didn't have the tools to succeed. But it would be absolutely insidious to let ongoing discrimination prevent potential talent from developing.

It's telling to bring the focus back to college admissions, and one instance in which "affirmative action" worked for white men, and no one complained. Brandeis University in Massachusetts first opened its doors in 1948; the graduating class four years later was 52 percent male, 48 percent female. But when admissions officers analyzed the student pool before admitting any students to the brand-new school, they found something shocking—if they made admissions based on test scores and aptitude tests alone, the school would have been 70 percent female. They chose to make gender—in this case, the male gender—a positive criterion for admission. Duster writes, "Yet, at no time did we hear the anguished cries from [conservatives] Nathan Glazer and Irving Kristol that less qualified Jewish males were getting into Brandeis unfairly bumping more qualified females."

Today's equivalent of Brandeis's male affirmative action is the system of "legacy" admission, which offers a crystal-clear advantage to the children of alumni, most from privileged backgrounds. In 1992, a group of Asian Americans asked the U.S. Department of Education to see if they were being rejected for less qualified whites. Investigators found that the children of alumni, as well as athletes, consistently received what they termed a "special preference" over other applicants at elite schools, including Harvard, Yale, and Stanford. Harvard's legacies were more than twice as likely to be admitted to the school than other applicants—even though their average SAT score was 35 points lower than the average admit. The most damning evidence came from the notes of admissions officers. In one case, a Harvard admissions officer posted this note in a folder: "Without lineage, there would be little case. With it, we will keep looking . . ." There's no evidence that Harvard follows a quota system for legacies colleges ("quotas" being the evil affirmative action foes protest the hardest)—but Notre Dame, for example, has a quota decreeing that 25 percent of each class be children of alumni. Legacy status, regional diversity, disability, and socioeconomics are all routinely considered when it comes to evaluating who's admitted to schools. None of them speak to the questions of who has the highest SAT scores or grades—to the (already unattainable) idea of a pure meritocracy—but all of them are part of the process of picking and choosing who it is in the school's, and perhaps society's, best interest to have attend. All, that is, except race. ■

Working with the Text

1. Midway through her chapter, Chideya asks, "Do we even know what affirmative action is?" The term "affirmative action" has been used to refer to a wide range of policies in diverse institutional settings for almost forty years. Investigate the meanings of "affirmative action" by summarizing various perspectives and definitions of affirmative action that Chideya encounters in the course of her reporting. You can expand your research by conducting your own campus poll, asking other students for their personal working definitions, and by talking with or emailing the person on campus responsible for monitoring or administering local affirmative action programs.

2. Chideya argues, "In a nutshell, affirmative action hinges on two issues: the inherent quality of the student (or worker) and the readiness to get the education (or job)." Explore your own attitudes and those of others in the class towards the mix of preparation and potential necessary for college success on your campus. Based on your experiences, what would you say are the keys to doing well in college? You might compare your own ideas with those of faculty, or expand your discussion to the workplace by interviewing local employers on what qualities they most look for in people they hire.

3. Chideya is sympathetic to the continuing need for affirmative action. Consider the kinds of evidence she offers: statistical information; personal stories and biographies; examples of other preferential policies, such as "legacies"; logical analysis. Which do you find personally most convincing and why? What are the different audiences you think she is appealing to with these various strategies? How might they relate to her assertion that beyond logic, our individual "history, our current socioeconomics" shapes our understanding of these issues?

Working with Connections

1. Both the stories of Frederick Douglass and Nina Saltman tell of people who faced barriers of race and gender. Locate some examples from these stories that you find most supportive or most challenging to Chideya's positions on affirmative action. How might some of the different people Chideya interviews interpret these stories based on their own attitudes and opinions?

2. Jean Anyon examines the impact of social class on educational opportunities and the structure of schooling in "Social Class and the Hidden Curriculum of Work" (in Chapter 3, Education and Work/Education as Work). What new perspectives could her discussion of class-based education have on the "preparation/potential" argument that Chideya sees as the heart of the debate over affirmative action?

3. Look at the charts taken from the report by the Population Reference Bureau entitled *America's Diversity: On the Edge of Two Centuries* and consider how they might be used as part of the debate and discussion on affirmative action. As you do so, consider how visual presentations of statistical information can function as arguments in themselves. Speculate on what explicit and implicit points of view we might see represented in these charts. How would other ways of presenting this information visually allow us to emphasize or de-emphasize different aspects of the data?

SHELLEY DONALD COOLIDGE
On the Job, It's English or the Pink Slip

Most people would probably identify the United States as an English-speaking country. Yet almost 9 percent of the population speaks Spanish, and one million Americans speak French, just to choose two European languages. Some linguists estimate that there are over 175 different languages spoken in the United States, some by only a small population, others by thousands of people. Given the fact that the United States was created by immigrants from Europe, Africa, and Asia inhabiting a land already populated by a million native peoples who spoke hundreds of different languages themselves, this linguistic diversity should not be surprising, yet this same wealth of languages is seen by some as a threat to unity and a hindrance to communication, especially in the workplace.

In this newspaper story written for The Christian Science Monitor, *reporter Shelley Donald Coolidge reports on the controversy over companies creating "English Only" workplace rules and the specific cases of workers whose firings may have been related to their speaking in a language other than English on the job. The creation of "English Only" policies in the workplace raises important questions of just how much control an employer may exercise over employees as well as how closely issues of language use (including writing) are tied to our senses of identity, family, community, and history.*

The occasional "que pasa?" probably won't hurt you. But carrying on a full-blown conversation in any language other than English could someday cost you your job.

For reasons of safety and employee unity, businesses are increasingly adopting English-only rules for the workplace.

That means idle chatter in the wrong tongue on the factory floor, at the check-out counter, or even on the street a block away from the office is becoming grounds for dismissal at some US firms.

As a result, a growing number of workers—whose native languages include Spanish, Chinese, Vietnamese, and French Creole—are filing discrimination suits over the new rules.

The rise in such restrictions comes at a time when nearly two dozen states have declared English as the official language. Some say the trend reflects a larger ambivalence in society over the acceptance of immigrants in a nation built by immigrants—one that often considers diversity a strength.

Many businesses, in fact, seek out bilingual employees and welcome less-costly workers—from Mexican strawberry pickers to Russian software engineers. Yet, increasingly, that may only be on certain terms.

As the American workplace diversifies, the flap over what language is legal around the water cooler will likely only intensify.

"This is not only a legal question. It is also a question of how do you manage a diverse work force?" says Ed Chen, a lawyer at the American Civil Liberties Union in California.

English-only rules are not new. Yet lawyers and activists say companies are placing more demands on when and where workers must speak English, and they are enacting harsher penalties on employees who don't comply.

The US Equal Employment Opportunity Commission (EEOC), which only started tracking complaints about English-only rules in 1996, says they are rising. Maria Quinones and Evelyn Silverman, for example, say they were dismissed in May 1995 shortly after their supervisor at a New York City home-care agency met with them to discuss "speaking Spanish on the job."

The two women, who speak English and Spanish, allege that the company prohibits employees from speaking Spanish during breaks, lunch in the cafeteria, and within one city block of their office building. An attorney for their former employer, Long Life Home Care, contends that "there was no English-only rule in effect at the company and the [two workers] were fired for just cause." The EEOC filed a lawsuit a year ago in US District Court in New York against the company.

Companies—from retailers to financial institutions—say they adopt such policies because speaking a language that customers or coworkers don't understand is inefficient and can create distrust. "It's not so much that companies don't want workers speaking Spanish or German in the workplace," says Barry Lawrence of the Society for Human Resource Management in Alexandria, Va. "But sometimes it defeats the purpose of trying to build synergy."

In some workplaces, such as air-traffic-control towers and on assembly lines, clear communication can also be a critical safety issue. But civil libertarians argue that these rules stem from a growing anti-immigration sentiment and don't respect cultural and language diversity in the workplace.

"We see people being reprimanded not for violating safety laws, but because they are talking to a fellow employee in the elevator," says William Tamayo, an EEOC lawyer in San Francisco.

Mr. Tamayo argues that English-only rules reinforce the "erroneous perception" that when people speak in another language it is meant to demean someone who only speaks English.

In many cases, lawyers say, companies don't have policies in writing. Rather a supervisor, without direct corporate approval, is prohibiting workers from speaking other languages.

Still, the legality of English-only policies and how far companies can go in implementing them remains unclear. The EEOC maintains that English-only rules discriminate against workers based on national origin, and it is therefore illegal to require all employees to speak English at all times. Under the guidelines, however, an employer may have a rule requiring employees to speak only in English at certain times where the employer can show the rule is "justified by business necessity."

The problem, say the ACLU's Mr. Chen and others, is that while courts reviewing English-only laws are supposed to refer to the EEOC guidelines in making a ruling, they are not required to accept them. In 1993, for example, the US Ninth Circuit Court of Appeals in San Francisco put aside the guidelines and upheld the English-only rules of a local meat-packing plant. The court said such rules are invalid only if an employee proves that they create an atmosphere of "inferiority, isolation, and intimidation."

Still, of the five companies the EEOC has sued in the past four years, all have ended their English-only policies, says Mr. Tamayo. In 1995, two American Red Cross laboratories in Rockville, Md., abandoned such a rule after the EEOC sued on behalf of Chinese employees who were prohibited from speaking English and Chinese interchangeably to each other during office hours and telephone conversations to family members.

"Language is a very emotional subject," says Marielena Hincapie, a lawyer at the Employment Law Center in San Francisco. "A lot of the arguments companies are making [for English-only policies] are not logical or legal, but are coming from inside." ■

Working with the Text

1. Reflect on and write about your own experiences with language diversity, whether on the job, at school, or in the community. Can you think of specific stories that you can use to illustrate

your personal connection to language diversity? Tell these stories, using as much detail as possible, especially about your reactions at the time and now. Share and discuss these stories as a class in order to explore the different perspectives and attitudes of people in the class to language and language diversity.

2. What are the main reasons given for instituting "English Only" rules as described in Coolidge's story? Can you think of other reasons? Which reasons do you find most persuasive? How well do these reasons fit the Equal Employment Opportunity Commission guidelines that an English Only rule needs to be "justified by business necessity"?

3. What are the main criticisms of English Only rules as described in Coolidge's story? Can you think of other possible objections to these kinds of policies? Which criticisms do you find most valid and why?

4. According to Marielena Hincapie, a lawyer for the Employment Center in San Francisco who is quoted in the story, "'Language is a very emotional subject,'" and "'a lot of arguments companies are making [for English Only policies] are not logical or legal, but are coming from inside.'" What might these emotional aspects of the English Only debate be? How would Hincapie explain the motivations of companies for instituting these policies? What examples of arguments "coming from inside" can you find in the stories you wrote in response to question one above?

Working with Connections

1. As a class, discuss different ways issues of language diversity can and are incorporated into the college writing classroom. What guidelines, for example, could you suggest for writers in thinking about using a variety of languages in a particular piece of writing? You can extend this discussion to include both languages other than English and the many varieties of English itself, which varies by geographic region, ethnicity, social class, and context. Which languages feel most at home to you, and what issues and questions do you face in making language use decisions in school and on the job?

2. Many of the readings in Chapter 8, Work in the Global Economy, discuss issues relating to the increasingly interna-

tional nature of modern commerce, where a single corporation may employ people around the world who will need to communicate effectively with one another. What impact does the global economy have on questions of language diversity in the workplace?

DALTON CONLEY

The Cost of Slavery

From the sixteenth century until the end of the Civil War, millions of Africans and Americans of African descent were forced to work without pay or freedom as enslaved laborers. Even though slavery was abolished by the 13ᵗʰ Amendment to the Constitution, its legacy continues with us today, including enduring disparities in economic opportunity between African- and European-Americans. Some have argued that abolishing slavery was not enough, and that formerly enslaved Americans and their descendants have never been compensated for the injuries done to them with the consent of the US government prior to 1865. The issue of reparations for slavery—cash payments made by the government to the families descended from those enslaved—has become a controversial and fiercely debated issue, with some arguing that America has a moral responsibility to apologize and atone for what is now generally regarded as a crime against humanity, and others countering that those most directly harmed by slavery are now dead and that providing compensation to their descendants would be costly, difficult, and socially divisive.

In this essay originally published in the New York Times, *Dalton Conley enters the debate over reparations to offer what he sees as a new way of understanding the lasting economic harm done by slavery to African Americans and the enduring economic benefits of slavery to many white Americans.*

Dalton Conley is a sociology professor and director of the Center for Advanced Social Research at New York University. He is the author of Honky, *a memoir recounting his experiences growing up as a white child in a low-income primarily African-American and Latino neighborhood on the lower east side of Manhattan.*

Marching across the South in 1865, Union soldiers seized up to 900,000 acres of "abandoned property." Some radical Northerners hoped to use this land to provide freed slaves with the now-legendary "40 acres and a mule" as restitution for slavery. Their hopes were obviously dashed. But the argument for reparations lives on nearly 140 years later.

While few doubt that slavery was a great wrong, the challenge before us is how to make things right through financial restitution. But just how would we devise a practical formula to determine who gets what?

Most assessments start with the notion of payment for lost wages. One researcher took 1860's prices for slaves as an estimate of their labor value and applied compound interest. The result: $2 trillion to $4 trillion. Six generations after slavery's demise, such approaches present serious difficulties. There are issues of what to do with whites (and blacks) who immigrated here after slavery ended. What about descendants of blacks who lived freely during the antebellum period? Does someone who is born to a white parent and a black parent cancel out? It would take Solomon to solve this.

Perhaps the issue needs to be looked at differently. One way is to recognize slavery as an institution upon which America's wealth was built. If we take this view, it is not important whether a white family arrived in 1700 or in 1965. If you wear cotton blue jeans, if you take out an insurance policy, if you buy from anyone who has a connection to the industries that were built on chattel labor, then you have benefited from slavery. Likewise, if you are black—regardless of when your ancestors arrived—you live with slavery's stigma.

Extending the reparations argument this broadly frees one to move beyond the issue of lost wages and seek out other factors on which to base a formula. If there were one statistic that captured the persistence of racial inequality, it would be net worth.

The typical white family enjoys a net worth that is more than eight times that of its black counterpart, according to the economist Edward Wolff. Even at equivalent income levels, gaps remain large. Among families earning less than $15,000 a year, the median African-American family has a net worth of zero, while the corresponding white family has $10,000 in equity. The typical white family earning $40,000 annually has a nest egg of around $80,000. Its black counterpart has about half that amount.

This equity inequity is partly the result of the head start whites enjoy in accumulating and passing on assets. Some economists estimate that up to 80 percent of lifetime wealth accumulation results from gifts from earlier generations, ranging from the down payment on a home to a bequest by a parent. If the government used such net-worth inequality as a basis, and then factored in measures like population size, it could address reparations by transferring about 13 percent of white household wealth to blacks. A two-adult black family would receive an average reparation of about $35,000.

What would be the effect of wealth redistribution on such a vast scale? My own research—using national data to follow black and white adolescents into adulthood—shows that when we compare families with the same net worth, blacks are more likely to finish high school than whites and are equally likely to complete a bachelor's degree. Racial differences in welfare rates disappear. Thus, one generation after reparations were paid, racial gaps in education should close—eliminating the need for affirmative action.

The unpopularity of this radical plan would no doubt be unprecedented. There are also no guarantees that reparations would be a magic bullet for lingering racial problems. That said, it remains vital to explore formulas and keep the reparations debate alive. It is important because each resulting dollar amount implies a theory of race, history and equal opportunity. That includes the figure implicit in our current policy—zero—which rests on the most absurd assumption of all: that slavery didn't matter. ■

Working with the Text

1. Before you read Conley's essay, did you have an opinion about reparations for slavery? If so, what was it, and what caused you to think about the issue in this way? How does Conley's argument affect your thinking about the issue? What do you find most and least persuasive about his essay?

2. How does Conley redefine the basic argument over reparations for slavery away from the idea of "payment for lost wages"? In what ways might his new way of looking at the issue help change the opinions of those who might otherwise oppose reparations?

3. What does Conley mean by "wealth" and "net worth"? Why does Conley find the idea of net worth so powerful in understanding differences in economic opportunity linked to race? What was your own reaction to his assertion that "up to 80 percent of lifetime wealth accumulation results from earlier generations"? How does this idea change our attitudes about the relationship between individual effort and inherited advantage in achieving economic success?

4. Conley published this essay as an opinion piece during Black History Month (February) 2003. To what extent do you see his argument as a serious public policy proposal? To what extent do you see it as a provocative way of challenging readers to rethink the issue of reparations for slavery as well as the continuing economic gaps based on race in the United States today?

Working with Connections

1. Conley argues that according to his own research, when blacks and whites are compared on the basis of similar net worth, differences in educational achievement disappear. "Thus," he writes, "one generation after reparations were paid, racial gaps in education should close—eliminating the need for affirmative

action." How would Conley's approach to the topic of reparations for slavery affect the arguments over affirmative action discussed in the excerpt from *The Color of Our Future* by Farai Chideya? Who might welcome or challenge his point of view and why?

2. If Conley's research is accurate suggesting that differences in educational achievement are more closely linked to net worth than income level or race, how would this enrich the analysis of the connections between social class and education that Jean Anyon conducts in "Social Class and the Hidden Curriculum of Work" (in Chapter 3, Education and Work/Education as Work)? How might your family's net worth affect lifestyle, behavior, and attitudes toward education even more than the kinds of work done by family members?

Reading the Web

Ragged Edge Magazine Online

Ragged Edge Magazine Online <http://www.disabilityrag.org> *is the web version of a magazine published by disability rights activists in order to highlight issues of concern to the disability rights community and to help organize political activities. One key area of their focus is the 1990 Americans with Disabilities Act, a landmark law that forbids workplace discrimination against people with disabilities. Since its passage, the law has both improved working conditions for people with disabilities and created dialogue and debate over definitions of disability and the responsibilities of employers to accommodate the physical and psychological needs of workers. As you discuss the home page from late 2002 reproduced here, consider the question of audience. While the magazine is aimed primarily at the disability community, it also hopes to educate and persuade those who do not identify as disabled as well.*

MAKE THEM GO AWAY

TELL-US-YOUR-STORY.COM
DISABILITY DISCUSSION FORUM
finding what we have in common one story at a time

The Disability Rag's
R A G G E D   E D G E   M A G A Z I N E   O N L I N E

BUY THIS BOOK!

NEWS
CURRENT ISSUE
ARCHIVES
SUBSCRIBE
CONTACT US
CARTOONS
ADVOCADO PRESS
BOOKSTORE
Text-only version

Hi
Please support
Ragged Edge
magazine!

Click to Give

Amazon honor system

Many more titles!

About the Advocado
Press

NEWS from the Disability Rights NATION
Disability groups file brief for woman with brain injury Over a dozen national disability rights groups today filed a friend-of-the-court brief supporting Terri Schiavo's right to food, water and rehabilitation FULL STORY | MORE NEWS

Ragged Edge EXTRA!
'Daredevil': One older crip reviews another "If the image of The Supercrip bugs you, this film might make you grind your teeth," writes **RUS COOPER-DOWDA**. Yet, she says, the script plays with stereotypes in interesting ways. MORE.

Google™ ○ Search www.raggededgemagazine.com ○ Search WWW   [Google Search]

From our PRINT EDITION
Inspiration Human interest "supercrip" stories, ubiquitous in newspapers and on TV newscasts, have long made disability rights activists uneasy, writes **JOHN KELLY**. So why are they so beloved by reporters and editors? Just what do normals get out of the whole inspiration routine? READ ARTICLE | TABLE OF CONTENTS

Visitability: Becoming a national issue? "One day in 1986 I was driving around in Atlanta, Georgia, my home city, and I passed though a large development of new homes," says **ELEANOR SMITH**, founder of the U.S. visitability movement. Suddenly it came to her, she says: "These homes could have *all* had access!" READ STORY | TABLE OF CONTENTS

Ragged Edge EXTRA!
Superman to the rescue in Australia? "When Christopher Reeve flies back to the U.S. this week, he leaves behind people with disabilities who are once more cast into a medical model of 'disability as tragedy,'" writes **ERIK LEIPOLDT** -- "again publicly cast as victims of our impairments." MORE.

NEWS from the Disability Rights NATION
CA activists announce 'March in March to save *Olmstead*!' A new Americans with Disabilities Act case to be heard by U.S. Supreme Court in March may gut the Court's 1999 *Olmstead* decision, say advocates. They are planning a major national march on March 15 and 16 in Sacramento to send a message. FULL STORY. | MORE NEWS

From our LAST ISSUE
Ripples, A Tide, An Ocean "At first, Lee Larsen's case was private, between her and her family. Then other people got involved: teachers, social workers, interpreters, lawyers," writes **CAL MONTGOMERY**. "As the pressures on her mounted to shape her deaf sons to make them less Deaf, more hearing, she started ripples. Flowing out, like in water, so that everyone could feel them." READ STORY | TABLE OF CONTENTS

NEWS from the Disability Rights NATION

San Diego, other cities abandon Sacramento's Supreme Court sidewalk access fight Disability activists have gotten San Diego and some smaller Calif. cities to do an about-face and remove themselves from a brief they signed onto last fall, supporting Sacramento in its petition to the U.S. Supreme Court. Sacramento insists it is not required under the Americans with Disabilities Act to ensure its sidewalks are passable and usable by people in wheelchairs. New York, Phoenix and Denver are among the hundreds of cities that remain signed onto the suit. FULL STORY | MORE NEWS

From our LAST ISSUE

Café Solo with an Old Horn "She was earnest, the woman who approached," writes poet **STEPHEN KUUSISTO.** "She was offering to cure me." READ ESSAY | TABLE OF CONTENTS

LOST DISABILITY CLASSICS: The Sterilization Spectre Oklahoma's law authorizing sterilization was the talk of inmates at its Eastern state hospital when it was passed early in the 20th century. **MARION MARLE WOODSON,** known as "Inmate, Ward 8," offers an exceptional first-person account of the fears of his fellow inmates. FULL STORY | TABLE OF CONTENTS

Wishing for kryptonite when he watched the ABC television documentary, *Christopher Reeve, Courageous Steps,* "I too wished I could will my body to move," writes **WILLIAM J. PEACE.** "Had I been able to, I would have locked my TV." More

How Bruce Springsteen Showed Up Jerry Lewis's Big Lie: September 11th Fundraising vs. The MDA Labor Day Telethon Will this be the year Lewis and the MDA get called big-time on their big ol' lie? That's up to you and me, says **RUS COOPER-DOWDA** who saw a new way from The Boss — and liked it. More.

WHAT DO YOU THINK of these stories?
Click to tell us

The Supreme Court's Catch 22
Jerry Lewis tells crips, "stay in your house!"
The Supreme Court Garrett Decision
Eugenics: Making a Comeback?
'Disabled for A Day,' Reporter Finds Frustration and Stigma

Clint Eastwood's unnoticed loss

MORE.

WHO WE ARE: Ragged Edge magazine is successor to the award-winning periodical, The Disability Rag. In Ragged Edge, and on this website, you'll find the best in today's writing about society's "ragged edge" issues: medical rationing, genetic discrimination, assisted suicide, long-term care, attendant services. We cover the disability experience in America — what it means to be a crip living at the start of the 21st century.

E-MAIL US

Ragged Edge magazine and Ragged Edge online are publications of The Advocado Press, Inc. a nonprofit 501(c)3 organization founded in 1981 to publish materials on disability rights.

This Disability Studies Web Ring site maintained by Mary Johnson, Editor.

[Prev 5 Sites | Skip Previous | Previous | Next |
Skip Next | Next 5 Sites | Random | List Sites]

Join the Disability Studies Web Ring ●

*Note: All sites will be reviewed for appropriateness.

Working with the Text

1. *Ragged Edge* is known for its blunt, assertive tone, exemplified by its mission statement: "We cover the disability experience in America—what it means to be a crip living at the start of the 21st century." The defiant use of "crip," a word that originated as a slur against those perceived as disabled, suggests a willingness on the part of the magazine to challenge the attitudes of its readers about disability issues. How might such rhetoric challenge a reader to rethink assumptions about disabilities? What are the risks and benefits of such an approach? What kinds of attitudes does the rhetoric of *Ragged Edge Online* convey to the multiple potential audiences for the site? For example, how might readers new to disability rights issues react versus members of the disability rights community?

2. While *Ragged Edge* covers a wide variety of issues, employment and workplace concerns are certain to be featured in whatever current edition of the magazine you access. What are the ways that the web transforms our understanding of disability rights? How does working on the web potentially change our understanding of the concepts of "ability" and "disability"?

3. One of the "edgiest" parts of *Ragged Edge* is its inclusion of cartoons by John Lytle, John Callahan, Sharon Wachsler, and other cartoonists and writers who embrace what they describe as "sick humor" about the lives of disabled and chronically ill people. After reading some of these cartoons at the *Ragged Edge* web site, explore your reactions by writing about them. Do you find them funny? Can you relate to them? Are you shocked by any of them? How do your reactions connect to your feelings about using humor and satire as a way of exploring important issues? How does your own ability status affect your reactions?

Working with Connections

1. Compare the more confrontational language and attitude used by *Ragged Edge* with another disability rights site such as the *American Association of People with Disabilities* <http://www.aapd-dc.org>, not to determine which approach is "right" or "wrong," but to engage in a discussion of the different language choices faced by political activists. What are the advantages and disadvantages of these different approaches? Imagine how the editors of each site would explain their rhetorical strategies and those of the other site.

2. Explore further the ways the Internet itself along with the information economy offer new opportunities and new contexts for thinking about issues related to disability rights and work by reading an essay in Chapter 9, Work in the Information Age/The Future of Work such as "An Age of Optimism" by Nicholas Negroponte from the perspective of disability rights issues. Based on these connections, write about what opportunities and challenges you think the future workplace may hold for questions of ability.

Stories of Work

FREDERICK DOUGLASS ■

From *Narrative of the Life of Frederick Douglass, An American Slave, Written by Himself*

In the long history of the struggle for workers' rights in America, there is no chapter more violent or more heroic than the fight of enslaved Africans and African Americans to win their freedom. Of the countless stories of resistance against and escape from enslavement, the autobiography of Frederick Douglass is among the most well known. Douglass was born into slavery in Maryland in 1818, the son of Harriett Bailey, an enslaved woman, and what he always suspected was a white man. After escaping slavery in 1838, Douglass first worked as a laborer but went on to become one of the nation's most famous abolitionist speakers, writers, and political activists, whose influence reached the White House of Abraham Lincoln. As part of his antislavery efforts, Douglass wrote and published three different versions of his life story, the first of which, Narrative of the Life of Frederick Douglass, An American Slave, Written by Himself, appeared in 1845 and contains the excerpt included here.

In this famous passage from Chapter 10, Douglass recalls both his lowest point as an enslaved person and the decisive moment that steeled his resolution to escape and win his freedom. Sent to work as a field hand at age sixteen, Douglass found himself under the brutal supervision of Edward Covey, a poor white man whose job was to oversee and discipline the work of enslaved agricultural workers. In this excerpt, Douglass tells of his suffering under Covey's harsh system of work and punishment and of his inability to find relief from his owner after a particularly violent beating from Covey. Faced with the prospect of continued beatings, Douglass finally resolves to fight back against Covey, risking his life but also making a bold stand for his dignity and self-respect.

I lived with Mr. Covey one year. During the first six months, of that year, scarce a week passed without his whipping me. I was seldom free from a sore back. My awkwardness was almost always his excuse for whipping me. We were worked fully up to the point of endurance. Long before day we were up, our horses fed, and by the first approach of day we were off to the field with our hoes and ploughing teams. Mr. Covey gave us enough to eat, but scarce time to eat it. We were often less than five minutes taking our meals. We were often in the field from the first approach of day till its last lingering ray had left us; and at saving-fodder time, midnight often caught us in the field binding blades.

Covey would be out with us. The way he used to stand it, was this. He would spend the most of his afternoons in bed. He would then come out fresh in the evening, ready to urge us on with his words, example, and frequently with the whip. Mr. Covey was one of the few slaveholders who could and did work with his hands. He was a hard-working man. He knew by himself just what a man or a boy could do. There was no deceiving him. His work went on in his absence almost as well as in his presence; and he had the faculty of making us feel that he was ever present with us. This he did by surprising us. He seldom approached the spot where we were at work openly, if he could do it secretly. He always aimed at taking us by surprise. Such was his cunning, that we used to call him, among ourselves, "the snake." When we were at work in the cornfield, he would sometimes crawl on his hands and knees to avoid detection, and all at once he would rise nearly in our midst, and scream out, "Ha, ha! Come, come! Dash on, dash on!" This being his mode of attack, it was never safe to stop a single minute. His comings were like a thief in the night. He appeared to us as being ever at hand. He was under every tree, behind every stump, in every bush, and at every window, on the plantation. He would sometimes mount his horse, as if bound to St. Michael's, a distance of seven miles, and in half an hour afterwards you would see him coiled up in the corner of the wood-fence, watching every motion of the slaves. He would, for this purpose, leave his horse tied up in the woods. Again, he would sometimes walk up to us, and give us orders as though he was upon the point of starting on a long journey, turn his back upon us, and make as though he was going to the house to get ready; and, before he would get half way thither, he would turn short and crawl into a fence-corner, or behind some tree, and there watch us till the going down of the sun.

Mr. Covey's *forte* consisted in his power to deceive. His life was devoted to planning and perpetrating the grossest deceptions. Every thing he possessed in the shape of learning or religion, he made conform to his disposition to deceive. He seemed to think himself equal to deceiving the Almighty. He would make a short prayer in the morning, and a long prayer at night; and, strange as it may seem, few men would at times appear more devotional than he. The exercises of his family devotions were always commenced with singing; and, as he was a very poor singer himself, the duty of raising the hymn generally came upon me. He would read his hymn, and nod at me to commence. I would at times do so; at others, I would not. My non-compliance would almost always produce much confusion. To show himself independent of me, he would start and stagger through with his hymn in the most discordant manner. In this state of mind, he prayed with more than ordinary spirit. Poor man! such was his disposition, and success at deceiving, I do verily believe that he sometimes deceived himself into the solemn belief, that he was a sincere worshipper of the most high God; and this, too, at a time when he may be said to have been guilty of compelling his woman slave to commit the sin of adultery. The facts in the case are these: Mr. Covey was a poor man; he was just commencing in life; he was only able to buy one slave; and, shocking as is the fact, he bought her, as he said, for *a breeder.* This woman was named Caroline. Mr. Covey bought her from Mr. Thomas Lowe, about six miles from St. Michael's. She was a large, able-bodied woman, about twenty years old. She had already given birth to one child, which proved her to be just what he wanted. After buying her, he hired a married man of Mr. Samuel Harrison, to live with him one year; and him he used to fasten up with her every night! The result was, that, at the end of the year, the miserable woman gave birth to twins. At this result Mr. Covey seemed to be highly pleased, both with the man and the wretched woman. Such was his joy, and that of his wife, that nothing they could do for Caroline during her confinement was too good, or too hard, to be done. The children were regarded as being quite an addition to his wealth.

If at any one time of my life more than another, I was made to drink the bitterest dregs of slavery, that time was during the first six months of my stay with Mr. Covey. We were worked in all weathers. It was never too hot or too cold; it could never rain, blow, hail, or snow, too hard for us to work in the field. Work, work, work, was scarcely more the order of the day than of the night. The longest days were too short for him, and the shortest nights too long for him. I was somewhat unmanageable when I first went there, but a few months of this discipline tamed me. Mr. Covey succeeded in breaking me. I was broken in body, soul, and spirit. My natural elasticity was crushed, my intellect languished, the disposition to read departed, the cheerful spark that lingered about my eye died; the dark night of slavery closed in upon me; and behold a man transformed into a brute!

Sunday was my only leisure time. I spent this in a sort of beast-like stupor, between sleep and wake, under some large tree. At times I would rise up, a flash of energetic freedom would dart through my soul, accompanied with a faint beam of hope, that flickered for a moment, and then vanished. I sank down again, mourning over my wretched condition. I was sometimes prompted to take my life, and that of Covey, but was prevented by a combination of hope and fear. My sufferings on this plantation seem now like a dream rather than a stern reality.

Our house stood within a few rods of the Chesapeake Bay, whose broad bosom was ever white with sails from every quarter of the habitable globe. Those beautiful vessels, robed in purest white, so delightful to the eye of freemen, were to me so many shrouded ghosts, to terrify and torment me with thoughts of my wretched condition. I have often, in the deep stillness of a summer's Sabbath, stood all alone upon the lofty banks of that noble bay, and traced, with saddened heart and tearful eye, the countless number of sails moving off to the mighty ocean. The sight of these always affected me powerfully. My thoughts would compel utterance; and there, with no audience but the Almighty, I would pour out my soul's complaint, in my rude way, with an apostrophe to the moving multitude of ships:—

"You are loosed from your moorings, and are free; I am fast in my chains, and am a slave! You move merrily before the gentle gale, and I sadly before the bloody whip! You are freedom's swift-winged angels, that fly round the world; I am confined in bands of iron! O that I were free! O, that I were on one of your gallant decks, and under your protecting wing! Alas! betwixt me and you, the turbid waters roll. Go on, go on. O that I could also go! Could I but swim! If I could fly! O, why was I born a man, of whom to make a brute! The glad ship is gone; she hides in the dim distance. I am left in the hottest hell of unending slavery. O God, save me! God, deliver me! Let me be free! Is there any God? Why am I a slave? I will run away. I will not stand it. Get caught, or get clear, I'll try it. I had as well die with ague as the fever. I have only one life to lose. I had as well be killed running as die standing. Only think of it; one hundred miles straight north, and I am free! Try it? Yes! God helping me, I will. It cannot be that I shall live and die a slave. I will take to the water. This very bay shall yet bear me into freedom. The steamboats steered in a north-east course from North Point. I will do the same; and when I get to the head of the bay, I will turn my canoe adrift, and walk straight through Delaware into Pennsylvania. When I get there, I shall not be required to have a pass; I can travel without being disturbed. Let but the first opportunity offer, and, come what will, I am off. Meanwhile, I will try to bear up under the yoke. I am not the only slave in the world. Why should I fret? I can bear as much as any of them. Besides, I am but a boy, and all boys are bound to some one. It may be that my misery in slavery will only increase my happiness when I get free. There is a better day coming."

Thus I used to think, and thus I used to speak to myself; goaded almost to madness at one moment, and at the next reconciling myself to my wretched lot.

I have already intimated that my condition was much worse, during the first six months of my stay at Mr. Covey's, than in the last six. The circumstances leading to the change in Mr. Covey's course toward me form an epoch in my humble history. You have seen how a man was made a slave; you shall see how a slave was made a man. On one of the hottest days of the month of August, 1833, Bill Smith, William Hughes, a slave named Eli, and myself, were engaged in fanning wheat. Hughes was clearing the fanned wheat from before the fan, Eli was turning, Smith was feeding, and I was carrying wheat to the fan. The work was simple, requiring strength rather than intellect; yet, to one entirely unused to such work, it came very hard. About three o'clock of that day, I broke down; my strength failed me; I was seized with a violent aching of the head, attended with extreme dizziness; I trembled in every limb. Finding what was coming, I nerved myself up, feeling it would never do to stop work. I stood as long as I could stagger to the hopper with grain. When I could stand no longer,

I fell, and felt as if held down by an immense weight. The fan of course stopped; every one had his own work to do; and no one could do the work of the other, and have his own go on at the same time.

Mr. Covey was at the house, about one hundred yards from the treading-yard where we were fanning. On hearing the fan stop, he left immediately, and came to the spot where we were. He hastily inquired what the matter was. Bill answered that I was sick, and there was no one to bring wheat to the fan. I had by this time crawled away under the side of the post and rail-fence by which the yard was enclosed, hoping to find relief by getting out of the sun. He then asked where I was. He was told by one of the hands. He came to the spot, and after looking at me awhile, asked me what was the matter. I told him as well I could, for I scarce had strength to speak. He then gave me a savage kick in the side, and told me to get up. I tried to do so, but fell back in the attempt. He gave me another kick, and again told me to rise. I again tried, and succeeded in gaining my feet; but, stooping to get the tub with which I was feeding the fan, I again staggered and fell. While down in this situation, Mr. Covey took up the hickory slat with which Hughes had been striking off the half-bushel measure, and with it gave me a heavy blow upon the head, making a large wound, and the blood ran freely; and with this again told me to get up. I made no effort to comply, having now made up my mind to let him do his worst. In a short time after receiving this blow, my head grew better. Mr. Covey had now left me to my fate. At this moment I resolved, for the first time, to go to my master, enter a complaint, and ask his protection. In order to [do] this, I must that afternoon walk seven miles; and this, under the circumstances, was truly a severe under-taking. I was exceedingly feeble; made so as much by the kicks and blows which I received, as by the severe fit of sickness to which I had been subjected. I, however, watched my chance, while Covey was looking in an opposite direc-tion, and started for St. Michael's. I succeeded in getting a considerable distance on my way to the woods, when Covey discovered me, and called after me to come back, threatening what he would do if I did not come. I disregarded both his calls and his threats, and made my way to the woods as fast as my feeble state would allow; and thinking I might be overhauled by him if I kept to the road, I walked through the woods, keeping far enough from the road to avoid detection, and near enough to prevent losing my way. I had not gone far before my little strength again failed me. I could go no farther. I fell down, and lay for a considerable time. The blood was yet oozing from the wound on my head. For a time I thought I should bleed to death; and think now that I should have done so, but that the blood so matted my hair as to stop the wound. After lying there about three quarters of an hour, I nerved myself up again, and started on my way, through bogs and briers, barefooted and bareheaded, tearing my feet sometimes at nearly every step; and after a journey of about seven miles, occu-pying some five hours to perform it, I arrived at master's store. I then presented an appearance enough to affect any but a heart of iron. From the crown of my head to my feet, I was covered with blood. My legs and feet were torn in sundry places with briers and thorns, and were also covered with blood. I suppose I looked like a man who had escaped a den of wild beasts, and barely escaped them. In this state I appeared before my master, humbly entreating him to interpose his authority for my protection. I told him all the circumstances as well as I could, and it seemed, as I spoke, at times to affect him. He would then walk the floor, and seek to justify Covey by saying he expected I deserved it. He asked me what I wanted. I told him, to let me get a new home; that Covey would surely kill me; he was in a fair way for it. Master Thomas ridiculed the idea that there was any danger of Mr. Covey's killing me, and said that he knew Mr. Covey; that he was a good man, and that he could not think of taking me from him; that, should he do so, he would lose the whole year's wages; that I belonged to Mr. Covey for one year, and that I must go back to him, come what might; and that I must not trouble him with any more stories, or that he would himself *get hold of me*. After threatening me thus, he gave me a very large dose of salts, telling me that I might remain in St. Michael's that night (it being quite late) but that I must be off back to Mr. Covey's early in the morning; and that if I did not, he would *get hold of me*, which meant that he would whip me. I remained all night, and, according to his orders, I started off to Covey's in the morning, (Saturday morning,) wearied in body and broken in spirit. I got no supper that night, or breakfast that morning. I reached Covey's about nine o'clock; and just as I was getting over the fence that divided Mrs. Kemp's fields from ours, out ran Covey with his cowskin, to give me another whipping. Before he could reach me, I succeeded in getting to the cornfield; and as the corn was very high, it afforded me the means of hiding. He seemed very angry, and searched for me a long time. My behavior was altogether unaccountable. He finally gave up the chase, thinking, I suppose, that I must come home for something to eat; he would give himself no further trouble in looking for me. I spent that day mostly in the woods, having the alternative before me,—to go home and be whipped to death, or stay in the woods and be starved to death. That night, I fell in with Sandy Jenkins, a slave with whom I was somewhat acquainted. Sandy had a free wife who lived about four miles from Mr. Covey's; and it being Saturday, he was on his way to see her. I told him my circumstances, and he very kindly invited me to go home with him. I went home with him, and talked this whole matter over, and got his advice as to what course it was best for me to pursue. I found Sandy an old adviser. He told me, with great solemnity, I must go back to Covey; but that before I went, I must go with him into another part of the woods, where there was a certain *root*, which, if I would take some of it with me, carrying it *always on my right side*, would render it impossible for Mr. Covey, or any other white man, to whip me. He said he had carried it for years; and since he had done so, he had never received a blow, and never expected to while he carried it. I at first rejected the idea, that the simple carrying of a root in my pocket would have any such effect as he had said, and was not disposed to take it; but Sandy impressed the necessity with much earnestness, telling me it could do no harm, if it did no good. To please him, I at length took the root, and, according to his direction, carried it upon my right side. This was Sunday morning. I immediately started for home; and upon entering the yard gate, out came Mr. Covey on his way to meeting. He spoke to me very kindly, made me drive the pigs from a lot near by, and passed on towards the church. Now, this singular conduct of Mr. Covey really made me begin to think that there was something in the *root* which Sandy had given me; and had it been on any other day than Sunday, I could have attributed the conduct to no other cause than the influence of that root; and as it was, I was half inclined to think the *root* to be something more than I at first had taken it to be. All went well till Monday morning. On this morning, the virtue of the *root* was fully tested. Long before daylight, I was called to go and rub, curry, and feed the horses. I obeyed, and was glad to obey. But whilst thus engaged, whilst in the act of throwing down some blades from the loft, Mr. Covey entered the stable with a long rope; and just as I was half out of the loft, he caught hold of my legs, and was about tying me. As soon as I found what he was up to, I gave a sudden spring, and as I did so, he holding to my legs, I was brought sprawling on the stable floor. Mr. Covey seemed now to think he had me, and could do what he pleased; but at this moment—from whence came the spirit I don't know—I resolved to fight; and, suiting my action to the resolution, I seized Covey hard by the throat; and as I did so, I rose. He held on to me, and I to him. My resistance was so entirely unexpected, that Covey seemed taken all aback. He trembled like a leaf. This gave me assurance, and I held him uneasy, causing the blood to run where I touched him with the ends of my fingers. Mr. Covey soon called out to Hughes for help. Hughes came, and, while Covey held me, attempted to tie my right hand. While he was in the act of doing so, I watched my chance, and gave him a heavy kick close under the ribs. This kick fairly sickened Hughes, so that he left me in the hands of Mr. Covey. This kick had the effect of not only weakened Hughes, but Covey also. When he saw Hughes bending over with pain, his courage quailed. He asked me if I meant to persist in my resistance. I told him I did, come what might; that he had used me like a brute for six months, and that I was determined to be used so no longer. With that, he strove to drag me to a stick that was lying just out of the stable door. He meant to knock me down. But just as he was leaning over to get the stick, I seized him with both hands by his collar, and brought him by a sudden snatch to the ground. By this time, Bill came. Covey called upon him for assistance. Bill wanted to know what he could do. Covey said, "Take hold of him, take hold of him!" Bill said his master hired him out to work, and not to help whip me; so he left Covey and myself to fight our own battle out. We were at it for nearly two hours. Covey at length let me go, puffing and blowing at a great rate, saying that if I had not resisted, he would not have whipped me half so much. The truth was, that he had not whipped me at all. I considered him as getting entirely the worst end of the bargain; for he had drawn no blood from me, but I had from him. The whole six months afterwards, that I spent with Mr. Covey, he never laid the weight of his finger upon me in anger. He would occasionally say, he didn't want to get hold of me again. "No," thought I, "you need not; for you will come off worse than you did before."

This battle with Mr. Covey was the turning-point in my career as a slave. It rekindled the few expiring embers of freedom, and revived within me a sense of my own manhood. It recalled the departed self-confidence, and inspired me again with a determination to be free. The gratification afforded by the triumph was a full compensation for whatever else might follow, even death itself. He can only understand the deep satisfaction which I experienced, who has himself repelled by force the bloody arm of slavery. I felt as I never felt before. It was a glorious resurrection, from the tomb of slavery, to the heaven of freedom. My long-crushed spirit rose, cowardice departed, bold defiance took its place; and I now resolved that, however long I might remain a slave in form, the day had passed forever when I could be a slave in fact. I did not hesitate to let it be known of me, that the white man who expected to succeed in whipping, must also succeed in killing me.

From this time I was never again what might be called fairly whipped, though I remained a slave four years afterwards. I had several fights, but was never whipped.

It was for a long time a matter of surprise to me why Mr. Covey did not immediately have me taken by the constable to the whipping-post, and there regularly whipped for the crime of raising my hand against a white man in defence of myself. And the only explanation I can now think of does not entirely satisfy me; but such as it is, I will give it. Mr. Covey enjoyed the most unbounded reputation for being a first-rate overseer and negro-breaker. It was of considerable importance to him. That reputation was at stake; and had he sent me—a boy about sixteen years old—to the public whipping-post, his reputation would have been lost; so, to save his reputation, he suffered me to go unpunished. ■

Working with the Text

1. Based on Douglass's story, write a job description for Edgar Covey's position. What seem to you the main requirements for his line of work? How differently would his job be described by a slave owner, Covey himself, and an enslaved person?

2. In addition to his use of physical brutality, Covey is described by Douglass as a man whose *"forte* consisted in his power to deceive." Why does Douglass find Covey so effective in his use of deception?

3. Before describing his crucial confrontation with Covey, Douglass writes, "You have seen how a man was made a slave; you shall see how a slave was made a man." Looking carefully at the language Douglass uses in recounting his fight with Covey as well as in other parts of this excerpt, explain as specifically as possible how Douglass is defining manhood, especially in relation to work.

4. After besting Covey in their fight, Douglass says that the overseer "never laid the weight of his finger upon me in anger" and never reported Douglass's defiance to the man who claimed ownership of Douglass. Douglass speculates that perhaps Covey

wished to retain his good reputation as a "slavebreaker." What other reasons can you think of for Covey's change in attitude and behavior toward Douglass? How had their working relationship changed?

Working with Connections

1. Douglass's story is part of a long line of American autobiographies tracing the rise of a person from humble beginnings to social prominence and importance. Many scholars point to Benjamin Franklin's *Autobiography* (from Chapter 2, Work, Labor, and Career: The Meaning of Work) as one of the first examples of such an inspirational life story. How well do the recommendations Franklin makes in his autobiography apply to Douglass's situation? How might Douglass reply to Franklin's advice from the perspective of an enslaved worker?

2. Herman Melville's short story "Bartleby, the Scrivener" (in Chapter 2, Work, Labor, Career: the Meaning of Work) was written during the same time period as Douglass's autobiography and describes the working conditions among the supposedly free workers of the north. Compare the depiction of work in these two stories to explore what ideas like slavery and freedom meant in relation to work in the nineteenth century. How do you think our own definitions of these terms have been affected by this historical background?

LALO GUERRERO ■

Corrido de César Chávez

The corrido is a type of ballad folk song that developed in Mexico and the Spanish language cultures of the American southwest in the late nineteenth century. Like all ballads, corridos function in part as a form of popular storytelling, and in the U.S. border areas most associated with the corrido, many of these stories relate the experiences and struggles of Latino peoples living in dominant Anglo-American societies, often focusing on the exploits of a heroic figure such as Gregorio Cortez. Like all folk traditions, most early corridos were composed anonymously and passed along orally, with different singers in different areas and at different times creating their own versions of the song. Again like other kinds of folk music, however, the corrido survives as a form that contemporary musicians use to comment on more recent historical events.

Lalo Guerrero's "Corrido de César Chávez" (reprinted here in both its original Spanish and an English translation) celebrates the life and achievements of César Chávez (1927–1993), the Chicano-American labor leader who was a founder of the United Farm Workers union that fought to improve the working conditions and lives of the largely Latino agricultural workers in California and other states from the 1960s until today. In particular, the corrido *commemorates Chávez's twenty-five-day fast in 1968 as part of a strike against grape growers in Delano, California. As the* corrido *notes, Senator and then-presidential candidate Robert Kennedy appeared with Chávez when the strike ended on March 10, only three months before Kennedy was assassinated in Los Angeles.*

Lalo Guerrero is himself a legend in the world of Chicano music, a pioneer in increasing the visibility and popularity of Mexican-American music and culture from the 1930s to the present. In 1997, he was awarded the National Medal of the Arts.

CORRIDO DE CÉSAR CHÁVEZ

Detente mi corazón,
En el pecho no me cabe
El regocijo y orgullo
Al cantarle a César Chávez.

Inspiración de mi gente,
Protector del campesino
El es un gran mexicano
Ese sería su destino.

De muy humildes principios
Organizaste a la gente;
Y a los hacendados ricos
Te paraste frente a frente.

Injustamente te acusan
Que intentaste usar violencia
Ayunaste veinticinco días
Pa' probar tu inocencia.

En el estandarte que lleva
Mi Virgen de Guadalupe,
En tu incesante labor
De bendiciones te tuve.

A los venticinco días
El ayuno terminó

En el parque de Delano
Una misa celebró.

Junto con ocho mil almas
Bobby Kennedy asistió;
Admiración y cariño
Nuestra gente le brindó.

Vuela de aquí de me seno,
Paloma, vete a Delano;
Y por si acaso no sabes
Allí vive César Chávez.

BALLAD OF CÉSAR CHÁVEZ[*]

Stop, my heart,
In my breast there is no room
For the joy and pride
Of singing of César Chávez.

Inspiration of my people,
Protector of the farm worker,
He is a great Mexican;
This would be his destiny.

From very humble beginnings
You organized your people;
And against the rich ranchers
You stood face to face.

Unjustly they accuse you
Of intending to use violence.
You fasted for twenty-five days
In order to prove your innocence.

On the standard that carries
My Virgin of Guadalupe,
In whose presence you came to worship,
I esteemed you with my praise.

[*]Head of the United Farm Workers, 1965–1993.

After twenty-five days
The fast ended;
In the park in Delano
A mass was celebrated.

Together with eight thousand souls
Bobby Kennedy attended;
Admiration and affection
Our people offered him a toast.

Fly from my breast,
Dove, go to Delano;
And if perhaps you don't know,
There lives César Chávez. ■

Working with the Text

1. What do you think the advantages are of telling history in the form of a folk song as opposed to nonmusical forms of story-telling? Who do you think the intended audiences might be, and what would be their relationship to the song? Why would a *corrido* be especially appropriate for celebrating the life of César Chávez? Can you think of examples of other types of folk songs that also comment on contemporary events? If you are familiar with *corridos*, write about the different kinds of effects they have on listeners.

2. What are the most important impressions and ideas about César Chávez that you think Guerrero is trying to make with his *corrido*? Pick out specific passages and phrases that you think are most important in the *corrido*.

3. Folk traditions such as the *corrido* can represent a way for stories to be told that otherwise wouldn't be included in "official" histories or of conveying alternative points of view. Choose a recent historical event that you feel hasn't received enough attention, a point of view that you think hasn't been fully expressed, or a person seen as heroic by an oppressed or marginalized community and try writing your own ballad version of the event or person. As you do, think about who your specific audiences will be and the most effective ways of communicating to them ballad form.

Working with Connections

1. In writing this *corrido*, Guerrero is taking part in a long tradition in Chicano culture. Locate recordings of other *corridos*, of both recent and historic origins, and study three or four of them to identify patterns in how *corridos* tell stories and in the kinds of emotions conveyed by their musical performances. Then write about how your experience of listening to other examples of the *corrido* tradition affects your reaction to "Corrido de César Chávez" and your understanding of the choices Guerrero made in telling this story.

2. As a research project, find out more about César Chávez, the United Farm Workers (UFW) union, and the strike in 1968 that inspired Guerrero's *corrido*. What different points of view do you encounter in looking at various sources about Chávez and the UFW? For example, compare versions of the 1968 strike as told by the UFW on their web site and in their publications, in materials prepared by educators, in encyclopedias, and in newspaper accounts from 1968. Locate Guerrero's interpretation of Chávez within these different versions, considering both questions of accuracy but also how different interpreters highlight different factual events or describe them differently to convey different impressions to the readers.

3. In addition to referring to specific historical incidents, Guerrero also refers to cultural beliefs and values in "Corrido de César Chávez" as a way of identifying and connecting with his listeners. Locate some of these key cultural markers (such as the Virgin of Guadalupe) and explore how these markers affect the meanings of the *corrido*, whether you write as an insider for whom these markers are a part of your own cultural identity or as someone who is new to these markers. You may also include research, involving both written and oral sources (such as interviews with family or other community members) as part of your exploration.

WANDA COLEMAN

Office Politics

Poet Wanda Coleman was born in the Watts neighborhood of Los Angeles in 1946 and has been writing poetry since the early 1970s. She has been an editor, journalist, and scriptwriter, but she has also worked as a medical secretary. Her poem, "Office Politics," reflects both her experiences working in a business office as well as her interest in exploring and exposing the racialized ways of thinking in American society.

the white boss

stops at my desk to see how i'm doing. it's something, what a
good strong work horse i am. nothing like those lazy mexicans
and them power hungry jews can't be trusted
who knows what's on the oriental mind
but we negroes understand what the white man is about
we understand that his best interest is ours
that's why we've always made such fine employees

the jewish foreman

stops at my desk to say how's it going. we are soul mates
after all we have much more in common than other races
my slavery and his death camp. not like those greasy mexicans
or clannish orientals. there are jews in the NAACP
and Harlem was once a jewish ghetto
if it weren't for jews the negroes would be
worse off

the white feminist co-worker

brands men subhuman, as her black "sister" don't i understand
our oppression is the same? what is the difference
between being lynched and being man-handled?
and didn't white female abolitionists play a major role
in our emancipation? and black men are
the same as white men. they are men aren't they?

the mexican co-worker

confides outrage. the white boy's days are numbered
california & texas will be spanish-speaking again and soon
we will not allow the red herring of jobs
to set us at each other's throats. the white boy and
the jew can only buy the illusion of loyalty from us
never the reality

the japanese accountant

passes by my desk to his
does not say a word
when everyone else
is out of the office
save me and him

he goes into his attaché case
for the flask of scotch
and bottoms up
without offering me
a sip

my black co-worker

comes over to my desk, looks deep
into my eyes. opens his mouth. moans
shakes his head
and goes back to work ■

Working with the Text

1. Write about which of the characterizations of her fellow office workers you found most surprising, funny, or shocking and why.

2. While it might be safe to assume that Coleman's poem draws on her experiences as an office worker, we can also view the poem as a kind of story, with the narrator of the poem as much a created character as the other employees described here. Write a description of what you think the narrator is like based on her observations here. Who do you think the narrator might be speaking to?

3. In each character sketch the narrator focuses on a kind of self-justifying story that each person in the office tells in order to connect with the narrator. Based on your reading of these stories, why does each character want to try to connect with the narrator around issues of race and ethnicity? What subtexts about guilt, anger, and suspicion can you find in each portrait? How might each of the narrator's coworkers respond to "Office Politics"?

Working with Connections

1. The workers in Coleman's poem not only represent different racial and ethnic identities, they also inhabit different positions in the office hierarchy, from the "boss" to the foreman to coworkers to the "accountant," whose rank and position in relation to the speaker of the poem are not specified. How do you see rank and status affecting your reading of the narrator's descriptions of

office politics? How can you use ideas about social class from readings in Chapter 4, Work and Social Class, such as the excerpt from *The Working-Class Majority* by Michael Zweig as well as "Media Magic: Making Class, Invisible" by Gregory Mantsios to explore the relationships among social class, race, and ethnicity in the workplace?

2. "Office Politics" can be seen as a form of satire, in this case raising questions about what is often called "identity politics," stereotyping, and the difficulties of communicating across perceived barriers of race, ethnicity, and class. As is common with satire as a rhetorical strategy, Coleman presents us with different attitudes and points of view as perceived by the narrator of the poem, but the question remains as to the author's own ideas and beliefs in relation to the views expressed in the poem. Explore your own ideas about what you think Coleman's opinions are by first writing about your initial reaction to the poem. Widen your discussion by learning more about Wanda Coleman through reading interviews and essays she has written. Learn more about the complex ways different readers interpret writing by asking a variety of people outside the class to read and comment on the poem. Collect these responses and write about what patterns you see in terms of the different reactions the poem evokes.

NINA SALTMAN

Carpenter Foreman

The association of certain jobs with certain genders is often thought of as a matter of "common sense." Perhaps, many people might say, women can perform equally to men in an office, but men definitely have the advantage in work that also demands physical exertion and stamina. Often what we mean by "common sense," though, is a collection of unexamined and untested beliefs that raise as many questions as they answer. What do we mean by "stamina" and "strength," for example? What about the varieties of physical size and ability among men and women as well as between them?

In this account from the collection Hard Hatted Women: Stories of Struggles and Success in the Trades *edited by Molly Martin, Nina Saltman tells how she became a carpenter in the construction industry and eventually rose to the position of foreman. In so doing, she addresses many of the unexamined prejudices and beliefs we may have about "blue collar" work and whether gender should really be as much of a qualification as ability and desire.*

No girl born in the fifties was born to be a carpenter. Just ask anybody. Carpenters are boys; born with tools in their hands, digits exactly one inch long and the uncanny ability to see level at twenty yards. How then, could I, a midwestern Jewish girl born in 1950, end up as a carpenter? I certainly wasn't told by my high school counselor to "try a hand" at the trades. Not by a long shot. I was a typical female student at a public high school. I took sewing and cooking, as was required for girls, due to our obvious genetic qualities that facilitate our usage of ladles instead of levels. I was on a college-bound track with an emphasis on English, drama and art. I loved art, and if the truth be known, I loved sewing. (I still do, although now, I never seem to get past mending my coveralls.) So where was the transition? What was the impetus for a career outside my track?

It must have been something to do with my Great-Uncle Borach who was a carpenter in Lithuania. I guess the genes got passed down to me instead of my brothers. Perhaps the fact that I find great similarities between building and sewing and art has had an effect on my career decisions. Or, maybe, it's my love of seeing something created out of nothing, and made beautifully and skillfully. I have always loved working with my hands. It gives me a sense of accomplishment to create a thing of beauty, be it a work of art or a well-hung door.

As typical as my schooling was, my work history has not been. After graduating college with a BA in English Lit and a minor in Drama, as well as a teaching credential for secondary education (good in thirty states I'd never consider for residence), I left the States and traveled to Europe. I lived in Amsterdam for a year working as a leather crafts artisan in a snazzy, hip leather boutique on the shopping street, the Nieuwendijk. I remember my dirty hands and the feeling of creativity. I was also the shop "go-fer," and often had to carry heavy leather skins back to the shop on the streetcar. My first effort at physical labor, and I loved it. I also loved the way people would look at me carrying these heavy items . . . what a woman. . . .

After two and a half years of living and working abroad, I came back to the States and moved to California. It was 1974 and I was ready to try anything. I took a number of odd jobs from housepainting to more leather work. While housepainting, I met a couple of friends of friends who were working at a cooperative food warehouse. The slogan was "Food for People, Not for Profit." I liked that a lot. I also liked the fact that the warehouse was relatively new at that time, and the business was just starting to blossom. I ended up working there fulltime and becoming a member of the collective. As the warehouse grew, our collective consciousness changed. We had lengthy discussions about workers versus management, worker control, trade unions and general organization, as well as how to run our business. So, in addition to building myself up physically by doing manual labor forty hours a week, I learned, ironically enough, management skills, group organization and general business skills. By the end of four years I could lift and heave one-hundred pound sacks with the best of them. I also learned how to operate a forklift and qualified for a Class II license by driving a ten-wheeler truck. I was, however, tiring of the long hours of political discussion while the business failed . . . I was ready for a new job. Oh, and did I mention the salary??

I quit the warehouse and took a vacation. When I returned, I went to the Women in Apprenticeship Program (WAP) office in San Francisco. I was interested in getting into the ILWU or the Teamsters, preferably as a warehouser, but I was open to anything. After a few weeks, I received a call from WAP that Union Carbide in South San Francisco was looking for a woman in their industrial gas plant. Union Carbide had federal contracts to honor, and was being pressured to comply with affirmative action requirements. There was a woman working there, but she was leaving. They needed to fill her spot. I went down and had an interview. I was asked to demonstrate that I could handle a hand truck and was physically able. I started as a Teamster for twice what I had been making at the warehouse. During my time at U.C. I learned how to deal with a lot of insults, smutty pictures and imbecilic behavior, as well as a somewhat boring job.

After about a year, it was time to move on. I knew a couple of other women who had started apprenticeships in various trades and had talked to them about the work, the atmosphere and the men. Although I knew I would have to put up with the same childish behavior from my co-workers that I experienced at U.C., I also had confidence that I would end up with a marketable skill and a stimulating job.

I approached the trades using what I now refer to as the "blitz" method: sign up for all tests and all trades, and whichever pans out first gets the prize: me. I had taken one test for operating engineers and signed up for the electrical and sheet metal tests when I started to look for carpentry jobs. Carpentry had always been my first choice. The idea of building buildings and being able to work on my own place had definite appeal. I started looking into the cabinet shops in the area. I went to about fifteen with no luck whatsoever . . . they were, in fact, a big turn off. The shops were nearly all white and completely male. They didn't want to have anything to do with me. By the time I had visited most of the shops, I felt the same way about them. I was undaunted, though, and my search continued.

I started visiting big construction sites in the city. It was rainy season and many of the jobs were muddy holes in the ground. When I visited a Dinwiddie Construction site downtown (now Saks Fifth Avenue), Dean, the general foreman, looked at me, looked at the muddy hole in the ground, and asked, "Would you be able to handle working in this?" "Sure, why not?" I said . . . and he told me who to call. I set up an "interview" for the next day with a superintendent of another jobsite. When I got there the next day, instead of an interview, I got a little speech that was becoming all too familiar.

"Well, uh, er, we have had other girls work here before. (PUFF, PUFF on the cigar.) And, uh, er, they just haven't been able to handle the work."

TRANSLATION: We don't really want you broads here, but we're being forced to hire you. The other women couldn't take the abuse . . . will you?

"One girl missed a lot of time, and another didn't want to do the heavy work."

TRANSLATION: Your period is no excuse . . . and you're gonna get the shittiest, dirtiest jobs we've got. You're gonna have to work twice as hard as the men if you want to stick around.

The "Everywoman" speech. Ah, yes, I'd heard it before. Did all these guys get together and practice it? I had heard it at Union Carbide, at the Sheet Metal union office, and from some of the cabinet makers. I was hearing it from Dinwiddie, and would later hear it from others. I wondered how many men ever got these "interviews." My answer to their speech was sort of pat, by now, too. "Try me out, and judge me on my own merits," or words to that effect. What I shoulda said was "!@#$%&*0!!!°°!" Anyway, I got hired and started my apprenticeship.

I worked for Dinwiddie for the next two years, went to apprenticeship school in the evenings and started to feel like a real carpenter. I was fairly active in my union and also got involved with the local women carpenters' committee, meeting many wonderful and able women carpenters. It was unusual to be steadily employed, and I felt very fortunate. I also realized this reality: that I am white, heterosexual, well-educated, physically fit and very mouthy. Unfortunately, most employers are not known for their efforts to combat racism and sexism, not to mention homophobia in their hiring practices. In addition, I was in the right place at the right time. There had been a couple of other women that had worked for Dinwiddie, so I wasn't the first woman that most of these men had seen in a tool belt. I don't want to minimize the fact that I busted my butt. I worked very hard, was never late, and rarely missed a day of work. I fell in love with the trade and had an intense desire to be a proficient craftsperson.

After two years of building concrete forms for high-rise construction with Dinwiddie, I decided I needed to expand my knowledge of the trade and work for another contractor. I quit Dinwiddie, took a vacation and came back to town ready to work for someone else. That's one of construction's best perks: the opportunity to take long vacations between jobs. With the help of a friend, I got hired by an extremely reputable remodeling contractor, Plant Builders. They needed women on a redevelopment job, so, after an interview, and an "Everywoman" speech, I started for work for Plant.

The new work was varied, and I was finally doing something besides concrete. The men I was working with seemed decent and friendly. Once again, I had the advantage of a woman predecessor. As in my jobs at U.C. and at Dinwiddie, there had been women working with the crew before my arrival. They had, in each of their ways, broken in the crew for me, to the extent that I had it better than the women before me (but not so good as those who followed). The one other woman working for Plant at that time was a very good carpenter that all the men respected. Besides this woman carpenter, there were (are) rarely other women on my jobs. Despite this fact, I kept fairly content at my new job. I learned a lot, and Plant was training well. Unlike a lot of other women apprentices, I was being given some responsibility at work. For the most part the men were willing to share their expertise without any apparent prejudice. I had to put up with occasional badgering not only because I was a woman and therefore an easy mark, but also because I was an apprentice.

After two years of working for Plant, as I approached the end of my apprenticeship, I started to get a little apprehensive. I knew that I would be expected to know everything the day after I "turned out." Magically one goes from apprentice to journey status in one day. Once one is paid the same as other journeylevel workers, one is expected to produce the same, even though, clearly, the experience is NOT the same. Fortunately, because I'd been working for the same company for awhile, they were aware of my capabilities. I probably felt more pressure from myself than from bosses or co-workers to perform better or faster. To this day, I am probably my own worst critic.

After a few months of work as a journeywoman, I started working on what was referred to as the Service Truck. Plant had and still has a lot of clients who require follow-up work, or pick-up work at the end of jobs. I had a company truck, a beeper and a purchase book. My partner on the truck was one of my favorite carpenters in the company, and he broke me in to the ins and outs of service calls. It seemed clear to me that this position was a training ground for future foremen or women, as the case may be. I had to fill out time cards, daily reports and lumber lists, as well as plan small projects and deal with clients.

After six months on the truck, I worked on a couple of different projects as a regular carpenter, and was then given my first job as a fore . . . woman. I was flattered, but also worried. What if I screwed up? Was this a set-up? I had never really wanted to run work. Remember? I was the one who worked in a collective, with no bosses. Now, I was gonna be a boss? Oh, irony of ironies!

The job was a relatively easy one to run. There were no plans and only a couple of subcontractors. Plus, the real clincher was that my immediate boss was the owner of the company, Mr. Plant, himself. Hmmm, was he just checking me out? Or what? Or, maybe, they didn't think I could handle it, so they made sure that I couldn't screw it up too much. The thoughts that went through my head. . . . Needless to say, though, the job went off without a hitch.

The ribbing I got from some of my co-workers was incessant. "Hey Saltman. I thought you didn't want to be a foreman! Hah! ForePERSON Nina . . . Hey Boss. . . ." Then, of course, there were a few people who probably had a lot to say behind my back . . . oh, to be that fly on the wall.

I think that the nature of this particular company has had a positive effect on my success in the trade. Plant hires carpenters from the union or the field, and if they work out, they keep on working. If they continue to work and can take on added responsibility, they start to run work. I feel fortunate to be a "company person"—Plant has treated me fairly and generously and I doubt that I would be running work were it not for the fact that I work for them. As far as I know, I am the only woman who has run a job in the capacity of superintendent the size of my most recent one. I marvel at the speed with which I have been given this amount of responsibility. After all, I've been in the trade less than ten years. Still, when people ask me what I do, I sometimes hesitate, and say, "I'm working as a carpenter." Not that I am a carpenter, for I don't always feel like I am. After all, I wasn't born with tools in my hand. Sometimes I feel like an impostor. "Who is this person wearing these coveralls?" I ask myself.

Since my first job as fore ... MAN ("forewoman" isn't a recognized term—yet), I've run four other jobs of some magnitude. Two of them were twelve-week jobs, and one was a nine-week butt-kicker. Sometimes the shorter the job, the more hectic the pace. The first two jobs were finished on time and within budget. The third job was not so smooth, and the fourth was a whole novel in and of itself.

All four of these jobs were in historical landmarks of one kind or another. The first one was at the only Frank Lloyd Wright building in San Francisco. I found out during the job that part of the reason that I had been given the job was because, being a woman, they thought that I would take care of the building, and make sure that nothing happened to it that wasn't supposed to. A woman's touch. . . . This is, I think, part of the rationale when I have been chosen to do a particular project. Women are more careful than men . . . Nina is a woman, therefore she will take better care of this building! In some cases this may be a warranted consideration, but definitely not always. I did respect the Wright building, no question about it; the job went well and I have felt close to Frank Lloyd ever since.

After that job I had nine months or so of working on a crew again. This was fine with me, as I felt (and still do) that there is a lot for me to learn. I arrived on one jobsite and found a crew composed of some old and new faces. After a coffee break, one of my buddies, Uncle Harry, as he is affectionately called, came over to me and started to laugh.

"Nina, you see that guy over there? (Points to a carpenter I'd never met before.) He asked me if you were a journeyman or an apprentice. I told him, 'Yeah, she's a journeyman all right . . . In fact she's a foreman!' The guy looked at me in shock, 'You mean she's a foreman?!' Yeah, he just couldn't believe it. I thought you'd get a kick out of that, so I wanted to tell you."

I sure did.

I like the fact that some carpenters (men) don't quite know how to relate to me. I like the feeling I get when a tradesperson comes on to my jobsite and asks who is in charge, and I can say, "Me!" There are also some aspects of being a foreman that have their drawbacks. When I'm on another person's job, and I make a mistake, the response is usually, "I thought you were a foreman." Or, now that I'm a little more experienced at running work, invariably, during the course of the job, I'm bound to hear, "Is this your first job?" at least a few times. I don't know if this is because of something missing from my performance or if it is just so unusual to see a woman in charge.

After a summer project at an all-girls school, I ran the nine week butt-kicker. It was a tenant-improvement job with a high pressure schedule and an unrealistic budget. I was doomed before I started. The owner's agent was an ex-marine sergeant, a woman with no sense of humor and a penchant for putting the blame on somebody. I'm sure she saw me as a likely scapegoat. I had a number of exercises in personal diplomacy. I really learned what it meant to literally bite your tongue. I must say that this aspect of running work—the politics of being a foreman—is one of a number of things I don't like. I am in between a rock and a hard place, namely the workers and the management. My attitude is not necessarily supportive of management all the time. I don't like being put in the position of having to defend an unrealistic schedule, for example, or a decision on the work that may lack integrity. I don't see the point of lying about the work. This can cause conflict, needless to say, when the project manager has a different agenda.

That job was the only one, so far, where I had a real blowout with a subcontractor. The aforementioned project manager was pushing the schedule hard, which meant pushing me to push the subs. One of the subs was responding in a very lackadaisical fashion and was not responding to my daily barrage of phone calls, so the project manager sent him a telegram. For some reason the subs hate this, and it never fails to get them pissed off. On the other hand, it does usually produce results.

It certainly did in this case. The two workers for this sub were working overtime to compensate us, and they and I had worked out a plan for them to proceed. Their boss came onto the job, obviously very uptight, and started barking orders to them, contrary to what we had just worked out. He then came over to me, all red in the face, and got right up in my face, and says, "You send me a telegram that I have to have such and such done and you're not even ready for us and how can you do this and you better have A B and C ready in five minutes or BLAH BLAH BLAH. . . ." It really shook me up; I knew he would never have related to a man like that. At that moment I really wished I had been six-foot-four and weighed two hundred and sixty pounds. I walked away from him, so furious that I started to cry.

This same jerk came over to me about fifteen minutes later and asked me if I would accept an apology. He told me that his crew explained that we had already worked everything out. Reluctantly, I said I would consider accepting the apology. Grrrr. . . . It was at the end of this job that I really started to evaluate how I felt about running work. It is definitely different from being a regular carpenter. There are endless challenges and it's become clear that the skills needed to run work are not always the same ones needed to be a good carpenter.

Aside from the stress factor, which is my number one complaint about the position of foreman, there are a lot of things that I *do* like about running work. My day is scheduled by me. I decide when and how to get my daily work done, as well as everybody else's work. Despite the fact that I have a project manager, who is, officially, my boss, I have a lot of autonomy on the job.

Though very active, it is not as physically demanding as the trade itself. Rarely will I have to do physical labor. After all, I am the boss. I can get someone else to do the grunt work. What I do do, though, is run around a lot: checking everybody's work, answering the phone, answering billions of questions like "How do you want this done?" trying to mediate differences between the subs, ordering materials, scheduling people in and out of the job in the proper sequence, and dealing with all the personalities from architects to cops. The trade has been, in general, a stimulating test of my will and endurance. Being a foreman has heightened the challenge of the test, and it can be an exhilarating feeling to meet it head on.

Meeting the challenge on my most recent job was much more than I bargained for. The building was the first high-rise built on the West Coast (1897). The first three floors of exterior façade were to be stripped off, and new façade was to be engineered and re-attached. The new look would be 1980s Art Deco. It was an extremely interesting project, with every known building material in the world on the new façade, and I learned a tremendous amount. Not only did I learn a lot about construction, but about people, too, myself included.

The job was started by another foreman, a friend of mine. After about a month on the job, he and the project manager, a guy who I had worked with before, were not getting along and my friend was ready to quit. I was working on another job, happy as a clam to be using my tools again, when I got a phone call from this project manager asking me to take over the job. I called my friend to check out what the deal was. He explained that the job was a tough one: the client was difficult (a woman, of course), the estimates had been all wrong so there was no money in the job, the schedule was a mess, the plans were incomplete because the architects were inexperienced, and he thought that the project manager was a horse's ass.

Needless to say I was not anxious to get involved. It meant working with a difficult project manager, which I wasn't looking forward to. It also meant taking on a very large, long-term (seven months), already confused job. All this equaled a lot of overtime, and a *lot* of stress. For the extra dollar-fifty an hour foreman's pay, it didn't seem worth it. However, after a conversation with Mr. Plant I was convinced (coerced?) to help out and take the job.

It was everything I had expected and more. There were more than fourteen subcontractors on the job, each with three to twelve people on a crew, as well as our own crew of carpenters and laborers. From the second I hit the jobsite in the morning until I left, which was rarely a mere eight hours, I was on the go. There were a number of days when I literally did not have time to pee. The jobsite was large and it was difficult to keep track of what everyone was doing at all times.

Like, for instance, the time that the ironworkers were up on the second floor putting in their structural steel. Apparently they had to keep stepping over this phone line. Little did they realize that the travel agent next door was connected to that line. The effort to step over this wire must have simply seemed too much of a burden, so they just took their snips and . . . snipped it! All hell broke loose. I was summoned to the office of the owner and scolded. After all, I was responsible, because the ironworkers were a subcontractor of the general contractor on the job. I was also responsible, of course, when these same ironworkers were using the women's restroom on one of the occupied floors. Oh those ironworkers. . . .

Some of the moments of frustration were offset by funnier ones. There was this young guy who came to the jobsite looking for work. He must have talked to someone in another part of the site and then came in to the area of my job shack. He approached me and asked, or so I thought, "Where's the chick?"

I flew out of my office in a rage, and said, "If you're looking for a job here, you better think twice about referring to me as a chick. I am not a chick. I am a woman, and I am also the foreman here . . . so you better ask again."

The guy was flabbergasted. "I thought your name was 'Chick.' One of the guys over there told me I should go to the office and ask for Chick. I'm really sorry . . . I would never . . . if I had known. . . ."

The fire department must have shown up at this job at least four different times because tenants in the building would smell smoke from our welding or burning and think we were all on fire. Each time I would have to apologize to the chief and show him what we were doing, and then have to deal with the owner, tenants and my project manager. One morning, after I had worked until 11:30 the night before, I walked onto the job, dealt with a couple of problems a sub was having and heard the fire trucks pull up. I went around the corner, and there were two trucks with their lights flashing and sirens going. My project manager pulled up to the job just at that same moment. . . . We both walked over to the fire trucks and the fire chief says, "Who's in charge here?"

At the same moment we both started to say "I am." I looked at the project manager like, "Who the hell do you think you are?" and he says to the chief, "She is."

Through all the stress and tension, and all the years leading up to it, I have neglected to say how big a role the support of friends and family has been. Without that support and positive feedback, I doubt I would have had the singular strength to survive. My companion James, for example, has been great about being a friend and listener when I've had a rough day. He says, "I don't have a choice!" Of course, he benefits—I do a lot of carpentry work around the house. My family has also been very supportive. I think that they get a kick out of the fact that their sister/daughter is a tradeswoman. How unique! Of course, they *also* like it when I come to visit and fix a few things around the house. My mom recently commented that she thought my four years of apprenticeship were at least as difficult as the medical school my brother has gone through. Many friends gave me the encouragement to go on. And the fact is that some of my co-workers have also given me a lot of encouragement, telling me that I was all right and as good as the next person . . . and not to be afraid to "turn out" or run work.

Having a network of tradeswomen is also invaluable. Any woman involved in a trade or occupation where she is isolated can benefit from the camaraderie and strength of networking with other women in their field.

I don't know when or if I will be running another job. I will undoubtedly accept the new job, if and when it's offered. I plan to try to expand my expertise in carpentry no matter what my position. I really love the craft and the trade.

The seemingly impenetrable old-boy network has, at least, been punctured, if not thoroughly pierced. I have no illusion that I have made it in their world. Rather, I have met my own challenge and thereby weakened their hold, just a bit. Little by little each one of us must make our mark, meet our respective challenges and take charge of our lives. With time it will make a difference. ■

Working with the Text

1. Why does Saltman say, "No girl born in the fifties was born to be a carpenter"? What kinds of work did her early upbringing prepare her for? What do you see as the most important factors in her life that allowed her to follow what she had been raised to think of as an inappropriate career path for girls?

2. What attracted Saltman the most to carpentry and construction? How do these qualities relate to what Saltman seems to be looking for in a job and career in general?

3. Before you read the essay, what would you have guessed would be the biggest stumbling blocks in terms of Saltman's survival and success in the male-dominated world of construction? Did she encounter these problems, and if so how did she handle them? What problems or situations did you find most surprising?

4. In several places Saltman credits the pioneering women who preceded her in the building trades. How did these earlier tradeswomen help Saltman in her career? What effect does Saltman see her own career having on future women in the building trades?

Working with Connections

1. Are you or do you know a women working in what has traditionally been considered a man's line of work, whether in construction or some other area? Compare your own experience or interview the woman you know and compare her experiences with Saltman's. What common experiences and attitudes do you find? What points of convergence? Saltman's story was published in 1988; what changes have the ensuing years made in the situation of women in jobs like Saltman's?

2. In one area, Saltman wonders whether her gender might have been an advantage in being chosen for certain jobs involving the

restoration of architecturally significant buildings. She speculates that the building owners might think, "Women are more careful than men . . . Nina is a woman, therefore she will take better care of this building!" In what ways could Saltman's speculation connect with Alice Kessler-Harris's question in *Women Have Always Worked* (in Chapter 5, Work and Family): "Is it possible for women simultaneously to join the work force on an equal basis with men and to alter it in ways that accord with their own sensibilities?" On the other hand, in what ways could the assumption that "women are more careful than men" function as another limiting stereotype about gender?

3. Molly Martin, the editor of the collection from which Saltman's essay is taken, is herself an electrician who also is a part of Tradeswomen, Inc., an organization of "ironworkers, electricians, carpenters, pipefitters, stone masons, surveyors, and other union members, who are working together to provide fair and safe conditions for women who work in the building trades." Visit their web site at <http://www.tradeswomen.org/index.html> to learn more about contemporary issues facing women in the trades and other traditionally male-identified professions.

Media Images

Fast Food Restaurant Job Advertisement

While issues such as affirmative action remain controversial, most major corporations have embraced the concept of diversity as part of both their marketing campaigns and hiring practices. As celebrations of diversity and multiculturalism become more and more common in advertising and corporate policy statements, cultural critics debate how much this embracing of a diverse workforce represents a genuine commitment to a more equal society or a shrewd sales strategy (and since corporations are large, complex institutions, these motives are not necessarily mutually exclusive).

This mock job advertisement and application is typical of one used by a fast food restaurant. In trying to attract job applicants, the advertisement displays photos of employees (or models portraying employees) on the job at the restaurant. As you study the advertisement, consider the visual messages you think are being sent, how those messages interact with the words, and who the target audiences for the ad might be.

Working with the Text

1. As with all advertisements, the designers of this ad want to create a positive impression, in this case of just what it is like to work at a fast food restaurant. They also know that the readers of the ad will already have a great deal of familiarity with fast food restaurants (in fact, ads like this are often distributed to customers). Before you looked at the ad for the first time, what was your general impression of fast food restaurants, both as places to eat and as potential places to work? What positive and negative associations did you have? How well do the images and words in the ad reinforce your positive associations and counteract any negative ones? Which specific images were most and least effective?

2. What images of diversity in the workplace does the advertisement offer? What specific audiences do you think the ad is trying to reach, and how might these images of diversity attract different viewers? As a research project, you could visit various local fast food restaurants and do diversity inventories based on the images in the ad.

3. One particular aspect of diversity featured in the advertisement is age diversity. The employees range in age from teenagers to retirement age. The issue of fast-food restaurants recruiting older workers has sparked some debate over whether this represents a healthy social development. What are the potential plusses and minuses of workers fifty-five and older becoming a new work force in the fast food industry? What might be the reasons older people take these jobs? What might be the reasons fast-food restaurants are interested in hiring them?

Working with Connections

1. Locate actual fast food restaurant job advertisements, either in the restaurants themselves or on the web. Identify common rhetorical strategies among the ads as well as ways the ads have changed over time. How frequently is workplace diversity featured in the ads? What variations on the theme of diversity do you find, and what different purposes do these variations serve?

2. Fast food restaurants are an entry points to the paid work force for millions of Americans. It is likely that you, someone in your class, or someone you know has worked at or is working at a fast food restaurant. Locate a current or former employee and ask them to look at the ad and comment on it. Record their reactions and write about what you think they reveal about the ad and the rhetorical strategy behind the ad. How do responses vary depending on whether the person had a generally positive or negative experience of working at a fast food restaurant? What do they find most and least accurate about the representation of the restaurant workplace in the ad?

THE WORK OF WRITING/WRITING AS WORK: DIVERSITY INVENTORY

One way that colleges, business, and other organizations assess their progress on diversity issues is by hiring consultants to visit the organization and write an assessment of how well that organization is reaching its diversity goals. As a class project, act as consultants and prepare a diversity inventory for your college campus as a workplace. Among the tasks to consider:

1. Identify the specific diversity categories and issues you wish to focus on in your inventory. As you consider this question, keep in mind the particular issues of importance to the local community in which your school is located. Some issues to consider could include:

   - Race and ethnic diversity
   - Gender diversity
   - Ability issues
   - Sexual orientation
   - Linguistic diversity

2. Locate institutional information about the demographic makeup of the people who work for your college, including faculty staff and administrators. What diversity categories is your school keeping track of in terms of the workforce? Try and locate information that connects demographic information with job rank and status.

3. Locate and identify existing college affirmative action, equal employment, and other policies related to the diversity of the campus workforce. What are your college's stated diversity goals?

4. In addition to gathering empirical information about the workforce and college diversity policies, use observation and interviews to gauge the diversity "atmosphere" on campus. How welcome or unwelcome might employees from different backgrounds feel on campus? For example, if there are employee associations and groups on campus centered on diversity issues, such as an African-American faculty and staff association, some class members might meet with them to discuss their views on how inviting the campus feels. Based on these interviews and your own assessment of the campus culture, how prevalent are forms of social prejudice such as racism or homophobia? You

can also conduct tours of campus to determine how accessible the campus is from the standpoint of physical ability. Are there adequate ramps? Electric doors? What kind of impressions do posters and art on campus make in terms of the diversity climate?

5. Finally, work as a class to synthesize and analyze the information you gather and identify areas of achievement in terms of campus workplace diversity and areas that need further work. Prepare a written and/or web version of your findings to present to the chief administrator of the college. In consultation with your instructor, you can then decide whether to actually submit the report.

CHAPTER 7

The Ethics of Work/
The Work Ethic

- It's the bottom of the ninth inning, and the home team is losing by a run. The bases are loaded, and there are two outs. A base hit will score two runs and win the game. The batter at the plate hits a low fly ball dropping into left field. The left fielder dives to try and make a shoe-string catch, but can only catch the ball on one hop after it hits the ground. The umpire, however, thinks it was a clean catch and signals out. The left fielder knows that if he keeps quiet, his team wins. Should he tell the umpire that he didn't really catch the ball?

- Even though her company has been consistently making a profit, the CEO knows that she can increase profits even further by shutting down a local manufacturing plant and moving it to another country where labor costs are lower. The loss of the plant, however, will mean the loss of jobs for hundreds of workers and the economic devastation of the town in which it is located. The stockholders, however, judge the CEO by how well she maximizes profits. Should she keep the plant open, or should she go for higher profits?

- A paper on the Great Depression is due tomorrow morning in history class. The student scans the Internet looking for source materials and comes across an essay that seems perfect for the assignment, so perfect, in fact, that it could be copied and turned in as is. What should the student do?

Each of these situations presents us with a different kind of ethical dilemma, the question of judging the impact our behavior has on other people and our society. Often, ethical dilemmas concern a conflict between benefiting ourselves and harming others. In some ways, they result from the potential contradictions involved in our ideas and ideals of success. On the one hand, we admire "winners," people who come out on top, whether that means winning a championship, acquiring wealth and status, or achieving fame. But the idea of winners also implies the existence of losers and the fact that success can sometimes come at the expense of others. And what about taking shortcuts? Is what's important how you play the game, or whether you win or lose? What would each of us rather be: wealthy or good? Are these two ideals compatible?

In his *Autobiography* (part of which can be found in Chapter 2, Work, Labor, and Career: The Meaning of Work), Benjamin Franklin suggested that there is no conflict between the desire to be good and the desire to be prosperous. According to Franklin, traditional moral rules were designed to help us succeed: "vicious Actions are not hurtful because they are forbidden, but forbidden because they are hurtful, the Nature of Man alone consider'd: That it was therefore every one's Interest to be virtuous, who wish'd to be happy even in this World." Similarly, the early economist Adam Smith (whose work can be found in Chapter 4, Work and Social Class), resolved the potential conflict between a society based on every person looking to advance his or her own personal interests and the interests of society as a whole by suggesting that "an invisible hand" made sure that as each of us tries to get ahead individually, society as a whole benefits.

But is, as Franklin also said, "honesty the best policy"? Does our society really reward the most virtuous and honest with the greatest wealth and success? The recent scandals involving Enron, WorldCom, and other corporations suggest a different value system, one in which the desire to acquire wealth supersedes all other ethical considerations. In confronting ethical dilemmas of your own, is doing the right thing always obvious?

This chapter asks you to think about the relationship of values, success, and ethics, both in school and on the job, especially insofar as the classroom is seen as training for the workplace. The chapter in fact includes a subsection on cheating in school. As you prepare to read these selections, you might consider the following questions and issues:

1. Define what the phrase "work ethic" means to you. What inherent value do you see in work? What value does society see?

2. Write about an ethical dilemma you had to face either on the job or in school. What made the choices so difficult? What did you eventually decide and why? What was the outcome? How do you feel about your decision in retrospect?

3. Brainstorm recent ethical conflicts and dilemmas in the news that could form the basis for research projects, such as the Enron scandal or the debate over copying music on the Internet. What specific ethical issues are raised in each case?

Foundational Readings

MAX WEBER

■

From *The Protestant Ethic and the Spirit of Capitalism*

Max Weber (1864–1920) was a German scholar and a founder of the discipline of sociology. In one of his most famous works, The Protestant Ethic and the Spirit of Capitalism, *first published in 1905, Weber tackled the question of why contemporary capitalism had developed in Europe and the United States rather than in the ancient civilizations of Asia. His much-discussed and much-debated answer was that cultural forces, and specifically the rise of Protestant Christianity, created an ethical belief system about the relationship of the individual to work and the acquisition of wealth that led to the growth of the modern market economy. In the years since Weber first proposed his ideas, the phrase "Protestant work ethic" has entered the popular vocabulary as shorthand for the belief that it is one's duty to work as hard as possible to increase personal wealth while also living frugally and simply. In this way, so the idea goes, the apparent selfishness of an economic system based on the making of profit is balanced by an ethic of self-denial and hard work.*

Most sociologists and economists today would challenge Weber's argument as the true explanation for the economic development of Europe and the United States, but the idea of the Protestant work ethic remains with us, as does the general social concern over the ethical conflict between personal greed and the public good.

In the title of this study is used the somewhat pretentious phrase, the *spirit* of capitalism. What is to be understood by it? The attempt to give anything like a definition of it brings out certain difficulties which are in the very nature of this type of investigation.

If any object can be found to which this term can be applied with any understandable meaning, it can only be an historical individual, i.e. a complex of elements associated in historical reality which we unite into a conceptual whole from the standpoint of their cultural significance.

Thus, if we try to determine the object, the analysis and historical explanation of which we are attempting, it cannot be in the form of a conceptual definition, but at least in the beginning only a provisional description of what is here meant by the spirit of capitalism. Such a description is, however, indispensable in order clearly to understand the object of the investigation. For this purpose we turn to a document of that spirit which contains what we are looking for in almost classical purity, and at the same time has the advantage of being free from all direct relationship to religion, being thus, for our purposes, free of preconceptions.

* * * * *

"Remember, that *time* is money. He that can earn ten shillings a day by his labour, and goes abroad, or sits idle, one half of that day, though he spends but sixpence during his diversion or idleness, ought not to reckon *that* the only expense; he has really spent, or rather thrown away, five shillings besides.

"Remember, that *credit* is money. If a man lets his money lie in my hands after it is due, he gives me the interest, or so much as I can make of it during that time. This amounts to a considerable sum where a man has good and large credit, and makes good use of it.

"Remember, that money is of the prolific, generating nature. Money can beget money, and its offspring can beget more, and so on. Five shillings turned is six, turned again it is seven and threepence, and so on, till it becomes a hundred pounds. The more there is of it, the more it produces every turning, so that the profits rise quicker and quicker. He that kills a breeding-sow, destroys all her offspring to the thousandth generation. He that murders a crown, destroys all that it might have produced, even scores of pounds."

"Remember this saying, *The good paymaster is lord of another man's purse.* He that is known to pay punctually and exactly to the time he promises, may at any time, and on any occasion, raise all the money his friends can spare. This is sometimes of great use. After industry and frugality, nothing contributes more to the raising of a young man in the world than punctuality and justice in all his dealings; therefore never keep borrowed money an hour beyond the time you promised, lest a disappointment shut up your friend's purse for ever.

"The most trifling actions that affect a man's credit are to be regarded. The sound of your hammer at five in the morning, or eight at night, heard by a creditor, makes him easy six months longer; but if he sees you at a billiard-table, or hears your voice at a tavern, when you should be at work, he sends for his money the next day; demands it, before he can receive it, in a lump.

"It shows, besides, that you are mindful of what you owe; it makes you appear a careful as well as an honest man, and that increases your credit.

"Beware of thinking all your own that you possess, and of living accordingly. It is a mistake that many people who have credit fall into. To prevent this, keep an exact account for some time both of your expenses and your income. If you take the pains at first to mention particulars, it will have this good effect: you will discover how wonderfully small, trifling expenses mount up to large sums, and will discern what might have been, and may for the future be saved, without occasioning any great inconvenience."

"For six pounds a year you may have the use of one hundred pounds, provided you are a man of known prudence and honesty.

"He that spends a groat a day idly, spends idly above six pounds a year, which is the price for the use of one hundred pounds.

"He that wastes idly a groat's worth of his time per day, one day with another, wastes the privilege of using one hundred pounds each day.

"He that idly loses five shillings' worth of time, loses five shillings, and might as prudently throw five shillings into the sea.

"He that loses five shillings, not only loses that sum, but all the advantage that might be made by turning it in dealing, which by the time that a young man becomes old, will amount to a considerable sum of money."

It is Benjamin Ferdinand who preaches to us in these sentences, the same which Ferdinand Kürnberger satirizes in his clever and malicious *Picture of American Culture* as the supposed confession of faith of the Yankee. That it is the spirit of capitalism which here speaks in characteristic fashion, no one will doubt, however little we may wish to claim that everything which could be understood as pertaining to that spirit is contained in it. Let us pause a moment to consider this passage, the philosophy of which Kürnberger sums up in the words, "They make tallow out of cattle and money out of men". The peculiarity of this philosophy of avarice appears to be the ideal of the honest man of recognized credit, and above all the idea of a duty of the individual toward the increase of his capital, which is assumed as an end in itself. Truly what is here preached is not simply a means of making one's way in the world, but a peculiar ethic. The infraction of its rules is treated not as foolishness but as forgetfulness of duty. That is the essence of the matter. It is not mere business astuteness, that sort of thing is common enough, it is an ethos. *This* is the quality which interests us.

When Jacob Fugger, in speaking to a business associate who had retired and who wanted to persuade him to do the same, since he had made enough money and should let others have a chance, rejected that as pusillanimity and answered that "he (Fugger) thought otherwise, he wanted to make money as long as he could", the spirit of his statement is evidently quite different from that of Franklin. What in the former case was an expression of commercial daring and a personal inclination morally neutral, in the latter takes on the character of an ethically coloured maxim for the conduct of life. The concept spirit of capitalism is here used in this specific sense, it is the spirit of modern capitalism. For that we are here dealing only with Western European and American capitalism is obvious from the way in which the problem was stated. Capitalism existed in China, India, Babylon, in the classic world, and in the Middle Ages. But in all these cases, as we shall see, this particular ethos was lacking.

Now, all Franklin's moral attitudes are coloured with utilitarianism. Honesty is useful, because it assures credit; so are punctuality, industry, frugality, and that is the reason they are virtues. A logical deduction from this would be that where, for instance, the appearance of honesty serves the same purpose, that would suffice, and an unnecessary surplus of this virtue would evidently appear to Franklin's eyes as unproductive waste. And as a matter of fact, the story in his autobiography of his conversion to those virtues, or the discussion of the value of a strict maintenance of the appearance of modesty, the assiduous belittlement of one's own deserts in order to gain general recognition later, confirms this impression. According to Franklin, those virtues, like all others, are only in so far virtues as they are actually useful to the individual, and the surrogate of mere appearance is always sufficient when it accomplishes the end in view. It is a conclusion which is inevitable for strict utilitarianism. The impression of many Germans that the virtues professed by Americanism are pure hypocrisy seems to have been confirmed by this striking case. But in fact the matter is not by any means so simple. Benjamin Franklin's own character, as it appears in the really unusual candidness of his autobiography, belies that suspicion. The circumstance that he ascribes his recognition of the utility of virtue to a divine revelation which was intended to lead him in the path of righteousness, shows that something more than mere garnishing for purely egocentric motives is involved.

In fact, the *summum bonum* of this ethic, the earning of more and more money, combined with the strict avoidance of all spontaneous enjoyment of life, is above all completely devoid of any eudæmonistic, not to say hedonistic, admixture. It is thought of so purely as an end in itself, that from the point of view of the happiness of, or utility to, the single individual, it appears entirely transcendental and absolutely irrational. Man is dominated by the making of money, by acquisition as the ultimate purpose of his life. Economic acquisition is no longer subordinated to man as the means for the satisfaction of his material needs. This reversal of what we should call the natural relationship, so irrational from a naïve point of view, is evidently as definitely a leading principle of capitalism as it is foreign to all peoples not under capitalistic influence. At the same time it expresses a type of feeling which is closely connected with certain religious ideas. If we thus ask, *why* should "money be made out of men", Benjamin Franklin himself, although he was a colourless deist, answers in his autobiography with a quotation from the Bible, which his strict Calvinistic father drummed into him again and again in his youth: "Seest thou a man diligent in his business? He shall stand before kings" (Prov. xxii. 29). The earning of money within the modern economic order is, so long as it is done legally, the result and the expression of virtue and proficiency in a calling; and this virtue and proficiency are, as it is now not difficult to see, the real Alpha and Omega of Franklin's ethic, as expressed in the passages we have quoted, as well as in all his works without exception. ■

Working with the Text

1. Before you read this selection, how would you have defined the goals of a modern business person? What ethical questions did you see involved in those goals? What would you have said were the main ethical or moral conflicts a person was likely to face in business?

2. Weber begins his attempt to define "the spirit of capitalism" by including several quotations from Benjamin Franklin, which

Weber says contain that spirit "in almost classical purity." Working individually or in groups, choose one or two of these quotations and discuss what you think Weber would say represents the "spirit of capitalism" in them?

3. Weber defines the Protestant work ethic as "the earning of more and more money, combined with the strict avoidance of all spontaneous enjoyment of life." Based on this definition, can you find modern examples of successful businesspeople who fit this definition? How would you comment on the state of the Protestant work ethic today?

4. Part of the work ethic that Weber describes is based on utilitarianism, or the belief that the value of anything is determined by its usefulness. As a result, Weber says that the "spirit of capitalism" does not regard honesty as a virtue in itself, but only insofar as it leads to a good credit rating. In fact, he says, that "where, for instance, the appearance of honesty serves the same purpose, that would suffice." How do you respond to the idea that sometimes appearing honest is enough, and that maintaining honesty beyond where it is immediately useful is a kind of wastefulness?

Working with Connections

1. Weber offers Benjamin Franklin as a model of the work ethic he is describing. Based on your reading of the excerpts from his *Autobiography* (in Chapter 2, Work, Labor, and Career: The Meaning of Work), how would Franklin respond to Weber? With what would he agree or disagree?

2. In "Summertime Dues," Walter Kirn writes about what he thinks teenagers really learn from summer jobs, often in contrast to the character-building values that are usually promoted as the reason for young people to work for pay. Based on Kirn's testimony, how well does the work ethic Weber describes fit the kinds of part-time jobs you or others in the class may have had?

3. The advertisement for The Phoenix Companies, Inc. (in Chapter 4, Work and Social Class) addresses the anxieties and problems wealthy people face in dealing with their success. Use Weber's definition of the Protestant ethic as "the earning of more and more money, combined with the strict avoidance of all spontaneous enjoyment of life" to explore the potential ethical and personal conflicts expressed in the ad.

JOHN B. JUDIS   ■

Value-Free

We have all heard the complaints at one time or another from someone older than ourselves: people today don't work as hard as they did in the past; they don't know how to save their money, only spend it; they are less respectful and less moral than they used to be. It seems that people have always had a tendency to look back at the "good old days" and lament a decline in moral character. In part, this nostalgia stems from the uncertainty that accompanies all social and historic change. But do the people criticizing the present also have a point? Are we less hard-working and more self-centered in the present than in the past?

In this essay written for The New Republic *magazine in 1999, John B. Judis examines the charge that America has lost its work ethic. He traces the changes that have occurred since the nineteenth century, when the work ethic was closely linked to Protestant religious beliefs and the nature of early manufacturing (the conditions that led Max Weber to develop his concept of the "Protestant work ethic"), through the twentieth century and the advent of more efficient means of production, to the present day. Along the way, he argues that our working goals have shifted from a desire for happiness in a life to come to a search for a meaningful and satisfying lifestyle in the here and now.*

John B. Judis is a journalist and a senior editor of The New Republic. *He went to college at the University of California, Berkeley in the 1960s and was a member of Students for a Democratic Society. His work has appeared in many publications and he is the author of several books on American politics and society.*

Hardly a day goes by when we don't hear a politician, preacher, or pundit bemoaning the decline in the nation's morals. But it is not just Gary Bauer decrying the "virtue deficit." The *San Antonio Express-News* editorialized earlier this year: "The 1980s were known as the decade of self-indulgence and trickle-down economics. The 1990s will be known as the decade of moral decline." A *Washington Post* survey last August found that 78 percent of Americans believe that the "morals of young Americans have declined."

America has had its prophets of moral doom since the Pilgrims landed. But, interestingly, the current culture war is not about how extensively Americans are violating accepted moral standards but about what those standards should be. It's not whether teenagers are having sex but whether they think it is wrong to do so.

Morality is, of course, an elusive and difficult subject, but at the center of contemporary concerns about moral decline is a familiar complex of issues about work, leisure, sex, love family, the role of women, the place of religion, and the importance of self-denial. Should the goal of life be to achieve happiness or to please God? Should the goal of work be to make as much money as possible or to improve the situation of one's fellow humans? Should divorce be discouraged? Should abortion be permitted? Should homosexuality be tolerated? Is morality based upon religion? These debates herald a time of national moral and religious transition.

America's moral flux can be explained, at least in part, by everything from the introduction of birth control pills to the rise in life expectancy. But the fundamental explanation has to do with the relationship—noted by both Karl Marx and Max Weber—between the moral imperatives economic life generates and our broader moral and religious beliefs. As this basic relationship has changed during the twentieth century, it has undermined traditional morality and religion, contributing to the moral uncertainty in which we now find ourselves. And the change hinges on the meaning of saving and self-denial.

From the 1850s through the early decades of the twentieth century, the United States experienced an industrial revolution. During this period of capital accumulation, businessmen didn't consume their profits; they saved them and invested them in new plants, machinery, and raw materials in order to produce more goods at a lower cost. The accumulation of capital depended on saving. In an 1889 textbook, Francis Walker, the president of MIT, wrote: "At every step of its progress capital follows one law. It arises solely out of saving. It stands always for self-denial and abstinence." And what applied to the businessmen's income also applied to workers' wages. If businessmen paid their workers more than a subsistence wage, businesses would not have sufficient profit to invest and expand production. Workers accepted this, and, in this sense, their self-denial was also essential to industrialization.

This system of production was seen to be normal and necessary, according to certain religious and moral precepts that were rooted in the dissenting Protestant denominations that dominated the Northern colonies. For these Protestant groups, the goal of life was salvation in the afterlife. Success in work was an indication that a person would be saved. The aim of work was not to accumulate riches per se but to contribute to God's glory. This meant accumulating, rather than spending, what one earned and expanding its value. Work itself was a means of purifying the self against the sinful pleasures of the body. Indulgence in bodily pleasures—from sex outside of procreation to social dancing—was a sin. Idleness was a temptation to sin. As John Wesley, the founder of Methodism, put it, "We must exhort all Christians to gain all they can and to save all they can."

These tenets became central to Americans' work ethic. In 1701, Cotton Mather enjoined his parishioners, "Away to your business, lay out your strength in it, put forth your skill in it." One hundred and fifty years later, Henry Ward Beecher warned that "the indolent mind is not empty, but full of vermin." Secular as well as religious thinkers invoked the connection between economics and morals. William Graham Sumner, the foremost American disciple of Herbert Spencer, wrote in 1885: "The only two things which really tell on the welfare of man on earth are hard work and self-denial (in technical language, labor and capital), and these tell most when they are brought to bear directly upon the effort to earn an honest living, to accumulate capital, and to bring up a family of children to be industrious and self-denying in their turn."

In the first half of the twentieth century, the system of production that this Protestant work ethic sustained was utterly transformed. From 1900 to 1930, industrial productivity rose about twice as fast as it did from 1870 to 1900, largely because of the introduction of scientific management and the replacement of steam power by electricity. By the 1920s, as historian Martin Sklar has documented, it had become possible to increase output while decreasing the total number of workers engaged in goods production. During the '20s, overall manufacturing output increased 64 percent, but the number of manufacturing workers dropped by 300,000. This changed the role of saving.

Why? the industrial revolution depended upon the fact that both consumer goods workers and their employers would lay aside a certain portion of those goods (in the form of wages and profits, respectively) to be consumed by new workers hired to produce machines and other capital goods. In the '20s, however, it became possible to expand the production of consumer goods without increasing the number of workers engaged in goods production. In fact, the number of capital goods workers actually fell during the '20s, from 3.3 million to 2.9 million. This meant that goods producers no longer had to lay aside an additional part of their income for new workers. They no longer had to save as much as they had saved before.

By way of analogy, imagine an office in 1985 that produced greeting cards on a mini-computer that cost $50,000 and required several trained technicians to operate. Seven years later, the company could have taken a small percentage of the money it had put away to replace that machine and bought a new computer for $5,000 that would produce more cards with much less expensive labor. There would be no new net investment, merely the replacement of an older machine with a new one. If you imagine such a process taking place in the economy as a whole, you can get some idea of how the American economy changed in the '20s.

A similar paradox affected workers' self-denial. In the nineteenth century, wages had to be kept down to provide profits to invest in the newly growing capital goods industries. The growth of these industries required new workers who created new demand for consumer goods, which caused the consumer goods industries to make new investments, reigniting the process of accumulation. But, in the '20s, the process broke down because, again, the capital goods sector stopped growing. When new workers weren't hired, new demand for consumer goods dwindled. Consumer goods industries became so productive that they reduced the demand for their own goods every time they expanded production.

This created a crisis of overproduction that contributed to the depth and persistence of the Depression in the 1930s. Rising productivity led to an accumulation of profits that, in the absence of new investment outlets, found its way into the overvalued stock market. Workers' self-denial resulted not in new investment but in a lack of effective demand for the goods they produced. It was what Keynes called the "fallacy of saving."

In the early '30s, many Americans feared that capitalism had become obsolete and that there was no way to overcome the threat of overproduction that the new productivity had created. They were wrong: American capitalism recovered and flourished for the next 60 years by creating new outlets for investment and new demand for the goods that were produced. But these measures also undermined the foundations of the older Protestant work ethic.

The government subsidized both consumer demand and the demand for capital goods through welfare programs, public works, guaranteed loans for housing, highway construction, and military spending. Businesses acceded to wage increases and used various forms of easy consumer credit to encourage spending. Advertising also exploded, especially after the introduction of television. But, more important, businesses vastly expanded into realms that had been either unexplored or previously reserved for upper-class luxuries. They now sold fun and leisure and mental and physical health to the working class; they marketed not merely edible food but gourmet delights and prepackaged and frozen food. They sold fashion and not merely clothes.

They sold these new goods and services through advertising, but the advertising itself had to create new needs and a new conception of what Americans should want to have and want to be. Advertising, along with popular entertainment, promoted the idea of a new American quite unlike the older American of the Protestant work ethic. For this new American, the goal of life was not salvation in the afterlife but happiness now. The goal of work was a comfortable and pleasurable life for yourself and for your family. Physical pleasure, through sex, sports, social activity, entertainment, and eating was an integral part of happiness. Leisure was a reward for having worked, and the enjoyment of leisure was an important part of happiness.

The older life had been based on saving and self-denial; the new one was based on spending and self-fulfillment—the "good life." In the '60s, Americans began to look for the right "lifestyle." The older American had inherited his identity; the new American chose his identity, constructed his appearance (through diet, fashion, and cosmetics), created a personality (through education and even psychotherapy), and selected a career. One achieved happiness by choosing the right lifestyle.

This obsession with lifestyle has been reflected in the books Americans have read. For the past three decades, the nonfiction best-seller lists have been dominated by books explaining how to achieve happiness through adopting a certain lifestyle—from Thomas A. Harris's *I'm OK-You're OK* to Nancy Friday's *My Mother, My Self* down to Stephen Covey's *The Seven Habits of Highly Effective People* to Suze Orman's current best-seller, *The Courage to be Rich*.

Orman, who has become a superstar on public television, tells her own story of achieving the good life. After working for seven years as a waitress after college, she decided to get a job as a stockbroker. "I remember how proud my mom was when, years later, I was able to buy my first luxury car," she writes.

She then decided to start her own financial group, but, after only a year, someone stole all her client records. She went deeply into debt. She then describes a Bunyanesque "turning point" in her life. Sitting in a Denny's restaurant, she "looked closely at the woman waiting on me, and it dawned that she surely had more money than I did. I might have looked richer, wearing my designer clothes and with my fancy car parked outside. But I knew that the only wealth that I had at this point was a negative, drawn in red ink. Looking again, I could see clearly that this waitress was also happier than I was, and more honest. I was the poor one, inside and out. Where would I find the courage I needed, the courage to change?"

In the standard Christian tale, the rich man realizes that the beggar is more virtuous and will be rewarded in the afterlife. But, in Orman's morality tale, both virtue and the promise of eternal life have disappeared. What Orman realizes is that her wealth is superficial because her business is in arrears and that the waitress actually has more money than she does and is therefore happier. Orman's "fancy car" couldn't bring her happiness because the bank still owned it. Seized with this insight into her true condition, she rebuilds her business—a business that consists of telling people how to manage their Roth IRAs—and regains the "courage to be rich."

The new capitalism has transformed religion itself into primarily a social and therapeutic activity. Shorn of its promise of otherworldly salvation, religion has become a lifestyle strategy—from Norman Vincent Peale's 1952 best-seller, *The Power of Positive Thinking,* to televangelist Robert H. Schuller's best-selling 1988 guide to make it, *Success Is Never Ending, Failure Is Never Final.* Last year, the host of a sports talk show was questioning a Dallas Cowboys representative about whether star player Deion Sanders's newfound commitment to religion was simply another "fad" that he was embracing. The rep became indignant at this slight to Sanders. "Being a Christian," he explained to the incredulous host, "has become Deion's lifestyle."

The "culture war" of the past decades has pitted descendants of the movements of the '60s against conservative Republicans and members of the religious right. It has had all the trappings of the final battle between good and evil on Armageddon, but it is really being fought on the much more prosaic terrain of modern capitalism. The two sides have much in common. They share not only a goal of worldly success but also a rejection of the purely individual strategy for salvation favored by Orman or Covey. They stand for visions of the good society and not simply the good life.

The counterculture of the '60s was part of the new capitalism but was also a reaction to the form it had taken after World War II. It fused cultural experimentation with politics: the search for the good life with the crusade for a good society. It featured communes, widespread use of drugs, and sexual liberation, but it also gave rise to the feminist, environmental and consumer movements. The feminist movement was an attempt to secure not merely economic equality but equal opportunity to define one's existence; the environmental and consumer movements aimed to include safe cars and healthy food and clean air and water in the definition of the good life.

The religious right was descended from the Fundamentalists and Pentecostals of the early twentieth century who counseled Christians to save themselves before the world's end. These early Fundamentalists represented the last stand of the old Protestantism. Today's religious activists of the Christian Coalition have become worldly in their aims. They seek not to save their own souls but to reform present-day America. And they have expanded their own purview from restoring prayer in public school to cutting capital gains taxes.

Though not a fundamentalist Christian himself, William Bennett illustrates the trend. Bennett (like Orman) embraces the older virtues for newer ends. In *The Spirit of America* for instance, he touts frugality as a virtue, but not for the same reasons that Wesley did. "In our modern age of easy credit and consumer debt, of great affluence and great decadence," he writes, "it is important to recall that industry and frugality are the sources not only of material success but of good and satisfactory living as well."

If you look at this culture war not from the perspective of the moment but from the sweep of two centuries, it looks like a family quarrel. One could imagine the adherents of the counterculture and the religious right as passengers in a spaceship furiously debating which direction it should go, when, unbeknownst to them, it is primarily being directed from below by remote control. Its overall direction is already mapped out. The best that the critics can do is steer it to the right or the left.

So, does the replacement of the older Protestant *work ethic* represent a decline in morality, as some conservatives insist? I would suggest that it is far preferable to worry about how to achieve happiness on earth than to tolerate unhappiness and even misery in the pursuit of an imagined afterlife. It is also a decided advance that the average citizen can now take advantage of activities and opportunities once reserved for a wealthy few—like travel, education, psychotherapy, athletics, and preventive medicine. Most Americans can now enjoy the aesthetic dimension of fine clothes and food. And they can participate in sexual activities that were formerly performed secretly under a burden of crippling guilt.

Within this given framework, one can still find ample room for questioning whether certain kinds of behavior represent, if not a decline in morality, a departure from it. These include not simply obvious examples of criminal behavior but also the egregious pursuit of luxury that Robert Frank documents in his new book, *Luxury Fever*—from face-lifts to castles in the Hamptons—and the rabid intolerance of social differences (yes, lifestyles!) that is fueled by Bauer, Pat Buchanan, and others who claim the mantle of God. One can also find justification for encouraging social rather than purely individual solutions to the achievement of the good life—an objective that liberal and Christian right movements share but that they seek to achieve in very different ways. What is at stake is not the decline of morality but its redefinition—a process in which all Americans, from born-again to New Age to agnostic, are already participating. ■

Working with the Text

1. What does Judis see as the main differences between the work ethic of the past and the work ethic of the present? How does he say employers and workers of the past defined their goals? What goals do we have today?

2. Explain what the changes were in economic production and government policies from the 1920s to the end of World War II that Judis says brought about a change in the work ethic. How effective is his analogy of the company that produces greeting cards on a minicomputer in explaining these changes? Can you come up with your own analogies?

3. Overall, Judis sees the changes in the modern attitudes toward work as changes for the better. What does he see as most positive about these changes? What do others find most disturbing about these changes? How much are you convinced by Judis's argument?

Working with Connections

1. Use the discussion of the work ethic found in both Weber and Judis in a discussion of Bob Black's radical manifesto, "The Abolition of Work" (in Chapter 2, Work, Labor, and Career: The Meaning of Work). Compare the interpretations of history found in Black with those in Judis and Weber. Where do they agree and disagree? What might Judis's response to Black be?

2. Judis argues, "the new capitalism has transformed religion itself into primarily a social and therapeutic activity. Shorn of its promise of otherworldly salvation, religion has become a lifestyle strategy." Explore the validity of Judis's argument about the role of religion in contemporary life by interviewing others about what their religious beliefs mean to them. What connections do people see between their religious faith, if any, and their ideas and attitudes toward work?

3. Given the impact that the changing economy of the past has had on our work ethic, according to Judis, what do you see as some possible effects of the many changes occurring now in the workplace? Use an essay that speculates on the future of work such as "An Age of Optimism" by Nicolas Negroponte (in Chapter 9, Work in the Information Age: The Future of Work) as the basis for your speculation.

WALTER KIRN

Summertime Dues

Part-time summer jobs used to be how many young people entered the for-pay work force for the first time. Today, however, more and more high school and college students work before- and after-school jobs as well. In addition to providing spending or tuition money, these first jobs have also been seen as crucial preparation for adult work by helping to build responsibility, character, and a strong work ethic. But is there a gap between what a young worker is supposed to learn and what he or she actually encounters in the world of work? In this essay written for the New York Times Sunday Magazine, *Walter Kirn says that his part-time summer jobs did teach him about the real values and ethics governing the world of work, but what he actually learned was very different than what he was supposed to have learned.*

Walter Kirn is a writer and critic who grew up in Minnesota and now lives in Montana. He is the literary editor of GQ Magazine *and is the author of three novels,* She Needed Me, Thumbsucker, *and* Up in the Air.

On my first summer job I learned to cheat. I was working in one of those cute, old-timey ice cream shops where the sundaes are decorated with toothpick flags and the staff sings "Happy Birthday" to the customers. The day I clocked in, the owner showed me how to scoop up a generous-looking ball of ice cream that was perfectly hollow in the center. The trick was in the wrist, and it took practice, but eventually I mastered the subterfuge and was serving up great gobs of rocky road that weighed, according to a hidden kitchen scale, exactly 1.5 ounces. I felt rotten. Kids would come in holding flimsy dollar bills—all the money they'd ever had, it seemed—and in return I would give them globes of air that collapsed inward the moment they were licked. I complained to the owner, who threatened to let me go and accused me of being a secret "heavy scooper" who didn't understand the ways of business.

Like millions of other American teenagers, I was doing what was expected of me that summer: preparing myself for the world of work by holding down a minimum-wage job that conveyed no special skills or knowledge but did breed a certain early cynicism. Like prom night and graduation, a summer job was a rite of passage in my town. Whether or not we needed the money or felt we had better uses for our time than topping off radiators at the mini-lube or repainting the foul lines on the city tennis courts, we teenagers labored straight through to Labor Day, emerging strengthened and toughened at summer's end.

That was two decades ago, another time. These days, according to several recent reports, the summer-job tradition is in decline. Fewer and fewer kids, the experts tell us, are showing an interest in whiling away their holidays folding boxes and weed-whipping cracked sidewalks.

What's more, the once-popular government programs that subsidized such jobs are drying up, the victims of a prosperous economy and a shrinking pool of applicants. A troubling development? Perhaps. Then again, if my own experience means anything, maybe not.

Summer jobs are supposed to build character in teenagers—the question is, What sort of character? A lot of the jobs, let's face it, are pure make-work: clearing dead-end trails through national forests, planting violets around school flagpoles. They're the sort of duties assigned to prison inmates and pensioners in the Soviet Union, and what they mainly teach is the necessity of appearing busy for the boss while doing something that no one really needs done. At the end of the week there's a paycheck, small but helpful, which you promptly pump into the gas tank of your car or blow on Christina Aguilera tickets. The jobs are entitlement programs, basically, or political schemes to keep rambunctious kids out of the way of adults and off the streets.

Not that learning to look busy isn't valuable. One of my own summer jobs was moving books between two floors of a college library. My supervisor was barely in his 20's, a member of one of those upbeat New Age movements that preach prosperity through optimism. He called me and my coworkers his "team" and referred to our simple duties as "the mission." What he failed to notice, though, in his zeal to convert us to his beliefs, was that, after only four weeks on the job, we'd finished moving every single book. There was no more to do, and two more months to do it. The team made a decision then: say nothing. The job was so easy and the pay so generous that we agreed to keep a good thing going. We emptied half of the shelves that we'd just filled, carried the books downstairs, and started over.

Better training for corporate life would be hard to find. In that sense, the library job fulfilled its promise. I not only learned to work, I also learned when not to work. I learned to protect my friends and even my boss, who might have been laid off had someone realized that he'd fulfilled his objective prematurely. These lessons have come in handy ever since. In office after office, I've seen the price paid by those who complete assignments early, only to be handed yet more work in a continual, exhausting spiral that ends in hospitalization or unemployment. Such eager beavers tend to burn out early, perhaps because they never had summer jobs that taught them how to conserve their vital energy.

The kids who are eschewing summer work in favor of more broadening pursuits like travel, athletics and daily moviegoing may find themselves at a disadvantage someday. There's so much they won't know. Like when to steal. I learned to steal while working at a gas station. I resisted at first, but my manager pushed hard, and since he was the nephew of the proprietor, I found him persuasive. The guy stole everything, from cans of Dr. Pepper to tanks of gas, explaining that they belonged not to the station but to a multinational oil company. What's more, he said, if I tattled to his uncle he'd blame me for the thefts. I'd lose my job.

Summer work is important. Hop to it, kids. There are some things you just can't learn in school. ■

Working with the Text

1. What was the first for-pay job you had or the closest experience to it? Write about what you anticipated about your experience, including your hopes and fears. What were you most and least surprised by about the experience? What exceeded your expectations? What disappointed you the most? What would you say were the biggest ethical conflicts you faced? What did you learn from the experience, and how does that compare with what Kirn learned?

2. If you had been a friend of Kirn's when he faced one of his ethical challenges at his part-time job, what advice would you have given him?

3. Kirn writes that his early "minimum-wage" jobs "conveyed no special skills or knowledge but did breed a certain early cynicism." How realistic do you find the lessons that Kirn draws from his experiences? To what extent do you agree that part-time jobs can make a person more cynical about work?

4. Among the lessons Kirn took with him from his part-time experiences are "when to steal" and that "eager beavers tend to burn out early." While Kirn is critical of summer jobs for reinforcing negative work habits, he also claims that these same work habits are useful survival skills. How seriously do you take Kirn when he says, "There are some things you just can't learn in school"?

Working with Connections

1. In his use of sarcasm and his distinction between what work is supposed to teach and what it actually does, Kirn uses strategies similar to Kathryn Carmony in "Surfing the Classifieds" (in Chapter 2, Work. Labor, and Career: The Meaning of Work). Using the example of Kirn and Carmony and your own experiences, write your own satirical "Guide to Workplace Ethics" aimed at teenagers entering the job market for the first time. As you work on your piece, think about the actual message about ethics and work that you want to convey.

2. Some of the workplace situations and pressures that Kirn describes are similar to school situations, such as figuring out what to do when you complete a task before the allotted time is

up or when (and if) to "pad" the ice-cream serving with air. In what ways do traditional classroom practices foster the same kinds of cynicism that Kirn describes? What are the resulting ethical challenges facing students? How could these potential pressures to cut corners or disguise work relate to the issues discussed below in the special section on plagiarism?

3. Imagine Kirn writing as a teenage worker to Randy Cohen's "Ethicist" column (in the section on "Stories of Work" below) describing one of the ethical dilemmas he confronted on the job. How do you think Cohen would answer him? How would his answer compare to the answer you would give?

Focus on School Work and Ethics: Plagiarism and Cheating

In 2001, the news media reported that two prominent historians—Stephen J. Ambrose and Doris Kearns Goodwin—had been accused of copying from other historians in writing their best-selling books. In both cases, the two writers had listed the sources they used in their books, but they had not indicated with quotation marks and specific citations the actual words and phrases they copied from the originals. That same year in Kansas, a controversy erupted when twenty-eight high school students were said by their teacher to have copied and pasted material from the Internet into their biology essays without citing their sources. The teacher flunked the students on the assignment; the local school board later reduced the penalty for most of the students, and the teacher resigned in protest.

Both of these cases address one of the key ethical challenges facing student writers: plagiarism. In simple terms, plagiarism is defined as claiming someone else's work as your own. In real-life situations, however, the question of plagiarism can get more complicated. In a research writing project, for example, your task is to draw on the work and writing of others in creating your own essay. You may borrow ideas, information, and even specific language from your sources, as long as you cite them properly. But what if 90 percent of your writing is borrowed from other sources, even if those sources are cited? What if you paraphrase ideas? What are the best ways for showing your readers when the ideas you borrow from another end and your own begin? How can you tell the difference yourself between your own ideas and those of your sources? It can be easy for an inexperienced research writer to make mistakes without meaning to cheat.

The question of deliberate cheating, of course, is an even more serious matter. With the advent of the Internet, many faculty worry about how easy it has become to simply copy and paste material from a web site to a student's paper, or even to download entire essays. Teachers' concerns range from how to detect plagiarism and cheating to the even thornier question of understanding what might motivate cheating in the first place and how to address the factors that might lead students to plagiarize, either accidentally or deliberately.

The readings in this minisection bring up several issues related to plagiarism and cheating: the definition of the term *plagiarism*, a news story claiming that cheating is becoming more acceptable, and a story from *The Chronicle of Higher Education* about the growth of web sites featuring downloadable papers. Before you begin reading and writing about this section, consider these questions:

1. How would you define plagiarism in your own words? What is your school's official definition of plagiarism, and how does it compare to your own? What most confuses you or concerns you about plagiarism?
2. How prevalent do you think cheating is among students, and how concerned do you think faculty and administrators should be? Interview students anonymously on campus about cheating and plagiarism. How widespread do others believe it to be? How seriously do students regard cheating as an ethical issue?
3. What are the specific procedures and possible penalties at your school for dealing with plagiarism? Do they seem fair and effective to you? What suggestions would you have for improving these policies?

RICHARD A. POSNER

On Plagiarism

How do we define plagiarism, and is all plagiarism equal or equally wrong? In this essay from The Atlantic Monthly Magazine, *Richard A. Posner comments on the plagiarism cases mentioned in the introduction to this minisection and draws some distinctions he sees in different kinds of plagiarism. Making such distinctions is part of what Posner does for a living. He is a judge in the U.S. Seventh Circuit Court of Appeals, a law professor, and a writer on issues involving the law and society.*

Recently two popular historians were discovered to have lifted passages from other historians' books. They identified the sources in footnotes, but they failed to place quotation marks around the purloined passages. Both historians were quickly buried under an avalanche of criticism. The scandal will soon be forgotten, but it leaves in its wake the questions What is "plagiarism"? and Why is it reprobated? These are important questions. The label "plagiarist" can ruin a writer, destroy a scholarly career, blast a politician's chances for election, and cause the expulsion of a student from a college or university. New computer search programs, though they may in the long run deter plagiarism, will in the short run lead to the discovery of more cases of it.

We must distinguish in the first place between a plagiarist and a copyright infringer. They are both copycats, but the latter is trying to appropriate revenues generated by property that belongs to someone else—namely, the holder of the copyright on the work that the infringer has copied. A pirated edition of a current best seller is a good example of copyright infringement. There is no copyright infringement, however, if the "stolen" intellectual property is in the public domain (in which case it is not property at all), or if the purpose is not an appropriation of the copyright holder's revenue. The doctrine of "fair use" permits brief passages from a book to be quoted in a book review or a critical essay; and the parodist of a copyrighted work is permitted to copy as much of that work as is necessary to enable readers to recognize the new work as a parody. A writer may, for that matter, quote a passage from another writer just to liven up the narrative; but to do so without quotation marks—to pass off another writer's writing as one's own—is more like fraud than like fair use.

"Plagiarism," in the broadest sense of this ambiguous term, is simply unacknowledged copying, whether of copyrighted or uncopyrighted work. (Indeed, it might be of uncopyrightable work—for example, of an idea.) If I reprint *Hamlet* under my own name, I am a plagiarist but not an infringer. Shakespeare himself was a formidable plagiarist in the broad sense in which I'm using the word. The famous description in *Antony and Cleopatra* of Cleopatra on her royal barge is taken almost verbatim from a translation of Plutarch's life of Mark Antony: "on either side of her, pretty, fair boys appareled as painters do set forth the god Cupid, with little fans in their hands, with which they fanned wind upon her" becomes "on each side her / Stood pretty dimpled boys, like smiling Cupids, / With divers-colour'd fans, whose wind did seem / To glow the delicate cheeks which they did cool." (Notice how Shakespeare improved upon the original.) In *The Waste Land*, T. S. Eliot "stole" the famous opening of Shakespeare's barge passage, "The barge she sat in, like a burnish'd throne, / Burn'd on the water" becoming "The Chair she sat in, like a burnished throne, / Glowed on the marble."

Mention of Shakespeare brings to mind that *West Side Story* is just one of the links in a chain of plagiarisms that began with Ovid's Pyramus and Thisbe and continued with the forgotten Arthur Brooke's *The Tragical History of Romeus and Juliet*, which was plundered heavily by Shakespeare. Milton in *Paradise Lost* plagiarized Genesis, as did Thomas Mann in *Joseph and His Brothers*. Examples are not limited to writing. One from painting is Edouard Manet, whose works from the 1860s "quote" extensively from Raphael, Titian, Velásquez, Rembrandt, and others, of course without express acknowledgment.

If these are examples of plagiarism, then we want more plagiarism. They show that not all unacknowledged copying is "plagiarism" in the pejorative sense. Although there is no formal acknowledgement of copying in my examples, neither is there any likelihood of deception. And the copier has added value to the original—this is not slavish copying. Plagiarism is also innocent when no value is attached to originality; so judges, who try to conceal originality and pretend that their decisions are foreordained, "steal" freely from one another without attribution or any ill will.

But all that can be said in defense of a writer who, merely to spice up his work, incorporates passages from another writer without acknowledgment is that the readability of his work might be impaired if he had to interrupt a fast-paced narrative to confess that "a predecessor of mine, _____, has said what I want to say next better than I can, so rather than paraphrase him, I give you the following passage, indented and in quotation marks, from his book _____." And not even that much can be said in defense of the writer who plagiarizes out of sheer laziness or forgetfulness, the latter being the standard defense when one is confronted with proof of one's plagiarism.

Because a footnote does not signal verbatim incorporation of material from the source footnoted, all that can be said in defense of the historians with whom I began is that they made it easier for their plagiarism to be discovered. This is relevant to how severely they should be criticized, because one of the reasons academic plagiarism is so strongly reprobated is that it is normally very difficult to detect. (In contrast, Eliot and Manet *wanted* their audience to recognize their borrowings.) This is true of the student's plagiarized term paper, and to a lesser extent of the professor's plagiarized scholarly article. These are particularly grave forms of fraud, because they may lead the reader to take steps, such as giving the student a good grade or voting to promote the professor, that he would not take if he knew the truth. But readers of popular histories are not professional historians, and most don't care a straw how original the historian is. The public wants a good read, a good show, and the fact that a book or a play may be the work of many hands—as, in truth, most art and entertainment are—is of no consequence to it. The harm is not to the reader but to those writers whose work does not glitter with stolen gold. ■

Working with the Text

1. What distinctions does Posner make among the terms "plagiarism," "copyright infringement," and "fair use"? In what ways do his distinctions clarify the issue of plagiarism for you? In what ways do they raise further questions?

2. "If these are examples of plagiarism," Posner writes, referring to Shakespeare, T. S. Eliot, Thomas Mann, Edouard Manet, and others,

"then we want more plagiarism." Why does Posner approve of these forms of "plagiarism"? Do you agree with him? How would more contemporary forms of cultural texts such as hip-hop music that feature extensive borrowing from various sources relate to his argument about "desirable" forms of plagiarism? What would a counterargument be?

3. Why does Posner believe that academic forms of plagiarism, whether by students or faculty, are so "grave"? What specific kinds of harm does he see these kinds of plagiarism creating? To what extent do you agree with his assessment of the damage done by academic plagiarism? Where would you agree or disagree?

KATHY SLOBOGIN ■

Survey: Many Students Say Cheating's OK

We all know what cheating is, and we all know that it is wrong. But is the issue as simple as that? This article from early 2002 written for the CNN web site by reporter Kathy Slobogin suggests that many students see the issue of cheating as more complicated than a clear-cut case of right and wrong. In fact, Slobogin finds evidence that students and teachers do not always agree about what constitutes cheating. This article asks you to consider whether the students Slobogin talks to are simply making excuses for bad behavior or reflecting the contradictory pressures of a success-oriented society.

Kathy Slobogin has been a professional writer and reporter since 1974. Before joining CNN, she has worked for the New York Times, ABC News, *and* CBS News.

(CNN) —"Cheating is a shortcut and it's a pretty efficient one in a lot of cases."

That's not exactly the lesson most people want students to be learning in high school, but it's what 17-year-old Alice Newhall, a senior in a top high school in northern Virginia, says she believes. There's growing evidence she's not alone.

- A national survey by Rutgers' Management Education Center of 4,500 high school students found that 75 percent of them engage in serious cheating.
- More than half have plagiarized work they found on the Internet.
- Perhaps most disturbing, many of them don't see anything wrong with cheating: Some 50 percent of those responding to the survey said they don't think copying questions and answers from a test is even cheating.

Newhall, a B student at George Mason High School, says students have very little sense of moral outrage about cheating. For many, she says, the pressure to do well academically and compete for good colleges has made cheating a way to survive high school.

"What's important is getting ahead," says Newhall. "The better grades you have, the better school you get into, the better you're going to do in life. And if you learn to cut corners to do that, you're going to be saving yourself time and energy. In the real world, that's what's going to be going on. The better you do, that's what shows. It's not how moral you were in getting there."

ACCESS TO INFO

Some say the Internet has exacerbated the problem, making electronic plagiarism as easy as having a modem and a credit card. There are many Web sites like schoolsucks.com where you can download a paper on nearly any subject for $9.95 per page.

Schools have begun to fight Internet plagiarism with the students' own weapons.

George Mason High School is one of thousands of schools that have contracted with a company called turnitin.com, which allows teachers to submit student papers. The company then searches the Web for matching prose. Within 48 hours, the teacher gets the paper back, color-coded for plagiarism.

Turnitin.com representatives say about a third of the papers they receive have some amount of plagiarism.

SURVEYING THE SHIFTY

"Students today find it so much easier to rationalize their cheating," says Donald McCabe, the Rutgers professor who conducted the nationwide survey on high school cheating.

McCabe polled the students in his survey for reasons they cheat. Beside academic pressure, he says he found the most common response was that the adult world sets such poor examples.

"I think kids today are looking to adults and society for a moral compass," he says, "and when they see the behavior occurring there, they don't understand why they should be held to a higher standard."

Of course, not all students cheat. Mike Denny, also a senior at George Mason High School, thinks it's simply wrong. But he says a sense of honor that would prevent cheating seems lacking in high school.

"Honor seems like it's a concept of the past," says Denny. "Something like chivalry and knights and maybe a Victorian passe thing that no one really believes in any more."

Denny also blames a high school culture where grades and test scores are more important than integrity.

"By now many of us are so jaded we feel like our whole life has just been taught for one test," he says. "Things such as who you are and standing by your word and what not, that's something that we haven't really been taught."

Companies like turnitin.com may be part of the solution, but Donald McCabe says he thinks such policing action is just a Band-Aid for a moral deficit that schools and parents should address.

"I subscribe to the theory that suggests we'd be much better off promoting integrity among our students rather than trying to police their dishonesty," says McCabe. ■

Working with the Text

1. According to the survey quoted by Slobogin, "50 percent of those responding to the survey said they don't think copying questions and answers from a test is even cheating." Does this response surprise you? How do you and others in the class define cheating? As a way of exploring this question further, work in groups to come up with a series of scenarios that might be considered cheating and interview faculty and other students on campus for their opinions on what constitutes "cheating."

2. Alice Newhall, one of the students interviewed in the article, frames the question of cheating as a case of efficiency versus ethics. "'In the real world,'" she says, "'that's what's going to be going on. The better you do, that's what shows. It's not how moral you were in getting there.'" What are your reactions to Newhall's statement? Whether you approve of her own ethical reasoning, to what extent do you agree or disagree with her judgment of what counts in "the real world"?

3. The professor who conducted the survey on cheating, Donald McCabe, tells Slobogin "'we'd be much better off promoting integrity among our students rather than trying to police their dishonesty.'" How would you explain the distinction that McCabe is trying to make in your own words? How much do you agree with his position? Can you come up with any ideas for practical ways to promote integrity among students?

4. What overall impressions about contemporary high school and college students does this article convey? What key passages create this impression? Who do you see as the main audiences for this article, based both on how the article is written and what you know about the viewership of CNN? How could the same information be presented to create a different impression, or how would it be presented to different audiences, such as college students?

KELLY MCCOLLUM ■

Term-Paper Web Site Has Professors Worried About Plagiarism

The rise of the Internet has proved a boon to researchers, especially students, by offering thousands of readily available sources of information from around the world. At the same time, however, the Internet has also created new concerns about academic cheating, especially plagiarism.

With the aid of a computer mouse and a keyboard, passages can be cut and pasted or whole papers downloaded with a few clicks. In this 1996 article from The Chronicle of Higher Education, *the leading news magazine covering college and university issues, Kelly McCollum reports on the development of web sites offering term papers for students to download, both for free and for pay, and the fears faculty have that such Internet resources will lead to an epidemic of cheating. The section on "Reading the Web" below will give you the opportunity to examine the web site, "schoolsucks.com," referred to in this article as well as "turnitin.com," a web site based on detecting Internet plagiarism.*

A new library on the World-Wide Web may prove to be a valuable resource—mainly for dishonest students.

The Web site, called "School Sucks," was created last month by Kenneth A. Sahr, a student at Florida International University. Mr. Sahr says the library will eventually include thousands of college-level research papers on all kinds of topics—all free to any student who visits the site.

The site's slogan, "Download your workload," suggests that it is an electronic version of the term-paper mills advertised in the back pages of magazines—except that most of those services charge for their products. Mr. Sahr says that his site is not intended to promote plagiarism and that offering students papers without charge makes the library more of a service for professors than for students.

He describes the site as a "checks-and-balances system" for coping with plagiarism. Students have open access to the archive, but so do professors, who can check the texts on the site against papers about which they have suspicions, he notes. Mr. Sahr boasts that pay-for-paper services, to which professors generally don't have access, will be driven out of business by his site.

The library has created a stir among professors in several on-line discussion groups. A "Plagiarism Websource Alert" was circulated across the Internet on faculty mailing lists soon after the site was announced. "That got me more publicity than a two-page ad in *The New York Times*," Mr. Sahr says. Eric W. Crump, a graduate student at the University of Missouri at Columbia who edits an on-line writing journal, has created a Web site with dozens of messages from mailing lists where the topic was debated.

Most of the 20 or so works currently available on the site seem best suited—in topic and quality—for introductory English courses. A few papers are more specialized, such as a business essay about the soft-drink industry. Mr. Sahr says he has received about 50 other submissions.

He hopes the service will eventually offer hundreds of papers, in many subject areas—and that it will draw advertising dollars, which, he says, will allow him to expand the service.

Missouri's Mr. Crump agrees with Mr. Sahr's defense of the archive. "It's a very visible version of the underground paper mills that exist and thrive on many college campuses. Its visibility brings attention to the practice."

The most important check, Mr. Sahr argues, is on professors themselves. Faculty members who assign overly broad topics for term papers invite students to go shopping in paper mills, he argues. On the other hand, he says, assignments that are closely related to classroom discussions are not easily filled with plagiarized papers.

Here Mr. Crump disagrees. "I don't think the problem has so much to do with how broad or narrow the topic is," he says. In fact, a sufficiently large archive could provide papers on any topic, he says.

"What defeats plagiarism is not increasing particularity in assignments, but increasing self-motivation as the force driving writing," Mr. Crump says. Students who are truly interested in a subject and are engaged in the class, he adds, "will find plagiarism utterly irrelevant to their work."

So far, much of the negative reaction to the site has been aimed at its irreverent name. According to Mr. Sahr, the site's name and the "Download your workload" motto were meant simply to get people's attention. "I don't mean it literally," he says.

But if "School Sucks," or sites like it, do grow, Mr. Crump says, plagiarism will be easy for willing students. "When I was an undergraduate student, I wouldn't have known who to ask, even if I'd wanted to borrow a paper," he says. "Now, anybody with a computer and Net access can find paper mills with a quick and easy search of the Web." ■

Working with the Text

1. The developer of "School Sucks," Kenneth A. Sahr, denies that he created his web site to promote cheating. He points to the fact that he offers many papers for free, and that the web site can function as a "'checks-and-balances system'" by allowing students to access term papers and permitting teachers to check for suspected plagiarism. How convincing do you find Sahr's arguments? What might his motivations be in creating such a web site?

2. In speculating about what might tempt students to plagiarize and what might keep them from doing so, Sahr and Eric Crump, a college writing teacher, offer different explanations. Sahr suggests that when teachers assign topics that are overly broad or general it allows students to more easily find online papers that can fit the assignment. Crump points to the importance of "'increasing self-motivation'" among students by coming up with topics that the students feel a personal connection to. How well do each of these possible explanations fit in with

your own experiences as a student writer? What situations would you say offer the greatest temptations to plagiarism? What suggestions would you make to writing teachers in terms of combating plagiarism?

3. Sahr says that the name of his web site was simply designed "to get people's attention." Anticipating the section on Reading the Web below, write about how the name "School Sucks" gets your attention. What would your expectations be about such a web site? Whose attention do you think the name would most attract and why?

Reading the Web

Schoolsucks.com and *Turnitin.com*

What are the ethical responsibilities of students and teachers? What are the motives that lead students to plagiarize? What can teachers do to prevent it? Has the Internet created a new epidemic of cheating, or has it brought out into the open ethical issues about education that already existed? The two web sites featured here, Schoolsucks.com and Turnitin.com, are both evidence of and responses to the ethical questions surrounding schoolwork, plagiarism, and the Internet.

Schoolsucks.com is the web site featured in the article, "Term-Paper Web Site Has Professors Worried About Plagiarism," featured in the "Focus on School Work and Ethics: Plagiarism and Cheating" section above. It was started in 1996 by Kenneth Sahr, and while critics of the site charge Sahr with promoting plagiarism and cheating for a profit, Sahr claims that his main motive is to encourage improved education by exposing poor teaching practices and poor student results.

Turnitin.com was also started in 1996 as a for-pay service that screens all papers submitted to a given course for similarities to documents appearing on the Internet. Each student's essay is then given an "Originality Report" assessing the degree to which the paper may have been plagiarized. If any directly plagiarized material is found, it is highlighted in the report. Turnitin.com promotes itself as an effective means to fight plagiarism and encourage academic honesty among students, although in charging for their service and automatically placing every student's paper under suspicion, a question arises as to whether the main impact of the site will be to promote classroom honesty or to make a business out of policing student behavior.

Welcome back to School Sucks!! Ya ready?
Time to get out those dusty notebooks, the whoopie cushions, the notes you got from the kid who took the same classes last year and get your asses back to school.

We're ready.

We got a new site for you. A chat room so you can talk homework with students from all over the world. Message boards, games and polls. If you sign up, you can send instant messages.

We're giving a $250 high school scholarship this semester. But you have to prove that you're not an A student to participate!

Let us know what you think and keep spreading the word:

School Sucks!

I hereby agree that School Sucks

Email your comments to schoolsucks@schoolsucks.com
Press Inquires: (International) +972-55-755-849
Business Inquires: (International) +972-53-420-194
Yes, that means you have to dial 011 from the U.S

©1996 - 2003 School Sucks. All Rights Reserved

Working with the Texts

1. Compare the graphic presentations of the two sites in terms of the main audiences you think the sites want to appeal to. Why, for example, might the creator of *Schoolsucks.com* boast about how "ugly" his site is? Why does *Turnitin.com* use college images from the early twentieth century in their web site?

2. Explore the different rationale that Kenneth Sahr offers for the existence of *Schoolsucks.com* to students and teachers. What do you find most and least convincing about his explanations? How does the fact that the site offers access both to free papers and to sites that sell papers affect your opinion of the site? Do you agree with Sahr that the visibility of *Schoolsucks.com* to teachers and students alike actually discourages cheating?

3. Read some of the comments posted to *Schoolsucks.com* by people claiming to be students. How common or valid do you think their opinions are in relation to how you and other students feel about school? Would you agree that whether students find

school interesting and relevant is a key factor in determining their behavior and their ethical relationship toward school?

4. Review the materials that introduce *Turnitin.com* to students and teachers. What different approaches do they take? How do they explain the need and the importance of *Turnitin.com*?

5. What reactions would you have if your instructors began using the *Turnitin.com* service? What is your reaction and the reactions of others in the class to the idea of reviewing every student paper for signs of plagiarism? You can expand this assignment by interviewing students and faculty on campus for their views on such a service. If your school or course already uses a service like *Turnitin.com*, write about what your reactions have been and those of others in the class.

6. How effective do you think *Turnitin.com* would be in cutting down on plagiarism? How effective would it be in promoting a stronger ethical sense in students? What would be the plusses and minuses of using such a system?

7. As a way of coming to some conclusions on the subject of School Work and Ethics, create a web site, either individually or as a class, on the subject of classroom ethics and plagiarism. You can direct your web site to students, teachers, or both. You can include definitions of plagiarism, a discussion of a code of ethics for the classroom, and advice for both students and teachers on how to prevent plagiarism and cheating and how to deal with cheating and the Internet.

Stories of Work

RANDY COHEN ■

Letters from The Ethicist

Advice columns are almost as old as newspapers themselves. Most are practical in nature, such as columns offering gardening or home repair tips. The most well-known, however, such as Dear Abby and Ann Landers, feature people seeking the columnist's advice about personal problems and life issues. As a matter of course, these columns often deal with questions of ethics. In 1999, the New York Times *hired Randy Cohen to write an advice column specifically dedicated to ethical questions. Called "The Ethicist" in the* Times *and "Everyday Ethics" in newspapers across the* country, the column prints ethical dilemmas sent in by readers along with Cohen's responses. As you might expect, many of these questions have to do with workplace ethics. In 2002, Cohen collected and commented on his column in the book The Good, The Bad, and The Difference: How to Tell Right from Wrong in Everyday Situations, from which the following questions are taken.

In the following pages, you will find four questions from the section on work in Cohen's book. Cohen's answers to those questions follow. Before you read his responses, though, try your hand, at first individually and then as a class, at answering the letters. Then, compare your responses to Cohen's as you consider the Working with the Text questions at the end.

Before writing "The Ethicist," Randy Cohen published short stories and worked as a television writer for Late Night with David Letterman and The Rosie O'Donnell Show. He also publishes frequently in other magazines.

PROPRIETARY INFO?

I work for a small dot-com that is developing a service that will be available in three to five months. I have been courted by a much larger dot-com, and during our meetings I learned that they will launch a similar service in two months, decimating the one offered by my current employer. I have not yet signed with the larger company. Do I tell my current employer about their plans?

—C. M., AUSTRALIA

MODERNITY LEAVE

My wife and I excitedly expect a child this year. Her employer provides paid maternity leave. But she is unsure whether she will want to return to work after the child arrives. Would it be proper for her to take the paid leave and then quit the job without returning? Should she, in that event, repay any of the money she received?

—ANONYMOUS, ATLANTA, GEORGIA

TEMPORARY INSANITY

I am a recruiter for a temp agency. Many companies that use us practice nationality-, sex-, age-, or race-based discrimination. I can cooperate, making me personally guilty and legally liable. I can dispatch applicants solely on ability, knowing they are not welcome. Or I can cease to deal with such clients, forfeiting revenue. Is there a positive alternative to simply leaving the industry?

—ANONYMOUS, NORTH CAROLINA

INDECOROUS DECORATOR

> When I worked for myself as an interior designer, I registered with a carpet store that offered me a 10 percent commission on any business I referred them. Now I work for someone who was unaware of this store until I told him about it. Recently I sent that carpet store a customer who placed a big order. Can I keep the commission or must I split it with my boss?
>
> —S. R., LONG ISLAND, NEW YORK

PROPRIETARY INFO?

You should alert your current employer to this powerful threat lurking over the horizon. You might save your boss a lot of money and help your coworkers keep their jobs. Unless the interviewers asked you to hold the conversation in confidence, you are free to discuss it; they certainly know where you work.

If you plan to jump to the big dot-com, you may be tempted to keep this information to yourself rather than help what will soon be a rival. However, as long as you work for the small dot-com, you should show some consideration for its fate. In any case, if the big dot-com is as big as you say, you'll do it no harm by warning your current boss.

And consider the tiny Hitchcockian possibility that the big dot-com is nowhere near perfecting that new service and is using you to carry disinformation behind enemy lines and scare your boss from the field. One misstep and you could be an innocent man swept into a whirlpool of intrigue.

MODERNITY LEAVE

Since your wife is unsure about her future, she should take the leave without the least hesitation. In such a life-changing situation, few of us can be absolutely certain how we'll feel six months later. Circumstances change—emotional ones as well as financial ones. Right now she may think she'll itch for her old desk, only to discover later that she yearns to have another child. Or vice versa: Maybe she'll end up wanting two or three more desks.

Should she ultimately decide not to return to work, your wife has no moral obligation to return any of the money (unless, of course, her company has a policy that requires her to so). Her situation is analogous to a worker out with an injury who, upon recovering his health, decides not to return to his job. Certainly no one expects him to return his disability payments.

If your wife were certain she'd never return, then she doesn't want leave, she wants to quit, and she should tell her boss as much. First, she owes him an honest account of her situation so he can plan accordingly. And second, she should consider the other workers who will be affected by her actions. Some employers are reluctant to offer paid maternity leave (the Family and Medical Leave Act mandates only unpaid leave), fearing that their employees will never come back. Were your wife to hide her intentions, it would reinforce this negative view of pregnant workers. One hopes that upon learning of her situation, your wife's boss will still grant her a paid leave in the same spirit as she'd be given her accrued vacation time.

One caution: You may want to check with a lawyer to make sure that, under the provision of your wife's particular leave, she is not obliged to repay any benefits should she decide not to return.

TEMPORARY INSANITY

What you describe is not only unethical, it is criminal. "This has been illegal since July 1965," says Daniel Pollitt, the Kenan Professor of Law Emeritus at the University of North Carolina. "Title VII of the Civil Rights Act of 1964 forbids most of this. Age and disability discrimination were added later."

While it is difficult for a single individual to resist such pervasive iniquity, passive acceptance is not an honorable option. Fortunately, there is the positive solution you seek. Call the Equal Employment Opportunity Commission, the federal agency charged with enforcing Title VII. And, Pollitt adds, the E.E.O.C. is conveniently located: "They've got offices in Charlotte and in Raleigh."

INDECOROUS DECORATOR

Neither of you should take the commission. The kind term for this practice is "conflict of interest." Rather than direct your client to the store where she'd get the best product at the best price, you sent her to the place where you'd make a profit. That she is happy with the carpet is neither here nor there. She'd be even happier if the 10 percent price reduction went to her, not you. The unkind term for this practice is "kick-back."

That said, the "Code of Ethics and Professional Conduct" of the American Society of Interior Designers permits such commissions as long as the client knows about them and forbids only "undisclosed compensation" from those with whom you do business. (Then again, this is a code of ethics that allows you to put a red velvet sofa in a lime green room.)

In some professions and many parts of the world the payment of such commissions and fees (what many Americans would call "bribes") is standard procedure, but just because a practice is commonplace does not exempt it from ethical scrutiny. ■

Working with the Text

1. Where did you most and least agree with Cohen's answers? Did you ever come up with the same answer but for different reasons? Which of Cohen's answers did you find most surprising? In comparing class responses with Cohen's to each of the questions, where do you see the possibility for more than one correct answer?

2. Cohen mixes a serious reply with humor in his answers. Consider this mixture in terms of the tone Cohen creates. What kind of self-presentation is he making to his readers? How does his persona add to or detract from the persuasiveness of his answers?

3. From where does Cohen derive his authority as an ethicist? What most persuades you to take his answers seriously? Whom do you usually regard as ethical experts and why? What do you think the qualifications should be for someone giving ethical advice?

Working with Connections

1. Create your own version of "The Ethicist" focused on school and classroom issues. Either write questions yourself or solicit questions from other students focusing on what you or other students feel to be the most pressing ethical dilemmas facing contemporary students. Then work individually and as a class framing answers to these questions.

2. Herman Melville's story "Bartleby, the Scrivener" (from Chapter 2, Work, Labor, and Career: The Meaning of Work) features a narrator confronted with an ethical problem in the form of his silent employee who "prefers not to" respond to any of the narrator's requests. Frame a letter to Cohen's column from Melville's narrator as well as what you would take to be Cohen's response. How would it differ from or resemble your own response? How does the narrator analyze the ethical situation? What do you infer Melville thinks the "correct" ethical response should be?

3. According to John B. Judis in "Value-Free," our working goals and ethics have changed over the last 150 years. Using the information in Judis's essay, imagine what responses based in nineteenth-century ethics might be to the questions discussed here. Extend the discussion further back in time by speculating on what Benjamin Franklin's answers might be.

Images of Work

World Trade Center Rescue Worker

On September 11, 2001, 343 firefighters and 87 police officers lost their lives attempting to evacuate people from the World Trade Center towers. In the days that followed, surviving firefighters and police from New

York City, along with others from across the country, meticulously searched the ruins for any survivors, at great personal risk. Part of the national reaction to this tragedy included a renewed appreciation for the work and work ethic of firefighters, police, emergency medical personnel, and others who work in public service. This image of a firefighter from photographer Joe McNally's book Faces of Ground Zero focuses on one person who worked at ground zero.

Jason Cascone, 22
Jason finished his training on September 10, 2001. The next morning his mother woke him up and said there was a fire at the World Trade Center. He remembers being transported to his first assignment with 50 other firefighters. "There was this chaplain on the bus and he was giving absolution to everyone."

Working with the Text

1. How would you explain why the work of people like Jason Cascone has so resonated with the public? In addition to the personal bravery exhibited by the rescue workers, what about their attitudes toward work and the work ethic would people find inspiring?

2. Why do you think McNally posed Cascone like this? What is the effect of having him stand with his uniform on, staring straight into the camera? What mood is he trying to create, and how does he want you to feel about his subject?

3. Write an essay in response to this photograph entitled "Reflections on the Work Ethic," using your reading of this picture to explain what you think it says about the idea of a work ethic.

4. Working individually or in groups, construct your own photo montage about the work ethic. Either locate images of workers or take your own photographs to illustrate your idea of "the work ethic."

THE WORK OF WRITING/WRITING AS WORK: STUDENT ETHICS HANDBOOK

Every college and university has ethical guidelines. They go by various names—Student Code of Responsibility; Student Honor Code; College Policy on Classroom Ethics—but they all define the ethical guidelines students and faculty are expected to follow as well as the penalties for violating the policy. How familiar are students at your school with these policies? Where are they published? Were they covered at orientation? What parts of the policy are typically found on course syllabi? What questions do students and faculty most often have about the ethics policy?

One means of addressing these questions can be the creation of a student ethics handbook. While some schools already feature some such handbook, fewer offer guidance created by students for students. As a group or class project, research your college's ethics policy and construct a variety of texts from the student's point of view aimed at addressing student questions about campus ethics. Alternatively, you could focus your project on your school's writing program in particular and the specific ethical questions associated with writing courses.

As part of research for your project, you should:

■ Familiarize yourself with your school's or writing program's existing ethics policies. Who created them? How are they revised? What role do students play in the revision and/or implementation of the ethics policy? What questions do you have as you review the policy, and who would be the best person to address such questions to?

■ Interview someone in the Dean of Students office, a member of a student honor council, or the administrator responsible for your school's writing program to find out which specific ethical problems are most common on your campus and what the most typical responses and penalties are. Such information will be useful in organizing your handbook.

Among the types of publications you might consider writing are a handbook, a brief pamphlet, and a web site. As you begin to organize your handbook, consider how to prioritize the information you have collected. Rather than simply reprinting the existing ethics code, decide the most effective ways to introduce this material to students. What key issues should they keep in mind? What might be some warning signs that a student may be in danger of unethical behavior?

In considering how best to clarify the school's or writing program's policies to your fellow student readers, consider the following options:

- Specific examples
- Scenarios either made up or based on actual cases
- A Question and Answer or Frequently Asked Questions (FAQ) section
- A list of most common ethical issues or problems

If you would like to offer your handbook for distribution or list your web site as a student resource, you will need to work with your instructor to submit a draft for feedback from various interested readers: administrators charged with ethics oversight; student honor code members; other students. Use this feedback to check for the accuracy of your information and to see how helpful your potential audience finds the material.

CHAPTER 8

Work in the Global Economy

Whether you have lived in the United States a short time or your entire life, you are connected with people and places around the world. Just go through your closet at home and check to see where the clothes you wear every day come from. Chances are you will find the names of countries from Italy to Indonesia. In fact, take a look at all the products around your home. How many were made just in the United States? Even if a person drives an "American" car, it's likely that many of the parts of that car were made overseas; conversely, the owner of a "Japanese" car may be driving a vehicle manufactured in the Midwest.

As the ability to travel around the world continues to become faster and easier, both physically and electronically, the lives of people around the world are becoming more intertwined and interdependent, especially in terms of economics, work, and commerce. You've probably heard the term *globalization* used as a shorthand way to refer to this increasing interdependence along with a wide range of issues and controversies that are associated with it. For some, globalization means the creation of new economic opportunities and the possibility of spreading the benefits of economic development around the world. To others, globalization suggests an ever-increasing exploitation of poor workers as businesses seek cheaper labor markets and fewer restrictions on how workers or the environment are treated.

Although you will sometimes hear this debate expressed in terms of whether someone is "for" or "against" globalization, most of those involved in the debate would agree that an increasingly international economic world is inevitable; the real arguments are over how globalization will continue to develop, who should have a say in these developments, and the positive and negative prospects for different developments. As the attacks of September 11, 2001, demonstrated, these issues are not merely academic. While the factors that led to that horrific day are complex, the targets included a global workplace, the World Trade Center, filled with workers from around the globe living in a great international city, involved the main means of international travel, commercial jet aircraft, and stemmed at least in part from anger and rage connected to the spread and influence of international commerce.

In this chapter, you will encounter different opinions about the benefits and dangers different writers find in the global economy, including a particular focus on the issue of "sweatshop" labor. Before you begin your reading of this chapter, explore your present ideas about globalization with these exercises:

■ When you hear people mention "globalization" or "the global economy," what specific issues and ideas come to mind? Where did you learn about these issues? What opinions, if any, do you have about them?

■ Do a "globalization" inventory in your class by listing as many different countries of origin as you can find for the products and clothes that you and your classmates have with you or are wearing. What are the most frequently mentioned countries? What do you know about working conditions in those countries? What reactions do you have to these different countries of origin and why?

■ Can you see a "global" dimension to the job you may have now? If there are any people in class who cannot immediately see global dimensions to the work they do, work in groups to brainstorm what different global connections there might be to these jobs.

■ Write about the future careers you are considering for yourself and the impact you think the global economy will have on those careers.

Foundational Readings

Declaration Concerning the Aims and Purposes of the International Labour Organization

The birth of the International Labour Organization (ILO) dates back to the end of World War I and the creation of the League of Nations, one of the first attempts at creating a global alliance of nations that would seek to resolve disputes between nations without resorting to war and that would also try to set international standards for human rights. Although the original League of Nations failed, a second effort after World War II to create such a global organization resulted in the United Nations, which included the International Labour Organization as its first specialized agency. The ILO is charged with setting international standards for the treatment of workers, and at its general conference held in

Philadelphia in the 1940s the ILO adopted the following "Declaration of the aims and purposes of the International Labour Organization and the principles which should inspire the policy of its members."

Before you begin reading, brainstorm as a class what you think the essential rights of workers and employees all over the world should be. What basic conditions should every worker expect?

The General Conference of the International Labour Organization meeting in its Twenty-sixth Session in Philadelphia, hereby adopts this tenth day of May in the year nineteen hundred and forty-four the present Declaration of the aims and purposes of the International Labour Organization and of the principles which should inspire the policy of its Members.

I

The Conference reaffirms the fundamental principles on which the Organization is based and, in particular, that—

- (a) labour is not a commodity;
- (b) freedom of expression and of association are essential to sustained progress;
- (c) poverty anywhere constitutes a danger to prosperity everywhere;
- (d) the war against want requires to be carried on with unrelenting vigor within each nation, and by continuous and concerted international effort in which the representatives of workers and employers, enjoying equal status with those of governments, join with them in free discussion and democratic decision with a view to the promotion of the common welfare.

II

Believing that experience has fully demonstrated the truth of the statement in the Constitution of the International Labour Organization that lasting peace can be established only if it is based on social justice, the Conference affirms that—

- (a) all human beings, irrespective of race, creed or sex, have the right to pursue both their material well-being and their spiritual development in conditions of freedom and dignity, of economic security and equal opportunity;
- (b) the attainment of the conditions in which this shall be possible must constitute the central aim of national and international policy;
- (c) all national and international policies and measures, in particular those of an economic and financial character, should be judged in this light and accepted only in so far as they may be held to promote and not to hinder the achievement of this fundamental objective;
- (d) it is a responsibility of the International Labour Organization to examine and consider all international economic and financial policies and measures in the light of this fundamental objective;
- (e) in discharging the tasks entrusted to it the International Labour Organization, having considered all relevant economic and financial factors, may include in its decisions and recommendations any provisions which it considers appropriate.

III

The Conference recognizes the solemn obligation of the International Labour Organization to further among the nations of the world programmes which will achieve:

- (a) full employment and the raising of standards of living;
- (b) the employment of workers in the occupations in which they can have the satisfaction of giving the fullest measure of their skill and attainments and make their greatest contribution to the common well-being;
- (c) the provision, as a means to the attainment of this end and under adequate guarantees for all concerned, of facilities for training and the transfer of labour, including migration for employment and settlement;
- (d) policies in regard to wages and earnings, hours and other conditions of work calculated to ensure a just share of the fruits of progress to all, and a minimum living wage to all employed and in need of such protection;
- (e) the effective recognition of the right of collective bargaining, the cooperation of management and labour in the continuous improvement of productive efficiency, and the collaboration of workers and employers in the preparation and application of social and economic measures;
- (f) the extension of social security measures to provide a basic income to all in need of such protection and comprehensive medical care;
- (g) adequate protection for the life and health of workers in all occupations;
- (h) provision for child welfare and maternity protection;
- (i) the provision of adequate nutrition, housing and facilities for recreation and culture;
- (j) the assurance of equality of educational and vocational opportunity.

IV

Confident that the fuller and broader utilization of the world's productive resources necessary for the achievement of the objectives set forth in this Declaration can be secured by effective international and national action, including measures to expand production and consumption, to avoid severe economic fluctuations to promote the economic and social advancement of the less developed regions of the world, to assure greater stability in world prices of primary products, and to promote a high and steady volume of international trade, the Conference pledges the full cooperation of the International Labour Organization with such international bodies as may be entrusted with a share of the responsibility for this great task and for the promotion of the health, education and well-being of all peoples.

V

The conference affirms that the principles set forth in this Declaration are fully applicable to all peoples everywhere and that, while the manner of their application must be determined with due regard to the stage of social and economic development reached by each people, their progressive application to peoples who are still dependent, as well as to those who have already achieved self-government, is a matter of concern to the whole civilized world. ■

Working with the Text

1. Compare the list of rights you came up with in class with the aims and purposes listed in the Declaration. Where do you find points of agreement, even if the specific language might be different? What did you include that you don't find in the Declaration, and vice versa?

2. As its first fundamental principle, the Declaration states, "labour is not a commodity." Why do you think this principle was listed first? What would it mean to think of labor as a commodity? Try and come up with a concrete example to illustrate the point you think the Declaration is trying to make here.

3. Form into a small group and choose one or two of the goals of the ILO listed in Section 3. Investigate and discuss as a group how well you think that goal is being met in your community and the nation as a whole. How about in the international community? Meet again as a class to compare your findings and determine which goals you think have been most nearly met and which are furthest from being achieved.

Working with Connections

1. What kind of a document is a "declaration"? Who are the intended audiences for this document, and what are its purposes? How does the wording of the declaration reflect these goals and audiences? Explore these questions by looking at examples of other declarations and manifestos, such as Karl Marx and Friedrich Engels's *The Communist Manifesto* or the Declaration of Independence.

2. While the ILO Declaration seeks to define basic workers' rights, Bob Black in "The Abolition of Work" (in Chapter 3, Work, Labor, and Career: The Meaning of Work) issues his own manifesto against the concept of work itself. In what ways and in which areas do you think Black would agree or disagree with the ideals of the ILO Declaration? What additions or corrections might he make?

The Global Village Finally Arrives

"Made in the USA." "American Owned and Operated." Businesses and products that carry these labels can mean many things by them and appeal to a range of ideas and emotions on the parts of consumers, from a desire to support the local community to a fear of money and jobs going to "outsiders." But what do local and global, domestic and foreign, mean in the twenty-first century? How meaningful are borders—whether geographic, psychological, or cultural—in the contemporary world? To what extent are we citizens of a nation and/or members of a global community?

In "the Global Village Finally Arrives," Pico Iyer explores the many ways in which the more traditional ideas of national and cultural identity do not fit the increasingly globalized culture of today. In so doing, he asks us to think about the future of the global village and what that will mean in terms of how we identify our communities and ourselves. Pico Iyer is the writer of several books, including The Global Soul: Jet Lag, Shopping Malls, and the Search for Home; Falling Off the Map: Some Lonely Places of the World; *and* The Lady and the Monk: Four Seasons in Kyoto. *He is also a frequent contributor to* Time *magazine.*

This is the typical day of a relatively typical soul in today's diversified world. I wake up to the sound of my Japanese clock radio, put on a T shirt sent me by an uncle in Nigeria and walk out into the street, past German cars, to my office. Around me are English-language students from Korea, Switzerland and Argentina—all on this Spanish-named road in this Mediterranean-style town. On TV, I find, the news is in Mandarin; today's baseball game is being broadcast in Korean. For lunch I can walk to a sushi bar, a tandoori palace, a Thai café or the newest burrito joint (run by an old Japanese lady). Who am I, I sometimes wonder, the son of Indian parents and a British citizen who spends much of his time in Japan (and is therefore—what else?—an American permanent resident)? And where am I?

I am, as it happens, in Southern California, in a quiet, relatively uninternational town, but I could as easily be in Vancouver or Sydney or London or Hong Kong. All the world's a rainbow coalition, more and more; the whole planet, you might say, is going global. When I fly to Toronto, or Paris, or Singapore, I disembark in a world as hyphenated as the one I left. More and more of the globe looks like America, but an America that is itself looking more and more like the rest of the globe. Los Angeles famously teaches 82 different languages in its schools. In this respect, the city seems only to bear out the old adage that what is in California today is in America tomorrow, and next week around the globe.

In ways that were hardly conceivable even a generation ago, the new world order is a version of the New World writ large: a wide-open frontier of polyglot terms and postnational trends. A common multiculturalism links us all—call it Planet Hollywood, Planet Reebok or the United Colors of Benetton. *Taxi* and *hotel* and *disco* are universal terms now, but so too are *karaoke* and *yoga* and *pizza*. For the gourmet alone, there is *tiramisù* at the Burger King in Kyoto, echt angel-hair pasta in Saigon and enchiladas on every menu in Nepal.

But deeper than mere goods, it is souls that are mingling. In Brussels, a center of the new "unified Europe," 1 new baby in every 4 is Arab. Whole parts of the Paraguayan capital of Asunción are largely Korean. And when the prostitutes of Melbourne distributed some pro-condom pamphlets, one of the languages they used was Macedonian. Even Japan, which prides itself on its centuries-old socially engineered uniculture, swarms with Iranian illegals, Western executives, Pakistani laborers and Filipina hostesses.

The global village is defined, as we know, by an international youth culture that takes its cues from American pop culture. Kids in Perth and Prague and New Delhi are all tuning in to [1980s American soap opera] *Santa Barbara* on TV, and wriggling into 501 jeans, while singing along to Madonna's latest in English. CNN (which grew 70-fold in its first 13 years) now reaches more than 140 countries; an American football championship pits London against Barcelona. As fast as the world comes to America, America goes round the world—but it is an America that is itself multi-tongued and many hued, an America of Amy Tan and Janet Jackson and movies with dialogue in Lakota.

For far more than goods and artifacts, the one great influence being broadcast around the world in greater numbers and at greater speed than ever before is people. What were once clear divisions are now tangles of crossed lines: there are 40,000 "Canadians" resident in Hong Kong, many of whose first language is Cantonese. And with people come customs: while new immigrants from Taiwan and Vietnam and India—some of the so-called Asian Calvinists—import all-American values of hard work and family closeness and entrepreneurial energy to America, America is sending its values of upward mobility and individualism and melting-pot hopefulness to Taipei and Saigon and Bombay.

Values, in fact, travel at the speed of fax; by now, almost half the world's Mormons live outside the U.S. A diversity of one culture quickly becomes a diversity of many: the "typical American" who goes to Japan today may be a third-generation Japanese American, or the son of a Japanese woman married to a California serviceman, or the offspring of a Salvadoran father and an Italian mother from San Francisco. When he goes out with a Japanese woman, more than two cultures are brought into play.

None of this, of course, is new: Chinese silks were all the rage in Rome centuries ago, and Alexandria before the time of Christ was a paradigm of the modern universal city. Not even American eclecticism is new: many a small town has long known Chinese restaurants, Indian doctors and Lebanese grocers. But now all these cultures are crossing at the speed of light. And the rising diversity of the planet is something more than mere cosmopolitanism: it is a fundamental recoloring of the very complexion of societies. Cities like Paris, or

Hong Kong, have always had a soigné, international air and served as magnets for exiles and émigrés, but now smaller places are multinational too. Marseilles speaks French with a distinctly North African twang. Islamic fundamentalism has one of its strongholds in Bradford, England. It is the sleepy coastal towns of Queensland, Australia, that print their menus in Japanese.

The dangers this internationalism presents are evident: not for nothing did the Tower of Babel collapse. As national borders fall, tribal alliances, and new manmade divisions, rise up, and the world learns every day terrible new meanings of the word Balkanization. And while some places are wired for international transmission, others (think of Iran or North Korea or Burma) remain as isolated as ever, widening the gap between the haves and the have-nots, or what [writer] Alvin Toffler has called the "fast" and the "slow"' worlds. Tokyo has more telephones than the whole continent of Africa.

Nonetheless, whether we like it or not, the "transnational" future is upon us: as Kenichi Ohmae, the international economist, suggests with his talk of a "borderless economy," capitalism's allegiances are to products, not places. "Capital is now global," Robert Reich, the [former] Secretary of Labor, has said, pointing out that when an Iowan buys a Pontiac from General Motors, 60% of his money goes to South Korea, Japan, West Germany, Taiwan, Singapore, Britain and Barbados. Culturally we are being re-formed daily by the cadences of world music and world fiction: where the great Canadian writers of an older generation had names like Frye and Davies and Laurence, now they are called Ondaatje and Mistry and Skvorecky.

As space shrinks, moreover, time accelerates. This hip-hop mishmash is spreading overnight. When my parents were in college, there were all of seven foreigners living in Tibet, a country the size of Western Europe, and in its entire history the country had seen fewer than 2,000 Westerners. Now a Danish student in Lhasa is scarcely more surprising than a Tibetan in Copenhagen. Already a city like Miami is beyond the wildest dreams of 1968; how much more so will its face in 2018 defy our predictions of today?

It would be easy, seeing all this, to say that the world is moving toward the *Raza Cósmica* (Cosmic Race), predicted by the Mexican thinker José Vasconcelos in the '20s—a glorious blend of mongrels and mestizos. It may be more relevant to suppose that more and more of the world may come to resemble Hong Kong, a stateless special economic zone full of expats and exiles linked by the lingua franca of English and the global marketplace. Some urbanists already see the world as a grid of 30 or so highly advanced city-regions, or technopoles, all plugged into the same international circuit.

The world will not become America. Anyone who has been to a baseball game in Osaka, or a Pizza Hut in Moscow, knows instantly that she is not in Kansas. But America may still, if only symbolically, be a model for the world. *E Pluribus Unum*, after all, is on the dollar bill. As Federico Mayor Zaragoza, the director-general of UNESCO, has said, "America's main role in the new world order is not as a military superpower, but as a multicultural superpower."

The traditional metaphor for this is that of a mosaic. But Richard Rodriguez, the Mexican-American essayist who is a psalmist for our new hybrid forms, points out that the interaction is more fluid than that, more human, subject to daily revision. "I am Chinese," he says, "because I live in San Francisco, a Chinese city. I became Irish in America. I became Portuguese in America." And even as he announces this new truth, Portuguese women are becoming American, and Irishmen are becoming Portuguese, and Sydney (or is it Toronto?) is thinking to compare itself with the "Chinese city" we know as San Francisco. ■

Working with the Text

1. Iyer begins his essay with a description of the global aspects of a typical day in a Southern California city. Write your own description of a typical day for you that focuses on what you see as the most global aspects of the community you live in.

2. As Iyer describes the increasingly "transnational" aspects of modern life, do you as a reader find his examples to be mainly positive or negative? That is, what impression does he create about whether he see these developments as good or bad based on the examples he chooses and the way he describes them?

3. In the final paragraph, Iyer suggests that cultural identity may become even more fluid in the future by quoting the writer Richard Rodriguez, who says he "became Irish in America, I became Portuguese in America." In what senses do you think Rodriguez (and Iyer) mean this? Can you relate their description of multiple identities to experiences from your own life living in multicultural America?

Working with Connections

1. How does Iyer's vision of the globalization of contemporary life fit with or offer a different perspective on the two opposing developments that Benjamin Barber describes as "Jihad vs. McWorld"? Which writer seems more optimistic, which more concerned, and why? How does the concept of the "*Raza Cósmica* (Cosmic Race)" apply to the possible futures Barber envisions?

2. What implications does Iyer's vision of a globalized community with more fluid identities have for the debate over affirmative action described in Farai Chideya's *The Color of Our Future* (from Chapter 6: Work and Diversity)? Do you think, for example,

that race-based discrimination will decrease as the world becomes more globalized, or will prejudice persist? How do you think the different interview subjects in the chapter from Chideya's book would react to Iyer's essay?

BENJAMIN R. BARBER ■

Jihad vs. McWorld

Rather than seeing globalization as a single, unified process creating an increasingly uniform world, the political scientist Benjamin Barber argues that we can best understand contemporary geopolitical developments as a conflict between two different trends: "McWorld," or the ever-widening spread of consumer culture and market capitalism, and "Jihad," or the desire to preserve traditional and local ways of life and beliefs. This conflict connects to the gap between the haves and the have-nots, between those who benefit most from the global economy and those who feel most victimized by it. Both McWorld and Jihad, Barber argues, present potential threats to the development of democratic political institutions and work practices. As the tragedy of September 11, 2001, and the subsequent wars in Afghanistan and Iraq have demonstrated, these forces can also produce dramatic and violent consequences.

Benjamin R. Barber is a professor of political science at Rutgers University in New Jersey. He has worked with international and national government agencies and has written many articles and books, including Jihad Versus McWorld, *based on this essay, which originally appeared in* The Atlantic Monthly *magazine.*

Just beyond the horizon of current events lie two possible political futures—both bleak, neither democratic. The first is a retribalization of large swaths of humankind by war and bloodshed: a threatened Lebanonization of national states in which culture is pitted against culture, people against people, tribe against tribe—a Jihad in the name of a hundred narrowly conceived faiths against every kind of interdependence, every kind of artificial social cooperation and civic mutuality. The second is being borne in on us by the onrush of economic and ecological forces that demand integration and uniformity and that mesmerize the world with fast music, fast computers, and fast food—with MTV, Macintosh, and McDonald's, pressing nations into one commercially homogenous global network: one McWorld tied together by technology, ecology, communications, and commerce. The planet is falling precipitantly apart *AND* coming reluctantly together at the very same moment.

These two tendencies are sometimes visible in the same countries at the same instant: thus Yugoslavia, clamoring just recently to join the New Europe, is exploding into fragments; India is trying to live up to its reputation as the world's largest integral democracy while powerful new fundamentalist parties like the Hindu nationalist Bharatiya Janata Party, along with nationalist assassins, are imperiling its hard-won unity. States are breaking up or joining up: the Soviet Union has disappeared almost overnight, its parts forming new unions with one another or with like-minded nationalities in neighboring states. The old interwar national state based on territory and political sovereignty looks to be a mere transitional development.

The tendencies of what I am here calling the forces of Jihad and the forces of McWorld operate with equal strength in opposite directions, the one driven by parochial hatreds, the other by universalizing markets, the one re-creating ancient subnational and ethnic borders from within, the other making national borders porous from without. They have one thing in common: neither offers much hope to citizens looking for practical ways to govern themselves democratically. If the global future is to pit Jihad's centrifugal whirlwind against McWorld's centripetal black hole, the outcome is unlikely to be democratic—or so I will argue.

MCWORLD, OR THE GLOBALIZATION OF POLITICS

Four imperatives make up the dynamic of McWorld: a market imperative, a resource imperative, an information-technology imperative, and an ecological imperative. By shrinking the world and diminishing the salience of national borders, these imperatives have in combination achieved a considerable victory over factiousness and particularism, and not least of all over their most virulent traditional form—nationalism. It is the realists who are now Europeans, the utopians who dream nostalgically of a resurgent England or Germany, perhaps even a resurgent Wales or Saxony. Yesterday's wishful cry for one world has yielded to the reality of McWorld.

The Market Imperative

Marxist and Leninist theories of imperialism assumed that the quest for ever-expanding markets would in time compel nation-based capitalist economies to push against national boundaries in search of an international economic imperium. Whatever else has happened to the scientistic predictions of Marxism, in this domain they have proved farsighted. All national economies are now vulnerable to the inroads of larger, transnational markets within which trade is free, currencies are convertible, access to banking is open, and contracts are enforceable under law. In Europe, Asia, Africa, the South Pacific, and the Americas such markets are eroding national sovereignty and giving rise to entities—international banks, trade associations, transnational lobbies like OPEC and Greenpeace, world news services like CNN and the BBC, and multinational corporations that increasingly lack a meaningful national identity—that neither reflect nor respect nationhood as an organizing or regulative principle.

The market imperative has also reinforced the quest for international peace and stability, requisites of an efficient international economy. Markets are enemies of parochialism, isolation, fractiousness, war. Market psychology attenuates the psychology of ideological and religious cleavages and assumes a concord among producers and consumers—categories that ill fit narrowly conceived national or religious cultures. Shopping has little tolerance for blue laws, whether dictated by pub-closing British paternalism, Sabbath-observing Jewish Orthodox fundamentalism, or no-Sunday-liquor-sales Massachusetts puritanism. In the context of common markets, international law ceases to be a vision of justice and becomes a workaday framework for getting things done—enforcing contracts, ensuring that governments abide by deals, regulating trade and currency relations, and so forth.

Common markets demand a common language, as well as a common currency, and they produce common behaviors of the kind bred by cosmopolitan city life everywhere. Commercial pilots, computer programmers, international bankers, media specialists, oil riggers, entertainment celebrities, ecology experts, demographers, accountants, professors, athletes—these compose a new breed of men and women for whom religion, culture, and nationality can seem only marginal elements in a working identity. Although sociologists of everyday life will no doubt continue to distinguish a Japanese from an American mode, shopping has a common signature throughout the world. Cynics might even say that some of the recent revolutions in Eastern Europe have had as their true goal not liberty and the right to vote but well-paying jobs and the right to shop (although the vote is proving easier to acquire than consumer goods). The market imperative is, then, plenty powerful; but, notwithstanding some of the claims made for "democratic capitalism," it is not identical with the democratic imperative.

The Resource Imperative

Democrats once dreamed of societies whose political autonomy rested firmly on economic independence. The Athenians idealized what they called autarky, and tried for a while to create a way of life simple and austere enough to make the polis genuinely self-sufficient. To be free meant to be independent of any other community or polis. Not even the Athenians were able to achieve autarky, however: human nature, it turns out, is dependency. By the time of Pericles, Athenian politics was inextricably bound up with a flowering empire held together by naval power and commerce—an empire that, even as it appeared to enhance Athenian might, ate away at Athenian independence and autarky. Master and slave, it turned out, were bound together by mutual insufficiency.

The dream of autarky briefly engrossed nineteenth-century America as well, for the underpopulated, endlessly bountiful land, the cornucopia of natural resources, and the natural barriers of a continent walled in by two great seas led many to believe that America could be a world unto itself. Given this past, it has been harder for Americans than for most to accept the inevitability of interdependence. But the rapid depletion of resources even in a country like ours, where they once seemed inexhaustible, and the maldistribution of arable soil and mineral resources on the planet, leave even the wealthiest societies ever more resource-dependent and many other nations in permanently desperate straits.

Every nation, it turns out, needs something another nation has; some nations have almost nothing they need.

The Information-Technology Imperative

Enlightenment science and the technologies derived from it are inherently universalizing. They entail a quest for descriptive principles of general application, a search for universal solutions to particular problems, and an unswerving embrace of objectivity and impartiality.

Scientific progress embodies and depends on open communication, a common discourse rooted in rationality, collaboration, and an easy and regular flow and exchange of information. Such ideals can be hypocritical covers for power-mongering by elites, and they may be shown to be wanting in many other ways, but they are entailed by the very idea of science and they make science and globalization practical allies.

Business, banking, and commerce all depend on information flow and are facilitated by new communication technologies. The hardware of these technologies tends to be systemic and integrated—computer, television, cable, satellite, laser, fiber-optic, and microchip technologies combining to create a vast interactive communications and information network that can potentially give every person on earth access to every other person, and make every datum, every byte, available to every set of eyes. If the automobile was, as George Ball once said (when he gave his blessing to a Fiat factory in the Soviet Union during the Cold War), "an ideology on four wheels," then electronic telecommunication and information systems are an ideology at 186,000 miles per second—which makes for a very small planet in a very big hurry. Individual cultures speak particular languages; commerce and science increasingly speak English; the whole world speaks logarithms and binary mathematics.

Moreover, the pursuit of science and technology asks for, even compels, open societies. Satellite footprints do not respect national borders; telephone wires penetrate the most closed societies. With photocopying and then fax machines having infiltrated Soviet universities and *samizdat* literary circles in the eighties, and computer modems having multiplied like rabbits in communism's bureaucratic warrens thereafter, *glasnost* could not be far behind. In their social requisites, secrecy and science are enemies.

The new technology's software is perhaps even more globalizing than its hardware. The information arm of international commerce's sprawling body reaches out and touches distinct nations and parochial cultures, and gives them a common face chiseled in Hollywood, on Madison Avenue, and in Silicon Valley. Throughout the 1980s one of the most-watched television programs in South Africa was *The Cosby Show*. The demise of apartheid was already in production. Exhibitors at the 1991 Cannes film festival expressed growing anxiety over the "homogenization" and "Americanization" of the global film industry when, for the third year running, American films dominated the awards ceremonies.

America has dominated the world's popular culture for much longer, and much more decisively. In November of 1991 Switzerland's once insular culture boasted best-seller lists featuring *Terminator 2* as the No. 1 movie, *Scarlett* as the No. 1 book, and Prince's *Diamonds and Pearls* as the No. 1 record album. No wonder the Japanese are buying Hollywood film studios even faster than Americans are buying Japanese television sets. This kind of software supremacy may in the long term be far more important than hardware superiority, because culture has become more potent than armaments. What is the power of the Pentagon compared with Disneyland? Can the Sixth Fleet keep up with CNN? McDonald's in Moscow and Coke in China will do more to create a global culture than military colonization ever could. It is less the goods than the brand names that do the work, for they convey life-style images that alter perception and challenge behavior. They make up the seductive software of McWorld's common (at times much too common) soul.

Yet in all this high-tech commercial world there is nothing that looks particularly democratic. It lends itself to surveillance as well as liberty, to new forms of manipulation and covert control as well as new kinds of participation, to skewed, unjust market outcomes as well as greater productivity. The consumer society and the open society are not quite synonymous. Capitalism and democracy have a relationship, but it is something less than a marriage. An efficient free market after all requires that consumers be free to vote their dollars on competing goods, not that citizens be free to vote their values and beliefs on competing political candidates and programs. The free market flourished in junta-run Chile, in military-governed Taiwan and Korea, and, earlier, in a variety of autocratic European empires as well as their colonial possessions.

The Ecological Imperative

The impact of globalization on ecology is a cliche even to world leaders who ignore it. We know well enough that the German forests can be destroyed by Swiss and Italians driving gas-guzzlers fueled by leaded gas. We also know that the planet can be asphyxiated by greenhouse gases because Brazilian farmers want to be part of the twentieth century and are burning down tropical rain forests to clear a little land to plough, and because Indonesians make a living out of converting their lush jungle into toothpicks for fastidious Japanese diners, upsetting the delicate oxygen balance and in effect puncturing our global lungs. Yet this ecological consciousness has meant not only greater awareness but also greater inequality, as modernized nations try to slam the door behind them, saying to developing nations, "The world cannot afford your modernization; ours has wrung it dry!"

Each of the four imperatives just cited is transnational, transideological, and transcultural. Each applies impartially to Catholics, Jews, Muslims, Hindus, and Buddhists; to democrats and totalitarians; to capitalists and socialists. The Enlightenment dream of a universal rational society has to a remarkable degree been realized—but in a form that is commercialized, homogenized, depoliticized, bureaucratized, and, of course, radically incomplete, for the movement toward McWorld is in competition with forces of global breakdown, national dissolution, and centrifugal corruption. These forces, working in the opposite direction, are the essence of what I call Jihad.

JIHAD, OR THE LEBANONIZATION OF THE WORLD

OPEC, the World Bank, the United Nations, the International Red Cross, the multinational corporation . . . there are scores of institutions that reflect globalization. But they often appear as ineffective reactors to the world's real actors: national states and, to an ever greater degree, subnational factions in permanent rebellion against uniformity and integration—even the kind represented by universal law and justice. The headlines feature these players regularly: they are cultures, not countries; parts, not wholes; sects, not religions; rebellious factions and dissenting minorities at war not just with globalism but with the traditional nation-state. Kurds, Basques, Puerto Ricans, Ossetians, East Timoreans, Quebecois, the Catholics of Northern Ireland, Abkhasians, Kurile Islander Japanese, the Zulus of Inkatha, Catalonians, Tamils, and, of course, Palestinians—people without countries, inhabiting nations not their own, seeking smaller worlds within borders that will seal them off from modernity.

A powerful irony is at work here. Nationalism was once a force of integration and unification, a movement aimed at bringing together disparate clans, tribes, and cultural fragments under new, assimilationist flags. But as Ortega y Gasset noted more than sixty years ago, having won its victories, nationalism changed its strategy. In the 1920s, and again today, it is more often a reactionary and divisive force, pulverizing the very nations it once helped cement together. The force that creates nations is "inclusive," Ortega wrote in *The Revolt of the Masses*. "In periods of consolidation, nationalism has a positive value, and is a lofty standard. But in Europe everything is more than consolidated, and nationalism is nothing but a mania . . ."

This mania has left the post-Cold War world smoldering with hot wars; the international scene is little more unified than it was at the end of the Great War, in Ortega's own time. There were more than thirty wars in progress last year, most of them ethnic, racial, tribal, or religious in character, and the list of unsafe regions doesn't seem to be getting any shorter. Some new world order!

The aim of many of these small-scale wars is to redraw boundaries, to implode states and resecure parochial identities: to escape McWorld's dully insistent imperatives. The mood is that of Jihad: war not as an instrument of policy but as an emblem of identity, an expression of community, an end in itself. Even where there is no shooting war, there is fractiousness, secession, and the quest for ever smaller communities. Add to the list of dangerous countries those at risk: In Switzerland and Spain, Jurassian and Basque separatists still argue the virtues of ancient identities, sometimes in the language of bombs. Hyperdisintegration in the former Soviet Union may well continue unabated—not just a Ukraine independent from the Soviet Union but a Bessarabian

Ukraine independent from the Ukrainian republic; not just Russia severed from the defunct union but Tatarstan severed from Russia. Yugoslavia makes even the disunited, ex-Soviet, nonsocialist republics that were once the Soviet Union look integrated, its sectarian fatherlands springing up within factional mother-lands like weeds within weeds within weeds. Kurdish independence would threaten the territorial integrity of four Middle Eastern nations. Well before the current cataclysm Soviet Georgia made a claim for autonomy from the Soviet Union, only to be faced with its Ossetians (164,000 in a republic of 5.5 million) demanding their own self-determination within Georgia. The Abkhasian minor-ity in Georgia has followed suit. Even the good will established by Canada's once promising Meech Lake protocols is in danger, with Francophone Quebec again threatening the dissolution of the federation. In South Africa the emer-gence from apartheid was hardly achieved when friction between Inkatha's Zulus and the African National Congress's tribally identified members threat-ened to replace Europeans' racism with an indigenous tribal war. After thirty years of attempted integration using the colonial language (English) as a unifier, Nigeria is now playing with the idea of linguistic multiculturalism—which could mean the cultural breakup of the nation into hundreds of tribal fragments. Even Saddam Hussein has benefited from the threat of internal Jihad, having used renewed tribal and religious warfare to turn last season's mortal enemies into reluctant allies of an Iraqi nationhood that he nearly destroyed.

The passing of communism has torn away the thin veneer of international-ism (workers of the world unite!) to reveal ethnic prejudices that are not only ugly and deep-seated but increasingly murderous. Europe's old scourge, anti-Semitism, is back with a vengeance, but it is only one of many antagonisms. It appears all too easy to throw the historical gears into reverse and pass from a Communist dictatorship back into a tribal state.

Among the tribes, religion is also a battlefield. ("Jihad" is a rich word whose generic meaning is "struggle"—usually the struggle of the soul to avert evil. Strictly applied to religious war, it is used only in reference to battles where the faith is under assault, or battles against a government that denies the practice of Islam. My use here is rhetorical, but does follow both journalistic practice and his-tory.) Remember the Thirty Years War? Whatever forms of Enlightenment uni-versalism might once have come to grace such historically related forms of monotheism as Judaism, Christianity, and Islam, in many of their modern incar-nations they are parochial rather than cosmopolitan, angry rather than loving, proselytizing rather than ecumenical, zealous rather than rationalist, sectarian rather than deistic, ethnocentric rather than universalizing. As a result, like the new forms of hypernationalism, the new expressions of religious fundamentalism are fractious and pulverizing, never integrating. This is religion as the Crusaders knew it: a battle to the death for souls that if not saved will be forever lost.

The atmospherics of Jihad have resulted in a breakdown of civility in the name of identity, of comity in the name of community. International relations have sometimes taken on the aspect of gang war—cultural turf battles featuring tribal factions that were supposed to be sublimated as integral parts of large national, economic, postcolonial, and constitutional entities.

THE DARKENING FUTURE OF DEMOCRACY

These rather melodramatic tableaux vivants do not tell the whole story, however. For all their defects, Jihad and McWorld have their attractions. Yet, to repeat and insist, the attractions are unrelated to democracy. Neither McWorld nor Jihad is remotely democratic in impulse. Neither needs democracy; neither promotes democracy.

McWorld does manage to look pretty seductive in a world obsessed with Jihad. It delivers peace, prosperity, and relative unity—if at the cost of independence, community, and identity (which is generally based on difference). The primary political values required by the global market are order and tranquillity, and freedom—as in the phrases "free trade," "free press," and "free love." Human rights are needed to a degree, but not citizenship or participation—and no more social justice and equality than are necessary to promote efficient economic production and consumption. Multinational corporations sometimes seem to prefer doing business with local oligarchs, inasmuch as they can take confidence from dealing with the boss on all crucial matters. Despots who slaughter their own populations are no problem, so long as they leave markets in place and refrain from making war on their neighbors (Saddam Hussein's fatal mistake). In trading partners, predictability is of more value than justice.

The Eastern European revolutions that seemed to arise out of concern for global democratic values quickly deteriorated into a stampede in the general direction of free markets and their ubiquitous, television-promoted shopping malls. East Germany's Neues Forum, that courageous gathering of intellectuals, students, and workers which overturned the Stalinist regime in Berlin in 1989, lasted only six months in Germany's mini-version of McWorld. Then it gave way to money and markets and monopolies from the West. By the time of the first all-German elections, it could scarcely manage to secure three percent of the vote. Elsewhere there is growing evidence that glasnost will go and perestroika—defined as privatization and an opening of markets to Western bidders—will stay. So understandably anxious are the new rulers of Eastern Europe and whatever entities are forged from the residues of the Soviet Union to gain access to credit and markets and technology—McWorld's flourishing new currencies—that they have shown themselves willing to trade away democratic prospects in pursuit of them: not just old totalitarian ideologies and command-economy production models but some possible indigenous experiments with a third way between capitalism and socialism, such as economic cooperatives and employee stock-ownership plans, both of which have their ardent supporters in the East.

Jihad delivers a different set of virtues: a vibrant local identity, a sense of community, solidarity among kinsmen, neighbors, and countrymen, narrowly conceived. But it also guarantees parochialism and is grounded in exclusion. Solidarity is secured through war against outsiders. And solidarity often means obedience to a hierarchy in governance, fanaticism in beliefs, and the obliteration of individual selves in the name of the group. Deference to leaders and intolerance toward outsiders (and toward "enemies within") are hallmarks of tribalism—hardly the attitudes required for the cultivation of new democratic women and men capable of governing themselves. Where new democratic experiments have been conducted in retribalizing societies, in both Europe and the Third World, the result has often been anarchy, repression, persecution, and the coming of new, noncommunist forms of very old kinds of despotism. During the past year, Havel's velvet revolution in Czechoslovakia was imperiled by partisans of "Czechland" and of Slovakia as independent entities. India seemed little less rent by Sikh, Hindu, Muslim, and Tamil infighting than it was immediately after the British pulled out, more than forty years ago.

To the extent that either McWorld or Jihad has a natural politics, it has turned out to be more of an antipolitics. For McWorld, it is the antipolitics of globalism: bureaucratic, technocratic, and meritocratic, focused (as Marx predicted it would be) on the administration of things—with people, however, among the chief things to be administered. In its politico-economic imperatives McWorld has been guided by laissez-faire market principles that privilege efficiency, productivity, and beneficence at the expense of civic liberty and self-government.

For Jihad, the antipolitics of tribalization has been explicitly antidemocratic: one-party dictatorship, government by military junta, theocratic fundamentalism—often associated with a version of the *Fuhrerprinzip* that empowers an individual to rule on behalf of a people. Even the government of India, struggling for decades to model democracy for a people who will soon number a billion, longs for great leaders; and for every Mahatma Gandhi, Indira Gandhi, or Rajiv Gandhi taken from them by zealous assassins, the Indians appear to seek a replacement who will deliver them from the lengthy travail of their freedom.

THE CONFEDERAL OPTION

How can democracy be secured and spread in a world whose primary tendencies are at best indifferent to it (McWorld) and at worst deeply antithetical to it (Jihad)? My guess is that globalization will eventually vanquish retribalization. The ethos of material "civilization" has not yet encountered an obstacle it has been unable to thrust aside. Ortega may have grasped in the 1920s a clue to our own future in the coming millennium.

"Everyone sees the need of a new principle of life. But as always happens in similar crises—some people attempt to save the situation by an artificial intensification of the very principle which has led to decay. This is the meaning of the 'nationalist' outburst of recent years. . . . things have always gone that way. The last flare, the longest; the last sigh, the deepest. On the very eve of their disappearance there is an intensification of frontiers—military and economic."

Jihad may be a last deep sigh before the eternal yawn of McWorld. On the other hand, Ortega was not exactly prescient; his prophecy of peace and internationalism came just before blitzkrieg, world war, and the Holocaust tore the old order to bits. Yet democracy is how we remonstrate with reality, the rebuke our aspirations offer to history. And if retribalization is inhospitable to democracy, there is nonetheless a form of democratic government that can accommodate parochialism and communitarianism, one that can even save them from their defects and make them more tolerant and participatory: decentralized participatory democracy. And if McWorld is indifferent to democracy, there is nonetheless a form of democratic government that suits global markets passably well—representative government in its federal or, better still, confederal variation.

With its concern for accountability, the protection of minorities, and the universal rule of law, a confederalized representative system would serve the political needs of McWorld as well as oligarchic bureaucratism or meritocratic elitism is currently doing. As we are already beginning to see, many nations may survive in the long term only as confederations that afford local regions smaller than "nations" extensive jurisdiction. Recommended reading for democrats of the twenty-first century is not the U.S. Constitution or the French Declaration of Rights of Man and Citizen but the Articles of Confederation, that suddenly pertinent document that stitched together the thirteen American colonies into what then seemed a too loose confederation of independent states but now appears a new form of political realism, as veterans of Yeltsin's new Russia and the new Europe created at Maastricht will attest.

By the same token, the participatory and direct form of democracy that engages citizens in civic activity and civic judgment and goes well beyond just voting and accountability—the system I have called "strong democracy"—suits the political needs of decentralized communities as well as theocratic and nationalist party dictatorships have done. Local neighborhoods need not be democratic, but they can be. Real democracy has flourished in diminutive settings: the spirit of liberty, Tocqueville said, is local. Participatory democracy, if not naturally apposite to tribalism, has an undeniable attractiveness under conditions of parochialism.

Democracy in any of these variations will, however, continue to be obstructed by the undemocratic and antidemocratic trends toward uniformitarian globalism and intolerant retribalization which I have portrayed here. For democracy to persist in our brave new McWorld, we will have to commit acts of conscious political will—a possibility, but hardly a probability, under these conditions. Political will requires much more than the quick fix of the transfer of institutions. Like technology transfer, institution transfer rests on foolish assumptions about a uniform world of the kind that once fired the imagination of colonial administrators. Spread English justice to the colonies by exporting wigs. Let an East Indian trading company act as the vanguard to Britain's free parliamentary institutions. Today's well-intentioned quick-fixers in the National Endowment for Democracy and the Kennedy School of Government, in the unions and foundations and universities zealously nurturing contacts in Eastern Europe and the Third World, are hoping to democratize by long distance. Post Bulgaria a parliament by first-class mail. Fed Ex the Bill of Rights to Sri Lanka. Cable Cambodia some common law.

Yet Eastern Europe has already demonstrated that importing free political parties, parliaments, and presses cannot establish a democratic civil society; imposing a free market may even have the opposite effect. Democracy grows from the bottom up and cannot be imposed from the top down. Civil society has to be built from the inside out. The institutional superstructure comes last. Poland may become democratic, but then again it may heed the Pope, and prefer to found its politics on its Catholicism, with uncertain consequences for democracy. Bulgaria may become democratic, but it may prefer tribal war. The former Soviet Union may become a democratic confederation, or it may just grow into an anarchic and weak conglomeration of markets for other nations' goods and services.

Democrats need to seek out indigenous democratic impulses. There is always a desire for self-government, always some expression of participation, accountability, consent, and representation, even in traditional hierarchical societies. These need to be identified, tapped, modified, and incorporated into new democratic practices with an indigenous flavor. The tortoises among the democratizers may ultimately outlive or outpace the hares, for they will have the time and patience to explore conditions along the way, and to adapt their gait to changing circumstances. Tragically, democracy in a hurry often looks something like France in 1794 or China in 1989.

It certainly seems possible that the most attractive democratic ideal in the face of the brutal realities of Jihad and the dull realities of McWorld will be a confederal union of semi-autonomous communities smaller than nation-states, tied together into regional economic associations and markets larger than nation-states—participatory and self-determining in local matters at the bottom, representative and accountable at the top. The nation-state would play a diminished role, and sovereignty would lose some of its political potency. The Green movement adage "Think globally, act locally" would actually come to describe the conduct of politics.

This vision reflects only an ideal, however—one that is not terribly likely to be realized. Freedom, Jean-Jacques Rousseau once wrote, is a food easy to eat but hard to digest. Still, democracy has always played itself out against the odds. And democracy remains both a form of coherence as binding as McWorld and a secular faith potentially as inspiriting as Jihad. ■

Working with the Text

1. Summarize Barber's concepts of "McWorld" and "Jihad" in your own words. What do you see as the key ideas in each?

2. What do you think people find most attractive about each of the tendencies that Barber describes? What is most potentially dangerous about each? Which do you find yourself most attracted to and why?

3. Barber refers to the need for a "participatory and direct form of democracy that engages citizens in civic activity and civic judgment and goes well beyond voting and accountability." What do you think Barber means by this "direct" form of democracy? Using Barber's definitions, how democratic is your community? Your workplace? Leaving voting aside, in what ways would you say you most participate in direct democracy? What local ways can you imagine to create more direct democracy?

Working with Connections

1. In "The Global Village Finally Arrives," Pico Iyer says, "Values . . . travel at the speed of fax," and Barber argues that American "software"—or popular culture—may be "more potent than armaments" in creating a "McWorld." If the cultural "software" Barber refers to is one powerful way American "values" are sent around the world, how would we describe these values? What do you see American popular culture and products telling the world about life in the United States and about American values? What do you see as the positive and negative aspects of American cultural "software"?

2. Many people argue about whether the protests held at international meetings of the World Trade Organization represent a version of the direct democracy Barber advocates or a "Jihad"-like reaction to the global economy. What ideas in Barber's essay can help you understand, criticize, or defend the aims of the protesters? Do you think Barber would approve of them? As a research project, learn more about Barber's work to see if he comments on the protests.

3. Based on this essay, how do you think Barber might respond to the two essays on sweatshops in the minisection that follows? Where would he see evidence of "McWorld" and "Jihad"?

Focus on Work and the Global Economy: The Debate Over Sweatshops

The term *sweatshop* can evoke images of a century or more ago, with poor workers, including children, forced to labor long hours in uncomfortable and unsafe conditions doing work that is repetitive and often dangerous for little pay. The section of poetry on the Triangle Shirtwaist

Factory fire of 1911 (in Chapter 4, Work and Social Class) pays tribute to the mainly young women who perished as the result of such unsafe sweatshop work. This tedious, manual labor seems out of keeping with contemporary media reports about the new, computer-based information economy, where critical thinking skills are supposed to replace physical labor.

Factory and production work of all kinds, however, remains an integral part of the world of work, on both the local and global levels, and arguments over the ethics and prevalence of sweatshops are as much with us at the turn to the twenty-first century as they were at the beginning of the twentieth. All around the world, including in the United States, people still work for ten or more hours a day, six to seven days a week, processing food products, making clothing, toys, CD players, sports equipment, even the microchips and computers that are driving the information economy. As transportation costs decrease and the flow of information and goods becomes easier, manufacturers can travel the world seeking people who will work for the lowest possible wages with the least amount of regulation or interference from governments or labor unions, then ship their products to consumers around the world looking for the best bargains.

Are sweatshops an inevitable part of the economic development of poor countries, or do they represent the exploitation of human misery for profit and cheap consumer goods? Who bears responsibility for the human costs of sweatshop work? Factory owners? Governments? Consumers? What can be done to improve working conditions in sweatshops without depriving workers the chance to earn a living? These questions and more are part of an international debate over sweatshop work and form the basis for this section on the sweatshop question. In the following pages you will find two essays, each arguing for a different understanding of the sweatshop issue. The excerpt from William Greider's *One World, Ready or Not* describes "the worst industrial fire in the history of capitalism" in order to bring to light the tragic record of death and injury in sweatshops around the world. In "Two Cheers for Sweatshops," Nicholas Kristoff and Sheryl WuDunn make the counterargument that in spite of their excesses, sweatshops have also meant the arrival of relative prosperity and economic development to people in poor countries. The section on Reading the Web then spotlights the specific controversy over the use of low-wage workers overseas to manufacture Nike shoes and products. As you prepare to read this section, consider the following questions and exercises:

- What images and working conditions come to mind when you hear the word *sweatshop*? Write them down and then collaborate as a class to come up with a group impression. Where do these images and ideas come from?

- Brainstorm as a class about sweatshop controversies you have heard of or are familiar with (such as the Kathy Lee Gifford line of clothing) and do research to find out more about the issues involved.

- Choose an article of clothing or other consumer product that you own and use the web to try to trace back to how it was manufactured. What information are you able to find? Did this information come from company web sites or from sites run by labor activists? Does the information you find reassure you or cause concern?

- See if there is a campus student organization focused on international labor or sweatshop issues. Interview members of the group or invite them to class to discuss why they feel it is important for college students to take an interest in these issues and what they can do.

WILLIAM GREIDER

from *One World, Ready or Not: The Manic Logic of Global Capitalism*

After the Triangle Shirtwaist Fire in 1911 claimed the lives of 146 young women sweatshop workers, thousands took to the streets of New York to protest the working conditions that led to this tragedy. After the 1993 Kader Industrial Toy Company fire in Bangkok killed 188 young women, reports William Greider, the event barely registered in U.S. and European media. Yet the fire highlights how many of the inexpensive consumer goods we take for granted, from the shoes on our feet to the stuffed animals we buy for our children, are manufactured in harsh, unsafe conditions, often by young women and even children. Why does a system of labor many Americans believe disappeared long ago still flourish, and what is the responsibility of those who benefit from sweatshop labor? These are a few of the questions that Greider explores in this excerpt of a chapter from his book One World, Ready or Not: The Manic Logic of Global Capitalism.*

William Greider is the national-affairs reporter for The Nation *and has written several books on politics and the economy, including* Secrets of the Temple: How the Federal Reserve Runs the Country *and* Who Will Tell the People: The Betrayal of American Democracy.

On May 10, 1993, the worst industrial fire in the history of capitalism occurred at a toy factory on the outskirts of Bangkok and was reported on page 25 of the *Washington Post.* The *Financial Times* of London, which styles itself as the daily newspaper of the global economy, ran a brief item on page 6. The *Wall Street Journal* followed a day later with an account on page 11. The *New York Times* also put the story inside, but printed a dramatic photo on its front page: rows of small shrouded bodies on bamboo pallets—dozens of them—lined along the damp pavement, while dazed rescue workers stood awkwardly among the corpses. In the background, one could see the collapsed, smoldering structure of a mammoth factory where the Kader Industrial Toy Company of Thailand had employed three thousand workers manufacturing stuffed toys and plastic dolls, playthings destined for American children.

The official count was 188 dead, 469 injured, but the actual toll was undoubtedly higher since the four-story buildings had collapsed swiftly in the intense heat and many bodies were incinerated. Some of the missing were never found; others fled home to their villages. All but fourteen of the dead were women, most of them young, some as young as thirteen years old. Hundreds of the workers had been trapped on upper floors of the burning building, forced to jump from third- or fourth-floor windows, since the main exit doors were kept locked by the managers, and the narrow stairways became clotted with trampled bodies or collapsed.

When I visited Bangkok about nine months later, physical evidence of the disaster was gone—the site scraped clean by bulldozers—and Kader was already resuming production at a new toy factory, built far from the city in a rural province of northeastern Thailand. When I talked with Thai labor leaders and civic activists, people who had rallied to the cause of the fire victims, some of them were under the impression that a worldwide boycott of Kader products was under way, organized by conscience-stricken Americans and Europeans. I had to inform them that the civilized world had barely noticed their tragedy.

As news accounts pointed out, the Kader fire surpassed what was previously the worst industrial fire in history—the Triangle Shirtwaist Company fire of 1911—when 146 young immigrant women died in similar circumstances at a garment factory on the Lower East Side of Manhattan. The Triangle Shirtwaist fire became a pivotal event in American politics, a public scandal that provoked citizen reform movements and energized the labor organizing that built the International Ladies Garment Workers Union and other unions. The fire in Thailand did not produce meaningful political responses or even shame among consumers. The indifference of the leading newspapers merely reflected the tastes of their readers, who might be moved by human suffering in their own communities but were inured to news of recurring calamities in distant places. A fire in Bangkok was like a typhoon in Bangladesh, an earthquake in Turkey.

The Kader fire might have been more meaningful for Americans if they could have seen the thousands of soot-stained dolls that spilled from the wreckage, macabre litter scattered among the dead. Bugs Bunny, Bart Simpson and the Muppets. Big Bird and other *Sesame Street* dolls. Playskool "Water Pets." Santa Claus. What the initial news accounts did not mention was that Kader's Thai factory produced most of its toys for American companies—Toys "R" Us,

Fisher-Price, Hasbro, Tyco, Arco, Kenner, Gund and J. C. Penney—as well as stuffed dolls, slippers and souvenirs for Europe.

Globalized civilization has uncovered an odd parochialism in the American character: Americans worried obsessively over the everyday safety of their children, and the U.S. government's regulators diligently policed the design of toys to avoid injury to young innocents. Yet neither citizens nor government took any interest in the brutal and dangerous conditions imposed on the people who manufactured those same toys, many of whom were mere adolescent children themselves. Indeed, the government position, both in Washington and Bangkok, assumed that there was no social obligation connecting consumers and workers, at least none that governments could enforce without disrupting free trade or invading the sovereignty of other nations.

The toy industry, not surprisingly, felt the same. Hasbro Industries, maker of Playskool, subsequently told the *Boston Globe* that it would no longer do business with Kader, but, in general, the U.S. companies shrugged off responsibility. Kader, a major toy manufacturer based in Hong Kong, "is extremely reputable, not sleaze bags," David Miller, president of the Toy Manufacturers of America, assured *USA Today.* "The responsibility for those factories," Miller told ABC News, "is in the hands of those who are there and managing the factory."

The grisly details of what occurred revealed the casual irresponsibility of both companies and governments. The Kader factory compound consisted of four interconnected, four-story industrial barns on a three-acre lot on Buddhamondhol VI Road in the Sampran district west of Bangkok. It was one among Thailand's thriving new industrial zones for garments, textiles, electronics and toys. More than 50,000 people, most of them migrants from the Thai countryside, worked in the district at 7,500 large and small firms. Thailand's economic boom was based on places such as this, and Bangkok was almost choking on its own fantastic growth, dizzily erecting luxury hotels and office towers.

The fire started late on a Monday afternoon on the ground floor in the first building and spread rapidly upward, jumping to two adjoining buildings, all three of which swiftly collapsed. Investigators noted afterwards that the structures had been cheaply built, without concrete reinforcement, so steel girders and stairways crumpled easily in the heat. Thai law required that in such a large factory, fire-escape stairways must be sixteen to thirty-three feet wide, but Kader's were a mere four and a half feet. Main doors were locked and many windows barred to prevent pilfering by the employees. Flammable raw materials—fabric, stuffing, animal fibers—were stacked everywhere, on walkways and next to electrical boxes. Neither safety drills nor fire alarms and sprinkler systems had been provided.

Let some of the survivors describe what happened.

A young woman named Lampan Taptim: "There was the sound of yelling about a fire. I tried to leave the section but my supervisor told me to get back to work. My sister who worked on the fourth floor with me pulled me away and insisted we try to get out. We tried to go down the stairs and got to the second floor; we found that the stairs had already caved in. There was a lot of yelling and confusion. . . . In desperation, I went back up to the windows and went back and forth, looking down below. The smoke was thick and I picked the best place to jump in a pile of boxes. My sister jumped, too. She died."

A young woman named Cheng: "There is no way out [people were shouting], the security guard has locked the main door out! It was horrifying. I thought I would die. I took off my gold ring and kept it in my pocket and put on my name tag so that my body could be identifiable. I had to decide to die in the fire or from jumping down from a three stories' height." As the walls collapsed around her, Cheng clung to a pipe and fell downward with it, landing on a pile of dead bodies, injured but alive.

An older woman named La-iad Nada-nguen: "Four or five pregnant women jumped before me. They died before my eyes." Her own daughter jumped from the top floor and broke both hips.

Chauweewan Mekpan, who was five months pregnant: "I thought that if I jumped, at least my parents would see my remains, but if I stayed, nothing would be left of me." Though her back was severely injured, she and her unborn child miraculously survived.

An older textile worker named Vilaiwa Satieti, who sewed shirts and pants at a neighboring factory, described to me the carnage she encountered: "I got off work about five and passed by Kader and saw many dead bodies lying around, uncovered. Some of them I knew. I tried to help the workers who had jumped from the factory. They had broken legs and broken arms and broken heads. We tried to keep them alive until they got to the hospital, that's all you could do. Oh, they were teenagers, fifteen to twenty years, no more than that, and so many of them, so many."

This was not the first serious fire at Kader's factory, but the third or fourth. "I heard somebody yelling 'fire, fire,'" Tumthong Podhirun testified, ". . . but I did not take it seriously because it has happened before. Soon I smelled smoke and very quickly it billowed inside the place. I headed for the back door but it was locked. . . . Finally, I had no choice but to join the others and jumped out of the window. I saw many of my friends lying dead on the ground beside me."

In the aftermath of the tragedy, some Bangkok activists circulated an old snapshot of two smiling peasant girls standing arm in arm beside a thicket of palm trees. One of them, Praphai Prayonghorm, died in the 1993 fire at Kader. Her friend, Kammoin Konmanee, had died in the 1989 fire. Some of the Kader workers insisted afterwards that their factory had been haunted by ghosts, that it was built on the site of an old graveyard, disturbing the dead. The folklore expressed raw poetic truth: the fire in Bangkok eerily resembled the now-forgotten details of the Triangle Shirtwaist disaster eighty years before. Perhaps the "ghosts" that some workers felt present were young women from New York who had died in 1911.

Similar tragedies, large and small, were now commonplace across developing Asia and elsewhere. Two months after Kader, another fire at a Bangkok shirt factory killed ten women. Three months after Kader, a six-story hotel collapsed and killed 133 people, injuring 351. The embarrassed minister of industry ordered special inspections of 244 large factories in the Bangkok region and found that 60 percent of them had basic violations similar to Kader's. Thai industry was growing explosively—12 to 15 percent a year—but workplace injuries and illness were growing even faster, from 37,000 victims in 1987 to more than 150,000 by 1992 and an estimated 200,000 by 1994.

In China, six months after Kader, eighty-four women died and dozens of others were severely burned at another toy factory fire in the burgeoning industrial zone at Shenzhen. At Dongguan, a Hong Kong–owned raincoat factory burned in 1991, killing more than eighty people (Kader Industries also had a factory at Dongguan where two fires have been reported since 1990). In late 1993, some sixty women died at the Taiwanese-owned Gaofu textile plant in Fuzhou Province, many of them smothered in their dormitory beds by toxic fumes from burning textiles. In 1994, a shoe factory fire killed ten persons at Jiangmen; a textile factory fire killed thirty-eight and injured 160 at the Qianshan industrial zone.

"Why must these tragedies repeat themselves again and again?" the *People's Daily* in Beijing asked. The official *Economic Daily* complained: "The way some of these foreign investors ignore international practice, ignore our own national rules, act completely lawlessly and immorally and lust after wealth is enough to make one's hair stand on end."

America was itself no longer insulated from such brutalities. When a chicken-processing factory at Hamlet, North Carolina, caught fire in 1991, the exit doors there were also locked and twenty-five people died. A garment factory discovered by labor investigators in El Monte, California, held seventy-two Thai immigrants in virtual peonage, working eighteen hours a day in "sub-human conditions." One could not lament the deaths, harsh working conditions, child labor and subminimum wages in Thailand or across Asia and Central America without also recognizing that similar conditions have reappeared in the United States for roughly the same reason.

Sweatshops, mainly in the garment industry, scandalized Los Angeles, New York, and Dallas. The grim, foul assembly lines of the poultry-processing industry were spread across the rural South; the *Wall Street Journal*'s Tony Horwitz won a Pulitzer Prize for his harrowing description of this low-wage work. "In general," the U.S. Government Accounting Office reported in 1994, "the description of today's sweatshops differs little from that at the turn of the century."

That was the real mystery: Why did global commerce, with all of its supposed modernity and wondrous technologies, restore the old barbarisms that had long ago been forbidden by law? If the information age has enabled multinational corporations to manage production and marketing spread across continents, why were their managers unable—or unwilling—to organize such mundane matters as fire prevention?

The short answer, of course, was profits, but the deeper answer was about power: Firms behaved this way because they could, because nobody would stop them. When law and social values retreated before the power of markets, then capitalism's natural drive to maximize returns had no internal governor to check its social behavior. When one enterprise took the low road to gain advantage, others would follow.

The toy fire in Bangkok provided a dramatic illustration for the much broader, less visible forms of human exploitation that were flourishing in the global system, including the widespread use of children in manufacturing, even forced labor camps in China or Burma. These matters were not a buried secret. Indeed, American television had aggressively exposed the "dark Satanic mills" with dramatic reports. ABC's *20/20* broadcast correspondent Lynn Sherr's devastating account of the Kader fire; CNN ran disturbing footage. Mike Wallace of CBS's *60 Minutes* exposed the prison labor exploited in China. NBC's *Dateline* did a piece on Wal-Mart's grim production in Bangladesh. CBS's *Street Stories* toured the shoe factories of Indonesia.

The baffling quality about modern communications was that its images could take us to people in remote corners of the world vividly and instantly, but these images have not as yet created genuine community with them. In terms of human consciousness, the "global village" was still only a picture on the TV screen.

Public opinion, moreover, absorbed contradictory messages about the global reality that were difficult to sort out. The opening stages of industrialization presented, as always, a great paradox: the process was profoundly liberating for millions, freeing them from material scarcity and limited life choices, while it also ensnared other millions in brutal new forms of domination. Both aspects were true, but there was no scale on which these opposing consequences could be easily balanced, since the good and ill effects were not usually apportioned among the same people. Some human beings were set free, while others lives were turned into cheap and expendable commodities.

Workers at Kader, for instance, earned about 100 baht a day for sewing and assembling dolls, the official minimum wage of $4, but the constant stream of new entrants meant that many at the factory actually worked for much less—only $2 or $3 a day—during a required "probationary" period of three to six months that was often extended much longer by the managers. Only one hundred of the three thousand workers at Kader were legally designated employees; the rest were "contract workers" without permanent rights and benefits, the same employment system now popularized in the United States.

"Lint, fabric, dust and animal hair filled the air on the production floor," the International Confederation of Free Trade Unions based in Brussels observed in its investigative report. "Noise, heat, congestion and fumes from various sources were reported by many. Dust control was nonexistent; protective equipment inadequate. Inhaling the dust created respiratory problems and contact with it caused skin diseases." A factory clinic dispensed antihistamines or other drugs and referred the more serious symptoms to outside hospitals. Workers paid for the medication themselves and were reimbursed, up to $6, only if they had contributed 10 baht a month to the company's health fund.

A common response to such facts, even from many sensitive people, was: yes, that was terrible, but wouldn't those workers be even worse off if civil standards were imposed on their employers since they might lose their jobs as a result? This was the same economic rationale offered by American manufacturers a century before to explain why American children must work in the coal mines and textile mills. U.S. industry had survived somehow (and, in fact, flourished) when child labor and the other malpractices were eventually prohibited by social reforms. Furthermore, it was not coincidence that industry always assigned the harshest conditions and lowest pay to the weakest members of a society—women, children, uprooted migrants. Whether the factory was in Thailand or the United States or Mexico's *maquiladora* zone, people who were already quite powerless were less likely to resist, less able to demand decency from their employers.

Nor did these enterprises necessarily consist of small, struggling firms that could not afford to treat their workers better. Small sweatshops, it was true, were numerous in Thailand, and I saw some myself in a working-class neighborhood of Bangkok. Behind iron grillwork, children who looked to be ten to twelve years old squatted on the cement floors of the open-air shops, assembling suitcases, sewing raincoats, packing T-shirts. Across the street, a swarm of adolescents in blue smocks ate dinner at long tables outside a two-story building, then trooped back upstairs to the sewing machines.

Kader Holding Company, Ltd., however, was neither small nor struggling. It was a powerhouse of the global toy industry—headquartered in Hong Kong, incorporated in Bermuda, owned by a wealthy Hong Kong Chinese family named Ting that got its start after World War II making plastic goods and flashlights under procurement contracts from the U.S. military. Now Kader controlled a global maze of factories and interlocking subsidiaries in eight countries, from China and Thailand to Britain and the United States, where it owned Bachmann toys.

After the fire Thai union members, intellectuals and middle-class activists from social rights organizations (the groups known in developing countries as nongovernmental organizations, or NGOs) formed the Committee to Support Kader Workers and began demanding justice from the employer. They sent a delegation to Hong Kong to confront Kader officials and investigate the complex corporate linkages of the enterprise. What they discovered was that Kader's partner in the Bangkok toy factory was actually a fabulously wealthy Thai family, the Chearavanonts, ethnic Chinese merchants who own the Charoen Pokphand Group, Thailand's own leading multinational corporation.

The CP Group owns farms, feed mills, real estate, air-conditioning and motorcycle factories, food-franchise chains—two hundred companies worldwide, several of them listed on the New York Stock Exchange. The patriarch and chairman, Dhanin Chearavanont, was said by *Fortune* magazine to be the seventy-fifth richest man in the world, with personal assets of $2.6 billion (or 65 billion baht, as the *Bangkok Post* put it). Like the other emerging "Chinese multinationals," the Pokphand Group operates through the informal networks of kinfolk and ethnic contacts spread around the world by the Chinese diaspora, while it also participates in the more rigorous accounting systems of Western economies.

In the mother country, China, the conglomerate nurtured political-business alliances and has become the largest outside investor in new factories and joint ventures. In the United States, it maintained superb political connections. The Chearavanonts co-sponsored a much-heralded visit to Bangkok by ex-president George Bush, who delivered a speech before Thai business leaders in early 1994, eight months after the Kader fire. The price tag for Bush's appearance, according to the Bangkok press, was $400,000 (equivalent to one month's payroll for all three thousand workers at Kader). The day after Bush's appearance, the Chearavanonts hosted a banquet for a leading entrepreneur from China—Deng Xiaoping's daughter.

The Pokphand Group at first denied any connection to the Kader fire, but reformers and local reporters dug out the facts of the family's involvement. Dhanin Chearavanont himself owned 11 percent of Honbo Investment Company and with relatives and corporate directors held majority control. Honbo, in turn, owned half of KCP Toys (KCP stood for Kader Charoen Pokphand), which, in turn, owned 80 percent of Kader Industrial (Thailand) Company. Armed with these facts, three hundred workers from the destroyed factory marched on the Pokphand Group's corporate tower on Silom Road, where they staged a gentle sit-down demonstration in the lobby, demanding just compensation for the victims.

In the context of Thai society and politics, the workers' demonstration against Pokphand was itself extraordinary, like peasants confronting the nobility. Under continuing pressures from the support group, the company agreed to pay much larger compensation for victims and their families—$12,000 for each death, a trivial amount in American terms but more than double the Thai standard. "When we worked on Kader," said Professor Voravidh Charoenloet, an economist at Chulalongkorn University, "the government and local entrepreneurs and factory owners didn't want us to challenge these people; even the police tried to obstruct us from making an issue. We were accused of trying to destroy the country's reputation."

The settlement, in fact, required the Thai activists to halt their agitation and fall silent. "Once the extra compensation was paid," Voravidh explained, "we were forced to stop. One of the demands by the government was that everything should stop. Our organization had to accept it. We wanted to link with the international organizations and have a great boycott, but we had to cease."

The global boycott, he assumed, was going forward anyway because he knew that international labor groups like the ICFTU and the AFL-CIO had investigated the Kader fire and issued stinging denunciations. I told him that aside from organized labor, the rest of the world remained indifferent. There was no boycott of Kader toys in America. The professor slumped in his chair and was silent, a twisted expression on his face.

"I feel very bad," Voravidh said at last. "Maybe we should not have accepted it. But when we came away, we felt that was what we could accomplish. The people wanted more. There must be something more."

In the larger context, this tragedy was not explained by the arrogant power of one wealthy family or the elusive complexities of interlocking corporations. The Kader fire was ordained and organized by the free market itself. The toy industry—much like textiles and garments, shoes, electronics assembly and other low-wage sectors—existed (and thrived) by exploiting a crude ladder of desperate competition among the poorest nations. Its factories regularly hopped to new locations where wages were even lower, where the governments would be even more tolerant of abusive practices. The contract work assigned to foreign firms, including thousands of small sweatshops, fitted neatly into the systems of far-flung production of major brand names and distanced the capital owners from personal responsibility. The "virtual corporation" celebrated by some business futurists already existed in these sectors and, indeed, was now being emulated in some ways by advanced manufacturing—cars, aircraft, computers.

Over the last generation, toy manufacturers and others have moved around the Asian rim in search of the bottom-rung conditions: from Hong Kong, Korea and Taiwan to Thailand and Indonesia, from there to China, Vietnam and Bangladesh, perhaps on next to Burma, Nepal or Cambodia. Since the world had a nearly inexhaustible supply of poor people and supplicant governments, the market would keep driving in search of lower rungs; no one could say where the bottom was located. Industrial conditions were not getting better, as conventional theory assured the innocent consumers, but in many sectors were getting much worse. In America, the U.S. diplomatic opening to Vietnam was celebrated as progressive politics. In Southeast Asia, it merely opened another trapdoor beneath wages and working conditions.

A country like Thailand was caught in the middle: if it conscientiously tried to improve, it would pay a huge price. When Thai unions lobbied to win improvements in minimum-wage standards, textile plants began leaving for Vietnam and elsewhere or even importing cheaper "guest workers" from Burma. When China opened its fast-growing industrial zones in Shenzhen, Dongguan and other locations, the new competition had direct consequences on the factory floors of Bangkok.

Kader, according to the ICFTU, opened two new factories in Shekou and Dongguan where young people were working fourteen-hour days, seven days a week, to fill the U.S. Christmas orders for Mickey Mouse and other American dolls. Why should a company worry about sprinkler systems or fire escapes for a dusty factory in Bangkok when it could hire brand-new workers in China for only $20 a month, one fifth of the labor cost in Thailand?

The ICFTU report described the market forces: "The lower cost of production of toys in China changes the investment climate for countries like Thailand. Thailand competes with China to attract investment capital for local toy production. With this development, Thailand has become sadly lax in enforcing its own legislation. It turns a blind eye to health violations, thus allowing factory owners to ignore safety standards. Since China entered the picture, accidents in Thailand have nearly tripled."

The Thai minister of industry, Sanan Kachornprasart, described the market reality more succinctly: "If we punish them, who will want to invest here?" Thai authorities subsequently filed charges against three Kader factory managers, but none against the company itself nor, of course, the Chearavanont family.

In the aftermath, a deputy managing director of Kader Industrial, Pichet Laokasem, entered a Buddhist monastery "to make merit for the fire victims," *The Nation* of Bangkok reported. Pichet told reporters he would serve as a monk until he felt better emotionally. "Most of the families affected by the fire lost only a loved one," he explained. "I lost nearly two hundred of my workers all at once."

The fire in Bangkok reflected the amorality of the marketplace when it has been freed of social obligations. But the tragedy also mocked the moral claims of three greta religions, whose adherents were all implicated. Thais built splendid golden temples exalting Buddha, who taught them to put spiritual being before material wealth. Chinese claimed to have acquired superior social values, reverence for family and community, derived from the teachings of Confucius. Americans bought the toys from Asia to celebrate the birth of Jesus Christ. Their shared complicity was another of the strange convergences made possible by global commerce. ■

Working with the Text

1. Had you or any members of the class heard of the Kader Industrial Toy Company fire before you read Greider's chapter? What was your reaction? Why do you think this tragedy is not better known? How would you explain why our ability to see images of people from around the world has "not as yet created genuine community with them"?

2. Greider asserts, "Americans worried obsessively over the everyday safety of their children, and the U.S. government's regulators diligently policed the design of toys to avoid injury to young innocents. Yet neither citizens nor government took any interest in the brutal and dangerous conditions imposed on the people who manufactured those same toys, many of whom were mere adolescent children themselves." How would you respond to or explain Greider's observation? What responsibility do you think you have as a consumer in terms of how the products you buy are made?

3. According to Greider, "A country like Thailand was caught in the middle: if it conscientiously tried to improve, it would pay a huge price," mainly in the form of companies simply moving their manufacturing to other countries. What would you hope the government of Thailand would do? What role could other countries play in addressing this situation? What do you think Greider would recommend?

NICHOLAS D. KRISTOF AND SHERYL WUDUNN

Two Cheers for Sweatshops

Sweatshop work can seem hard, dangerous, and exploitive, particularly when wages amount to only one or two dollars per day. Yet for poor families in many countries, that one or two dollars might mean survival and even a step up in standard of living. And for nations struggling to modernize and develop their economies, sweatshops can be a source of investment and jobs. In this article written for the Sunday New York Times Magazine, *reporters Nicholas D. Kristof and Sheryl WuDunn argue that while sweatshop work is hard work and can foster abuse and exploitation, it is a mistake to judge sweatshops by American standards. They conclude that for all the negatives associated with them, sweatshops have led the way to increased social prosperity and economic progress for many poor nations, especially in Asia.*

Nicholas D. Kristof and Sheryl WuDunn are Pulitzer Prize–winning reporters for the New York Times *who have written extensively about Asia, including the books* Thunder from the East: Portrait of a Rising Asia *and* China Wakes: The Struggle for the Soul of a Rising Power.

It was breakfast time, and the food stand in the village in northeastern Thailand was crowded. Maesubin Sisoipha, the middle-aged woman cooking the food, was friendly, her portions large and the price right. For the equivalent of about 5 cents, she offered a huge green mango leaf filled with rice, fish paste and fried beetles. It was a hearty breakfast, if one didn't mind the odd antenna left sticking in one's teeth.

One of the half-dozen men and women sitting on a bench eating was a sinewy, bare-chested laborer in his late 30's named Mongkol Latlakorn. It was a hot, lazy day, and so we started chatting idly about the food and, eventually, our families. Mongkol mentioned that his daughter, Darin, was 15, and his voice softened as he spoke of her. She was beautiful and smart, and her father's hopes rested on her.

"Is she in school?" we asked.

"Oh, no," Mongkol said, his eyes sparkling with amusement. "She's working in a factory in Bangkok. She's making clothing for export to America." He explained that she was paid $2 a day for a nine-hour shift, six days a week.

"It's dangerous work," Mongkol added. "Twice the needles went right through her hands. But the managers bandaged up her hands, and both times she got better again and went back to work."

"How terrible," we murmured sympathetically.

Mongkol looked up, puzzled. "It's good pay," he said. "I hope she can keep that job. There's all this talk about factories closing now, and she said there are rumors that her factory might close. I hope that doesn't happen. I don't know what she would do then."

He was not, of course, indifferent to his daughter's suffering; he simply had a different perspective from ours—not only when it came to food but also when it came to what constituted desirable work.

Nothing captures the difference in mind-set between East and West more than attitudes toward sweatshops. Nike and other American companies have been hammered in the Western press over the last decade for producing shoes, toys and other products in grim little factories with dismal conditions. Protests against sweatshops and the dark forces of globalization that they seem to represent have become common at meetings of the World Bank and the World Trade Organization and, this month, at a World Economic Forum in Australia, livening up the scene for Olympic athletes arriving for the competition. Yet sweatshops that seem brutal from the vantage point of an American sitting in his living room can appear tantalizing to a Thai laborer getting by on beetles.

Fourteen years ago, we moved to Asia and began reporting there. Like most Westerners, we arrived in the region outraged at sweatshops. In time, though, we came to accept the view supported by most Asians: that the campaign against sweatshops risks harming the very people it is intended to help. For beneath their grime, sweatshops are a clear sign of the industrial revolution that is beginning to reshape Asia.

This is not to praise sweatshops. Some managers are brutal in the way they house workers in firetraps, expose children to dangerous chemicals, deny bathroom breaks, demand sexual favors, force people to work double shifts or dismiss anyone who tries to organize a union. Agitation for improved safety conditions can be helpful, just as it was in 19th-century Europe. But Asian workers would be aghast at the idea of American consumers boycotting certain toys or clothing in protest. The simplest way to help the poorest Asians would be to buy more from sweatshops, not less.

On our first extended trip to China, in 1987, we traveled to the Pearl River delta in the south of the country. There we visited several factories, including one in the boomtown of Dongguan, where about 100 female workers sat at workbenches stitching together bits of leather to make purses for a Hong Kong company. We chatted with several women as their fingers flew over their work and asked about their hours.

"I start at about 6:30, after breakfast, and go until about 7 p.m.," explained one shy teenage girl. "We break for lunch, and I take half an hour off then."

"You do this six days a week?"

"Oh, no. Every day."

"Seven days a week?"

"Yes." She laughed at our surprise. "But then I take a week or two off at Chinese New Year to go back to my village."

The others we talked to all seemed to regard it as a plus that the factory allowed them to work long hours. Indeed, some had sought out this factory precisely because it offered them the chance to earn more.

"It's actually pretty annoying how hard they want to work," said the factory manager, a Hong Kong man. "It means we have to worry about security and have a supervisor around almost constantly."

It sounded pretty dreadful, and it was. We and other journalists wrote about the problems of child labor and oppressive conditions in both China and South Korea. But, looking back, our worries were excessive. Those sweatshops tended to generate the wealth to solve the problems they created. If Americans had reacted to the horror stories in the 1980's by curbing imports of those sweatshop products, then neither southern China nor South Korea would have registered as much progress as they have today.

The truth is, those grim factories in Dongguan and the rest of southern China contributed to a remarkable explosion of wealth. In the years since our first conversations there, we've returned many times to Dongguan and the surrounding towns and seen the transformation. Wages have risen from about $50 a month to $250 a month or more today. Factory conditions have improved as businesses have scrambled to attract and keep the best laborers. A private housing market has emerged, and video arcades and computer schools have opened to cater to workers with rising incomes. A hint of a middle class has appeared—as has China's closest thing to a Western-style independent newspaper, Southern Weekend.

Partly because of these tens of thousands of sweatshops, China's economy has become one of the hottest in the world. Indeed, if China's 30 provinces were counted as individual countries, then the 20 fastest-growing countries in the world between 1978 and 1995 would all have been Chinese. When Britain launched the Industrial Revolution in the late 18th century, it took 58 years for per capita output to double. In China, per capita output has been doubling every 10 years.

In fact, the most vibrant parts of Asia are nearly all in what might be called the Sweatshop Belt, from China and South Korea to Malaysia, Indonesia and even Bangladesh and India. Today these sweatshop countries control about one-quarter of the global economy. As the industrial revolution spreads through China and India, there are good reasons to think that Asia will continue to pick up speed. Some World Bank forecasts show Asia's share of global gross domestic product rising to 55 to 60 percent by about 2025— roughly the West's share at its peak half a century ago. The sweatshops have helped lay the groundwork for a historic economic realignment that is putting Asia back on its feet. Countries are rebounding from the economic crisis of 1997-98 and the sweatshops—seen by Westerners as evidence of moribund economies—actually reflect an industrial revolution that is raising living standards in the East.

Of course, it may sound silly to say that sweatshops offer a route to prosperity, when wages in the poorest countries are sometimes less than $1 a day. Still, for an impoverished Indonesian or Bangladeshi woman with a handful of kids who would otherwise drop out of school and risk dying of mundane diseases like diarrhea, $1 or $2 a day can be a life-transforming wage.

This was made abundantly clear in Cambodia, when we met a 40-year-old woman named Nhem Yen, who told us why she moved to an area with particularly lethal malaria. "We needed to eat," she said. "And here there is wood, so we thought we could cut it and sell it."

But then Nhem Yen's daughter and son-in-law both died of malaria, leaving her with two grandchildren and five children of her own. With just one mosquito net, she had to choose which children would sleep protected and which would sleep exposed.

In Cambodia, a large mosquito net costs $5. If there had been a sweatshop in the area, however harsh or dangerous, Nhem Yen would have leapt at the chance to work in it, to earn enough to buy a net big enough to cover all her children.

For all the misery they can engender, sweatshops at least offer a precarious escape from the poverty that is the developing world's greatest problem. Over the past 50 years, countries like India resisted foreign exploitation, while countries that started at a similar economic level—like Taiwan and South Korea—accepted sweatshops as the price of development. Today there can be no doubt about which approach worked better. Taiwan and South Korea are modern countries with low rates of infant mortality and high levels of education; in contrast, every year 3.1 million Indian children die before the age of 5, mostly from diseases of poverty like diarrhea.

The effect of American pressure on sweatshops is complicated. While it clearly improves conditions at factories that produce branded merchandise for companies like Nike, it also raises labor costs across the board. That encourages less well established companies to mechanize and to reduce the number of employees needed. The upshot is to help people who currently have jobs in Nike plants but to risk jobs for others. The only thing a country like Cambodia has to offer is terribly cheap wages; if companies are scolded for paying those wages, they will shift their manufacturing to marginally richer areas like Malaysia or Mexico.

Sweatshop monitors do have a useful role. They can compel factories to improve safety. They can also call attention to the impact of sweatshops on the environment. The greatest downside of industrialization is not exploitation of workers but toxic air and water. In Asia each year, three million people die from the effects of pollution. The factories springing up throughout the region are far more likely to kill people through the chemicals they expel than through terrible working conditions.

By focusing on these issues, by working closely with organizations and news media in foreign countries, sweatshops can be improved. But refusing to buy sweatshop products risks making Americans feel good while harming those we are trying to help. As a Chinese proverb goes, "First comes the bitterness, then there is sweetness and wealth and honor for 10,000 years." ◼

Working with the Text

1. What do Kristof and WuDunn see as the most important benefits of sweatshops? How would you rank them in order of importance and why?

2. Both Kristof and WuDunn initially react with concern upon learning that fifteen-year-old Darin Latlakorn is working nine hours a day in a dangerous factory instead of attending school, but her father is proud of her. What was your own reaction to the story of Darin? How would you define the importance of work and education? When should one take precedence over the other?

3. Kristof and WuDunn refer to the "different perspective" governing how many sweatshop workers in Asia understand their jobs versus how the readers of the *New York Times* view sweatshop labor. Explore your own perspective by describing your own expectations for a job. What limits do you have in terms of minimal working conditions? What would make you change your perspective?

Debating the Question

1. Although they refer to many of the same places in their articles (Thailand, Dongguan in China), Greider in *One World, Ready or Not* and Kristof and WuDunn in "Two Cheers for Sweatshops" offer descriptions of sweatshop labor that emphasize very different aspects of the working conditions involved and the resulting social impact. As journalists, they both rely on the use of specific examples and stories to make their points. Which specific examples from both articles did you find most effective and why? How might the writers respond to the examples in the articles of the other?

2. Write a letter to the editor from the point of view of Greider responding to Kristof and WuDunn's article, or vice versa. You can extend this exercise into constructing a dialogue/debate on the issue of sweatshops between them, either in a paper, as a part of an online discussion, or in the form of an oral debate.

3. In Greider's article, he describes the disappointment of Thai labor activists that Americans and Europeans were not taking part in a boycott against Kader toys. In Kristof and WuDunn's article, they argue that the best thing consumers in the United States can do is "buy more from sweatshops, not less." After

reading both articles, write an essay explaining your opinions about what U.S. consumers should do about products manufactured in sweatshop factories. To develop the assignment further, use your essay as the basis for further research into the topic. You might start with the Nike situation explored in Reading the Web below, or you might focus on a different boycott or controversy.

Reading the Web

The Controversy Over Nike

Nike has become one of the most well known brand names in the world, as famous for its "swoosh" logo and expensive advertising campaigns as its line of athletic shoes and clothing. Like many U.S. shoe and apparel companies, Nike pays to have its products manufactured in factories outside America, mainly in Asian countries like Indonesia and Vietnam. Typically, these factories are not owned directly by Nike or other manufacturers; instead, Nike contracts with overseas factories to make their products. Over the last ten to fifteen years, social activists and workers groups around the world have brought attention to the working conditions in these factories. As a high-profile company, Nike has drawn special scrutiny. Various boycotts have been organized against Nike, and Nike has both defended its labor practices and formulated policies designed to encourage humane working conditions in the companies with which it contracts.

The growth of what has come to be known as the "anti-sweatshop" movement has paralleled the rapid development of the Internet, and a significant part of the protest and counterprotest over factory working conditions has taken place via web sites. Since athletic shoes and apparel are particularly popular with traditional-age college students, college campuses have been another focal point for this kind of activism. One prominent student activist group is United Students Against Sweatshops, and one of their most visible campaigns has centered on urging colleges and universities to make sure that their official school logo clothing be manufactured under decent working conditions. They have also been active in various actions involving Nike.

united students against sweatshops

What's New?

corporate responsibility

Working with the Text

1. How effective do you find Nike's mission statement? What does the term *sourcing* mean? Why would this be an important term for Nike to use?

2. The photos included on the Nike web site do not have explanatory captions. How did you read the pictures? Who did you think the people were? What were they doing? What impression do they leave of Nike's work practices?

3. Take a close look at the logo used by United Students Against Sweatshops. How do you interpret who the people are in the logo and what they are doing? Why would this be an effective logo to appeal to college students?

4. The USAS web site includes the following quotation:

   If you have come to help me, you are wasting your time;
   But if you've come because your liberation is bound up with mine,
   Then let us work together.
   —aboriginal activist sister

   What is the significance of this quotation for an organization of American college students interested in improving working conditions in factories around the world? What attitudes is it trying to encourage and discourage?

5. Explore both web sites for specific information about protests involving Nike and Nike's responses. How does this information further reinforce or modify the issues of exploitation versus development outlined in *One World, Ready or Not* by William Greider and "Two Cheers for Sweatshops" by Nicholas Kristof and Sheryl WuDunn?

Stories of Work

WOODY GUTHRIE ■

Deportee (Plane Wreck at Los Gatos)

Although "globalization" is often thought of as a new phenomenon, the colonizing of the Americas and the history of the United States can be seen as the product of the early global economy, as Europeans exported raw materials from the lands they conquered. As European colonies grew and the United States was formed, a network of global economic exchanges, from fur trading to cotton to the traffic in enslaved workers, fueled the expansion of the new nation. And just as American companies operate factories around the world, so the United States still imports workers from around the world, whether legally or illegally.

U.S. agriculture is especially dependent on the importation of farm workers from countries like Mexico. In the 1940s, the United States and Mexico set up a "bracero" program that allowed Mexican agricultural workers to cross the border as temporary visitors; the program was discontinued in the early 1960s. Another 1940s program said that foreign farm workers in the United States illegally could apply for work visas after being deported. Some U.S. farm owners began deliberately "deporting" their Mexican workers in order to bring them back with these work permits. Although both programs allowed some poor Mexican workers the ability to work in the United States legally, these workers had little power and few rights and were subject to exploitation.

In early 1948, the legendary folk singer and labor activist Woody Guthrie read a newspaper account of a plane crash in California that killed 28 Mexican farm workers being deported to Mexico and was inspired to write a song in tribute to these men and in protest of the treatment of seasonal migrant farm workers.

The crops are all in and the peaches are rott'ning,
The oranges piled in their creosote dumps;
They're flying 'em back to the Mexican border
To pay all their money to wade back again

CHORUS:
Goodbye to my Juan, goodbye, Rosalita,
Adios mis amigos, Jesus y Maria;
You won't have your names when you ride the big airplane,
All they will call you will be "deportees"

My father's own father, he waded that river,
They took all the money he made in his life;
My brothers and sisters come working the fruit trees,
And they rode the truck till they took down and died.

Some of us are illegal, and some are not wanted,
Our work contract's out and we have to move on;
Six hundred miles to that Mexican border,
They chase us like outlaws, like rustlers, like thieves.

We died in your hills, we died in your deserts,
We died in your valleys and died on your plains.
We died 'neath your trees and we died in your bushes,
Both sides of the river, we died just the same.

The sky plane caught fire over Los Gatos Canyon,
A fireball of lightning, and shook all our hills,
Who are all these friends, all scattered like dry leaves?
The radio says, "They are just deportees"

Is this the best way we can grow our big orchards?
Is this the best way we can grow our good fruit?
To fall like dry leaves to rot on my topsoil
And be called by no name except "deportees"? ■

Working with the Text

1. Some of the lines in the song are from the point of view of one of the men being deported, and some are from the point of view of the songwriter. Identify which lines are which and to whom you think each speaker is addressing his words. How does Guthrie's mix of these points of view affect your understanding of the song? How do you understand Guthrie's rhetorical strategy?

2. Based on your reading of the lyrics, whom do you see Guthrie as holding responsible for the plane crash? One way of exploring this question is by looking at his use of pronouns in the song. In the fourth verse, for example, the speaker says, "we died in your deserts," and the fifth verse says that the plane crash "shook all our hills." How do you understand who is meant by "your" in "we died in your hills" and "our" in "shook all our hills"? What are the possibilities? Are these the same groups of people?

3. The final verse is composed of rhetorical questions: "Is this the best way we can grow our big orchards?/Is this the best way we can grow our good fruit?" It seems clear that the speaker is asking listeners to consider alternative work arrangements and practices. Based on your initial reading of the lyrics, brainstorm some possible alternatives. You can then use the ideas as the starting point of longer research projects that investigate the question of

agricultural labor and various proposals for dealing with some of the problems described in the song.

4. Locate and listen to a recorded version of this song, either online or on a CD. What emotional and rhetorical emphases are created by the melody and the way the song is sung?

Working with Connections

1. Compare Guthrie's "Deportee (Plane Wreck at Los Gatos)" with Lalo Guerrero's "Corrido de César Chávez" (in Chapter 6, Work and Diversity) celebrating the life of César Chávez, the leader of the United Farm Workers, who focused on improving the working conditions of both Mexican-American and Mexican farm workers. What similarities and differences in audience do you see? How do these similarities and differences affect the tone of the lyrics and the overall rhetorical strategy?

2. Learn more about the life of Woody Guthrie and write about why you think he was particularly interested in writing about this tragedy. What other songs did he write that conveyed similar ideas and themes? What connections can you draw between Guthrie's background in the Oklahoma farm country and the lives of the workers he wrote about in this song?

MICHAEL MOORE

Interview with Phil Knight, CEO of Nike, Inc.

In his 1997 documentary The Big One, *the journalist and filmmaker Michael Moore interviewed the founder and Chief Executive Officer of Nike, Phil Knight, about labor practices in the Indonesian factories that manufacture Nike athletic shoes. Knight had invited Moore to interview him after hearing Moore on a Portland, Oregon talk radio program. Over the course of their conversation, Moore challenged Knight on a variety of issues related to globalization, including why Nike does not make shoes in the United States and what responsibility a corporation has for the safety and well-being of its overseas workers.*

On his web site publicizing the film, Moore includes the following transcripts of portions of the interview with Knight that were not included in the film, in part in response to charges from Nike that Knight's views had been misrepresented by Moore. In these transcripts, Knight defends the use of 14-year-old workers against Moore's arguments that these young people should be in schools rather than in factories. The exchange is as much a debate as an interview, and both Moore and Knight are aware that they are being filmed. As they attempt to counter one another's positions, they are also making appeals to the viewing audience.

In addition to The Big One, *Michael Moore is also well known as the maker of the provocative documentaries* Roger and Me *and* Bowling for Columbine. Bowling for Columbine *received the Academy Award for Best Documentary feature in 2003.*

Michael Moore: When I left you the two things I asked for, two very simple things I asked for is that you build a factory in Flint and provide some jobs for the people there, the people that you said would not want to make shoes. And the second thing was to raise the minimum age. That I said that the watchdog groups said there are 12-year-olds who work in your factories and you said, 'no, they're 14,' and you said, 'well, I've never really thought about that issue.' Have you thought about it?

Phil Knight: I have thought about it.

Michael Moore: And what do you want to do about it?

Phil Knight: I think that it's . . . I think it's, I don't wanna say stupid, but I'll say stupid because essentially what it is it's that somebody—

Michael Moore: What's stupid?

Phil Knight: The idea of raising the minimum age from 14 to 18. It's somebody sitting in New York City saying this is what's good for the Indonesians or the Vietnamese. Basically, there is a United Nations standard and there is a standard in each of these countries and it says the age for somebody to work is 14 and that basically is trying to balance the needs of a family in those countries, which they know better than we know, sitting over here, 10,000 miles away. If you want to take that argument to the extreme, why don't you raise the minimum age to 25 and then you'll have a whole nation of PhDs. It isn't just necessarily a situation where you say, 'OK, a guy has to be 18 before he goes to work in a shoe factory, that therefore he's gonna go to school.' It just isn't that simple.

Michael Moore: But a kid is a kid is a kid. A 14-year-old here is a 14-year-old there in terms of their body development, their growing up. They shouldn't be working full-time in a manufacturing facility.

Phil Knight: Well, I mean, tell it to the United Nations.

Michael Moore: No, I'm telling it to you. See you, you're actually bigger than the United Nations in this case, because you own the factories and you could actually make this decision. As we sit here.

Phil Knight: But basically they have certain economic needs as well. I mean, one of the arguments, I mean basically when we said 'OK, that we're going to enforce the United Nations standard in Pakistan,' they said 'well, these families will be economically deprived.' So obviously there's a balance that has to be worked out between that and the balance that really is consistent all through the underdeveloped world and with the Untied Nations standard is that a person can go to work when they're 14.

Michael Moore: But is that right?

Phil Knight: I think so, I think you—

Michael Moore: Do you have kids?

Phil Knight: Yes.

Michael Moore: Would you want your kid working full time at 14 years old?

Phil Knight: Well, but—

Michael Moore: In a manufacturing facility?

Phil Knight: But you're trying to impose, and this is where the problem always comes. You're trying to impose US standards in a different part of the world, which is terribly different than what it is in the United States.

Michael Moore: We do that all the time. Did you think that apartheid was wrong in South Africa?

Phil Knight: But of course.

Michael Moore: Of course. And that was imposing our standard because we believe that black citizens should have equal rights.

Phil Knight: That's right. But you have, you have a situation in the underdeveloped world where they—basically in the United States it wasn't always you had to be 18 to get a job. But basically you know in the early years of this country, that 14-year-olds were working. So basically it's position in terms of economic development and what the standard should be and I think the United Nations and that the governments all those governments in those countries, they're not all bad and they basically have set the standard at 14.

Michael Moore: And you're gonna stick with that?

Phil Knight: Yes, we are.

Michael Moore: But you're in charge, you're the boss—

Phil Knight: Yeah, I'm in charge of it, basically—

Michael Moore: Just tell 'em, no one under 16, just like our shoe factories. Just tell em. You're Phil Knight.

Phil Knight: Well, actually, I think that over, within a fairly short period of time you'll see some of that, but it won't happen, it won't happen over the next six months probably.

Michael Moore: But you're committed.

Phil Knight: No, no, we want good labor practices in all these countries. We try to be the best citizen we can be.

Michael Moore: So you're telling me now that you're committed to not having people work in your factories under the age of 16?

Phil Knight: That's true in the shoe factories in Indonesia . . .

Dusty Kidd: (*Nike's labor relations chief*) We are one of 20 or 30 customers in our apparel factories, so we can't dictate to them nearly to the extent—

Michael Moore: Is it safe to say that's your goal? Is it safe to say that's your goal—to not have people—

Phil Knight: We can impose that and will do that in those apparel factories that we basically have the dominant position in. But we can't do that when we're just a minor buyer.

Michael Moore: But, anything that you control, you're going to, you're goal—

Phil Knight: In Indonesia, in Indonesia, we're moving towards age 16. ■

Working with the Text

1. This interview raises the question of responsibility. Who or what is to blame for the fact that 14-year-olds are working in shoe factories? Should we even be concerned about this situation? Make two lists showing how Michael Moore and Phil Knight each would respond to these questions. With whom do you most agree and why?

2. In addition to trying to convince one another, both Moore and Knight are also making their cases to the larger audience that will hear or read this interview. Based on their responses, speculate about which particular listeners or readers each man is trying to persuade and why. Conversely, discuss how you think different groups of listeners or readers would respond to their interchange. These groups might include factory workers (both in the US and Indonesia), consumers of Nike products, investors, and teenagers (and of course these can be overlapping groups as well).

3. Watch a video of *The Big One* to see the full interview sequence involving Moore and Knight. What larger issues related to the globalizing economy does the film bring up? What do you find to be Moore's most and least effective interview and argument strategies? What opinion of Phil Knight are you left with and why?

Working with Connections

1. How do the arguments Knight and Moore make about the minimum age for factory work compare with those made by William Greider, Nicholas Kristoff, and Sheryl WuDunn in the Debate Over Sweatshops section? Where do you stand on the question of whether different contexts and social situations make it difficult to compare the experiences of a 14-year-old in Indonesia and one in the United States versus Moore's assertion that "a kid is a kid" and that all 14-year-olds share similar developmental needs?

2. Working individually or in groups, research what the current situation is in regards to Nike's (or any other international company's) use of factory labor in third world countries. How has the situation changed? What are the current arguments and debate? What trends do you see developing?

Media Images

■

Undocumented Workers Lost in the World Trade Center

Most of the approximately three thousand people killed in the attack on the World Trade Center and Pentagon were on the job at the time they died, from stockbrokers to firefighters and police officers, from the airline pilots and flight crews to secretarial staffs, from military personnel to the servers and kitchen help working in the restaurants. As the name of the buildings destroyed on September 11 indicate, New York is a center of the global economy as well, and the workers who died that day came from countries all around the world, including many undocumented workers who make up a crucial part of the economic infrastructure of New York. These workers, mostly though not exclusively men, traveled to New York alone or in some cases with their families, and they worked making deliveries, busing tables in restaurants, cleaning and maintaining the buildings, preparing food, and doing other jobs in the World Trade Center and in the surrounding neighborhoods.

For people in Mexico and throughout Latin America who had families working in New York, September 11 brought silence, fear, and dread. In their attempts to find out what happened to their loved ones, they face obstacles such as the lack of employment records, official papers and visas, and even DNA samples. This photo of Felix Martinez from the New York Times *magazine along with her story illustrates how a tragedy that has brought people together across borders of nation and culture has also revealed barriers that still exist in the globalizing economy.*

As preparation for learning about Felix Martinez, write about the feelings created in you by the events of September 11. Next, focus your exploration by writing and discussing the World Trade Center attacks as a workplace tragedy.

Felix Martinez: "My husband Jose worked in one of those very huge buildings. He called my cousin in Chicago when the planes hit. He tried to talk, but my cousin heard an explosion. Two days later, I left my four children and went to look for Jose, thinking New York was like here, a small town with shacks. I don't even understand how I did it. I can't read or write. I went to a coyote, and he crossed me over. Once I was in New York, I met a woman who helped me. She was from Puebla, near me, and said I could live with her because she didn't have a husband, either. She told me that it was going to be difficult to find Jose because people here don't know each other, so I told her I wanted a job so I could make money to return to my country. My daughter, Wendy Daniels, was born on Jan. 25 in Brooklyn. Now we're back home in Zaragoza. The baby makes me feel closer to him, but it's not the same."
(Photograph by Jennifer Szymaszek)

Working with the Text

1. Before reading the caption underneath the photo of Martinez, write about the thoughts, feelings, and reactions produced by this image that originally appeared as part of a collection entitled,

"Registering the 9/11 Dead: Mexican families left behind by the undocumented workers who died in the World Trade Center." How does the picture relate to your preconceptions or associations with terms such as *undocumented workers*? How familiar do you feel you are with the experiences of undocumented workers? How does this familiarity or lack of familiarity affect your initial reaction to this photograph?

2. After reading the caption, how did your thoughts and feelings about the photograph change? What ideas and impressions were reinforced, and what were altered? Use your reactions to questions one and two to consider why the photographer Jennifer Szymaszek composed the photograph in the way she did. What reactions do you think she was hoping to create in the viewers? How does the information in the caption and the specific way in which the caption is written work to create an overall impression?

3. Why do you think the plight of the undocumented workers in the World Trade Center tragedy has not received greater media attention than it has? What do you think the most effective strategies would be for fostering greater U.S. public awareness and attention to the situation described here?

4. The story of the Martinez family presented here evokes the hopes and dreams of undocumented workers (for example, the desire to earn enough money to send children to college) as well as a sense of powerlessness at not being able to receive any final word of what happened to the workers lost. Use the example of the Martinez family as the start of a longer research project on the fate of undocumented workers in the World Trade Center tragedy. In what ways do their stories help us understand and illustrate the debate over the positive and negative affects of globalization?

THE WORK OF WRITING/WRITING AS WORK: LANGUAGE AND THE GLOBAL ECONOMY

Language and communication issues are at the center of the global economy. As more and more people around the world become economically interdependent on one another, the challenges and opportunities represented by the need to talk and write to each other in a multilingual, multicultural world will only increase. The projects described following recognize two seemingly contradictory yet parallel developments related to language use in the global economy.

On the one hand, as corporations become global rather than national, they find themselves dealing with and employing people who speak hundreds of different languages. Closer to home, the United States itself remains a multilingual society, with newcomers arriving every day who bring their own language and cultural traditions with them. On the other hand, as almost any experience surfing the web will demonstrate, English is increasingly becoming the language of world business and trade, and while it is not the only language spoken by Americans, it remains the most widely used.

The common link in these two developments is that the necessity and advantages of knowing more than one language have never been greater, and schools of all kinds, especially colleges and universities, are natural centers for helping to meet these needs. As writing students studying the power and complexity of language use, your developing skills and knowledge can help with this educational project.

Project One: Encouraging the Study of a Second Language

Depending on your college or university, you may or may not have a language requirement. Whether studying a second language is mandatory or not, not every student will see the need or understand the usefulness of learning another language. As a writing class project, review the promotional and informational materials (brochures, web sites, catalog copy, etc.) about language instruction at your school and consult with language instruction faculty about revising or producing texts written by students for students making the case for the importance and usefulness of studying another language. In keeping with the topic of this chapter, you may wish to focus primarily on the work and career benefits of language instruction, always a powerful motive for college students, but you need not limit yourself to them. As you work on the project, consider the following issues and subprojects:

- Survey students on campus to learn more about their attitudes toward studying a language. For the students who enjoy or persist at learning languages, what are the most powerful motives and incentives? For students who resist language study, what are their primary objections? What benefits would they find most persuasive?

- Taking your local campus climate into account is crucial in devising your rhetorical strategy. For example, how language diverse is your campus student body and surrounding community? Are students likely to hear several different languages during the course of a typical day, or do they seldom encounter a language other than English? How many students are bi- or multilingual before they arrive on campus? Which languages other than English are of most importance in the local area?

- Are students on campus planning to stay in the local area after graduation? How many come from other areas of the country or the world? How do the answers to these questions relate to the most popular choice of second-language study on campus?

- What would be the most effective ways to deliver your materials to students? Via the Internet? At a campus orientation? At cultural or arts events? Through classroom visits?

Project Two: Volunteering in an ESL Program

While preconceptions persist that non-English-speaking immigrants to the United States are reluctant to learn English, the reality is that newcomers to the United States acquire English-language skills more rapidly today than in the past. Often, programs offering instruction in English as a Second Language, whether at schools or community centers, struggle to meet the demand of those wishing to learn or improve their language skills. Working with your instructor or campus service-learning representative, locate ESL programs in your area that need volunteer tutors. (The National Institute for Literacy and Partners has a web site that can help you locate ESL programs in your area. Go to http://www.literacydirectory.org/default.asp.) As you become involved in volunteering, you will discover:

- Tutoring is a skill that you can learn and improve.
- Helping others study language is a great way to develop your own understanding of language.
- Work in ESL education can be an interesting career choice.

CHAPTER 9

Work in the Information Age/The Future of Work

In 1888, the American writer Edward Bellamy wrote a novel entitled *Looking Backward* that imagined the United States in the year 2000. In Bellamy's utopian vision, he guessed at technological innovations such as radio broadcasts and even credit cards, but he also described a world where the problems of poverty and hunger had been solved, where people worked, lived, and ate together in harmony under the leadership of a benevolent government that had evolved beyond politics and conflict. To be fair, Bellamy meant his novel to be as much a plea for how the world of the future should be as a prediction. Since Bellamy's time, however, the project of predicting the future has remained a source of interest and fascination, and not just in the realm of fiction and entertainment.

The visions of Bellamy and other writers about the future, whether artists, scholars, political figures, or experts of various kinds, are a response to the constant change—social, technological, and economic—that has defined modern life for the last two centuries. While none of us is sure what the world will be like in ten, twenty, or thirty years, we are sure that it will be different in crucial ways from the world we have now. Nowhere is this truer than in the world of work. At the turn of the twentieth century, the largest percentage of American workers were still involved in agricultural labor of some kind, and more people lived in rural rather than urban areas. At the turn of the present century, the situation has almost reversed. Most people in the United States live in cities or, more likely, suburban areas surrounding cities, and fewer and fewer people are involved in farming-related work. Where only a tiny percentage of Americans attended college in 1900, by 2000 a college degree of some kind had come to be seen by many as crucial to career success and mobility.

In addition, the computer revolution of the last twenty years has suggested to many people that we may be at the dawn of a radical change in the economic structure of society similar in its impact to the industrial revolution of the nineteenth century: the rise of the Information Age. You've probably heard speculation, for example, about how the Internet will change our lives; such predictions range from the modest (we'll be able to buy plane tickets more easily) to the radical (the Internet will completely reshape how we understand work and our place in society). Whoever is right, it does seem clear that computer technology and the Internet culture it has created are here to stay, and that they will become an increasingly important part of the world of work. The texts in this chapter explore some ideas about what work will be like in the next twenty-five years or so. For some of you, this will be the time you embark on what you hope to be your lifetime careers; for others, this will be a world that may make you wonder about how your existing skills and experiences will serve you in the second half of your working lives. In any case, we all have a vested interest in the world of the future.

Before you begin reading, prepare by responding to these exercises:

1. When you think of the world of work over the next twenty-five years, what dominant changes come to mind? What kinds of skills do you think it will be most important to have?

2. How would you define the Information Age? In what ways has it affected your life so far? Does it make you feel more hopeful or anxious about the future?

3. Think about your current career plans or possible career plans. How do you think these kinds of work will be affected by information technology? How might they change over the next two decades?

4. Interview a parent or grandparent about the biggest changes in the world of work they have experienced in their lifetimes. What surprised them the most? Which changes do they feel were for the better? For the worse? How well do they think their educations prepared them for these changes?

Foundational Readings

NICHOLAS NEGROPONTE ▬

An Age of Optimism

More than being simply another new technology, computers and the Internet are often described as creating a whole new lifestyle or way of being. While the increasing pervasiveness of computer culture intimidates many people, others see in what is called "the digital age" the promise of freedom and human empowerment. Some of the most enthusiastic proponents of computer culture compare it to the Renaissance in terms of the impact it will have on society and its potential for benefit.

Nicholas Negroponte has written extensively about the promises of the digital age, most famously in Being Digital, *his analysis of the many ways computers and computer culture are changing the way we work and interact with one another. In the epilogue to that book, Negroponte offers his reasons for feeling optimistic about the future benefits of the digital age, while also recognizing the costs involved. While he discusses the economic impact of the digital age, he points to the changes in attitude and worldview that the Internet may promote as the main reasons for his optimism.*

Nicholas Negroponte teaches media technology and directs the Media Laboratory at the Massachusetts Institute of Technology.

I am optimistic by nature. However, every technology or gift of science has a dark side. Being digital is no exception.

The next decade will see cases of intellectual property abuse and invasion of our privacy. We will experience digital vandalism, software piracy, and data thievery. Worst of all, we will witness the loss of many jobs to wholly automated systems, which will soon change the white-collar workplace to the same degree that it has already transformed the factory floor. The notion of lifetime employment at one job has already started to disappear.

The radical transformation of the nature of our job markets, as we work less with atoms and more with bits, will happen at just about the same time the 2 billion–strong labor force of India and China starts to come on-line (literally). A self-employed software designer in Peoria will be competing with his or her counterpart in Pohang. A digital typographer in Madrid will do the same with one in Madras. American companies are already outsourcing hardware development and software production to Russia and India, not to find cheap manual labor but to secure a highly skilled intellectual force seemingly prepared to work harder, faster, and in a more disciplined fashion than those in our own country.

As the business world globalizes and the Internet grows, we will start to see a seamless digital workplace. Long before political harmony and long before the GATT talks can reach agreement on the tariff and trade of atoms (the right to sell Evian water in California), bits will be borderless, stored and manipulated with absolutely no respect to geopolitical boundaries. In fact, time zones will probably play a bigger role in our digital future than trade zones. I can imagine some software projects that literally move around the world from east to west on a twenty-four-hour cycle, from person to person or from group to group, one working as the other sleeps. Microsoft will need to add London and Tokyo offices for software development in order to produce on three shifts.

As we move toward such a digital world, an entire sector of the population will be or feel disenfranchised. When a fifty-year-old steelworker loses his job, unlike his twenty-five-year-old son, he may have no digital resilience at all. When a modern-day secretary loses his job, at least he may be conversant with the digital world and have transferrable skills.

Bits are not edible; in that sense they cannot stop hunger. Computers are not moral; they cannot resolve complex issues like the rights to life and to death. But being digital, nevertheless, does give much cause for optimism. Like a force of nature, the digital age cannot be denied or stopped. It has four very powerful qualities that will result in its ultimate triumph: decentralizing, globalizing, harmonizing, and empowering.

The decentralizing effect of being digital can be felt no more strongly than in commerce and in the computer industry itself. The so-called management information systems (MIS) czar, who used to reign over a glass-enclosed and air-conditioned mausoleum, is an emperor with no clothes, almost extinct. Those who survive are usually doing so because they outrank anybody able to fire them, and the company's board of directors is out of touch or asleep or both.

Thinking Machines Corporation, a great and imaginative supercomputer company started by electrical engineering genius Danny Hillis, disappeared after ten years. In that short space of time it introduced the world to massively parallel computer architectures. Its demise did not occur because of mismanagement or sloppy engineering of their so-called Connection Machine. It vanished because parallelism could be decentralized; the very same kind of massively parallel architectures have suddenly become possible by threading together low-cost, mass-produced personal computers.

While this was not good news for Thinking Machines, it is an important message to all of us, both literally and metaphorically. It means the enterprise of the future can meet its computer needs in a new and scalable way by populating its organization with personal computers that, when needed, can work in unison to crunch on computationally intensive problems. Computers will literally work both for individuals and for groups. I see the same decentralized mind-set growing in our society, driven by young citizenry in the digital world. The traditional centralist view of life will become a thing of the past.

The nation-state itself is subject to tremendous change and globalization. Governments fifty years from now will be both larger and smaller. Europe finds itself dividing itself into smaller ethnic entities while trying to unite economically. The forces of nationalism make it too easy to be cynical and dismiss any broad-stroke attempt at world unification. But in the digital world, previously impossible solutions become viable.

Today, when 20 percent of the world consumes 80 percent of its resources, when a quarter of us have an acceptable standard of living and three-quarters don't, how can this divide possibly come together? While the politicians struggle with the baggage of history, a new generation is emerging from the digital landscape free of many of the old prejudices. These kids are released from the limitation of geographic proximity as the sole basis of friendship, collaboration, play, and neighborhood. Digital technology can be a natural force drawing people into greater world harmony.

The harmonizing effect of being digital is already apparent as previously partitioned disciplines and enterprises find themselves collaborating, not competing. A previously missing common language emerges, allowing people to understand across boundaries. Kids at school today experience the opportunity to look at the same thing from many perspectives. A computer program, for example, can be seen simultaneously as a set of computer instructions or as concrete poetry formed by the indentations in the text of the program. What kids learn very quickly is that to know a program is to know it from many perspectives, not just one.

But more than anything, my optimism comes from the empowering nature of being digital. The access, the mobility, and the ability to effect change are what will make the future so different from the present. The information superhighway may be mostly hype today, but it is an understatement about tomorrow. It will exist beyond people's wildest predictions. As children appropriate a global information resource, and as they discover that only adults need learner's permits, we are bound to find new hope and dignity in places where very little existed before.

My optimism is not fueled by an anticipated invention or discovery. Finding a cure for cancer and AIDS, finding an acceptable way to control population, or inventing a machine that can breathe our air and drink our oceans and excrete unpolluted forms of each are dreams that may or may not come about. Being digital is different. We are not waiting on any invention. It is here. It is now. It is almost genetic in its nature, in that each generation will become more digital than the preceding one.

The control bits of that digital future are more than ever before in the hands of the young. Nothing could make me happier. ■

Working with the Text

1. Negroponte begins his epilogue entitled "An Age of Optimism" with a discussion of some of the costs and damage associated with the rise of the digital age. What are these costs? Who are the people most likely to be affected positively and negatively by the advent of Internet technology in the world and in the workplace?

2. Negroponte describes the digital age as having a "decentralizing" effect on business, social, and political relationships. Explore his ideas about decentralization by first defining what you think he means by the concept in your own words. Next, apply the concept to a kind of work or social institution, such as school, a community group, or even the family, that you are familiar with. In what ways could these activities or institutions be further decentralized? What do you see as the positive and negative effects? To expand this project further, do research to find examples of the kinds of decentralization you are thinking and writing about.

3. Much of Negroponte's optimism for the future rests on the effects of "being digital" on young people. For example, he suggests that young people growing up in the digital age will be "free of many of the old prejudices" and will "experience the opportunity to look at the same thing from different perspectives" because of the

impact of the Internet and computer culture. Test the validity of Negroponte's ideas by talking with younger people and children. How "digital" are they? To what extent have their computer-related experiences produced the effects that Negroponte describes? Do you find yourself sharing or qualifying Negroponte's optimism?

Working with Connections

1. How are or aren't the kinds of changes computer technology is bringing to college education related to the positive effects of the digital age that Negroponte describes? Compare Negroponte's essay with the discussions in Focus on the Future of College Work: The Role of Technology in Higher Education (from Chapter 3, School as Work/The Work of School). In what ways does distance learning, for example, positively embody the qualities of "decentralizing, globalizing, harmonizing, and empowering"? In what ways might distance learning frustrate these goals?

2. How well does Jonathan Lebed, the young man who used the Internet to trade stocks and stock tips in Michael Lewis's "Jonathan Lebed's Extracurricular Activities" exemplify the optimistic qualities that Negroponte sees in young people growing up in the digital age? In what ways does Lebed's experience provide a note of caution?

LYNNELL HANCOCK ————————————————————— ■

The Haves and the Have-Nots

It has become a truism to say that computer skills and Internet savvy are key workplace skills in the twenty-first century. But computer technology is expensive. Even though electronic goods tend to become relatively cheaper over time, a home computer system can still represent a month's wages or more to many families. What is more, given how rapidly computer hardware changes, even a state-of-the-art system will most likely be obsolete before a year is through. Add to these expenses the cost of software and Internet subscription fees, and the result is a technology growing in social importance that is still out of the financial reach of millions of Americans.

In "The Haves and the Have-Nots," LynNell Hancock explores what has been described as the "digital divide" between those families and schools who can afford computer technology and those who cannot. The developments that Hancock explores suggest that rather than increasing access to information and empowering its users, computer technology may also be reinforcing divisions of social class and social privilege.

LynNell Hancock teaches journalism at the Columbia University Graduate School of Journalism and has written as a reporter for many publications. She is the author of Hands to Work: The Stories of Three Families Racing the Welfare Clock. *"The Haves and the Have-Nots" was originally published in* Newsweek.

Aaron Smith is a teenager on the techno track. In America's breathless race to achieve information nirvana, the senior from Issaquah, a middle-class district east of Seattle, has the hardware and hookups to run the route. Aaron and 600 of his fellow students at Liberty High School have their own electronic-mail address. They can log on to the Internet every day, joining only about 15 percent of America's schoolchildren who can now forage on their own for documents in European libraries or chat with experts around the world. At home, the 18-year-old e-mails his teachers, when he is not prowling the World Wide Web to track down snowboarding conditions on his favorite Cascade mountain passes. "We have the newest, greatest thing," Aaron says.

On the opposite coast, in Boston's South End, Marilee Colon scoots a mouse along a grimy Apple pad, playing a Kid Pix game on an old black-and-white terminal. It's Wednesday at a neighborhood center, Marilee's only chance to poke around on a computer. Her mom, a secretary at the center, can't afford one in their home. Marilee's public-school classroom doesn't have any either. The 10-year-old from Roxbury depends on the United South End Settlement Center and its less than state-of-the-art Macs and IBMs perched on mismatched desks. Marilee has never heard of the Internet. She is thrilled to double-click on the stick of dynamite and watch her teddy-bear creation fly off the screen. "It's fun blowing it up," says the delicate fifth grader, twisting a brown ponytail around her finger.

Certainly Aaron was born with a stack of statistical advantages over Marilee. He is white and middle class and lives with two working parents who both have higher degrees. Economists say the swift pace of high-tech advances will only drive a further wedge between these youngsters. To have an edge in America's job search, it used to be enough to be well educated. Now, say the experts, it's critical to be digital. Employees who are adept at technology "earn roughly 10 to 15 percent higher pay," according to Alan Krueger, chief economist for the U.S. Labor Department. Some argue that this pay gap has less to do with technology than with industries' efforts to streamline their work forces during the recession. . . . Still, nearly every American business from Wall Street to McDonald's requires some computer knowledge. Taco Bell is modeling its cash registers after Nintendo controls, according to Rosabeth Moss Kanter. The "haves," says the Harvard Business School professor, will be able to communicate around the globe. The "have-nots" will be consigned to the "rural backwater of the information society."

Like it or not, America is a land of inequities. And technology, despite its potential to level the social landscape, is not yet blind to race, wealth and age.

The richer the family, the more likely it is to own and use a computer, according to 1993 census data. White families are three times as likely as blacks or Hispanics to have computers at home. Seventy-four percent of Americans making more than $75,000 own at least one terminal, but not even one third of all Americans own computers. A small fraction—only about 7 percent—of students' families subscribe to online services that transform the plastic terminal into a telecommunications port.

At least in public schools, the computer gap is closing. More than half the students have some kind of computer, even if it's obsolete. But schools with the biggest concentration of poor children have the least equipment, according to Jeanne Hayes of Quality Education Data. Ten years ago schools had one computer for every 125 children, according to Hayes. Today that figure is one for 12.

Though the gap is slowly closing, technology is advancing so fast, and at such huge costs, that it's nearly impossible for cash-strapped municipalities to catch up.

Seattle is taking bids for one company to wire each ZIP code with fiber optics, so everyone—rich or poor—can hook up to video, audio and other multimedia services. Estimated cost: $500 million. Prosperous Montgomery Country, Md., has an $81 million plan to put every classroom online. Next door, the District of Columbia public schools have the same ambitious plan but less than $1 million in the budget to accomplish it.

New ideas—and demands—for the schools are announced every week. The '90s populist slogan is no longer "A chicken in every pot" but "A computer on every desk." Vice President Al Gore has appealed to the telecommunications industry to cut costs and wire all schools, a task Education Secretary Richard Riley estimates will cost $10 billion. House Speaker Newt Gingrich stumbled into the discussion with a suggestion that every poor family get a laptop from Uncle Sam. Rep. Ed Markey wants a computer sitting on every school desk within 10 years. "The opportunities are enormous," Markey says.

Enormous, yes, but who is going to pay for them? Some successful school projects have relied heavily on the kindness of strangers. In Union City, N.J., school officials renovated the guts of a 100-year-old building five years ago, overhauling the curriculum and wiring every classroom in Christopher Columbus Middle School for high tech. Bell Atlantic provided wiring free and agreed to give each student in last year's seventh-grade class a computer to take home. Even parents, most of whom are South American immigrants, can use their children's computers to e-mail the principal in Spanish. He used translation software and answers them electronically. The results have shown up in test scores. In a school where 80 percent of the children are poor, reading, math, attendance and writing scores are now the best in the district. "We believe that technology will improve our everyday life," says principal Bob Fazio. "And that other schools will piggyback and learn from us."

Still, for every Christopher Columbus, there are far more schools like Jordan High School in South-Central Los Angeles. Only 30 computers in the school's lab, most of them 12 to 15 years old, are available for Jordan's 2,000 students, many of whom live in the nearby Jordan Downs housing project. "I am teaching these kids on a system that will do them no good in the real world when they get out there," says Robert Doornbos, Jordan's computer-science instructor. "The school system has not made these kids' getting on the Information Highway a priority."

Donkey Kong: Having enough terminals to go around is one problem. But another important question is what the equipment is used for. Not much beyond rote drills and word processing, according to Linda Roberts, a technology consultant for the U.S. Department of Education. A 1992 National Assessment of Educational Progress survey found that most fourth-grade math students were using computers to play games, "like Donkey Kong." By the eighth grade, most math students weren't using them at all.

Many school officials think that access to the Internet could become the most effective equalizer in the educational lives of students. With a modem attached, even most ancient terminals can connect children in rural Mississippi to universities in Asia. A Department of Education report last week found that 35 percent of schools have at least one computer with a modem. But only half the schools let students use it. Apparently administrators and teachers are hogging the Info Highway for themselves.

There is another gap to be considered. Not just between rich and poor, but between the young and the used-to-be-young. Of the 100 million Americans who use computers at home, school or work, nearly 60 percent are 17 or younger, according to the census. Children, for the most part, rule cyberspace, leaving the over-40 set to browse through the almanac.

The gap between the generations may be the most important, says MIT guru Nicholas Negroponte, author of the new book "Being Digital." Adults are the true "digitally homeless, the needy," he says. In other words, adults like Debbie Needleman, 43, an office manager at Wallpaper Warehouse in Natick, Mass., are wary of the digital age. "I really don't mind that the rest of the world passes me by as long as I can still earn a living," she says.

These aging choose-nots become a more serious issue when they are teachers in schools. Even if schools manage to acquire state-of-the-art equipment, there is no guarantee that trained adults will be available to understand them. This is something that tries Aaron Smith's patience. "A lot of my teachers are quite illiterate," says Aaron, the fully equipped Issaqua teenager. "You have to explain it to them real slow to make sure they understand everything." Fast or slow, Marilee Colon, Roxbury's fifth-grade computer lover, would like her chance to understand everything too. ■

Working with the Text

1. Hancock's article was originally published in 1995. How have the statistics she quoted then about the extent of computer use changed?

2. Hancock's story points out that many schools have limited and/or outdated computer resources, and that even in schools with some kind of computers available to students, they may be used only for "rote" exercises or to play computer games. How "wired" are the schools in your community? Contact several of them in different areas to compare and contrast student access to computers. If possible, travel to a local school to observe how computers are used in the classroom.

3. What is the main evidence that Hancock uses to persuade us that the digital divide she describes is a serious problem? What did you find to be the most effective examples and statistics and why?

Working with Connections

1. Hancock quotes Nicholas Negroponte in her article on the age gap in computer familiarity and experience. In his "Age of Optimism," Negroponte argues that a familiarity with computer culture among young people offers hope for the future. How does the digital divide described by Hancock affect Negroponte's argument? How could you combine information from Negroponte's and Hancock's essays to craft your own argument about what should be done about the digital divide and why?

2. Jean Anyon's essay "Social Class and the Hidden Curriculum of Work" (from Chapter 3, School as Work/The Work of School) was written largely before the rise in importance of personal computers and computing skills. Use Hancock's essay to update the concerns expressed by Anyon. Beyond the lack of financial resources, how well or poorly do the kinds of curricula described by Anyon address the differences in experience and skills that Hancock examines in her article?

PAULA SPAN ■

The On-Line Mystique

Think of the stereotype of the "computer nerd" and what image comes to mind? Chances are, whatever other specific details you pictured, your nerd was probably male. From Bill Gates to the Lone Gunmen on TV's The X-Files, we are surrounded by media images that reinforce the idea of the computer and Internet as largely male domains and, judging by the evidence cited by journalist Paula Span in her article "The On-Line Mystique," there are statistics that suggest this perception may have a lot of truth to it. On the other hand, proponents of the Internet such as Nicholas Negroponte have claimed that "a new generation is emerging from the digital landscape free of many of the old prejudices," including traditional ideas about gender roles and identities. After all, everyone is equal in cyberspace, or at least that was the promise.

In her article written for The Washington Post *in 1994, Span explores some possible reasons why a gender divide has persisted in the digital age. Recognizing the importance of computer skills and familiarity in the world and workplace of the twenty-first century, Span goes on to consider the prospects and obstacles for greater gender equity in cyberspace.*

The love affair between men and computers was something I knew about but didn't really get, until that morning at the local coffee shop. My pal Pam and I were gabbing in the front booth when in walked Michael, a friend and journalist about to take a leave from his newspaper to write a book. His first step, naturally, was to sink a significant chunk of his book advance into a shiny new computer. It was a beauty: worked faster than a speeding locomotive, boasted many megabytes of RAM, brewed cappuccino, etc.

Pam and I exchanged glances. This sounded familiar. She had written several books on an Apple so antediluvian that the company no longer manufactures it, and abandoned it only when it got damaged by clumsy movers. Yet her husband was about to invest in a pricey new CD-ROM rig, making unconvincing noises about how useful their daughter would find it for schoolwork. My own husband, as it happened, was also taking advantage of a new work assignment and plunging computer prices to replace the system he'd purchased just two years before, though his new machine wasn't as powerful as Michael's. ("Mike could fly to Chicago with that thing" he would later remark, wistfully.)

More speed. Better performance. With names like Quadra and Performa, computers even sound like cars these days. (Quick, is it a fastback or a sedan?) The women I know, who all primarily use these things for work, don't give them two seconds' thought unless they encounter some problem. On the other hand, a lot of the men I know ogle weird software in MacWarehouse catalogue and always seem to require some new $200 gizmo that quacks.

"It's a guy thing," Pam and I decided, virtually in unison. Women treat computers like reliable station wagons: Learn how to make them take you where you want to go, and as long as they're functioning properly, who cares about pistons and horsepower? Computers are useful but unexciting. When something goes wrong, you call a mechanic.

Whereas guys, even those who never learned how to change an oil filter, are enamored of computers, want to play with them, upgrade them, fix them when they falter, compare theirs with the other guys'.

As an admitted technoklutz, I initially figured this observation might simply reflect my own prejudice, not to mention a small sample size. Computers, after all, were initially thought to be a field in which women would triumph.

Computers had no history of discrimination. They had no history at all. They did not require biceps. They wouldn't be, to adopt the social science term, gendered.

Well. It turned out—as I started looking into the whole evolving subject of women, computers, on-line communications and other matters I had previously been unconcerned about—that computing is even more of a guy thing than I knew. That's worth paying attention to, not only for women but for our daughters (mine's 12). Yet I would also learn, as I ventured hesitantly into the computer communications realm dubbed cyberspace, that things don't have to stay this way.

Warning: The following article contains assorted generalizations and risks gender stereotyping.

For there are, no question, numerous males who are phobic about or merely uninterested in computing. And there are plenty of techie females, women who know their algorithms, who run major software companies, and who can clean the cat hair out of a trackball in 30 seconds or less.

But it's hard to overlook the stats. Who studies computer science? The *Chronicle of Higher Education's* latest numbers show that fewer than 30 percent of the people getting bachelor's and master's degrees are women and that fewer than one in seven doctorates is earned by a woman.

Who works in the industry? The Bureau of Labor Statistics reports that the percentage of women who are computer systems analysts and scientists has barely budged in a decade. It's still under 30 percent, even though nearly half a million more people have entered the field. Fewer than a third of computer programmers are women, as well, another statistic little changed since 1983.

Who pants over those fat, glossy computer magazines (*PC World, Byte, MacUser*) whose lust-inspiring displays of software and laptops have been dubbed, by writer James Fallows, compuporn? Eighty percent of their readers are male, says the research firm Simmons MRI. (So are 85 percent of those who buy the newer and hipper *Wired*.)

Millions of women use computers at their jobs, of course, though often in routinized ways that leave the machines' more intriguing possibilities unexplored. But home computers, which after several years of significant growth still are found in only 31 percent of American homes, remain largely a male preserve. (And a middle-class preserve, but that's another story.) LINK Resources, a New York consulting firm, has found that in only a quarter of those homes is the primary user a woman.

As for cyberspace, about which more later, no one's hung a "No Girls Allowed" sign on the door. It's often a male clubhouse nonetheless, one girls can enter provided they are willing and able to scramble through the briers, shinny up the tree, ignore the skinned knees and announce that they can spit a watermelon seed just as far as the guys inside can. Figuratively speaking.

All of this reflects attitudes toward computers that form at unnervingly young ages.

Ten years ago, not long after *Time* magazine had declared the computer its Person of the Year, education journals started to fill with reports about the way schoolaged boys embraced computers while girls avoided them. Boys were more likely to have home computers and use them, to enroll in computer camps and summer programs, to take advantage of school computer labs, to elect high school computer courses. Academics who pay attention to these things say they haven't seen much dramatic change since.

So much for parents' assuring themselves that kids who've grown up in the Super Mario Era won't inherit their elders' anxieties and biases. The old patterns show considerable staying power. As early as first grade, according to a 1990 study in the Journal of Research and Development in Education, computer use is seen, by both boys and girls, as masculine. Reading and writing, on the other hand, have no perceived gender associations.

Researchers offer various explanations, including the well-documented aversion that many girls develop to math and science, the ever-popular lack-of-role-models theory, and the fact that many boys are introduced to computers through those kill-and-maim computer and video games that girls very sensibly disdain. (Who dubbed the control a joystick, anyway?) The disparity, however triggered, intensifies with age: by high school, girls may use computers to write their term papers (tests show that they're as competent at it as the guys), but deeper interest is suspect.

Computing's male aura may be one of the enduring legacies of the mythic hackers and nerds who patched together the early personal computers, hammered out breakthrough programs and invented computer bulletin boards. (A notorious few also dabbled in phone and credit-card-fraud.) They were true trailblazers. In addition, they and their descendants are, as a subculture, so unappetizing—pale geeks without social skills who lose themselves in binary code, sci-fi sagas and chess gambits—that women develop "computational reticence" in response.

This, at least, is the theme developed by well-known MIT sociologist Sherry Turkle in an essay that's part of a 1988 collection called *Technology and Women's Voices*. Basing her analysis on interviews with college women who were doing well in computer courses but resisted identifying themselves as "computer science types," Turkle says that women "observe [the hackers'] obsessions, observe their anti-sensuality, observe the ways in which they have put things rather than people at the center of their lives and count themselves out."

It's not hard to understand why an adolescent boy might find computing seductive. At a time when sexual pressures and social demands loom threateningly large, the hacker culture offers autonomy, mastery, safety. "The hook is the feeling of power that it gives you: You control a world of your own making," says my friend Steve Adamczyk, an MIT grad who owns a software company called the Edison Design Group. (I'd call Steve a former nerd except that, he explains, "it's like being an alcoholic: You're always a nerd but you're a recovering nerd.") Staying up all night coding software in FORTRAN, as Steve did in high school, was "terrifically appealing to people who don't do so well at controlling the real world, maintaining relationships and all that."

Girls, though of course also buffeted by adolescence, have by that point been culturally programmed to maintain relationships. And those who withdraw generally seem to find safe havens other than computer labs.

As a small but influential cadre, hackers are also something of an alien species to non-nerd men. But men, Turkle writes, are apt to view hackers' achievements with admiration. Women, however many magazine stories they read about Bill Gates's net-worth, are more likely, to bolt.

The good news is that unlike some stubborn power imbalances requiring generations to redress (the composition of the U.S. Congress comes to mind), computer attitudes appear to be rather dramatically revisable. And such attempts are underway: This year, the National Science Foundation has more than tripled its funding for programs aimed at pulling girls and women into science, math and engineering. The boys-will-be-nerds paradigm "is just a throwback to separate spheres, simply a vestigial anachronism," announces Jo Sanders, of the Center for Advanced Study, City University of New York.

Sanders ran the NSF-funded Computer Equity Expert Project. A 30-month-long guerrilla campaign to increase girls' participation in math, science and technology by, well, gently but firmly smashing sexism. Sanders convened 200 teachers and administrators, representing every state, for week-long seminars on the causes and consequences of the gender gap and strategies for closing it. Back in their middle and high schools, these people taught computer equity workshops to their own faculties and recruited girls with everything from guest speakers to pizza parties.

The project, which ended last year, got results with startling speed. Reports flooded in: Within a year, an all-male advanced PASCAL class in Virginia turned 50 percent female and an all-male elective computer course in Oklahoma was nearly a third female, while a West Virginia computer club increased its female membership tenfold. "When you change attitudes," Sanders concludes, "the resistance just evaporates."

As for us grown-up women no longer facing math and science requirements, our resistance is also susceptible to change. What has been missing until recently, however, isn't just spine-stiffening; it's a motivation, some reason to acquire or cozy up to a computer, an incentive to struggle past the inevitable glitches.

For years, if you didn't need a computer for work, it has been hard to see what it would do for you. No one really needs to make that sort of investment in time and money to balance her checkbook, file her recipes (to cite one early personal-computer application that was supposed to turn us on) or handle ordinary correspondence. The love of gadgetry and tinkering that draws some men to computers as a hobby hasn't had much measurable impact on women.

What's been missing is the Killer App.

That's the term Silicon Valley types use for the breakthrough use, the irresistible application that finally makes a technological advance not just a toy but a useful tool, so that ordinary people look at it and say, "We need one of those." The Killer App for the desktop computer itself was the Lotus 1-2-3 spreadsheet.

The Killer App for microwave ovens, now in 80 percent of homes, was probably reheating leftovers, or maybe popping corn.

The Killer App that draws women into computer use in significant numbers, researchers tell me will be communication. With a cheap modem and a few commands that connect you to a network, you can reach out and touch people you know and hundreds of thousands of people you don't and discuss everything from breastfeeding to foreign policy. This isn't technology, this is expression, relationships, community, all the things women are taught to be skilled at.

Cyberspace isn't as brave-new-world as the name makes it sound. Reva Basch, whom I've recently met-by-modem on a computer conferring system called the WELL, told me this story: "My mother-in-law, who's 80, was visiting and expressed curiosity about the WELL. I showed it to her, showed her some of the conferences. She said, 'Why, honey, it's just talking, isn't it?' She got it."

My daughter, Emma, was my guide at first. Growing up with parents who use computers (however rudimentary) and encourage her to do likewise, plus hours of playing Nintendo and computer games with friends who are boys, seems to have immunized her against computer-aversion. She's not fascinated by the things, exactly, but she's entirely unthreatened by them. So, six weeks before I began writing this essay, I nervously sat down at the Macintosh bequeathed to her when my husband, partly for that very reason, bought his latest. She patiently showed me now to log on to America Online, the country's third largest computer communications system.

America Online is easy to use, even for a neophyte. It has a welcoming "interface," a display of onscreen symbols to point to and click at, so that you can read highlights from *USA Today* and the *Atlantic*, send electronic mail ("E-mail") to friends and strangers, scroll through 406 messages from fans of Smashing Pumpkins and add your own in the RockLink Forum, or join as many as 22 other users all typing away at each other in "real time" in each of dozens of "lobbies" and "chat areas." It's gotten so popular and grown so fast that the system grew temporarily choked and sluggish this winter from overuse by its 600,000 subscribers.

I found AOL reassuringly simple but not particularly simpatico and so, two weeks later, I logged onto the WELL, a Sausalito-based network founded in 1985 by the folks who published the Whole Earth Catalogue. This was not simple, and resulted in the humiliation of repeatedly having to dash down two flights of stairs to ask my husband (already a WELLbeing), "How do you get to an OK prompt?," then dash back up. But I've figured out enough to be able to send and receive E-mail and join in the conversation. I've entered cyberspace.

It's become part of the daily routine: I brush my teeth; I go to my aerobics class; I dial the WELL. Once there, I check my E-mail box (an on-line friend from Massachusetts says revisions on her novel are going well; an on-line friend and new dad in California says the baby slept five hours last night). I usually visit Women on the WELL first (no guys allowed) to learn the latest depressing or exhilarating details of the lives of women I've never met but am coming to know anyway, to commiserate or cheer them on, to complain that I've gained three pounds.

Then I venture out to see who's arguing about what topic in the media con-ference and who's soliciting advice in the parenting conference. If I care to, I add my own comments stories, jokes, requests for information and general two cents worth. If I had hours to spend at this, as some folks seem to, I could join conferences where people are yakking about politics, bicycling, sex, Judaism, AIDS, the Grateful Dead and a zillion other passions and problems.

I haven't yet dared the next step, which is using the WELL to access the Internet, the vast global aggregation of computer networks that would allow me to use countless libraries and databases, join hundreds more conferences, and tell *millions* of people that I've gained three pounds. But I could. And someday, depending on how much of the prattling about the "information superhighway" and its services one chooses to believe, I'll use a computer (attached discreetly to my television) to make rental movies pop up on my TV screen, buy everything from groceries to mutual funds, take the courses I need to finish my master's degree. It all looks quite prosaic at this point—just lines of text appearing on my screen—but it feels very exciting.

At the moment, cyberspace is populated primarily by—did you guess this?—men. The WELL has only about 15 to 18 percent women among its 8,000 sub-scribers, its managers believe, a proportion considered representative of most con-ferencing or "bulletin board" systems (BBSs). Even the big on-line services that spend bundles on advertising and direct mail have drawn few female subscribers (though they believe that many women and children log on using men's accounts). Most of CompuServe's 1.5 million subscribers are guys (90 percent) and so are most of America Online's (85 percent); Prodigy claims to be the most egalitarian of the big on-line services with a 30 percent female membership.

Yet these are numbers that could change quickly and dramatically, as women learn that even those who don't know bauds from broads can use a BBS (believe me when I tell you) and—more significantly—learn that there are reasons to.

I give you Sarah Randolph, the poet who co-hosts the WELL's writers confer-ence, who lives in a small seaside town and was "just really hungry for conver-sation and life" when she bought a modem and joined this odd little commu-nity. Through it she's made friends, picked up writing jobs, and learned how to increase her garden's broccoli yield. It isn't a substitute for having real people around, yet it has its own rewards. "In the real world, there's your body. Your body is shy and needs something to hold on to at a party," she muses. On-line, "I feel fairly transparent . . . I feel like I can go anywhere in that world."

I give you Patrizia DiLucchio, who read about the WELL a few years ago while writing her dissertation "on an extremely dry topic" and thought "it sounded like having pen pals . . . like putting messages in bottles and sending them out to alien shores." Now, because she lives in the San Francisco area, the WELL's home port, "half the people I hang out with in real life I met on the WELL." She also had a heavy-duty romance of several years' duration with a fel-low WELLperson, and she's hardly the only one: "To some extent, all bulletin boards are interactive personals ads."

I give you Ellen Pack, president of a new on-line service that reverses the usual stats (10 percent of its members are male) called Women's Wire. Along with the databases on women's health, the updates on legislation and such, Women's Wire lets Pack, a San Franciscan, stay in touch with her parents and sisters in New York via E-mail. "My mom is 65 and not particularly computer-literate, but I got her a Mac and now she logs on," Pack reports. "It doesn't replace face-to-face or the occasional phone call, but I communicate with them so much more now because it's sooo easy." E-mail is cheaper and more convenient than long distance telephoning, and Pack points out, "it lets you have all the incremental communications, things you wouldn't pick up the phone for."

I give you, moreover, my friend Pam, who sallied into cyberspace about the same time I did and is busily researching her new book via America Online. We agree that our most serious current problem with computer networks is that work and family obligations can really cut into the time we spend on-line.

And yet. The thing about cyberspace is that although sometimes it feels like a sophisticated graduate seminar or a good-natured pub, it can also, for women, feel like a walk past a construction site or a wrong turn down a dark street. Like life itself, it requires tactical decisions about how to proceed in a not-always-welcoming sphere: Do you opt for a strategic retreat into protected bunkers? Lobby for reform? Take a deep breath and wade in swinging?

For cyberspace is not an alternate, genderless universe. College women report dopey sexist limericks and images of breasts sent via computer nets. Women can be publicly propositioned or stalked by E-mail suitors who hurl abuse when they get rejected. My daughter, visiting an America Online gathering called Teen That, is regularly invited by the teenaged boys who predominate therein to enter a private "room." Sometimes she sees whether they have anything interesting to say. Sometimes she Just Types No.

I have watched as someone named Stacy logged onto an AOL book discussion group, introduced herself as a newcomer, then disappeared from the screen for a while. She came back long enough to type out, "What are all these messages?" She'd been flooded "with IMs—instant messages directed only to her. The other women in the group pointed out that her female ID had made her a target for attention. It was at this point that, although I had not encountered such treatment, I changed my own ID to something offering no gender clues. The problem, hardly limited to America Online, is widely reported. "You seek out your friends and places you know are safe and harassment-free," an AOL subscriber named Citywoman tells me via E-mail.

You don't have to sit still for such annoyances, of course. Many on-line systems have some sort of recourse, hosts or monitors who chastise offenders, or policies that can toss a persistent harasser off the net. On the WELL , a "bozofilter" command allows you to simply never hear from a given user again, an option I'd find useful in everyday existence. You can change an ID like Citywoman to a string of numbers or to JackSpratt. You can confront jerks.

Still, if cyberspace were a workplace, this stuff would qualify as creating a hostile environment. "Hearing that incidents happen probably discourages some women who haven't even tried going on-line," worries Reva Basch, who co-hosts the cozy Women on the WELL conference. "They'll say, 'Oooh, you'll get cruised and hit on. Who needs it? I get enough of that on my job.'"

It was Basch who alerted the WELL at large to another way in which cyberspace can mirror life: the discovery last summer that a "cybercad" had been romancing several WELLwomen simultaneously, exchanging erotic E-mail with each of them without the other's knowledge, going so far as to visit one woman using a plane ticket she helped pay for. The incident, first reported in this newspaper, sparked weeks of heated discussion about whether and how this sort-of community should respond. The cad eventually resigned his account voluntarily, but left behind a lot of unanswered questions about what the differences between behavior on-line and behavior IRL (in real life) are and ought to be.

And if it's tough to figure out what to do about virtual knavery, what to do about a virtual rape? It happened in a computer-generated environment developed by Xerox researchers in Palo Alto, Calif., reachable through the Internet and called LambdaMOO. In this fantasy domain, a kind of multi-authored fictional work-in-progress known to its denizens as "the MOO," a motley array of characters glide through many rooms, doing and saying what users sitting at their terminals (mostly college and graduate students in their late teens and early twenties, three-fourths of them male) tell them to do and say. Last year, in an incident vividly reported in the *Village Voice*, a crude jester named Mr. Bungle sexually assaulted several other LambdaMOO characters in a rampage of intensifying verbal violence. The ensuing sociopolitical debate was fierce and prolonged.

Civilization—as designed by Pavel Curtis, who heads the Xerox Social Virtual Reality Project—has now come to the MOO. An arrangement of petitions and ballots allows users to modify the system, request arbitration, seek justice. In the on-line world, Curtis concludes, "the medium is different, but the people are the same."

Less dramatic than rape or harassment, but a deterrent nevertheless to bringing women into cyberspace, is the matter of style. Here again, the hackers of yore have left their fingerprints all over the world they helped create. Hackers were known for a strong anti-authoritarian streak, a libertarian philosophy that resisted rules, controls, the restrictive codes of real life. They also adopted online a style of expression that reflected all the maturity, nuance and nurturing qualities of 17-year-old boys. (A recent press release about a book on women and information technology, for example, posted on a University of Illinois network, brought immediate and snarky attacks on the woman who'd written the release, "Who is she, a cow who belongs to NOW?" "A member of Dykes on Bikes?")

This is the clubhouse atmosphere that greets the tentative newcomer of either gender. Nets and conferences have their own varying personalities, but many of them offer no-holds-barred arguments and aggressive put-downs, a rambunctious interplay (known as "flaming") in which women, vastly outnumbered, find their contributions derided or simply ignored. Academics analyzing "netiquette" have pointed out that both men and women respond more to men's messages. Some women charge in and give as good as they get: others retreat.

The WELL, for instance, seems a reasonably civil place with an egalitarian tradition, where conflict-avoidance abbreviations like "imho" (in my humble opinion) and "YMMV" (your mileage may vary) abound. Yet even here, there are women who feel more comfortable in the supportive confines of the women's conference and rarely leave it (though others find it earnest and too polite and rarely enter). During an on-line flap about "male discourse," a woman named Tigereye kept the history conference at a boil for weeks with remarks about the "traditional male style of communication involving gratuitous oneupmanship, insult and posturing we can readily observe on the WELL."

What if women dominated the net and set the tone? To find out, Nancy Baym, a University of Illinois doctoral candidate, has immersed herself in a Usenet group called re.arts.tv.soaps, devoted to discussion of soap operas. (And referred to as RATS, which is why Baym hopes to title her dissertation "Of RATS and Women.") Its participants are largely female engineers, techies and academics who like to break up their workdays with discussions on such topics as, "Is Dixie a Ho?"

Wading through 7,000 posted messages on the subject of "All My Children," Baym found a language of elaborate courtesy. "They use a lot of politeness strategies to make disagreement nonthreatening," she reports. "They'll try to build the esteem of the person they're disagreeing with: 'Jane, I see your point of view, but I must say . . .' Alternately, they'll diminish the force of their disagreement, qualify things: 'I could be wrong but . . .' In the soap group, the netiquette is, don't insult people. If you look at groups discussing 'Star Trek,' they'll say, 'Stay off the 'Net, you Nazi!'"

Groans all around. Somewhere between enforcing Nice Networks for women, and having women set upon by wolf packs roaming the Internet, there must be a workable middle ground. I count myself among the optimists, partly because there are systems that demonstrate the possibility of egalitarianism. It doesn't happen by accident, but it does happen.

ECHO, a New York-based bulletin board, is more than 50 percent female, an achievement attributed to its founder's determination to lure women in by means of tutorials, a mentoring program and reduced rates. Arlington's Metasystems Design Group operates the Meta Network, a conferencing system that is also more than half female—and aspires to be a no-flame zone.

"We do all the things good moderators do in person," says Metasystems partner Lisa Kimball. On the Meta Net, new members get buddies, flamers get a private talking-to, welcomes are issued the first time someone speaks up online, yet the opinions fly. "It's like arriving at a big party with lots of people," Kimball says. "One issue is finding out where the bar is, but it's even better when the hostess says, 'I'm so glad you're here. There's someone over on the other side of the room I think you'd like to meet.'"

One of the elders of cyberspace, who has founded bulletin boards in many places, is Dave Hughes, a k a the Cursor Cowboy. He now runs the Old Colorado City Electronic Cottage, based in Colorado Springs, from which perspective he can see the analogy between that onetime frontier and this one. "It's the same as going into the gold rush towns," the Cowboy observes. "Males jump onto their horses, set up these roistering places, saloons and all. As soon as you begin to approach one-third to one-half of the population being women . . . you still have the saloons and the hoop-de-doo, but you also have the schools.

"It's the same in the on-line world, dominated by men, their language, their interests. . . . The moment a woman goes on-line, she's a target for all sorts of things, like the gal that came into town on the stage. . . . [On-line women] have to be like frontier women, a little tougher-skinned. . . . They have to master all kinds of skills they didn't know before. But as the numbers increase, the language changes, the subjects begin to reflect a more balanced society.

Does it matter? I vote yes.

True, people of either gender can still live meaningful lives without computers. If I never progressed beyond the half-dozen commands necessary to send my stories to *The Washington Post,* I might suffer little handicap. I don't think that will be true for my daughter, though, or any of our daughters. They're entering a world in which card catalog drawers have already vanished from the public library, replaced by terminals and keyboards.

Perhaps they won't need to be whiz-bang programmers (though it wouldn't hurt). But they can't afford to see computers as toys for boys, to see ignorance as feminine, to wring their hands over the keyboard and worry that they'll break something.

"A sense of yourself as a technologically competent person is no small shakes in this world," Jo Sanders of City University says. "It builds confidence in yourself as a problem-solver. It's important on a résumé whether or not the job you're interested in uses computers. . . . It's proof that you are able to learn things, a certificate of capability."

I recall, 20 years ago—as women were trying to free themselves from a set of social expectations that has already changed startlingly—a brief vogue for feminist courses in auto repair. Whether or not you could afford to have someone change your oil or your tire, a sense of independence and mastery of the world demanded that you take on the guy things. You wanted to demonstrate to yourself and others that you could change spark plugs even if, once having proven it, you went back to dropping your VW Bug off at the local garage.

More and more, the computer world feels like that. Women have to be in it because incompetence is an unattractive trait. Women have to be in it because decisions about language and culture and access are being made and we should be involved in making them. Women have to be in it because, although nobody really knows what form all this technology will take, there shouldn't be any clubhouse we're afraid to climb into.

I think that because of timely early intervention, Emma will handle the club-house just fine.

As for myself, I'm not afraid of the guys inside, but I dread the technical challenge of climbing the tree. Still, a couple of weeks ago, I logged on and typed in "support" and ordered the WELL User's Manual, Version 5.1a. It arrived recently, a fat and daunting volume that tells you when to use "lsz-a*" as opposed to "lxm stky my*." I'm sure there are dozens of elegant functions in it that I don't need and may never master, just as I doubt that I'll ever drool over the compu-porn in Byte or order RAM-doublers by mail.

But I need to know how to download. I've got to learn how to move files around. So I'm going to wade in. It was sort of a kick, late the other night, when Tigereye taught me, via E-mail, how to extract. It wasn't so difficult; I just typed "!extract -u tigereye history" and the stuff poured forth in waves. ■

Working with the Text

1. What does Span see as the main obstacles to greater interest in and participation by women in cyberspace and on the Internet? Create different categories for classifying and sorting these obstacles; for example, some may have to do with hostile environments and sexual harassment, others with stereotypes or traditional ideas about gender roles. Which obstacles seem the most and least difficult to overcome?

2. Write about your own experiences with gender and the web. What about Internet culture has struck you as friendly or unfriendly to either men or women? If you have participated in online discussions of any kinds, to what extent have you noticed the interpersonal dynamics that Span describes, such as immature sexual references, flaming, or the desire to avoid confrontation and hurt feelings? In which areas of cyberspace have you felt more or less comfortable on the basis of gender and why?

3. One reason Span considers for why more women are not participating in computer culture is the lack of a "killer app," or a use for the Internet that would make it indispensable in everyday life. Span tries out the WELL and other discussion sites as possibilities for a more gender-inclusive "killer app." Use the idea of the "killer app" to discuss how you think gender issues have changed in cyberspace since 1994, for both better or worse. For example, how well might the rise of instant messaging fit the bill of a "killer app" that is more attractive to girls and women?

Working with Connections

1. In *Women Have Always Worked* (from Chapter 5, Work and Family), Alice Kessler-Harris wonders whether

   > [t]he kind of work women have done over the past two hundred years has created sensibilities that differ from those of men. Can women now leave their own sphere without giving up what is best in their lives? Is it possible for women simultaneously to join the work force on an equal basis with men and to alter it in ways that accord with their own sensibilities?

   Similarly, Span asks, "What if women dominated the web and set the tone?" Use Kessler-Harris's and Span's essays to consider the question of how much women and girls will have to change to fit into the computer culture or how much computer culture should change to meet the needs of many women (and men)?

2. The Personal Daily Assistant (PDA) depicted in "Media Images" on pages 482–483 has proven popular with women as well as men. Using ideas from Span's article, write about why you think the PDA might be appealing to women. Expand the discussion by suggesting ways that computer manufacturers could make the Internet and computer culture more gender inclusive.

3. In "An Age of Optimism," Nicholas Negroponte argues that the greatest effects of the digital age will be a "decentralizing, globalizing, harmonizing, and empowering" of human society. How would Span respond to Negroponte's essay based on the evidence she presents here? What would most lend support to Negroponte's claims? What would cast most doubt upon them?

Reading the Web

■

Charting Changes in the Web: The Internet Archive

Although it seems today that everything and everybody has a web site, and web-based research is quickly becoming the preferred first option for student writers, less than ten years ago the Internet was largely the domain of a small group of computer enthusiasts and experts. The rapid expansion of the World Wide Web since then is testament to its growing importance to cultural and economic life. Even after the burst of the "dot com" bubble at the end of the 1990s, the web remains an essential component of the future world of work. Likewise, writing on and for the web is increasing in importance as a rhetorical skill, and the concept of "professional writing" is coming to replace the older categories of "business" and "technical" writing.

Because web-based writing is so dynamic, the conventions informing and shaping it are themselves constantly changing. You can trace these changes in the development of web-based writing using the resources of *The Internet Archive* http://www.archive.org. *The Internet Archive* describes itself as a "digital library," and among its holdings are examples of web sites going back to the mid-1990s (ancient history in the compressed time frame of the World Wide Web). Using the "Wayback" collections, you can follow the changes in a particular web site (for example, Yahoo.com)

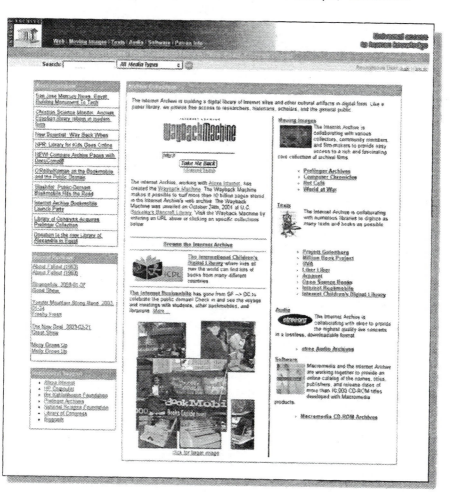

from 1996 to the present, taking note of what aspects of design and presentation have remained the same and which have changed.

As a research project into how the rhetoric of the web has evolved, choose a web site with which you are familiar that is cataloged in the Internet Archive collections (you can type in a URL or choose from one of their highlighted collections). You can probably find your school's web site archived here as well. Once you have found a site, choose three or four examples of that site from different times that illustrate the major changes and developments in the presentation of that site. Use these sample pages to explore the following issues and questions:

1. Describe the overall biggest change you have observed in the design and presentation of the web site over its history.
2. What are some factors that might have influenced those changes? Among things to consider are the changing audience for the site, the changing rhetorical needs and purposes for the site, and the changes in web site design technology.
3. Do you notice any changes that were tried and discontinued? Speculate about why these changes were not kept.
4. Is the current site your favorite version of the site? Why or why not?
5. Use your observations about how the site has changed to create some principles for effective web site design. After doing this individually, work together as a class to combine your ideas into a class consensus about principles for effective web site design.

Stories of Work

MICHAEL LEWIS ■

Jonathan Lebed's Extracurricular Activities

In the year 2000, the Securities and Exchange Commission announced that it had reached a settlement in a stock market fraud case against Jonathan Lebed. As part of the deal, Lebed agreed to give the government $285,000 he had made from his stock trading while keeping half a million dollars. What made this case of particular interest, even to those who don't follow news from Wall Street, is that Jonathan Lebed was a 15-year-old high school student operating from his bedroom computer.

In "Jonathan Lebed's Extracurricular Activities," reporter Michael Lewis tells the story of how a boy, not old enough to get a driver's license, managed to draw the attention and concern of the most powerful financial regulatory agency in the federal government. In addition to explaining the wrongdoing Lebed was accused of, Lewis also expresses skepticism about whether in fact Lebed had done anything wrong. Lewis *explores what Lebed's story says about how the Internet has the poten-tial to change our most basic notions of identity and authority. Lewis describes a world in which the expertise and skills of children surpass those of their parents and other adults, suggesting that the rules govern-ing the economic and social structure of the 20th century may need to be completely rewritten for the 21st.*

Michael Lewis is a journalist who has written extensively on the Information Age and the new economy, including the books Next: The Future Just Happened *and* Liar's Poker: Rising Through the Wreckage on Wall Street.

On Sept. 20, 2000, the Securities and Exchange Commission settled its case against a 15-year-old high-school student named Jonathan Lebed. The S.E.C.'s news release explained that Jonathan—the first minor ever to face pro-ceedings for stock-market fraud—had used the Internet to promote stocks from his bedroom in the northern New Jersey suburb of Cedar Grove. Armed only with accounts at A.O.L. and E*Trade, the kid had bought stock and then, "using multiple fictitious names," posted hundreds of messages on Yahoo Finance message boards recommending that stock to others. He had done this 11 times between September 1999 and February 2000, the S.E.C. said, each time triggering chaos in the stock market. The average daily trading vol-ume of the small companies he dealt in was about 60,000 shares; on the days he posted his messages, volume soared to more than a million shares. More to the point, he had made money. Between September 1999 and February 2000, his smallest one-day gain was $12,000. His biggest was $74,000. Now the kid had agreed to hand over his illicit gains, plus interest, which came to $285,000.

When I first read the newspaper reports last fall, I didn't understand them. It wasn't just that I didn't understand what the kid had done wrong; I didn't understand what he had done. And if the initial articles about Jonathan Lebed raised questions—what did it mean to use a fictitious name on the Internet, where every name is fictitious, and who were these people who traded stocks naïvely based on what they read on the Internet?—they were trivial next to the questions raised a few days later when a reporter asked Jonathan Lebed's lawyer if the S.E.C. had taken all of the profits. They hadn't. There had been many more than the 11 trades described in the S.E.C.'s press release, the lawyer said. The kid's take from six months of trading had been nearly $800,000. Initially the S.E.C. had demanded he give it all up, but then backed off when the kid put up a fight. As a result, Jonathan Lebed was still sitting on half a million dollars.

At length, I phoned the Philadelphia office of the S.E.C., where I reached one of the investigators who had brought Jonathan Lebed to book. I was maybe the 50th journalist he'd spoken with that day, and apparently a lot of the others had had trouble grasping the finer points of securities law. At any rate, by the time I asked him to explain to me what, exactly, was wrong with broadcasting one's private opinion of a stock on the Internet, he was in no mood.

"Tell me about the kid."

"He's a little jerk."

"How so?"

"He is exactly what you or I hope our kids never turn out to be."

"Have you met him?"

"No. I don't need to."

Cedar Grove is one of those Essex County suburbs defined by the fact that it is not Newark. Its real-estate prices rise with the hills. The houses at the bottom of each hill are barely middle class; the houses at the top might fairly be described as opulent. The Lebeds' house sits about a third of the way up one of the hills.

When I arrived one afternoon not long ago, the first person to the door was Greg Lebed, Jonathan's 54-year-old father. Black hair sprouted in many directions from the top of his head and joined together somewhere in the middle of his back. The curl of his lip seemed designed to shout abuse from a bleacher seat. He had become famous, briefly, when he ordered the world's media off his front lawn and said, "I'm proud of my son." Later, elaborating on "60 Minutes," he said, "It's not like he was out stealing the hubcaps off cars or peddling drugs to the neighbors."

He led me to the family dining room, and without the slightest help from me, worked himself into a lather. He got out a photocopy of front-page stories from *The Daily News*. One side had a snapshot of Bill and Hillary Clinton beside the headline "Insufficient Evidence' in Whitewater Case: CLINTONS CLEARED"; the other side had a picture of Jonathan Lebed beside the headline "Teen Stock Whiz Nailed." Over it all was scrawled in Greg's furious hand, "U.S. Justice at Work."

"Look at that!" he shouted. "This is what goes on in this country!"

Then, just as suddenly as he had erupted, he went dormant. "Don't bother with me," he said. "I get upset." He offered me a seat at the dining-room table. Connie Lebed, Jonathan's 45-year-old mother, now entered. She had a look on her face that as much as said: "I assume Greg has already started yelling about something. Don't mind him; I certainly don't."

Greg said testily, "It was that goddamn computer what was the problem."

"My problem with the S.E.C.," said Connie, ignoring her husband, "was that they never called. One day we get this package from Federal Express with the whatdyacallitt, the subpoenas inside. If only they had called me first." She will say this six times before the end of the day, with one of those marvelous harmonicalike wails that convey a sense of grievance maybe better than any noise on the planet. If only they'da caaaawwwwlled me.

"The wife brought that goddamn computer into this house in the first place," Greg said, hurling a thumb at Connie. "Ever since that computer came into the house, this family was ruined."

Connie absorbed the full frontal attack with an uncomprehending blink, and then said to me, as if her husband had never spoken: "My husband has a lot of anger. He gets worked up easily. He's already had one heart attack."

She neither expects nor receives the faintest reply from him. They obey the conventions of the stage. When one of them steps forward into the spotlight to narrate, the other recedes and freezes like a statue. Ten minutes into the conversation, Jonathan slouched in. Even that verb does not capture the mixture of sullenness and truculence with which he entered the room. He was long and thin and dressed in the prison costume of the American suburban teenager: pants too big, sneakers gaping, a pirate hoop dangling from one ear. He looked away when he shook my hand and said "Nice to meet you" in a way that made it clear that he couldn't be less pleased. Then he sat down and said nothing while his parents returned to their split-screen narration.

At first glance, it was impossible to link Jonathan in the flesh to Jonathan on the Web. I have a file of his Internet postings, and they're all pretty bombastic. Two days before the FedEx package arrived bearing the S.E.C.'s subpoenas, for instance, he logged onto the Internet and posted 200 separate times the following plug for a company called Firetector (ticker symbol FTEC):

"Subj: THE MOST UNDERVALUED STOCK EVER

"Date: 2/03/00 3:43pm Pacific Standard Time

"From: LebedTGI

"FTEC is starting to break out! Next week, this thing will EXPLODE. . . .

"Currently FTEC is trading for just $2 1/2! I am expecting to see FTEC at $20 VERY SOON.

"Let me explain why. . . .

"Revenues for the year should very conservatively be around $20 million. The average company in the industry trades with a price/sales ratio of 3.45. With 1.57 million shares outstanding, this will value FTEC at . . . $44.

"It is very possible that FTEC will see $44, but since I would like to remain very conservative . . . my short-term target price on FTEC is still $20!

"The FTEC offices are extremely busy. . . . I am hearing that a number of HUGE deals are being worked on. Once we get some news from FTEC and the word gets out about the company . . . it will take-off to MUCH HIGHER LEVELS!

"I see little risk when purchasing FTEC at these DIRT-CHEAP PRICES. FTEC is making TREMENDOUS PROFITS and is trading UNDER BOOK VALUE!!!"

And so on. The author of that and dozens more like it now sat dully at the end of the family's dining-room table and watched his parents take potshots at each other and their government. There wasn't an exclamation point in him.

Not long after his 11th birthday, Jonathan opened an account with America Online. He went onto the Internet, at least at first, to meet other pro-wrestling fans. He built a Web site dedicated to the greater glory of Stone Cold Steve Austin. But about the same time, by watching his father, he became interested in the stock market. In his 30-plus years working for Amtrak, Greg Lebed had worked his way up to middle manager. Along the way, he accumulated maybe $12,000 of blue-chip stocks. Like half of America, he came to watch the market's daily upward leaps and jerks with keen interest.

Jonathan saved him the trouble. When he came home from school, he turned on CNBC and watched the stock-market ticker stream across the bottom of the screen, searching it for the symbols inside his father's portfolio. "Jonathan would sit there for hours staring at them," Connie said, as if Jonathan is miles away.

"I just liked to watch the numbers go across the screen," Jonathan said.

"Why?"

"I don't know," he said. "I just wondered, like, what they meant."

At first, the numbers meant a chance to talk to his father. He would call his father at work whenever he saw one of his stocks cross the bottom of the television screen. This went on for about six months before Jonathan declared his own interest in owning stocks. On Sept. 29, 1996, Jonathan's 12th birthday, a savings bond his parents gave him at birth came due. He took the $8,000 and got his father to invest it for him in the stock market. The first stock he bought was America Online, at $25 a share—in spite of a lot of adverse commentary about the company on CNBC.

"He said that it was a stupid company and that it would go to 2 cents," Jonathan chimed in, pointing at his father, who obeyed what now appeared to be the family rule and sat frozen at the back of some mental stage. AOL rose five points in a couple of weeks, and Jonathan had his father sell it. From this he learned that a) you could make money quickly in the stock market, b) his dad didn't know what he was talking about and c) it paid him to exercise his own judgment on these matters. All three lessons were reinforced dramatically by what happened next.

What happened next was that CNBC—which Jonathan now rose at 5 every morning to watch—announced a stock-picking contest for students. Jonathan had wanted to join the contest on his own but was told that he needed to be on a team, and so he went and asked two friends to join him. Thousands of students from across the country set out to speculate their way to victory. Each afternoon CNBC announced the five top teams of the day.

To get your name read out loud on television, you obviously opted for highly volatile stocks that stood a chance of doing well in the short term. Jonathan's team, dubbing itself the Triple Threat, had a portfolio that rose 51 percent the first day, which put them in first place. They remained in the Top 3 for the next three months, until in the last two weeks of the contest they collapsed. Even a fourth-place finish was good enough to fetch a camera crew from CNBC, which came and filmed the team in Cedar Grove. The Triple Threat was featured in *The Verona-Cedar Grove Times* and celebrated on television by the Cedar Grove Township Council.

"From then, everyone at work starting asking me if Jonathan had any stock tips for them," said Greg.

"They still ask me," said Connie.

By the Spring of 1998, Jonathan was 13, and his ambitions were growing. He had glimpsed the essential truth of the market: that even people who called themselves professionals are often incapable of independent thought and that most people, though obsessed with money, have little ability to make decisions about it. He knew what he was doing, or thought he did. He had learned to find everything he wanted to know about a company on the Internet; what he couldn't find, he ran down in the flesh. It became part of Connie Lebed's life to drive her son to various corporate headquarters to make sure they existed. He also persuaded her to open an account with Ameritrade. "He'd done so well with the stock contest, I figured, Let's see what he can do," Connie said.

What he did was turn his $8,000 savings bond into $28,000 inside of 18 months. During the same period, he created his own Web site devoted to companies with small market capitalization—penny stocks. The Web site came to be known as Stock-dogs.com. ("You know, like racing dogs.") Stock-dogs.com plugged the stocks of companies Jonathan found interesting or that people Jonathan met on the Internet found interesting. At its peak, Stock-dogs.com had maybe 1,500 visitors a day. Even so, the officers of what seemed to Jonathan to be serious companies wrote to him to sell him on their companies. Within a couple of months of becoming an amateur stock-market analyst, he was in the middle of a network of people who spent every waking hour chatting about and trading stocks on the Internet. The mere memory of this clearly upset Greg.

"He was just a little kid," he said. "These people who got in touch with him could have been anybody."

"How do you know?" said Jonathan. "You've never even been on the Internet."

"Suppose some hacker comes in and steals his money!" Greg said. "Next day, you type in, and you got nothing left."

Jonathan snorted. "That can't happen." He turned to me. "Whenever he sees something on TV about the Internet, he gets mad and disconnects my computer phone line."

"Oh, yeah," Connie said, brightening as if realizing for the first time that she lived in the same house as the other two. "I used to hear the garage door opening at 3 in the morning. Then Jonathan's little feet running back up the stairs."

"I haven't ever even turned a computer on!" Greg said. "And I never will!"

"He just doesn't understand how a lot of this works," explained Jonathan patiently. "And so he overreacts sometimes."

Greg and Connie were born in New Jersey, but from the moment the Internet struck, they might as well have just arrived from Taiwan. When the Internet landed on them, it redistributed the prestige and authority that goes with a general understanding of the ways of the world away from the grown-ups and to the child. The grown-ups now depended on the child to translate for them. Technology had turned them into a family if immigrants.

"I know, I know," Greg said, turning to me. "I'm supposed to know how it works. It's the future. But that's his future, not mine!"

"Anyway," Connie said, drifting back in again. "That's when the S.E.C. called us the first time."

The first time?

Jonathan was 14 when Connie agreed to take him to meet with the S.E.C. in its Manhattan offices. When he heard the news, Greg, of course, hit the roof and hopped on the high-speed train to triple bypass. "He'd already had one heart attack," Connie explained and started to go into the heart problems all over again, inspiring Greg to mutter something about how he wasn't the person who brought the computer into the house and so it wasn't his responsibility to deal with this little nuisance.

At any rate, Connie asked Harold Burk, her boss at Hoffmann-La Roche, the drug company where she worked as a secretary, to go with her and Jonathan. Together, they made their way to a long conference table in a big room at 7 World Trade Center. On one side of the table, five lawyers and an examiner from the S.E.C.; on the other, a 14-year-old boy, his mother and a bewildered friend.

This is how it began:

S.E.C.: Does Jonathan's father know he's here today?

Mrs. Lebed: Yes.

S.E.C.: And he approves of having you here?

Mrs. Lebed: Right, he doesn't want to go.

S.E.C.: He's aware you're here.

Mrs. Lebed: With Harold.

S.E.C.: And that Mr. Burk is here.

Mrs. Lebed: He did not want to—this whole thing has upset my husband a lot. He had a heart attack about a year ago, and he gets very, very upset about things. So he really did not want anything to do with it, and I just felt like— Harold said he would help me.

The S.E.C. seemed to have figured out quickly that they are racing into some strange mental cul-de-sac. They turned their attention to Jonathan or, more specifically, his brokerage statements.

S.E.C.: Where did you learn your technique for day trading?

Jonathan: Just on TV, Internet.

S.E.C.: What TV shows?

Jonathan: CNBC mostly—basically CNBC is what I watch all the time

S.E.C.: Do you generally make money on your day trading?

Jonathan: I usually don't day trade; I just try to—since I was home these days and I was very bored, I wanted something to do, so I was just trading constantly. I don't think I was making money. . . .

S.E.C.: Just looking at your April statement, it looks like the majority of your trading is day trading.

Jonathan: I was home a lot that time.

Mrs. Lebed: They were on spring vacation that week.

Having established and then ignored the boy's chief motive for trading stocks—a desire to escape the tedium of existence—the authorities then sought to discover his approach to attracting attention on the Internet.

S.E.C.: On the first page [referring to a hard copy of Jonathan's Web site, Stock-dogs.com] where it says, "Our 6- to 12-month outlook, $8," what does that mean? The stock is selling less than 3 but you think it's going to go to 8.

Jonathan: That's our outlook for the price to go based on their earnings potential and a good value ratio. . . .

S.E.C.: Are you aware that there are laws that regulate company projections?
Jonathan: No.

Eventually, the S.E.C. people crept up on the reason they had noticed Jonathan in the first place. They had been hot on the trail of a grown-up named Ira Monas, one of Jonathan Lebed's many Internet correspondents. Monas, eventually jailed on unrelated charges, had been employed in "investor relations" by a number of small companies. In that role, he had fed Jonathan Lebed information about the companies, some of which turned out to be false and some of which Jonathan had unwittingly posted on Stock-dogs.com.

The S.E.C. asked if Monas had paid Jonathan to do this and thus help to inflate the price of his company's stocks. Jonathan said no, he had done it for free because he thought the information was sound. The S.E.C. then expressed its doubt that Jonathan was being forthright about his relationship with Monas. One of the small companies Monas had been hired to plug was a cigar retail outlet called Havana Republic. As a publicity stunt, Monas announced that the company—in which Jonathan came to own 100,000 shares—would hold a "smoke-out" in Midtown Manhattan.

The S.E.C. now knew that Jonathan Lebed had attended the smoke-out. To the people across the table from Jonathan, this suggested that his relationship with a known criminal was deeper than he admitted.

S.E.C.: So you decided to go to the smoke-out?
Jonathan: Yes.
S.E.C.: How did you go about that?
Jonathan: We walked down the street and took a bus.
S.E.C.: Who is "we"?
Jonathan: Me and my friend Chuck.
S.E.C.: O.K.
Jonathan: We took a bus to New York.
S.E.C.: You cut school to do this?
Jonathan: It was after school. Then we got picked up at Port Authority, so then my mother and Harold came and picked us up and we went to the smoke-out.
S.E.C.: Why were you picked up at the Port Authority?
Jonathan: Because people like under 18 across the country, from California. . . .
Mrs. Lebed: They pick up minors there at Port Authority.
S.E.C.: So the cops were curious about why you were there?
Jonathan: Yes.
S.E.C.: And they called your mother?
Jonathan: Yes.
S.E.C.: And she came.
Jonathan: Yes.
S.E.C.: You went to the smoke-out.
Jonathan: Yes.
S.E.C.: Did you see Ira there?
Jonathan: Yes.

S.E.C.: Did you introduce yourself to Ira?

Jonathan: No.

Here, you can almost hear the little sucking sound on the S.E.C.'s side of the table as the conviction goes out of this line of questioning.

S.E.C.: Why not?

Jonathan: Because I'm not sure if he knew my age, or anything like that, so I didn't talk to anyone there at all.

This mad interrogation began at 10 in the morning and ended at 6 in the evening. When it was done, the S.E.C. declined to offer legal advice. Instead, it said, "The Internet is a grown-up medium for grown-up-type activities." Connie Lebed and Harold Burk, both clearly unnerved, apologized profusely on Jonathan's behalf and explained that he was just a naïve child who had sought attention in the wrong place. Whatever Jonathan thought, he kept to himself.

When I came home that day, I closed the Ameritrade account," Connie told me.

"Then how did Jonathan continue to trade?" I asked.

Greg then blurted out, "The kid never did something wrong,"

"Don't ask me!" Connie said. "I got nothing to do with it."

"All right," Greg said, "here's what happened. When Little Miss Nervous over here closes the Ameritrade account, I open an account for him in my name with that other place, E*Trade."

I turned to Jonathan, who wore his expression of airy indifference.

"But weren't you scared to trade again?"

"No."

"This thing with the S.E.C. didn't even make you a little nervous?"

"No."

"No?"

"Why should it?"

Soon after he agreed to defend Jonathan Lebed, Kevin Marino, his lawyer, discovered he had a problem. No matter how he tried, he was unable to get Jonathan Lebed to say what he really thought. "In a conversation with Jonathan, I was supplying too many of the ideas," Marino says. "You can't get them out of him." Finally, he asked Jonathan and his parents each to write a few paragraphs describing their feelings about how the S.E.C. was treating Jonathan. Connie Lebed's statement took the form of a wailing lament of the pain inflicted by the callous government regulators on the family. ("I am also upset as you know that I was not called.") Greg Lebed's statement was an angry screed directed at both the government and the media.

Jonathan's statement—a four-page e-mail message dashed off the night that Marino asked for it—was so different in both tone and substance from his parents' that it inspired wonder that it could have been written by even the most casual acquaintance of the other two.

It began:

"I was going over some old press releases about different companies. The best performing stock in 1999 on the Nasdaq was Qualcomm (QCOM). QCOM was up around 2000% for the year. On December 29th of last year, even after QCOM's run from 25 to 500, Paine Webber analyst Walter Piecky came out and issued a buy rating on QCOM with a target price of 1,000. QCOM finished the day up 156 to 662. There was nothing fundamentally that would make QCOM worth 1,000. There is no way that a company with sales under $4 billion should be worth hundreds of billions. . . . QCOM has now fallen from 800 to under 300. It is no longer the hot play with all of the attention. Many people were able to successfully time QCOM and make a lot of money. The ones who had bad timing on QCOM lost a lot of money.

"People who trade stocks, trade based on what they feel will move and they can trade for profit. Nobody makes investment decisions based on reading financial filings. Whether a company is making millions or losing millions, it has no impact on the price of the stock. Whether it is analysts, brokers, advisors, Internet traders, or the companies, everybody is manipulating the market. If it wasn't for everybody manipulating the market, there wouldn't be a stock market at all. . . ."

As it happens, those last two sentences stand for something like the opposite of the founding principle of the United States Securities and Exchange Commission. To a very great extent, the world's financial markets are premised on a black-and-white mental snapshot of the American investor that was taken back in 1929. The S.E.C. was created in 1934, and the big question in 1934 was, How do you reassure the public that the stock market is not rigged? From mid-1929 to mid-1932, the value of the stocks listed on the New York Stock Exchange had fallen 83 percent, from $90 billion to about $16 billion. Capitalism, with reason, was not feeling terribly secure.

To the greater public in 1934, the numbers on the stock-market ticker no longer seemed to represent anything "real," but rather the result of manipulation by financial pros. So, how to make the market seem "real"? The answer was to make new stringent laws against stock-market manipulation—aimed not at ordinary Americans, who were assumed to be the potential victims of any manipulation and the ones who needed to be persuaded that it was not some elaborate web of perceptions, but at the Wall Street elite. The American financial elite acquired its own police force, whose job it was to make sure their machinations did not ever again unnerve the great sweaty rabble. That's not how the S.E.C. put it, of course. The catch phrase used by the policy-making elites when describing the SEC's mission was "to restore public confidence in the securities markets." But it amounted to the same thing. Keep up appearances, so that the public did not become too cautious. It occurred to no one that the public might one day be as sophisticated in these matters as financial professionals.

Anyone who paid attention to the money culture could see its foundation had long lay exposed, and it was just a matter of time before the termites got to it. From the moment the Internet went boom back in 1996, Web sites popped up in the middle of nowhere—Jackson, Mo.; Carmel, Calif.—and began to give away precisely what Wall Street sold for a living: earning forecasts, stock recommendations, market color. By the summer of 1998, Xerox or AT&T or some such opaque American corporation would announce earnings of 22 cents a share, and even though all of Wall Street had predicted a mere 20 cents and the company had exceeded all expectations, the stock would collapse. The amateur Web sites had been saying 23 cents.

Eventually, the Bloomberg News Service commissioned a study to explore the phenomenon of what were now being called "whisper numbers." The study showed the whisper numbers, the numbers put out by the amateur Web sites, were mistaken, on average, by 21 percent. The professional Wall Street forecasts were mistaken, on average, by 44 percent. The reason the amateurs now held the balance of power in the market was that they were, on average, more than twice as accurate as the pros—this in spite of the fact that the entire financial system was rigged in favor of the pros. The big companies spoon-fed their scoops directly to the pros; the amateurs were flying by radar.

Even a 14-year-old boy could see how it all worked, why some guy working for free out of his basement in Jackson, Mo;, was more reliable than the most highly paid analyst on Wall Street. The companies that financial pros were paid to analyze were also the financial pros' biggest customers. Xerox and AT&T and the rest needed to put the right spin on their quarterly earnings. The goal at the end of every quarter was for the newspapers and the cable television shows and the rest to announce that they had "exceeded analysts' expectations." The easiest way to exceed analysts' expectations was to have the analysts lower them. And that's just what they did, and had been doing for years. The guy in Carmel, Calif., confessed to Bloomberg that all he had to do to be more accurate on the earnings estimates than Wall Street analysts was to raise all of them 10 percent.

A year later, when the Internet bubble burst, the hollowness of the pros only became clearer. The most famous analysts on Wall Street, who just a few weeks before had done whatever they could to cadge an appearance on CNBC or a quote in The Wall Street Journal to promote their favorite dot-com, went into hiding. Morgan Stanley's Mary Meeker, who made $15 million in 1999 while telling people to buy Priceline when it was at $165 a share and Healtheon/WebMD when it reached $105 a share, went silent as they collapsed toward zero.

Financial professionals had entered some weird new head space. They simply took it for granted that a "financial market" was a collection of people doing their best to get onto CNBC and CNNfn and into the Heard on the Street column of The Wall Street Journal and the Lex column of The Financial Times, where they could advance their narrow self-interests.

To anyone who wandered into the money culture after, say, January 1996, it would have seemed absurd to take anything said by putative financial experts at face value. There was no reason to get worked up about it. The stock market was not an abstraction whose integrity needed to be preserved for the sake of democracy. It was a game people played to make money. Who cared if anything anyone said or believed was "real"? Capitalism could now afford for money to be viewed as no different from anything else you might buy or sell.

Or, as Jonathan Lebed wrote to his lawyer:

"Every morning I watch Shop at Home, a show on cable television that sells such products as baseball cards, coins and electronics. Don West, the host of the show, always says things like, 'This is one of the best deals in the history of Shop at Home! This is a no-brainer folks! This is absolutely unbelievable, congratulations to everybody who got in on this! Folks, you got to get in on the line, this is a gift, I just can't believe this!' There is absolutely nothing wring with him making quotes such as these. As long as he isn't lying about the condition of a baseball card or lying about how large a television is, he isn't committing any kind of a crime. The same thing applies to people who discuss stocks."

Right from the start, the SEC treated the publicity surrounding the case of Jonathan Lebed at least as seriously as the case itself. Maybe even more seriously. The Philadelphia office had brought the case, and so when the producer from "60 Minutes" called to say he wanted to do a big segment about the world's first teenage stock market manipulator, he called the Philadelphia office. "Normally we call the top and get bumped down to some flack," says Trevor Nelson, the "60 Minutes" producer in question. "This time I left a message at the S.E.C.'s Philadelphia office, and Arthur Levitt's office called me right back." Levitt, being the S.E.C. chairman, flew right up from Washington to be on the show.

To the S.E.C., it wasn't enough that Jonathan Lebed hand over his winnings: he had to be vilified; people had to be made to understand that what he had done was a crime, with real victims. "The S.E.C. kept saying that they were going to give us the name of one of the kid's victim so we could interview him," Nelson says. "But they never did."

I waited a couple of months for things to cool off before heading down to Washington to see Arthur Levitt. He was just then finishing up being the longest-serving chairman of the S.E.C. and was taking a victory lap in the media for a job well done. He was now 69, but as a youth, back in the 1950's and 1960's, he had made a lot of money on Wall Street. At the age of 62, he landed his job at the S.E.C.—in part, because he had raised a lot of money on the street for Bill Clinton—where he set himself up to defend the interests of the ordinary investor. He had declared war on the financial elite and pushed through rules that stripped it of its natural market advantages. His single bravest act was Regulation FD, which required corporations to release significant information about themselves to everyone at once rather than through the Wall Street analysts.

Having first determined I was the sort of journalist likely to see the world exactly as he did, he set out to explain to me the new forces corrupting the financial markets. "The Internet has speeded up everything," he said, "and we're seeing more people in the markets who shouldn't be there. A lot of these new investors don't have the experience or the resources of a professional trader. These are the ones who bought that [expletive] that Lebed was pushing."

"Do you think he is a sign of a bigger problem?"

"Yes, I do. And I find his case very disturbing . . . more serious than the guy who holds up the candy store. . . . I think there's a considerable risk of an anti-business backlash in this country. The era of the 25-year-old billionaire represents a kind of symbol which is different from the Horatio Alger symbol. The 25-year-old billionaire looks lucky, feels lucky. And investors who lose money buying stock in the company of the 25-year-old billionaire. . . ."

He trailed off, leaving me to finish the thought.

"You think it's a moral issue."

"I do."

"You think Jonathan Lebed is a bad kid?"

"Yes, I do."

"Can you explain to me what he did?"

He looked at me long and hard. I could see that this must be his meaningful stare. His eyes were light blue bottomless pits. "He'd go into these chat rooms and use 20 fictitious names and post messages. . . ."

"By fictitious names, do you mean e-mail addresses?"

"I don't know the details."

Don't know the details? He'd been all over the airways decrying the behavior of Jonathan Lebed.

"Put it this way," he said. "He'd buy, lie and sell high." The chairman's voice had deepened unnaturally. He hadn't spoken the line; he had acted it. It was exactly the same line he had spoken on "60 Minutes" when his interviewer, Steve Kroft, asked him to explain Jonathan Lebed's crime. He must have caught me gaping in wonder because, once again, he looked at me long and hard. I glanced away.

"What do you think?" he asked.

Well, I had my opinions. In the first place, I had been surprised to learn that it was legal for, say, an author to write phony glowing reviews of his book on Amazon but illegal for him to plug a stock on Yahoo just because he happened to own it. I thought it was—to put it kindly—misleading to tell reporters that Jonathan Lebed had used "20 fictitious names" when he had used four AOL e-mail addresses and posted exactly the same message under each of them so that no one who read them could possibly mistake him for more than one person. I further thought that without quite realizing what had happened to them, the people at the S.E.C. were now lighting out after the very people—the average American with a bit of money to play with—whom they were meant to protect.

Finally, I thought that by talking to me or any other journalist about Jonathan Lebed when he didn't really understand himself what Jonathan Lebed had done, the chairman of the S.E.C. displayed a disturbing faith in the media to buy whatever he was selling.

But when he asked me what I thought, all I said was, "I think it's more complicated than you think."

"Richard—call Richard!" Levitt was shouting out the door of his vast office. "Tell Richard to come in here!"

Richard was Richard Walker, the S.E.C.'s director of enforcement. He entered with a smile, but mislaid it before he even sat down. His mind went from a standing start to deeply distressed inside of 10 seconds. "This kid was making predictions about the prices of stocks," he said testily. "He had no basis for making these predictions." Before I could tell him that sounds a lot like what happens every day on Wall Street, he said, "And don't tell me that's standard practice on Wall Street," so I didn't. But it is. It is still O.K. for the analysts to lowball their estimates of corporate earnings and plug the stocks of the companies they take public so that they remain in the good graces of those companies. The S.E.C. would protest that the analysts don't actually own the stocks they plug, but that is a distinction without a difference: they profit mightily and directly from its rise.

"Jonathan Lebed was seeking to manipulate the market," said Walker.

But that only begs the question. If Wall Street analysts and fund managers and corporate C.E.O.'s who appear on CNBC and CNBCfn to plug stocks are not guilty of seeking to manipulate the market, what on earth does it mean to manipulate the market?

"It's when you promote a stock for the purpose of artificially raising its price."

But when a Wall Street analyst can send the price of a stock of a company that is losing billions of dollars up 50 points in a day, what does it mean to "artificially raise" the price of a stock? The law sounded perfectly circular. Actually, this point had been well made in a recent article in *Business Crimes Bulletin* by a pair of securities law experts, Lawrence S. Bader and Daniel B. Kosove. "The casebooks are filled with opinions that describe manipulation as causing an 'artificial' price," the experts wrote. "Unfortunately, the casebooks are short on opinions defining the word 'artificial' in this context. . . . By using the word 'artificial,' the courts have avoided coming to grips with the problem of defining 'manipulation'; they have simply substituted one undefined term for another."

Walker recited, "The price of a stock is artificially raised when subjected to something other than ordinary market forces."

But what are "ordinary market forces"?

An ordinary market force, it turned out, is one that does not cause the stock to rise artificially. In short, an ordinary market force is whatever the S.E.C. says it is, or what it can persuade the courts it is. And the S.E.C. does not view teenagers' broadcasting their opinions as "an ordinary market force." It can't. If it did, it would be compelled to face the deep complexity of the modern market—and all of the strange new creatures who have become, with the help of the Internet, ordinary market forces. When the Internet collided with the stock market, Jonathan Lebed became a market force. Adolescence became a market force.

I finally came clean with a thought: the S.E.C. let Jonathan Lebed walk away with 500 grand in his pocket because it feared that if it didn't , it would wind up in court and it would lose. And if the law ever declared formally that Jonathan Lebed didn't break it, the S.E.C. would be faced with an impossible situation: millions of small investors plugging their portfolios with abandon, becoming in essence professional financial analysts, generating embarrassing little explosions of unreality in every corner of the capital markets. No central authority could sustain the illusion that stock prices were somehow "real" or that the market wasn't, for most people, a site of not terribly productive leisure activity. The red dog would be off his leash.

I might as well have strolled into the office of the drug czar and lit up a joint.

"The kid himself said he set out to manipulate the market," Walker virtually shrieked. But, of course, that is not all the kid said. The kid said everybody in the market was out to manipulate the market.

"Then why did you let him keep 500 grand of his profits?" I asked.

"We determined that those profits were different from the profits he made on the 11 trades we defined as illegal," he said.

This, I already knew, was a pleasant fiction. The amount Jonathan Lebed handed over to the government was determined by haggling between Kevin Marino and the S.E.C.'s Philadelphia office. The S.E.C. initially demanded the $800,000 Jonathan had made, plus interest. Marino had countered with 125 grand. They haggled a bit and then settled at 285.

"Can you explain how you distinguished the illegal trades from the legal ones?"

"I'm not going to go through the case point by point."

"Why not?"

"It wouldn't be appropriate."

At which point, Arthur Levitt, who had been trying to stare into my eyes as intently as a man can stare, said in his deep voice, "This kid has no basis for making these predictions."

"But how do you know that?"

And the chairman of the S.E.C., the embodiment of investor confidence, the keeper of the notion that the numbers gyrating at the bottom of the CNBC screen are "real," drew himself up and said, "I worked on Wall Street."

Well. What do you say to that? He had indeed worked on Wall Street—in 1968.

"So did I," I said.

"I worked there longer than you."

Walker leapt back in. "This kid's father said he was going to rip the [expletive] computer out of the wall."

I realized that it was my turn to stare. I stared at Richard Walker. "Have you met Jonathan Lebed's father?" I said.

"No, I haven't," he said curtly. "But look, we talked to this kid two years ago, when he was 14 years old. If I'm a kid and I'm pulled in by some scary government agency, I'd back off."

That's the trouble with 14-year-old boys—from the point of view of the social order. They haven't yet learned the more sophisticated forms of dishonesty. It can take years of slogging to learn how to feign respect for hollow authority.

Still! That a 14-year-old boy, operating essentially in a vacuum, would walk away from a severe grilling by six hostile bureaucrats and jump right back into the market—how did that happen? It occurred to me, as it had occurred to Jonathan's lawyer, that I had taken entirely the wrong approach to getting the answer. The whole point of Jonathan Lebed was that he had invented himself on the Internet. The Internet had taught him how hazy the line was between perception and reality. When people could see him, they treated him as they would treat a 14-year-old boy. When all they saw were his thoughts on financial matters, they treated him as if he were a serious trader. On the Internet, where no one could see who he was, he became who he was. I left the S.E.C. and went back to my hotel and sent him an e-mail message, asking him the same question I asked the first time we met: why hadn't he been scared off?

Straight away he wrote back:

"It was about 2-3 months from when the S.E.C. called me in for the first time until I started trading again. The reason I didn't trade for those 2-3 months is because I had all of my money tied up in a stock. I sold it at the end of the year to take a tax loss, which allowed me to start trading again. I wasn't frightened by them because it was clear that they were focused on whether or not I was being paid to profile stocks when the fact is I was not. I was never told by them that I was doing something wrong and I was never told by them not to do something."

By September 1999, Jonathan Lebed was playing at the top of his game. He had figured out the advantage, after he had bought shares in a small company, in publicizing his many interests. "I came up with it myself," he said of the idea. "It was obvious from the newspapers and CBNC. Of course stocks respond to publicity!"

After he had picked and bought his stock, he would write a single message about it and stick it up in as many places on Yahoo Finance as he could between 5 and 8 in the morning, when he left home for school. There were no explicit rules on Yahoo Finance, but there were constraints The first was that Yahoo limited the number of messages he could post using one e-mail address. He would click onto Yahoo and open an account with one of his four AOL screen names; a few minutes later, Yahoo, mysteriously, would tell him that his messages could no longer be delivered. Eventually, he figured out that they must have some limit that they weren't telling people about. He got around it by grabbing another of his four AOL screen names and creating another Yahoo account. By rotating his four AOL screen names, he found he could get his message onto maybe 200 Yahoo message boards before school.

He also found that when he went to do it the next time, with a different stock, Yahoo would no longer accept messages from his AOL screen names. So he was forced to create four more screen names and start over again. Yahoo never told him he shouldn't do this. "The account would be just, like, deleted," he said. "Yahoo never had a policy; it's just what I figured out." The S.E.C. accused Jonathan of trying to seem like more than one person when he promoted his stocks, but when you see how and why he did what he did, that is clearly false. (For instance, he ignored the feature on Yahoo that enables users to employ up to seven different "fictitious names" for each e-mail address.) It's more true to say that he was trying to simulate an appearance on CNBC.

Over time, he learned that some messages had more effect on the stock market than others. "I definitely refined it," he said of his Internet persona. "In the beginning, I would write, like, very professionally. But then I started putting stuff in caps and using exclamation points and making it sound more exciting. That worked better. When it's more exciting, it draws people's attention to it compared to when you write like, dull or something." The trick was to find a stock that he could get excited about. He sifted the Internet chat rooms and the shopping mall with three things in mind: 1) "It had to be in the area of the stock market that is likely to become a popular play"; 2) "it had to be undervalued compared to similar companies"; and 3) "it had to be undiscovered—not that many people talking about it on the message boards."

Over a couple of months, I drifted in and out of Jonathan Lebed's life and became used to its staccato rhythms. His defining trait was that the strangest things happened to him, and he just thought of them as perfectly normal—and there was no one around to clarify matters. The threat of being prosecuted by the U.S. Attorney in Newark and sent away to a juvenile detention center still hung over him, but he didn't give any of it a second thought. He had his parents, his 12-year-old sister Dana and a crowd of friends at Cedar Grove High School, most of whom owned pieces of Internet businesses and all of whom speculated in the stock market. "There are three groups of kids in our school," one of them explained to me. "There's the jocks, there's the druggies and there's us—the more business oriented. The jocks and the druggies respect what we do. At first, a lot of the kids are, like, What are you doing? But once kids see money, they get excited."

The first time I heard this version of the social structure of Cedar Grove High, I hadn't taken it seriously. But then one day I went out with Jonathan and one of his friends, Keith Graham, into a neighboring suburb to do what they liked to do most when they weren't doing business, shoot pool. We parked the car and set out down an unprosperous street in search of the pool hall.

"Remember West Coast Video?" Keith said drolly.

I looked up. We were walking past a derelict building with "West Coast Video" stenciled on its plate glass.

Jonathan chuckled knowingly. "We owned, like, half the company."

I looked at him. He seemed perfectly serious. He began to tick off the reasons for his investment. "First, they were about to open an Internet subsidiary; second, they were going to sell DVD's when no other video chain. . . ."

I stopped him before he really got going. "Who owned half the company?"

"Me and a few others. Keith, Michael, Tom, Dan."

"Some teachers, too," Keith said.

"Yeah, the teachers heard about it," Jonathan said. He must have seen me looking strangely at him because he added: "It wasn't that big a deal. We probably didn't have a controlling interest in the company, but we had a fairly good percentage of the stock."

"Teachers?" I said. "The teachers followed you into this sort of thing."

"Sometimes," Jonathan said.

"All the time," Keith said. Keith is a year older than Jonathan and tends to be a more straightforward narrator of events. Jonathan will habitually dramatize or understate some case and emit a strange frequency, like a boy not quite sure how hard to blow into his new tuba, and Keith will invariably correct him. "As soon as people at school found out what Jonathan was in, everybody got in. Like right way. I was, like, if Jonathan's in on it, it must be good." And then the two boys moved on to some other subject, bored with the memory of having led some teachers in the acquisition of shares of West Coast Video. We entered the pool hall and took a table, where we were joined by another friend, John. Keith had paged him.

My role in Jonathan Lebed's life suddenly became clear: to express sufficient wonder at whatever he has been up to that he is compelled to elaborate.

"I don't understand," I said. "How would other kids find out what Jonathan was in?"

"It's high school," said Keith, in a tone reserved for people over 35. "Four hundred kids. People talk."

"How would the teachers find out?"

Now Keith gave me a look that told me that I'm the most prominent citizen of a new nation called Stupid. "They would ask us!" he said.

"But why?"

"They saw we were making money," Keith said.

"Yeah," said Jonathan, who, odd as it sounds, exhibits none of his friend's knowingness. He just knows. "I feel, like, that most of my classes, my grades would depend not on my performance but on how the stocks were doing."

"Not really," Keith said.

"O.K.," Jonathan said. "Maybe not that. But, like, I didn't think it mattered if I was late for class."

Keith considered that. "That's true," he said.

"I mean," Jonathan said, "they were making like thousands of dollars off the trades, more than their salaries even. . . ."

"Look," I said, "I know this is a stupid question. But was there any teacher who, say, disapproved of what you were doing?"

The three boys considered this, plainly for the first time in their lives.

"The librarian," Jonathan finally said.

"Yeah," John said. "But that's only because the computers were in the library, and she didn't like us using them."

"You traded stocks from the library?"

"Fifth-period study hall was in the library," Keith said. "Fifth-period study hall was like a little Wall Street. But sometimes the librarian would say the computers were for study purposes only. None of the other teachers cared."

"They were trading," Jonathan said.

The mood had shifted. We shot pool and pretended that there was no more boring place to be than this world we live in. "Even though we owned like a million shares," Jonathan said, picking up the new mood. "It wasn't that big a deal. West Coat Video was trading at like 30 cents a share when we got in."

Keith looked up from the cue ball. "When you got in," he said. "Everyone else got in at 65 cents; then it collapsed. Most of the people lost money on that one."

"Hmmm," Jonathan said, with real satisfaction. "That's when I got out."

Suddenly I realized the S.E.C. was right: there were victims to be found from Jonathan Lebed's life on the Internet. They were right here in New Jersey. I turned to Keith. "You're Jonathan's victim."

"Yeah, Keith," Jonathan said, laughing. "You're my victim."

"Nah," Keith said. "In the stock market, you go in knowing you can lose. We were just doing what Jon was doing, but not doing as good a job at it." ■

Working with the Text

1. In the second paragraph of the article, Michael Lewis states, "When I first read the newspaper reports [about the Jonathan Lebed case], I didn't understand them. It wasn't just that I didn't understand what the kid had done wrong; I didn't understand what he had done." Part of Lewis's task in this article is to explain to the general audience the specific financial activities Lebed used to make hundreds of thousands of dollars as a teenager. Check your own understanding of what Lebed did by explaining it in your own words. Develop your explanation even further by writing a version of this story for a junior high school audience (the age of Lebed when he began trading stocks).

2. Part of Lewis's article involves an argument he has with the Securities and Exchange Commission, especially Arthur Levitt, the chairman of the SEC, about whether what Lebed did was criminal or dangerous behavior. How would you explain the positions of Lewis and the SEC regarding Lebed's activities? What does Lewis see as the primary points of contention? Which case do you find most persuasive?

3. In explaining how he was able to convince Internet investors that his advice was worth following, Lebed says, "'In the beginning, I would write, like, very professionally. But then I started putting stuff in caps [capital letters] and using exclamation points and making it sound more exciting. That worked better. When it's more exciting, it draws people's attention to it compared to when you write, like, dull or something.'" You may find that Lebed's advice contradicts what you have learned about writing in school, particularly in regard to the use of many exclamation points or words in all capital letters. How do you respond as a reader to visual cues like exclamation points? Do you find yourself responding differently in different reading situations? Use the example of Lebed's Internet writing as well as the information in Chapter 1 under "Working with Words and Images/Words as Images: Reading in a Visual Culture" to come up with your own

guidelines on when and when not to use dramatic punctuation and visual cues in your writing.

4. Lewis writes, "The whole point of Jonathan Lebed was that he had invented himself on the Internet. The Internet had taught him how hazy was the line between perception and reality." Lebed's success as a stock market analyst on the Internet raises interesting questions about writing and personal identity in cyberspace. Had those reading his postings to discussion boards known that he was only 13 or 14 years old, they may have been reluctant to follow his advice. By learning how to write like an Internet stock analyst, though, Lebed managed to acquire authority comparable to a Wall Street veteran. Explore the connections between writing and identity through the use of a class discussion board. Have each member of the class come up with an online identity different in a crucial way from his or her "real" one. Gender is a good place to start. Then, conduct a discussion on the discussion board and try to convince the other participants of your online identity. You will quickly discover that relying on stereotypes isn't very useful. (You can even conduct this discussion among different sections of the same course.) Reflect on the experience and how successful or unsuccessful you were.

Working with Connections

1. In explaining to Lewis why he thinks Jonathan Lebed sets such a dangerous example, SEC Chairman Arthur Levitt says, "'And I find his case very disturbing . . . more serious than the guy who holds up the candy store. . . . I think there's a considerable risk of an anti-business backlash in this country. The era of the 25-year-old billionaire represents a kind of symbol which is different from the Horatio Alger symbol. The 25-year-old billionaire looks lucky, feels lucky.'" Respond to Levitt's concerns by examining your own reactions to the Lebed case, and by comparing the story of Lebed with the excerpt from Horatio Alger's novel *Ragged Dick* (in Chapter 2, Work, Labor, Career: The Meaning of Work). Why do you think Levitt so greatly fears the association of luck and success? What do you think he means by "the Horatio Alger symbol"? Do you find Lebed's story frightening? Amusing? Inspiring?

2. Although Jonathan Lebed's parents argue over the wisdom of buying him a computer and helping him open up a stock trading account, their ability to provide Lebed with hardware and

Internet access were essential to his ability to become a successful stock trader. How does Lebed's story fit into the discussion of the digital divide found in LynNell Hancock's "The Haves and the Have-Nots"? How could the example of Lebed be used in a discussion of the relation between social class and Internet access?

3. In their debate about Nike's overseas labor practices (in Chapter 8: Work in the Global Economy), Michael Moore and Nike CEO Phil Knight argue about whether a 14-year-old belongs in school or in the workplace. How does the case of the 14-year-old Jonathan Lebed complicate their discussion? Is what Lebed was doing child labor, or does Lebed's story force us to reexamine what we mean by "child" or "adult" labor?

4. In "Summertime Dues" (in Chapter 7, The Ethics of Work/The Work Ethic), Walter Kirn describes the real lessons he learned about the world of work from his summer jobs as a teenager, lessons different from those his parents thought he would learn. Using Kirn's essay as a model, write about what you think Lebed has learned about the world of work from his even more dramatic experiences.

Media Images

The Personal Daily Assistant ■

Around the turn of the twenty-first century, a new electronic device began appearing in the workplace. Instead of the leather-bound organizers that became a consumer icon of the 1990s, more and more people began carrying Personal Daily Assistants (PDAs for short): small, hand-held computers. Initially, PDAs filled the same function as the nonelectronic organizer: keeping track of appointments and phone numbers, storing lists of things to do. As their popularity spread, however, so did the functions included in them, from making telephone calls to answering e-mails to surfing the web. For all their high-tech status, PDAs do feature one old-fashioned technology: the ability to make entries by writing on the screen using the cursor and a special alphabet.

The addition of the pencil-like cursor points to the importance of design and presentation in addition to sheer functionality in the PDA. As a successful consumer product, the design of the PDA reflects larger attitudes and even anxieties about technology, work, and the future. Examine the PDA pictured here; if possible, see if one can be brought into class for closer inspection in preparation for the discussion questions that follow.

Working with the Text

1. Consider the name of the product: the Personal Daily Assistant. Why do you think this name was chosen? What attitudes toward work and technology might it express? What fears or anxieties might it soothe? Brainstorm other possible names for a product like this, and write about the different values implied by the different names.

2. In "The On-Line Mystique," Paula Span examines how computer technology and culture reflects different ideas about gender and

gender roles. How can you read the design of the PDA in terms of gender? Do you think they would mainly appeal to men or women and why? In what different ways might they appeal?

3. One aspect of the idea of an "assistant" is that the user must be in a position of authority. What jobs or lines of work does the PDA seemed designed to appeal to? In which do you think the product would or could be useful? How might the PDA be redesigned to appeal to people in a wider variety of work situations?

THE WORK OF WRITING/WRITING AS WORK: OVERCOMING THE DIGITAL DIVIDE

In "The Haves and the Have-Nots," LynNell Hancock writes about a growing gap between those students who have the financial and educational resources to compete in the computer culture of the information economy and those who do not, a gap that could widen divisions of social and economic opportunity. Since the 1990s, many organizations have appeared to address the problem of the digital divide, including the U.S. Department of Commerce and the Digital Divide Network http://www.digitaldividenetwork.org/. There are also many local community- and school district–based projects as well.

Working with your instructor, identify what if any projects exist in your community addressing the problem of the digital divide. Contact them to see how your class can participate in the project. Among the ideas you might consider:

- Set up an e-mail discussion list with students at local schools taking part in the project about the digital divide.
- Work on developing written materials, from a handbook to a web site, describing the key computer-based writing skills and knowledge you think high school students should have before coming to college.
- Draft proposals for your college or university to be more involved with the project, whether making computer lab time available to area students, offering classes, or donating computers.

If no project currently exists, work as a class to do research on other projects across the country. Contact local school districts to assess their computing skills needs. Use this information to draft a proposal for the creation of a local project. What should the key components of the project be? Who needs to be involved? What funding sources have others used? Work with your instructor on determining the most effective place to send your proposal.

Epilogue

The Joy of Work

I n his song, "Into the Fire," Bruce Springsteen writes from the perspective of the spouse of a firefighter or police officer who perished on September 11, 2001:

> The sky was falling and streaked with blood
> I heard you calling me, then you disappeared into the dust
> Up the stairs, into the fire
> Up the stairs, into the fire
> I need your kiss, but love and duty called you someplace higher
> Somewhere up the stairs, into the fire

Rather than focusing on courage and bravery, Springsteen, who has written many songs about the meaning and importance of work, chooses to describe the sacrifice of the emergency worker as one of "love and duty." As a result, in the chorus he is able to transform a song of mourning into one of hope and inspiration:

> May your strength give us strength
> May your faith give us faith
> May your hope give us hope
> May your love give us love

We can look at Springsteen's elegy as a commentary on the kind of life's work many of us hope to find, a work that goes beyond the idea of a "job" and instead approaches nearer to the older spiritual idea of a "calling." This kind of work is motivated less by the demands of practical necessity or the lure of financial reward than a sense of "love and duty," a feeling that what we do has deep meaning for ourselves and others, a meaning that can integrate our most deeply held values and beliefs with our work in the world.

As a capstone to your course-long thinking and writing about work, this epilogue asks you to reflect on and synthesize your thinking and experiences about work into the simple yet complex idea of work as a source of joy and fulfillment. What follows are a series of artworks that illustrate three examples of joyful work. They range from a Renaissance engraving of an imagined scene from the life of St. Jerome to a contemporary portrait of the scientist Mary Hodgkin. As you view these images, think about the ways each might evoke a different aspect of the "joy of work" as you define it.

ALBRECHT DÜRER

St. Jerome in His Study

In this engraving from 1514, Albrecht Dürer, the great German Renaissance artist, creates an imaginary scene from the life of St. Jerome, a fifth-century saint. Dürer is trying to evoke the unusual sense of calling and deep commitment we associate with the work of a saint, but by placing Jerome quietly at work in his study, Dürer asks us to consider an extraordinary person in a very ordinary setting and occupation.

Working with the Text

1. What are the main emotional responses you find Dürer evoking in this engraving? Try connecting these emotional responses to specific details in the drawing.

2. You may have had a pet quietly snoozing in your room while you have worked on your writing, and the same is true for St. Jerome, although his animal companions may be more exotic than your own. What is your response to the sleeping lion in Dürer's engraving?

3. Name at least three qualities you associate with "the joy of work" that you find in Dürer's engraving.

MAGGI HAMBLING

Dorothy Mary Crowfoot Hodgkin

The British chemist Mary Hodgkin won the Nobel Prize in Chemistry in 1964 for her work in describing the structure of vitamin B-12. She was also a humanitarian deeply committed to issues of peace and the needs of children living in poverty. In 1985, the artist Maggi Hambling painted Hodgkin at work in her office. At first glance, this subtle painting seems a straightforward portrait, until we look closely, when intriguing details begin to emerge.

Working with the Text

1. Although she depicts Hodgkin seated at her desk, Hambling still manages to create a sense of motion and activity. What key details and techniques does Hambling use to help visualize the energetic life of the mind that characterizes Hodgkin at work?

2. What sense of Hodgkin's personality do you take away from this work? Which details and aspects of the painting convey this sense of Hodgkin as a person to you?

3. Name at least three qualities you associate with the "joy of work" that you find in Hambling's painting.

Working with Connections

1. Locate someone you know who represents the "joy of work" to you and interview them about their life's work. Which aspects of these three works of art best relate to your understanding of what work means to this person?

2. Find your own image, whether a painting, photograph, drawing, or a work you create yourself, that you feel best expresses the joy of work and write an essay explaining your choice.

3. Write a capstone essay to the course entitled "The Joy of Work" describing the specific qualities you are looking for in your life's work. If you think you know what that work is, you can explain why you have made this choice. To create a more extended essay, you can make reference to those essays, images, and other cultural texts that you have encountered in this course that have most influenced your thinking.

Credits

CHAPTER 1

Marge Piercy, "To Be of Use" from *Circles on the Water.* Copyright © 1982 by Marge Piercy. Used by permission of Alfred A. Knopf, a division of Random House, Inc.

CHAPTER 2

Aristotle, *The Politics,* Book VII, Part IX, translated by Benjamin Jowett. Copyright © 2000 Dover Publications. Used with permission.

monster.com screen capture, Copyright © TMP Interactive Inc. All rights reserved.

Kathryn Carmony, "Surfing the Classifieds." First printed in *Lumpen*, Vol. 3, No. 28, April 28, 1995. Copyright © 1994 Kathryn L. Carmony. Used with permission.

Dilbert, reprinted by permission of United Feature Syndicate, Inc.

CHAPTER 3

Jean Anyon, "Social Class and the Hidden Curriculum of Work," *Journal of Education*, Vol. 162, No. 1, Winter 1980. Copyright © 1980 Jean Anyon. Reprinted by permission of the author.

Ron Nixon, "Caution: Children at Work," *The Progressive*, Aug. 1996, p. 30. Copyright © 1996 Ron Nixon. Used with permission.

Robert Cwiklik, "A Different Course," *Wall Street Journal*, November 16, 1998. Copyright © 1998 Dow Jones & Co. Inc. Used with permission.

James Traub, "The Next University. Drive-Thru U: Higher Education for People Who Mean Business" *New Yorker*, 1997. Copyright © 1997 James Traub. Used with permission of the author.

Neal Postman, "Of Luddites, Learning, and Life" *Technos Quarterly*, Winter, 1993. Copyright © 1993 Agency for Instructional Technology.

University of Phoenix screen capture, Copyright © 2003 University of Phoenix. All rights reserved.

Portland State University screen capture, Copyright © 2003 Portland State University. All rights reserved.

Mt. San Antonio College screen capture, Copyright © 2002 Mt. San Antonio College. Used with permission.

Life in School, © 1983 by Matt Groening. All rights Reserved.

Mike Rose, from *Lives on the Boundary: The Struggles and Achievements of America's Underprepared.* Reprinted with the permission of The Free Press, a Division of Simon & Schuster Adult Publishing Group. Copyright © 1989 by Mike Rose.

CHAPTER 4

Adam Smith, from *An Inquiry into the Nature and Causes of the Wealth of Nations,* pp. 13–24, edited by Skinner, Campbell & Todd. Copyright © 1976 Clarendon Press. Used with permission.

Gregory Mantsios, "Media Magic: Making Class Invisible" from *Race, Class & Gender in the U.S.: An Integrated Study,* 5/e, edited by Paula Rothenberg. Copyright © 2001 Gregory Mantsios. Reprinted by permission.

Barbara Ehrenreich, *Nickel and Dimed: On (Not) Getting By in America.* © 2001 by Barbara Ehrenreich. Reprinted by permission of Henry Holt and company, LLC.

Justice for Janitors screen capture, www.seiu.org/building/janitors Copyright © SEIU. Used with permission.

Bertolt Brecht, "Questions from a Worker Who Reads" in *Bertolt Brecht, Poems 1913–1956.* Copyright © 1976. Reproduced by permission of Routledge, Inc., part of The Taylor & Francis Group.

Mary Fell, "Havdallah" from *Persistence of Memory.* Copyright © 1975, 1976, 1977, 1978, 1979, 1980, 1981, 1982, 1983, 1984 by Mary Fell. Used by permission of Random House, Inc.

Carol Tarlen, "Sisters in the Flames" from *Women's Studies Quarterly,* Vol. 23, Nos. 1 & 2, Spring/Summer 1995, pp. 70–71. Copyright © 1995 by Carol Tarlen, by permission of the Feminist Press at the City University of New York, www.feministpress.org.

Safiya Henderson-Holmes, "Colors of Spring" from *Madness and a Bit of Hope,* © 1990 Harlem River.

Chris Llewellyn, "SEAR" from *Fragments from the Fire,* © 1997 Chris Llewellyn. Published by Penguin Putnam, Inc.

Michael Zweig, from *The Working Class Majority: America's Best Kept Secret,* pp.9–35. Copyright © 2000 by Michael Zweig. Used by permission of the publisher, Cornell University Press.

The Phoenix Companies, Inc. advertisement. ©The Phoenix Companies, Inc.

CHAPTER 5

Alice Kessler-Harris, from *Women Have Always Worked.* Copyright © 1983 by Alice Kessler-Harris, by permission of the Feminist Press at the City University of New York, www.feministpress.org.

Stephanie Coontz, "The American Family." Copyright © 2000 Stephanie Coontz. Reprinted by permission of the author.

Juliet B. Schor, from *The Overworked American: The Unexpected Decline of Leisure.* Copyright © 1991 by BasicBooks. Reprinted by permission of Basic Books, a member of Perseus Books, L.L.C.

Ellen Galinsky, "Do Working Parents Make the Grade?" from *Ask the Children.* Copyright © 1999 by Ellen Galinsky. Reprinted by permission of HarperCollins Publishers Inc.

Families and Work Institute screen capture, © Families and Work Institute. www.familiesandwork.org. Used with permission.

Deb Casey, "ZOOOOOM: A Familiar Story: Drop-Off/Pick-Up Panic," *Calyx*, Vol. 12, No. 3, Summer 1990, pp. 69–70. Copyright © Deb Casey. Used by permission.

Annie Downey, "Is There Life After Welfare?" *Hip Mama*, Autumn 1997. Copyright © 1997 by Annie Downey. Used with permission.

Annie Downey, "The Journey to Not" *Hip Mama*. Copyright © Annie Downey. Used with permission.

Working Mother.com screen capture, Copyright © 2003 Working Mother.

Dadmag.com screen capture, Copyright © 2003 Dadmag.com.

CHAPTER 6

"The Majority of Immigrants" (Graph) from *Population Reference Bureau Reports on America,* Vol.1, No. 2,May 1999. Copyright © 1999 Population Reference Bureau. Used with permission.

Lisa Belkin, "Showdown at Yazoo Industries" *New York Times Sunday Magazine*, January 21, 1996. Copyright © 1996 Lisa Belkin. Reprinted by permission.

Shelley Donald Coolidge, "On the Job, It's English or the Pink Slip," *Christian Science Monitor*, January 15, 1998. Copyright © 1998 The Christian Science Moniotr (www.csmonitor.com). All rights reserved. Reproduced with permission.

Ragged Edge screen capture, Copyright © 2003 Advocado Press. Used with permission.

Lalo Guerrero, "Corrido de Cesar Chavez." Published by Barrio Libre Music. Copyright © 1968 Lalo Guerrero. All rights reserved.

Wanda Coleman, "Office Politics" copyright © 1990 by Wanda Coleman. Reprinted from *African Sleeping Sickness* by Black Sparrow Press (imprint of David Godine, Publisher, Inc.), with the permission from the author.

Molly Martin, "Nina Saltman: Carpenter Foreman" from *Hard-Hatted Women*, pp. 122–134. Copyright © 1997 Seal Press.

Farai Chideya, *The Color of Our Future*. Copyright © 1999 by Farai Chideya. Reprinted by permission of HarperCollins publishers, Inc.

Dalton Conley, "The Cost of Slavery" *New York Times*, 2/15/2003. Copyright © 2003, The New York Times. Reprinted by permission.

Fast food employee photos courtesy of: © Don Smetzer/Stone. © Michael Newman/Photo Edit. © Spencer Grant/Photo Edit. © Rubberball Productions/Rubberball Productions/PictureQuest. © Ariel Skelley/CORBIS.

CHAPTER 7

Max Weber from *The Protestant Ethic and the Spirit of Capitalism*. Copyright Pearson Education. Reprinted by permission of Pearson Education, Inc, Upper Saddle River, NJ.

John Judis, "Value Free" *New Republic*, 4/26/99. Reprinted by permission of The New Republic, © 1999, The New Republic, LLC.

Walter Kirn, "Summertime Dues" *New York Times Sunday Magazine*, 7/9/00. Copyright © 2000 Walter Kirn. Reprinted by permission.

Richard Posner, "On Plagiarism" *Atlantic Monthly*, April 2002. Copyright © 2002 Richard Posner. Used with permission from the author.

Kathy Slobbogin, "Survey: Many Students Say Cheating's OK" from CNN.com, April 5, 2002. Copyright © 2002. Used with permission.

Kelly McCollum, "Term-Paper Web Site Has Professors Worried about Plagiarism" *Chronicle of Higher Education*, August 2, 1996. Copyright © 1996 The Chronicle of Higher Education. Reprinted with permission.

School Sucks.com screen capture, Courtesy of School Sucks.

Turnitin.com screen capture, © 2003 iParadigms. Used with permission from iParadigms, LLC.

Randy Cohen, from *The Good, the Bad, and the Difference*. Copyright © 2002 by Randy Cohen. Used by permission of Doubleday, a division of Random House, Inc.

Joe McNally, *Faces of Ground Zero*. Copyright © 2002 Joe McNally.

CHAPTER 8

"Declaration Concerning the Aims and Purposes of the International Labour Organization" Copyright © International Labour Organization 1998. Used with permission.

Pico Iyer, "The Global Village Finally Arrives," *Time*, Vol. 42, No. 21, 1993, pp. 86–87. © 1993 Time Inc. Reprinted by permission.

Benjamin Barber, "Jihad vs. McWorld." Published originally in *The Atlantic Monthly*, March 1992 as an introduction to the *Jihad vs. McWorld* (Ballantine paperback, 199) a volume that discusses and extends the themes of the original article. Used with permission of the author.

William Greider, from *One World Ready or Not*. Reprinted with the permission of Simon & Schuster. Copyright © 1997 by William Greider.

Nicholas Kristof and Sheryl WuDenn, "Two Cheers for Sweatshops" *New York Times Sunday Magazine*, September 24, 2000. Copyright © 2000 Nicholas Kristof and Sheryl WuDunn. Reprinted by permission.

United Students Against Sweatshops screen capture, Copyright © 2003 USAS. Used with permission.

Nike screen capture, Copyright © 2003 Nike, Inc. All rights reserved.

Woody Guthrie, *Plane Wreck at Los Gatos (Deportee)*. Words by Woody Guthrie; Music by Martin Hoffman. TRO—© Copyright 1961 (Renewed) 1963 (Renewed) Ludlow Music, Inc., New York, NY. Used by permission.

Silvana Paternostro, "Registering the 9/11 Dead," *New York Times Magazine*, June 23, 2002. Copyright © 2002 Silvana Paternostro. Reprinted with permission.

Felix Martinez photo. Copyright © 2002 Jennifer Szymaszek.

Michael Moore, "Interview with Phil Knight, CEO of Nike." Copyright © Michael Moore.

CHAPTER 9

Nicholas Negroponte, "An Age of Optimism" from *Being Digital*. Copyright © 1995 by Nicholas Negroponte. Used by permission of Alfred A. Knopf, a division of Random House, Inc.

Lynnell Hancock, "The Haves and the Have Nots" *Newsweek*, February 1995. Copyright © 1995 Newsweek, Inc. All rights reserved. Reprinted by permission.

Paula Span, "Women and Computers: Is There Equity in Cyberspace?" in The Online Mystique" *Washington Post Magazine*, February 27, 1994. Copyright © 1994, The Washington Post. Reprinted with permission.

Internet Archive screen capture, Copyright © 2003 Internet Archive. All rights reserved.

Michael Lewis, "Jonathan Lebed's Extracurricular Activities" *New York Times Sunday Magazine*, February 25, 2001. Copyright © 2001 Michael Lewis. Reprinted with the permission of Writers House, LLC.

Handspring screen capture, Copyright © Handspring, Inc. All rights reserved.

EPILOGUE

Bruce Springsteen, "Into the Fire." Copyright © 2002 Bruce Springsteen. All rights reserved. Reprinted by permission of Grubman Indursky & Schindler.

Albrecht Duerer, "Saint Jerome in his Study" (woodcut). Reprinted with permission of Scala/Art Resource, NY.

Maggi Hambling, Portrait of "Dorothy Mary Crowfoot Hodgkin." By courtesy of the National Portrait Gallery, London.

Index